AF173202

Communications
in Computer and Information Science   2372

Series Editors

Gang Li, *School of Information Technology, Deakin University, Burwood, VIC, Australia*

Joaquim Filipe, *Polytechnic Institute of Setúbal, Setúbal, Portugal*

Zhiwei Xu, *Chinese Academy of Sciences, Beijing, China*

Rationale

The CCIS series is devoted to the publication of proceedings of computer science conferences. Its aim is to efficiently disseminate original research results in informatics in printed and electronic form. While the focus is on publication of peer-reviewed full papers presenting mature work, inclusion of reviewed short papers reporting on work in progress is welcome, too. Besides globally relevant meetings with internationally representative program committees guaranteeing a strict peer-reviewing and paper selection process, conferences run by societies or of high regional or national relevance are also considered for publication.

Topics

The topical scope of CCIS spans the entire spectrum of informatics ranging from foundational topics in the theory of computing to information and communications science and technology and a broad variety of interdisciplinary application fields.

Information for Volume Editors and Authors

Publication in CCIS is free of charge. No royalties are paid, however, we offer registered conference participants temporary free access to the online version of the conference proceedings on SpringerLink (http://link.springer.com) by means of an http referrer from the conference website and/or a number of complimentary printed copies, as specified in the official acceptance email of the event.

CCIS proceedings can be published in time for distribution at conferences or as post-proceedings, and delivered in the form of printed books and/or electronically as USBs and/or e-content licenses for accessing proceedings at SpringerLink. Furthermore, CCIS proceedings are included in the CCIS electronic book series hosted in the SpringerLink digital library at http://link.springer.com/bookseries/7899. Conferences publishing in CCIS are allowed to use Online Conference Service (OCS) for managing the whole proceedings lifecycle (from submission and reviewing to preparing for publication) free of charge.

Publication process

The language of publication is exclusively English. Authors publishing in CCIS have to sign the Springer CCIS copyright transfer form, however, they are free to use their material published in CCIS for substantially changed, more elaborate subsequent publications elsewhere. For the preparation of the camera-ready papers/files, authors have to strictly adhere to the Springer CCIS Authors' Instructions and are strongly encouraged to use the CCIS LaTeX style files or templates.

Abstracting/Indexing

CCIS is abstracted/indexed in DBLP, Google Scholar, EI-Compendex, Mathematical Reviews, SCImago, Scopus. CCIS volumes are also submitted for the inclusion in ISI Proceedings.

How to start

To start the evaluation of your proposal for inclusion in the CCIS series, please send an e-mail to ccis@springer.com.

Michele Dassisti · Kurosh Madani ·
Hervé Panetto

Editors

Innovative Intelligent Industrial Production and Logistics

5th International Conference, IN4PL 2024
Porto, Portugal, November 21–22, 2024
Proceedings, Part I

 Springer

Editors
Michele Dassisti
Polytechnical University of Bari
Bari, Italy

Kurosh Madani
University of Paris-EST Créteil
Créteil, France

Hervé Panetto 🆔
University of Lorraine
Vandoeuvre-les-Nancy, France

ISSN 1865-0929　　　　　　ISSN 1865-0937 (electronic)
Communications in Computer and Information Science
ISBN 978-3-031-80759-6　　　　ISBN 978-3-031-80760-2 (eBook)
https://doi.org/10.1007/978-3-031-80760-2

This Springer imprint is published by the registered company Springer Nature Switzerland AG
The registered company address is: Gewerbestrasse 11, 6330 Cham, Switzerland

If disposing of this product, please recycle the paper.

Preface

This book contains the proceedings of the 5th International Conference on Innovative Intelligent Industrial Production and Logistics. This year, IN4PL was held in Porto, Portugal, on November 21–22, 2024. It was sponsored by the Institute for Systems and Technologies of Information, Control and Communication (INSTICC), co-sponsored by the International Federation of Automatic Control (IFAC), and technically co-sponsored by the IEEE Industry Applications Society.

This conference focuses on research and development involving innovative methods, software and hardware, whereby intelligent systems are applied to industrial production and logistics. This is currently related to the concept of Industry 5.0 - an expression describing the new wave that extends the trend towards automation and data exchange in manufacturing technologies and processes - including cyber-physical systems, the industrial internet of things, industrial robotics, cloud computing, cognitive computing and artificial intelligence - towards the new role of human resources cooperating with these technologies.

IN4PL 2024 received 76 paper submissions from 23 countries of which 15 (21%) were accepted and published as full papers. A double-blind paper review was performed for each submission by at least 2 but usually 3 or more members of the International Program Committee, which was composed of established researchers and domain experts.

The high quality of the IN4PL 2024 program was enhanced by the keynote lectures delivered by distinguished speakers who are renowned experts in their fields: Georg Weichhart (Primetals Technologies, Austria), Jose Barata (Universidade Nova De Lisboa, Portugal) and Fazleena Badurdeen (University of Kentucky, USA).

The conference was complemented by a Special Session on Industrial AI at the Edge, organised by Ander Garcia and Xiao Lin, and the 18th IFAC/IFIP Workshop on Enterprise Integration, Interoperability and Networking, chaired by Hervé Panetto, Qing Li and Yannick Naudet.

All presented papers will be submitted for indexing by DBLP, Google Scholar, EI-Compendex, INSPEC, Japanese Science and Technology Agency (JST), Norwegian Register for Scientific Journals and Series, Mathematical Reviews, SCImago, Scopus, zbMATH and Web of Science/Conference Proceedings Citation Index.

As recognition for the best contributions, several awards based on the combined marks of paper reviewing, as assessed by the Program Committee, and the quality of the presentation, as assessed by session chairs at the conference venue, were conferred at the closing session of the conference.

The program for this conference required the dedicated effort of many people. Firstly, we must thank the authors, whose research efforts are herewith recorded. Next, we thank the members of the Program Committee and the auxiliary reviewers for their diligent and professional reviewing. We would also like to deeply thank the invited speakers for their invaluable contribution and for taking the time to prepare their talks. Finally, a word of appreciation for the hard work of the INSTICC team; organizing a conference of this level is a task that can only be achieved by the collaborative effort of a dedicated and highly competent team.

We hope you all had an exciting and inspiring conference. We hope to have contributed to the development of our research community, and we look forward to having additional research results presented at the next edition of IN4PL, details of which are available at https://in4pl.scitevents.org.

November 2024

Michele Dassisti
Kurosh Madani
Hervé Panetto

Organization

Conference Co-chairs

Kurosh Madani   University of Paris-Est Créteil, France
Hervé Panetto   University of Lorraine, France

Program Chair

Michele Dassisti   Polytechnic University of Bari, Italy

Program Committee

António Abreu   Polytechnic University of Lisbon, Portugal
Anna Adamik   Lodz University of Technology, Poland
Cláudio Alves   Universidade do Minho, Portugal
Allison Barnard Feeney   National Institute of Standards and Technology, USA
Giuseppe Berio   University of South Brittany, France
Hing Kai Chan   University of Nottingham Ningbo China, China
Tin-Chih Toly Chen   National Chiao Tung University, Taiwan
Ferdinando Chiacchio   University of Catania, Italy
Law Chong Seng   Southern University College, Malaysia
Mauro Dell'Amico   University of Modena and Reggio Emilia, Italy
Xavier Delorme   École Nationale Supérieure des Mines de Saint-Etienne, France
William Derigent   Université de Lorraine, France
Alejandro Escudero-Santana   University of Seville, Spain
Åsa Fast-Berglund   Stena Recycling, Sweden
Piotr Gaj   Silesian University of Technology, Poland
Ander Garcia   Vicomtech, Spain
Virginie Goepp   Institut National des Sciences Appliquées de Strasbourg, France
Gil Gonçalves   University of Porto, Portugal
Marvin Gonzalez   College of Charleston, USA
Cathal Heavey   University of Limerick, Ireland
Petri Helo   University of Vaasa, Finland

François Vernadat	University of Lorraine, France
Ramon Vilanova	Universitat Autònoma de Barcelona, Spain
Georg Weichhart	Primetals Technologies, Austria
Morteza Yazdani	Vilnius Tech, Lithuania
Yuehwern Yih	Purdue University, USA

Additional Reviewers

Dylan Molinié	University Paris Est Creteil, France
Kanishka Tyagi	Aptiv Advanced Engineering Center, USA

Invited Speakers

Georg Weichhart	Primetals Technologies, Austria
Jose Barata	Universidade Nova De Lisboa, Portugal
Fazleena Badurdeen	University of Kentucky, USA

Keynotes

Digital Transformation in Steel Industry

Georg Weichhart

Digital Transformation, Primetals Technologies, Austria

Abstract. Steel is an important resource in today's world. It can be found almost everywhere. With appropriate processing, steel gets properties that allows to use it in many products ranging from cutlery over cars to buildings. The steel industry is facing megatrends that require a respond. An aging society together with Gen Z entering the workforce, require knowledge-transfers and new workplace designs. Decarbonization of the industry is a particular challenge for this industrial sector. Digitalization and data driven technologies are becoming more important to improve the production processes. Primetals Technologies is a leading engineering and steel plant construction company with locations worldwide. It operates as a full liner, capable of delivering production machines and automation for the full metals process ranging from beneficiation, direct reduction, oxygen steelmaking, electric steelmaking, continuous casting, over hot and cold rolling, to final processing. Future machines for this industry will be maintained for more that 20 years and hence have to meet the demands imposed by the megatrends. In this talk a few examples of current innovations at Primetals Technologies are presented.

Brief Biography

Georg Weichhart studied Business Informatics at Vienna University, Lund University and received a PhD and a Venia Docendi from Johannes Kepler University, Linz. He was leading innovation projects and teams at universities, and production companies across Europe. His work in academia and industry focuses on approaches to integration and interoperability of cyber physical production systems, including Distributed Artificial Intelligence, IT/OT Convergence, digital tools for collaboration and Digital Transformation to name a few. In his current role as Digital Transformation Manager at Primetals Technologies he supports the development of innovative solutions for the green transition of the metals industry.

The Long Road Towards SMART Manufacturing: Challenges and Future Prospects

Jose Barata

DEEC, Universidade Nova De Lisboa - Uninova, Monte Da Caparica, Portugal

Abstract. The main objective of this keynote is to discuss the evolution of manufacturing since the first industrial revolution in the 17th century until the current 4th industrial revolution. During this period several manufacturing paradigms have been identified and accepted as important shifts that transform the way manufacturing was being managed and operated with the corresponding impact on how shop floors and supporting activities were operated or controlled. There are two important aspects to discuss in this presentation. The first one is how society, economy and technology determined the requirements and challenges throughout the time, which in turn directly affected the way manufacturing control systems were developed and implemented, or saying it in another way, the prevalent manufacturing paradigm for a certain period. This is to emphasise that the different control systems paradigms used by manufacturing systems are not technologically only driven but very dependent on external factors and, consequently, one can understand better all temporal evolution, and grasp how the technological approaches used by control systems have evolved. Manufacturing paradigm shifts than occur mainly when these external causes provoke breakthroughs that lead to radically new methods and approaches in the manufacturing domain. The second one is discussing the contributions of the author in the road towards the current SMART Manufacturing and Digitalisation paradigm and which were the main keypoints in this endeavor. The presenter has participated in relevant research areas that directly contributed to many of the current main manufacturing trends, in particular the aspects related with considering that a manufacturing system is intrinsically modular and composed of intelligent entities that can be composed to create highly adaptable and reconfigurable production systems. All the current trends such as the Internet of Things (IOT) and Cyber Physical Systems (CPS) are very much related to this aspect. After going through this long road towards SMART Manufacturing current and future prospects will be detailed and analysed.

Brief Biography

Jose Barata is Full Professor at the Electrical and Computing Engineering, Member of the Scientific Committee of the Doctoral Program in Electrical and Computing Engineering at the NOVA-FCT, where he is currently responsible for the courses units Robotics, Systems Integration, Telerobotics and Autonomous Systems, and Robotics Systems and

CIM. He is senior researcher at the CTS – Centre of Technology and Systems at the UNI-NOVA Institute, where he is also coordinating the research group RICS – Robotics and Industrial Complex Systems (http://rics.uninova.pt), that develops research in the areas of service robots and smart industry. RICS has more than 20 members, including 4 PhDs, 8 Phd Students, Master Students, and Technicians. Together with his RICS group he has won the INCM (Mint House and Official Print) INNOVATION Prize that was awarded in May 2018. He is currently the scientific coordinator of the Collaboratory Laboratory aiming to boost Digital Innovation in Agriculture: the SFCOLAB: Smart Farm Collaborative Laboratory. His main research interests are in the area of SMART Manufacturing (Industry 4.0) with particular focus on Complex Adaptive Systems, involving intelligent manufacturing devices, and Robotics systems, focused on multi robot interactions. For Industry 4.0 he has contributed to some of the basic concepts behind Industry 4.0, namely about intelligent modular components or cyber physical systems, and participated in some of the initial industrial demonstrators of these concepts, together with companies such as FESTO, SIEMENS, PHILIPS, and ELECTROLUX. For the Robotics area he has contributed to the development of all terrain, aerial, and surface vehicles. He has published over 250 original papers in international journals and international conferences. He is a member of the IEEE technical committees on Industrial Agents (IES), Self-Organisation and Cybernetics for Informatics (SMC), and Education in Engineering and Industrial Technologies (IES). He is also a member of the IFAC technical committee 4.4 (Cost Oriented Automation). He has more than 7000 citations ((https://scholar.google.pt/citations?user=4G8tKCsAAAAJ&hl=en).

Advancing Supply Chain Resilience and Sustainability Through Novel Metal Additive Manufacturing

Fazleena Badurdeen

University of Kentucky, USA

Abstract. Supply chain competitiveness hinges on the ability to operate successfully under dynamic market conditions and during disruptions caused by events such as geopolitical uncertainties, regional conflicts, and the COVID-19 pandemic. Concurrently, the increased emphasis on the circular economy and sustainable manufacturing necessitates the adoption of better practices to enhance resource conservation, reduce environmental impacts, and value creation for all stakeholders. Technology plays a pivotal role in enhancing supply chain resilience and sustainability. Additive manufacturing (AM), a core technology within the Industry 4.0 portfolio, offers numerous capabilities to address challenges encumbering supply chain competitiveness. AM can enable enhancing supply chain resilience and flexibility while providing opportunities for increased product, process, and system sustainability. Recent advances in solid-state AM (SSAM) technologies for metallic part production offer significant advantages over conventional fusion-based methods including superior product quality, increased functional life, reduced lead time, and cost advantages. This presentation will explore SSAM technologies such as Additive Friction Stir Deposition (AFSD) and Cold Spray AM (CSAM), examining their characteristics, benefits, and potential for advancing various aspects of supply chain operations to enhance resilience and sustainability. The ability to transform existing supply chains, particularly in the domain of large-scale rapid component manufacturing, and the increasing opportunities for customization, while simultaneously offering cost and sustainability benefits, will be discussed.

Brief Biography

Fazleena Badurdeen is the Earl Parker Robinson Chair Professor in Mechanical Engineering at the University of Kentucky (UK). She is the Director for the Online Manufacturing Systems Engineering MS program and a core faculty of UK's Institute for Sustainable Manufacturing. Prof. Badurdeen's research interests are in sustainable and circular product design, measurement systems for circularity and sustainability evaluation, and modeling and analysis of manufacturing systems and supply chains. She has served as principal investigator (PI)/Co-PI for externally funded research in excess of $16 million and has published over 150 peer-reviewed papers. Prof. Badurdeen is the founding Chair of the International Forum on Sustainable Manufacturing and is an Editor for the Resources, Conservation, and Recycling journal and serves on the editorial boards of a number of other journals. Prof. Badurdeen is a Fellow of IISE. She received her PhD in Integrated (Industrial and Mechanical) Engineering and MS in Industrial Engineering, both from Ohio University, USA. She also holds an MBA from the Postgraduate Institute of Management, Sri Lanka and BS in Engineering from the University of Peradeniya, Sri Lanka.

Contents – Part I

Main Event

Contents – Part II

Main Event

**18th International Workshop on Enterprise Integration,
Interoperability and Networking**

Special Session on Industrial AI at the Edge

Main Event

Multi-Agent Deep Q-Network with Layer-Based Communication Channel for Autonomous Internal Logistics Vehicle Scheduling in Smart Manufacturing

Mohammad Feizabadi[1], Arman Hosseini[2], and Zakaria Yahouni[1(✉)]

[1] Univ. Grenoble Alpes, CNRS, Grenoble INP G-SCOP, 38000 Grenoble, France
zakaria.yahouni@grenoble-inp.fr
[2] Systems Engineering, University of Virginia, Charlottesville, VA 22903, USA

Abstract. In smart manufacturing, scheduling autonomous internal logistic vehicles is crucial for optimizing operational efficiency. This paper proposes a multi-agent deep Q-network (MADQN) with a layer-based communication channel (LBCC) to address this challenge. The main goals are to minimize total job tardiness, reduce the number of tardy jobs, and lower vehicle energy consumption. The method is evaluated against nine well-known scheduling heuristics, demonstrating its effectiveness in handling dynamic job shop behaviors like job arrivals and workstation unavailabilities. The approach also proves scalable, maintaining performance across different layouts and larger problem instances, highlighting the robustness and adaptability of MADQN with LBCC in smart manufacturing.

Keywords: Autonomous Internal Logistics · AIV Scheduling · Dynamic Flexible Job Shop · Multi-Agent Deep Q-Network (MADQN) · Layer-Based Communication Channel (LBCC)

1 Introduction

Internal Logistics Vehicles (ILVs) are crucial in enhancing the performance of manufacturing systems by facilitating the movement of products within manufacturing facilities [1]. With the advent of Industry 4.0 technologies, the automation of these movements has been driven by multiple factors, including the improvement of production capacity and the reduction of injuries among human operators who traditionally moved heavy products. Notable technologies in this domain include Automated Guided Vehicles (AGVs) and Autonomous Intelligent Vehicles (AIVs), which autonomously transport products while considering workshop constraints and layouts.

© The Author(s), under exclusive license to Springer Nature Switzerland AG 2025
M. Dassisti et al. (Eds.): IN4PL 2024, CCIS 2372, pp. 3–22, 2025.
https://doi.org/10.1007/978-3-031-80760-2_1

The implementation of these systems presents several challenges that require careful consideration. Key among these challenges is the task of determining the priority for transporting products and selecting the appropriate vehicle for each transportation task. Moreover, these scheduling activities must account for various constraints, including delivery times, vehicle capacity and battery charging requirements, handling breakdowns of vehicles and machines, addressing urgent jobs, etc. Effective vehicle management is therefore crucial to align internal logistics with manufacturing objectives, such as minimizing tardiness of orders, achieving a balanced workload among workstations and vehicles, and optimizing the energy consumption of vehicles. To address these challenges, scheduling strategies consist of a set of rules designed to allocate vehicles to transportation requests while accounting for these complex constraints.

This paper addresses these challenges by introducing a multi-agent deep reinforcement learning approach along with a layer-based communication channel to dynamically allocate vehicles to transportation requests within a dynamically changing environment. Drawing from insights discussed in prior research by [2], which implemented a deep Q-network technique, this study makes several notable contributions. In the proposed multi-agent system, each job is instantiated as an individual agent, operating in a decentralized manner. These agents interact with one another to optimize their reward policies within a deep Q-network algorithm. By leveraging this multi-agent framework, the system gains enhanced capabilities to navigate the complexities inherent in a dynamic manufacturing environment, characterized by the dynamic arrival of jobs and occurrences of workstation breakdowns/unavailabilities.

The principal manufacturing objectives targeted by this approach encompass the minimization of total job tardiness, number of tardy jobs and the reduction of vehicle energy consumption. To assess the efficacy of our proposed methodology, we conducted a comparative analysis against various heuristic methods. Results from this evaluation demonstrate the superior performance of our multi-agent deep reinforcement learning method over traditional heuristics for the considered objectives.

The paper is structured as follows: Sect. 2 delves into the literature, exploring related work regarding scheduling ILVs. Section 3 encompasses the problem description. Section 4 outlines the proposed multi-agent deep reinforcement learning approach. The subsequent sections are devoted to the experimental results, conducting analysis, and drawing conclusions.

2   Related Work

In this section, the state of the art in shop scheduling with intelligent transporters is first presented. Following this, the evolution and application of artificial intelligence and machine learning methods in these problems are reviewed. Finally, the current state of multi-agent systems applied to intelligent transporter scheduling in manufacturing shops is examined, with emphasis on the importance of communication between different agents and the integration of multi-agent systems with machine learning.

2.1 Integrated Shop and Transporters Scheduling

Integrated shop and transporter scheduling is a comprehensive approach aimed at optimizing both the production schedule within a manufacturing shop and the logistics of material handling and transport. This approach considers the interdependencies between the resource assignment for production tasks to workstations and the transfer of jobs via vehicles such as AGV or AIV.

In the study [3], the authors addressed two-machine flow shop and open shop scheduling problems where workpieces are transported via a single vehicle. For each problem, they proposed a heuristic algorithm aimed at minimizing the makespan. Notably, the transporter's capacity is assumed to be sufficient to transport any number of jobs, thereby neglecting the potential capacity constraints of vehicles in real-world scenarios.

More recent studies have increased the complexity of interstage transportation by considering multiple vehicles available in the field. This added complexity aims to better reflect real-world scenarios where multiple vehicles are used to transport workpieces between machines. The study [4], tackled the multi-AGV flow shop scheduling problem using Q-learning to optimize makespan and minimize average job delays. However, this study does not consider the charging consumption of AGVs, which is a significant limitation in real-world scenarios. In [5], authors explored the impact of AGV charging constraints on the scheduling of flexible manufacturing units with multiple AGVs. A genetic algorithm was employed to minimize the completion time while balancing AGV loads and reducing charging times. Their model effectively schedules AGVs to complete tasks and reduces charging wait times. However, this study overlooks the variations in job weights and their effects on transfer time and AGV charging consumption.

In real-world scenarios, another significant challenge complicating AGV scheduling is their load capacity, which is often overlooked in most studies. In [6], authors considered transporter capacity limitations and layout rearrangement, proposing an improved non-dominated sorting genetic algorithm with hybrid local search (INSGA-HLS). Their approach successfully minimized exit time, labor cost, worker workload, and transportation time.

2.2 Artificial Intelligence Application in Scheduling

In the past few decades, there has been substantial growth in artificial intelligence (AI) applications within manufacturing, largely attributed to the accessibility of data facilitated by the Internet of Things (IoT). Supervised learning and reinforcement learning are among the most used methods in scheduling problems [7]. Supervised learning relies on sample data, requiring data collection through real-world cases or simulations. A combination of supervised learning and linear programming was presented by [8]. A mixed-integer linear programming was initially employed to obtain the optimal solution, which served as the foundation for the supervised learning training. Subsequently, a random forest classifier was introduced to predict the priority of jobs. However, the study does not address the adaptability of the algorithm in dynamic environments with factors like machine breakdowns or stochastic processing times. The authors [9] employed multiple linear regression to predict the optimal scheduling rule at each decision step in a dynamic job shop with a single AIV transporter. Their proposed method outperformed heuristic approaches in minimizing the makespan. It is important to note that supervised learning methods require substantial data collection and are not well-suited for real-time decision-making processes.

Among the array of advancements in machine learning techniques, Deep Q-Networks stand out for their simplicity in implementation and their capacity to tackle complex problems by amalgamating deep learning with Q-learning [10]. Reinforcement learning (RL) is recognized as a broader framework encompassing decision-making tasks [11]. A key distinction between RL and other AI algorithms lies in the learning mechanism, where RL learns through interactions with a dynamic environment, contrasting with supervised and unsupervised learning methods that rely on sample data for their learning process.

The authors [12], employed a Deep Q Network (DQN) to improve adaptive scheduling in dynamic job shops. The DQN algorithm selects actions from a set of ten heuristic dispatching rules. Their method demonstrated superior performance compared to single dispatching rules and traditional Q-learning. However, it is important to note that this work focused on a single performance indicator-total job tardiness-thereby overlooking the complexity of managing multiple objectives, which is more representative of real-world manufacturing environments.

The study [13], utilized Deep Q-network (DQN) for online scheduling of a job shop, aiming to optimize multiple objectives including makespan, production cost, and machine utilization. Their approach effectively handled dynamic system behaviors such as urgent orders and machine failures and outperformed common scheduling methods such as Shortest Processing Time (SPT) heuristic and genetic algorithm. However, this study overlooked a significant complexity of real-world production systems: the optimization of job transportation. Modern manufacturing sites are equipped with intelligent vehicles, introducing new challenges for the production system. In study [14], the authors addressed transportation optimization on a flexible shop floor. They employed a Deep Q-Network (DQN) to schedule multiple AGVs in real-time, with the aim of minimizing the delay ratio and makespan. Two main decisions were handled: dispatching jobs and AGV selection. Their method outperformed previous approaches like AHP dynamic scheduling and traditional RL methods such as Q-learning and Sarsa. However, the study did not consider optimizing AGV charging consumption as an objective, nor did it address realistic limitations related to AGV charging, such as recharging times and policies, due to their added complexities.

In summary, the literature review highlights the significant advancements and applications of artificial intelligence, particularly in manufacturing scheduling. Several gaps are identified, including the optimization of multiple transportation vehicles with specific capacity constraints, considering their recharging times and policies, addressing multiple objectives, and accounting for unforeseen events such as machine breakdowns for robust optimization.

To address these challenges, DQN offer a robust solution, merging deep learning with Q-learning to address complex scheduling challenges. Given its simplicity in implementation and proven effectiveness across various scheduling scenarios, our study adopts the DQN approach. The principles and workings of the Deep Q-Network are elaborated in the subsequent subsection.

2.3 Deep Q-Network

Deep Q-Network (DQN) agent learns through experimenting within an environment[15]. The base framework for such interaction is the Markov Decision Process which is represented by the tuple (S, A, R) where:

S: Stands for the state space, $s_t \in S$ represents the state at time t

A: Stands for the action space, $a_t \in A$ represents action taken at time t considering s_t

R: stands for the reward function, $r_t \in R(s_t, a_t)$ represents the reward received by the agent after taking action a_t in the state s_t

At each time step t, the agent takes the action a_t and transitions from state s_t to state s_{t+1}. The agent receives an immediate reward $r_t = R(s_t, a_t, s_{t+1})$ upon reaching state s_{t+1} which indicates the performance of the agent. The objective of an RL algorithm is to maximize the cumulative rewards [16]. To achieve this objective, a DQN algorithm aims to approximate an optimal Q function of a given environment. The optimal Q function $Q^*(s, a)$ represents the maximum expected cumulative reward that agent can obtain. Formally the Q function can be defined as:

$$Q(s, a) = \mathbb{E}\left[\sum_{t=0}^{\infty} \gamma^t r_{t+1} \mid s_0 = s, a_0 = a\right] \tag{1}$$

Where $\mathbb{E}$ denotes the expected value, γ is the discount factor which lies in range [0,1], determining the importance of future rewards. And r_{t+1} is the expected reward at the next time step. The optimal Q function $Q^*(s, a)$ is formulated as:

$$Q^*(s, a) = \max_{\pi} Q^{\pi}(s, a) \tag{2}$$

To approximate $Q^*(s, a)$, DQN uses a deep neural network parametrized by θ, which is denoted by $Q^{\theta}(s, a)$. The network takes the state s_t as input and outputs the Q values for all possible actions in the space. The Q function is approximated using the temporal difference (TD) loss function [17]. The main idea is to minimize the difference between the predicted Q values and the target Q values, which are computed using the following equation:

$$Loss_{DQN}(\theta) = \mathbb{E}_{(s_t, a_t, r_t, s'_{t+1})}[y - Q^{\theta^-}(s_t, a_t)]^2 \tag{3}$$

Where $y = r_t + \gamma * max_{a'}(Q(s'_{t+1}, a'; \theta^-))$is the target value , γ is the discount factor and θ^- represents the parameters of the target network, which are copied periodically from the primary network to stabilize training.

2.4   Multi Agent Systems

The review study conducted by [18] investigated the use of multi-agent reinforcement learning in smart factories, suggesting that multi-agent systems, when combined with AI techniques are the most appropriate for such environments. Furthermore, [19] provides a general background on single-agent and multi-agent deep reinforcement learning, highlighting the challenges and advantages of multi-agent systems over single-agent ones, particularly in wireless communications.

One of the prominent challenges of Multi-Agent Deep Reinforcement Learning is the non-stationarity of the environment, which refers to the consistent variations in other agents' parameters. In the study [20], authors targeted communication efficiency in multi-UAV cooperative trajectory planning. They applied a Double Stream Attention Multi-Agent Actor-Critic (DSAAC) algorithm. The study needs to enhance the algorithm's adaptability to a broader range of dynamic scenarios and complex operational conditions.

In the study [21], a Multi-Agent Reinforcement Learning algorithm, specifically DQN, was employed to optimize operations. The agents within this system leverage Internet of Things (IoT) technology to facilitate inter-agent communication. The primary objectives of the study are to minimize the makespan and balance the total workload across the system. The results indicate that the distributed architecture inherent to the proposed approach effectively manages the high dimensionality characteristic of smart factory environments, outperforming traditional centralized methods.

The authors [22] introduced a novel decentralized multi-agent system approach incorporating capacity constraints for AGVs. The agents collaborate in a decentralized manner to assign product transport tasks to each other and determine their routes. The results demonstrate that te proposed approach yields competitive outcomes compared to the Mixed-Integer Linear Programming model, highlighting its potential as a promising decentralized approach. However, the study primarily focuses on capacity constraints related to the weight of products, rather than the effects of transporting multiple products with a single AGV. In the study [23], the authors address a job scheduling problem in a resource preemption environment using a policy-based Multi-Agent Reinforcement Learning approach. In this method, each job is considered an intelligent agent, utilizing a separate policy network. Additionally, a shared mixed Q-network is proposed to compute the global loss, fostering cooperation among the agents. Nevertheless, This study need to investigate the integration of diverse multi-agent scheduling algorithms to tackle a wider range of Job Shop Scheduling Problems (JSSPs) and to enhance model generalization through advanced representation learning techniques.

In summary, the literature review underscores the significant advancements and applications of AI in manufacturing scheduling, with a particular focus on the efficacy of multi-agent techniques and Deep Q-Networks in addressing complex challenges. Given the proven benefits of DQNs, our approach leverages multi-agent DQN to optimize Internal Logistics Vehicles scheduling.

3   Problem Description

For illustrative purposes, a case study is presented of a manufacturing system consisting of four assembly workstations (WS1, WS2, WS3, and WS4), a storage location, two charging stations, and two AIVs. These vehicles are utilized to transport raw materials from storage to workstations and to facilitate the movement of subassemblies and products between workstations.

Four types of products (P1, P2, P3, and P4) are considered, each requiring processing at specific set of workstations. Each product undergoing processing at a workstation is referred to as an operation (the term job is also used for a product, which consists of a set of operations). The manufacturing shop floor is structured as a flexible job shop, where each product follows its own unique routing through the workstations. Additionally, the flexibility of the job shop allows certain operations to be handled by any one of several possible workstations rather than a single designated workstation. Table 1 provides an overview of the different routings and workstation possibilities for each product operation.

Table 1. Routing of each product.

Products	Routs of Products
P1	(WS1/WS3) -> (WS3/WS4) -> (WS2/WS3)
P2	(WS1/WS4) -> (WS1/WS4) -> (WS2/WS3)
P3	(WS4/WS5) -> (WS1/WS5) -> (WS2/WS3)
P4	(WS1/WS4) -> (WS1/WS2) -> (WS3/WS4)

In real-world scenarios, manufacturing shops are not static; they must accommodate dynamic events such as the continuous arrival of jobs and the potential breakdowns of machines at workstations. These dynamic factors are considered in our problem.

The goal of this study is to avoid tardiness to prevent penalty payments and optimize the use of AIVs to minimize energy consumption costs. As these orders arrive, each job (product) is scheduled individually, necessitating two key decisions as illustrated in Fig. 1:

1. For each operation of a product, assign a workstation when multiple options are available.
2. For each product transfer to the designated workstation, assign an AIV

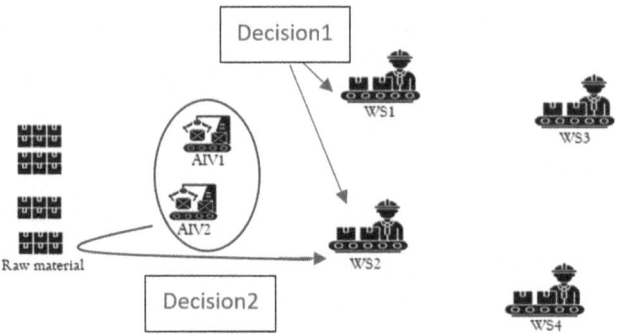

Fig. 1. Illustration of the two decisions.

These two decisions must account for several constraints, including the remaining energy of each AIV, its loading capacity, the urgency of orders, the availability of AIVs, and the need to handle unexpected events such as the unavailability of workstations. Therefore, taking these two decisions ensures that products arrive at the workstations in a specific order and can be then processed. Transportation is influenced by the location and status of the AIVs. Consequently, these decisions directly impact the tardiness of jobs and the energy consumption of the AIVs. By optimizing these allocations, job tardiness can be effectively reduced, and energy usage minimized, thereby enhancing overall operational efficiency.

The job shop scheduling problem is known to be NP-hard [24], and the additional complexity of allocating AIVs further exacerbates the problem. The challenge lies in determining the optimal allocation of AIVs and workstations such that the scheduling of jobs at workstations is optimal, all while managing the transportation and dynamic constraints. Consequently, advanced strategies are essential to effectively balance the multiple objectives and constraints inherent in this problem.

4   Multi-Agent Deep Q-Network (MADQN) Approach with Layar-Based Communication Channel (LBCC)

In this section, a decentralized multi-agent Deep Q-Network (MADQN) approach is proposed to solve the illustrated problem described in Sect. 3 involving AIV transporters. Furthermore, a layer-based communication channel (LBCC) is introduced and employed to deal with the non-stationarity of the multi-agent system. The primary objectives are to minimize total job tardiness, the number of tardy jobs, and AIVs energy consumption. This approach addresses two types of decisions: *workstation-selection* and *AIV-selection*. Each job is considered an agent equipped with two deep Q-networks, one for each decision type.

All available jobs interact with the workshop environment simultaneously, resulting in the formation of queues for both AIVs and workstations. It is noteworthy that the queues for each AIV and workstation are managed based on a First-In-FirstOut (FIFO) policy, wherein jobs that are requested earlier are given priority.

For each job agent, two Deep Q-networks (DQN) are developed: one for *workstation-selection* and the other for *AIV-selection*. Each DQN is designed based on a Partially Observable Markov Decision Process. Status of each job are illustrated in Fig. 2.

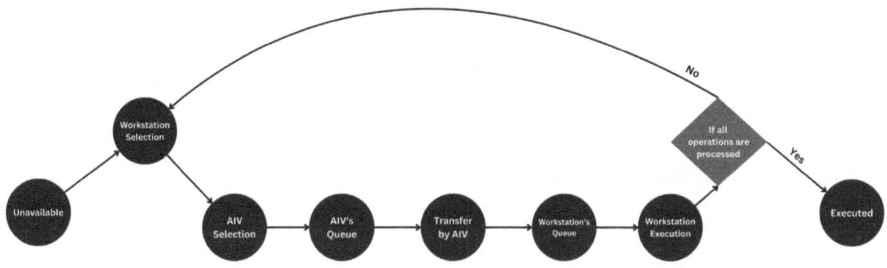

Fig. 2. Graphical representation of the job's status.

The observations for each DQN are provided as follows:

Workstation-Selection DQN Observation:

- Queue length of workstations
- Distance of workstations from the job
- Workstations' busy time percentage
- Job's next processing time
- Job's current tardiness
- Job's remaining processing time
- Current time step

AIV-Selection DQN Observation:

- Queue length of AIVs
- Distance of AIVs from the job
- AIVs' battery percentage
- Job's current tardiness
- Job's remaining processing time
- Current time step

4.1   DQN Characteristics: Actions, Rewards, Neaural Network Features

The action of the *workstation-selection* DQN is to select the appropriate work-station for each available job. Similarly, the action of the *AIV-selection* DQN is to select the appropriate AIV for transferring the job to the selected worksta-tion. It is crucial to manage the variation in the action space dimension for the *workstation-selection* DQN at each step, which necessitates the use of a mask for the current operation. This mask delineates the feasible actions (workstations) available. For instance, if product/job P1 can only be processed on workstations WS2 or WS4 for its first operation among all m workstations, other workstations are masked out except WP2 and WP4. Consequently, the network's output is adjusted to $-\infty$ where no viable action exists (masked options). This adjust-ment to $-\infty$ is advantageous as it allows the objective function, which employs an argmax, to disregard the masked options.

At each step, two immediate rewards are allocated to the agent, one to the *AIV-selection* DQN and another to the *workstation-selection* DQN. The *AIV-selection* DQN receives a reward immediately upon completing the transfer of a product to the designated workstation. This reward is computed based on the energy consumption of the AIV, encompassing the period from when the AIV commences the job pick-up process until it delivers the product. This reward is assigned a negative value. The *workstation-selection* DQN obtains a reward immediately after completing the execution of the product's operation. This reward is calculated based on the current tardiness of the product upon finishing that operation, which is computed as follows for each product:

$$CurrentTardiness_i = max(0, k_i \times RPT_i + CT - DueDate_i), \quad i = 1, 2, \ldots, n; \tag{4}$$

Where RPT_i stands for the Remaining Processing Time of $product_i$, CT is the current time of the simulation, and k is a coefficient used to account for the transfer times of the job. This reward, given as a negative value, reflects the deviation from the due date, thereby incentivizing the minimization of prod-uct/job tardiness.

Moreover, a final reward is assigned to each job agent for both DQNs when the product is executed completely (i.e., all operations of the product are com-pleted). The *final reward* is calculated based on the lateness of each product after the product is executed. For each $product_i$ lateness is defined as:

$$Lateness_i = CompletionTime_i - DueDate_i \quad i = 1, 2, \ldots, n; \tag{5}$$

$$FinalReward_i = Lateness_i \times (-1) \quad i = 1, 2, \ldots, n; \tag{6}$$

The structure of all networks is identical. A fully connected deep neural network with five hidden layers is utilized, with each layer consisting of 10 nodes and employing the Tanh activation function. It is noteworthy that all inputs for the agents are normalized. Stochastic Gradient Descent is employed to optimize the Mean Squared Error loss function. The learning rates are uniformly set to 0.01, and the discount factors are set to 0.9.

4.2   Layer Base Communication Channel (LBCC)

A key advantage of multi-agent systems lies in their capacity for inter-agent communication, which substantially enhances system performance. In the proposed approach, the uniform structure of all agents facilitates the creation of a communication channel across corresponding layers. This communication channel is integrated into the networks of the job agents' DQNs (*workstation-selection* and *AIV-selection*). Specifically, within each hidden layer of a job agent's network, the input to that hidden layer, originating from the output of the preceding layer, is combined with the output of the same hidden layer from all other job agents. This design ensures that each job agent is aware of the outputs of other agents at the same level of the hidden layer. Such an integrated communication mechanism promotes effective information sharing and coordination among agents, enhancing overall system efficiency. The mathematical representation of the communication channel is provided below:

$$h_{out,i}^{(l)} = \tanh\left(W^{(l)} \cdot \left(h_{in,i}^{(l)} \cup H^{(l)}\right) + b^{(l)}\right) \quad i = 1, 2, \ldots, n; \quad (7)$$

Where:

- $h_{out,i}^{(l)}$ is the output of l-th layer of the i-th job agent.
- $W^{(l)}$ is the weight matrix for the l-th layer.
- $h_{in,i}^{(l)}$ is the input to the l-th layer of the i-th agent.
- $H^{(l)} = \cup_{j\neq i} h_j^{(l)}$ represents the union of the outputs from the same hidden layer l of all other job agents j except i.
- $b^{(l)}$ is the bias vector for the l-th layer.
- tanh is the Tanh activation function applied to the linear combination of the inputs, weights, and biases.

As an example, Fig. 3 illustrates the communication mechanism within the *workstation-selection* networks of job agents at the third hidden layer. Specifically, for job J_k, the input to its third hidden layer is integrated with the outputs from the third hidden layer of all other jobs, ranging from J_1 to J_n and $1 < k < n$.

5   Experimentation and Results

5.1   Case Study Data

The case study described in Sect. 3, which involves four products and four workstations, is used to experiment the MADQN approach. In this example, each product can have various numbers of job arrivals (each job represent one product). It is assumed that the number of jobs for all product types is equal. For instance, in the case of a total of 60 job arrivals, each of the four product types has 15 job arrivals. The time between the arrival of jobs is assumed to follow an exponential distribution with a rate parameter of $\lambda = 5$ time units.

Dealing with tardiness as two of the three objectives requires having due dates for each job. In this case study, a due date generator is used based on the

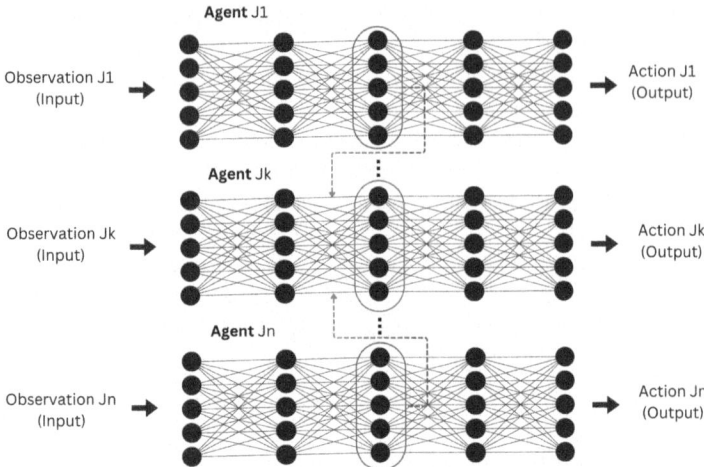

Fig. 3. Communication channel example for the third layer of *workstation-selection* network.

work of [25] for each job. The due date of job i is computed as shown in the following equation:

$$DueDate_i = ArrivalTime_i + T \sum MeanProcessingTime_i, \quad i = 1, 2, \dots, n;$$

(8)

Essentially, the due date is equal to the arrival time of the job plus the total required processing time for that job. T is a coefficient to take into account the transfer time of jobs between workstations. This coefficient follows a normal distribution with parameters defined as follows :

$$\mu = \frac{Nb\_Jobs}{4} \quad , \quad \sigma = 4$$

As the problem is a flexible job shop, jobs have the flexibility to be processed on different workstations for their various operations. Therefore, the processing time for each operation of the job is determined by the mean of the processing times of that operation on the possible workstations. For example, if one operation can be processed on either workstation WS1 with a processing time of 8 or on workstation WS2 with a processing time of 4 min, $MeanProcssingTime$ for that operation will be 6 min.

To enhance the dynamic behavior of the job shop, machine breakdowns or in this case workstation unavailabilities are also considered. An exponential distribution is applied for both the time interval between two unavailabilities (TBI) and the time required for fixing the problem (workstation to be available) (TRF) [26]. The parameters for TBI (time between two inspections) and TRF (time required for fixing) are set to $\lambda_{\text{TIB}} = 200$ and $\lambda_{\text{TRF}} = 50$.

Another important aspect is the layout of the job shop, which is defined by the distances between workstations, the raw material storage location, and the charging stations. To generate different layouts, a uniform random variable between 10 and 50 is used for each transfer time, reflecting various possible distances and assuming that both AIVs have the same speed.

Each of the two AIVs is set with a loading capacity of two, and each job/product occupies one out of the two capacity units of the AIVs. In other words, AIVs are capable of transferring two products simultaneously. The transfer policy is that AIVs fill their capacity if there are enough requests; otherwise, they collect the available requests, carry all picked-up products to their destinations, and then become idle at the last destination, ready for the next transfer.

There are two charging stations each with a capacity of one AIV at the same time. AIVs are sent to the charging station when their battery level falls below 40%. The location of the charging stations can vary across different layout setups. The charging consumption of the AIVs is assumed to correlate with their status (moving or stopped) and the number of product they are carrying. The energy consumption percentage pattern of AIVs is provided in Table 2.

Table 2. AIV Consumption Based on Carrying Load.

Condition	Consumption
Not moving	0.01%
Moving, carrying 0 product	0.02%
Moving, carrying 1 product	0.05%
Moving, carrying 2 products	0.10%

5.2   Results

The proposed case study is unique and novel due to the added complexities, constraints, and dynamic events. Since there is no existing solution in the literature to compare our approach with, nine heuristics are provided to evaluate the performance of the proposed MADQN method. These heuristics are generated by mixing three dispatching rules for *workstation-selection* and three rules for *AIV-selection*. The three dispatching heuristics for *workstation-selection* are as follows:

– **SPT (Shortest Processing Time).** Workstation with the Shortest Processing Time is selected for each product. It is worth noting that the processing time of each operation varies depending on the workstation performing the process.
– **SQL (Shortest Queue Length).** Workstation with the shortest queue length has priority.

- **SWL$_W$ (Shortest Workload).** Workstation with the Shortest Workload or shortest percentage of busy time has priority.

The three dispatching rules for *AIV-selection* are:

- **MC (Most Charge).** Select the AIV with the most remaining charge.
- **STT (Shortest Transfer Time).** Select the AIV with the Shortest Transfer Time (from its current location to the location of the first product to pick up).
- **SWL$_A$ (Shortest Workload).** Choose the AIV with the Shortest Workload or shortest percentage of busy time.

The effectiveness of the proposed approach is evaluated based on jobs scalability. Scalability is typically assessed by evaluating the method across different ranges of arriving products. As the number of products increases, the complexity of the scheduling problem also arises, making it more challenging to optimize the three objectives. A set of simulations with an increasing number of jobs (20, 40, 60, 80, and 100) is conducted. For each job count, a unique layout is considered, which is based on the transfer times between workstations and process times of operations on workstations. This layout remains consistent for each specific job count but varies between different job counts. The simulation is executed 100 times (each time with different values of processing times and time arrivals of products/jobs).

The objectives of the problems are set to the total tardiness of all products, the number of tardy products, and the total AIVs' charging consumption. For each objective, the mean results of all 100 simulations are collected for each job count. Based on Tables 3, 4, and 5, where best results are highlighted in bold, the proposed MADQN method outperforms all nine heuristic combinations across all three objectives. Importantly, the results remain stable as the number of jobs increases, even when the job shop layouts change and different processing times are used. This stability demonstrates the scalability of the proposed approach.

Table 3. Mean of total tardiness for each 100 simulation of n jobs.

Jobs	STT.SPT	STT.SQL	STT.SWL$_W$	SWL$_A$.SPT	SWL$_A$.SQL	SWL$_A$.SWL$_W$	MC.SPT	MC.SQL	MC.SWL$_W$	MADQN
20	4084.7	3755.9	5382.5	4537.6	3626.2	5134.3	7385.0	4068.2	5148.8	**2586.7**
40	33520.4	30683.9	31601.8	21104.5	34829.9	30927.5	28467.1	37616.1	38026.5	**7917.2**
60	46410.3	57723.2	74085.8	26591.7	13932.4	43301.0	32431.8	28510.7	57797.8	**10229.2**
80	96602.7	146211.9	198746.6	35938.4	58552.9	83505.9	41344.1	48923.0	75331.7	**14546.6**
100	45686.28	110800.91	134116.17	32336.17	80030.2	80112.83	38905.59	77558.05	91913.11	**19363.87**

To provide a comprehensive comparison between the distribution of results obtained by MADQN and other heuristics, box plots for all three objectives are presented for a product count of 40. Due to space constraints, plots for other product counts are not included. Figures 4, 5, and 6 demonstrate the notable disparity in the distribution of results between MADQN and other heuristics. Regarding total tardiness, a comparison of the median values reveals

Table 4. Mean of number of tardy jobs for each 100 simulation of n jobs.

Jobs	STT.SPT	STT.SQL	STT.SWLw	SWLA.SPT	SWLA.SQL	SWLA.SWLw	MC.SPT	MC.SQL	MC.SWLw	MADQN
20	14.76	14.32	16.20	16.53	14.45	17.49	17.95	15.63	17.01	**12.40**
40	32.99	37.91	38.44	34.52	38.20	37.28	34.28	36.81	36.46	**19.32**
60	42.75	42.54	47.77	42.41	30.94	48.54	42.64	36.98	48.46	**24.39**
80	58.10	71.99	74.80	47.61	58.32	64.85	47.10	50.78	56.51	**36.74**
100	62.56	70.96	74.64	57.4	74.13	74.16	56	66.15	67.67	**43.61**

Table 5. Mean of total energy consumptions for AIVs for each 100 simulation of n jobs.

Jobs	STT.SPT	STT.SQL	STT.SWLw	SWLA.SPT	SWLA.SQL	SWLA.SWLw	MC.SPT	MC.SQL	MC.SWLw	MADQN
20	95.77	92.37	102.12	98.15	91.19	105.33	103.71	88.80	101.64	**76.86**
40	235.24	262.89	261.62	236.13	283.86	270.66	241.24	270.53	273.47	**166.76**
60	320.55	341.63	393.10	320.58	281.60	370.85	319.18	291.34	392.81	**240.97**
80	444.40	457.23	562.18	395.93	444.85	508.96	399.52	417.69	476.92	**323.53**
100	410.69	508.54	537.94	401.46	498.74	511.77	403.18	488.30	518.54	**348.04**

that MADQN is centered around 5000 time-units, while the best-performing heuristic, $SWL_A.SPT$, is centered around 20000 time-units. This approximate 15000 time-unit gap in tardiness, can have a significant impact on manufacturing delay costs. Furthermore, the small variations in values for MADQN are reflected in the box plot, which shows that quartiles are close together. This minimal variation underscores the reliability and stability of the results across the 100 experiments.

For the second objective as shown in Fig. 5, the number of tardy jobs, MADQN values are clustered around 18, while the best performing heuristic in this regard $STT.SPT$, centers around 33. With 40 jobs, employing MADQN enables the timely delivery of approximately 15 more jobs compared to the best heuristic, which can have a substantial impact on the costs associated with tardy jobs.

In the case of the third objective, total AIV energy consumption, MADQN results center around 163% of battery percentage consumption, whereas heuristics, $STT.SPT$ and $SWL_A.SPT$, centers around 235% (Fig. 6). This difference not only indicates energy savings but also translates into time savings within the job shop.

According to the recharging policy assumption, AIVs are sent to the charging station when their battery level falls below 40%. In other words, each 60% battery consumption necessitates a recharge. With the $SWL_A.SPT$ heuristic, approximately 4 recharging instances are required, while with MADQN, only around 2 recharges occur. Considering that each recharge takes approximately 30 time units and temporarily suspends transfers between workstations, the reduced number of recharges with MADQN contributes to lower job tardiness.

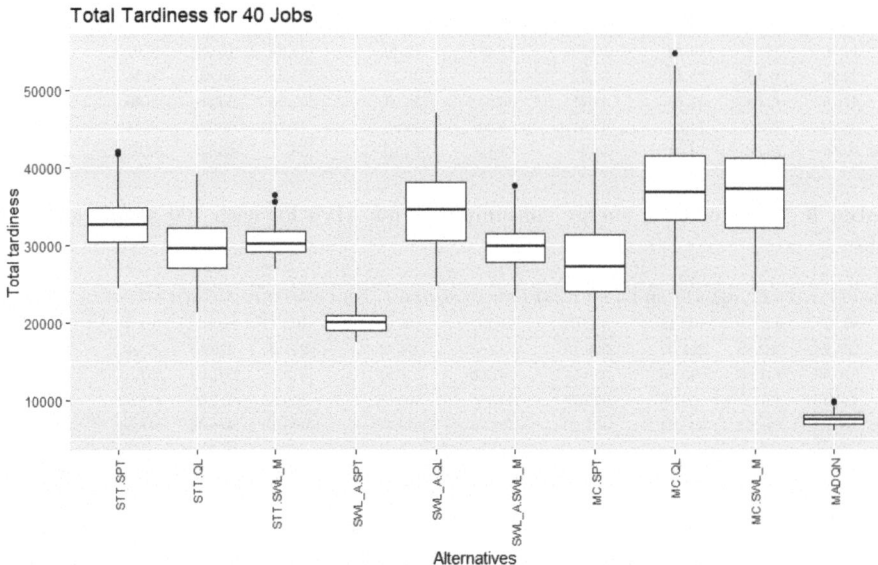

Fig. 4. Total tardiness of 40 product counts.

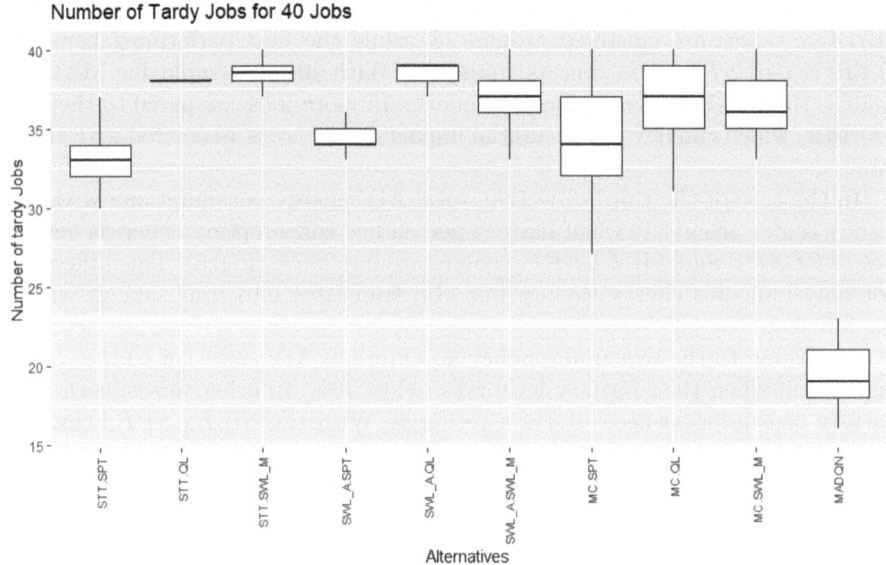

Fig. 5. Number of tardy jobs of 40 product counts.

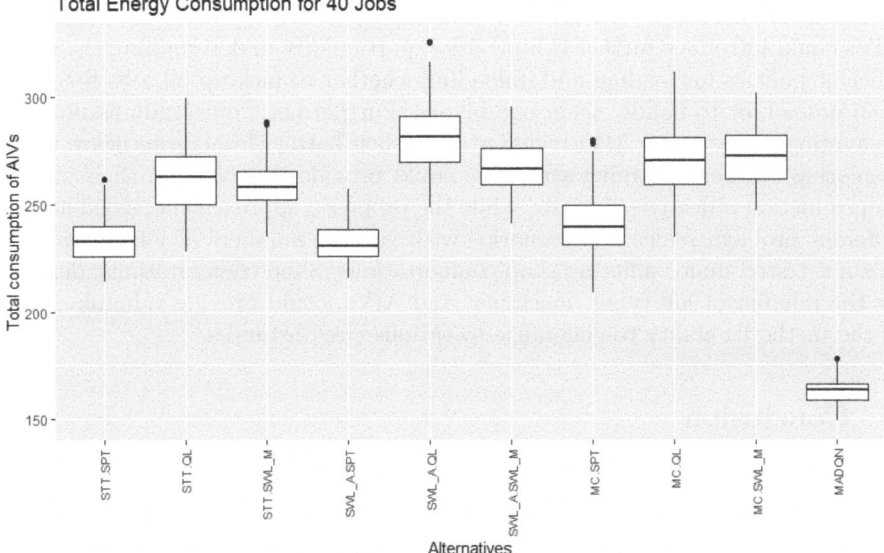

Fig. 6. AIVs total energy consumption.

5.3   Discussion

The proposed approach effectively addresses several key challenges in real-world production systems, particularly in flexible job shop scheduling where multiple routing options and dynamic events, such as machine breakdowns, stochastic job arrivals, and variable processing times, complicate decision-making. The integration of Autonomous Intelligent Vehicles (AIVs) for material handling, while enhancing efficiency, introduces constraints like energy management and battery recharging. Notably, our study incorporates the often-overlooked capability of AIVs to handle multiple jobs simultaneously, which significantly improves both energy efficiency and job tardiness.

Our application of reinforcement learning, specifically the Multi-Agent Deep Q-Network (MADQN), demonstrates the method's suitability for real-time scheduling, offering a rapid response to dynamic changes. While it may not match the precision of exact optimization methods, it provides a favorable balance between speed and accuracy, particularly in large-scale problems.

However, this study has limitations. The uniqueness of the case study, with its complex constraints, meant there was no established benchmark, such as linear programming or metaheuristics, for direct comparison. We only tested one reinforcement learning method, DQN, though other methods like policy-based approaches could be worth exploring. Additionally, we employed a layer-based communication structure between agents, but other communication methods, such as Graph Neural Networks (GNN) or attention mechanisms, which are increasingly applied in the literature, could also be considered.

While we accounted for AIVs with a capacity of two jobs, higher-capacity AIVs could introduce further complexities, particularly in determining the most efficient policies for loading and unloading-whether to pick up all jobs first and then unload, or to handle them one by one. Furthermore, our study assumed a recharging policy where AIVs recharge when their battery level drops below 40%. Exploring different charging strategies could provide insights into their effects on production objectives. Finally, while the proposed approach succeeded across different problem scales and scenarios with varying numbers of job arrivals, it was not tested under differing shop configurations. Shop configurations, defined by the number of job types, machines, and AIVs, could provide valuable proof of the method's ability to generalize to various circumstances.

6   Conclusion

This study presents a solution for scheduling autonomous internal logistic vehicles in smart manufacturing environments using multi-agent deep Q-network (MADQN) with a layer-based communication channel (LBCC). The proposed approach effectively addresses three key objectives: minimizing the total tardiness of jobs, reducing the number of tardy jobs, and decreasing the total energy consumption of vehicles. Our comprehensive analysis, comparing the method against nine well-known heuristics, highlights the superior performance and adaptability of the MADQN with LBCC.

The method's compatibility with flexible job shops exhibiting dynamic behaviors, such as dynamic job arrivals and workstation unavailabilities, underscores its practical applicability. Furthermore, the proposed approach ensures consistent results across various job shop layouts and larger problem instances, making it an adaptable tool for real-world applications. For practical applications, it is recommended to integrate the proposed method into fleet management software. This integration allows the algorithm to offer decision recommendations each time a new order is received. These recommendations can be reviewed by experts to finalize vehicle and machine selection decisions, thereby improving both the efficiency and reliability of the decision-making process.

Despite the promising results of this study, several avenues for future research are evident. Future work should explore a broader range of reinforcement learning methods, including policy-based approaches, to enhance the robustness of the proposed solution. Additionally, investigating alternative communication methods for multi-agent systems, such as attention mechanisms, could provide new insights and improve performance. The study focused on AIVs with a capacity of two jobs, but exploring higher-capacity AIVs could address new challenges in optimizing loading and unloading strategies. Different recharging policies for AIVs should also be evaluated to assess their impact on production efficiency. Lastly, testing the proposed approach across various shop configurations, defined by different numbers of job types, machines, and AIVs, could validate its generalizability and effectiveness in diverse settings.

References

1. Soufi, Z., David, P., Yahouni, Z.: Generation of material handling system alternatives: a constraints satisfaction problem approach. Comput. Ind. **155**, 104045 (2024)
2. Hosseini, A., Feizabadi, M., Yahouni, Z.: Integrated dynamic flexible job shop and AIV scheduling: deep reinforcement learning approach considering AIV charging and capacity constraints. In: Thürer, M., Riedel, R., von Cieminski, G., Romero, D. (eds.) Advances in Production Management Systems. Production Management Systems for Volatile, Uncertain, Complex, and Ambiguous Environments, pp. 522–536. Springer, Cham (2024). https://doi.org/10.1007/978-3-031-71645-4_35
3. Lee, C.-Y., Strusevich, V.A.: Two-machine shop scheduling with an uncapacitated interstage transporter. IIE Trans. **37**(8), 725–736 (2005)
4. Xue, T., Zeng, P., Yu, H.: A reinforcement learning method for multi-AGV scheduling in manufacturing. In: 2018 IEEE International Conference on Industrial Technology (ICIT), pp. 1557–1561. IEEE (2018)
5. Li, J., Cheng, W., Lai, K.K., Ram, B.: Multi-AGV flexible manufacturing cell scheduling considering charging. Mathematics **10**(19), 3417 (2022)
6. Li, Y., Chen, X., An, Y., Zhao, Z., Cao, H., Jiang, J.: Integrating machine layout, transporter allocation and worker assignment into job-shop scheduling solved by an improved non-dominated sorting genetic algorithm. Comput. Ind. Eng. **179**, 109169 (2023)
7. Seeger, P.M., Yahouni, Z., Alpan, G.: Literature review on using data mining in production planning and scheduling within the context of cyber physical systems. J. Ind. Inf. Integr. **28**, 100371 (2022)
8. Jun, S., Lee, S., Chun, H.: Learning dispatching rules using random forest in flexible job shop scheduling problems. Int. J. Prod. Res. **57**(10), 3290–3310 (2019)
9. Hosseini, A., Yahouni, Z., Feizabadi, M.: Scheduling AIV transporter using simulation-based supervised learning: a case study on a dynamic job-shop with three workstations. IFAC-PapersOnLine **56**(2), 8591–8597 (2023)
10. Hafiz, A.M.: A survey of deep q-networks used for reinforcement learning: state of the art. In: Intelligent Communication Technologies and Virtual Mobile Networks: Proceedings of ICICV 2022, pp. 393–402 (2022)
11. Wei, D., Ding, S.: A survey on multi-agent deep reinforcement learning: from the perspective of challenges and applications. Artif. Intell. Rev. **54**(5), 3215–3238 (2021)
12. Zhao, Y., Wang, Y., Tan, Y., Zhang, J., Hongxia, Yu.: Dynamic jobshop scheduling algorithm based on deep Q network. IEEE Access **9**, 122995–123011 (2021)
13. Zhou, T., et al.: Reinforcement learning for online optimization of job-shop scheduling in a smart manufacturing factory. Adv. Mech. Eng. **14**(3), 16878132221086120 (2022)
14. Hu, H., Jia, X., He, Q., Fu, S., Liu, K.: Deep reinforcement learning based AGVs real-time scheduling with mixed rule for flexible shop floor in Industry 4.0. Comput. Ind. Eng. **149**, 106749 (2020)
15. Arulkumaran, K., Deisenroth, M.P., Brundage, M., Bharath, A.A.: Deep reinforcement learning: a brief survey. IEEE Sig. Process. Mag. **34**(6), 26–38 (2017)
16. Clifton, J., Laber, E.: Q-learning: theory and applications. Ann. Rev. Stat. Appl. **7**, 279–301 (2020)
17. Hao, J., et al.: Exploration in deep reinforcement learning: from single-agent to multiagent domain. IEEE Trans. Neural Netw. Learn. Syst. (2023)

18. Bahrpeyma, F., Reichelt, D.: A review of the applications of multi-agent reinforcement learning in smart factories. Front. Robot. AI **9**, 1027340 (2022)
19. Feriani, A., Hossain, E.: Single and multi-agent deep reinforcement learning for AI-
enabled wireless networks: a tutorial. IEEE Commun. Surv. Tut. **23**(2), 1226–1252
(2021)
20. Ao, T., Zhang, K., Shi, H., Jin, Z., Zhou, Y., Liu, F.: Energy-efficient multi-UAVs
cooperative trajectory optimization for communication coverage: an MADRL approach. Remote Sens. **15**(2), 429 (2023)
21. Zhou, T., Tang, D., Zhu, H., Zhang, Z.: Multi-agent reinforcement learning for
online scheduling in smart factories. Robot. Comput. Integr. Manuf. **72**, 102202
(2021)
22. Maoudj, A., Kouider, A., Christensen, A.L.: The capacitated multi-AGV scheduling problem with conflicting products: model and a decentralized multi-agent approach. Robot. Comput. Integr. Manuf. **81**, 102514 (2023)
23. Wang, X., Zhang, L., Lin, T., Zhao, C., Wang, K., Chen, Z.: Solving job scheduling
problems in a resource preemption environment with multi-agent reinforcement
learning. Robot. Comput. Integr. Manuf. **77**, 102324 (2022)
24. Yahouni, Z., Mebarki, N., Sari, Z.: Evaluation of a new decision-aid parameter for
job shop scheduling under uncertainties. RAIRO Oper. Res. **53**(2), 593–608 (2019)
25. Adibi, M.A., Zandieh, M., Amiri, M.: Multi-objective scheduling of dynamic job
shop using variable neighborhood search. Exp. Syst. Appl. **37**(1), 282–287 (2010)
26. Shahrabi, J., Adibi, M.A., Mahootchi, M.: A reinforcement learning approach to
parameter estimation in dynamic job shop scheduling. Comput. Ind. Eng. **110**,
75–82 (2017)

Digital Twin Data Broker with Assisted Mapping into a Knowledge Base

Thomas Schmeyer[1(✉)], Kai Krämer[1], Anna-Lena Peh[2], Boris Brandherm[1], Margarita Chikobava[1], and Gian-Lucca Kiefer[1]

[1] German Research Center for Artificial Intelligence, Cognitive Assistence Systems, 66123 Saarbrücken, Germany
{Thomas.Schmeyer,Kai.Kramer,Boris.Brandherm,Margarita.Chikobava, Gian-Lucca.Kiefer}@dfki.de

[2] Fraunhofer IOSB, Angewandte Systemtechnik, 98693 Ilmenau, Germany
Anna-Lena.Peh@iosb-ast.fraunhofer.de

Abstract. The frequent usage of digital twins to communicate between physical objects is resulting in more complex cyber-physical systems. To simplify the individual components' integration and to optimize their usage, a data broker is being developed. Therefore, digital twins need to be semantically organized in an ontology that provides the advantage of reasoning methods. An assisted workflow is being developed to automatically enter subgraphs into an ontology. As a digital twin representation, the Asset Administration Shell format is used to have an international standard technology. Based on this, a new domain-specific language is developed, allowing experts to configure the generation process. This process maps the digital twin's information into a graph representation of the ontology. The preconfigured generation process enables the user to efficiently register new digital twins without having expert knowledge of the underlying ontology. Additionally, a Large Language Model vector embedding and text reasoning support is implemented analysing the digital twin to create entity suggestions. The presented data broker is an automation tool for bridging the gap between semantic descriptions and digital twin formats in order to unite the advantages of both representations.

Keywords: Digital twin · Asset administration shell · Ontology · Automation · Cyber-physical system

1 Introduction

This thesis aims to make digital twins semantically interoperable by using the Asset Administration Shell (AAS) [1] format with a domain-specific language to enable a semi-automatic mapping to the Open Energy Ontology (OEO) [2]. This mapping ensures a precise and uniform description of resources and thus enables the efficient use and searchability of the digital twins on a digital marketplace for energy-related goods.

© The Author(s), under exclusive license to Springer Nature Switzerland AG 2025
M. Dassisti et al. (Eds.): IN4PL 2024, CCIS 2372, pp. 23–40, 2025.
https://doi.org/10.1007/978-3-031-80760-2_2

Industry 4.0 needs software solutions to create more flexible and effective workflows. However, the heterogeneous integration of these software solutions is leading to increasingly complex cyber-physical systems. Managing these systems requires in-depth specialist knowledge. This also affects the energy sector.

An intelligent and interactive energy system is needed to enable the efficient use of energy from volatile renewable energy sources such as solar panels and wind turbines and through electric heating systems or electric personal transport. This includes the generation of synthetic data of households [3] and forecasting methods [4] to estimate the energy consumption and production of electrical grids. An approach combining these methods into one cyber-physical system is used to protect only sparsely monitored low-voltage grids [5].

The European Commission released a strategy to accelerate the digital transformation of the European Energy System [6]. Especially the innovation of Digital Twin (DT) technology and Artificial Intelligence of Things (AI-IoT) of the Horizon Europe program should be transferred to the energy infrastructure. There is a whole range of DT applications with various use cases in different energy sector industries [7] that need to be managed in a system critical infrastructure and in heterogeneous systems.

Hence, there is a need to semantically annotate digital twins for their specific task. This can simplify the integration of digital twins into production. It also helps to find suitable digital twins on an external marketplace for digital goods. Therefore a data broker application is developed that provides an assistance system to transfer a digital representation of an asset automatically into an ontology, see Fig. 1. The used base ontology in this use case scenario is the OEO [2]. Some new properties extend the OEO to integrate descriptions of DTs. Enhancing the scalability of the data broker, the extended ontology is transferred from the OWL format to a graph database, see Sect. 3.

The DTs must be integrated interoperably into existing software systems. An international standard technology for describing and exchanging information about DTs is the AAS [1]. An AAS-JSON file is used as base representation of DTs managed by the broker. Such a shell contains the information and functional aspect of an asset in submodels. An assisted mapping of submodels to the ontology is developed.

Therefore, suitable asset descriptions are extracted. They are analyzed via a large language model (LLM) and classical text mining algorithms to propose to the user some suggestions for ontology classes. This is described in Sect. 4.1. Then the submodels of the AAS file are matched against saved template models, with a configured automized graph generation. This generation is configured by a newly developed domain-specific language (DSL). If such a match is recognized, the configured DSL code is executed to generate a subgraph. This is added to the knowledge base. The process takes already existing entries into account to prevent data duplication.

In the next section, a summary is given on related work. It is followed by a detailed description of the OEO with the new developed extension in Sects. 2 and 3 to explain the application's theoretical background. In Sect. 4 the data broker application is described in detail, focusing on the assistance system. Followed by a discussion in Sect. 5 with an outlook.

2   Related Work

In [8] a so-called Semantic Asset Administration Shell (SAAS) is presented that maps the AAS model to Resource Description Framework (RDF). This is used to build a validation model of AAS exchange data specified in the Shapes Constraint Language (SHACL).

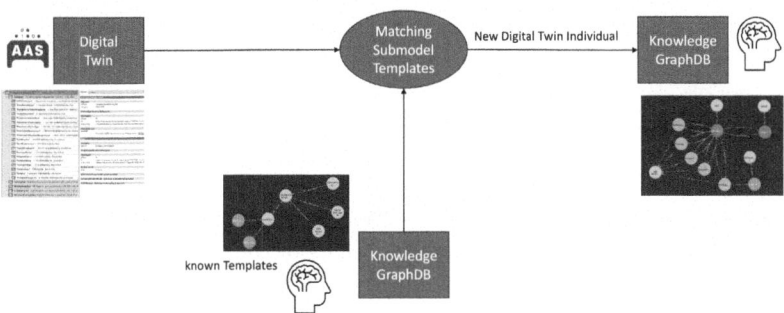

Fig. 1. The main idea of the assistance system.

An approach to enable semantic interoperability with an ontology is demonstrated in [9]. The Authors use a transformation from OWL to Unified Modeling Language (UML) using a concept that maps between different transformations to generate AAS stereotypical descriptions. The AAS files are then annotated to this UML description and then vice versa remapped to an ontology.

Another approach, in which ontology is used as a semantic description, is shown in [10]. The authors transform RDF ontologies to AAS template files without losing the ontology URL reference. They provide an algorithm to rebuild the RDF graph from an instance file of an AAS and an algorithm to select such an annotated file with the standard AAS environment methods.

An approach to bridge the gap between different versions of control software is developed in [11]. The authors used a hierarchical domain-specific language that has direct access to the AAS environment to inject the right software version to control industrial machines.

In [12], the authors use an LLM to enrich some properties of a so-called semantic node with textual information. Therefore, they read a textual input of a user and extract the preliminary properties, like name, value, initial descriptions. This information is combined with an enhanced ECLASS search from a generative LLM Agent to a semantic node. As shown in [10], such a node can then be referenced by an AAS Submodel or used by other agents.

An approach that uses an AAS environment in combination with a graph database is presented in [13]. The authors used a specialized AAS hazard model and transferred them into a knowledge graph. Using the query language of the database they detect hazards in a worker environment.

3 OEO and AAS

The Open Energy Ontology (OEO) has been developed to facilitate collaboration and information exchange in the field of energy systems analysis. It was created with the aim of improving scientific exchange and reflecting the complexity of the research field. Ambiguous terminologies of energy systems analyses and related fields have been collected, linked and structured. Like ontologies in other fields, the OEO helps to replace heterogeneous data, different definitions and incompatible models. By annotating information with the OEO, it becomes reusable, searchable, exchangeable, comparable, linkable and semantically interoperable [2]. As far as possible, the OEO follows a taxonomic structure in which each class has exactly one parent class in a so-called monohierarchy.

The OEO is defined in expressive OWL2 semantics, which allows implicit knowledge to be inferred. The top-level ontology of the OEO is the Basic Formal Ontology (BFO) [15]. The OEO resources are being developed and are available on GitHub.

3.1 Extension of OEO by AAS Digital Twin Information

The natural OEO has no structure to describe the AAS technology. Therefore, an additional part is added, using a similar structure like [8] and [14] to describe AAS structure, see Fig. 2. As base description the concepts of asset, AAS and submodels are added. An asset represents exactly one AAS. Such an AAS can have multiple submodels. It is defined that a submodel has only one AAS as a parent, see Fig. 2. More detailed information can be saved as data properties in the database for further use. The new classes are set as subclasses of the 'content entity'-class and the connection is from the relative loose relation 'has information content entity' from the OEO. Submodels of a shell are also stored if they fulfill standards. Such standardized submodel templates are provided by the Industrial Digital Twin Association (IDTA), for example. The IDTA is a central point for standardization for digital twins to enhance interoperability and also provide such submodel templates, [16]. Such templates specify the structure of how certain submodels should look.

For scalability, the ontology was imported to a Neo4J graph database. Therefore, the Neosemantic plugin is used [17]. It allows the import of RDF and associated vocabularies like OWL to Neo4J Graph Databases. In order to simplify the import and have the possibility to change the underlying ontology, the import functionality is automatized via a shell script. So the application can adapted easily to another use case.

Another reason is the flexibility of stored objects. It enables a wider range of graph-based analyses, such as vector similarities, directly via the database. An example application is shown in Sect. 4.1.

4   Digital Twin Data Broker

The application architecture is separated into backend, middleware and frontend, see Fig. 3. The architecture is containerized, so that all parts are easily portable.

The backend contains the graph database storing the knowledge base of the OEO with the newly developed extensions. It also contains a large language model (LLM) to transform AAS asset descriptions and labels into a vector embedding, which allows fast similarity matching.

The middleware is designed as a REST service and has three main functionalities. A query service to provide and aggregate data about the stored DTs in the database for the user. Then there is an AAS register template service, which gives a domain ontology expert the possibility to configure the automatized generation of knowledge base subgraphs for predefined templates. The configuration is done by a newly developed DSL presented in Sect. 4.3.

These configured templates are used in a DT register service to provide the user an assistance system to register DTs. It checks if the uploaded AAS file's submodels correspond to template standards. In addition, it also provides an

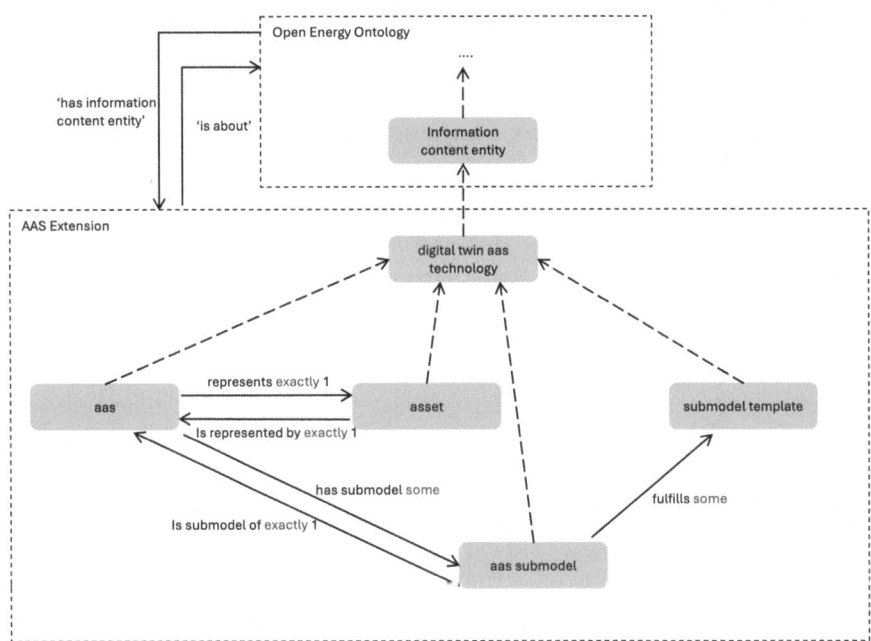

Fig. 2. Overview of the new developed extensions added to the OEO. The dotted arrows are 'is subclass of' properties. The slide arrows show the class description.

interface to analyze AAS files to suggest to the user where to assign the asset to the knowledge graph. Additionally, an automatization was developed to transfer the properties of matched submodels into the knowledge base. The following section will focus on this automatization procedure/service.

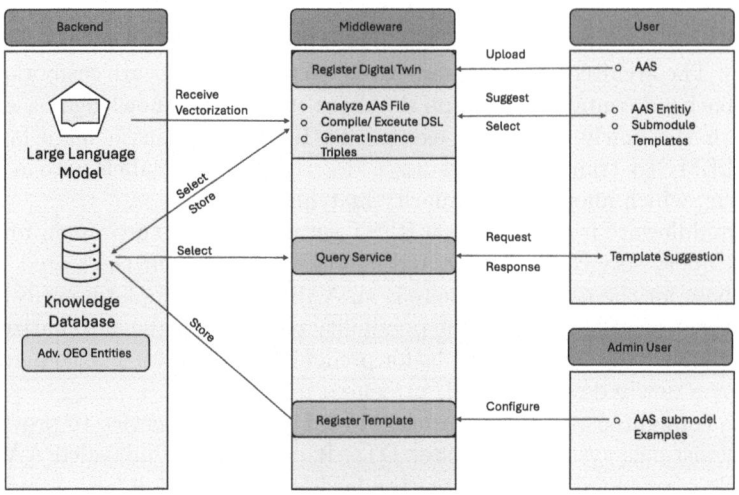

Fig. 3. Service Architecture Overview.

4.1   Labelmapping with Large Language Models and Jaccard Index

The functionality presented is intended to help an external user to correctly assign their digital twin in the ontology. A LLM is used to examine the uploaded AAS file of the digital twin. For this purpose, an interface was provided that segments the stored class label string into tokens and calculates the semantic embedding of the LLM as a vector. This is stored as a property of the class in the database so that it is available for further mathematical methods.

In order to suggest to the user the best possible matches, the descriptions of the asset are extracted from the uploaded file. Therefore, the standard description field of the AAS format is used, which is always available. Other descriptions of standardized formats are taken into account if available, such as the nameplates of the IDTA and HSU.

The description's embedding vectors are then computed with the LLM and matched against the label vectors with the cosine similarity

$$S_c(v_1, v_2) = \frac{< v_1, v_2 >}{||v_1||_2 \cdot ||v_2||_2}, \tag{1}$$

where $v_1, v_2 \in \mathbf{R}^n$ are embedding vectors with $n \in \mathbf{N}$, $< \cdot, \cdot >$ the standard dot product and $|| \cdot ||_2$ the l_2-norm to normalize the vectors [18]. The results of different descriptions of one OWL class label are then merged as mean value. The suggestions are then presented in descending order of the computed similarity value.

As an example of a description, a solar heat plant is analysed. It is described as "A solar heat plant is a heat plant that has solar heat units as parts." in a comment of the OEO. As LLM the pretrained BERT-base-uncased [19] without adaption of the weights is used to analyse the description. The result is presented in Table 1. Because of the lack of a large corpus of AAS sample descriptions an interface is implemented to get additional descriptions of the ontology itself. These embedding vectors are then computed and compared with the cosine similarity (1) to provide a guess of the accuracy of the used LLM. In order to test the abstraction ability of the LLM the descriptions are additionally modified by substituting the single words of a label by a placeholder like thing a, thing b .... This is done for all combinations.

Using the not adapted BERT-base-uncased model it shows that only 639 of 1145 entities has a hit in the first 20 suggested results. The best similarity match was about $0.9 \in [0; 1]$ with the natural description and about 0.6 in mean with replaced label word combinations.

The results show that there is a need to retrain a LLM to a specific scenario to enhance the accuracy of matching labeled entities. Because of that, the application provides the user, besides the manual search, some classical approaches. A Jaccard Index based algorithm has been implemented counting the matched words of the label. The result of the previous example is shown in Table 2.

When looking at the result Tables 1 and 2 of the example above, both algorithms select the correct label. While the Jaccard algorithm naturally has advantages if the label is named directly in the description, COS-Similarity can also make suggestions abstracted from the description using LLM word embedding.

Table 1. Resulting LLM suggestions of the label solar heat plant ordered by cossimilarity.

Label	COS-Similarity
solar heat plant	0.609
solar heat unit	0.604
solar power plant	0.601
solar thermal heat technology	0.587
solar thermal power unit	0.578
solar thermal energy transformation	0.572
geothermal heat plant	0.568
solar energy	0.567
rooftop photovoltaic power plant	0.563
solar thermal power technology	0.560

Table 2. Resulting jaccard suggestions for the user ordered by the count of words.

Label	Count
solar heat plant	7
heat plant	5
geothermal heat plant	5
solar heat unit	5
combined heat and power plant	5
solar thermal heat technology	5
solar power plant	4
plate heat exchanger	3
heat transfer unit	3

4.2   Class Description Mapping of OEO

In ontologies, classes can include general class axioms or descriptions, which are logical statement and readable in Protégé. In Neo4j databases, these statements become very difficult to read, see Figs. 4 and 5. The Neo4j plugin Neosemantics provides some reasoning methods but no functionality to make these descriptions readable. In order to provide such class descriptions to users, a mapping algorithm is implemented solving the OWL class descriptions and equivalences properties. This uses the standardised web ontology referenced in [20], especially the class properties. As a simple example with two restrictions, the graph of the previous example of a solar heat pump is given in Fig. 4. These restrictions are mapped to the following semantic sentences:

1. solar heat plant has part some solar heat unit
2. solar heat plant participates some solar thermal energy

A more complicated example is the graph of an electric vehicle, see Fig. 5. Since it is a subgraph that describes the equivalences, the mapping algorithm must handle intersections to solve the logical expression. The equivalences and the restrictions are mapped to following semantic sentences:

1. electric vehicle is equivalent to (vehicle and has part some electric traction motor)
2. electric vehicle has energy input some electrical energy

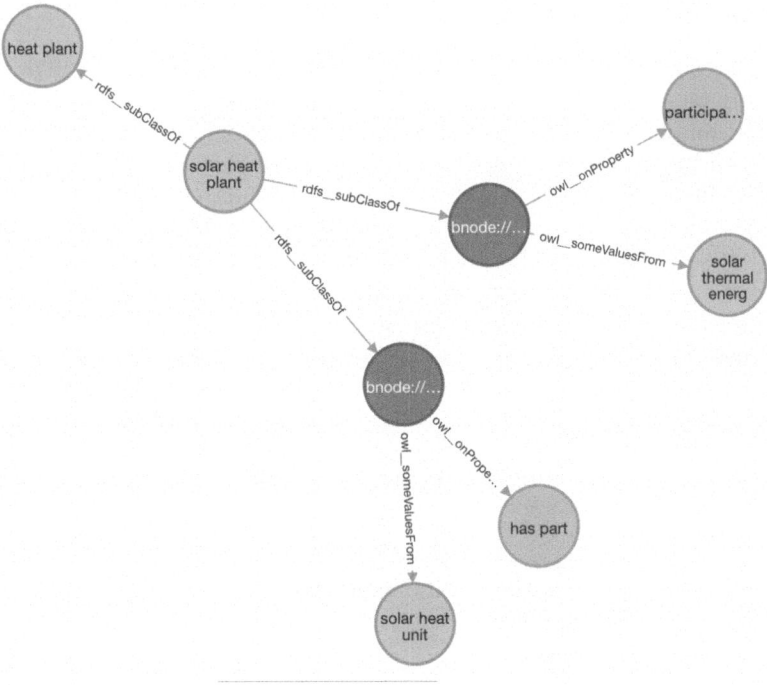

Fig. 4. Solar Heat Pump class descriptions as graph stored in the database.

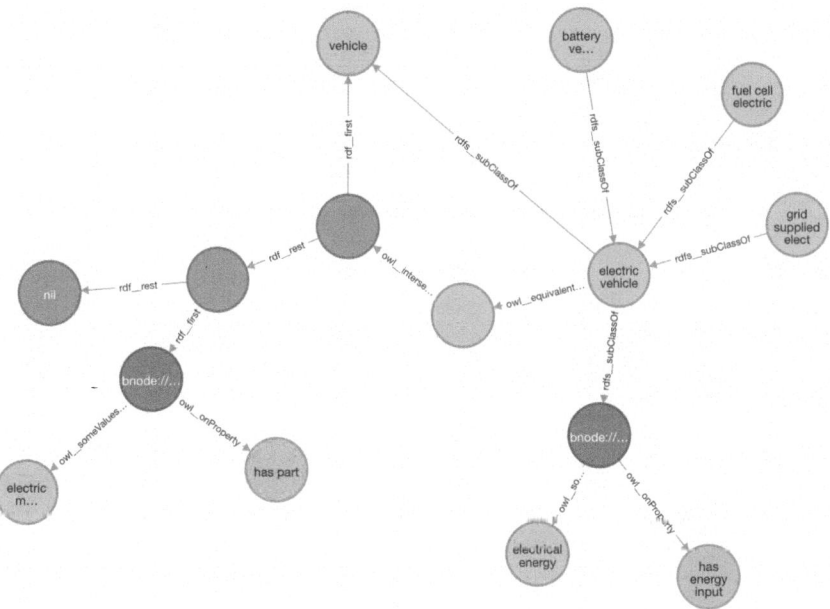

Fig. 5. Electric Vehicle class descriptions as graph stored in the database.

4.3   Domain Specific Language

In contrast to relational databases, which can be easily queried with SQL, there is currently no standardized query mechanism in the AAS. To address this limitation and simplify the configuration logic on a matching AAS templates, a DSL is developed. It analyse AAS files based on the hierarchical structure of the submodel templates. The DSL syntax is based on lambda expressions introduced with "=¿". The access operator is $ followed by the variable name whose value is accessed. It serves as a placeholder for the object that is successively changed by the lambda operators. Without any variable name, the root object is accessed, in this use case an AAS submodel format.

One base functionality of the DSL is the usage of JMESPath expressions, a JSON query language [21] to filter and extract JSON fields. This gives the user a set of tools to process JSON files. This is done by the function

$$\textbf{jmespath}(\text{expression, flag}). \qquad (2)$$

The flags can be set as

1. *Natural* $= 0$ interpreted the natural expression,
2. *TypeName* $= 1$ selects the type name,
3. *Value* $= 2$ selects the value,
4. *ShortId* $= 4$ selects the short id,
5. *IdPath* $= 8$ selects the object of the id path.

For example, the following code snippet is explained. To give an essential example only the *Natural* flag is used. If the root is { "a": {b: "foo" }} then the code

```
1        v = $
2        => jmespath(a,0)
3        v_2 = $v
4        => jmespath(b,0)
5        => exist()
```

assigns the value {b: "foo" } to v. Then it is checked if the extracted value foo of the JSON field b of variable v exists and assigns the boolean value true to v_2.

The AAS has a fixed formated structure of subelements of a submodel. A simplified JSON example

```
1   [
2     {
3       "value":
4       [
5         {
6           "value":[
7             {
8               "shortId":"baz",
9               "value":"Hello",
10              "modelType":{"name":"string"}
11            }
12          ],
13          "shortId":"bar",
14          "modelType":
15          {
16            "name":"subElementCollection"
17          }
18        }
19      ],
20      "shortId":"foo",
21      "modelType":
22      {
23        "name":"subElementCollection"
24      }
25    }
26  ]
```

is given to show the need for AAS specialized functionalities of the DSL. Using the operator (2) with the flag *IdPath*, a functionality is implemented to extract the last object of a list of short ids separated by ".". The listing is translated to a natural expression to filter the submodel element collections structure of the submodel iterative by short id names. Using *foo.bar.baz* as an expression, it is interpreted as follows

$$exp = \{$$
$$\text{r:}[?\text{shortId}==\text{'foo'}][]$$
$$.\text{value}[?\text{shortId}==\text{'bar'}][]$$
$$.\text{value}[?\text{shortId}==\text{'baz'}][]$$
$$\}.r[0]$$

a natural JMESPath expression. It filters an array of elements with the short id *foo* and gets the value fields. This is repeated with the short id *bar*. Then the last element with the short id *baz* of the JSON array is extracted. In the example above, the expression for this object is evaluated:

```
1  {
2       "shortId":"baz",
3       "value":"Hello",
4       "modelType":{"name":"string"}
5  }.
```

The examples show that the integration of JMESPath in the DSL creates a powerful tool to process JSON AAS structures. The DSL is very flexible and can be easily enhanced with more features. Therefore, there are functionalities to check a value of existent, get the value or value type of a submodel etc. Planned but not yet implemented is a regular expression functionality for mapping JSON fields and some auto type conversion patterns.

4.4 Automatic Graph Generation Algorithm

In this section, the Graph Generation Algorithm is described. The different strategies to process AAS submodels are configured in the template instances of the Database. The DSL code preprocesses the AAS file and native queries are stored there. Furthermore, multiple decision-making processes are configured. They are made of selection and creation strategies using the native queries and the DSL. An overview is given in Fig. 6.

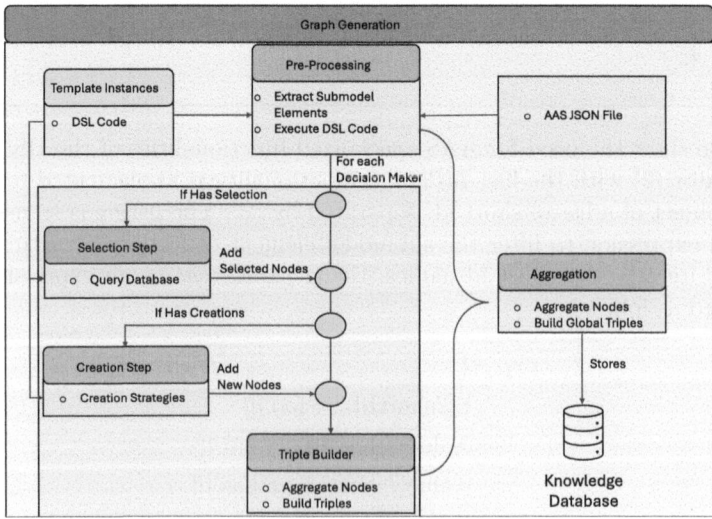

Fig. 6. Graph Generation Algorithm Structure.

As a precondition, the parameter of the global URL of the asset is set as an identifier of the asset shell to register. First in a pre-processing step the Submodel

Elements are extracted from the AAS file. Then they are processed using the DSL to build a dictionary of variables as keys to aggregated properties. This dictionary is then used as a base data set for the decision-making processes.

Then for each configured decision maker a selection step to query existing entries of the database and a creation step to build new individual structures. Both aggregate the nodes of the new shell knowledge graph but only one of them must be configured. For each node it is necessary to have the aggregated information of the following described fields:

1. **url**: The global URL as identifier of the node.
2. **label**: The human readable label of the node.
3. **subclass url**: The identifier URL of the OWL entity, the node of which is a subclass.
4. **node name**: The node name as a short identification.
5. **properties**: A JSON dictionary with properties of the node to store.

Therefore, the selection step requires that the executed query returns a list of rows containing these fields.

In the creation step, strategies are configured to generate the values for each of the required fields, using the aggregated information from pre-processing and selection. Each strategy can be configured by the DSL but there are various native strategies. For example, there is a native strategy to attach a path to the asset or server URL to have a valid directory structure. This strategy transfers the asset shell structure to the knowledge database and guarantees an easy-to-query identifier.

The aggregated nodes are then processed in a triple builder to connect them with labeled edges. However, before a new edge is created it is checked if one of the connected nodes is a newly created node. If not, it is checked if such a connection already exists. In this step, all local duplicates are removed.

Then all nodes and edges are gathered and aggregated. In particular, the individual entries that are a subclass of categories asset, AAS and their associated submodels are generated. The removal of duplicate nodes and edges of graphs generated by different submodels, guarantees a coherent graph of the asset.

4.5 Generated Examples

For example, two shells are migrated into the knowledge base ontology. The submodel templates utilized are IDTA-Nameplating and IDTA-TimeSeries. The previously described functionalities store the structure of submodels data properties in their corresponding nodes. The corresponding graph of a nameplating is presented in Fig. 7. It shows an asset that is represented by an AAS and its submodels including the submodel with IDTA-Nameplate structure. The producer of the asset is mapped as an organization in the knowledge graph.

The second example is a time series that fulfills the IDTA template. A part of the corresponding knowledge graph is shown in Fig. 8, depicts the AAS and its corresponding typical metadata like resolution, start and end time and the measurement units.

Both examples show that the stored information of the AAS is semantically annotated and accessible to the user. Particularly in the area of time series,

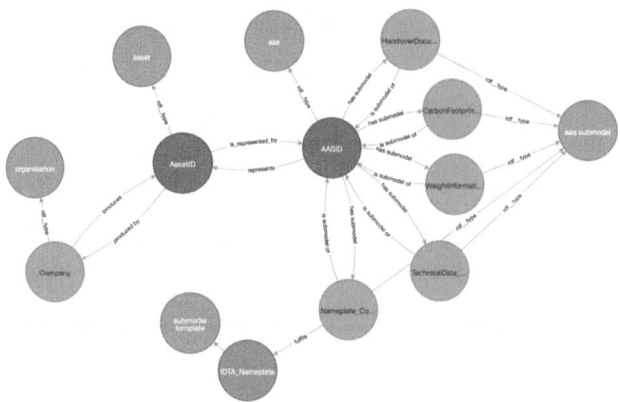

Fig. 7. Transferred AAS with submodels and a Company as 'organisation' that produced the asset. The orange nodes are classes and the rest are Individuals.

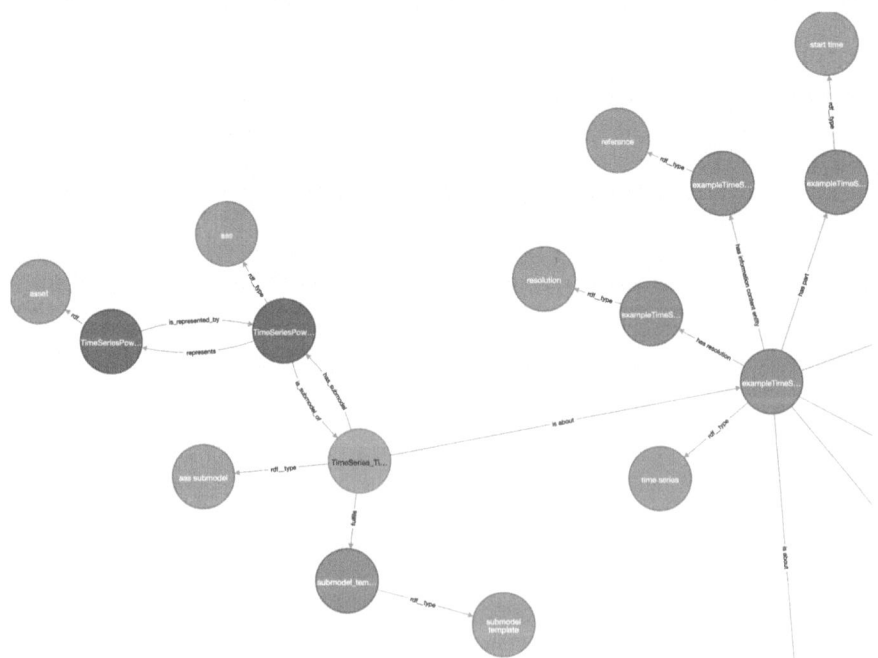

Fig. 8. IDTA-TimeSeries AAS transferred into the extended OEO partial graph. The orange nodes are classes and the rest are Individuals. (Color figure online)

the data broker makes it possible to offer these to the user in an AAS industry standard format. This is of great value for the market for digital goods, as data sets are precisely specified and can thus facilitate the modeling and training of neural networks.

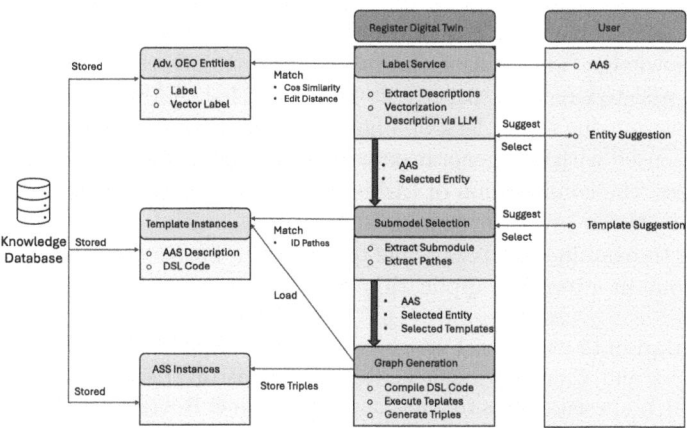

Fig. 9. Overview over the assisted digital twin register process.

5   Conclusion

In summary, it is shown that DT descriptions of AAS and an ontology knowledge base can be combined to have the advantages of both. With the transfer of the knowledge base to a graph database a wide range of mathematical tools is enabled. So it can be shown that LLM text mining algorithms assist the user. The data broker application is also more scalable, especially concerning cloud technologies that use cooperative data spaces like Gaia-X [22]. Semantic interoperability makes it possible to search the offers in a targeted manner.

It is also shown that the mapping algorithm from Sect. 4.1, it works without losing class description information and the newly developed DSL presented in Sect. 4.3 is a tool to bridge the gap between the knowledge of a normal user and an ontology domain expert. It has a direct application in the configuration of the templates as a configuration tool for the automatized process of registering DTs, see Fig. 9.

6   Discussion

The registering process based only on JSON files is no restriction because the tools of generation AAS exchange format files, like the AASX package explorer

[23], have the functionality to convert the shell of an asset into a JSON representation. However, integrating the newly developed client technology of the AAS environment of the BaSyx project [24] can help to enable new promising features having direct access to the digital twins.

Another aspect is the integration of semantic ids shown in [9] and [12]. It can enhance the mapping process of an AAS file to a specific template. However, since there is no effective restriction on semantic IDs it requires a lot of specific domain knowledge. This will be the subject of future works.

In the assisted register process it is shown that AAS can be analysed by LLMs. However, due to the lack of a large data corpus, classical approaches cannot be dispensed with and generation without the help of the user is not possible. Nevertheless, the combination of LLMs, text mining, semantic descriptions and reasoning methods gives developers a lot of possibilities. As future work, it is interesting to examine if it is possible to transfer a native description to a query like it is done in a tourism application [25].

Acknowledgments. This work has been founded by the Federal Ministry for Economic Affairs and Climate Action in the context of the Project IdFlexNetz (FKZ 03EI6067A-E). Special thanks to Julia Bayer and Daniel Rohrbach for corrections and to our project partners VSE AG, Schneider Electric and Spherity.

References

1. Grüner S., Neidig J., Orzelski A., Pollmeier S.: Asset administration shell reading guide, March 2023. https://industrialdigitaltwin.org/wp-content/uploads/2022/11/2022-11-03_IDTA_AAS-Reading-Guide.pdf. Accessed 12 Apr 2024
2. Booshehri M., Emele L., et al.: Introducing the open energy ontology: enhancing data interpretation and interfacing in energy systems analysis. Energy AI **5**, 100074 (2021). ISSN 2666-5468. https://doi.org/10.1016/j.egyai.2021.100074
3. Meiser M., Duppe B., Zinnikus I.: Generation of meaningful synthetic sensor data - evaluated with a reliable transferability methodology. Energy AI **15** (2023). https://doi.org/10.1016/j.egyai.2023.100308
4. Brandherm, B., Deru, M., Ndiaye, A, Kiefer, G., Baus, J., Gampfer, R.: Integration of renewable energies—AI-based prediction methods for electricity generation from photovoltaic systems. In: Barton, T., Müller, C. (eds.) Apply Data Science: Introduction, Applications and Projects, GER 2023, pp. 137–158. Springer Fachmedien, Wiesbaden, Germany (2023). ISBN 978-3-658-38798-3. https://doi.org/10.1007/978-3-658-38798-3_9
5. Schmeyer, T.A., et al.: Assistance system for ai-based monitoring and prediction in smart grids. In: 2023 Human Computer Interaction International Conferences (HCII-2023). Springer, Cham (2023). https://doi.org/10.1007/978-3-031-36001-5_65
6. European Commission: Accelerating the digital transformation of the European energy system. https://digital-strategy.ec.europa.eu/en/policies/digitalisation-energy. Accessed 12 Apr 2024

7. Ismail, F.B., Al-Faiz, H., Hasini, H., Al-Bazi, A., Kazem, H.A.: A comprehensive review of the dynamic applications of the digital twin technology across diverse energy sectors. Energy Strategy Rev. **52**, 101334 (2024). ISSN 2211-467X. https://doi.org/10.1016/j.esr.2024.101334

8. Bader, S., Maleshkova, M.: The semantic asset administration shell (2019). https://doi.org/10.1007/978-3-030-33220-4_12

9. Huang Y., Dhouib S., Medinacelli L. P., Malenfant J.: Enabling semantic interoperability of asset administration shells through an ontology-based modeling method. In: Proceedings of the 25th International Conference on Model Driven Engineering Languages and Systems: Companion Proceedings, MODELS 2022, pp. 497–502. Association for Computing Machinery, New York, NY, USA (2022). https://doi.org/10.1145/3550356.3561606

10. Rongen, S., Nikolova, N., van der Pas, M.: Modelling with AAS and RDF in Industry 4.0. Comput. Ind. **148**, 103910 (2023). ISSN 0166-3615. https://doi.org/10.1016/j.compind.2023.103910

11. Lehnert, C., Engel, G., Steininger, H., Drath, R., Greiner, T.: A hierarchical domain-specific language for cyber-physical production systems integrating asset administration shells. In: IEEE 26th International Conference on Emerging Technologies and Factory Automation (ETFA), Vasteras, Sweden, SWE, pp. 01–04 (2021)

12. Xia, Y., Xiao, Z., Jazdi, N., Weyrich, M.: Generation of asset administration shell with large language model agents: towards semantic interoperability in digital twins in the context of Industry 4.0, March 2024. https://arxiv.org/abs/2403.17209

13. Luxenburger, A., Porta, D., Knoch, S., Mohr, J., Schwartz, T.: A service infrastructure for Industrie 4.0 testbeds based on asset administration shells. In: IEEE 28th International Conference on Emerging Technologies and Factory Automation (ETFA), Sinaia, Romania, ROU, pp. 1–8 (2023). https://doi.org/10.1109/ETFA54631.2023.10275335

14. Industrial Digital Twin Association e.V., AAS-Specs: Resource Description Framework. https://github.com/admin-shell-io/aas-specs/tree/master/schemas/rdf. Accessed 29 May 2024

15. Spear, A., Ceusters, W., Smith, B.: Functions in basic formal ontology. Appl. Ontol., 103–128 (2016)

16. Industrial Digital Twin Association: IDTA Submodel Templates published. https://industrialdigitaltwin.org/en/news-dates/publication-of-idta-submodel-templates-4071. Accessed 03 Jun 2024

17. Neo4j: neosemantics (n10s): Neo4j RDF & Semantics toolkit. https://neo4j.com/labs/neosemantics/. Accessed 16 May 2024

18. Singhal, A., Google, Inc.: Modern information retrieval: a brief overview. IEEE Data Eng. Bull. **24**, 35–44 (2021)

19. Hugging Face: BERT-base-uncased. https://huggingface.co/google-bert/bert-base-uncased. Accessed 17 May 2024

20. Bechhofer, S., et al.: W3C-OWL web ontology language reference. https://www.w3.org/TR/owl-ref/. Accessed 17 May 2024

21. Saryerwinnie, J.: JMESPath: JMESPath Libraries. https://jmespath.org/libraries.html. Accessed 23 May 2024

22. National Academy of Science and Engineering: Gaia-X Hub Germany. https://gaia-x-hub.de/en/. Accessed 23 May 2024

23. Eclipse: GitHub: AASX Package Explorer. https://github.com/eclipse-aaspe/package-explorer. Accessed 24 May 2024

24. Eclipse BaSyx^{TM}: GitHub: eclipse-basyx. https://github.com/eclipse-basyx. Accessed 24 May 2024

25. Chase, A., et al.: Multimodales Fenster in die Vergangenheit der ehemaligen Vauban-Festung Saarlouis mittels ChatGPT. In: Barton T., Müller C. (eds.) Angewandte Wirtschaftsinformatik - Generative KI im Kontext der Wirtschaftsinformatik, December 2024, pp. 1–19, Springer Vieweg, Wiesbaden, Germany, GER (2024, to appear)

An Out-of-Sample Clustering Ensemble Method for Defect Detection and Classification in Metal Additive Manufacturing

Sylvain Chabanet[1,2](✉) ⓘ, Adil Han Orta[1,2] ⓘ, and Mathias Kersemans[1] ⓘ

[1] Mechanics of Materials and Structures (MMS), Department of Materials, Textiles and Chemical Engineering, Ghent University, Technologiepark 46, 9052 Zwijnaarde, Belgium
sylvain.chabanet@ugent.be
[2] SIM-STREAM, Technologiepark 48, 9052 Zwijnaarde, Belgium

Abstract. Unsupervised learning methods, and in particular clustering algorithms, have found many applications in manufacturing, ranging from customer segmentation to quality monitoring. It has, however, been demonstrated that no clustering algorithm can be suitable for all applications and data structures. Ensembles of clustering algorithms have emerged as a partial answer to this limitation, aiming at increasing the robustness of clustering algorithms by aggregating partitions discovered by many models. This robustness, however, comes at the cost of increased computational requirements to generate and aggregate partitions. The ability to quickly predict a cluster for new, out-of-sample data points without having to recompute the whole clustering algorithm from scratch is, therefore, a desirable property for many real-world applications. Such out-of-sample methods, however, are not straightforward in the context of clustering ensemble, and few models include one. As a step toward filling this gap, this article proposes a novel out-of-sample method for clustering ensemble algorithms following the median consensus framework. An application of this method is proposed for the detection and classification of defects in metal parts produced by additive manufacturing processes. The proposed method is compared with state-of-the-art algorithms on both artificial and experimental datasets, demonstrating its high performance and robustness.

Keywords: Clustering ensemble · Resonance testing · Additive manufacturing · Out-of-sample

1 Introduction

Machine Learning (ML) is an increasingly important cornerstone of industry digitalization in the context of Industry 4.0. One of the most famous examples of this trend is deep learning models which have encountered great successes in image and natural language processing. Most of these models, however, fall under the umbrella of supervised learning and often require massive amounts of data points to be trained on. Importantly, they require these data points to be labeled, i.e., they need to have access to pairs of input X

© The Author(s), under exclusive license to Springer Nature Switzerland AG 2025
M. Dassisti et al. (Eds.): IN4PL 2024, CCIS 2372, pp. 41–58, 2025.
https://doi.org/10.1007/978-3-031-80760-2_3

and ground truth labels y. The obtention of these ground truth labels often requires the intervention of human experts, computation-intensive simulation, and eventually time-consuming tests on expensive equipment. In practice, this labeling process is a bottleneck of many ML pipelines.

Alternatives to supervised learning, such as semi-supervised or unsupervised learning have, however, been extensively studied by the machine learning community. A common unsupervised learning task, in particular, is clustering. Clustering models aim at finding meaningful structures in data by dividing datasets into groups of objects, so that objects placed in the same group, or cluster, are similar to each other while objects placed in different groups are not. Clustering algorithms have found many applications in manufacturing. For example, the authors of [1] propose a clustering model to characterize geometric deviations in additive manufacturing parts and link them to production conditions. Similarly, the authors of [2] introduce an unsupervised fault detection method based on gaussian mixtures to detect gear-wear in industrial robots. The authors of [3] present a digital shadow of a machine-tool used in the aerospace industry, including a clustering model to detect critical tool failures.

It is, however, well known that clustering is an ill-posed optimization problem. No algorithm can perform well on all applications and data geometries. Clustering ensembles, i.e., ensembles of clustering models, have been proposed to increase the robustness of clustering algorithms by combining the results of different models [4].

Clustering ensemble algorithms can, generally, be decomposed into two steps. The first step is the generation of the ensemble by running clustering algorithms with different sources of variability. This variability can, for example, come from different representations of the data points being clustered, different hyperparameters of the models, or different types of clustering algorithms. Each base-clustering model generates a partition. The ensemble can eventually be reduced by selecting only high-quality partitions [5]. The second step is the aggregation of all the partitions into one by a consensus function. A general drawback of clustering ensemble methods is, however, the increased computational cost, owing to both the need to generate many base-partitions, and the aggregation step which often requires to solve an additional optimization problem.

A useful addition to any clustering algorithm is an out-of-sample extension. Given a previously unseen data point, such a method aims at allocating it to an existing cluster without recomputing the full clustering algorithm. Out-of-sample extensions are necessary for the online exploitation of the defined cluster structure. Such methods are used, for example, by the authors of [3] to allow fault detection in new instances using precomputed clusters. Some clustering algorithms naturally possess such out-of-sample methods. For example, gaussian mixtures, a type of probabilistic clustering model, can allocate new points to the cluster to which they belong with maximum probability. The transition to clustering ensembles is, however, not straightforward due to the aggregation step, and very few clustering ensemble models augmented with out-of-sample methods have been published in the literature.

The main contribution of this article is a novel out-of-sample extension algorithm for an ensemble clustering algorithm, as a step toward bridging this gap in the literature. This includes both a novel out-of-sample extension for the base-clustering model used, and a method to aggregate them to obtain a consensus. An application of this algorithm to quality control in additive manufacturing is additionally developed. The objective is to detect and classify defects in 3D printed metal parts.

The remainder of this article is organized as follows. Section 2 first reviews related works in the field of ensemble clustering. The proposed clustering method and out-of-sample extension are detailed in Sect. 3, and results of a first numerical evaluation on artificial datasets are presented in Sect. 4. Section 5 details the additive manufacturing application and presents numerical results on two use-cases. Lastly, Sect. 6 concludes this article and presents avenues for future research.

2   Related Works

2.1   Clustering Ensemble

Clustering ensemble algorithms are algorithms aggregating many base-partitions into a final consensus to increase the robustness and quality of the final partition. Many strategies have been proposed to solve this aggregation problem. The authors of [4] categorize these strategies into two groups: the co-occurrence approach and the median-partition approach.

One of the simplest co-occurrence approaches is the relabeling and voting strategy. This method first relabels the partitions found by each member of the ensemble so that a label corresponds to similar clusters across the ensemble. This can, for example, be solved using the Hungarian algorithm [6]. The consensus partition is then obtained through voting, an object being allocated the label it is given the most by ensemble members. The main drawback of this approach is that solving the label reassignment problem requires all base-partitions to share the same number of clusters. This parameter is, however, generally unknown in advance. A popular strategy to bypass this issue is the co-association method, introduced in [7]. These methods first define a similarity matrix M between the clustered objects using the base-partitions. Another clustering algorithm is then used to generate a consensus function from this dissimilarity matrix. The original similarity between two objects O_i and O_j introduced in [7], in particular, is the number of co-occurrences of two points in the same cluster:

$$M_{ij} = S(O_i, O_j) = \sum_q^m \mathbb{I}_{\{l_{iq}=l_{jq}\}}$$ (1)

With M_{ij} the coefficient ij of the matrix M. $\mathbb{I}_{\{l_{iq}=l_{jq}\}}$ is the function taking the value 1 if the label l_{iq} of the object O_i in the partition q is equal to the label l_{jq} of the object O_j in the same partition, and taking the value 0 otherwise. m is the number of members in the ensemble.

Contrary to co-occurrence approaches, median-partition approaches define a similarity $S(P_i, P_j)$ between pairs of base-partition P_i and P_j. A consensus partition P is then searched as the partition maximizing the average similarity toward members of the ensemble:

$$C = \underset{P}{\mathrm{argmax}} \frac{1}{m} \sum_{i=1}^m S(P, P_i)$$ (2)

With $(P_1, \ldots, P_m)$ the base-partitions. Similarity functions that have been used for this problem include the Adjusted Rand Index (ARI) and the Normalized Mutual Information (NMI), [8]. This optimization problem, however, is NP-hard in general and heuristics have to be defined to find an approximate solution. The authors of [9], in particular, propose several such heuristics, including selecting the partition from the ensemble maximizing (2) and moving objects from cluster to cluster to improve the cost.

3 Proposed Method

This section first outlines the clustering ensemble algorithm designed for this study, and then presents the proposed out-of-sample extension. The clustering ensemble algorithm is a median partition method based on the HDBSCAN clustering algorithm [10]. The out-of-sample extension, therefore, requires an extension for HDBSCAN itself, followed by a strategy to aggregate the predictions of the base-models.

3.1 Outline of the Clustering Ensemble Algorithm

The clustering ensemble algorithm defined in the following of this study uses HDBSCAN to generate base partitions. HDBSCAN is a clustering algorithm based on estimates of the density distribution of the objects to be clustered. Clusters are considered to be areas of the feature space with high point density separated by areas with low point density and isolated points. HDBSCAN is a hierarchical algorithm. It generates a hierarchy of clusters organized as a tree, starting from the root being the cluster containing all points, then successively divides clusters until all points are isolated. A final partition is then extracted from the hierarchy, keeping the most stable clusters.

The hierarchy is computed as follows. The core distance of a point x, $d_c(x)$, is defined as the distance from x to its hth nearest neighbour, with h a user-defined parameter. The inverse of this core distance, $\lambda(x) = \frac{1}{d_c(x)}$ is an estimate of the local density in a neighbourhood of x. The mutual reachability distance between two points x and y is then computed as $\max(d_c(x), d_c(y), d(x, y))$, with $d(x, y)$ the distance between x and y. The mutual reachability distance is a regularized version of d that isolates points in groups smaller than h. The HDBSCAN algorithm first builds the distance graph whose vertices are data points and edges are the mutual reachability distance. In practice, this graph is reduced to its minimal spanning tree, greatly lowering the number of edges. A minimal spanning tree is a graph such that all points are connected, and the sum of all the edges weight is minimal [11]. As an example, Fig. 1 presents the minimal spanning tree, computed by the hdbscan python library [12] in a simple case with two small clusters. Edges are then cut sequentially from the largest to the lowest. Whenever a large enough group of points is isolated by a cut, a new cluster is added to the hierarchy, with apparition density the inverse of the weight of the last edge cut.

Several reasons have motivated the usage of this algorithm in this study. Firstly, it makes no assumption on the number of clusters present in the dataset. Secondly, it can find clusters of any shape. Lastly, it naturally handles isolated points, which is to say, points belonging to low-density areas and not associated with any cluster.

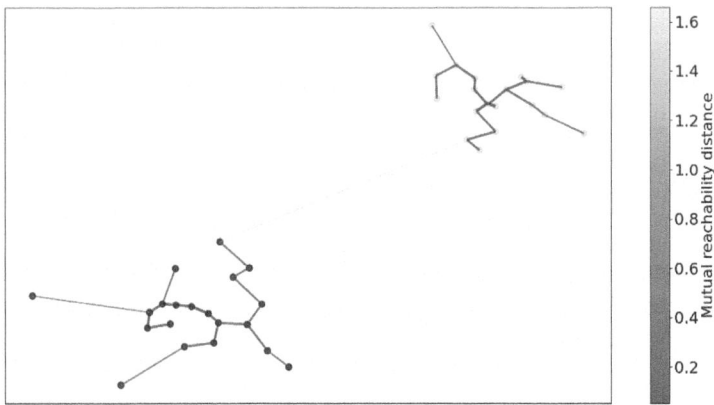

Fig. 1. Example of a minimum spanning tree, as computed by HDBSCAN. The points color corresponds to the clusters partition.

HDBSCAN is a fully deterministic algorithm. The structure of clusters and isolated points is, however, dependent on the nearest neighbor structure of the dataset. To ensure diversity in the ensemble, every base partition is, therefore, computed using a dataset perturbated by random gaussian noise. The standard deviation of this perturbation was selected through trial and error at 1% of the standard deviation of the feature it is added to.

m partitions $(P_1, \ldots, P_m)$ are generated this way with HDBSCAN. The base-partition maximizing the objective defined by Eq. (2) is then selected. The improved mutual information developed by the authors of [13] was selected to be the partitions similarity function S. Consider P_i and P_j two partitions, so that a_k count the number of objects in the kth group of the first partition, b_l the number of objects in the lth group of the first partition, and e_{kl} the number of objects in the intersection of these two groups. The similarity between these two partitions is computed as:

$$S(P_i, P_j) = \frac{1}{N} \sum_{k,l} c_{kl} \log(\frac{e_{kl} \times N}{a_k \times b_l}) - \frac{1}{N} \log(\Omega(P_i, P_j)) \qquad (3)$$

The first term of this equation is the usual mutual information between two partitions. However, this term is known to favor partitions with too many clusters. Therefore, the authors of [13] introduced the penalty term $\Omega(P_i, P_j)$ to penalize partitions with many clusters. Indeed, let R be the number of clusters in P_i and Q be the number of clusters in P_j. This penalty term is defined as:

$$\log(\Omega(P_i, P_j)) = (R - 1)(Q - 1)\log\left(N + \frac{QR}{2}\right)$$
$$+ \frac{1}{2}(R + \beta - 2) \sum_k \log(y_l)$$
$$\frac{1}{2}(Q + \alpha - 2) \sum_l \log(x_l)$$
$$\frac{1}{2}\log\left(\frac{\Gamma(\alpha R)\Gamma(\beta Q)}{(\Gamma(\alpha)\Gamma(R))^Q(\Gamma(\beta)\Gamma(Q))^R}\right)$$

with $w = \frac{N}{N + \frac{QR}{2}}$, $x_k - \frac{1-w}{R} + \frac{wa_k}{n}$, $y_l = \frac{1-w}{Q} + \frac{wb_l}{n}$, $\alpha = \frac{R+1}{R\sum y_l} - \frac{1}{R}$ and $\beta = \frac{Q+1}{Q\sum x_k} - \frac{1}{Q}$.

To find an approximate solution to the median partition problem, the partition of the ensemble maximizing the objective defined Eq. (2) is first found. This partition is then refined by moving objects from the group of isolated parts to clusters, if it improves the objective.

3.2 An Out-of-Sample Extension for HBDSCAN

The python implementation of HDBSCAN proposed by the authors of [12] contains an out-of-sample function, named Approximate Predict (AP). This function first finds the nearest neighbor of the new point that has to be allocated to a cluster. This nearest neighbor is defined with respect to the mutual reachability distance. The function then compares this mutual reachability distance to the apparition level of the cluster to which the neighbor belongs. If the mutual reachability distance between the new point and its neighbor is lower than the apparition threshold of the cluster, the point is allocated to it. Otherwise, it is considered an isolated point. In practice, however, this function can place points very far from any cluster into one of them. To understand why, consider the example presented in Fig. 2. This example has two well-separated clusters. In the cluster tree, the density at which the root cluster is divided into these two subsequent clusters is approximately proportional to the inverse of the distance between them. Therefore, points as far as this separating distance can be placed in these clusters.

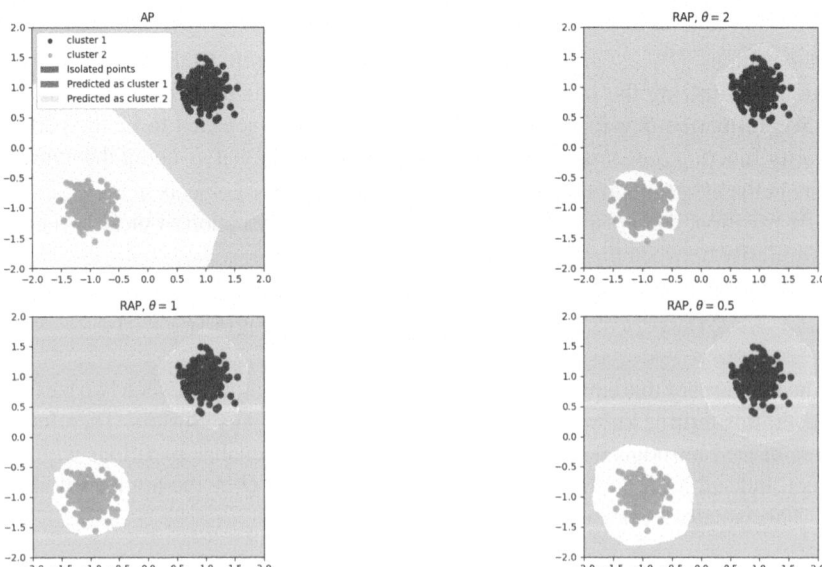

Fig. 2. Area of attraction of two clusters, as predicted by HDBSCAN implementation of AP and our implementation of RAP with three values of θ.

Therefore, we propose here a novel out-of-sample extension for HDBSCAN, referred to as Restricted Approximate Predict (RAP). RAP finds the nearest neighbor of the new point x, and gives it, at first, the same label. The mutual reachability distance $d_{mr}(x)$

between the new point and its nearest neighbor is then compared to the largest distance d_{max} observed between two points of the cluster in the minimum spanning tree used to compute the partition. It should be stressed that this distance is not the level of apparition of the cluster. It is always lower than it. The candidate label is kept if $d_{mr}(x) < \frac{\rho+1}{\rho\theta}d_{max}$, with θ a real valued, positive parameter and ρ the size of the cluster. The term $\frac{\rho+1}{\rho}$ is motivated by the expression of the unbiased estimator of a uniform distribution from a sample of size ρ with maximum v as $\frac{\rho+1}{\rho}v$. While a uniform distribution model is far from what is observed in practice, this correction term allows to be less restrictive for small clusters, for which the maximum estimate would be too approximative. The parameter θ governs the size of the area of attraction of the clusters. As can be seen from Fig. 2, in particular, a value of θ lower than 1 will increase this area of attraction beyond the boundaries of the clusters, while a value higher than 1 will only keep the core of the cluster.

3.3 An Out-of-Sample Extension for Median Partition Algorithms

Consider a general similarity function S to compare base partitions. According to Eq. (2), median partition algorithms aim at finding an approximate solution for the following optimization problem $C = \underset{P}{\mathrm{argmin}}\frac{1}{m}\sum_{i=1}^{m} S(P, P_i)$, with $(P_1, \ldots, P_m)$ the base partitions. Such a base partition P_i can be written as a vector of labels $P_i = (l_{i1}, \ldots l_{iN})$ with N the number of objects clustered and l_{ij} the label of the cluster to which belong the jth object. One of these labels can, eventually, be allocated to isolated points belonging to no cluster at all if the base clustering algorithm allows it. Consider $k \in [\![1, K]\!]$the labels in the median partion $C = (c_1, \ldots, c_N)$. Additionally, let's consider an out-of-sample method predicting a label l_{iN+1} for every base partition. We note $\widehat{P}_i = (l_{i1}, \ldots l_{iN}, l_{iN+1})$ the updated base partitions. Similarly, we note $C_k = (c_1, \ldots, c_N, k)$ the updated median partition placing the new point in the kth group. The final predicted cluster is then kept as the one maximizing the cost function:

$$c_{N+1} = \underset{k}{\mathrm{argmax}}\frac{1}{m}\sum_{i=1}^{m} S(C_k, P_i) \tag{4}$$

This method requires K calls to the cost function, which is, in general, significantly less than what would be needed to solve the whole optimization problem a second time.

4 First Evaluation on Artificial Datasets

This section presents a first comparative evaluation of the proposed method to artificial datasets generated as simplified models of what is observed in production batches from our use-cases. The proposed algorithm is, in particular, compared with the Voting method from [14] and the Support Vector method from [15], as well as with HDBSCAN. The dataset generation methods and evaluation procedure are presented first before numerical results are given and analyzed.

4.1 Datasets Generation

Because this study focuses on the out-of-sample extension rather than on the clustering algorithms themselves, datasets are generated to be voluntarily easy to cluster, as simplified models of what is observed on 3D printed batches of parts.

More precisely, each dataset is generated with two imbalanced anisotropic gaussian clusters, in dimension 2. To initialize the clustering algorithm, the first cluster gathers 900 data points, while the second gathers 100 data points. Both clusters share the same covariance matrix. One of the eigenvalues of this matrix is fixed to 1 while the other is sampled at random between 1 and 5.

For the evaluation of the out-of-sample extension, 100 points are sampled with the same probability law as the first cluster, and 100 points with the probability law of the second cluster. In addition, 100 additional points are sampled to form a link between both clusters, taken so that they are further than 3 standard deviations from each cluster center. As such, these points do not belong to any of the previously observed clusters and should be notified as such by the out-of-sample extension. A representative example is given Fig. 3.

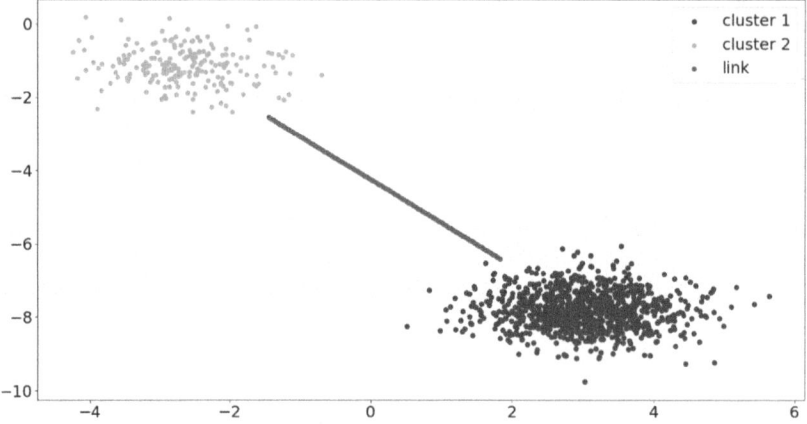

Fig. 3. A representative example of an artificial dataset composed of two clusters. The link points are only used for evaluation.

A hundred random datasets are generated in this manner.

4.2 Evaluation Scores

To evaluate the performances of the compared out-of-sampled method, the precision, recall, F_1 and Matthew coefficient are computed. These scores are first defined on classification tasks with only two labels, -1 and 1. Then:

- The number of True Positive (TP) is the number of data points whose real label is 1 and whose predicted label is 1.

- The number of True Negative (TN) is the number of data points whose real label is -1 and whose predicted label is -1.
- The number of False Positive (FP) is the number of data points whose real label is -1 and whose predicted label is 1.
- The number of False Negative (FN) is the number of data points whose real label is 1 and whose predicted label is -1.

The precision is the fraction of true positive among all data points predicted as positive:

$$\Pr = \frac{TP}{TP + FP}$$

Recall is the fraction of true positive among the data points that are indeed positive:

$$\mathrm{Rc} = \frac{TP}{TP + FN}$$

F_1 is the harmonic average of precision and recall and can be computed as:

$$F_1 = \frac{2TP}{2TP + FP + FN}$$

Lastly, Matthew coefficient is the correlation between the real and predicted labels, and can be computed as:

$$MC = \frac{TP \times TN - FP \times FN}{\sqrt{(TP + FP)(TP + FN)(TN + FP)(TN + FN)}}$$

In the case of precision, recall and F_1, the extension to the multiclass stage is done through macro-averaging. For every class, these scores are computed considering it as the positive class and all others as belonging to the negative class. The final precision recall and F_1 are computed as the average of these per-class scores.

The Matthew correlation extension to the multiclass stage is done through the method proposed by the authors of [16]. Consider a problem with K classes numbered from 1 to K. A label can be represented by a collection of binary variables δ_k taking value 1 if the real label is k and 0 otherwise. Similarly, $\hat{\delta}_k$ represents the predicted labels. The multiclass Matthew coefficient is then taken as:

$$\frac{\sum_k cov(\delta_k, \hat{\delta}_k)}{\sqrt{\sum_k cov(\delta_k, \delta_k) \sum_k cov(\hat{\delta}_k, \hat{\delta}_k)}}$$

With cov the usual covariance estimator.

Numerical Results

The evaluation scores of Voting, Support Vector, HDBSCAN and our proposed method for three decreasing values of θ (1, 0.75 and 0.5) are presented Table 1.

On these datasets, the best performing model for all scores is our proposed RAP with $\theta = 1$, followed by RAP ($\theta = 0.75$). They are then followed by the support vector model and by RAP ($\theta = 0.5$) in that order. HDBSCAN and the voting strategies have systematically the lowest average scores on these datasets.

To further analyses these results, pairwise student tests were run to compare the MC and F_1 scores of RAP ($\theta = 1$) with the second best models here, RAP ($\theta = 0.75$). The p-values of these tests are 3×10^{-6} for the F_1 score and 9×10^{-8} for the MC. RAP ($\theta = 1$) can therefore be considered significantly better than its competitors on these datasets. Interestingly, for the MC score, the support model cannot be considered significantly better than RAP ($\theta = 0.5$) because the p-value of the test comparing the two is 0.6. However, the difference is statistically significant for the F_1 score.

Table 1. Evaluation scores of HDBSCAN, Voting, Support Vector and our proposed method on artificial datasets, averaged over 100 runs. The standard deviations are given between brackets. The highest of each score is highlighted in bold.

	PRECISION	RECALL	F_1	MC
HDBSCAN	46.9 (9.5)	67.5 (4.7)	55.0 (7.1)	58.9 (5.9)
VOTING	44.4 (0.2)	66.6 (0.1)	53.3 (0.1)	57.7 (0.1)
SUPPORT VECTOR	92.6 (9.5)	90.4 (2.3)	90.4 (2.3)	86.8 (2.8)
OUR ($\theta = 1$)	**97.7 (6.1)**	**97.1 (5.5)**	**96.9 (6.8)**	**96.0 (6.9)**
OUR ($\theta = 0.75$)	95.4 (7.9)	95.9 (7.9)	94.2 (10.1)	93.1 (9.8)
OUR ($\theta = 0.5$)	91.2 (9.5)	89.4 (10.3)	87.5 (13.8)	86.0 (12.7)

Most of the differences between these models can be explained by how strict they are at allocating parts in previously observed clusters or predicting them as isolated. This is illustrated by Table 2 which presents the median precision and recall of each model on the simplified task of predicting if a point is in a previously observed cluster or not. For example, the Voting method does not have any way to predict a point out of previously observed clusters and has both precision and recall at zero. Similarly, HDBSCAN can differentiate between points that can be allocated to a previously seen cluster or not but has very large boundaries leading to low precision and recall on this task.

The cases of our proposed method and of the support vector model are more interesting. In particular, for RAP, as θ decreases, the precision increases and the recall decreases. This is because θ impact directly how tights cluster boundaries are. As θ decreases, points further and further from a cluster can be allocated to it, lowering the recall of isolated points. It also means that points predicted as isolated will be less and less likely to have been generated from the same process as the cluster, increasing precision. The support vector model has a rather different behavior. This model leads to extremely strict clusters boundaries. And consider many points on the edges of the gaussian clusters as isolated. This leads to a high recall but rather low precision.

While the most suitable model would of course depend on the use-case and user preference between precision and recall, our proposed RAP presents excellent precision and high recall.

Table 2. Median precision and recall of the six compared models, on the simplified task of predicting if a point belongs to a previously seen cluster or not.

	Precision	Recall
HDBSCAN	0.0	0.0
Voting	0.0	0.0
support vector	78.1	1.0
our ($\theta = 1$)	99.0	98.5
our ($\theta = 0.75$)	1.0	93.0
Our ($\theta = 0.5$)	1.0	78.5

5   An Application to Additive Manufacturing

Additive manufacturing is a term covering a large family of manufacturing processes producing parts through the addition of raw material, usually layer upon layer. These processes are often also called 3D printing. They include, for example, fused filament fabrication that produces parts by melting a filament of raw material through an extrusion nozzle, or powder bed fusion, where layers upon layers of raw material powder are melted by a localized heat source, typically a laser.

One of the main advantages of additive manufacturing processes is their ability to produce parts with complex geometries within a short development time. One of the main usages of these processes is rapid prototyping. However, they are complex processes that are difficult to control and lack repeatability and reliability. This large process variability impairs the large acceptance of these processes for cases with strict geometric and mechanical requirements, for example in the aerospace or medical sector [17]. In the case of powder bed fusion producing metal parts, for example, variations in the powder distribution or laser power can generate porosity or inclusion that degrade the mechanical properties of the parts. Such defects, however, cannot be detected through a simple visual inspection.

This exacerbates the need for fast and reliable quality control methods able to detect off-nominal parts. Resonance testing is one such promising method. It is a non-destructive testing process based on the measure of the resonance frequencies of a part. These resonance frequencies are linked to the mechanical properties of a part, such as its mass and stiffness. The presence of porosities in a part would, for example, lower its stiffness and produce a shift of these resonant frequencies toward the low frequencies.

In practice, however, several factors complexify the use of these methods in the context of additive manufacturing. The first one is the important process variability of these production methods, in particular on the geometries of the part produced, which also impact the resonant frequencies and can hide the presence of internal defects. One potential solution to this problem is the analysis of many different resonant frequencies and their interactions by ML algorithms. The authors of [18], for example, propose a supervised classification model based on a statistical measure of the distance of the parts from the standard behavior of healthy parts, paired with a metaheuristic optimization algorithm to find a threshold able to differentiate between nominal and off-nominal parts based on this distance.

The practical use of these models is, however, impaired by the typical usage of additive manufacturing for low-volume production. The training of such models requires many examples of both nominal and off-nominal parts, which might be too costly to generate for series of only a few hundred to a few thousand parts.

An alternative solution is to use unsupervised models, for example clustering algorithms, directly on produced batches. It would then be expected for nominal parts to be grouped into a single cluster, while defective parts would appear as small groups of parts with similar defects or as isolated points.

Considering that clustering, and in particular clustering ensemble methods, can be a lengthy and computationally costly processes, it is beneficial to pair such models with out-of-sample extensions to allow the fast allocation of new points to previously computed clusters, related to either nominal parts or known types of defects.

Two use cases are presented in the remainder of this paper, differing in their cluster structure. The first one is related to the clustering of titanium cylinders, some of which were willingly printed with internal defects. This dataset presents, by construction, a well-defined cluster structure and no isolated points. The second use-case studies the clustering of turbine blades. Contrary to the first use-case, this dataset was obtained through finite element simulation rather than from the measurement of real-parts. Some parts were simulated with the inclusion of defects localized at the center of the blade while some other present defects scattered at random all over the part. This configuration, therefore, generates a cluster of off-nominal parts surrounded by isolated points.

5.1   First Use-Case: Titanium Cylinders

This section presents the results of the proposed clustering and out-of-sample extension to detect and classify defects in 3D-printed titanium cylinders. Details of the experimental dataset are given first, followed by the evaluation procedure. Detailed results are then provided.

Dataset. This use-case focuses on a batch of 225 titanium cylinders printed simultaneously by powder bed fusion on the same machine by our industrial partner. These cylinders have a length of 40 mm and a diameter of approximately 5 mm. Of these 225 cylinders, 195 are known nominal parts. Ten parts were voluntarily printed with small, seeded defects, generated as small areas for which the power of the laser was reduced during printing. These areas cover approximately 0.1% of the parts. Ten more parts were similarly printed with larger seeded defects covering approximately 0.6% of the parts. The last ten parts correspond to parts printed on one row at one extremity of the printer. Eight out of these ten parts were confirmed to have a frequency response visibly different, from the naked eye, from other parts. Considering that this side of the printer can present uneven powder distribution, the whole raw was given its own question mark label. For defect detection and clustering, ten resonance frequencies of each part were measured in the 25 kHz–200 kHz range. Each part is also associated with one of four labels: nominal, small defects, large defects, and question marks.

Evaluation Procedure. To evaluate the ability of the out-of-sample extension to categorize nominal and defective parts, a leave-one-out strategy is used. 224 of the 225 parts are used to generate a partition, and the out-of-sample extension is used to allocate the last part to one of the found clusters. This part is then given the label appearing the most frequently in the cluster. In practice, this most frequent label would be unknown but could be approximated by carefully selecting a few core-points in each cluster and testing them. Such a method would then fall under the umbrella of active-learning algorithms which aim at training classifiers as efficiently as possible by labelling only part of a dataset. The authors of [19] propose a clear overview of these methods.

This process is repeated 225 times, isolating a different part every time. Classic classification metrics are used to evaluate the performance of the model. In particular, the precision, recall, F_1 and Matthew coefficient are provided. The confusion tables are also studied.

Table 3. Evaluation scores of HDBSCAN, Voting, Support Vector and our proposed method on the titanium cylinder use-case.

	PRECISION	RECALL	F_1	MC
HDBSCAN	0.74	0.80	0.76	0.94
VOTING	**0.95**	**1.0**	**0.97**	**0.96**
SUPPORT VECTOR	0.55	0.63	0.59	0.59
OUR ($\theta = 1$)	0.72	0.80	0.76	0.89
OUR ($\theta = 0.75$)	0.74	0.80	0.77	0.94
OUR ($\theta = 0.5$)	**0.95**	**1.0**	**0.97**	**0.96**

Numerical Results. Table 3 presents the performance scores of the six compared models. As can be seen from this table, the best evaluation scores are obtained simultaneously by the voting strategy and our proposed method, for $\theta = 0.5$. It should, however, be stressed out that Voting requires the expected number of clusters as input while ours does not. In particular, both models achieve extremely high MC, at 0.96 and F_1, at 0.97. They are followed by HDBSCAN and ours with $\theta = 0.75$, while Support Vector has the lowest evaluation scores on this use-case.

The performance of our proposed method is, however, once again highly dependent on the choice of θ. To further illustrate the impact of this parameter, Table 4 present the contingency tables of our proposed method for the $\theta = 1$ and $\theta = 0.5$. This tables indicate, in particular, how many of each type of part (healthy, damaged...) are allocated to which label by the evaluation strategy.

While these matrices should be interpreted with caution in particular due to the method used to determine the ground truth labels, their comparison illustrates that most of the difference between the two values of θ comes from how they are handling isolated points. A larger value of θ makes the allocation of parts to a cluster more restrictive, and

Table 4. Confusion matrix of our proposed method on the titanium cylinder use-case, for $\theta = 1$ on the left and $\theta = 0.5$ on the right.

Predicted \ Real	Healthy	Small damages	Large damages	Question marks
Healthy	193	0	0	1
Small damages	0	9	0	0
Large damages	0	0	9	0
Question marks	0	0	0	8
Isolated defects	2	1	1	1

Predicted \ Real	Healthy	Small damages	Large damages	Question marks
Healthy	195	0	0	2
Small damages	0	10	0	0
Large damages	0	0	10	0
Question marks	0	0	0	8
Isolated defects	0	0	0	0

some points on the edge of the clusters will rather be considered isolated. In particular, in this example, five parts are not allocated to any cluster for $\theta = 1$. On the other hand, the value $\theta = 0.5$ means that even parts relatively far from a cluster can be allocated to it. In this specific case, no parts are considered isolated by the algorithm. Considering that this specific use-case does not contain isolated points, a small value of θ can be safely selected.

5.2   Second Use-Case: Turbine Blades

This section presents results on the detection and classification of defects in a turbine blade. Contrary to the first use-case based on laboratory measurement of 3D printed parts, the dataset presented in this section is obtained through finite element simulation of the behavior of the blade. This, however, allows more flexibility in the composition of the clusters. The remainder of this section first presents the dataset used in these experiments, followed by numerical results.

Dataset. This dataset was generated through finite element analysis of turbine blades, such as presented Fig. 4. The 50 first resonant frequencies of blades with small variations in their geometry, global stiffness and density were computed. In particular, geometric variability was obtained by multiplying the part dimensions along each of the three main axis by a normal variable with mean 1 and standard deviation 0.1. A similar variation was used on the global part density, while its global stiffness parameters (the Young modulus and Poisson ratio) were multiplied by a normal variable with a standard deviation of 1%. It was validated that, in the case of cylinder geometry, this variation led to coefficients of variations of the resonant frequencies similar between the real and simulated data.

1000 parts were first simulated without defects. 100 additional parts were then simulated with defects localized at the center of the blades. These defects are areas with locally reduced stiffness, representing from 0.5% to 1% of the volume of the parts.

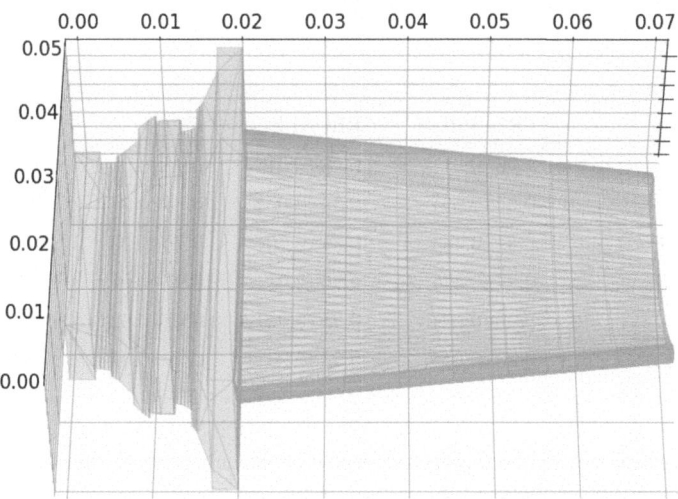

Fig. 4. Geometry of the turbine blade used as base for the finite element analysis.

Lastly, 200 additional parts were generated with similar defects, but scattered anywhere in the part, either in the root or blade.

Evaluation Method. To evaluate the performances of the out-of-sample extension to detect and classify defects, 200 nominal parts are first selected at random from the dataset. This batch is augmented with 20 parts with defects localized at the center of the blade and 20 parts with defects localized anywhere in the part. Contrary to the configuration from the first use-case with well-defined clusters and few isolated points, this configuration is expected to lead to two clusters surrounded by isolated points which are the defective parts with defects localized anywhere. The labels of all parts not belonging to the initial selection are then predicted. The precision, recall, F_1 and Matthew coefficients are then computed as defined in Sect. 4.2. To average out the effect of the selection of the initial batch, this procedure is repeated 30 times at random.

Numerical Results. The evaluation scores of HDBSCAN, Voting, Support Vector and our proposed method are presented Table 5, averaged over 30 runs. The highest scores are obtained for our proposed method with $\theta = 1$, with a MC of 0.96 and a F_1 of 0.97. It is followed by HDBSCAN, with a MC of 0.95 and a F_1 of 0.95. Contrary to the first use-case, however, Voting has, here, the lower evaluation scores. This is due to the inability of this method to predict points as isolated.

The thirty independent runs allow hypothesis testing to be used to verify the significance of the difference between the scores of the compared methods. In particular, paired Wilcoxon signed rank tests were performed to compare the F_1 and MC of our proposed method with $\theta = 1$, and HDBSCAN. This test evaluated the tendency of one of the algorithms to yield higher scores than the other. The p-values of these tests are 1.3×10^{-7} and 3.5×10^{-8} respectively, demonstrating the benefit of our proposed method on this application.

Table 5. Evaluation scores of HDBSCAN, Voting, Support Vector and our proposed method on the turbine blades use-case.

	PRECISION	RECALL	F_1	MC
HDBSCAN	0.96 (0.01)	0.95 (0.01)	0.95 (0.01)	0.95 (0.01)
VOTING	0.64 (0.09)	0.50 (0.03)	0.54 (0.06)	0.52 (0.08)
SUPPORT VECTOR	0.81 (0.14)	0.81 (0.16)	0.74 (0.23)	0.67 (0.29)
OUR ($\theta = 1$)	**0.97 (0.01)**	**0.96 (0.01)**	**0.97 (0.01)**	**0.96 (0.01)**
OUR ($\theta = 0.75$)	0.95 (0.02)	0.95 (0.02)	0.95 (0.02)	0.93 (0.02)
OUR ($\theta = 0.5$)	0.88 (0.04)	0.93 (0.04)	0.89 (0.04)	0.85 (0.04)

Table 6. Confusion matrix of our proposed method on the turbine blade use-case, for $\theta = 1$ on the left and $\theta = 0.5$ on the rignt

Predicted \ Real	Healthy	Center damaged	Isolated damages
Healthy	796	0	5
Center damaged	0	79	6
Isolated damages	3	0	168

$\theta = 1$

Predicted \ Real	Healthy	Center damaged	Isolated damages
Healthy	800	0	44
Center damaged	0	80	18
Isolated damages	0	0	158

$\theta = 0.5$

The evolution of the performances of our proposed method with θ is, however, different for this use-case than for the titanium cylinder. Once again, consider the confusion matrix of our proposed method with for $\theta = 1$ and for $\theta = 0.5$ presented in Table 6. These confusion matrices are averaged over thirty runs and rounded to the nearest integer for readability.

Once again, a smaller value of θ leads to fewer parts being considered isolated, and more parts being allocated to clusters. The high quantity of parts being simulated with isolated damages, however, means that, in that case, a more restrictive value of θ leads to higher evaluation score.

6 Conclusion

Out-of-sample extensions are an important addition to clustering algorithms, allowing the allocation of never-seen-before points to a cluster without recomputing fully a potentially costly algorithm. Very few out-of-sample extensions, however, have been proposed for the specific case of clustering ensemble algorithms.

As a step toward filling this gap in the literature, the present study proposes a novel out-of-sample extension for a median partition clustering ensemble algorithm. This extension is composed of, first, a novel out-of-sample extension for the base members of the ensemble, which are HDBSCAN models, and second, a general out-of-sample strategy for median consensus algorithms.

The performances of the proposed out-of-sample extension are evaluated on artificial datasets and further studied on two use-cases for the detection of internal defects in metal parts produced by powder bed fusion. The first use-case study 3D printed titanium cylinders while the second use-case study turbine blades, simulated through finite element method. The potential of the proposed method to outperform state-of-the-art competitors has been demonstrated in all cases.

An important limitation of the proposed method is, however, the choice of the parameter θ. While a careful inspection of the confusion matrices would point toward using values of θ close to one, with the minor risk of predicting some healthy parts as presenting isolated defects. The optimal value of θ, however, remains application dependent.

Future works will, therefore, focus on the development of unsupervised or semi-supervised methods to select this parameter. Similarly, an efficient active labelling strategy for the clusters will have to be designed. Extensive evaluation of the proposed strategy on multiple benchmark datasets from different fields of application will then be proposed.

Acknowledgments. The authors gratefully acknowledge the ICON RESONAM project which fits in the SIM re- 679 search program STREAM coordinated by Materialise and funded by SIM (Strategic Initiative 680 Materials in Flanders) and VLAIO (Flemish government agency Innovation & Entrepreneur- 681 ship).

References

1. Khanzadeh, M., Rao, P., Jafari-Marandi, R., et al.: Quantifying geometric accuracy with unsupervised machine learning: using self-organizing map on fused filament fabrication additive manufacturing parts. J. Manuf. Sci. Eng. **140**, 031011 (2018)
2. Cheng, F., Raghavan, A., Jung, D., et al.: High-accuracy unsupervised fault detection of industrial robots using current signal analysis. In: 2019 IEEE International Conference on Prognostics and Health Management (ICPHM), San Francisco, CA, USA, pp. 1–8. IEEE (2019)
3. Ladj, A., Wang, Z., Meski, O., et al.: A knowledge-based digital shadow for machining industry in a digital twin perspective. J. Manuf. Syst. **58**, 168–179 (2021)
4. Alqurashi, T., Wang, W.: Clustering ensemble method. Int. J. Mach. Learn. Cybern. **10**, 1227–1246 (2019)
5. Abbasi, S., Nejatian, S., Parvin, H., et al.: Clustering ensemble selection considering quality and diversity. Artif. Intell. Rev. **52**, 1311–1340 (2019)
6. Kuhn, H.W.: The Hungarian method for the assignment problem. Naval Res. Logist. Q. **2**, 83–97 (1955)
7. Fred, A.L.N., Jain, A.K.: Data clustering using evidence accumulation. In: Object Recognition Supported by User Interaction for Service Robots, Quebec City, Que, Canada, pp 276–280. IEEE Computer Society (2002)

8. Vega-Pons, S., Ruiz-Shulcloper, J.: A survey of clustering ensemble algorithms. Int. J. Pattern Recognit. Artif. Intell. **25**, 337–372 (2011)
9. Gionis, A., Mannila, H., Tsaparas, P.: Clustering aggregation. ACM Trans. Knowl. Discov. Data **1**, 4 (2007)
10. Campello, R.J.G.B., Moulavi, D., Zimek, A., Sander, J.: Hierarchical density estimates for data clustering, visualization, and outlier detection. ACM Trans. Knowl. Discov. Data **10**, 1–51 (2015)
11. Graham, R.L., Hell, P.: On the history of the minimum spanning tree problem. IEEE Ann. Hist. Comput. **7**, 43–57 (1985)
12. McInnes, L., Healy, J., Astels, S.: HDBSCAN: hierarchical density based clustering. JOSS **2**, 205 (2017)
13. Newman, M.E.J., Cantwell, G.T., Young, J.-G.: Improved mutual information measure for clustering, classification, and community detection. Phys. Rev. E **101**, 042304 (2020)
14. Chen, Y., Shi, J.: A cluster ensemble strategy for asian handicap betting. In: Leong Hou, U., Lauw, H.W. (eds.) PAKDD 2019. LNCS, vol. 11607, pp. 28–37. Springer, Cham (2019). https://doi.org/10.1007/978-3-030-26142-9_3
15. Park, S., Hah, J., Lee, J.: Inductive ensemble clustering using kernel support matching. Electron. Lett. **53**, 1625–1626 (2017)
16. Gorodkin, J.: Comparing two K-category assignments by a K-category correlation coefficient. Comput. Biol. Chem. **28**, 367–374 (2004)
17. Yang, H., Rao, P., Simpson, T., et al.: Six-sigma quality management of additive manufacturing. Proc. IEEE **109**, 347–376 (2021)
18. Cheng, L., Yaghoubi, V., Van Paepegem, W., Kersemans, M.: Mahalanobis classification system (MCS) integrated with binary particle swarm optimization for robust quality classification of complex metallic turbine blades. Mech. Syst. Signal Process. **146**, 107060 (2021)
19. Settles, B.: Active learning literature survey (2009)

Advanced Process Monitoring and OEE Metrics: Leveraging AASs for Efficiency

Aaron Zielstorff[1] , Dirk Schöttke[2]([⊠]) , Fiona Helena Büttner[2] ,
Thomas Kämpfe[2] , and Stephan Schäfer[2]

[1] Fraunhofer Institute for Experimental Software Engineering IESE,
Fraunhofer-Platz 1, 67663 Kaiserslautern, Germany
Aaron.Zielstorff@iese.fraunhofer.de
[2] Hochschule für Technik und Wirtschaft (HTW) Berlin, Wilhelminenhofstraße 75A,
12459 Berlin, Germany
dirk.schoettke@htw-berlin.de

Abstract. The article shows a way of collecting data to prepare the
Overall Equipment Effectiveness (OEE) using the asset administration
shell (AAS) in a case study. A systematic approach and the use of established methods are essential for this. The established KPI metric for
evaluating equipment effectiveness has proven itself and is used across
all industries for quantitative productivity measurement. The digitalization of systems generates a large amount of data from the production
environment, which forms the basis for modern analysis methods. These
enable, among other things, the detection of anomalies in the plant environment and an increase in machine effectiveness.

With the increasing establishment of the AAS, there is a need for
pragmatic integration of data that supports the process of asset evaluation and optimization. In this context, the use of the "Time Series Data"
submodel offers an effective solution. It defines a uniform standard for
the integration and semantic description of time series data.

The effective integration of time series data into the AAS environment, which enables the comprehensive use of generated process data, is
explained using an example.

Keywords: Asset administration shell · Time series data · Historic
data · OEE · Digital value creation

1 Introduction

Digitisation plays a central role in modern automation technology, particularly
in the integration and efficient use of data. In this context, the Asset Administration Shell (AAS) proves to be a crucial component. It enables the standardised
exchange of information regarding an asset across its entire life cycle [8]. The
rapid increase in data sources, especially through the use of smart sensors and
affordable storage options, leads to an exponential generation of time series data

M. Dassisti et al. (Eds.): IN4PL 2024, CCIS 2372, pp. 59–75, 2025.
https://doi.org/10.1007/978-3-031-80760-2_4

[21]. This data offers significant potential for value creation, providing deeper insight into operations and enabling the implementation of advanced analytics, predictive maintenance, quality control and process optimisation.

However, the challenge is not only to capture time series and historical data effectively, but also to make it available in a consistent manner. To address this, the *Time Series Data* Submodel Template provides a standard that facilitates the integration and semantic description of time series data within the AAS [13]. This interoperable description allows the interpretation and effective use of the generated data points throughout the lifecycle of an asset. Such a framework enables vendor-neutral integration with third-party systems, which can be used, for example, to calculate metrics such as Overall Equipment Effectiveness (OEE).

Based on the aspects outlined, the structure of this paper is as follows: Sect. 2 explains the fundamental concepts of OEE and the AAS, providing an overview of the subject matter and relevant technical background. Building on this, Sect. 3 presents an industrial use case that highlights the necessity of data collection to enable the optimisation of OEE-relevant processes. Section 4 details a method for data collection that utilises the Time Series Data Submodel along with tools for capturing metrics for time series databases. Additionally, a plugin mechanism is introduced to simplify the use of Submodels through a graphical interface. Finally, Sect. 5 illustrates how a prototypical AAS dashboard application can be implemented to visualise OEE data.

2   State of the Art

2.1   Overall Equipment Effectiveness (OEE)

The OEE is an established key performance indicator (KPI) that is used to comprehensively evaluate the effectiveness of a production plant. It measures the productivity of a plant and is used as a statistical indicator across all industries [22,23]. This key indicator enables companies to monitor progress and continuously improve production performance through regular benchmarking. In particular, the comparison of current OEE values with previous ones offers the opportunity to evaluate the effectiveness of optimisation measures that have been introduced. This comparison also allows for managing these measures in a targeted manner. OEE is therefore a key factor in identifying and eliminating efficiency deficiencies in production processes [16].

The OEE is calculated as a percentage value that represents the actual utilisation efficiency of a system compared to its theoretical maximum. The calculation comprises three main components: Availability (A), Performance (P) and Quality (Q). Availability measures what share of the planned production time is actually utilised for production. The performance efficiency evaluates how quickly the system produces in comparison to its maximum capacity. The quality rate indicates the amount of products that fulfil the quality standards without reworking. The OEE is calculated using the following formula [22]:

$$OEE = A \times P \times Q$$

where A, P and Q represent the availability, performance and quality as decimal values.

The calculation of the OEE is not limited to machine data measurement, but also includes the collection of operating data from manual activities. The aim is to recognise the potential of existing plants and operating areas and derive decisions for future investments [17]. The various OEE elements help to quantify potential deficits in the plant environment. The main deficits that can reduce the OEE include [6,7,12]:

1. Downtimes,
2. set up and adjustment processes,
3. idle times and short downtimes,
4. reduced speeds,
5. errors and rework,
6. reduced production during the start-up phase.

Figure 1 shows the OEE time loss model, which represents the various time losses in the context of the total production time. It takes into account both the operating time of the system components (the asset) and the unplanned downtimes. The production takes place during the operating time. Unplanned downtimes, which represent non-value-adding activities, include phases of machine failure and set up. In addition, speed losses and quality defects influence the effective operating time and therefore the overall performance of the system.

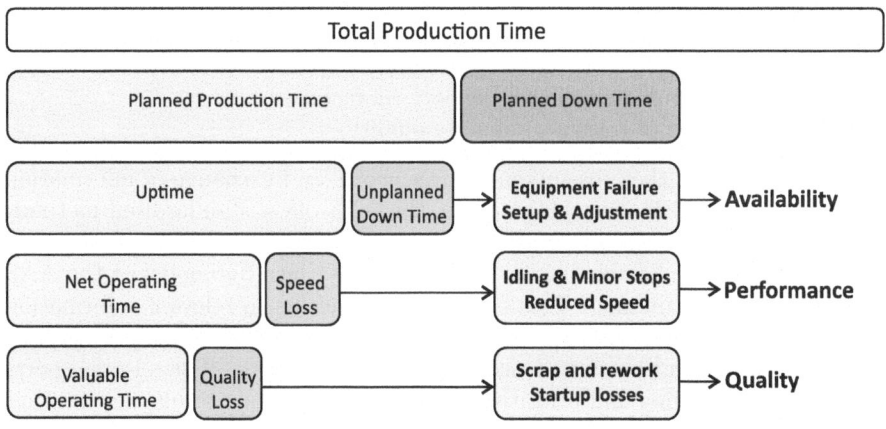

Fig. 1. OEE six big losses and time-loss model [26].

OEE solutions are established in large companies through the use of enterprise resource planning (ERP) systems, which support the identification of deficits and the uncovering of potential for value enhancement. Small and medium-sized enterprises (SMEs), on the other hand, are often still in the early stages of digitising their systems and processes. These SMEs rarely have the required software environments or the necessary knowledge of OEE factors. Moreover, there is usually a lack of understanding of how these factors can be influenced. A crucial starting point for improvements is to deeply understand the existing processes, their dependencies, and the people involved in controlling the production processes.

The fact that there is a lack of implementation knowledge for improving effectiveness was already pointed out in [18]. In [5], guidelines and steps for effective OEE implementation were presented, focusing on the classification and application of OEE as well as possible extensions. The following steps were highlighted for possible improvements:

1. Initiation of projects and team building,
2. Data collection and evaluation,
3. Prioritisation of OEE losses,
4. Analysing root causes and implementing improvements and
5. Validation, control and sustainability of improvements.

The collection and evaluation of data mentioned under point 2 is essential. Its relevance increases when it is integrated into continuous improvement processes. The main focus should be on areas that show potential for future improvements [24]. This is especially important when retrofitting existing systems.

In order to maximise the effectiveness of systems, the precise recording and analysis of machine data is crucial. The following data points are relevant for the calculation of the OEE:

- Changes to the machine status to determine availability,
- Causes of machine downtime to analyse availability losses,
- Time stamp for task start and stop to analyse machine performance,
- produced order quantity to analyse performance and
- produced amount of rejects to analyse quality.

One challenge is the cross-manufacturer access and exchange of information to determine the OEE. For this purpose, the AAS offers standardised methods for describing and providing the required data points. For example, time series data can be made available using the Time Series Data Submodel of the AAS in an interoperable manner. This enables direct access to relevant information for the calculation of the OEE. As a result, the performance level of systems can be evaluated and optimised over their entire life cycle. This also supports companies in analysing and prioritising OEE elements. As a result, deficits that impair the OEE can be determined in a targeted manner.

2.2 Asset Administration Shell (AAS)

The AAS is a standardised digital representation of a physical or logical object, the so-called asset [2]. The AAS can also be described as a digital model of the asset, which, based on metadata, serves as a machine-readable self-description of the corresponding physical or logical component. According to [3], the information model of an AAS consists of the following elements (excerpt):

- Metainformation on AASs, assets, Submodels, etc.,
- Asset-independent and asset-specific Submodels.

Submodels can represent certain aspects of the asset and contain both static and dynamic (or executable) elements. According to [11], an AAS comprises *Submodels* that are used to structure the information and functions of an AAS into distinct parts. Each Submodel refers to a clearly defined domain or subject. Submodels can be standardised and thus become submodel types. An AAS can refer to a Submodels Type, resulting in that submodel instance containing a guaranteed set of properties and functions. The class diagram shown in Fig. 2 gives a detailed impression of the structure of the AAS.

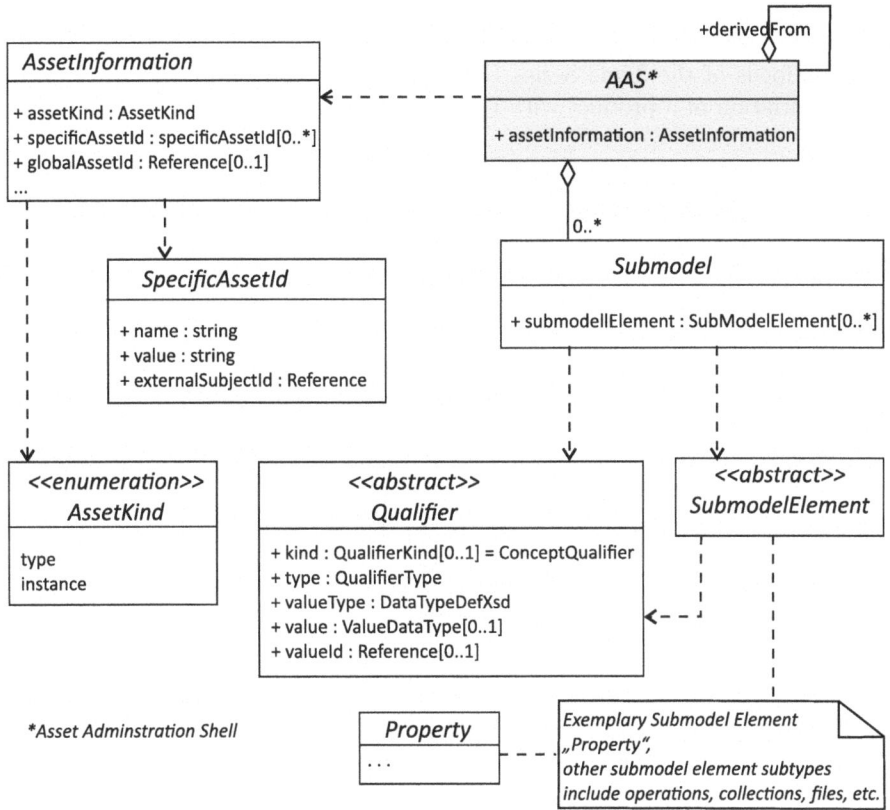

Fig. 2. Excerpt of a class diagram representing the structure of AASs [2].

The *SemanticId* attribute identifies elements of the AAS that contain machine-readable semantics. In addition to the unique identification of the AAS using the ID, a submodel is given a unique global identification. It can be used to reference submodels in information models. The Industrial Digital Twin Association (IDTA) defines a series of standardised Submodel Templates for AASs. These are data models that represent a semantically defined data structure for describing a specific context [3]. These Submodels include, for example, *Digital Nameplate*, *Handover Documentation* and *Time Series Data* [4].

2.3   Time Series Data Submodel Template

The Time Series Data Submodel represents an approach for the semantic description of time series data over the life cycle of an asset. In this respect, the specification defines the integration of external data sources (e.g. database systems) and the storage of time series data in the AAS itself [13]. The use of the Submodel begins in the engineering phase of an asset (asset type). In this phase, the Submodel is created based on metadata of the associated product type. However, the focus of the Time Series Data Submodel remains on the phase after the instantiation of a product with the storage of generated data records [13].

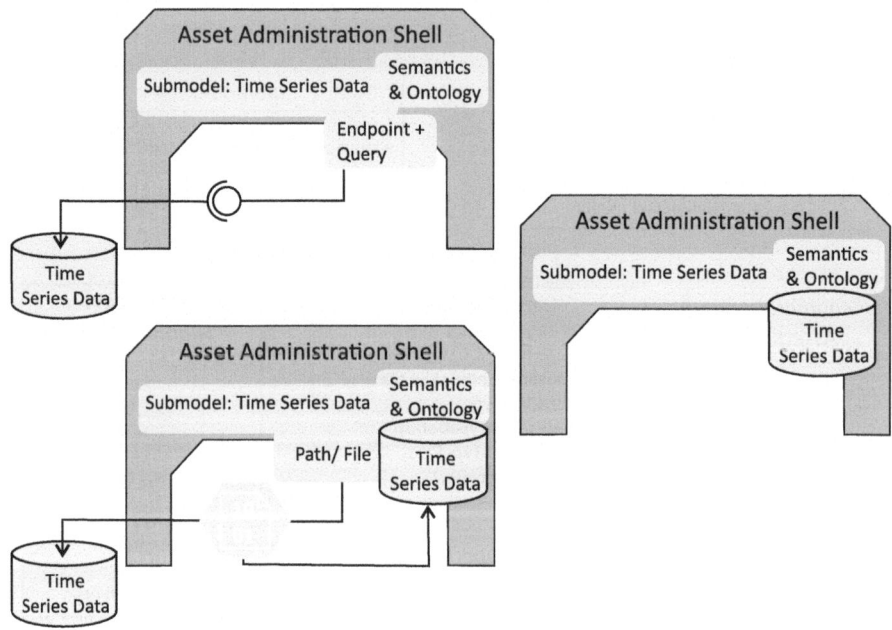

Fig. 3. Types of time series data segments [13].

The Submodel divides time series data into so-called time series segments. A time series segment is defined as a sequence of variables within a time series. A segment generally has a name, a description, a property for specifying the number of data records, a start time and an end time [13]. Other user-defined properties can also be embedded. The standard distinguishes between three types of time series segments [13]. Figure 3 shows the different types of time series segments:

- **InternalSegment.** This type allows managing the structure and content of time series data in the AAS itself. It is suitable for integrating a small number of data points or for integrating fewer data points, e.g. when transferring time series data using AASs.
- **LinkedSegment.** The linked segment enables an Industry 4.0 application to read the end point of an external system by specifying a query. In this case, the time series data is not managed by the AAS. Use cases include brownfield integration, which generates large volumes of data that can be dynamic, with continuous updates from the external system.
- **ExternalSegment.** The ExternalSegment type enables a data or BLOB file to be found in which the time series data is stored. The segment is used for static time series data (especially in brownfield integration). Another use case is the transfer of time series data with a generally low number of accesses to the data set.

3   Use Case: Optimizing OEE with AAS

A partner company that manufactures electromechanical components, among other things, is gradually digitizing its production processes using the administration shell (AAS). This concerns both areas of production as well as the area of checking the quality of the manufactured products. In addition to the objective of digitization, an overview of the resources used is to be prepared.

In this context, the relevant production processes, for example, as well as the specification of the machinery and equipment and their use had to be recorded. Their analysis and subsequent evaluation formed the basis for assessing overall efficiency, for example. This was based on the guidelines and necessary processes described in Chap. 2. The guidelines require the involvement of relevant employees in this process according to their role. In our case study, this mainly concerns those involved in the production process, such as the production manager, the machine operator and the quality engineer. This group of employees has extensive knowledge of

- Production plans and orders,
- machine status and performance,
- quality control reports,
- maintenance schedules and history,
- production capacities and material availability.

Before the employees of the partner company analyzed and evaluated their own systems, the topic of "OEE improvement" was methodically prepared in a virtual factory and test environment. Training on virtual plant components, which were configured to the company's use case, enabled the necessary knowledge to be gained and skills to be trained. The aim was to then mirror the knowledge on a real plant and demonstrate the improvement of the key figures. In the Visual Components environment [25], system components (see example in Fig. 4) of varying complexity were prepared for this purpose, which are controlled via various controllers (PLC).

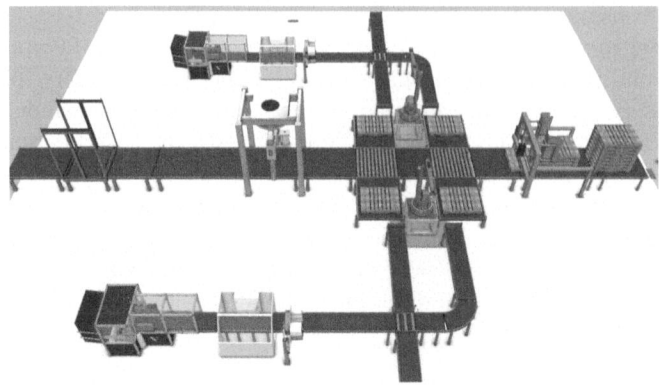

Fig. 4. Virtual factory (excerpt) in the Visual Components environment (example).

For example, the training environment used combines the virtual and real environments. The plant area shown in Fig. 4) shows extensive instrumentation and includes various conveyor belts, industrial robots and components for picking production orders. Here, the virtual area is enriched with real data from various sensors, for example. In addition, information on the resource consumption of real system components and environmental data is integrated as live data. The data is available to the industrial control systems and is processed for use in manufacturer-neutral environments. This also includes information on machine errors and set-up times. These are generated as models in the Visual Components environment. All data is mapped in a previously defined format and is therefore available via an MQTT broker, for example. Each MQTT client can subscribe to the data. In addition, the processed data is also offered via other communication protocols such as OPC UA.

In accordance with the guidelines and phases for optimizing the OEE, a profound understanding of the production processes and the use of the machinery has already been developed with the virtual factory. In this context, the add-ons available in the Visual Components environment should not be used to collect key figures, but rather the data should be collected externally using the real instrumentation and communication structures via administration shells. The controllers used include products from Schneider Electric, Wago and Beckhoff with their Codesys environment.

The analysis of the initial situation of the virtual plant environment resulted in a prioritization of those areas that have a decisive influence on productivity. In this context, the PPR method (product-process-resource) was used in particular to identify the dependencies between product, process and resources. The following differentiation is made [1]:

- A product describes an end product or a clearly identifiable intermediate product of the production system. Products are processed by resources.
- In a technical context, processes, on the other hand, describe the process of changes that are made to the product during production. Examples of this can be manufacturing, assembly or transportation processes.
- Resources describe hardware and software units integrated into the production process. For example, robots, processing machines and transport equipment are assigned to the group of resources.

This approach not only made it possible to map the current processes in detail, but also to obtain/derive relevant information for future optimizations. This data is crucial for the determination of OEE key figures for the continuous improvement of operational efficiency.

In addition to the analysis, data collection using standardized interfaces and their visualization was an essential task. The "AAS Starter Kit" was used here as an example. The "AAS Starter Kit" [10] was presented by the authors at the IDTA stand at the Hannover Messe 2024. It enables the simple preparation of administration shells in a productive environment and the use of standardized AAS interfaces.

The training phase was followed by the analysis and preparation of the initial situation of various production areas in the company. As in the virtual plant environment, the PPR approach was used here. Figure 5 shows an example of this context. In this context, the group of employees from maintenance who look after the plant areas were included in the process. They have knowledge of

- Maintenance plans and history,
- spare parts stocks and availability,
- machine and system specifications,
- diagnostic data and fault reports.

This knowledge allows a more in-depth evaluation of the environment, as the history of the system components can also be included here. The knowledge gained from the analysis forms the basis for the decision to completely retrofit one of the automatic riveting and welding machines involved. The machine is used in the company to manufacture contact springs for electromechanical components.

As illustrated in the Fig. 5, the machine has a continuous tool chain that transports spring plates along several processing stations at three-second intervals. The automatic provision and riveting of rivet switching pieces and the welding of a contact blade take place at these stations. Finally, the finished contact springs are formed and sorted. The retrofit aims to create the basic requirements for OEE optimization and to support the process of digitalizing production.

As part of the retrofit, relevant process information is systematically recorded with the new instrumentation in order to enable a well-founded evaluation and qualification of the production processes. In the case of automatic riveting and

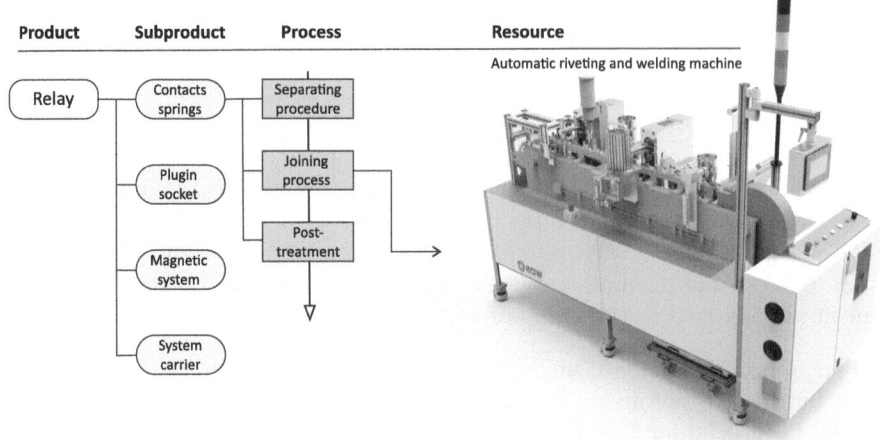

Fig. 5. Automatic riveting and welding machine from EAW Relaistechnik GmbH.

welding machines, this includes monitoring resource consumption, checking the supply, checking the cooling circuit and detecting good and reject parts. The information obtained should be accessible without direct intervention in the processes.

The aim is to implement a digital twin in the standardized form of AAS for effective process monitoring and the provision of information that contributes to the optimization of plant efficiency.

Using the AAS, various sub-models are prepared that promote the process of self-description and analysis. In particular, the Time Series Data submodel and the associated information are intended to drive production optimization. The riveting and welding machine is equipped with a large number of sensors that are used to generate the required time series data. These sensors record electrical parameters, operating hours, flow rates of the cooling system and the quality of production by detecting good/bad parts. In addition, a control concept based on state machines according to the OMAC PackML standard [20] was implemented, which enables a precise representation of system states. The recorded information is to be made available via the standardized interfaces of the AAS in order to enable a tool-neutral connection to OEE evaluation tools. It is also planned to semantically process recorded and aggregated data via the AAS and make it accessible to the actors involved in the process.

The project implementation pursues the following goals:

- Increasing overall system effectiveness by monitoring operating times and performance data,
- Optimization of processes through analysis of time series data, particularly in relation to product quality and material consumption,
- Analysis of energy consumption data to improve energy efficiency,
- Fault identification and diagnosis to minimize downtimes,

- Optimization of maintenance intervals based on actual wear values and usage patterns,
- Monitoring product quality,
- Prediction of tool wear for predictive maintenance and to avoid downtime.

4   Architecture and Implementation

To generate value from the operational data of the system described in the use case, it must first be persisted so that current and historical data can be accessed. In the use case, new data is constantly being generated. As the time series data is therefore not static in nature, it is advisable to use the *LinkedSegment* from the IDTA specification for integration into the AAS.

4.1   Architecture for the Integration of Dynamic Time Series Data

The implementation of the time series data Submodel requires two key architectural components that are important for the integration of time series data in the AAS. The first is the implementation of the AAS, including the Submodels and concept descriptions. Specifically, this is the so-called BaSyx AAS Environment, consisting of the AAS repository, the Submodel repository and the concept description repository [9]. On the other hand, a database system is required to store the time series data.

BaSyx, including its off-the-shelf components, represents a possible and open source implementation of the AAS. As a middleware, BaSyx implements the IDTA specifications regarding the AAS metamodel, the application programming interfaces (API) and the embedded data specifications. It provides the ability to execute runtime instances of AASs that can be read by Industry 4.0 applications using their APIs [9].

There are several dedicated database solutions for storing time series data. These are characterised by their performance in handling large amounts of data and high frequency generation of data points. An example of a time series database is *InfluxDB*. The advantages of InfluxDB are its low query latency, optimised data compression and the ability to query data via http/REST [14].

In order for previously recorded values from used sensors to be stored in the database, they must be connected to the application via connectors. BaSyx provides a possible component for connecting to various industrial protocols. The so-called *DataBridge* supports OPC UA, MQTT, Kafka and several other protocols [19]. However, the use case for the DataBridge has so far been limited to the transfer of live data between the asset and the AAS itself.

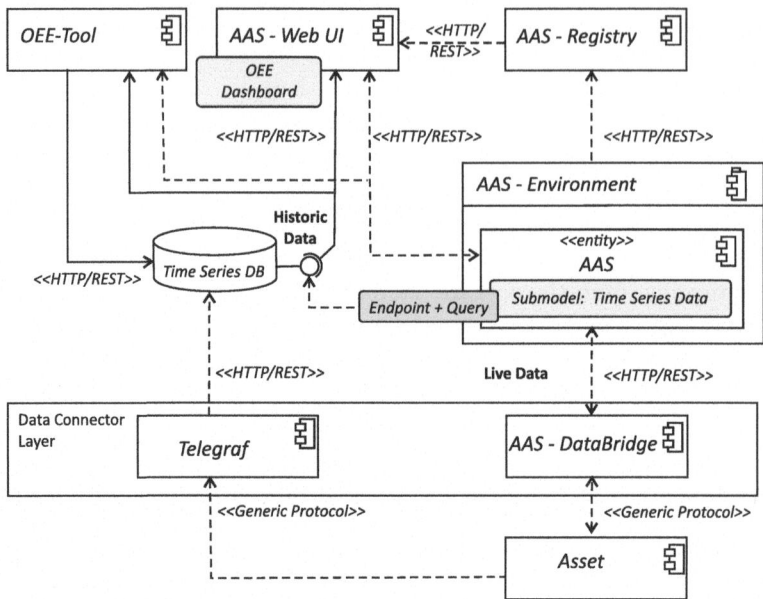

Fig. 6. Architecture for asset integration and integration of time series data.

4.2 Metrics Collection via Telegraf

Components that address this problem also exist in the area of database connectivity for assets. For example, *Telegraf* as a data connector for InfluxDB databases enables the collection of metrics and time series data. Similar to the DataBridge, various communication protocols are supported [15]. Examples include the MQTT protocol and OPC UA, which are being used in the use case described.

Figure 6 shows a component diagram for asset integration when using AAS during the operational phase of an asset. The right side shows the transfer of live data via the DataBridge. A database system (InfluxDB) and a metrics collection tool (Telegraf) are shown on the left-hand side of the diagram. These allow the retrieval and storage of time series data generated by an asset and its installed sensors. The time series data Submodel allows an Industry 4.0 application (here the BaSyx AAS Web UI and an external component for OEE calculation) to access the time series database and query a specific data set from the database using the endpoint and query term. Using a time series database makes it possible to store data points generated at different times. This means that even if a connection to an asset is lost, there are no runtime problems, only empty positions in the data series and its visualisation. Historical data can also be stored and analysed over long periods of time. This allows access to large databases for process analysis and optimisation.

To configure Telegraf to record time series data, a configuration file is first created that contains the connection credentials to the InfluxDB and details of the MQTT broker or OPC UA server used. The configuration file also defines the data to be recorded, including the frequency of data retrieval and the specific data points to be monitored. Once the configuration file is loaded into Telegraf, the component automatically starts collecting data and sending it to the InfluxDB.

4.3   Plugin Mechanism for the Time Series Data Submodel

As digitisation progresses, the need to present machine-readable, digital information in a role-specific way continues to grow. This applies to both the content and the form of visualisation. A plugin mechanism makes it possible to integrate customised user interfaces that are adapted to specific user requirements. This improves the accessibility and comprehensibility of the data by enabling user-oriented visualisation and interaction.

Plugins that address specific AAS Submodels can be easily integrated and shared across different organisations. This also applies to the time series data Submodel. This makes both accessing and visualising time series data more intuitive. Plugins are dynamically integrated by placing selected plugin files in a dedicated plugin folder in the BaSyx AAS Web UI application. This approach facilitates the extension and customisation of AAS systems without the need for extensive programming or changes to the AAS infrastructure.

To determine the availability of a plugin for a specific Submodel, its *SemanticId* is used to check if a suitable plugin exists. If a corresponding plugin exists, it is seamlessly retrieved and displayed in the BaSyx AAS Web UI. For example, the Time Series Data plugin enables the visualisation of time series data from an InfluxDB in the form of diagrams.

4.4   Calculation of OEE Characteristics

The Time Series Data Submodel can be used to retrieve all the base data required for the OEE calculation. This is done via the standardised http/REST interface of the AAS and the http/REST interface to the InfluxDB specified in the Submodel. A dedicated OEE component then processes the retrieved data and calculates the OEE metrics. This is done on the basis of user-defined specifications and configurations stored in the component. The three OEE factors, availability, performance and quality, must first be calculated and then aggregated into an overall metric:

- The availability is calculated from the actual operating time as a percentage of the planned operating time.
- The performance is calculated as the ratio of the actual production quantity to the maximum possible production quantity.
- Quality is calculated as the ratio of fault-free products to the total production quantity.

The OEE KPI is then calculated as a product of the three factors.

As all relevant data points are available in the InfluxDB at all times, the OEE can be continuously calculated and visualised. Both an integrated OEE plugin including dashboard visualisations in the BaSyx AAS Web UI itself and the connection to external OEE evaluation tools can be used. Both approaches shown in the top left of Fig. 6 are supported by the AAS interface in combination with the proprietary database interface.

5 Value Creation from Collected Metrics

The architecture described in Sect. 4 allows relevant information and time series data related to assets to be accessed in a tool-independent manner. As a result, operational data can be visualised in the form of diagrams. This includes, for example, the representation of energy consumption, production quantities or downtimes. The BaSyx AAS Web UI provides various visualisation formats such as bar charts, line charts and histograms. Thus, users can monitor the performance of their systems and manually identify anomalies if necessary.

The next step is to use this available data to calculate OEE metrics. Section 4.4 already describes how these metrics are calculated. Specifically, users first define the target values that form the basis for calculating the OEE factors: availability, performance and quality. The actual time series data is then retrieved from a database and fed into the calculation. This results in OEE calculation values that are now also available as aggregated time series data. These data points can be re-integrated into a time series database and made available again via the AAS in a vendor-neutral manner.

Within the BaSyx AAS Web UI, the Dashboard component allows users to combine their individually configured time series views into clear dashboard windows. These dashboards not only provide a concise and structured view of the data, but also allow views to be saved and reused. Of particular value is the ability to visualise live data for machine monitoring. It is also possible to display previously calculated OEE metrics to monitor and potentially improve the efficiency of plants and machines.

Figure 7 shows an example of a dashboard that visualises various time series and OEE data. It provides a detailed view of OEE metrics for different assets and equipment. Individual metrics, such as availability, can also be viewed over a longer period of time. In addition, it is possible to sort downtime by root cause, enabling the identification of triggers and the implementation of improvement actions.

Fig. 7. Dashboard for OEE monitoring in the BaSyx AAS Web UI.

6   Conclusion and Outlook

The integration of time series data into AAS via the time series data Submodel offers significant advantages over comparable proprietary solutions. A key value comes from the scaling effects that result from the use of this standard. The adoption of standardised and interoperable interfaces greatly simplifies the integration of information from heterogeneous data sources, reducing integration effort and costs in complex production environments.

In addition, the Submodel promotes the assurance of data quality and consistency through a harmonised and semantically unambiguous description of time series data. In contrast to proprietary solutions, which often create isolated data clusters, this standard facilitates cross-system and cross-company data integration. The AAS acts as a central interface for all asset-related information. This enables third-party applications for advanced analytics, such as predictive maintenance and OEE calculation, to gain optimised access to the data they need.

The architecture presented provides the basis for integrating underlying data from plant environments. It also includes the provision of the obtained data points for internal and external processing. As a result, the goal of efficient and tool-neutral OEE metrics determination was achieved.

Based on the continuous OEE calculation, reasons for efficiency shortfalls can be identified in the future and measures for improvement can be identified. The connection to tools with predictive maintenance functions that utilise machine learning is also possible. By integrating time series data into AASs, the potential of digitisation in production can be leveraged and further optimisation can be achieved.

Acknowledgments. This research work was funded in the project"Basys4Transfer" by the Federal Ministry of Education and Research BMBF under the number (01IS22089G). The authors would like to thank the support of the BaSys4Transfer team.

Disclosure of Interests. The authors have no competing interests to declare that are relevant to the content of this article.

References

1. Adler, P., Syniawa, D., Jakschik, M., Christ, L., Hypki, A., Kuhlenkötter, B.: Automatisierte Montage großskaliger Wasser-Elektrolyseure: Digitale Montageplanung für eine nachhaltige Wasserstoffwirtschaft auf Grundlage von Produkt, Prozess und Ressource. Industrie 4.0 Management **IM 38**(5), 12–16 (2022). https://doi.org/10.30844/IM_22-5_12-16
2. Bader, S., Barnstedt, E., Bedenbender, H., Berres, B., Billmann, M., Boss, B.: Details of the asset administration shell: part 1: the exchange of information between partners in the value chain of industrie 4.0, Technical report, Plattform Industrie 4.0 (2022)
3. Bedenbender, H., Bock, J., Boss, B., Diedrich, C., Garrels, K., Graf Gatterburg, A., et al.: Verwaltungsschale in der Praxis, Technical report, Plattform Industrie 4.0 (2020)
4. Belyaev, A., et al.: VWS-Referenzmodellierung: Exemplarische Modellierung einer fertigungstechnischen Anlage mit AASX Package Explorer auf Basis des VWS-Metamodells (2021)
5. Cheah, C.K., Prakash, J., Ong, K.S.: Overall equipment effectiveness: a review and development of an integrated improvement framework. Int. J. Prod. Qual. Manag. **30**(1), 46 (2020). https://doi.org/10.1504/ijpqm.2020.107240
6. da Costa, S., de Lima, E.: Uses and misuses of the overall equipment effectiveness for production management. In: IEEE International Engineering Management Conference, vol. 2, pp. 816 820 (2002). https://doi.org/10.1109/IEMC.2002.1038543
7. Dal, B., Tugwell, P., Greatbanks, R.: Overall equipment effectiveness as a measure of operational improvement - a practical analysis. Int. J. Oper. Prod. Manag. **20**(12), 1488–1502 (2000). https://doi.org/10.1108/01443570010355750
8. Drath, R., et al.: Diskussionspapier - Interoperabilität mit der Verwaltungsschale, OPC UA und AutomationML, Technical report
9. Eclipse BaSyx: BaSyx Java Server SDK. https://github.com/eclipse-basyx/basyx-java-server-sdk
10. Eclipse BàSyx: BaSyx Starter Kit. https://basyx.org/#/get-started/introduction
11. France: Ministry of Economy and Finances, Germany: Federal Ministry for Economic Affairs and Energy (BMWi), Italy: Ministero dello Sviluppo Economico: The Structure of the Administration Shell: TRILATERAL PERSPECTIVES from France, Italy and Germany, Technical report, Plattform Industrie 4.0 (2018)
12. Huang, S.H., et al.: Manufacturing productivity improvement using effectiveness metrics and simulation analysis. Int. J. Prod. Res. **41**(3), 513–527 (2003). https://doi.org/10.1080/0020754021000042391
13. Industrial Digital Twin Association: Time Series Data (IDTA 02008-1-1), Technical report (2023). https://industrialdigitaltwin.org/en/wp-content/uploads/sites/2/2023/03/IDTA-02008-1-1_Submodel_TimeSeriesData.pdf

14. Influx Data: InfluxDB Time Series Data Platform. https://www.influxdata.com/
15. Influx Data: Telegraf - Time Series Data Collection. https://www.influxdata.com/time-series-platform/telegraf/
16. Braglia, M., Castellano, D.M.F., Gallo, M.: Overall material usage effectiveness (OME): a structured indicator to measure the effective material usage within manufacturing processes. Prod. Plann. Control **29**(2), 143–157 (2018). https://doi.org/10.1080/09537287.2017.1395920
17. Muchiri, P., Pintelon, L.: Performance measurement using overall equipment effectiveness (OEE): literature review and practical application discussion. Int. J. Prod. Res. **46**(13), 3517–3535 (2008). https://doi.org/10.1080/00207540601142645
18. Nhaili, A.E., Meddaoui, A., Bouami, D.: Effectiveness improvement approach basing on OEE and lean maintenance tools. Int. J. Process Manag. Benchmarking **6**(2), 147 (2016). https://doi.org/10.1504/ijpmb.2016.075599
19. Schnicke, F., Haque, A., Kuhn, T., Espen, D., Antonino, P.O.: Architecture blueprints to enable scalable vertical integration of assets with digital twins. In: 2022 IEEE 27th International Conference on Emerging Technologies and Factory Automation (ETFA), pp. 1–8 (2022). https://doi.org/10.1109/ETFA52439.2022.9921728
20. Schäfer, S., Schöttke, D., Kämpfe, T., Lachmann, O., Zielstorff, A.: Synchronizing devices using asset administration shells. In: Smirnov, A., Panetto, H., Madani, K. (eds.) Innovative Intelligent Industrial Production and Logistics, pp. 70–92. Springer, Cham (2023). https://doi.org/10.1007/978-3-031-37228-5_5
21. Schütze, A., Helwig, N., Schneider, T.: Sensors 4.0 – smart sensors and measurement technology enable Industry 4.0. J. Sens. Sens. Syst. **7**(1), 359–371 (2018). https://doi.org/10.5194/jsss-7-359-2018
22. Seiichi, N.: Introduction to TPM: Total Productive Maintenance. Productivity Press (1988)
23. Sivakumar, A., Saravanan, K.: A Systemized operational Planning, implementation and analysis of robust framework for improvement of partial and total productivity in textile fabric industry: a research paper. Eur. J. Sci. Res. **53**(1), 385–399 (2011)
24. Stamatis, D.H.: The OEE Primer. Productivity Press, New York, NY (2010)
25. Visual Components: 3D manufacturing simulation software. https://www.visualcomponents.com/
26. Zhou, J., Wang, Y., Chua, Y.Q.: Real-time OEE for Industry 4.0 learning and practice Training. SSRN Electr. J. (2021). https://doi.org/10.2139/ssrn.3864886

Obsolescence Forecasting of Intel Processors: A Transformers Approach

Manelle Nouar[1,2(✉)], Amel Souifi[2], Bertrand Decocq[1], and Marc Zolghadri[2]

[1] Orange Innovation, Avenue de la République, Châtillon, France
manelle.nouar@orange.com
[2] Quartz Laboratory, Rue Fernand Hainaut, Saint-Ouen-sur-Seine, France

Abstract. This study investigates the issue of electronic product obsolescence, focusing on Intel processors within Orange's data centers. As digitization advances, managing stock and addressing supply chain disruptions become critical, particularly when dealing with the obsolescence of key components like servers. A proactive approach to obsolescence management is explored, emphasizing the importance of predicting the life cycle of server components to ensure operational continuity. The research highlights the use of advanced predictive techniques, specifically transformers, to forecast the life cycles of electronic devices. The study aims to provide insights into mitigating the risks associated with obsolescence, thereby aiding in the formulation of effective long-term strategies for maintaining and managing essential electronic components.

Keywords: Deep learning · Obsolescence · Life cycle stages · Predictive analysis · Transformers

1 Research Problem

In an increasingly digitized era, the specter of electronic product obsolescence looms large, posing significant challenges for future planning. Stock management becomes paramount in the face of recurrent disruptions in the supply chain across various sectors, often resulting in prolonged delays, such as extended waits for critical components like servers. Additionally, it is imperative to address the management of obsolete materials, requiring effective recycling strategies and alternatives for manufacturers to reclaim these resources [15].

The situation becomes more complex when essential equipment ceases production, leaving companies vulnerable to shortages and unavailability, compromising the operational continuity of their activities, primarily when dependent on obsolete components.

To mitigate the consequences of these challenges, proactive measures [1] are imperative. Proactive management adopts an anticipatory approach, where measures are taken to prevent or mitigate a potential problem before it arises. This may involve using mathematical models to predict future events and continuous system monitoring to detect and prevent problems before they reach a critical

M. Dassisti et al. (Eds.): IN4PL 2024, CCIS 2372, pp. 76–96, 2025.
https://doi.org/10.1007/978-3-031-80760-2_5

level. In contrast, reactive management is limited to responding to situations as they arise without planning or anticipation. This approach often results in immediate responses. Lastly, strategic management is characterized by a long-term vision and strategic planning to achieve defined objectives. This may involve the development of long-term strategies, establishing action plans, and other strategic initiatives [1].

This study, conducted in collaboration with Orange, a telecommunications company, explores the realm of processor obsolescence as a precursor to understanding server obsolescence within their data centers. The paper emphasizes the importance of individually analyzing server components before examining the entire server to achieve a comprehensive life cycle analysis.

2 Outline of Objectives

Obsolescence, unlike a breakdown, marks the end of the life of a piece of hardware or software [5]. A concrete example is that of a mobile phone, which, although obsolete, still functions but is no longer supported by its manufacturer for updates. This can have security implications, such as attack vulnerabilities, since the system is no longer updated. This is why it is essential to understand the issues related to obsolescence.

This study's main objective is to analyze and predict the obsolescence of Intel processors. Processors play a central role in server operation, which piqued Orange Group's interest in understanding the life cycle of these components in their data centers, given their significant impact on networks. In a data center, servers handle the commands and requests of different users, such as websites, applications, etc. Thus, the server's function is to store and process information and then deliver it back to the users. It is at the core of the entire computer system in the data center. With network virtualization, mobile core network functions are now software deployed on servers through a virtualization or containerization layer. Servers play a crucial role in mobile network resilience and availability of mobile services.

The main objective of this paper is to analyze the obsolescence dates of processors in the market to determine their lifespan. Understanding these obsolescence dates is crucial for businesses, as it allows them to anticipate potential problems related to product availability. Indeed, suppose a company foresees that its electronic components will become obsolete soon. In that case, it can then take measures such as negotiation to ensure the availability of necessary products. The company can anticipate maintaining the electronic components to ensure their proper functioning and avoid premature aging, which can lead to costly disruptions in their operations [7, 15].

The lifecycle begins with product introduction and ends with its phase-out, as illustrated in Fig. 1, where the y-axis represents sales [7].

The first phase is the introduction phase. This is when the product is first introduced to the market. Next comes the growth phase. At this stage, demand for the product is increasing, so sales and production experience significant growth.

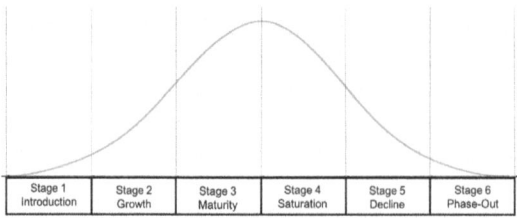

Fig. 1. Product life cycle model.

After the growth phase comes the maturity phase, when sales growth begins to slow down, competition becomes more intense, and competitive products start flooding the market. There is the saturation phase. At this stage, the market has become saturated, and demand for the product begins to decline. Companies face stiff competition and price pressure on the product, which can lead to a decline in profits.

In the decline phase, demand for the product significantly decreases, and companies begin to withdraw the product from the market. Finally, the product is abandoned in the phase-out phase and is no longer produced by the manufacturer.

These different stages of the life cycle of an electronic product are essential for understanding market evolution and making strategic decisions regarding product management.

We explore advanced predictive techniques to achieve this, focusing mainly on transformers. This document serves as an introduction to the use of transformers to predict the life cycle of electronic objects. While machine learning is often used [4,7,16] with algorithms such as random forests, support vector machines (SVM), and recurrent neural networks (LSTM), transformers remain underexplored in the field of obsolescence management. Thus, our goal is to propose an experimentation on transformers to open up new perspectives for future research in this area. Transformers offer several significant advantages for forecasting the lifecycle of electronic devices. Unlike traditional methods such as random forests, SVMs, and LSTMs, transformers demonstrate remarkable capability in capturing long-term dependencies in data sequences, which is crucial for modeling complex trends and patterns in the context of electronic product obsolescence [14].

3   State of the Art

In this state-of-the-art study, various prediction approaches utilizing both statistics and neural networks are explored to determine the most suitable method for anticipating the obsolescence of Intel processors.

3.1   Prediction Algorithms

Over the years, the immense amount of collected data has sparked a true revolution in prediction. Big Data has enabled collecting and analyzing colossal amounts of data, providing a better understanding of user behaviors. This has led to a significant increase in the utilization of machine learning and statistics for prediction, with increasingly advanced and accurate models.

However, it is essential to note that adopting prediction models does not come without challenges. Companies must be able to choose the most suitable prediction method for their needs (see Table 1), as well as the most efficient predictive algorithm, [4] and take into account the cost of deployment. It is also essential to have a good understanding of the limitations of prediction models to avoid errors.

Table 1. The most popular prediction algorithms.

No.	Prediction Algorithms
1	Gradient Boosting Machines
2	Naive Bayes
3	Random Forest
4	Support Vector Machine
5	Linear Regression
6	Logistic Regression
7	Decision Trees
8	k-Nearest Neighbors
9	Neural Network

Statistics and neural networks are two commonly used approaches for prediction.

Modeling time series involves the use of statistical or deep learning approaches. Statistical analysis consists of examining the variation of a variable over time, using techniques such as trend analysis, seasonal decomposition, and ARIMA models, cf. Sect. 3.2.2. Time series are utilized to predict short- and long-term trends.

Neural networks are deep learning models that use algorithms to recognize patterns in data. RNNs are used to predict trends and patterns from time-series data and are often applied to complex tasks such as image recognition, language translation, and word sequence prediction

3.2   Time Series Models

The prediction of time series involves forecasting future events based on past data. To achieve this, models are built from historical analysis, allowing us to track the evolution of a phenomenon over time and analyze trends, seasonal variations, and noise [2].

Autoregressive (AR) components predict future values based on a linear combination of past values within the series. Moving Average (MA) components forecast future values using past forecast errors. The ARMA model combines AR and MA components to model stationary time series with consistent statistical properties over time.

ARIMA integrates differencing to achieve stationarity and models trends and seasonal effects. SARIMA extends ARIMA by incorporating seasonal variations suitable for data with recurring patterns like seasonal sales fluctuations. SARIMAX extends SARIMA by including exogenous variables that influence the time series alongside seasonal trends. These models use ARMA terms for dependence on past values, integration terms for overall trends, and seasonal terms for periodic fluctuations [2,18].

3.3   Neural Networks

What Is a Neural Network? A neural network is a machine learning model used for various tasks such as prediction, classification, anomaly detection, etc. Inspired by the nervous system, a neural network employs mathematical and physical processes to simulate the functioning of neurons [13].

Unlike traditional prediction tools such as linear regression, which are limited by simplicity, neural networks excel in predictive analysis because they can learn from data nonlinearly and capture complex relationships. Neural networks consist of multiple interconnected layers that extract significant features from data and combine them to make predictions [13].

Gradient descent is employed to minimize the cost function, representing the difference between the value found by the neural network and the actual value. The goal is to reduce this difference so that the value the neural network predicts closely matches the exact value. The gradient descent method is used to minimize the cost function. This method determines the direction in which to update the network's weights, whether to increase or decrease the weights. It is called backpropagation because it updates the weights backward and then repeats the gradient descent method to minimize the cost function. This approach determines how the cost function evolves in a direction until it reaches its minimum [13].

Multilayer Perceptron. Multilayer Perceptrons (MLPs) are a neural network architecture designed to process data, including time series.

Unlike single-layer perceptrons with only an input and output layer, MLPs are characterized by their multilayer structure, including hidden layers. Each hidden layer can contain multiple neurons, allowing for a more complex representation of the data [12].

The significant advantage of MLPs lies in their flexibility: the number of hidden layers, the number of neurons in each layer, and the activation functions can be adjusted according to the specific needs of the problem and the data. This adaptability enables them to effectively model nonlinear relationships between variables, making it possible to solve complex tasks in machine learning [12].

To address nonlinear problems, MLPs use various activation functions such as sigmoid, hyperbolic tangent (tanh), or ReLU. These functions enable MLPs to learn complex patterns in the data, making them powerful tools for modeling and prediction [12].

However, it is essential to note that MLPs may require extended training times, especially when faced with large datasets due to the high number of parameters to adjust [12].

In summary, MLPs are a versatile neural network architecture that can be used in time series. They offer great flexibility and the ability to solve various problems in machine learning [12].

Recurrent Neural Networks for Prediction. In this sentence, "RNN" refers to "Recurrent Neural Networks", which are used to predict time series due to their ability to recognize and capture repeating patterns and trends over time. Unlike other neural networks, RNNs have built-in memory that allows them to consider the history of past data when predicting future values [6].

However, RNNs encounter a problem related to backpropagation through time. When RNNs are used to predict time series, they must consider the history of past data to make accurate predictions. However, when gradients propagate over long time sequences, their value can decrease significantly, making learning difficult. This gradient decay can decrease network performance as RNNs struggle to effectively capture long-term patterns and trends [6].

Variants of RNNs, such as LSTMs, have been developed to address this issue. LSTMs are recurrent neural networks designed to solve the problem of long-term information accumulation in data. LSTM networks stand out for their ability to handle time series data effectively, owing to their knack for capturing complex, nonlinear patterns and long-term dependencies among observations. In contrast to ARIMA and SARIMA models, which rely on autoregressive terms like moving averages to forecast future values, LSTMs leverage input time sequences to make predictions. A key distinction is that while ARIMA analyzes one variable at a time, LSTMs can process the entire dataset simultaneously. Specifically, ARIMA scrutinizes each time series in isolation, focusing on the temporal dependencies intrinsic to each series, with no regard for variable interactions. Conversely, LSTMs can implicitly incorporate inter-variable dependencies through their recurrent architecture, thus enabling the capture of nuanced relationships among different data series [6].

LSTMs are equipped with special mechanisms that allow them to control the flow of information within the network and remember relevant information for long-term time series prediction. They can decide how much information to retain or forget based on the importance of each piece of information [8].

AutoEncoder for Prediction. Autoencoders are neural networks designed for data compression and reconstruction. The architecture of autoencoders consists of two main parts.

The encoder part is responsible for compressing the input data into a reduced version called the "latent" representation. It uses neural layers to capture essential features of the data and reduce their dimensionality. This latent representation contains a condensed version of the data by removing noise, i.e., irrelevant information [6].

Once the data is compressed into the latent part, the decoder takes charge of decompressing and reconstructing the data to obtain a version close to the original input. The decoder uses another layer or set of neural layers to restore the original dimensions of the data. The decoding objective is to produce an output that closely resembles the initial input using only the information contained in the latent part [6].

When input data exhibits abnormal characteristics or does not match the usual transaction pattern, the autoencoder struggles to reconstruct it accurately. The difference between the decoded output and the original input is often used to measure the reconstruction error. Thus, when this error exceeds a predefined threshold, the autoencoder can identify this data as an anomaly, contributing to anomaly prediction or detection of unusual events [6].

Transformers for Prediction. Some research shows that Transformers is an effective method for predicting quantitative values [3,11,17], providing accurate results superior to other methods. This has made Transformers one of companies' most commonly used prediction approaches today [11].

Transformers are renowned for their use in natural language processing (NLP) [14] and computer vision. Their popularity in these fields stems from their ability to capture and understand complex relationships between data elements.

This method offers numerous advantages, including learning complex seasonal patterns, handling noise in data (such as outliers), and identifying and managing long-range dependencies.

Sequence Prediction. In language, the order of words is paramount to ensure effective communication, with sequences playing a crucial role in our expression. With the advent of transformers, sequence analysis has significantly expanded, allowing for more profound gradient optimization and granting more power to machines [14].

Sequence prediction is often associated with tasks such as translating sentences from one language to another, where each word in the source sequence is transformed into an equivalent target sequence. However, its scope is much broader. Indeed, sequence prediction also encompasses generative models (GANs) capable of producing images or text.

Classification and Regression. Transformers are suited for NLP tasks and have proven effective in analyzing quantitative data. [10,19,20] have adapted this algorithm to forecast univariate and multivariate time series. Transformers are used in regression and classification tasks. Several pre-trained models are available for automated tasks, including well-known models such as BERT, GPT, and N-BEATS, among others [17].

BERT is particularly renowned for its accurate results. However, its implementation is complex and requires substantial computing resources for training.

In Fig. 2, the algorithm for BERT is depicted [3].

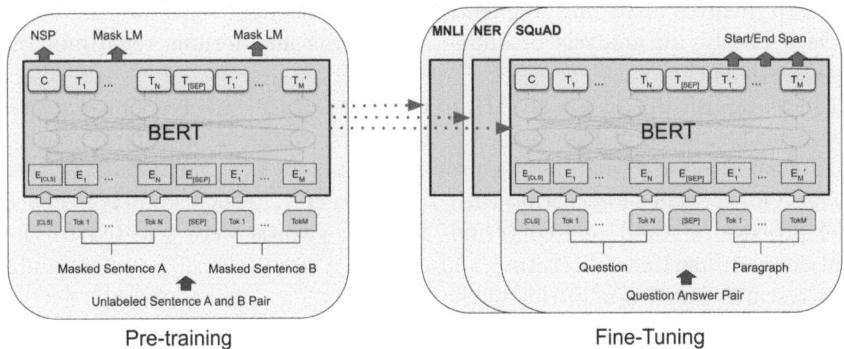

Fig. 2. Pre-training of Deep Bidirectional Transformers.

The purpose of this model, which is trained on unlabeled data, is to predict the output of a word based on the sentence context. BERT can be trained bidirectionally to have a sufficiently broad context to predict the next word more accurately. It considers the context of the word before and after each word [3]. The process consists of several phases. First, there is the pre-training phase on a massive text corpus. The model is trained on data without labels for which the answer is unknown. In our case, this involves processors whose obsolescence date is unknown, and the model will learn to predict when a processor will become obsolete. The model can rely on the product introduction date to estimate the end-of-life date [3].

Another phase is Fine-Tuning, which means that once our model is ready, its parameters must be adjusted to obtain more accurate results with the smallest possible margin of error. For this, processors with known end-of-life dates are provided to the model, which adjusts its weights for better adaptation.

In the Bidirectional Encoding phase, it considers the history of obsolete processors and those that are not to capture complex information in the data.

Regarding Multi-Head Attention, BERT selects the most relevant parts of the data to produce an accurate prediction.

4   Methodology

4.1   Keyword Search

Before delving into the study of Intel processor obsolescence, assessing existing research and work in this domain was crucial. Firstly, a search on Google Scholar is conducted to identify relevant articles in the field of processor obsolescence management. Next, a visualization is presented, illustrating publications referenced by Google Scholar on obsolescence prediction with transformers. The third step involves analyzing frequently asked questions by users during Google searches. Lastly, an analysis of online discussions and forums regarding Intel processors is performed.

To accomplish this, using an API to conduct keyword analyses proved indispensable. The choice of keywords was guided by the need to comprehensively capture the discourse surrounding processor obsolescence, encompassing terms such as "Obsolescence forecasting with Transformers", "processor obsolescence", "intel processors", and related terms. These keywords were selected to thoroughly explore pertinent literature and provide a comprehensive understanding of the research landscape in this field.

Table 2. Keyword search on Google Scholar.

Id	Title	Publication	Authors	Cited By Total	Date
1	Intermittent demand forecasting with transformer neural networks	Annals of Operations Research	GP Zhang	4	2023
2	Sparse Time Series Demand Forecasting for Intermittent Availability	Chalmers ODR	O Helgesson	1	2023
3	Electrical obsolescence management: How to spend $1 B efficiently	IEEE PCIC	R Pragale	1	2014
4	INFRANET: Forecasting intermittent time series using DeepNet with parameterized conditional demand and size distribution	ICDM Workshops	Diksha Shrivastava	0	2023
5	Obsolescence in urban energy infrastructures: the influence of scaling laws on consumption forecasting	Journal of urban technology	R Horta-Bernús	6	2015

The results of a keyword search on Google Scholar are presented in Table 2, highlighting the top five articles appearing at the forefront of this search. This preliminary step provided an overview of previous work, thus offering essential context to our analysis while also underscoring the growing interest in prediction research and the increased need to integrate Transformer neural networks into electronic object obsolescence management.

Next, Fig. 3 presents a histogram illustrating the publications referenced by Google Scholar on the theme of obsolescence forecasting with Transformers. The highest-ranked publications are arranged on the x-axis, while the corresponding number of citations is depicted on the y-axis. This visualization highlights

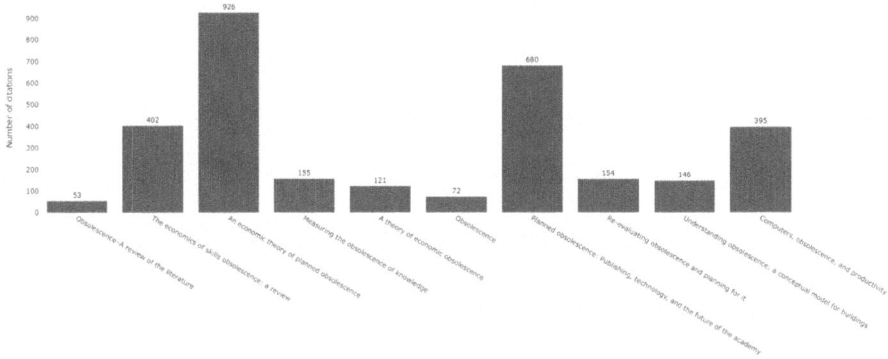

Fig. 3. The key papers on obsolescence forecasting with Transformers and their number of citations.

the relationship between the position of documents in search results and their impact, measured by the number of citations they have accumulated.

When conducting a Google search using the keyword "Obsolescence forecasting with Transformers", the most frequently asked questions appearing first are listed in Table 3. These questions represent users' initial concerns or common queries regarding obsolescence. These questions encapsulate various aspects of interest and concerns regarding the utilization of Transformers in this domain. They range from understanding the comparative performance of Transformers and LSTM models to discerning the differences between different recurrent neural network (RNN) architectures and Transformers for time series analysis. These inquiries signify the curiosity and exploration surrounding the effectiveness and suitability of Transformers in predictive modeling tasks.

Table 3. Top Frequently Asked Questions.

No.	Research Question (RQ)
RQ1	Can Transformers be used for time series forecasting?
RQ2	When to use LSTM instead of Transformer?
RQ3	Can Transformers give us better performance in time series forecasting than LSTM?
RQ4	What is the difference between RNN and Transformers for time series?

Table 4 presents the most frequent searches on Google associated with the keyword "Obsolescence forecasting with Transformers".

Table 4. Top Searches Related to Obsolescence on Google.

No.	Related Searches (RS)
RS1	Obsolescence forecasting with transformers pdf
RS2	Obsolescence forecasting with transformers github
RS3	Are transformers effective for time series forecasting?
RS4	Transformer for time series forecasting github
RS5	Itransformer: inverted transformers are effective for time series forecasting
RS6	Transformers for time series forecasting

Finally, Table 5 provides a detailed analysis of discussions held in online forums regarding Intel processors.

Table 5. Google Discussions and Forums API.

Id	Title	Source	Date
1	Why the older intel Core i series processors last so long and are still not obsolete, unlike the core 2 duos?	Reddit	8 months
2	TIL that all Intel processor are manufactured	Reddit	2 years
3	How do you compare different generations of Intel processors?	Ars Technica	4 years

4.2 Data Preparation

The first step, far from simple, involved retrieving data from the Intel processor's website. To do this, it was necessary to start by extracting the various links and collecting the data for each Intel processor using the UIpath tool. The data was collected in January 2024 from the Intel site and has not been updated since. The data collection process took an entire week.

Initially, an algorithm was developed to use the Firefox browser to retrieve the links to the pages containing the data for each processor. Once the links were retrieved, they were stored in an Excel sheet.

Next, another algorithm was designed to go through each link stored in the Excel file and extract the information related to the processors. For each link, the algorithm opened a new web page in Firefox, retrieved the detailed information for each processor from a specific table, and then saved it in a new Excel sheet. This process was repeated for each link present in the original Excel file.

The collected data comprises 257 unique features, including, for example, the number of cores corresponding to the number of independent processing cores in the processor. It also provides information such as thermal design power, which represents the maximum amount of heat that the processor cooling system must dissipate, cache memory, and base frequency, indicating the average operating clock speed of the processor, among many other characteristics. Each row of the table represents a processor.

4.3   Data Cleaning

After data collection, a crucial step involved formatting them for proper use.

The processor data table from Intel's website was not presented in a standard format, with variables arranged at the top of columns and observations for each processor aligned in rows. It was necessary to properly structure this data into a table by flipping rows and columns while delineating each processor. This data formatting task was accomplished using Python.

Next, following data collection, a crucial step involved transforming them to make them compatible and actionable. This entailed standardizing measurements on the same scale to make them comparable, converting data into different types such as integers, dates, floating-point numbers, or strings, and handling missing or outlier values as needed. Excel also proved very useful for standardizing data language. The data were in both English and French; for instance, for a feature, binary responses could be found in a column such as "yes", "oui", "no", or "non". Moreover, the feature names varied between translations, necessitating human intervention to visually identify the corresponding columns without relying on an algorithm. In summary, the goal was to make the data homogeneous and ready for subsequent analysis.

The final dataset includes an 'id' variable representing the processor references, the product launch date, the end-of-service date, the 'y' variable representing the product's lifespan (our target variable), and several quantitative exogenous variables such as the number of cores, base frequency, and Processor Designation Type (PDT), among others.

4.4   Data Analysis

This section, dedicated to data analysis, aims to delve deeply into Intel's dataset to better understand it, thus facilitating the subsequent selection of the most relevant features.

Figure 4 depicts the timeline of launches for four Intel processors. The x-axis indicates the launch dates of the processors, while the y-axis shows the number of processor variants for each collection launched on each date. A significant trend emerges: the production of the older Intel Core processor has steadily increased over the years, indicating a market presence since 2013. However, processors from the 7th Generation Intel Core i7, the Intel Xeon E3 v6 processor family, and the 8th Generation Intel Core i7 had fewer variants per collection. Between 2022 and 2023, no new versions with additional features were launched for these three processor families.

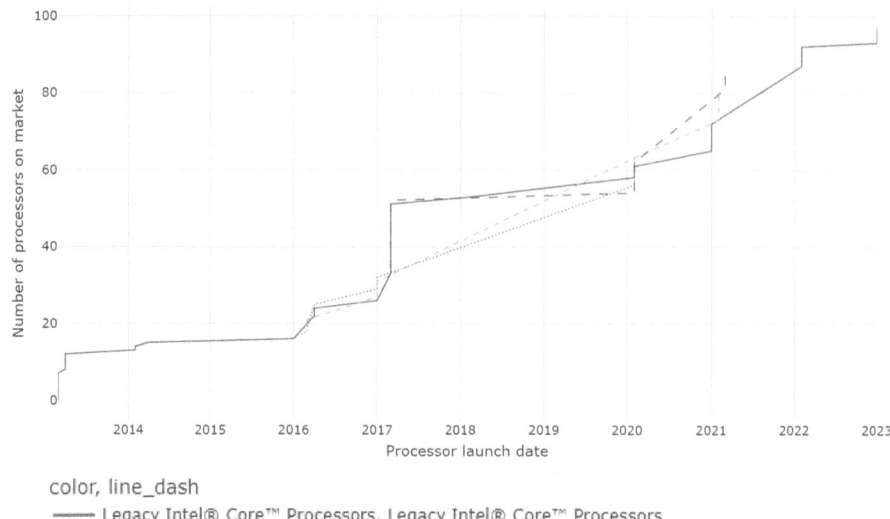

color, line_dash

    ──── Legacy Intel® Core™ Processors, Legacy Intel® Core™ Processors

    ····· 7th Generation Intel® Core™ i7 Processors, 7th Generation Intel® Core™ i7 Processors

    ── ── Famille de processeurs Intel® Xeon® E3 v6, Famille de processeurs Intel® Xeon® E3 v6

    ──── 8th Generation Intel® Core™ i7 Processors, 8th Generation Intel® Core™ i7 Processors

Fig. 4. Introducing Processors to the Market.

Figure 5 depicts the lifespan of five Intel processors. It highlights a notable disparity in the longevity of these components: some exhibit a lifespan of five years or less, while others endure beyond fifteen years. However, an intriguing aspect lies in the presence of outliers among processors with seemingly shorter lifespans yet persisting longer than expected in the market.

Several factors can explain this anomaly. For instance, these processors may benefit from sustained demand despite their seemingly inferior lifespan characteristics due to their competitive pricing or suitability for specific market needs. Additionally, external factors such as slower-than-anticipated technological advancements in the field or shifts in market trends could also contribute to keeping these processors on the market longer than initially expected.

In summary, while these outliers may appear counterintuitive, they underscore the complexity of factors influencing product lifespan in the market.

4.5   Constraint Identification

When identifying constraints, it was crucial to consider the 257 characteristics and determine the most relevant ones for predicting processor obsolescence. Another challenge was using a neural network despite a significant amount of missing data, totaling 585 291 values, and the low number of observations, amounting to 2 958 occurrences. These conditions can affect predictions by introducing a margin of error.

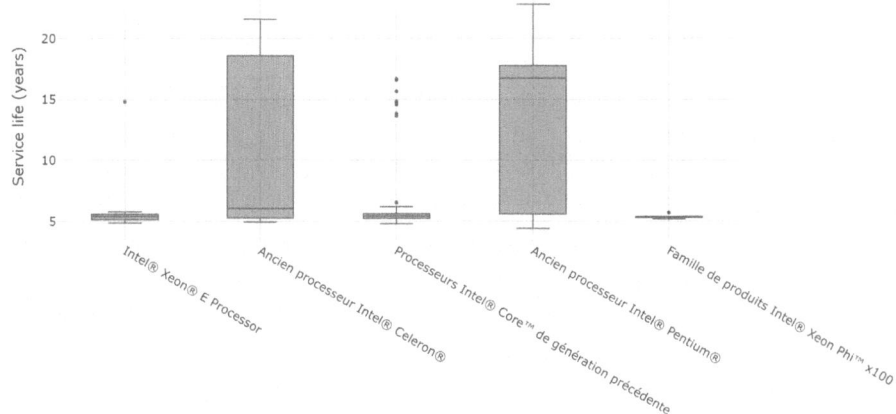

Fig. 5. Processor Lifespan (years).

Other factors can also influence predictions, such as periods of sharp recessions in Intel processor sales, often caused by increased competition. Competitive offerings in performance, price, or features can divert potential customers.

Additionally, market trends can influence processor sales and obsolescence. The emergence of new technologies like artificial intelligence and cloud computing can alter the demand for certain types of Intel processors.

These behavioral changes must be considered in the study as they can significantly affect prediction reliability.

4.6   Target System Approaches

Approaches concerning the target system aim to establish a robust forecasting model by leveraging historical data of processors currently on the market and those that have been phased out.

With this aim in mind, two main approaches have been considered:

– The first involves utilizing machine learning techniques to examine the commercial lifespan of processors on the market and those phased out.
– The second approach proposes developing a personalized recommendation system rooted in machine learning. A continuous data stream on obsolete processors and other relevant variables would fuel this system. By analyzing this data, the system could formulate specific recommendations tailored to observed behaviors during processor sales.

Following a thorough analysis of the advantages and constraints of each approach, the first one has been chosen.

The advantages of this first approach lie in the accuracy of the forecasts provided by the transformers. Neural networks are particularly effective at detecting complex trends in data. They adapt to variations, and the models can be continuously updated and adjusted, enabling them to remain relevant in the face of changes.

However, implementing these models poses particular challenges. Their creation and maintenance require advanced technical skills and significant computing resources. Moreover, the reliability of forecasts heavily depends on the quality and quantity of available historical data. Insufficient or poor-quality data can lead to unreliable predictions.

The advantage of the second approach lies in the customization of the recommendation system, which can provide specific suggestions tailored to individual needs. It is also beneficial for integrating various variables, such as processor market trends, customer preferences regarding features, and data on obsolete products, to provide relevant recommendations. These are pieces of information we don't have.

However, this approach also presents drawbacks. Developing and maintaining such a system can be costly and complex, requiring robust infrastructure and significant technical resources. Additionally, recommendation systems heavily rely on real-time data and require a continuous flow of up-to-date data to function correctly, which can be challenging to ensure.

Ultimately, developing a forecasting model provides a solid foundation for accurately and reliably anticipating fluctuations in the processor market.

5   Expected Outcome

5.1   Identification of Key Algorithms

N-BEATS is a transformer-based algorithm designed to make predictions on time series data [10].

It consists of multiple blocks called "Stacks", each comprised of two types of layers: "trend" layers and "seasonality" layers [10].

The "trend" layers are responsible for predicting the general trend of the time series. For example, in the context of processor sales over time, this layer aims to determine whether sales are increasing, decreasing, or remaining stable over a given period [10].

As for the "seasonality" layers, they are specifically designed to detect and predict cycles in the data. For instance, processor sales tend to increase during IT events or decrease during certain seasons like holidays.

The N-BEATS algorithm is trained on historical data using gradient descent, which adjusts the model's parameters to minimize the prediction error between actual and predicted values [10].

This model was chosen because it is based on transformer architecture, ensuring efficient sequential data processing. Its learning time is faster than that of traditional methods. Furthermore, this efficiency requires fewer data samples to be trained, which can be a significant advantage in contexts where data is limited or costly to collect. N-BEATS adapts to both long-term trends and short-term patterns, giving it great flexibility and adaptability to data [10].

To evaluate the effectiveness of transformers, we compared them to a linear regression model. Given that we aim to predict a continuous value over time and that linear regression is a simple model to implement, this comparison is particularly relevant.

Linear regression is a statistical method to model and predict the relationship between a dependent variable (y) and one or more independent variables (x). Simply put, it seeks to draw a straight line (or a hyperplane in the case of multiple independent variables) that best fits the available data [9].

The equation for simple linear regression is as follows:

$$y = a + bx$$

- y: dependent variable (what we want to predict).
- x: independent variable (what influences y).
- a: intercept (the y-value when x is 0).
- b: slope of the regression line, indicating the change in y for a one-unit change in x.

5.2 Experimentation of Algorithms

We conducted training sessions with the N-BEATS model using data from discontinued processors. Subsequently, we evaluated the model's performance on this data, for which we already knew the obsolescence dates and lifespans.

Predictions for the lifespan of discontinued Xeon processors are shown in Fig. 6. This plot compares the predicted commercial lifespan of the processors, shown in red, with the actual values in blue. According to the graph, the lifespan of processors is generally less than 6 years. However, some models significantly exceed this average, with longevity sometimes surpassing 6 years. These differences can be attributed to various factors, such as usage conditions, technological advancements, and strategies for updating or replacing components. Conversely, some processors have shorter lifespans, sometimes less than five years, often due to manufacturing defects. Generally, processors designed for servers have an average lifespan of around five years. The forecast for Xeon processors in the coming years is shown for 3 years in the graph.

To evaluate the model's performance (see Table 6), we used the Mean Squared Error (MSE), a commonly employed metric in regression models. In this context, we seek to determine the obsolescence date for a family of processors. The MSE measures the average of the squares of the errors, which is the average of the squares of the differences between the actual values (y_i) and the predicted values ($\hat{y}_i$). This metric indicates the magnitude of prediction errors.

$$\text{MSE} = \frac{1}{n} \sum_{i=1}^{n} (y_i - \hat{y}_i)^2$$

Table 6. Analysis of Discontinued Processor Performance.

Training Size (%)	MSE (Transformers)	MSE (Linear Regression)
50	0.0485	0.0527
60	0.0570	0.0665
70	0.0629	0.0723
80	0.0709	0.0804
90	0.0593	0.0991

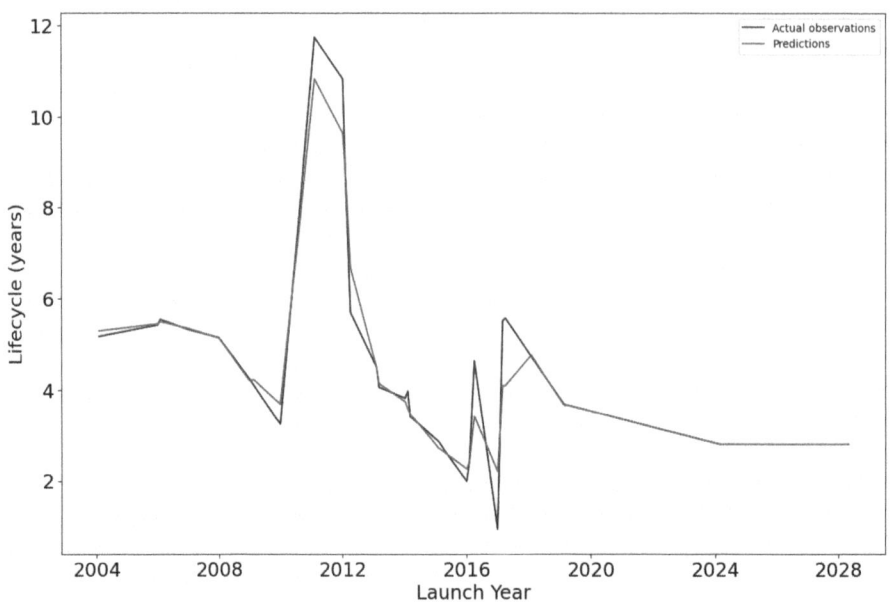

Fig. 6. Predictions of service life for discontinued processors.

This equation calculates the Mean Squared Error, where n is the number of data points, y_i represents the actual value of the i-th data point, and $\hat{y}_i$ represents the predicted value for the i-th data point.

The Table 6 presents the results of evaluating a Transformer-based model based on the size of the training dataset. It shows the impact of the proportion of training data on the model's Mean Squared Error (MSE). With 50% of the data used for training, the MSE is 0.0485, indicating relatively good performance. However, as the size of the training dataset increases to 60%, 70%, and 80%, the MSE rises to 0.0570, 0.0629, and 0.0709, respectively. This suggests that the model may struggle to effectively adapt to larger datasets or may begin to overfit the training data. Nevertheless, when the training data size is increased to 90%, the MSE slightly decreases to 0.0593. This slight improvement might indicate that the model benefits from exposure to a larger dataset, allowing it to generalize better.

Given these results, we chose to train the model using 70% of the dataset. This choice is based on the observation that 70% represents a balance between having a substantial amount of training data and avoiding potential overfitting that can occur with larger datasets. Training with 70% of the data provides a solid foundation for model learning while still maintaining a significant portion of data for validation and testing, ensuring a reliable evaluation of the model's performance.

Table 7. Comparative Analysis of Actual and Predicted Values.

Date	Actual	Predicted (Transformers)	Predicted (Linear Regression)
2012-02-01	8.660	8.749	9.637
2016-01-01	1.993	2.263	2.396
2019-02-01	3.734	3.712	3.665
2021-09-06	3.239	3.240	3.281

Table 7 presents an excerpt from a comparative analysis between actual and predicted values for specific dates in order to forecast the obsolescence of discontinued processors with known lifespans.

In this context, actual values correspond to empirical data on processor lifespans, while predicted values are based on analysis methods using the N-BEATS model.

The Table 7 lists specific dates along with their actual and predicted values using transformers. For example, on February 1, 2012, the actual lifespan of the processor was 8.660, and the value predicted by transformers was 8.749. Similarly, on January 1, 2016, the actual lifespan was 1.993, while the predicted value was 2.263.

These discrepancies between actual and predicted values highlight the overall accuracy of the N-BEATS model, despite some minor variations. The model demonstrates strong performance in forecasting processor lifespans, although small deviations can occur due to factors such as the inherent complexity of the data and external variables affecting processor durability.

In Table 6, we present an analysis of the performance of the linear regression model applied to discontinued processors. The table shows the Mean Squared Error (MSE) for different training set sizes, providing insights into the model's effectiveness based on data size.

Upon examining the table, it is clear that the performance of the linear regression model is inferior to that of the Transformers. For all training sample sizes, Transformers exhibit a significantly lower Mean Squared Error (MSE) compared to linear regression. For example, with 50% of the training data, the MSE for Transformers is 0.0485, while for linear regression it is 0.0527. This trend persists across all levels of training sample size. In summary, Transformers demonstrate a better ability to minimize prediction error compared to linear regression, especially as the training sample size increases.

In Table 7, significant differences are observed between the values predicted by linear regression and those predicted by Transformers. For example, on February 1, 2012, the value predicted by linear regression was 9.637, whereas the value predicted by Transformers was 8.749. Generally, the values predicted by Transformers appear to be closer to the actual values than those predicted by linear regression.

5.3 Conclusion

This document opens up significant perspectives regarding the obsolescence of electronic materials, particularly processors. From a practical point of view, predicting the commercial lifespan of the microprocessors used in servers enables the company to implement strategies to remedy future obsolescence and ensure uninterrupted customer service.

Each server component will be individually analyzed, along with the server's software, to enable Orange Group to determine their obsolescence dates. Once all predictions are made for each server component, the idea is to establish links between each hardware and software component of the server, aiming to assess the overall health status of the server by considering external factors. These factors depend not only on the software and hardware infrastructure but also on the environment where the servers are stored, cooling methods, air conditioning, etc.

These research efforts may lead to simulations of Orange's digital twins, providing an opportunity to test various maintenance and optimization strategies.

The simulations conducted in this paper with one of the transformer models have proven effective. In future studies, the aim would be to deepen prediction methods by exploring new models and refining the data used to enhance the accuracy of forecasts.

6   Stage of the Research

The primary objective of the PhD program is to design predictive models for the operational availability of systems affected by physical and software obsolescence. This entails creating a comprehensive obsolescence model and correlating it with networks and systems' maintainability and availability attributes.

The proposed work partially intersects with the domain of predictive maintenance. Yet, its innovation predominantly lies in integrating considerations of hardware or software obsolescence and scarcity and supply risks to enhance maintenance optimization.

An essential step was identifying one or more use cases where maintenance or resilience issues are paramount. Given the project's scope, data centers emerge as prime candidates, housing servers crucial for network functionalities, especially in expanding virtualization. Moreover, these facilities operate within intricate technical environments encompassing air conditioning, power supply, and network infrastructure.

Subsequently, selecting requisite data to assess the obsolescence of key components was imperative, followed by modeling the interplay and dependencies among various components. This process culminates in creating a predictive obsolescence model for hardware and software obsolescence.

The predictive model will be the cornerstone for constructing an optimization model for maintenance activities. These optimization models will incorporate a certain degree of uncertainty in the data, given that the predictive model can generate probabilistic estimates of obsolescence.

To validate these models, digital twins of the identified use cases will be developed for simulation purposes.

References

1. Bartels, B., Ermel, U., Sandborn, P., Pecht, M.G.: Strategies to the Prediction, Mitigation and Management of Product Obsolescence. Wiley (2012)
2. Box, G.E., Jenkins, G.M., Reinsel, G.C., Ljung, G.M.: Time Series Analysis: Forecasting and Control. Wiley (2015)
3. Devlin, J., Chang, M.W., Lee, K., Toutanova, K.: BERT: pre-training of deep bidirectional transformers for language understanding. arXiv preprint arXiv:1810.04805 (2018)
4. van Dinter, R., Tekinerdogan, B., Catal, C.: Predictive maintenance using digital twins: a systematic literature review. Inf. Softw. Technol. **151**, 107008 (2022)
5. Jang, E., Johnson, M., Burnell, E., Heimerl, K.: Unplanned obsolescence: hardware and software after collapse. In: Proceedings of the 2017 Workshop on Computing Within Limits, pp. 93–101 (2017)
6. Janiesch, C., Zschech, P., Heinrich, K.: Machine learning and deep learning. Electron. Mark. **31**(3), 685–695 (2021)
7. Jennings, C., Wu, D., Terpenny, J.: Forecasting obsolescence risk and product life cycle with machine learning. IEEE Trans. Compon. Packag. Manuf. Technol. **6**(9), 1428–1439 (2016)
8. Menculini, L., et al.: Comparing prophet and deep learning to ARIMA in forecasting wholesale food prices. Forecasting **3**(3), 644–662 (2021)
9. Montgomery, D.C., Peck, E.A., Vining, G.G.: Introduction to Linear Regression Analysis. Wiley (2021)
10. Oreshkin, B.N., Carpov, D., Chapados, N., Bengio, Y.: N-beats: neural basis expansion analysis for interpretable time series forecasting. arXiv preprint arXiv:1905.10437 (2019)
11. Paul, S., Chen, P.Y.: Vision transformers are robust learners. In: Proceedings of the AAAI Conference on Artificial Intelligence, vol. 36, pp. 2071–2081 (2022)
12. Popescu, M.C., Balas, V.E., Perescu-Popescu, L., Mastorakis, N.: Multilayer perceptron and neural networks. WSEAS Trans. Circ. Syst. **8**(7), 579–588 (2009)
13. Priddy, K.L., Keller, P.E.: Artificial Neural Networks: An Introduction, vol. 68. SPIE Press (2005)
14. Rothman, D.: Transformers for Natural Language Processing: Build, train, and fine-tune deep neural network architectures for NLP with Python, Hugging Face, and OpenAI's GPT-3, ChatGPT, and GPT-4. Packt Publishing Ltd. (2022)

15. Schulze, F.A., Arndt, H.K., Feuersenger, H.: Obsolescence as a future key challenge for data centers. In: Advances and New Trends in Environmental Informatics: Digital Twins for Sustainability. pp. 67–78. Springer, Heidelberg (2021)
16. Trabelsi, I., Zeddini, B., Zolghadri, M., Barkallah, M., Haddar, M.: Obsolescence prediction based on joint feature selection and machine learning techniques. In: ICAART, vol. 2, pp. 787–794 (2021)
17. Vaswani, A., et al.: Attention is all you need. Adv. Neural Inf. Process. Syst. **30** (2017)
18. Wang, S., Li, C., Lim, A.: Why are the ARIMA and SARIMA not sufficient (2021)
19. Wu, N., Green, B., Ben, X., O'Banion, S.: Deep transformer models for time series forecasting: the influenza prevalence case. arXiv preprint arXiv:2001.08317 (2020)
20. Wu, S., Xiao, X., Ding, Q., Zhao, P., Wei, Y., Huang, J.: Adversarial sparse transformer for time series forecasting. Adv. Neural. Inf. Process. Syst. **33**, 17105–17115 (2020)

Machine Learning Tool for Yield Maximization in Cream Cheese Production

Loïc Parrenin[1,2], Ambre Dupuis[3(✉)], Christophe Danjou[2], and Bruno Agard[1,2]

[1] Laboratoire en Intelligence des Données, Montréal, (QC), Canada
[2] Département de Mathématiques et de Génie Industriel, École Polytechnique de Montréal, Montréal, (QC), Canada
`{loic.parrenin,christophe.danjou,bruno.agard}@polymtl.ca`
[3] Département de Génie Industriel, Université du Québec à Trois-Rivières, Trois-Rivières, (QC), Canada
`ambre.dupuis@uqtr.ca`

Abstract. Artificial intelligence tools and data collection on the shop floor are enhancing flexibility and productivity in industry, addressing labor shortages and skills attrition by leveraging the tacit knowledge of workers. This study focuses on the cream cheese production sector, where operator expertise is essential for controlling the ultrafiltration concentration factor, a critical parameter affecting product moisture content. To ensure continuous and flexible production despite workforce challenges, a machine-learning tool was developed using the CRISP-DM approach to maximize cream cheese yield on a Canadian production line. A decision tree algorithm applied to real production and quality data yielded promising results, with an RMSE of 0.061 and an R^2 of 0.91 when predicting the ultrafiltration concentration factor used by an experienced operator to maximize yield while complying with quality standards. The implementation saw positive operator acceptance due to comprehensive training and an inclusive approach. This research marks a pioneering effort to harness tacit knowledge in the dairy industry for machine parameter control, highlighting data acquisition and quality as key areas for further investigation to enhance tool performance and adaptability.

Keywords: Machine learning · Tacit knowledge · Production flexibility · Operator expertise · Dairy industry

1 Introduction

Cheese production has come a long way since its origins in the early days of pastoralism, around 6500 BC. [8]. Since the Neolithic period it has become an integral component of the global economy with an estimated global cheese production of 21.3 million tons (representing between 65 and 68 billion U.S. dollars) in 2020 [26]. The cream cheese production is of growing economic importance in

M. Dassisti et al. (Eds.): IN4PL 2024, CCIS 2372, pp. 97–114, 2025.
https://doi.org/10.1007/978-3-031-80760-2_6

this industry since its global market is estimated to reach \$8.3 billion by 2026 [26]. To meet the ever-growing consumer demand for a wider variety of products at lower prices [19,27], the cheese industry must innovate with mechanization and automation [7].

To increase production efficiency while guaranteeing quality, membrane technologies such as ultrafiltration (UF) have been developed [7]. In the process of cream cheese production, the UF step is highly critical since it directly impacts quality, productivity and benefits [26]. The aim of UF is to concentrate fat and protein while reducing the amount of water, lactose and minerals in the final product. Membrane technologies has the potential to significantly improve plant capacity by making the process more efficient and limiting raw material wastage. Nevertheless, the full implementation of membrane treatment and the realization of its full potential remains to be done as it still faces major challenges: providing flexible production systems and procuring trained personnel [7]. The UF concentration factor varies due to multiple factors, including the milk quality properties which fluctuate over the year. Once this stage has been reached in the production system, it is no longer possible to effectively reduce the moisture content. Moisture content limits are imposed by law for the marketing of certain products, such as regular bricks [5], but also for quality specifications requested by the customer. Adjusting the UF factor becomes an important issue, as exceeding quality tolerances leads to rejects, while quality deviation below the maximum tolerance lead to volume loss. Experienced operators are therefore needed to control the UF concentration factor, to obtain the best yield/quality ratio. However, the current shortage of workers and skills puts production systems at risk and there is an urgent need to ensure that the expertise of a multi-generational workforce is put to good use [13]. It is then essential to develop tools to support production systems that must continue to operate despite significant risks of absenteeism and high turnover [25].

To meet the challenges of production system flexibility and robustness, the 21st century is seeing the emergence of the fourth industrial revolution, Industry 4.0. [9]. The dairy industry is entering this paradigm and generating large amounts of data [6] moving towards decision-making models using data analysis and digital twins [1]. The potential for AI to replicate human abilities, enabling it to learn and make decisions based on perceived environments [11,18], could facilitate sustainable food system transitions by automating food processing industries [6] and developing decision-support tools [24].

Thus, the objective of this research is to develop a data-driven tool for yield maximization in cream cheese production, using experience contained in historical data for UF concentration factor control.

The development of decision-support tools based on real manufacturing data aims to ensure the continuity of production despite the risk of losing expertise and the current shortage of manpower and helps knowledge transfer. In addition, the ability to maximize production yields while maintaining quality standards improves the profitability of an expensive production process and reduces food waste, contributing to the United Nations' Sustainable Development Goals 9 and 12 [10].

This paper makes a contribution to the integration of dairy industry operators' tacit knowledge with AI, thereby improving decision-making in fresh cheese production. It demonstrates the application of the CRISP-DM framework to develop a machine learning tool that optimizes the ultrafiltration process, achieving high accuracy in improving product quality and yield. Furthermore, it highlights the importance of operator acceptance and effective collaboration between man and machine through comprehensive training and inclusive practices.

A brief overview of the cream cheese production process is presented in Sect. 2. The proposed methodology is explained in Sect. 3 while the results obtained from its application on a case study are presented in Sect. 4. These results are discussed in Sect. 5 and Sect. 6 concludes the research.

2   Cream Cheese Production Process and the Ultrafiltration

Cheese production is an ancient activity whose earliest traces date back to the beginnings of pastoralism, around 6500 BC [8]. The transformation of milk into cheese represented a significant technological and cultural advancement in the history of food preservation. By making cheese, dairy products could be stored and transported easily for long periods without deteriorating. Furthermore, cheese enabled dairy products, particularly milk, to be consumed without any undesirable effects, such as bloating or digestive discomfort. This improvement in the digestive qualities of dairy products was due to a reduction in lactose content, largely as a result of the fermentation process into lactic acid, or the elimination of lactose as whey [8,20]. The production of cheese has undergone significant changes since the Neolithic period, becoming an integral component of the global economy. Global cheese production is estimated to be 21.3 million tons, representing a market value of between 65 and 68 billion U.S. dollars in 2020 [26]. With a global market estimated to reach $8.3 billion by 2026, the cream cheese production is growing economic importance in the food industry [26]. It was at the end of the 19th century (1870–1880) that the cream cheese was first produced in the United States [26]. Since that time, the manufacturing process has undergone significant evolution in order to meet the demands of mass production but the general process remains. It is described by [14,26] and illustrated in Fig. 1.

Fig. 1. Cream cheese general production process adapted from [14,26].

First, milk undergoes a series of standardization processes. These include the measurement of the protein and fat content, and subsequent adjustment to a specific ratio, dependent on the desired characteristics of the final product. Following this stage, the milk is subjected to homogenization through heat treatment and pasteurization, with specific parameters for each. The liquid is acidified to a specific pH level, thereby allowing the separation of the whey from the other components of the mixture.

Then, technologies such as the ultrafiltration (UF) allows to separate the whey of the acidified milk from its other components. To finalize the product, stabilizing agents and salt are then added to the concentrate. The product is then ready for cold packing.

Depending on the type of final product, the concentrate mixture may also undergo further processing steps, such as homogenization, shearing, blending of flavor ingredients and cooking.

The advent of technological innovations in cheese-making equipment and curd handling permitted the implementation of mechanization and automation, which were essential for the exponential growth in cheese production [7]. This resulted in the reduction in bacteriological contamination and the decrease in manufacturing costs [7]. It has also contributed to the production of a uniform product [7] required to meet quality standards. Indeed, with mass production comes the introduction of production standards. In 1994, the United States Department of Agriculture (USDA) implemented regulations governing the production of cream cheese. These regulations set strict quality requirements for cream cheese, including a minimum fat content and maximum moisture content of 33% and 55%, respectively [5, 12].

To increase production efficiency while guaranteeing quality, membrane technologies such as ultrafiltration have been developed [7]. In the process of cream cheese production, the UF step is highly critical since it directly impact quality, productivity and benefits [26].

The acidified milk passes through the UF, which filters the mixture to retain only the solid components, rich in fat and protein. The filtered solid components make up the concentrate, while the permeate (the liquid that has passed through the UF membranes) contains water, minerals and lactose. This filtration is controlled by a UF concentration factor and the result of the UF step is analyzed to determine the moisture content of the product [14, 26].

Should the moisture content of the product exiting the UF process exceed the tolerated moisture threshold, the UF concentration factor is increased, thus enabling the acidified mixture to be further filtered and the moisture content of the concentrate to be diminished. This decrease in moisture content leads to a reduction in the quantity of concentrate and an associated increase in the quantity of permeate.

As a result, membrane technology has the potential to significantly improve plant capacity by making the process more efficient and limiting raw material wastage. Nevertheless, the full implementation of membrane treatment and the realization of its full potential remains to be done. The current use of membrane treatment still faces major challenges: "Two of the challenges are procuring trained personnel to operate the equipment properly and adapting a manufacturing schedule to produce cheeses that meet the changing demands of the customer. Research and the education of employees that results from its implementation are still at the heart of proper cheese making" [7].

These challenges are not unique to the cheese industry. The manufacturing industry is well aware of the growing consumer demand for a wider variety of products at lower prices [19,27], and of the importance of experienced, well-trained personnel to guarantee production quality and efficiency [4]. The current shortage of workers and skills is therefore putting production systems at risk and there is an urgent need to ensure that the expertise of a multi-generational workforce is put to good use [13]. It is then essential to develop tools to support production systems that must continue to operate despite significant risks of absenteeism and high turnover [25].

To meet these challenges of production system flexibility and robustness, the 21st century is seeing the emergence of the fourth industrial revolution, Industry 4.0. [9]. It leverages the new capabilities of digital tools, such as cloud technology, massive data analytics and artificial intelligence (AI), the Internet of Things (IoT) and cyber-physical systems (CPS) [9], as well as the interconnectivity of production systems to create a manufacturing ecosystem capable of collecting, sharing, analyzing and using information to guide actions and decision-making [23]. Data is thus at the heart of Industry 4.0. since digital technologies are combined to collect and transmit information to monitor, control and even optimize production processes [9].

As mentioned by *Udugama et al.* [1], "the dairy industry is one of the more advanced food processing industries" with future trends revolving around decision-making using data analytics and digital twins. The dairy industry generates large amounts of data [6]. The industry needs new, reliable analytical tools to transform this vast amount of data into decisions and actions [9,23]. Data analytics using big data and artificial intelligence are, for example, used in real-time monitoring and decision making, or supply chain sustainability in dairy production [6]. The potential for AI to replicate human abilities, enabling it to learn and make decisions based on perceived environments [11,18], could facilitate sustainable food system transitions by automating food processing industries [6] and developing decision-support tools [24].

In this context, it is now up to develop the tools that may take advantage of such data to facilitate knowledge transfer and decision-making.

3 Methodology

This research has been conducted with an industrial partner in the cream cheese industry. The partner provided several years of production data (machine settings and quality of the final product). The context was one of diverse productivity outcomes observed while maintaining rigorous quality standards. In light of the rising cost of raw materials, it was imperative to identify way to make the milk transformation process more efficient.

To develop a machine learning tool for yield maximization in cream cheese production, a six-steps methodology illustrated in Fig. 2, is used. This methodology is adapted from the CRISP-DM approach [21] as depicted on the left part of the figure.

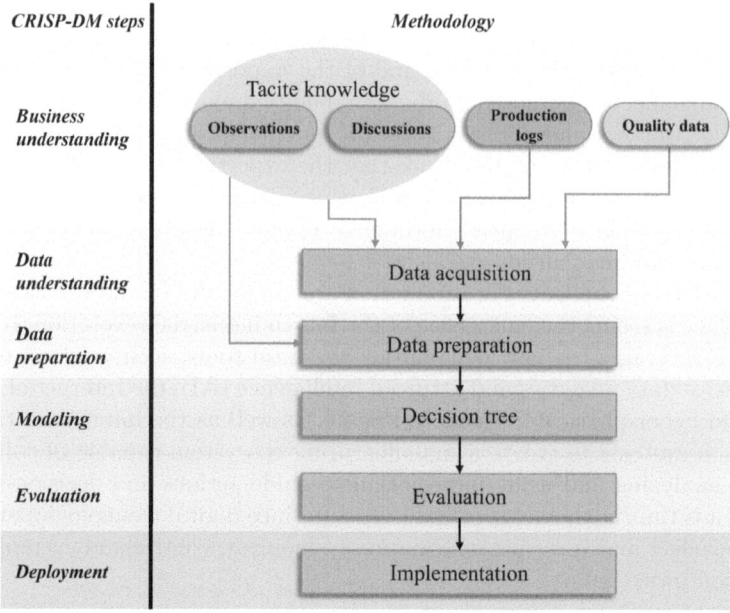

Fig. 2. Methodology for a data-driven tool maximizing yield through parameter tuning.

The first step in the CRISP-DM approach, the ***Business understanding*** step, aims to understand the business environment and the process under study [21,22]. In the proposed methodology, observations on the production floor and semi-structured discussions with operators are used to gather the tacit knowledge needed to operate the ultrafiltration step on the production line. The mapping of the available information present in the production logs and quality data is also gathered for further processing.

Once the business environment and the process under study have been characterized, the ***Data understanding*** step enables us to focus on the related data available. During the **Data acquisition** step, the tacit knowledge of operators is used to extract the attributes that affect the yield and quality of the ultrafiltration step from the production log and quality data. The ***Business understanding*** and the ***Data understanding*** steps are mutually reinforced until a representative set of data is acquired and can be prepared.

The **Data preparation** step is used to format the data to be used in the ***Modeling*** step. Once again, these two steps are interrelated and therefore need to be considered iteratively.

During the **Data preparation** step, Production run data are formatted into fixed-parameter production segments and Quality data are associated with each of them. outliers and missing values are managed using expert knowledge. Data are split into a train and a test set.

The *Modeling* step uses the prepared data to propose machine-learning models for predicting the yield of the ultra-filtration step based on the production attributes considered. **Decision trees** were chosen for their interpretability and ability to integrate tacit operator knowledge, making them well-suited for aligning AI predictions with human expertise in the production process. Additionally, they handle complex data effectively and are robust to outliers, ensuring reliable performance in industrial settings.

Once the model has been trained on the training set, its performance is evaluated in the **Evaluation** step using the *root mean squared error (RMSE)* described in Eq. 1 and the *coefficient of determination (R²)* metrics described in Eqs. 1 and 2 respectively.

$$\text{RMSE}(y, \hat{y}) = \sqrt{\frac{\sum_{i=1}^{N}(y_i - \hat{y}_i)^2}{N}} \tag{1}$$

$$R^2(y, \hat{y}) = 1 - \frac{\sum_{i=1}^{N}(y_i - \hat{y}_i)^2}{\sum_{i=1}^{N}(y_i - \bar{y})^2} \tag{2}$$

Where :

$y_i = $ *value real of the ith record of the test dataset*

$\hat{y}_i = $ *value predicted by the model for the ith record of the test dataset*

$\bar{y} = $ *mean value of y in the test dataset*

The **RMSE** is defined as the square root of the mean of the squared differences between the predicted values $(\hat{y}_i)$ and the actual values (y_i). As the **RMSE** scale is identical to the random variable, this metric can be employed to interpret errors and to compare models. Scale factors are practically normalized, which limits the occurrence of outliers. The **R²** metric is preferred to capture how well the model explains variations in the target variable [2].

Finally, the trained model is implemented in production during the **Deployment** step of the CRISP-DM approach. During the **Implementation** phase, an executable file is programmed to use the trained models directly from a graphical user interface (*GUI*). Furthermore, design tests have been conducted in conjunction with operator training on the production floor. These activities are aimed at improving the proposed decision-support tool and overcoming any resistance to change that may be inherent in the implementation of new technological tools on workstations.

4   Results

4.1   Case Study

The tool developed for yield maximization is designed to meet the needs of a company to gain competitiveness while reducing the risk of losing control of operability due to high staff turnover. The company specializes in the production of both large-format and small-format food products for a variety of customers, including grocery stores, restaurants and hotels. The automation of production processes has enabled production volumes to be increased, but their fine-tuning on the production floor due to variable raw material quality remains crucial to ensure an optimum yield and quality ratio throughout the year.

The proposed methodology was applied, using *Python 3.8*, to an empirical case study carried out at a cream cheese manufacturing facility in Quebec, Canada, between 2022 and 2023.

Data has been collected over a one-year period from rea data, supplied by the company. These data come from the PLCs equipment on the production floor, and from the information system grouping quality analysis tests. A more detailed description of the data is provided in Sect. 4.3.

4.2   Business Understanding

The system under study is illustrated in Fig. 3.

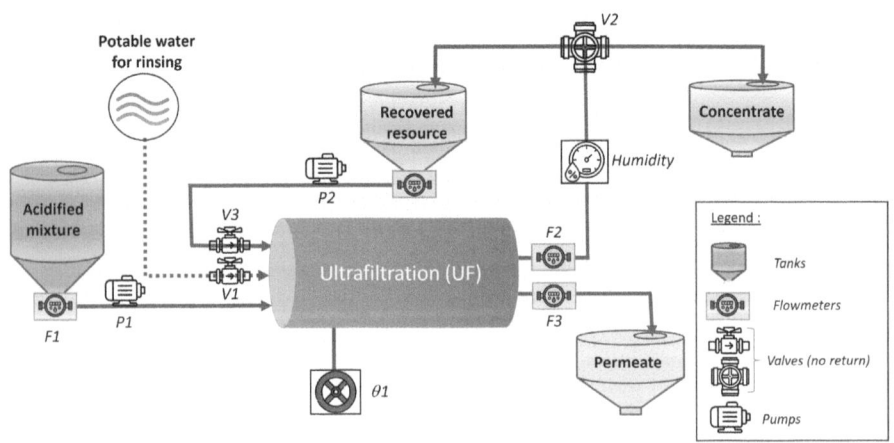

Fig. 3. Ultrafiltration process overview.

All the present equipment can be controlled manually via a digital interface. The UF concentration factor is represented by the $\theta 1$ parameter wich controls the amount of material filtered. It can vary from 1 to 7, where all material passes at $\theta 1 = 1$ and virtually no material at $\theta 1 = 7$. A concentration factor of level 7 implies the passage of 7 liters of input to produce 1 liter of output. Thus, the value of $\theta 1$ represents the liters of input required to produce 1 liter of output.

At the beginning of a production cycle, or when the moisture content exceeds the conformity threshold, the UF output stream is sent to the Recovered resource (RR) silo. This is continued until the $\theta 1$ parameter is correctly adjusted to the required moisture content to avoid any deterioration in product quality. When the required moisture content is reached, the output flow is redirected to the concentrate silo.

Once the production cycle is complete, a rinse is performed to recover the acidified mixture still present on the equipment walls and membranes before the cleaning operation. This rinse flow is directed to the recovered resource silo. The recovered resource can be reused in a new production course. The use of this resource results in variability in the performance of the ultrafiltration process due to the mixing of different products and the recovery of rinse water.

from interviews with operators, various factors have been mentioned to impact the $\theta 1$ parameter tuning to maximize yield depending on the product type being produced at time t.

Those factors are the duration of the production run *(D)*, the moisture content of the production *(H)* the quantity of acidified mixture and recovered resource (Qt_E) used as well as the quantity of concentrate (Qt_S) and recovered resource produced (Qt_{RR}).

At the UF stage, there are 6 different semi-finished products.

4.3   Data Acquisition

Once the influencing factors had been identified, various data sources were consulted to gather historical production and quality information.

The production data linked to the system's pumps *(P1, P2)*, valves *(V1, V2, V3)* and flow controllers *(F1, F2, F3)* provide millisecond-stamped information on material flows (Qt_E, Qt_{RR}, Qt_S).

The value of parameter $\theta 1$ is also provided, along with the timestamp of the value change in milliseconds, to track parameter changes during production.

Quality data is used to identify the moisture content H at a given timestamp of production.

Table 1. Statistical description of the production data.

Variable	$Qt_E(F1)$	Qt_S *(F2)*	Qt_{RR} *(F3)*	H *(%)*	$\theta 1$
Nb. samples	1.68e+06	1.27e+07	1.65e+06	5001	4238
Mean	14.67	4.88	9.18	58.26	2.18
Min	0.00	0.00	0.00	14.19	1.00
Max	85.62	50.00	60.00	77.49	7.00
σ	14.98	4.42	5.83	5.91	0.98

Material flows (Qt_E, Qt_{RR}, Qt_S), moisture content (H) and $\theta1$ are defined as continuous variables. Flows are measured in imperial gallons per minute. Their statistical description is presented in Table 1.

4.4   Data Preparation

As the objective of this research is to develop a data-driven tool for yield maximization through parameter control in cream cheese production, we seek to predict the parameter $\theta1$ from the historical production data previously collected.

To do so, the raw data described in Table 1 are prepared.

In this data preparation step, hypotheses were set:

- Raw material quality is not taken into account.
- The recovered resource is used up to 100% when used in a production run.
- The quantity of rinse water is used up to 100% when the recovered resource is consumed.

Each production run N is segmented according to $\theta1$ parameter changes, to extract the production and quality information that led the operator to make the change. For a better visualization of data preparation, Fig. 4 illustrates the segmentation of a production run according to changes in parameter $\theta1$.

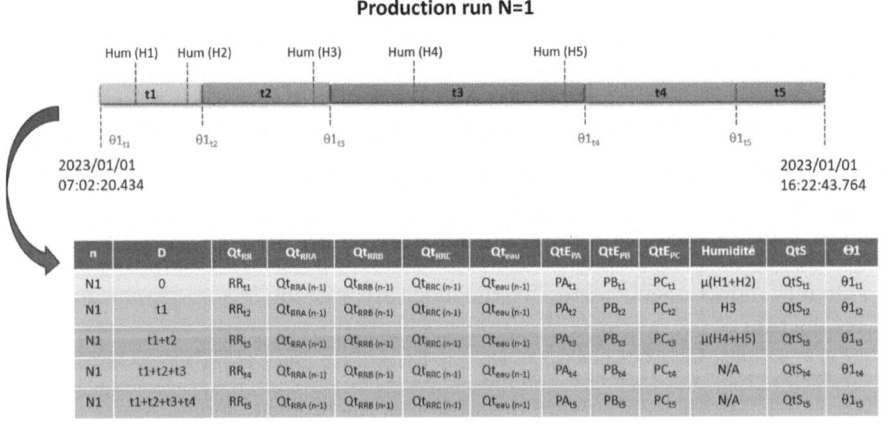

Fig. 4. Representation of the prepared data for the production run N=1.

For the sake of clarity, three different products are mentioned in Fig. 4, although all five were used in the development of the tool. These three products will be referred to as Product A, B and C. The 5 different colors represent the 5 time frames bounded by parameter adjustment of $\theta1$.

As illustrated in Fig. 4, the data table contains various variables.

- D represents the cumulative duration of the previous time frames.
- Qt_{RR} specifies the quantity of recovered resources used in a specific time frame t_i. The composition of the recovered resource used is given by the quantities of recovered resource of each product (Qt_{RRA}, Qt_{RRB}, Qt_{RRC}) and rinse water (Qt_{eau}) generated by previous runs.
- Qt_E is decomposed in QtE_{PA}, QtE_{PB}, QtE_{PC} representing the quantity of acidified mixture used during the time frame t_i for products A, B, and C respectively.
- H is the average of the moisture content tests performed over the time frame t_i. If no test is performed during this period, the time frame t_i is removed from the data.
- Qt_S is the quantity of concentrate produced over the time frame t_i.
- $\theta1$ corresponds to the $\theta1$ value after the adjustement performed at the beginning of the time frame t_i.

These data are completed by adding the production yield information. The production yield is calculated for each time frame t_i as the ratio between the quantity of acidified mixtures used in the ultrafiltration process (Qt_E) and the output quantity of concentrate produced (Qt_S) as illustrated by Eq. 3.

$$Yield = \frac{Qt_S}{Qt_E} \tag{3}$$

$$Where \; Qt_E = QtE_{PA} + QtE_{PB} + QtE_{PC}$$

The dataset is then split into training (75%) and test (25%) sets of 955 and 319 records respectively.

4.5   Modeling

Based on the structured data obtained above, a prediction model can be built to predict the parameter $\theta1$ configured according to the type and quantity of acidified mixture, the type and quantity of recovered resource, the quantity of rinsing water, the moisture content obtained and the calculated yield.

Due to the nonlinearity of the problem and the need to make the model explicable, a decision-tree-based model capable of handling continuous variables was developed.

Figure 5 illustrates the depth 2 decision tree obtained from the model. This representation provides the logical rules governing the model's predictions.

The nodes of the decision tree shown in Fig. 5 are colored according to the mean value of the $\theta1$ parameter. A dark orange shade indicates a high mean value of the independent variable at the node, while a lighter shade indicates a lower mean value. Figure 5 highlights that the most decisive attribute of the process, located at the root of the tree, is yield.

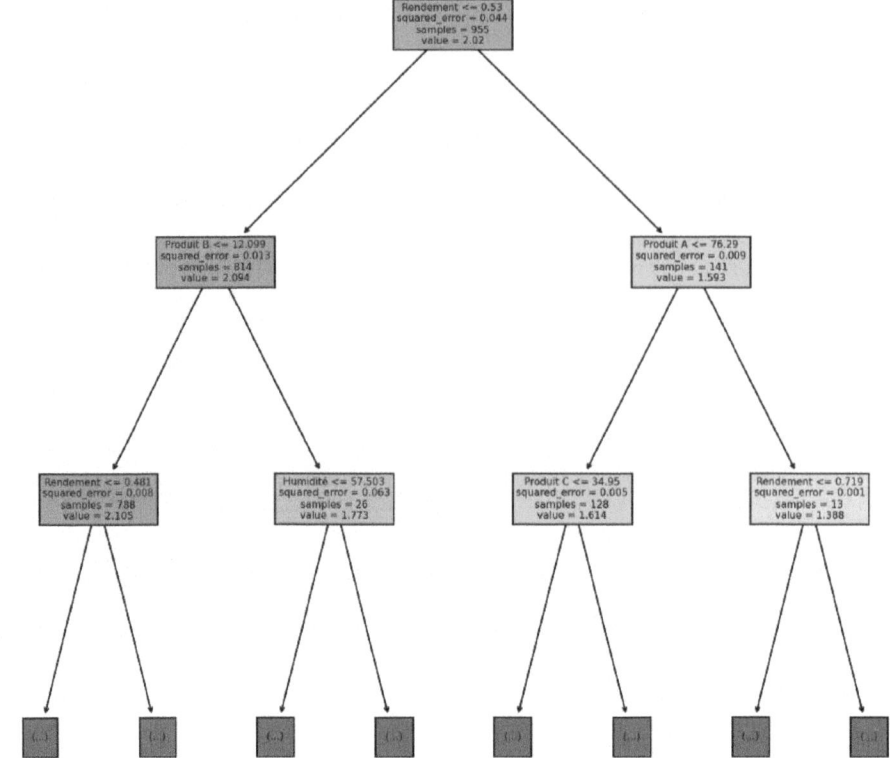

Fig. 5. Decision tree for predicting the $\theta1$ parameter of the UF process.

4.6   Evaluation

The model obtains a **RMSE** of 0.061 and a **R^2** of 0.91 when predicting the ultrafiltration concentration factor used by an experienced operator to maximize yield while complying with quality standards, and this, despite unbalanced data with a majority of records showing $\theta1 \geq 1.8$. This score means that the average model error is 0.061, depending on the unit of measurement of the $\theta1$ parameter. Significant accuracy in model predictions can be observed when yield exceeds 53% and the amount of acidified mixture used for product A exceeds 76.29 imperial gallons. In this branch, predictions are characterized by a **RMSE** of 0.001. By contrast, when the yield is less than 53% and the amount of acidified mixture used for product B exceeds 12.099 imperial gallons, the model suffers a degradation in performance and obtains an **RMSE** of 0.063.

To visualize the performance of the developed model, Fig. 6 shows the value predicted compared with the real value observed on the shopfloor.

From Fig. 6, 3 distinct groups are observed: (1) $\theta1 \leq 1.5$, (2) $1.5 < \theta1 < 1.8$ and (3) $\theta1 \geq 1.8$. A greater dispersion of prediction errors is observed when the parameter $\theta1$ is greater than 1.8 compared with predictions made when $\theta1$ is less

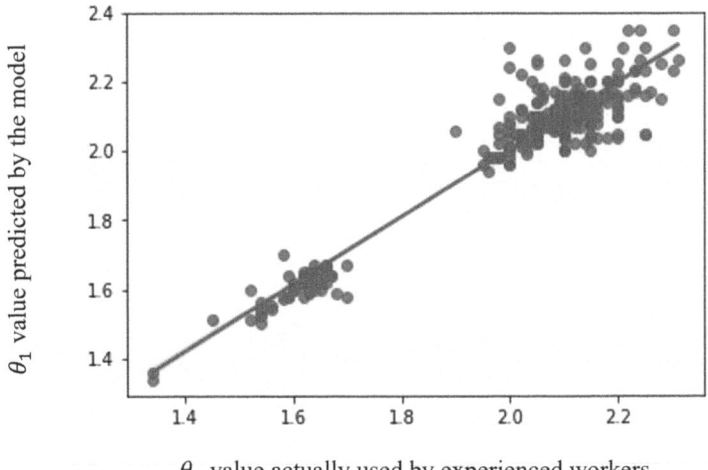

θ_1 value actually used by experienced workers

Fig. 6. Predicted vs. real values.

than 1.8. This shows that greater care needs to be taken when predicting the parameter $\theta 1 \geq 1.8$. The development of a tailored model, trained on extremum data, may be a potential solution to address this unique scenario.

4.7 Implementation

The convincing performance of the proposed model, with a **RMSE** of 0.061, allows us to envisage the development of a graphical user interface (GUI) for the development of an easy-to-use tool for all workstations linked to the UF operation.

As *Chiu et al.* [3] use GUIs to enable users to operate the intelligent preventive maintenance system, the GUI is here intended for users to easily operate the decision tool by modifying the configurations and recipe of production to get real-time parameter tuning.

Figure 7 illustrate the GUI used to collect information from operators and provide the predicted $\theta 1$ value based on the integrated trained model.

The GUI was built using the library *PysimpleGUI* [17]. Operators can first indicate the type of product in production. The target humidity (H) is also indicated. Finally, the use of the recovered resource (Qt_{RR}) and the type of product in it are specified. All the information is used as input to the trained model, which proposes a value of $\theta 1$ to be adjusted to obtain the highest yield.

Training documents were created to illustrate the tool's operation and maintenance procedures. These documents utilized screenshots and formal guidelines. Additionally, the location of source and executable files on the production environment was formally identified.

Additionally, operators have been informed of the potential for latency in the tool during practical training sessions on the production floor. These

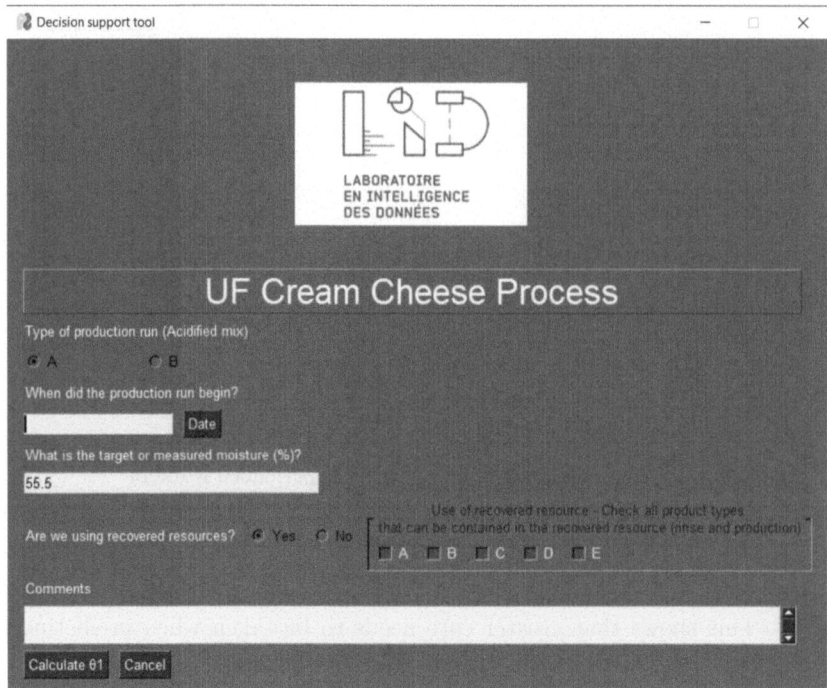

Fig. 7. GUI.

training sessions are essential for ensuring the tool's acceptability in production and for implementing effective change management among operators. This change management process involves, among other things, involving operators in the improvement of the tool. Thus, during the implementation phase on the production floor, some limitations and potential improvements were identified. These are discussed in the following section.

5   Discussion

The proposed methodology was used to develop a machine-learning tool for maximizing cream cheese production yield on a Canadian production line.

Although convincing results have been obtained on real production data, with an overall **RMSE** of 0.061 and an $\mathbf{R}^2$ of 0.91 when predicting the ultrafiltration concentration factor used by an experienced operator to maximize yield while complying with quality standards, as well as operator acceptance of the decision-support tool, some limitations persist.

The implementation phase revealed a difficulty in acquiring data concerning the specific quantity of products used in real-time. This information is difficult for operators to measure, but the presence or absence of each product in the recovered resources and acidified mixture is easily identifiable. Thus, a new data preparation replacing the quantities of each product QtE_{PA}, QtE_{PB} and QtE_{PC} as well as the attributes Qt_{RRA}, Qt_{RB}, Qt_{RRC} by binary variables would be relevant to specify only the presence or absence of each type of product. Thus, if the acidified mixture used is type A, QtE_{PA} will take the value 1, while QtE_{PB} and QtE_{PC} will take the value 0. On the other hand, if the acidified mixture used is type B, then QtE_{PB} will take the value 1, while QtE_{PA} and QtE_{PC} will take the value 0. For the recovered resource, if it contains product A and product C but no product B, then the values of Qt_{RRA}, Qt_{RRB} and Qt_{RRC} will be 1, 0 and 1 respectively. This change in data preparation would require new modeling and training of the decision tree, as well as a new performance evaluation.

The proposed model is based on the valuation of historical data. The results of the model therefore depend to a large extent on the quality of the data provided. The evaluation of data quality, its structuring in information systems and its acquisition should be the subject of further research. Also, other models and algorithms should be explored to identify the ideal tools for the specific process under study. In this study, decision trees were selected for their interpretability and effective integration with operator expertise, providing valuable insights into the production process. Neural networks and other advanced models could be promising options for future research if more data become available, as they have the potential to capture complex relationships and improve accuracy. However, the explicability of the model remains an important element of the methodology. Therefore, linear or quadratic regression models could be considered. Further studies should compare the performance and limitations of various machine learning tools in similar contexts to fully evaluate their effectiveness

Following observations and discussions on the production floor, the management of the $\theta1$ parameter changes when the process becomes faulty. Another avenue of research would be to integrate a real-time control map of the quality parameter measured using on-line NIR [15,16]. The evolution of the humidity variable H would enable us to detect the transition from controlled production to faulty production ($H \geq 55\%$) [12]. A new model should also be develop to specifically replicate the behavior of operators in a controlled and a faulty production mode. Once again, the data preparation step should be modified to take into account information gathered by operators in *faulty production mode*. For instance, the moisture content variable (H) should be transformed into the difference between it and the quality standard of 55% [12] since it is this deviation that operators use to correct the value of the $\theta1$ parameter more effectively. It is also important to consider the information provided by the online NIR, given the significance that operators attach to this information in correcting the $\theta1$ in the case of faulty production.

6   Conclusion

Artificial intelligence tools and data collection on the shop floor are opening up opportunities to improve flexibility and productivity in industry. Harnessing the tacit experience of workers on the shop floor is a rampart against the labor shortages and skills attrition currently experienced by organizations.

In the case of cheese production, and more specifically cream cheese production, the experience of operators is necessary to control the UF concentration factor, as this affects the moisture content of the product, to which strictly regulated. To ensure the continuity and flexibility of production lines despite an unfavorable job market and a high turnover rate, the proposed methodology used the CRISP-DM approach to develop a machine-learning tool for maximizing cream cheese production yield on a Canadian production line.

Convincing results have been obtained using a decision tree algorithm on real production and quality data, with an overall **RMSE** of 0.061 and an $\mathbf{R}^2$ of 0.91 when predicting the ultrafiltration concentration factor used by an experienced operator to maximize yield while complying with quality standards. The implementation step allowed to witness an acceptance of the tool by the operators, help by detailed training and an inclusive approach to limit resistance to change.

The scientific impact of this article lies in its advancement of Industry 4.0, as demonstrated by its illustration of how AI can address production challenges by harnessing the tacit knowledge of experienced workers. This approach has the potential to influence future research and applications in a number of sectors. It demonstrates the applicability and performance of machine learning tools in solving real-world production problems in the fresh cheese industry, which could pave the way for similar innovations in the dairy and food industries. Furthermore, it highlights the potential for the wider application of its methodologies in industries where tacit knowledge is essential, contributing to improved production efficiency and the development of human-centered AI systems.

However, there are a number of limitations, but these are also research opportunities to be exploited. Data acquisition and evaluation of data quality and quantity remain limiting factors that should be investigated to improve tool performance and usability. The development of tools for different production modes, e.g. for faulty production, should also be considered. The inclusion of new information, such as on-line NIR, could also improve the ability of the model to replicate the decisions of experienced operators.

Acknowledgments. We would like to thank our industrial partner for providing us with the data and the expert knowledge as well as MITACS Stage de stratégie d'entreprise (IT36475) for the support.

Disclosure of Interests. The authors have no competing interests to declare that are relevant to the content of this article.

References

1. Udugama, I.A., Kelton, W., Bayer, C.: Digital twins in food processing: a conceptual approach to developing multi-layer digital models. Digital Chem. Eng. **7**, 100087 (2023). https://doi.org/10.1016/j.dche.2023.100087
2. Abdel-Basset, M., Moustafa, N., Hawash, H.: Evaluating Deep Neural Networks, Chap. 4, pp. 77–102. Wiley (2022). https://doi.org/10.1002/9781119884170.ch4

3. Chiu, Y., Cheng, F., Huang, H.: Developing a factory-wide intelligent predictive maintenance system based on industry 4.0. J. Chin. Inst. Eng. **40**(7), 562–571 (2017). https://doi.org/10.1080/02533839.2017.1362357

4. Dupuis, A., Dadouchi, C., Agard, B.: A decision support system for sequencing production in the manufacturing industry. Comput. Ind. Eng. **185**, 109686 (2023). https://doi.org/10.1016/j.cie.2023.109686

5. Government of Canada: Food and drug regulations (C.R.C., c.870) – b.08.035 (1). cream cheese (2023). https://laws-lois.justice.gc.ca/eng/regulations/C.R.C.%2C_c._870/page-28.html

6. Hassoun, A., et al.: Birth of dairy 4.0: opportunities and challenges in adoption of fourth industrial revolution technologies in the production of milk and its derivatives. Curr. Res. Food Sci. **7**, 100535 (2023). https://doi.org/10.1016/j.crfs.2023.100535

7. Johnson, M.: A 100-year review: cheese production and quality. J. Dairy Sci. **100**(12), 9952–9965 (2017). https://doi.org/10.3168/jds.2017-12979

8. Kindstedt, P.: Cheese and Culture: A History of Cheese and its Place in Western Civilization. Chelsea Green Publishing, South West Asia and the Ancient Origins of Cheese (2012)

9. Kumar, A., Nayyar, A.: si3-Industry: A Sustainable, Intelligent, Innovative, Internet-of-Things Industry, pp. 1–21. Springer, Cham (2020). https://doi.org/10.1007/978-3-030-14544-6_1

10. Malekpour, S., et al.: What scientists need to do to accelerate progress on the SDGS. Nat. Comment **621**, 250–254 (2023). https://doi.org/10.1038/d41586-023-02808-x

11. Manning, L., et al.: Artificial intelligence and ethics within the food sector: developing a common language for technology adoption across the supply chain. Trends Food Sci. Technol. **125**, 33–42 (2022). https://doi.org/10.1016/j.tifs.2022.04.025

12. Ningtyas, D.W., Bhandari, B., Bansal, N., Prakash, S.: Effect of homogenisation of cheese milk and high-shear mixing of the curd during cream cheese manufacture. Int. J. Dairy Technol. **71**(2), 417–431. https://doi.org/10.1111/1471-0307.12482

13. OCDE: Retaining talent at all ages. OCDE (2023). https://doi.org/10.1787/00dbdd06-en

14. Phadungath, C.: Cream cheese products: a review. Songklanakarin J. Sci. Technol. **27**(1), 191–199 (2005)

15. Porep, J.U., Kammerer, D.R., Carle, R.: On-line application of near infrared (NIR) spectroscopy in food production. Trends Food Sci. Technol. **46**(2, Part A), 211–230 (2015). https://doi.org/10.1016/j.tifs.2015.10.002

16. Pu, Y.Y., O'Donnell, C., Tobin, J.T., O'Shea, N.: Review of near-infrared spectroscopy as a process analytical technology for real-time product monitoring in dairy processing. Int. Dairy J. **103**, 104623 (2020). https://doi.org/10.1016/j.idairyj.2019.104623

17. PySimpleSoft: Pysimplegui library (2018). https://www.PySimpleGUI.com

18. Ramirez-Asis, E., Vilchez-Carcamo, J., Thakar, C.M., Phasinam, K., Kassanuk, T., Navod, M.: A review on role of artificial intelligence in food processing and manufacturing industry. In: International Conference on Advances in Materials Science, Materials Today: Proceedings, vol. 51, pp. 2462–2465 (2022). https://doi.org/10.1016/j.matpr.2021.11.616

19. Salkin, C., Oner, M., Ustundag, A., Cevikcan, E.: A Conceptual Framework for Industry 4.0, pp. 3–23. Springer, Cham (2018). https://doi.org/10.1007/978-3-319-57870-5_1

20. Salque, M., et al.: Earliest evidence for cheese making in the sixth millennium BC in Northern Europe. Nature **493**(7433), 522–525 (2012). https://doi.org/10.1038/nature11698

21. Schröer, C., Kruse, F., Gómez, J.M.: A systematic literature review on applying Crisp-DM process model. Procedia Comput. Sci. **181**, 526–534 (2021). https://doi.org/10.1016/j.procs.2021.01.199

22. Schäfer, F., Zeiselmair, C., Becker, J., Otten, H.: Synthesizing crisp-dm and quality management: a data mining approach for production processes. In: 2018 IEEE International Conference on Technology Management, Operations and Decisions (ICTMOD), pp. 190–195 (2018). https://doi.org/10.1109/ITMC.2018.8691266

23. Sharma, A., Pandey, H.: Big Data and Analytics in Industry 4.0, pp. 57–72. Springer, Cham (2020). https://doi.org/10.1007/978-3-030-14544-6_4

24. Tsoukiàs, A.: From decision theory to decision aiding methodology. Eur. J. Oper. Res. **187**(1), 138–161 (2008). https://doi.org/10.1016/j.ejor.2007.02.039

25. Vahedi-Nouri, B., Tavakkoli-Moghaddam, R., Hanzalek, Z., Dolgui, A.: Workforce planning and production scheduling in a reconfigurable manufacturing system facing the COVID-19 pandemic. J. Manuf. Syst. **63**, 563–574 (2022). https://doi.org/10.1016/j.jmsy.2022.04.018

26. Wolfschoon Pombo, A.F.: Cream cheese: historical, manufacturing, and physico-chemical aspects. Int. Dairy J. **117**, 104948 (2021). https://doi.org/10.1016/j.idairyj.2020.104948

27. Womack, J., Jones, D., Roos, D.: The Machine that Changed the World. Simon & Schuster, New York (2007)

Comparative Evaluation of Irregular Shape Strip-Packing Algorithms

Niccolò Giovenali$^{(\boxtimes)}$, Giulia Bruno, and Paolo Chiabert

Politecnico di Torino, Turin, Italy
{niccolo.giovenali,giulia.bruno,paolo.chiabert}@polito.it

Abstract. The nesting problem of 2D shapes, which has impactful application in the cutting and packing fields, has been studied for many years. Previous papers are mainly focused on proposing new algorithms and prove their efficiency in terms of packing density or computation time. However, the results are reported only on few datasets and the comparison is done only with respect to few competing algorithms. The aim of the paper is to analyse and compare the results obtained by strip-packing algorithms published in the last 20 years. The results show that the effectiveness of the algorithms varies widely across different datasets, and there is a lack of comprehensive benchmarking that considers both the quality of solution and the computational time required to achieve it. Furthermore, since no algorithm clearly outperforms all the others, further methods to address the nesting problem with reinforcement learning and neural networks could be investigated to improve the generalization ability on the nesting problem.

Keywords: Irregular strip-packing · 2D nesting · Meta-heuristics · Combinatorial optimization · Packing · Cutting reinforcement learning · Artificial intelligence

1 Introduction

Two-dimensional irregular packing problems represent a significant challenge across various manufacturing industries, ranging from shipbuilding to clothing manufacturing. These industries are faced with the task of efficiently arranging irregularly shaped components or materials within a two-dimensional space, such as a sheet or container. The efficient packing of these materials is crucial for optimizing material utilization, reducing waste, and improving overall productivity [1].

One of the primary objectives of tackling 2D irregular packing problems is to maximize the utilization of available space while adhering to various constraints. In industries like shipbuilding and automotive production, where large and irregularly shaped parts are commonplace, efficient packing can significantly impact production costs and timelines. In clothing and furniture manufacturing, where irregularly shaped fabrics or components need to be arranged on cutting tables or within packaging, effective packing algorithms can streamline production processes, reduce material waste, and ultimately improve profitability [2]. Moreover, with the increasing adoption of automation and robotics in

© The Author(s), under exclusive license to Springer Nature Switzerland AG 2025
M. Dassisti et al. (Eds.): IN4PL 2024, CCIS 2372, pp. 115–127, 2025.
https://doi.org/10.1007/978-3-031-80760-2_7

manufacturing, efficient packing algorithms are essential for enabling autonomous systems to make real-time decisions regarding material handling and placement. This not only improves efficiency but also reduces the reliance on manual labor and minimizes the risk of human error [3]. By addressing these challenges, researchers can contribute to the development of more sustainable and cost-effective manufacturing practices, ultimately benefiting both industries and consumers alike.

We focus in one of the most general and more present case in the publications: the strip-packing (1 open dimension) of irregular (concave, possibly with holes) shapes, into one rectangular bin. Shapes are allowed to rotate of predetermined angles. The nesting is offline, meaning we already know in advance all the shapes to be nested, hence the order of placing can be chosen. Various approaches have been developed to tackle the 2D strip-packing problems. These include exact algorithms, heuristic methods, metaheuristic algorithms, and hybrid approaches that combine multiple techniques [4].

Previous papers are mainly focused on proposing new algorithms and prove their efficiency in terms of packing density or length of the solution. However, the results are reported only on few datasets and the comparison is done only with respect to few competing algorithms. Thus, it is difficult to have a proper analysis of strengths and limitations of each algorithm. The aim of the paper is to analyse and compare the results obtained by strip-packing algorithms published in the last 20 years. The research has two main objectives: (i) report the results and the trends of the algorithms, to see how the performance evolve over time, and (ii) highlight the main limitations and the possible improvements in the field.

2 Strip-Packing Problem

The strip-packing problem (SPP) involves arranging a set of irregular shaped items onto a larger rectangular strip with minimal wasted space [4]. The problem formulation aims to find the optimal arrangement of irregular shaped items within the strip, minimizing the horizontal space used while ensuring that none of the items overlap and that they fit within the bounds of the strip. Given a set of n irregular shaped items with a finite set of allowed angles of rotations, and a rectangular strip (bin) of fixed width and infinite length, the objective is to determine the placement and orientation of all the items that minimize the length of the utilized bin. The overlap constraint ensures that no two items overlap each other, while the boundary constraint ensure that all items fit within the dimensions of the bin.

The benchmarks instances on which the majority of authors test their algorithm are the Euro Special Interest Group on Cutting and Packing (ESICUP) 2D Irregular [5], composed of irregular polygons only.

Nesting algorithm frame the problem representing polygons as ordered collection of line segments, sometimes including primitives such as arc to extend the application to curved shapes. The space is often discretized by rasterization, transforming the problem formulation from a vectorized space to a discretized grid of points [9]. This approximation can be done with different resolution, and it's aimed to reduce the solution space, allowing a more efficient exploration.

Given a bin and the current item to be placed, the domain of positions of the item that do not overlap with other items and lays inside the bin must be determined. This constrain is usually satisfied with the use of geometrical tools such as the NFP, ψ-function, D-function, or direct trigonometry [6]. The no fit-polygon, is the most used tool in the literature due to the ease of calculation. Several methods to compute it have been developed, based on the principle of "sliding" the item around the borders of the bin and the already placed items. There is a trade-off between time complexity and the handling of irregular shapes and degenerated cases, such as handling holes, concave shapes, dealing with arcs, and with exact fit positions. ψ and D function, due to their nature, are more suitable to be used as constraints in a mathematical model especially when trying to handle continuous rotations, hence used sometimes in exact methods [7]. The algorithms analysed in this work make all use of the NFP, some of them develops new and more efficient methods to compute it.

3 Algorithm Classification

Various approaches have been developed to tackle the 2D nesting and strip-packing problems. They can be classified into two main categories: exact algorithms and meta-heuristic algorithms [8]. Each category can be further divided in sub-categories, as represented in Fig. 1.

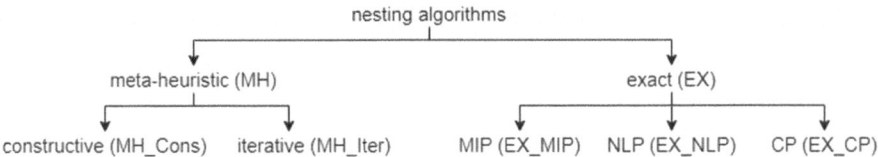

Fig. 1. Nesting algorithms approaches.

Exact algorithms (EX), such as integer linear programming formulations, aim to find the optimal solution by exhaustively exploring the solution space. While exact algorithms guarantee optimality, they may become computationally infeasible for large problem instances due to their exponential time complexity. Indeed, all the exact methods taken in consideration in this work introduce new and more efficient way of computing the constraints and modelling the problem with significantly less variables, allowing them to compute results for big instances, dealing with rotations as well. Various mathematical models have been proposed: mixed-integer linear programming (EX_MIP), non-linear programming (EX_NLP), and constraint programming (EX_CP). The specific characteristics of these models depend heavily on the geometric techniques employed [9].

Metaheuristic algorithms (MH), offer a balance between exploration and exploitation of the solution space. By incorporating probabilistic mechanisms and adaptive search strategies, metaheuristics can efficiently navigate complex problem landscapes and discover high-quality solutions. Some metaheuristic algorithms might as well include an optimization phase that is formulated as mathematical model, making use of the exact approach tools. In the literature, two main groups of meta-heuristic approaches exist for the polygon packing problem [10].

The first group, i.e., the constructive meta-heuristic algorithms [MH_Cons], uses a placement sequence of polygons and places them one at a time always in a valid position according to the placement rule. The solution quality is reliant on a heuristic placement rule and a meta-heuristic order and angle optimization.

The second group, i.e., the iterative meta-heuristic algorithms [MH_Iter], consists in finding an initial feasible solution with a simple heuristic and then iteratively optimise the position of polygons. A solution is found until each polygon satisfies the packing constraints. This approach permits overlap between polygons and penalises the overlap in the objective function, which creates a multi-objective problem. The two objectives, minimizing the length of the solution, and minimize overlap, are often handled with a separation and compaction scheme [11]. This approach can generate a smoother continuous solution space by allowing overlap between polygons, but its weakness is that it does not guarantee obtaining a feasible solution.

4   Literature Analysis

To identify relevant literature on strip packing algorithms, a comprehensive search was conducted on Scopus February 2024. The search query used was: *"TITLE-ABS-KEY ((nesting OR (strip-packing) OR (strip AND packing)) AND (irregular OR non-convex OR (non AND convex) OR concave) AND (shapes OR polygon))"*.

This query was refined limiting the results on the last 20 years, excluding book chapters, and limiting to the subjects of interest such as Computer Science, Engineering, Mathematics, Decision Sciences, Business Management and Accounting, Multidisciplinary, Material Science.

The filtered search returned 118 articles. From these results we selected the relevant strip-packing problem algorithms that could be fairly be compared among each other. The criteria for this selection have been that the algorithm was handling an offline nesting, with one open dimension, that handles irregular (non-convex) shapes with rotations, on a single bin, and were tested on at least 7 out if the 15 instances of the ESICUP dataset, found to be the wider common ground. Table 1 shows the instances belonging to that dataset, and their characteristics.

Figure 2 shows a packing example of the aforementioned instances with the intention to show the kind of shapes handled.

This reduction led us to 24 articles, collected in Table 2, classified accordingly to the categories described in Sect. 3. Particularly, 5 exact algorithms were retrieved (3 of type MIP, 1 NLP and 1 CP), and 19 meta-heuristics algorithms (8 of type Cons and 11 Iter).

Table 1. ESICUP Benchmark instances data. TNI: total number of items. NIT: number of item types. ANV: average number of vertices. AO: admissible orientations.

Instance	TNI	NIT	ANV	AO
Albano	24	8	7.25	0°, 180°
Dagli	30	10	6.30	0°, 180°
Dighe1	16	16	3.87	0°
Dighe2	10	10	4.70	0°
Fu	12	12	3.58	0°, 90°, 180°, 270°
Jakobs1	25	25	5.60	0°, 90°, 180°, 270°
Jakobs2	25	25	5.36	0°, 90°, 180°, 270°
Mao	20	9	9.22	0°, 90°, 180°, 270°
Marques	24	8	7.37	0°, 90°, 180°, 270°
Shapes0	43	4	8.75	0°
Shapes1	43	4	8.75	0°, 180°
Shapes2	28	7	6.29	0°, 180°
Shirts	99	8	6.63	0°, 180°
Swim	48	10	21.90	0°, 180°
Trousers	64	17	5.06	0°, 180°

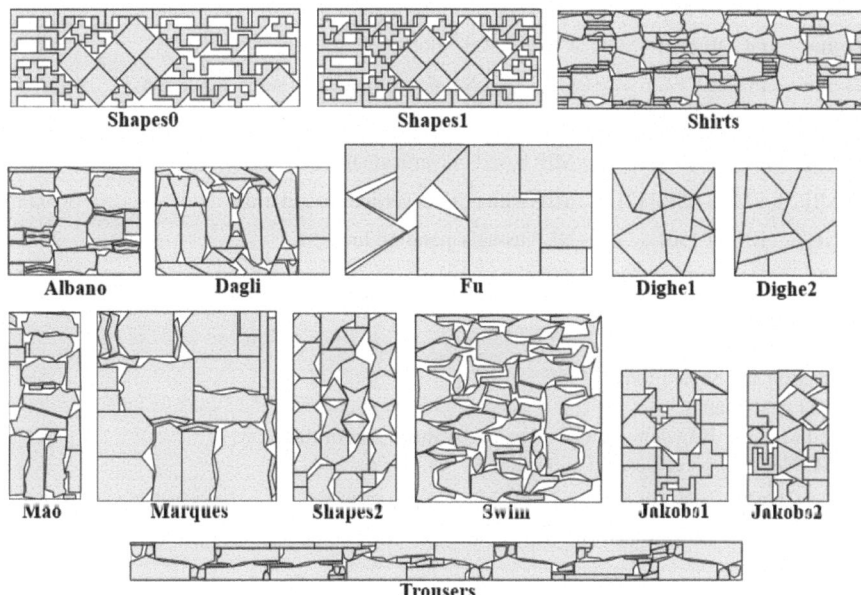

Fig. 2. Packing examples on the benchmark dataset.

Table 2. Selected algorithms.

Category	Name & reference	Main characteristics	year
MH_Cons	BLF [12]	Hill Climbing combined with TS[a]	2006
MH_Cons	BS [13]	Minimize functions of occupied space	2010
MH_Cons	BRKGA70 [14]	Bias Random Key GA[b]	2017
MH_Cons	EMCRL [15]	Reinforcement Learning: Every Visit Monte Carlo	2023
MH_Cons	μ-BRKGA [16]	Parametrized Bias Random Key GA[b]	2017
MH_Cons	H4NP [17]	Combines 6 placements heuristics	2018
MH_Cons	VS-NFP-MIP [18]	GA[b] improved with MIP constraints	2023
MH_Cons	FLD[10]	Space allocation problem solved by Ant Colony labor division	2017
MH_Iter	2DNest [19]	C&S[c]; GLS[d] along vert. and horiz. directions	2007
MH_Iter	FITS [20]	C&S[c]; GLS[d] along vert. and horiz. directions	2009
MH_Iter	CFREFP [21]	C&S[c]; SA for sequence position and orientation	2012
MH_Iter	SAHA [9]	C&S[c]; SA with LP to generate neighbors	2006
MH_Iter	ILSQN [22]	C&S[c]; GLS[d] and a swapping procedure	2009
MH_Iter	ELS [23]	C&S; overlap with L-BFGS[e]; items swap with TS[a]	2012
MH_Iter	GCS [24]	C&S[c]; GLS[d] and Cuckoo Search; Pairwise clustering	2013
MH_Iter	3PM [25]	3 phases: construction, VND[f], MIP	2016
MH_Iter	ROMA [11]	C&S[c]; GLS[d] rasterization with two resolutions	2019
MH_Iter	GCDH [26]	C&S[c]; GLS[d] along vert. and horiz. directions	2021
MH_Iter	FOMLS [27]	C&S[c]; GLS[d]; Fast obstruction map calculation	2023
EX_MIP	NFP-CM [28]	MIP	2016
EX_MIP	NFP-CM-VS [29]	MIP based on vertical slices and feasibility cuts	2023
EX_MIP	EM-2DISPP [2]	MIP with critical vertices calculation	2023
EX_NLP	IPOPT [30]	NLP using separation lines	2017
EX_CP	I1ODP-IGC [31]	CP with global constraints	2019

[a]Tabu Search.
[b]Genetic Algorithm.
[c]Compaction and Separation.
[d]Guided Local Search.
[e]Limited Memory Broyden–Fletcher–Goldfarb–Shanno algorithm.
[f]Variable Neighborhood Descent algorithm.

5 Results

5.1 Algorithm Performance Comparison

Given their iterative structure, strip-packing algorithms are usually evaluated by several runs on a specific dataset and the performance is identified by the best and average packing density and the corresponding computation times [12]. The packing density is defined as the area occupied by the figures (sum of the areas of all the polygons) over the total area of the bounding box that contains them all [12]. We have noticed that best and average packing density mostly goes hand in hand, and since the average was not always reported in the publications, we decided to focus on the best packing density for clarity. In fact, the computational time comparison is not significant since the algorithms are executed for an arbitrary time frame and results for smaller or bigger execution time were not provided. Figure 3 shows the best packing density obtained by the selected algorithms over the ESICUP datasets as reported in the author's publications.

Category	Algorithm	albano	dagli	dighe1	dighe2	fu	jakobs1	jakobs2	mao	marques	shapes0	shapes1	shapes2	shirts	swim	trousers
MH_Iter	GCS	89.6	89.5	100.0	100.0	92.4	89.1	87.7	85.4	90.6	68.8	76.7	84.8	89.0	75.9	91.0
MH_Iter	ROMA	89.1	88.7	100.0	100.0	92.3	89.1	87.7	86.1	91.0	68.8	76.7	83.6	88.5	75.7	91.1
MH_Cons	FLD	89.1	88.2	100.0	100.0	92.1	89.1	85.3	84.0	88.9	68.8	74.7		89.0	75.5	90.4
MH_Iter	FOMLS	85.7	87.6	100.0	100.0	94.0	93.8	86.2	79.3	90.8	69.5	78.6	83.1	87.9	69.3	91.0
MH_Iter	ELS	88.5	88.1	100.0	100.0	91.9	89.1	83.9	84.3	89.7	67.6	75.3	84.2	88.4	75.4	89.6
MH_Iter	CFREFP	89.2	88.4	100.0	100.0	92.0	89.1	84.8	84.2	90.0	67.6	72.5	83.3	87.6	71.8	90.1
MH_Iter	ILSQN	88.2	87.4	99.9	100.0	90.7	86.9	82.5	83.4	89.0	68.4	73.8	84.3	88.8	75.3	89.8
MH_Cons	mu-BRKGA	89.1		100.0	100.0	92.0	89.1	79.8		89.1	66.5	72.6			73.6	90.5
MH_Iter	FITS	87.6	86.4	99.9	100.0	91.2	89.1	80.8	83.7	89.2	66.5	73.9	81.7	86.9	74.5	89.4
MH_Cons	BS	87.9	88.0	100.0	100.0	90.3	86.0	80.4	84.1	88.9	64.4	72.6	81.3	89.7	75.0	90.4
MH_Iter	2DNest	87.4	86.0	99.9	100.0	91.8	89.1	80.4	85.2	89.2	67.1	73.8	81.2	86.3	71.5	89.8
MH_Iter	GCDH	88.2	86.3	97.6	97.3	90.8	88.0	79.5	84.8	90.4	66.1	72.4		84.3	74.1	88.3
MH_Iter	SAHA	87.4	87.2	100.0	100.0	91.0	75.9	77.3	82.5	88.1	66.5	71.3	83.6	86.8	74.4	90.0
EX_NLP	IPOPT	84.1	83.5			75.4	74.2		81.7				77.6	82.9	73.6	87.4
MH_Cons	BRKGA70	81.6	77.5	80.0	100.0	83.8	81.2	76.6	75.1	81.8	61.7	66.7	77.5	83.6	65.6	80.0
MH_Cons	BLF	84.6	83.7	77.4	79.4	86.9	82.6	74.8	79.5	86.5	67.6	60.5	66.5	84.6	68.4	88.5
MH_Iter	3PM	82.1				89.1	81.7	74.2	76.5	81.4	66.5	68.8	78.3			76.2
EX_MIP	EM-2DISPP	79.5	73.9	89.5	100.0	85.9	75.4	68.9	69.4	79.5	58.7					66.9
MH_Cons	VS-NFP-MIP	71.6	80.1			83.5	85.5	79.1	75.2		51.0				76.2	85.5
EX_MIP	NFP-CM-VS	79.0	74.5	100.0		86.0	81.7	68.9	19.9	83.3			75.7			
MH_Cons	EMCRL			77.4	100.0	77.0	76.1	67.9		80.4	56.5	58.2	70.8	81.4	64.2	77.5
MH_Cons	H4NP	80.7	77.1			75.4	68.4	71.4	82.7	62.2	65.0	74.7	81.8	66.1	78.8
EX_MIP	NFP-CM	67.6	71.2			81.7	62.7	67.6	74.8			70.8				
EX_CP	IIODP-IGC		72.3			83.8	37.0	33.9			61.4	58.7		78.7		

Fig. 3. Best packing density of the algorithms over the ESICUP instances, with gradient colouring based on performance over the instances. Result in bold are the best results for the instance.

It can be noticed that on two datasets (dighe1 and dighe2) the majority of algorithms reach a packing density of 100% meaning that the figures are placed perfectly in the bounding box. There is no algorithm that outperforms the others in all the instances, although 13 out of 15 best solutions are found by only 3 algorithms: GCS, ROMA, and

FOMLS. It also interesting to notice how BS and VS-NFP-MIP found the best solutions for shapes2 and swim, even if they don't perform at top on the majority of instances.

Heuristic algorithms seem more suited to address the nesting problem with a high number of shapes. Exact methods are usually tested on fewer datasets, mainly the smaller ones, even if they don't reach the performances of the heuristic algorithms.

To derive the coherent ranking of the algorithms, we compute the mean and standard deviation values of the packing densities over all the datasets for each algorithm. Table 3 shows the results, ordered by decreasing mean best packing density value.

From this analysis, we obtained that GCS has the biggest overall best packing density, even if ROMA and FLD obtain very close performance. Top performing algorithms (i.e., GCS, FLD, ROMA, FOMLS and ELS) are all based on meta-heuristic approaches. The standard deviation values are very similar, suggesting that the span of the performance over the different instances might be highly influenced by the single instance shapes characteristics.

Another interesting analysis is to study the evolution of algorithms over time. Figure 4 reports the average packing densities of the algorithms over the years. This analysis reveals that there is no clear evidence of a better approach. Constructive and iterative meta-heuristics algorithms share good performances, but surprisingly there's no trend of the better solutions over time.

The best performing algorithm, GCS, was published in 2013. It exploits a complex heuristic to generate the initial solution, and indeed is the only algorithm among the selected one that pre-process the data by constructing a similarity score among shapes, that influence the placement order. Furthermore, matching shapes, are moved together during the first 50% of the iterations.

5.2 Emerging Weakness and Possible Improvements of Algorithms

As in other NP-hard combinatorial problems, key points to address are the trade-off between the computational time and the quality of the solution, and the ability to perform consistently over a various set of instances. These two fields are still to be deeper investigated. All the algorithms in the literature are iterative, and the majority of articles reports the average and best solutions found over the time span, but don't report the quality of the solution over time, making it hard to compare them on the computational time field. It might be useful to know on average how quickly the solution gets close to the best found, since it's a relevant trade-off in many applications where time might become more important than space or material saving.

Another time aspect not consistently addressed is the computational time for the NFP calculation. It is usually calculated a priori for all couples of shapes of the instance, and then used in the algorithm. Therefore, its processing time does not impact the algorithm iterations, but at the same not much attention is given to how efficiently it has been calculated in the first place; that time is commonly not being reported in the execution time of the algorithm. This gives less relevance to the various and possibly more efficient ways of producing the NFPs [6], and ignores the relevance of it in real applications such as material cutting, where jobs with new shapes involved arrive at a given time and need to be nested and processed as soon as possible.

Table 3. Ranking of the algorithms showing the mean and standard deviation of best packing density (pd) over all the instances on which they algorithms were tested.

Category	Name	Mean best pd	St. dev. best pd	N. of instances
MH_Iter	GCS	87.4%	8.1%	15
MH_Iter	ROMA	87.2%	8.1%	15
MH_Cons	FLD	86.8%	8.5%	14
MH_Iter	FOMLS	86.4%	9.0%	15
MH_Iter	ELS	86.4%	8.4%	15
MH_Iter	CFREFP	86.0%	9.0%	15
MH_Iter	ILSQN	85.9%	8.3%	15
MH_Cons	μ-BRKGA	85.7%	10.6%	11
MH_Iter	FITS	85.4%	8.8%	15
MH_Cons	BS	85.3%	9.2%	15
MH_Iter	2DNest	85.2%	9.0%	15
MH_Iter	GCDH	84.9%	8.7%	14
MH_Iter	SAHA	84.1%	9.4%	15
EX_NLP	IPOPT	80.0%	4.7%	9
MH_Cons	BRKGA70	78.2%	8.8%	15
MH_Cons	BLF	78.1%	8.4%	15
MH_Iter	3PM	77.5%	6.3%	10
EX_MIP	EM-2DISPP	77.1%	11.1%	11
MH_Cons	VS-NFP-MIP	76.4%	10.0%	9
EX_MIP	NFP-CM-VS	74.3%	20.9%	9
MH_Cons	EMCRL	74.0%	11.2%	12
MH_Cons	H4NP	73.7%	6.7%	12
EX_MIP	NFP-CM	70.9%	5.6%	7
EX_CP	I1ODP-IGC	60.8%	18.0%	7
MH_Iter	GCS	87.4%	8.1%	15

Since no algorithm outperforms the others on all instances, thus there is no hint that heuristic methods have found generalization ability on the nesting problem, an interesting cue would be to address the nesting problem with reinforcement learning and neural networks [31]. Neural networks have already been shown to be competitive in solving combinatorial problems, in fact have been applied in the case of bin packing (rectangles) 3D or 2D, [3, 32, 33], showing strong generalization ability and stable results even when the number of rectangles or strip width differs from that during training.

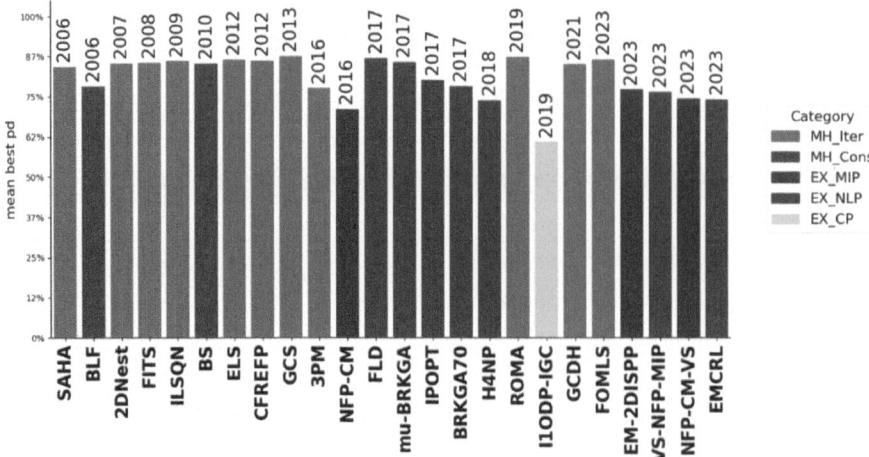

Fig. 4. Mean best packing density for each algorithm, ordered by publication year.

Among the selected algorithms, EMCRL utilises reinforcement learning to optimize the placement sequence, and place the shapes by a vanilla bottom-left heuristic [15]. The algorithm does not rank high, perhaps the overall structure of the algorithm with a BL placement isn't performing well. At the same time, it might highlight the fact that the dataset isn't large enough to apply learning techniques effectively, which are known to require a big amount of data. This suggests that irregular shape strip-packing might need larger dataset of shapes to show potential benefits of reinforcement learning techniques as in bin-packing, where boxes and rectangles are easily randomly generated.

6   Conclusion

The study of irregular strip packing remains a challenging area of combinatorial optimization due to the inherent complexity and variability of the problem instances, as well as its industrial relevance. While heuristic and exact algorithms offer potential solutions, the trade-off between computational time and solution quality is still a significant concern. The effectiveness of these algorithms varies widely across different datasets, and there is a lack of comprehensive benchmarking that considers both the quality of solutions and the computational time required to achieve them.

An important aspect highlighted in this study is the necessity of expressing the quality of solutions over time for a fair comparison of computational performance. This approach allows for a more nuanced understanding of how quickly and effectively different algorithms converge to high-quality solutions. By tracking the progression of solution quality throughout the computational process, researchers can better evaluate the efficiency of algorithms and their practical applicability in real-world scenarios.

The exploration of machine learning and deep learning techniques has shown promise, particularly in the context of bin packing, but their application to irregular strip packing requires larger datasets to fully demonstrate their potential. Future research should focus on developing more efficient algorithms for NFP calculation, investigating the use of learning-based approaches with larger and more diverse datasets, and providing more detailed performance metrics to facilitate better comparisons across different methods.

Acknowledgments. This publication is part of the project PNRR-NGEU which has received funding from the MUR – DM 352/2022.

Disclosure of Interests. The authors have no competing interests to declare that are relevant to the content of this article.

References

1. Gomes, A.M., Frias, R.: Irregular packing problems: industrial applications and new directions using computational geometry (2013)
2. Kimms, A., Király, H.: An extended model formulation for the two-dimensional irregular strip packing problem considering general industry-relevant aspects. Eur. J. Oper. Res. **306**(3), 1202–1218 (2023). https://doi.org/10.1016/j.ejor.2022.07.050
3. Hu, R., Xu, J., Chen, B., Gong, M., Zhang, H., Huang, H.: TAP-Net: transport-and-pack using reinforcement learning. ACM Trans. Graph. **39**(6) (2020). https://doi.org/10.1145/3414685.3417796
4. Guo, B., et al.: Two-dimensional irregular packing problems: a review. Front. Mech. Eng. **8** (2022). https://doi.org/10.3389/fmech.2022.966691
5. ESICUP dataset 2D Irregular. https://www.euro-online.org/websites/esicup/data-sets/#1535972088237-bbcb74e3-b507
6. Cox, W., While, L., Reynolds, M.: A review of methods to compute Minkowski operations for geometric overlap detection. IEEE Trans. Vis. Comput. Graph. **27**(8), 3377–3396 (2021). https://doi.org/10.1109/TVCG.2020.2976922
7. Stoyan, Y., Pankratov, A., Romanova, T.: Placement problems for irregular objects: mathematical modeling, optimization and applications. In: Butenko, S., Pardalos, P., Shylo, V. (eds.) Optimization Methods and Applications. SOIA, vol. 130, pp. 521–559. Springer, Cham (2017). https://doi.org/10.1007/978-3-319-68640-0_25
8. Sato, A.K., Castro Martins, T., Tsuzuki, M.S.G.: A study on GPU acceleration applied to 2D irregular packing problems. Int. J. Comput. Integr. Manuf. **35**(4–5), 427–443 (2022). https://doi.org/10.1080/0951192X.2022.2050302
9. Gomes, A.M., Oliveira, J.F.: Solving irregular strip packing problems by hybridising simulated annealing and linear programming. Eur. J. Oper. Res. **171**(3), 811–829 (2006). https://doi.org/10.1016/j.ejor.2004.09.008
10. Wang, Y., Xiao, R., Wang, H.: A flexible labour division approach to the polygon packing problem based on space allocation. Int. J. Prod. Res. **55**(11), 3025–3045 (2017). https://doi.org/10.1080/00207543.2016.1229070
11. Sato, A.K., Martins, T.C., Gomes, A.M., Tsuzuki, M.S.G.: Raster penetration map applied to the irregular packing problem. Eur. J. Oper. Res. **279**(2), 657–671 (2019). https://doi.org/10.1016/j.ejor.2019.06.008
12. Burke, E., Hellier, R., Kendall, G., Whitwell, G.: A new bottom-left-fill heuristic algorithm for the two-dimensional irregular packing problem. Oper. Res. **54**(3), 587–601 (2006). https://doi.org/10.1287/opre.1060.0293

13. Bennell, J.A., Song, X.: A beam search implementation for the irregular shape packing problem. J. Heuristics **16**(2), 167–188 (2010). https://doi.org/10.1007/s10732-008-9095-x
14. Mundim, L.R., Andretta, M., de Queiroz, T.A.: A biased random key genetic algorithm for open dimension nesting problems using no-fit raster. Expert Syst. Appl. **81**, 358–371 (2017). https://doi.org/10.1016/j.eswa.2017.03.059
15. Fang, J., Rao, Y., Zhao, X., Du, B.: A hybrid reinforcement learning algorithm for 2D irregular packing problems. Mathematics **11**(2) (2023). https://doi.org/10.3390/math11020327
16. Amaro Júnior, B., Pinheiro, P.R., Coelho, P.V.: A parallel biased random-key genetic algorithm with multiple populations applied to irregular strip packing problems. Math. Probl. Eng. **2017** (2017). https://doi.org/10.1155/2017/1670709
17. Mundim, L.R., Andretta, M., Carravilla, M.A., Oliveira, J.F.: A general heuristic for two-dimensional nesting problems with limited-size containers. Int. J. Prod. Res. **56**(1–2), 709–732 (2018). https://doi.org/10.1080/00207543.2017.1394598
18. Guo, B., Li, J., Zhang, Y., Wu, F., Peng, Q.: Efficient 2D irregular layout by vector superposition NFP and mixed-integer programming. Expert Syst. Appl. **230** (2023). https://doi.org/10.1016/j.eswa.2023.120548
19. Egeblad, J., Nielsen, B.K., Odgaard, A.: Fast neighborhood search for two- and three-dimensional nesting problems. Eur. J. Oper. Res. **183**(3), 1249–1266 (2007). https://doi.org/10.1016/j.ejor.2005.11.063
20. Umetani, S., Yagiura, M., Imahori, S., Imamichi, T., Nonobe, K., Ibaraki, T.: Solving the irregular strip packing problem via guided local search for overlap minimization. Int. Trans. Oper. Res. **16**(6), 661–683 (2009). https://doi.org/10.1111/j.1475-3995.2009.00707.x
21. Sato, A.K., Martins, T.C., Tsuzuki, M.S.G.: An algorithm for the strip packing problem using collision free region and exact fitting placement. CAD Comput. Aided Des. **44**(8), 766–777 (2012). https://doi.org/10.1016/j.cad.2012.03.004
22. Imamichi, T., Yagiura, M., Nagamochi, H.: An iterated local search algorithm based on nonlinear programming for the irregular strip packing problem. Discrete Optim. **6**(4), 345–361 (2009). https://doi.org/10.1016/j.disopt.2009.04.002
23. Leung, S.C.H., Lin, Y., Zhang, D.: Extended local search algorithm based on nonlinear programming for two-dimensional irregular strip packing problem. Comput. Oper. Res. **39**(3), 678–686 (2012). https://doi.org/10.1016/j.cor.2011.05.025
24. Elkeran, A.: A new approach for sheet nesting problem using guided cuckoo search and pairwise clustering. Eur. J. Oper. Res. **231**(3), 757–769 (2013). https://doi.org/10.1016/j.ejor.2013.06.020
25. Cherri, L.H., Carravilla, M.A., Toledo, F.M.B.: A model-based heuristic for the irregular strip packing problem. Pesqui. Oper. **36**(3), 447–468 (2016). https://doi.org/10.1590/0101-7438.2016.036.03.0447
26. Umetani, S., Murakami, S.: Coordinate descent heuristics for the irregular strip packing problem of rasterized shapes, April 2021. http://arxiv.org/abs/2104.04525
27. Sato, A.K., Mundim, L.R., Martins, T.C., Tsuzuki, M.S.G.: A separation and compaction algorithm for the two-open dimension nesting problem using penetration-fit raster and obstruction map. Expert Syst. Appl. **220** (2023). https://doi.org/10.1016/j.eswa.2023.119716
28. Cherri, L.H., Mundim, L.R., Andretta, M., Toledo, F.M.B., Oliveira, J.F., Carravilla, M.A.: Robust mixed-integer linear programming models for the irregular strip packing problem. Eur. J. Oper. Res. **253**(3), 570–583 (2016). https://doi.org/10.1016/j.ejor.2016.03.009
29. Lastra-Díaz, J.J., Ortuño, M.T.: Mixed-integer programming models for irregular strip packing based on vertical slices and feasibility cuts. Eur. J. Oper. Res. (2023). https://doi.org/10.1016/j.ejor.2023.08.009
30. Peralta, J., Andretta, M., Oliveira, J.F.: Solving irregular strip packing problems with free rotations using separation lines, July 2017. http://arxiv.org/abs/1707.07177

31. Cherri, L.H., Carravilla, M.A., Ribeiro, C., Toledo, F.M.B.: Optimality in nesting problems: new constraint programming models and a new global constraint for non-overlap. Oper. Res. Perspect. **6** (2019). https://doi.org/10.1016/j.orp.2019.100125

32. Liu, H., Zhou, L., Yang, J., Zhao, J.: The 3D bin packing problem for multiple boxes and irregular items based on deep Q-network. Appl. Intell. **53**(20), 23398–23425 (2023). https://doi.org/10.1007/s10489-023-04604-6

33. Li, D., Gu, Z., Wang, Y., Ren, C., Lau, F.C.M.: One model packs thousands of items with recurrent conditional query learning. Knowl. Based Syst. **235** (2022). https://doi.org/10.1016/j.knosys.2021.107683

An Inventory Management Support Tool Through Indirect Q-Value Estimation: A Combined Optimization and Forecasting Approach

Amanda Rodrigues Delfiol[1,2]($\boxtimes$), Camélia Dadouchi[1], Bruno Agard[1], and Philippe St-Aubin[2]

[1] Laboratoire en Intelligence des Données, École Polytechnique de Montréal, Montréal, (Québec), Canada
{amanda.rodrigues-delfiol,camelia.dadouchi,bruno.agard}@polymtl.ca
[2] Logistik Unicorp Inc, Saint-Jean-sur-Richelieu, (Québec), Canada
philippe_st-aubin@logistikunicorp.com

Abstract. Effective inventory management is crucial in manufacturing and wholesale businesses to reduce operation costs and meet service level guarantees. Due to the continuous increase in product catalogues and highly volatile demand, inventory management complexity continues to grow. This paper introduces a decision support tool designed to aid in inventory management through an indirect Q-value estimator technique. The proposed tool employs simulation, optimization and forecasting techniques to enable purchase actions evaluation for large horizons. By integrating both simulation and optimization into a supervised learning algorithm, the tool provides an easy to interpret cost estimation that can directly be used to make informed procurement decisions. A case study in the textile industry demonstrates its use and its performance in a single-echelon supply chain setting. This research presents a comprehensive step by step framework to support the creation of a decision support tool that can offer valuable aid for decision-making processes across different supply management contexts.

Keywords: Inventory management · Supervised learning · Decision making · Supply chain management

1 Introduction

In an increasingly competitive global landscape, companies operate with stricter margins and within intricate networks, striving to reduce costs and optimize operations. As such, businesses have started focusing even more on reducing transportation needs, saving on administrative resources, and automating non-value-added processes. With simultaneous growing demands and expectations for speed and efficiency, Supply Chain Management (SCM) becomes strategic, aiming to seamlessly combine product flow and production to meet market requirements.

A crucial part of SCM is Inventory Management (IM), in which decisions related to stock can strongly influence the cost of operations and directly affect company margins. It can be extremely challenging to take an informed decision when it comes to modern inventory systems as many of them grapple with stochastic demand and lead-time, variable fill-rates and a growing volume of personalized items [15]. As such, it is essential to have in place tools that can accurately evaluate supply chain scenarios with a great complexity, to allow for choices that will be the least costly in the long run.

In this article, we propose a novel way of processing inventory data through a combination of simulation, optimization and forecasting to choose an order quantity for a certain inventory state. As with classic inventory problems, we define our order quantity as one of the actions that minimize the incurred cost of our inventory management. This order quantity represents how many items will be ordered from the supplier and we evaluate the impact of this choice in the long-term. Another contribution of our model is the ability to reuse historical data as the input for our training set and be able to estimate the cost a plausible future scenario without going through multiple simulation and optimization loops.

The remainder of this paper is structured as follow, Sect. 2 presents a literature review presenting data analytics tools employed in supply chain management. Subsequently, the proposed methodology will be described with its three components of simulation, optimization and forecasting (3) as well as the experimental set-up (4). Following this, we demonstrate the tool's performance and possible improvements with a case study in the textile industry (5) and a discussion of the results (6). Finally, in section (7), we conclude with insights on generalized use cases and extensions of the proposed model.

2   State of the Art

Managing inventory flow has been modeled and studied across time using different approaches with the objective of lowering overall resource consumption. When it comes to stochastic inventories, there are two main models: the Economic Order Quantity models and the Newsvendor model [20]. The first one is based on known cycle stocks, which means both demand and supply are predictable and deterministic. In contrast, the Newsvendor model accounts for an unpredictable variability of demand by having safety stocks. The added complexity of stochastic inventories coupled with digitalization makes for complex supply chains that collect a great amount of data daily. As such, procurement decisions grapple with an extreme volatile and data-heavy environment which creates a difficult decision making scenario. To this end, data analytics techniques can be employed in different ways to help answer common questions, as seen in Fig. 1 [12, 25].

In **descriptive analytics**, the main objective is to better understand a current or past situation at hand through analysing and clustering data. Specifically

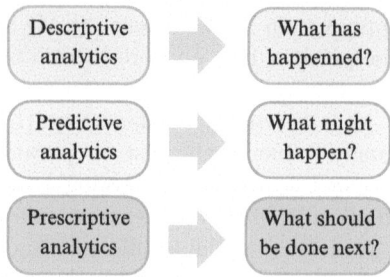

Fig. 1. Types of data analytics and their objectives.

in SCM, it can be used for vulnerability assessments to understand weaknesses in the supply chain design [6] and Selective Inventory Classification to allow for inventory prioritization [14]. Descriptive analytics can also be employed when wanting to recreate a system as is, by using simulation to retrace product flow and stock dynamics. In [17], simulation is used in a context of measuring an inventory policy for a multi-echelon supply chain problem.

In **predictive analytics**, the focus is on the future, on what might happen next following a specific situation. More specifically, supervised learning is the standard way to predict unknown future events from known past events. In our context, this type of learning has been used for performance indicators forecasting [25] and, in the more common use-case, demand forecasting [18,19]. In supervised learning, LightGBM (LGBM) is a commonly used tool, a Gradient Boosting Decision Tree [13]. This type of algorithm employs many weak learners called Decision Trees and boosts their performance by combining their outputs in the final estimation. In IM, LGBM is commonly employed in demand forecasting [18] but a few papers have had promising results in using it as an indirect solver for optimization problems [1,22]. This allows for a variety of new research, as directly solving an optimization problem can be computationally intensive, usually requiring more time than an LGBM prediction.

Optimization problems mostly fall on the **prescriptive analytics** category, where tools take a step further than predictive analytics and recommend a course of action for the future. To be considered prescriptive, a tool needs to answer the question "What should be done next?", see Fig. (1). In SCM, an example of action is an order that minimizes current and future costs of inventory [7]. In operational research, this can be known as the Newsvendor problem, where Newsvendor inventory dynamics are minimized while avoiding stockouts or excess inventory. In this context, one typically assumes a known demand distribution for traditional algorithms to work [5]. Knowing the real demand and its distribution parameters is a rare occurrence, which progressively prompted research on data-driven Newsvendor solutions. When dealing with more complex settings, traditional model-based approaches are outperformed by data-driven solutions, as they can better deal with more realistic settings [7]. An example of a data-driven approach used in IM is finding the best decision for a particular situation (state) determined from historical data, and compiling a large set of (state, optimal decision) pairs to train a machine learning model [23]. For this type of approach, an optimization problem can be transformed into a supervised learning one through Imitation Learning. Transforming a prescriptive optimization into a predictive algorithm can have advantages such as a smaller temporal and computational complexity, as supervised learning usually bypasses the need for simulation and complex mathematical models after training. In other words, the objective is to learn patterns through possible past decisions, such as how much was ordered following a certain base heuristic policy, and try to mimic past choices without having to redo simulations at every use. If the industrial objective is to take better actions than in the past, an Imitation Learning model can be limited in its performance and an approach that focuses on minimizing the cost of inventory instead of reproducing possible base stock policies might yield better results [23].

In prescriptive analytics, solving a Markov Decision Problem (MDP) is another classic way to find the optimal actions in a sequential decision problem with delayed consequences, which has been done in the context of IM [9]. An issue with this approach is that solving directly an MDP by Dynamic Programming can be intractable in many cases. Consequently, the field of Approximate Dynamic Programming was created (also known as Reinforcement Learning) where value functions and policies can be approximated [4]. In realistic SCM use-cases, Reinforcement Learning is still computationally expensive for hyper-parameter tuning and training, which might not make it a viable option for every company [10].

Trying to estimate a possible future is normally seen as a predictive problem. Nevertheless, with our proposed approach, we try to exploit a prescriptive objective through a predictive approach, namely through guiding procurement workers to find an optimal order action with a Q-value estimate. This estimate is the lowest possible cost that can be incurred from a specific action. While predictive learning can be limited in its most common use-cases ("What will be the next states of inventory?"), we will approach a more complex analytical problem ("How much should be ordered?") by automating the step before answering this question. Through a combination of simulation, optimization and forecasting, we will be able to estimate the minimal future inventory cost of an action at a certain inventory state, which can then be used to rank possible actions and, ultimately, choose an order quantity. Our tool will have a short training time unlike Reinforcement Learning and will be appropriate for complex stochastic and uncertain settings differently from optimization. Additionally, by using this method, the simulation and optimization will not be needed after training which can save computational power and time.

3   Method

The objective of the proposed tool is to offer an estimation for the present and future costs associated with an action. For this estimation, the state of inventory of a product is required. We define a state as the products in stock and the orders that are on the way - also known as open purchase orders - for a specific week in time. Inventory movements for that horizon are aggregated so that we have a single value for each week. In our scenario, we consider that orders always arrive at the end of the week and are only added to the stock of the following state. Furthermore, we simplify the inventory dynamics by considering that a product is shipped immediately after the demand is realized, without any delay of processing time or variable fill-rates. As such, the demand for the current state is used to generate the next stock. We characterize our inventory cost function C_t for a single product as the following (1), where $x^+ = \max\{x, 0\}$:

$$C_t = h(sk_t - d_t)^+ + b(d_t - sk_t)^+ + c\alpha_t + ua_t \tag{1}$$

Much like the newsvendor problem, the holding cost h and the back-order cost b are considered with their respective stocks [7]. Because the cost C_t is calculated at the end of the week, the demand d_t is known and is subtracts the current stock sk_t. If the total stock is positive, a holding cost is incurred and otherwise a backorder cost is. Moreover, a variable administrative cost c is added when an order is passed and when products arrive at the warehouse. The variable α_t is equal to one if an order is passed or arrives and zero otherwise. Finally, the unit cost of the item u is multiplied by how many units were ordered at a certain time stamp a_t.

A common issue with using a formula like C_t as the sole evaluator of an inventory cost is that it considers that only the present impacts our expenses, which is untrue. Our actions affect the current state but also the subsequent ones due to a delayed consequence, characterized in our problem as the variable lead-time from our suppliers where items arrive weeks after placing an order.

Instead of using a complex approach such as MDPs to evaluate the long-term effects of our decisions, we minimize a discounted cumulative cost function (2) and solve it by simulating possible future sequences of states. The parameter γ is in range (0,1) and serves to emphasize the significance of states closer to the present, as the further we move from $t = 0$, the less confident we are in the costs C_t and their impact in the present [8]. When choosing γ, the closer to 1, the more impactful future decisions are.

$$Q = \min_{a_1, a_2, \ldots, a_N} \sum_{t=0}^{N} \gamma^t C_t + V \tag{2}$$

The simulation parameters include ranges for items in inventory, demand, and lead-time, as well as a starting date and the trajectory horizon. All ranges are determined based off historical data. Moreover, a trajectory is the ensemble of states that follow a chronological order and represent the inventory evolution. The first action (a_0) is randomly generated from a range associated with the lead-time forecast minus the stock for that item. This a_0, along with the initial stock, future lead-times and demands are used to find the actions that will minimize Q through linear programming. The Q represents the minimal future cost incurred from a_0, considering all the next actions will be optimal and have an oracle-like behaviour of knowing future demands and lead-times. The V is a termination value with the objective of estimating the infinite horizon in this finite problem, which can be a backordering penalty at the end of the trajectory or selling all the stock on hand at a u cost [16]. Thus, our Q is a more complete measure of the total inventory costs obtained by taking an action, in contrast to C_t that only evaluates the present consequences.

The next step is to use the Q labelled trajectories for supervised learning using LGBM. Each state of a trajectory is treated as a separate point of a time-series where the input variables are the current stock, the open purchase orders and the actions taken. The output is an estimate of Q which can be used as a decision support tool when evaluating different actions for a specific state. The LGBM algorithm does not have access to any demands and lead-times, only the lead-time forecast, to mimic a real-life use scenario. Additionally, unlike for linear programming, there is no need to simulate future states as it has already been done when calculating the exact Q. This saves computational power and time so that the Q estimation can be quickly obtained without needing extra steps or algorithms. The goal of the predictive model is to be given a real state in the present and be able to predict the delayed consequences of an inventory order so that a procurement employee can make an informed decision.

4   Data and Experimental Setup

In this section we present the method proposed to develop the predictive tool for inventory management. The creation of the decision support tool follows the method described in Fig. 2.

Step 1. One or more products are selected, and historical data is sampled for a time period that is bigger than the size of the chosen trajectory horizon to allow for enough variety in estimating ranges. Demand and lead-time can oscillate according to the time of the year and exceptional circumstances such as a sanitary crisis or a driver strike. As such, it is essential that in the training data, a broad spectrum of situations is portrayed by sampling over a large horizon.

Step 2. consists of calculating the range for the three variables that will be simulated: initial stock, lead-time and demand. The same procedure is used for the three of them. Either historical data is inputted directly with an added Gaussian noise, or the past data is deseasonalized and when reused in a simulation, trend and season are readjusted according to the state's date.

Step 3. A simulator samples from the previously established ranges and outputs an initial stock, one array of demands and another of lead-times. The length of the output arrays is the number of weeks between the start date and the end of the horizon.

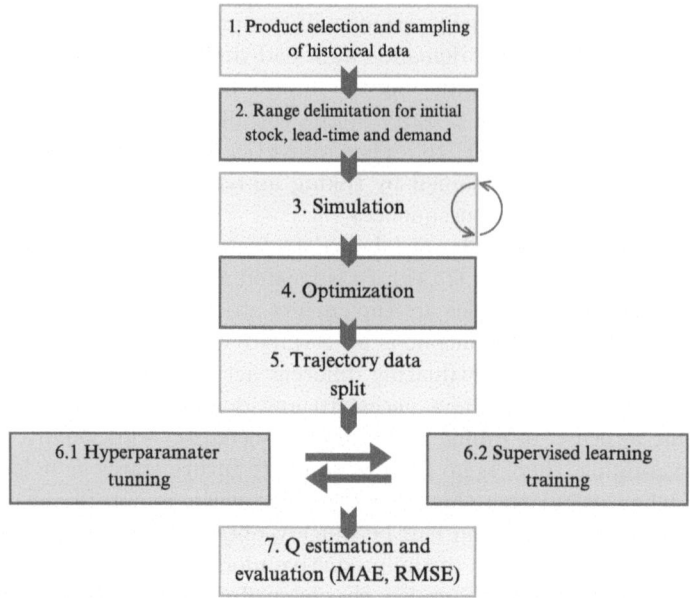

Fig. 2. Steps to obtain the Q estimator.

Step 4. An array of first actions is generated by taking the lead-time forecast and subtracting the initial stock. Lead-time forecast is obtained by adding a gaussian error to the lead-time demand. Each action in the array becomes part of a separate trajectory that is optimized to find the minimal Q after the first random step. The fourth step is repeated until there are no more possibilities of new samples or when enough data points have been gathered.

Step 5. is for the data split where full trajectories are placed either in a train, validate or test set.

Step 6.1. is for the tuning of the LGBM hyperparameters using a Bayesian optimization method over the training data to maximize accuracy, followed by the training of the regressor at **Step 6.2**.

Step 7. Lastly, the estimator's Q is outputted at step 7. We then compare our real cost with the forecasted one and calculate the errors to assess the quality of predictions. For the evaluation portion, mean average error (MAE) and root mean square error (RMSE) were chosen as complimentary indicators, as they are often used in forecasting with LGBM [2,3].

$$\text{MAE} = \frac{1}{n} \sum_{i=1}^{n} |y_i - \hat{y}_i| \qquad (3)$$

$$\text{RMSE} = \sqrt{\frac{1}{n} \sum_{i=1}^{n}(y_i - \hat{y}_i)^2} \tag{4}$$

For each state, y_i represents the real Q whereas $\hat{y}_i$ is the forecasted Q at times-tamp i. The variable n is the numbers of states that were predicted.

5   Case Study

In this section, a partner's textile company is used to showcase the performance of the presented tool. Their business model consists of a single-echelon supply chain with outsourced production. This production is then gradually sent to their warehouse by placing orders over time to meet weekly demand.

At step 1, for the case study, historical data from a single item in a warehouse was gathered, from August 2021 until October 2023. The selected item has a high-volume profile and an average demand of 744 items per week. At step 2, the simulated ranges are established following the procedure of manipulating historical data described in Sect. 4 (Table 1).

Table 1. Comparison of real and simulation statistics for various variables.

Variable	Real mean	Real std	Simulation mean	Simulation std
Demand (u)	744	826	1839	1122
Lead-time (weeks)	13.9	12.6	6.5	1.1
Initial stock (u)	2518	2502	9631	3999

For the lead-time, the past values were divided by two to enrich inventory dynamics by having more product arrivals in a single trajectory. At step 3, the simulation and the randomized action generate 50809 trajectories with a mean length of 86 weeks each. All trajectories are labelled by an optimized Q-value with an evaluation horizon of up to 52 weeks and a γ of 0.95 (step 4). At step 5, only the 34 first states are kept. This assures only trajectories where the Q was evaluated over one year are used. For training, validation and testing, 35566, 5081 and 10162 trajectories are assigned respectively. The data is split by whole trajectories instead of by date to allow the algorithm in training to grasp patterns for high and low inventory levels, as well as state transitions.

Before training the LGBM regressor, at step 6.1 some hyperparameters were tuned through Bayesian optimization based on Gaussian process regression [11]. The ranges given for each hyperparameter can be found in Table 2.

For each of the parameters above, the results were 128, 0.1, 0.4568, 10, 1000, 69, 1 and 28, respectively. The LGBM algorithm was trained (step 6.2) and the errors were calculated according to step 7's description. Both measures were also

Table 2. Hyperparameter ranges.

Parameter	Range
num_leaves	(2, 128)
learning_rate	$U(ln(10^{-3}), ln(10^{-1}))$
feature_fraction	(0.1, 1.0)
max_depth	(2, 10)
num_boost_round	(100, 1000)
early_stopping_rounds	(10, 100)
nthread	(1, 10)
min_child_samples	(1, 100)

Table 3. Case study errors for Q estimation.

Measure	Absolute	Relative (%)
MAE	109.33	0.26
RMSE	5850.58	15.11

divided by the mean real Q of the test set to better understand how they scale against our data (Table 3).

The MAE suggests that, on average, the model's predictions deviate of 109.33 from the actual Q-values. Meanwhile, the higher RMSE might represents that there are potential outliers and large errors as this metric is sensitive to such elements [24]. This shows the estimations are accurate enough to be used as action rankers and fulfil their purpose of an informative measure for procurement workers. Further results are needed to understand if the estimated Q's in the optimization function - and consequently the final forecasting model - closely represent reality and are an adequate representations of future costs.

6   Discussions

Following the results of the case study, the model offers enough of a prediction accuracy to be employed as an efficient decision tool. Because its usage is supposed to rank actions instead of providing the most accurate Q-value possible, buyers and inventory managers can confidently base their choices off the given forecast. This tool allows for an informed decision-making process with an estimation of the cumulative C_t after a first action. Due to its training, the prediction includes an estimation of the future inventory progression and the demand evolution, which is otherwise computationally expensive to obtain. Consequently, it isn't necessary to repeat the training simulations and optimization after getting to a satisfactory error rate. However, the model must be retrained if large gaps between current data and past data start to show in any of the variables used to build the simulations or if costs in the optimization function change.

7   Conclusion

This paper introduces a new way to indirectly estimate inventory costs and better procurement decisions by helping employees have a better visibility of impact of each decision. The Q-value estimation can offer a simple way to measure how placing (or not) an order at a certain week can impact future inventory states and, consequently, overall expenses. With this understanding, a complex supply-chain issue can be simplified. By using primarily an easily trainable algorithm such as LGBM and running simulations and optimizations only at training times, one can almost instantaneously produce complex estimates of future scenarios without a highly computationally expensive approach at the use phase. Additionally, the Q-value can potentially be used for decisions both in single-echelon and multi-echelon supply chains. For usage in multi-echelon supply chains, there needs to be additional simulation hypothesis and an optimization function that matches the constraints of this environment. The advantage of this methodology is that it can adapt to different constraints, such as restricting actions to comply with multiple order quantities and leveraging different models for different suppliers to aid in supplier selection. Another possible extension is to use it as the basis for an ABC SKUs rank, be either single or multi-criterion [21].

Lastly, an automatic action selection module would be a useful progression for this tool as it would allow for an even stronger automatization of procurement orders. This would shift our model from predictive to prescriptive and allow for a greater degree of user independence. A clear limitation is that quality of estimates strongly relies on clean historical data and accurate lead-time forecasting, which is not a given in all businesses. Nevertheless, this decision support tool can be a crucial element in reducing inventory costs by forecasting which actions will be the least costly on the long term.

Acknowledgments. This study was funded by MITACS Acceleration IT 25600.

Disclosure of Interests. The authors have no competing interests to declare that are relevant to the content of this article.

References

1. Abolghasemi, M., Abbasi, B., HosseiniFard, Z.: Machine learning for satisficing operational decision making: a case study in blood supply chain. Int. J. Forecast. (2023). https://doi.org/10.1016/j.ijforecast.2023.05.004
2. Ahakonye, L.A.C., Zainudin, A., Shanto, M.J.A., Lee, J.M., Kim, D.S., Jun, T.: A multi-MLP prediction for inventory management in manufacturing execution system. Internet Things **26**, 101156 (2024). https://doi.org/10.1016/j.iot.2024.101156
3. Ahmed, U., Mahmood, A., Tunio, M.A., Hafeez, G., Khan, A.R., Razzaq, S.: Investigating boosting techniques' efficacy in feature selection: a comparative analysis. Energy Rep. **11**, 3521–3532 (2024). https://doi.org/10.1016/j.egyr.2024.03.020
4. Bertsekas, D.: A Course in Reinforcement Learning. Athena Scientific, 1 edn. (2023)

5. Beutel, A.L., Minner, S.: Safety stock planning under causal demand forecasting. Int. J. Prod. Econ. **140**(2), 637–645 (2012). https://doi.org/10.1016/j.ijpe.2011. 04.017

6. Blackhurst, J., Rungtusanatham, M.J., Scheibe, K., Ambulkar, S.: Supply chain vulnerability assessment: a network based visualization and clustering analysis approach. J. Purch. Supply Manag. **24**(1), 21–30 (2018). https://doi.org/10.1016/j. pursup.2017.10.004

7. de Castro Moraes, T., Yuan, X.M.: Data-driven solutions for the newsvendor problem: a systematic literature review. In: Advances in Production Management Systems. Artificial Intelligence for Sustainable and Resilient Production Systems, pp. 149–158. Springer (2021)

8. Doshi-velez, F.: The infinite partially observable Markov decision process. In: Bengio, Y., Schuurmans, D., Lafferty, J., Williams, C., Culotta, A. (eds.) Advances in Neural Information Processing Systems, vol. 22. Curran Associates, Inc. (2009)

9. Giannoccaro, I., Pontrandolfo, P.: Inventory management in supply chains: a reinforcement learning approach. Int. J. Prod. Econ. **78**(2), 153–161 (2002). https:// doi.org/10.1016/S0925-5273(00)00156-0

10. Gijsbrechts, J., Boute, R.N., Van Mieghem, J.A., Zhang, D.J.: Can deep reinforcement learning improve inventory management? Performance on lost sales, dual-sourcing, and multi-echelon problems. Manuf. Serv. Oper. Manag. **24**(3), 1349–1368 (2022). https://doi.org/10.1287/msom.2021.1064

11. Head, T., Kumar, M., Nahrstaedt, H., Louppe, G., Shcherbatyi, I.: scikit-optimize/scikit-optimize (2020). https://github.com/scikit-optimize/scikit-optimize

12. Holsapple, C., Lee-Post, A., Pakath, R.: A unified foundation for business analytics. Decis. Support Syst. **64**, 130–141 (2014). https://doi.org/10.1016/j.dss.2014.05.013

13. Ke, G., et al.: LightGBM: a highly efficient gradient boosting decision tree. In: Advances in Neural Information Processing Systems, vol. 30, pp. 3146–3154 (2017)

14. Khanorkar, Y., Kane, P.: Selective inventory classification using ABC classification, multi-criteria decision making techniques, and machine learning techniques. Materials Today: Proceedings, 2nd International Conference and Exposition on Advances in Mechanical Engineering (ICoAME 2022), vol. 72, pp. 1270–1274 (2023). https://doi.org/10.1016/j.matpr.2022.09.298

15. Kosgoda, D., Perera, H.N., Aloysius, J.: Effective goal framing for managers using inventory management systems. Eur. J. Oper. Res. **316**(1), 138–151 (2024). https://doi.org/10.1016/j.ejor.2024.01.034

16. Madeka, D., Torkkola, K., Eisenach, C., Luo, A., Foster, D.P., Kakade, S.M.: Deep inventory management (2022)

17. Maheshwari, P., Kamble, S.: The application of supply chain digital twin to measure optimal inventory policy. IFAC-PapersOnLine **55**(10), 2324–2329 (2022). https://doi.org/10.1016/j.ifacol.2022.10.055

18. Makridakis, S., Spiliotis, E., Assimakopoulos, V.: M5 accuracy competition: results, findings, and conclusions. Int. J. Forecast. **38**(4), 1346–1364 (2022). https://doi. org/10.1016/j.ijforecast.2021.11.013

19. Panda, S.K., Mohanty, S.N.: Time series forecasting and modeling of food demand supply chain based on regressors analysis. IEEE Access **11**, 42679–42700 (2023). https://doi.org/10.1109/ACCESS.2023.3266275

20. Porteus, E.: Foundations of Stochastic Inventory Theory. Stanford University Press, 1 edn. (2002)

21. Ramanathan, R.: ABC inventory classification with multiple-criteria using weighted linear optimization. Comput. Oper. Res. **33**(3), 695–700 (2006). https://doi.org/10.1016/j.cor.2004.07.014
22. Ren, X., Gong, Y., Rekik, Y., Xu, X.: Data-driven analysis on anticipatory shipping for pickup point inventory. IFAC-PapersOnLine **55**(10), 714–718 (2022). https://doi.org/10.1016/j.ifacol.2022.09.491
23. St-Aubin, P.: Conception d'un système de gestion de l'inventaire pour un portefeuille de produits à profil de demande mixte, Ph.D. thesis, Polytechnique Montréal (2020)
24. St-Aubin, P., Agard, B.: Precision and reliability of forecasts performance metrics. Forecasting **4**(4), 882–903 (2022). https://doi.org/10.3390/forecast4040048
25. Zhang, T., Lauras, M., Zacharewicz, G., Rabah, S., Benaben, F.: Coupling simulation and machine learning for predictive analytics in supply chain management. Int. J. Prod. Res., 1–18 (2024). https://doi.org/10.1080/00207543.2024.2342019

Multiscale Clustering to Improve Anomaly Detection in Nuclear Equipments

Amaratou Mahamadou Saley[1,2]($\boxtimes$)(iD), Thierry Moyaux[2](iD), Aicha Sekhari[2](iD), Guillaume Bouleux[2](iD), Vincent Cheutet[2](iD), and Jean-Baptiste Danielou[1]

[1] INEO Nucláire, Lyon, France
[2] INSA Lyon, Université Lumiére Lyon 2, Université Claude Bernard Lyon 1, Université Jean Monnet Saint-Etienne, DISP, UR4570, 69621 Villeurbanne, France
amaratou.saley@equans.com

Abstract. In the nuclear industry, the relentless pursuit of operational excellence and reliability is paramount, especially considering the critical importance of safety and efficiency. This sector, a key component of global energy supply, is constantly driven to innovate and optimize its equipments. Early fault detection plays a central role in this endeavor, as it not only helps to prevent potential incidents, but also maximizes production. Traditional anomaly detection methods, primarily based on clustering algorithms, often overlook minor yet warning faults. Addressing this, our paper introduces a multiscale clustering approach, advancing beyond classical methods. This methods achieves a satisfactory classification of anomalies and culminates in a silhouette score of 90%. Additionally, it facilitates the computation of a preventive maintenance indicator.

Keywords: Predictive maintenance · Anomaly detection · Clustering methods · Time series · Nuclear industry

1 Introduction

The development of advanced information technologies, such as the Internet of Things, Cloud Computation and Artificial Intelligence (AI), enables the realization of the Industry 4.0 vision for the nuclear industry [10]. This digital transformation has facilitated the interaction between various equipments, systems and components [18]. Such inter-connectivity has revolutionized the way data is collected from facilities, greatly improving the monitoring of machines as well as the planning of their maintenance [13]. Consequently, the concept of anomaly detection has become increasingly pivotal as the ability to harness and analyze data opens new horizons in predictive maintenance and system reliability.

Anomaly detection has been an active area of research in the last decade [11]. Anomalies are patterns in data that do not conform to a well defined notion of normal behavior [18]. The goal of anomaly detection is to identify data samples

M. Dassisti et al. (Eds.): IN4PL 2024, CCIS 2372, pp. 140–154, 2025.
https://doi.org/10.1007/978-3-031-80760-2_9

that have abnormal behavior compared to the majority. Common techniques for this include statistical methods, data stream algorithm-based detection, and unsupervised learning-based machine learning methods [12]. Data mining and machine learning, in particular, have been extensively explored for their potential in anomaly detection, drawing considerable interest from the research community. Among the various strategies, the clustering method stands out as a key technique in data mining and machine learning for anomaly detection. These techniques are designed to group similar objects together while ensuring that dissimilar objects are placed in separate clusters [2]. Typically, this method employs traditional classification algorithms such as K-means, DBScan, and Hierarchical clustering.

However, various types of anomalies and the resulting high variability may limit the application of those traditional methods in practical scenarios [16], such as in the nuclear industry. The presence of diverse anomalies in nuclear systems, ranging from major incidents requiring maintenance to minor and predictive faults, poses a challenge for traditional clustering methods. They often *struggle with the heterogeneity of data, especially when minor anomalies (warning faults), which are crucial for preventive maintenance, are overshadowed by major ones.* In response, *multiscale clustering* has been introduced as an innovative solution. This method examines the data structure across various scales, ensuring a detailed and refined analysis of anomalies [9].

Thus, *this paper introduces a methodology that integrates multiscale clustering with domain knowledge, significantly improving anomaly detection in industrial time series data.* This strategy refines maintenance decision-making, crucial in the nuclear industry where precision and foresight are paramount. Our major contribution is the *application of multiscale clustering to improve anomaly detection in the context of nuclear maintenance*, which is a sector that has yet to explore this advanced technique.

The remainder of this paper is organized as follows. Section 2 explores related work, focusing on various clustering techniques used for anomaly detection. Section 3 details the methodology we propose. Section 4 discusses the results from our case study, showcasing the practical implications and effectiveness of our approach. Finally, Sect. 5 concludes.

2 Literature Review

2.1 Clustering Techniques For Anomaly Detection

The exploration of clustering techniques for anomaly detection has garnered significant attention within the research community. According to Web of Science database, 3,722 articles have been published on the thematic since 1991. Clustering [7] is used to group similar data instances into clusters. Clustering-based anomaly detection techniques can be categorized into three distinct groups, as outlined by [12]. The first category operates on the premise that normal (faultless) data instances are part of a cluster within the dataset, whereas anomalies do not belong to any cluster. Methods adhering to this principle employ established clustering algorithms, identifying instances that do not fit into any cluster as anomalous [4,5]. The second category is grounded in the observation that normal data instances are located close to their nearest cluster centrod, in comparison to anomalies which are positioned far from theirs [12,14]. The third category is based on the assumption that normal data instances are part of large and dense clusters, while anomalies are associated with either small or sparse clusters [1,12].

However, clustering-based techniques for anomaly detection face notable limitations [12]. Those techniques primarily struggle with accurately identifying the structure of normal instances and may not effectively detect anomalies that form their own clusters or are highly diverse. Additionally, the challenge of detecting minor anomalies, which are not easily distinguishable, further diminishes the effectiveness of these methods. This is compounded by the fact that several algorithms force every instance into a cluster, leading to a situation where anomalies could be wrongly considered normal if they get grouped into large clusters.

2.2   Anomaly Detection Enhanced by Multiscale Clustering

To address these limitations, the research community has delved into multiscale clustering, a topic covered by 4,015 articles on Web of Science database, across various areas, especially materials science and biology. A specific search on Web of Science using "Multiscale Clustering" and "Maintenance" as keywords reveals only 25 articles. These papers largely focus on multiscale data segmentation, feature extraction and construction.

For example, Zhang et al. [17] introduce a multiscale technique for creating features aimed at fault diagnosis, not at refining clustering algorithms to detect anomalies. This method focuses on constructing a fault feature matrix through entropy dispersion and principal component analysis. The main contribution of multiscale in this context is in the segmentation of data for feature construction.

Kim et al. [8] present an integrated framework to automatically detect anomalies and faults in underground transmission-line connectors. Their multiscale feature extraction module helps in distinguishing features of transmission-lines and their environments, coupled with a skip-layer fusion module that integrates distinct features from the extraction module. The major contribution of this work is the development of a multiscale feature extraction approach.

Despite these advancements, the specific application of multiscale clustering in the nuclear maintenance sector remains notably scarce. This gap is significant in an industry characterized by stringent regulatory requirements and the complexity of its operational technology, as highlighted in the literature and further underscored by the detailed review in [13]. The nuclear sector depends heavily on expert knowledge and historical operational data (feedback) for the effective surveillance and maintenance of its facilities, yet challenges in defect detection persist due to the intricate nature of the equipment.

To address these challenges, our research introduces a pioneering application of multiscale clustering tailored to nuclear maintenance, integrating crucial equipment knowledge. This approach not only seeks to enhance anomaly detection but also aims to refine the decision-making processes within nuclear facilities. By leveraging advanced data analysis techniques, our methodology promises transformative improvements in the accuracy and speed of detecting potential equipment failures.

Moreover, the incorporation of knowledge into our multiscale clustering framework enriches our models with decades of industry-specific experience. This integration leverages both state-of-the-art analytical techniques and deep sector-specific knowledge, markedly improving the reliability and efficiency of maintenance operations. Our innovative approach is poised to redefine the standards for predictive maintenance in the nuclear industry, aiming to enhance safety and reduce downtime by enabling more informed and precise maintenance strategies.

3   Proposed Methodology

This section details our multiscale clustering methodology for anomaly detection in nuclear systems. Our method is dividing into five parts (Fig. 1): Knowledge engineering, data preparation, coarse clustering, followed by multiscale clustering and downstream analysis with maintenance indicator computation.

3.1   Knowledge Engineering

This phase initiates our framework, aimed at extracting key knowledge from the equipment. We focus on obtaining explicit insights through a detailed functional analysis of the equipment. This analysis provides a comprehensive understanding of how the equipment behaves under various operational conditions. Based on this understanding, we develop a Rule-Based Knowledge (RBK) model employing classic "IF-THEN" logic.

The process for drafting these rules is well-established and comprises several critical steps to ensure accuracy and reliability: (i) initial exploration and classification of knowledge from functional analysis documents, (ii) implementation of the RBK model based on this classification, (iii) expert verification, enrichment, and validation conducted through technical review meetings, ensuring collaborative refinement. This process is iterative, allowing for necessary adjustments in response to feedback on the defined rules. (iv) The final approval of the rules is given by experts.

The RBK model systematically categorizes different operational scenarios, including normal operations, maintenance modes, and potential anomalies. The rules are highly reliable, as they are derived from documents authored by experienced equipment experts and validated by nuclear safety regulators. An annual review of these documents is conducted to minimize the risk of errors, enhancing the trustworthiness of the rules.

This approach goes beyond mere categorization of operations; it captures the essential behaviors of the equipment, providing a nuanced understanding that is crucial for guiding all steps of the anomaly detection process.

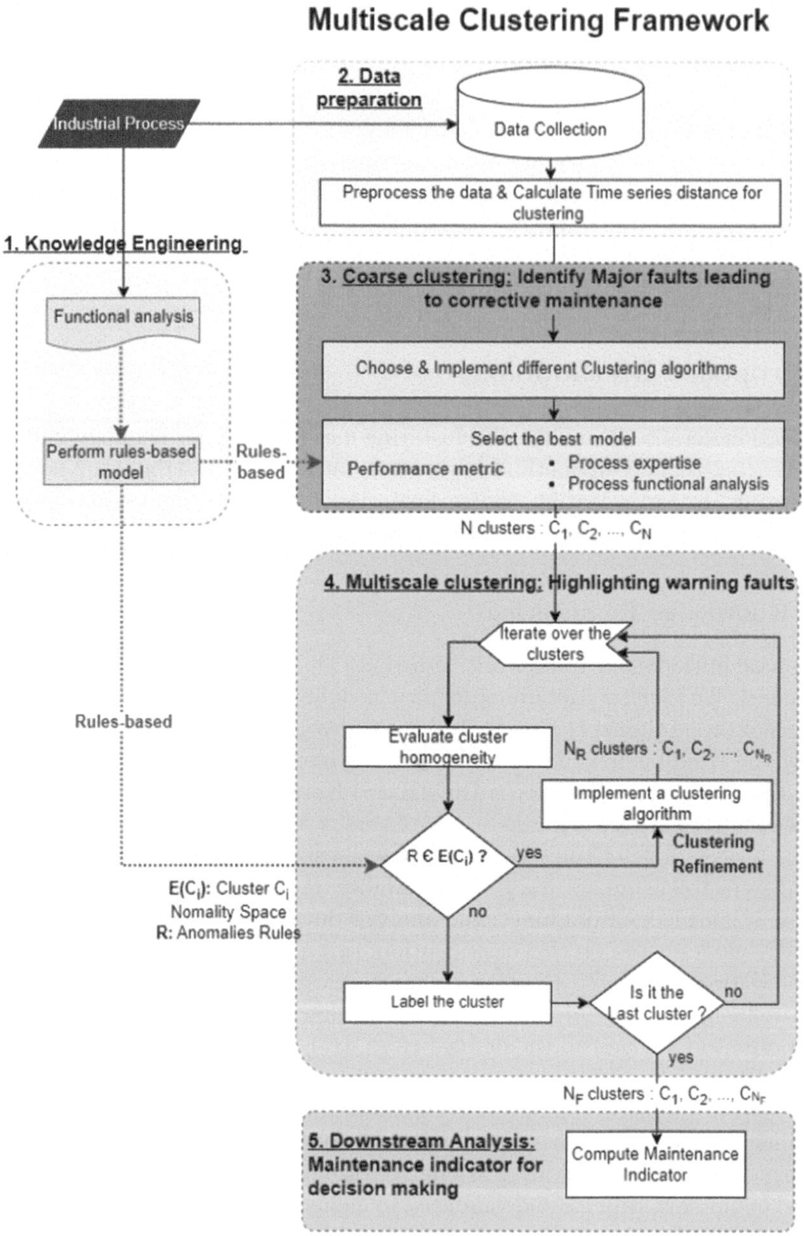

Fig. 1. Proposed methodology for anomaly detection

3.2   Data Preparation

The data derived from the industrial equipment are collected as time series characterized by their cyclic nature. In the framework, we consider that these cycles may vary in size. The preprocessing involves eliminating data from inactive equipment periods, incorporating equipment-specific knowledge, and rigorously addressing noise. This approach is in line with the strategies suggested by Cortes-Ibanes *et al.* [3], proposing a moving average technique to denoise the time series.

After preprocessing the data, selecting an appropriate distance metric for coarse clustering implementation becomes essential. This selection is heavily influenced by the attributes of time series, particularly the cycles size and variability [15].

3.3   Coarse Clustering

Next, we implement traditional clustering algorithms for anomaly detection, utilizing the previously computed distance and exploring different models before selecting the optimal one. Validating the best model entails two steps: choosing the top-performing classification model based on the highest performance metric, and assessing the quality of detected anomalies through our RBK model and expertise. This foundational clustering phase is pivotal, as it reveals patterns in the data, underscoring the necessity for a multiscale approach that adapts to diverse granularities of data for a more detailed analysis.

3.4   Multiscale Clustering

We focus here on the homogeneity of the resulting clusters, particularly assessing if anomalies coexist with normal cycles within the same cluster, based on our RBK. Non-homogeneous clusters, where anomalies and normal cycles are mixed, indicate the need for further refinement through a secondary clustering model. This iterative approach of re-clustering for in-depth data analysis underscores the essence of our multiscale clustering, ensuring a thorough and nuanced examination of the data structure.

3.5   Downstream Analysis

Implementing clustering models enable us to pinpoint anomalies within equipment data, a critical step towards developing a maintenance indicator. The aim is to define an optimal maintenance indicator that triggers efficient interventions, ideally before the apparition of any significant anomalies. To achieve this, we start with the industrial equipment maintenance plan, extracting the types of maintenance performed on the equipment. We then proceed to calculate an optimal indicator, leveraging the anomalies detected prior to each preventive intervention, thereby enhancing the effectiveness of maintenance operations.

4   Case Study

Our case study deals with a critical equipment in a nuclear facility, which is central to the facility's production. Any failure in this equipment halts production, incurring significant costs. The equipment operates in 'batch' mode, with each production cycle lasting around three days. The goal of the study is to detect deviations between two pressure sensors during a cycle. We focus on pressure measurements because maintenance experts recognize these sensors as the most sensitive indicators of system anomalies. Monitoring these pressure differences is crucial because it not only helps in early detection of operational deviations but also in scheduling preventive maintenance. By identifying when the pressure sensors start showing discrepancies, calibration can be conducted before the beginning of each cycle, thus minimizing the risk of sensor-related failures during critical operations. To achieve this, we compare two scenarios:

Scenario 1: A traditional clustering approach for anomaly detection without multiscaling.
Scenario 2: An approach with our multiscale clustering methodology.

4.1   Knowledge Engineering

Following the functional analysis of the equipment, we extract knowledge (K) by examining sequences of events leading to both faults and normal operational scenarios. Our analysis specifically focuses on the pressure difference (delta_P) between Sensors 1 and 2. Using this data, we develop a Rule-Based Knowledge (RBK) model. This model is validated with the support of expert equipment specialists to ensure the accuracy and relevance of our rules. The results of this model are presented in Table 1.

Table 1. Rules-based model

ID	Situation	IF (Condition)	THEN	CONSEQUENCES
1	Abnormal	IF $delta_P > 60\ hPa$	Major fault: Pressure 1 and Pressure 2 sensors are misaligned	Cycle interruption with corrective maintenance intervention
2	Abnormal	IF $30\ hPa < delta_P < 60\ hPa$	Warning fault	Cycle interruption and restart
3	Abnormal	IF $delta_P$ follows a regime change	Warning fault	Cycle interruption and restart
4	Normal	$delta_P < 30\ hPa$ and constant regime	No action, sensors are functioning properly	Cycle continuation

4.2   Data Preparation

For the analysis, we collect two years of historical data from the equipment, sampled every minute. The raw data are structured as time series for each production cycle. Our variable of interest is delta_P during the cycle.

Figure 2 zooms in on specific cycles of our time series data, highlighting their variability. We observe that the cycles exhibit different distributions.

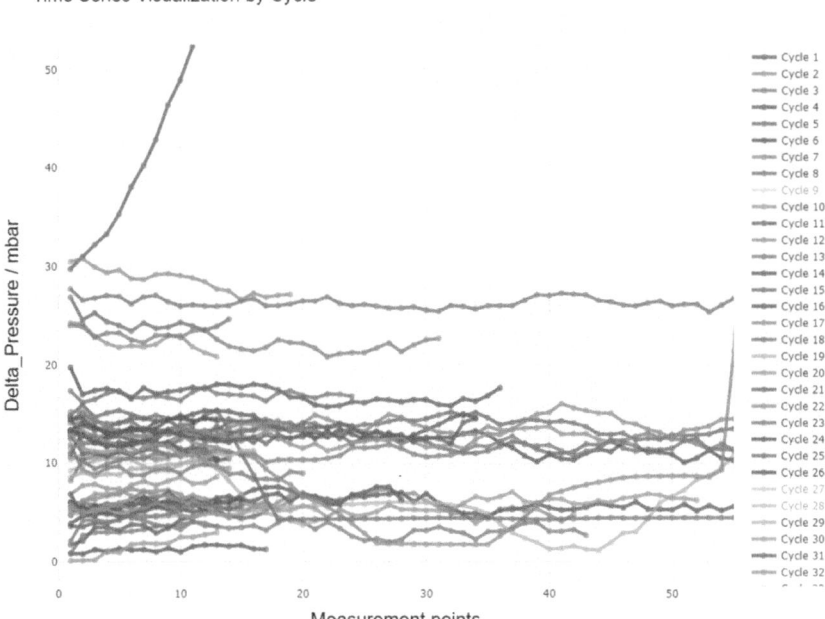

Fig. 2. Visualization of some time series for a specific time window

The preprocessing begins by excluding the machine downtime periods and setting a starting point (t0) for all cycles at 3 s post-cycle initiation, guided by the functional analysis and equipments experts. Lastly, noise within the cycles is reduced using the moving average technique. This equipment generate a total of 53 cycles for our analysis.

Given the variability of our cycles and their differing sizes, we opt for the Dynamic Time Warping (DTW) [6] distance for our case study. Figure 3 displays the DTW matrix for all cycles. The scatter plot in Fig. 3 has points spread across the Uniform Manifold Approximation and Projection (UMAP) dimensions in a manner that suggests variability in the different cycles, as measured by the DTW distances. Also, the points are not randomly distributed, indicating a pattern in the temporal evolution of the cycles. Distinct group of points along the diagonal may reflect cycles with similar temporal patterns, while the spread of points away from the diagonal could represent cycles with more unique or divergent characteristics.

4.3   Coarse Clustering

The DTW distance computed on the different cycles enables the implementation of two clustering algorithms: K-means and Agglomerative Hierarchical Clustering (AHC). The silhouette scores for both algorithms and our RBK results serves in selecting the best model. Initially, the silhouette score is high for $k = 2$ and decreases as the number of clusters increases. However, AHC maintains a comparatively high and stable score, proving to be the best choice for our data. we found it to be optimal for $k = 5$ clusters, achieving a silhouette score of 88.56%. Beyond 5 clusters, the silhouette score significantly decreases. Moreover, AHC shows a better ability to differentiate major (corrective) anomalies for $k = 5$ than K-means, although it does not detect all of them, according to our rules-based model. This insight leads us to choose AHC with $k = 5$ clusters for more detailed examination.

Figure 4 presents the results of the coarse clustering, using AHC with a setup of 5 clusters and guiding this process with our RBK model. The validation step emphasizes examining each cluster homogeneity, leveraging the rules from

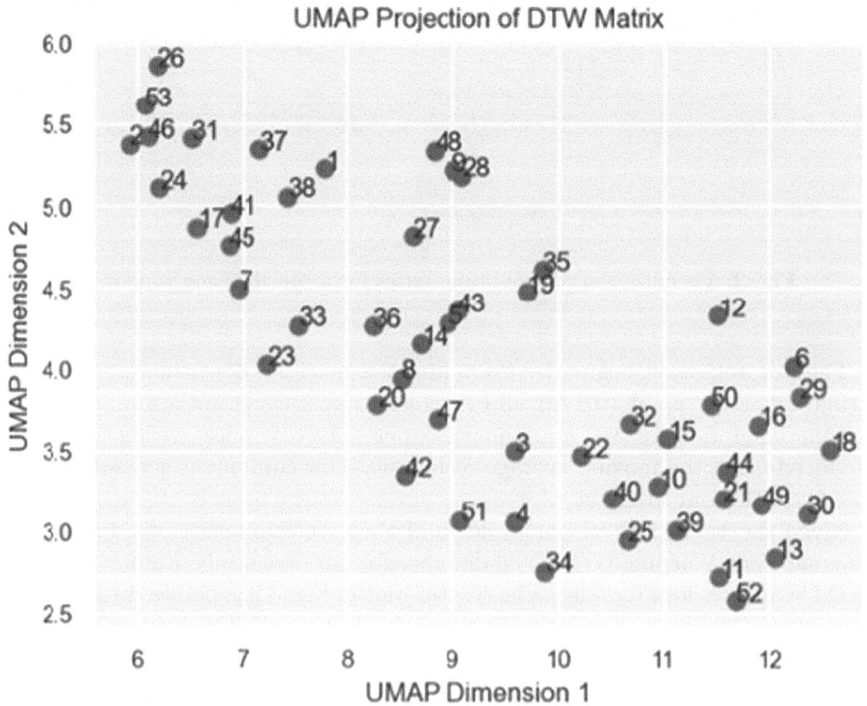

Fig. 3. UMAP-based visualization of data based DTW distance

our knowledge model to refine anomaly classification. As illustrated in Fig. 4, Clusters 1 through 4 are filled with cycles identified as abnormal, following Rule 1 from our knowledge model ($delta_P > 60\ hPa$), with a significant gap between the two sensors ranging widely from 100 to 3,000 hPa. However, Cluster_0 does not conform to the homogeneity criteria set by our RBK model. It comprises a mixture of both major (in red) and minor (in orange) anomalies as illustrated in Fig. 4, indicating that the anomaly classification was not fully effective.

4.4   Multiscale Clustering

At this stage, we first target the least homogeneous cluster, identified as Cluster_0 from the coarse clustering, due to its mixture of anomalies. To address this, another AHC algorithm is implemented, and through the silhouette score, we manage to segment into 4 clusters, achieving a silhouette score of 90%, effectively emphasizing the warning faults as described in our RBK model (Fig. 5).

This first stage of refinement leads to a homogeneous separation of our cycles, distinctly differentiating normal from abnormal cycles. This allows effectively identifying the warning faults, thanks to the validation carried out using the silhouette score and our RBK model. Therefore, at this point, we achieve our objective, indicating no further refinement was necessary. The stopping condition has been reached. Additionally, this analysis reveals two potential trends within the normal data, further enriching our understanding of the dataset patterns.

4.5   Discussion

Before continuing the process, this section compares the aforementioned two scenarios.

Scenario 1 involves increasing the number of clusters to improve coarse clustering classification, adjusting the number between 6 and 10. With 6 clusters (Fig. 6), we successfully identified all major anomalies (marked in red) in cluster_1, 2,3 and 4, while warning faults (marked in orange) in cluster_0 remain undetected, resulting in a silhouette score of 60%.

Beyond six clusters, cluster homogeneity decreased, with the silhouette score nearing zero. This highlights a significant limitation of this method: its capability to detect major but not the warning faults, prompting us to consider multiscale clustering as a more suitable solution.

Scenario 2 leverages our methodology to not only achieve a silhouette score of 90% but also to clearly identify both major (corrective) and warning faults, aligning with our RBK model. This success validates Scenario 2, as depicted in Fig. 5, demonstrating the effectiveness of our multiscale clustering approach in addressing both types of anomalies.

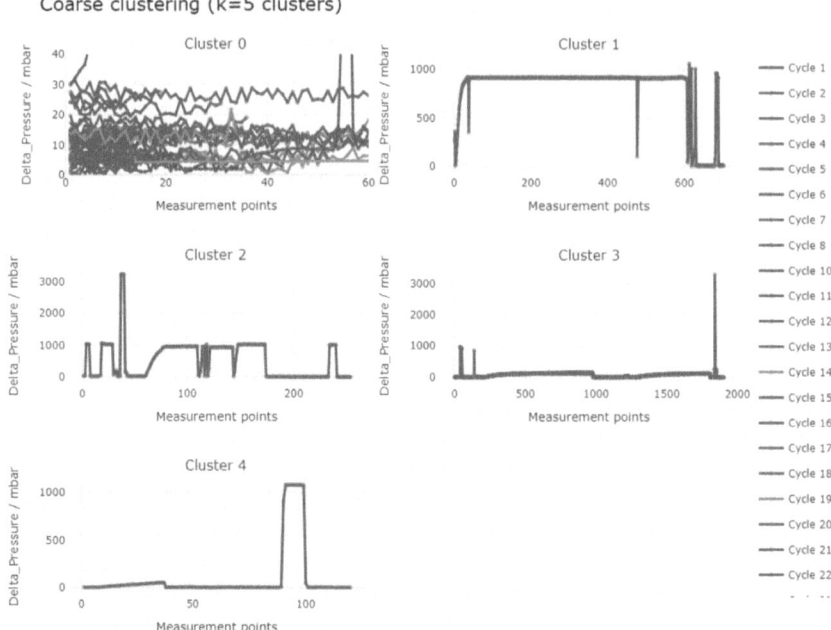

Fig. 4. Results of the AHC coarse clustering, with 5 clusters

4.6   Maintenance Indicator

After identifying and labeling the anomalies, we proceed to compute a preventive maintenance indicator for these critical sensors in the equipment. The Pareto analysis of the equipment failures indicates that sensors misalignment accounts for 20% of the failures, leading to 80% of the issues observed in sensors 1 and 2. Therefore, our aim is to determine the frequency of misalignment (both major and warning faults) per cycle before each scheduled preventive maintenance, which occurs every six months. From this analysis, we compute the average number of cycles after which preventive maintenance becomes most beneficial, rather than waiting for the next scheduled maintenance that does not guarantee the prevention of failures.

Figure 7 clearly shows how abnormal cycles are interspersed among normal ones and aligns with the scheduled preventive maintenance actions. It reveals that on average, abnormal cycles occur once every four cycles. This pattern underpins the recommendation that implementing preventive maintenance at this frequency may proactively mitigate issues, thus enhancing the overall reliability and efficiency of the maintenance strategy.

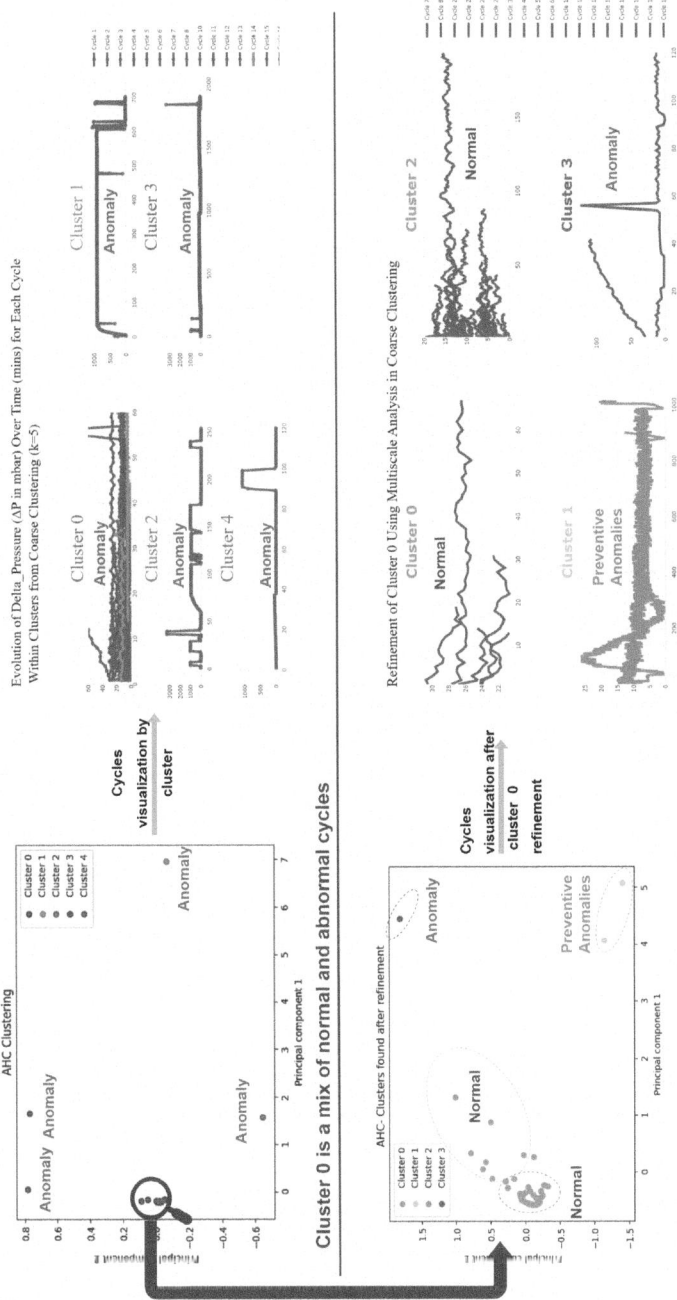

Fig. 5. Results of refined clustering applied on Cluster_0: on top the initial coarse clustering, below the refined results on the left the UMAP visualization, on the right the time series visualization

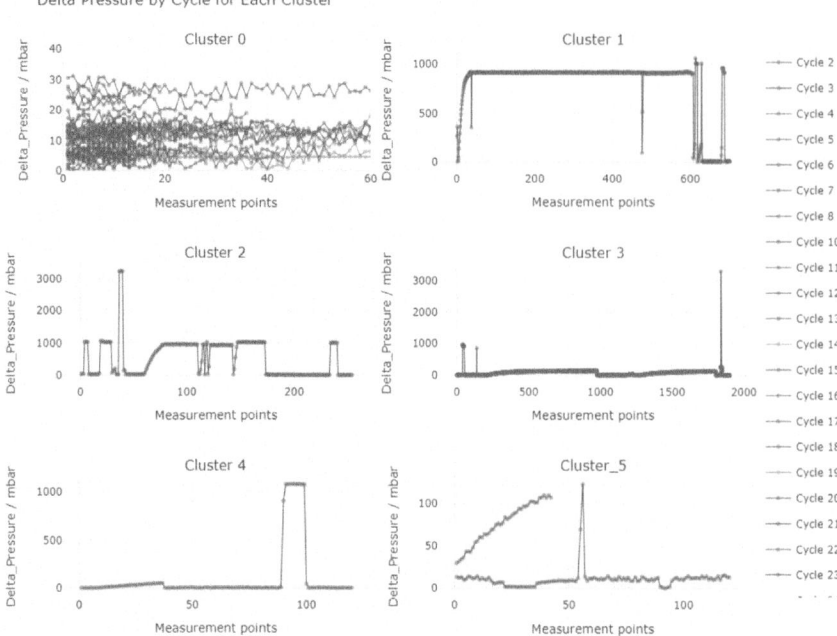

Fig. 6. Results of AHC coarse clustering with 6 clusters, dedicated to Scenario 1

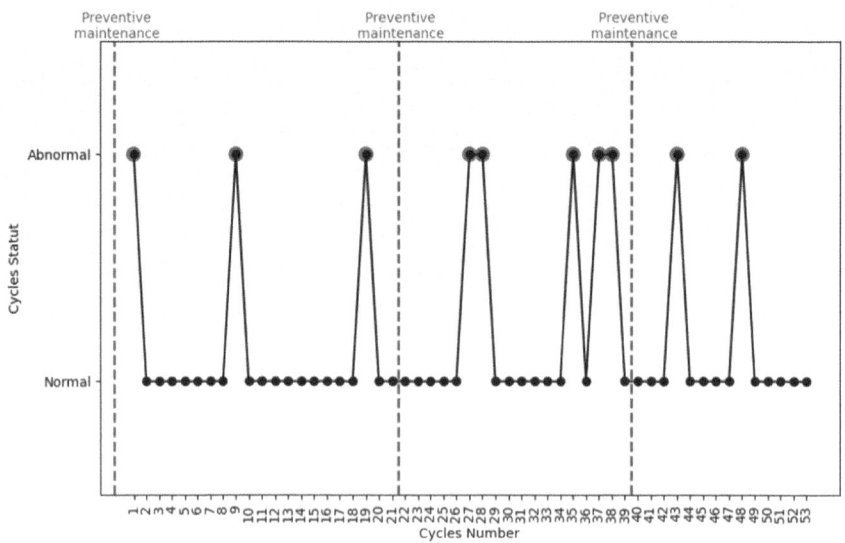

Fig. 7. Anomaly and preventive maintenance

5   Conclusion and Future Work

Industry 4.0 provides opportunities of increased flexibility, productivity, equipments availability for nuclear sector. Those benefits, however, are only achieved if the right solutions are introduced. Early anomaly detection is advantageous for facility operators as it allows for the prediction and preemption of potential failures, aligning with the objectives of predictive maintenance. However, conventional clustering-based techniques for detecting anomalies may not effectively capture all faults present in a dataset. This is particularly true in large-scale operations with varying point density, where such methods can erroneously identify anomalies as normal behavior.

To address this issue, this paper proposes a multiscale clustering approach that better distinguishes between minor (warning faults) and major anomalies, augmented by a RBK model. The application of this approach to real data from a nuclear facility validates the methodology, achieving an 90% silhouette score. Furthermore, it enables the calculation of a preventive maintenance indicator, recommending interventions every four cycles on average. This not only enhances maintenance accuracy but also contributes significantly to operational efficiency.

In the future, we plan to explore and test alternative distance metrics beyond Dynamic Time Warping (DTW) that are capable of representing time series of varying lengths. This expansion will allow for a comparative analysis of results and may potentially reveal more effective methods for anomaly detection over time. Additionally, as our current study focuses on pressure sensors-identified by experts as critical-we also plan to broaden our analysis to include other types of sensors within the equipment. This inclusion could provide a more scalability of our framework.

References

1. Chandola, V., Banerjee, A., Kumar, V.: Anomaly detection: a survey. ACM Comput. Surv. **41**(3) (2009). https://doi.org/10.1145/1541880.1541882
2. Chen, R., Zhao, S., Tian, Z.: A multiscale clustering approach for non-IID nominal data. Comput. Intell. Neurosci. (2021)
3. Cortés-Ibáñez, J.A., González, S., Valle-Alonso, J.J., Luengo, J., García, S., Herrera, F.: Preprocessing methodology for time series: an industrial world application case study. Inf. Sc. **514**, 385–401 (2020)
4. Ester, M., KriegelL, H.P., Sander, J., Xu, X.: A density-based algorithm for discovering clusters in large spatial databases with noise. Knowl. Discov. Data Min. (1996)
5. Fan, W., Miller, M., Stolfo, S.J., Lee, W., Chan, P.K.: Using artificial anomalies to detect unknown and known network intrusions. IEEE Comput. Soc. 123–130 (2001)
6. Guo, J., Si, Z., Liu, Y., Li, J., Li, Y., Xiang, J.: Dynamic time warping using graph similarity guided symplectic geometry mode decomposition to detect bearing faults. Reliab. Eng. Syst. Saf. **224**, 108533 (2022)
7. Jain, A.K., Dubes, R.C.: Algorithms for Clustering Data. Prentice-Hall, Hoboken (1988)

8. Kim, M.G., Jeong, S., Kim, S.T., Oh, K.Y.: Anomaly detection of underground transmission-line through multiscale mask DCNN and image strengthening. Mathematics **11**(14) (2023)

9. Li, S., Hou, S.: A machine learning method of accelerating multiscale analysis for spatially varying microstructures. Int. J. Mech. Sci. **266**, 108952 (2024)

10. Lu, C., et al.: Nuclear power plants with artificial intelligence in industry 4.0 era: top-level design and current applications-a systemic review. IEEE Access **8**, 194315–194332 (2020)

11. Maurya, C.K., Toshniwal, D.: Anomaly detection in nuclear power plant data using support vector data description. In: Proceedings of the 2014 IEEE Students' Technology Symposium, pp. 82–86 (2014)

12. Prasad, N.R., Almanza-Garcia, S., Lu, T.T.: Anomaly detection. Comput. Mater. Continua **14**(1), 1–22 (2009)

13. Saley, A.M., Marchand, J., Sekhari, A., Cheutet, V., Danielou, J.B.: State-of-art and maturity overview of the nuclear industry on predictive maintenance. In: Noël, F., Nyffenegger, F., Rivest, L., Bouras, A. (eds.) PLM 2022. IFIP AICT, vol. 667, pp. 337–346. Springer, Cham (2022). https://doi.org/10.1007/978-3-031-25182-5_33

14. Wang, H., Bah, M.J., Hammad, M.: Progress in outlier detection techniques: a survey. IEEE Access **7**, 107964–108000 (2019)

15. Warren Liao, T.: Clustering of time series data - a survey. Pattern Recogn. **38**(11), 1857–1874 (2005)

16. Yang, C., Wen, H., Hooi, B., Wu, Y., Zhou, L.: A multi-scale reconstruction method for the anomaly detection in stochastic dynamic networks. Neurocomputing **518**, 482–495 (2023)

17. Zhang, X., Zhang, M., Wan, S., He, Y., Wang, X.: A bearing fault diagnosis method based on multiscale dispersion entropy and gg clustering. Measurement **185**, 110023 (2021)

18. Zong, C., Huang, S., Liu, E., Yao, Y., Tang, S.Q.: Nowhere to hide methodology: application of clustering fault diagnosis in the nuclear power industry. IEEE Access **7**, 179864–179879 (2019)

Clustering Analysis for Forecasting Medicine Consumption

Douglas Mateus Machado[1], Zakaria Yahouni[1(✉)], Gülgün Alpan[1],
and Denis Koala[2]

[1] Univ. Grenoble Alpes, CNRS, Grenoble INP G-SCOP, 38000 Grenoble, France
douglas.mateus-machado@grenoble-inp.org,
{zakaria.yahouni,gulgun.alpan}@grenoble-inp.fr
[2] KLS-GROUP, 38240 Meylan, France
koala@kls-group.fr

Abstract. This study investigates machine learning for forecasting
medicine consumption in hospitals to optimize resource allocation and
logistics. We use two approaches: a unified approach that combines data
from multiple hospitals and a separated approach that forecasts for individual hospitals. We explored both K-means clustering and manual pair
clustering based on consumption trends. While K-means clustering did
not yield improvements, manual clustering identified specific pairs of
medicines with significantly enhanced forecast accuracy (e.g., Medicine
15 at Hospital 1: MAPE decreased from 19.70% to 3.30%). However, the
unified approach did not consistently benefit all hospitals (e.g., Medicine
9). This underscores the need to balance accuracy gains in some hospitals
against potential losses in others. Overall, manual clustering within the
separated approach shows promise. Future work should explore advanced
automated clustering techniques like Dynamic Time Warping (DTW)
and leverage larger datasets for further validation.

Keywords: Medicine consumption · Forecasting demand · Machine
learning · Clustering

1 Introduction

The healthcare sector, particularly in France is evolving within a complex and
dynamic environment [1]. With hospital budgets shrinking over the years, reducing logistics and process costs can profoundly impact the longevity and quality
of healthcare services. Therefore, optimizing resource management is essential
because of these ongoing budget constraints and the imperative to maintain high-
quality patient care [16]. Hospital's supplies and products, such as medicines,
represent a significant portion of healthcare expenditures [17,21]. Therefore,
pharmaceutical logistics, accounting for a significant portion of hospital budgets, is a critical area for optimization. Understanding hospital medicine demand
(consumption) is fundamental to achieving this optimization [9,22].

© The Author(s), under exclusive license to Springer Nature Switzerland AG 2025
M. Dassisti et al. (Eds.): IN4PL 2024, CCIS 2372, pp. 155–172, 2025.
https://doi.org/10.1007/978-3-031-80760-2_10

Various factors, including socio-demographic, socioeconomic, health-related, facility-related, staff-related aspects, inappropriate use of medication in some facilities, affect medicine consumption dynamics and are crucial for forecasting demand [3,4,12]. Furthermore, each region and country has its own cultural and specific factors that influence these dynamics. These findings align with the broader literature on healthcare supply chain management and the critical role of demand forecasting in optimizing pharmaceutical logistics [2,14,20].

When dealing with forecasting in healthcare sector, machine learning techniques have a good potential [15]. In this context, few works deal with forecasting medicine consumption such as [3,11]. In the work of [3] for instance, authors proposed prediction framework using short time-series. The consistency of the prediction was performed on data taken from 21 Italian regions. [12] in collaboration with a private sector company in France, highlighted and explored various factors influencing medicine consumption in French hospitals through qualitative analysis. A correlation analysis followed this to investigate key quantitative relationships [11]. Then, these factors were implemented in various techniques such as machine learning and Markov chain-based predictive approaches, to predict medicine consumption in French hospitals [13,22]. Our work relies on the data used in these studies.

The result of these previous studies showed that Machine Learning (ML) techniques offer innovative solutions for predicting medicine consumption patterns with good accuracy. However, as each medicine can be impacted differently by the identified factors [12], each medicine needs to have it specific ML model. Due to the limited data for each medicine, training and implementing a specific ML model for each medicine is not practical. Moreover, the accuracy of some ML algorithms for some medicines was not satisfactory, mostly due to a limited number of data. Our primary aim in this paper is to investigate clustering techniques in predicting medicine consumption. The aim is to propose a machine-learning model for a group of medicines instead of each medicine. This approach has two advantages that can cope with the literature gaps: first, reducing the number of models needed to forecast consumption accurately, and second, overcoming difficulties related to limited data.

To achieve this goal, and primarily the clustering aim, our study applies the K-means clustering technique. The effectiveness of these clusters is evaluated using the Random Trees Regressor model, which has demonstrated potential in previous research for handling complex datasets [6–8,19].

Forecasting medicine consumption based on clustered data proved challenging because of the limited data quantity and unknown factors linking consumption patterns across different hospitals. The classical clustering method (K-means clustering) did not yield satisfactory results during the forecasting phase. To explore an alternative approach, we manually compared all pairs of medicines to identify similarities based on consumption trends. This approach produced more satisfactory results than the baseline model, which involved creating a separate prediction model for each medicine from each hospital.

The goal is to develop robust forecasting tools that hospital administrators can use to plan and allocate resources more effectively. These improvements can lead to significant cost savings and more efficient allocation of resources, ultimately enhancing patient outcomes and operational efficiency.

The paper is structured as follows: as this section deals with the context background, Sect. 2 describes the dataset, the clustering and forecasting techniques used, and the methodology adopted. Sections 3 and 4 present the findings, including metrics and insights from the analysis, and compare different clustering approaches. Last section summarizes the key contributions of the study and suggests directions for future research.

2   Proposed Approach

Starting with the structured database developed in previous studies, we employed a systematic approach comprising the following steps: data format-

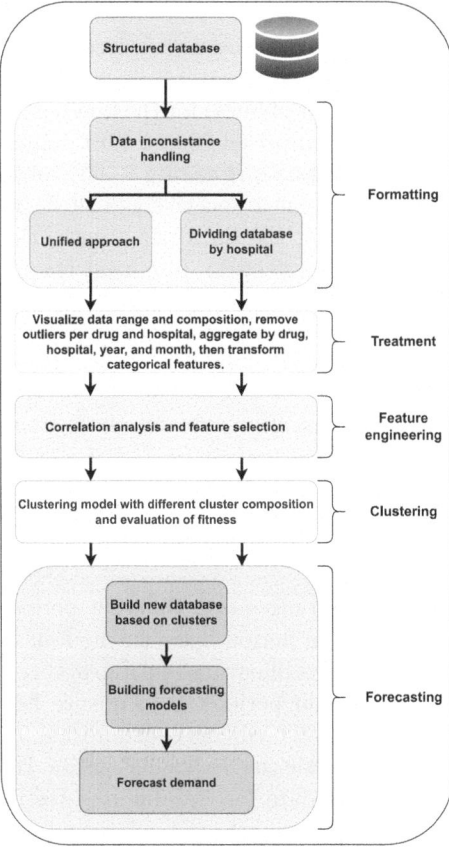

Fig. 1. Simplified pipeline of data processing, clustering and forecasting

ting, data treatment, feature manipulation and comprehension, clustering, and evaluation through forecasting.

The dataset included information on hospital size (number of departments), population served, year and month of consumption for each medicine. It required formatting and treatment before applying clustering and forecasting techniques.

Figure 1 illustrates the simplified steps leading to the creation of five treated databases. It also shows how the database was used to apply and evaluate clustering techniques, and subsequently analyze the clustering results for medicine consumption forecasting.

2.1   Data Formatting, Treatment and Feature Engineering

The dataset used in this research includes 21 of the most commonly consumed medicines in four different hospitals in France. 12 features were collected for each medicine, such as number of hospital medical units where the medicine is consumed, number of physician in the hospital, etc. All these features are taken from [11,12]. We add to these features, factors related to seasonality to find relationships between these factors and cluster different medicines. This approach can reduce the number of models required for accurate consumption forecasting.

The data distribution (number of lines) for the different hospitals is presented in Fig. 2. The original dataset comprised 75,684 data points ([11,12]). The first hospital contributed 22,725 inputs, representing 30.03% of the data. The second, third, and fourth hospitals represent respectively 20.40%, 36.45% and 13.12% of the total data. After aggregating the data per month, the input amount was 4072 with 1208 from hospital 1 (29.66%), 697 from hospital 2 (17.12%), 1397 from hospital 3 (34.31%) and 770 from hospital 4 (18.91%)

As presented in Fig. 1, different sub-steps were applied to test and validate two main approaches, leading to two sets of files (five databases):

– **Unified Approach:** In this approach, all data from four hospitals are grouped in a single database.
– **Dividing Database by Hospital:** Four databases are generated. Each one concerns one of the four hospitals. In this approach, all the next steps are applied to each of the four databases separately.

As data from four hospitals ranges over different periods, data was selected based on a common consumption period between the four hospitals to establish the same basis for comparison, as illustrated in Fig. 3.

The aim of selecting common periods is to ensure fair comparison across different hospitals when predicting medicine consumption. It's worth noting that the selected period does not include the SARS-CoV-2 era. However, these choices resulted in a limited amount of data for training and testing the models. After aggregating the data inputs per month and selecting a common period from March 2017 to March 2019, the distribution was as follows: the total number of data points was 1995. Hospital 1 had 459 entries (23.01%), Hospital 2 had 508

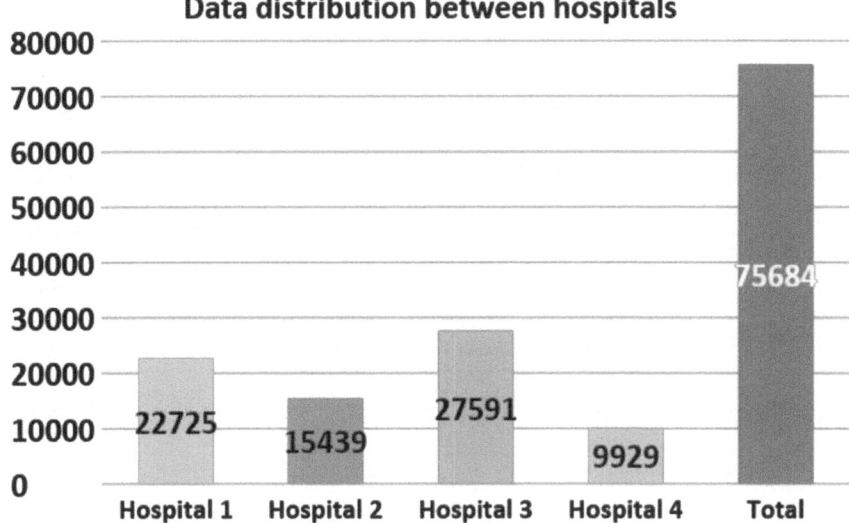

Fig. 2. Data distribution for the four different hospitals

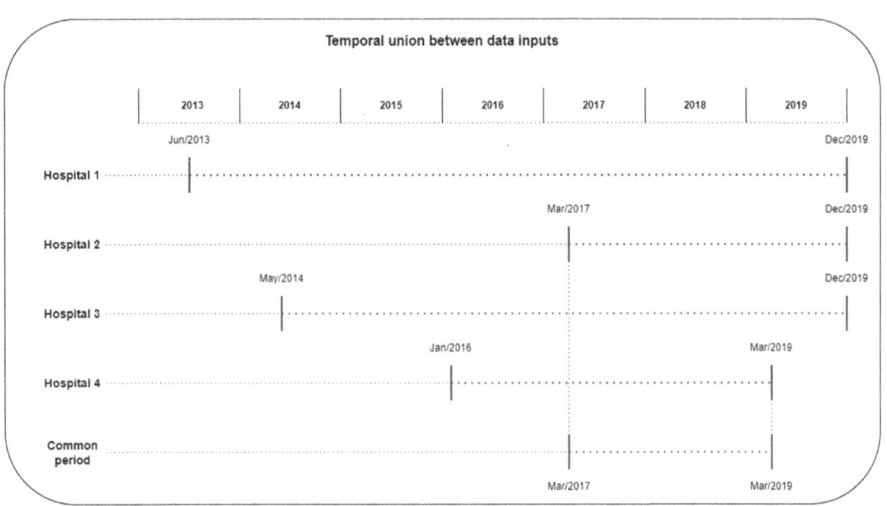

Fig. 3. Temporal union by a common period for the 4 hospitals

entries (25.46%), Hospital 3 had 524 entries (26.27%), and Hospital 4 had 504 entries (25.26%).

During these steps, inputs were aggregated by medicine, hospital, year, and month. Data were grouped by month of consumption because it is our targeted unit of prediction. Categorical features were transformed using one-hot encoding to facilitate the application of numerical methods.

In the feature engineering step, the correlation analysis between the different data of the treated dataset was performed in order to select the most relevant information to build the clustering and forecasting models. Multi-objective decision support techniques are appropriate for the identification of accurate and robust multivariate time series forecasting models [10]. For this work, seasonal decomposition was employed to gain a deeper understanding of the trends and time-related variations in medicine consumption [13,23]. The trends were later found to be very useful when applying the manual clustering method. Figure 4 presents an example of the created features.

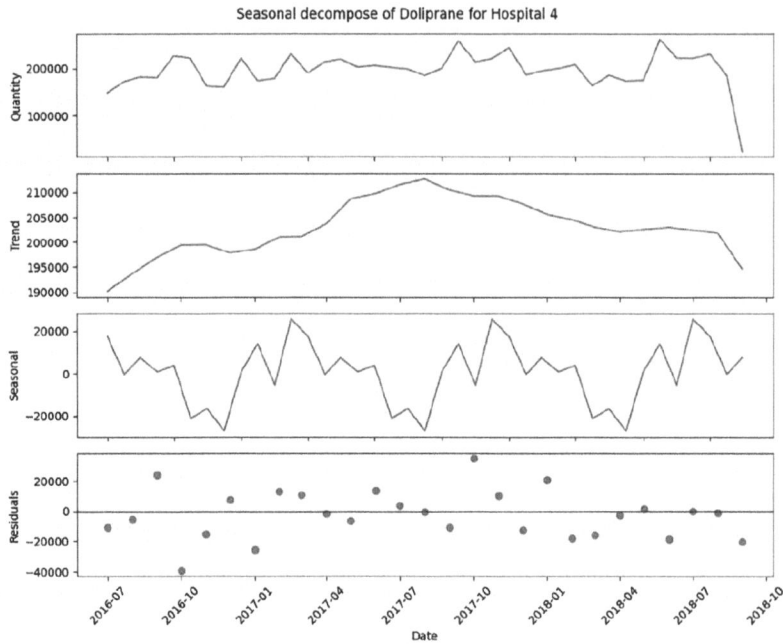

Fig. 4. Example of seasonal decomposition of time series for a medicine

Seasonal decomposition of the time series involved breaking down the consumption quantity of the medicine into four distinct components: quantity, trend, seasonal, and residual. The quantity represents the actual observed data over time. The trend component captures the long-term progression of the data, showing whether the consumption is generally increasing or decreasing. The seasonal component reflects the recurring patterns or cycles that repeat over a fixed period, such as monthly or yearly fluctuations in medicine usage. Last, the residual component accounts for the irregular or random variations in the data that are not explained by the trend or seasonal components. By analyzing these features, we can better understand the underlying factors influencing medicine consumption, enabling more accurate forecasting and informed decision-making.

The output of these steps is two sets of files: one containing combined data from all four hospitals, resulting in a larger dataset, and another set composed of four separate files, each corresponding to an individual hospital, resulting in fewer data entries per file.

2.2   Clustering

To achieve the clustering aim, an analytical causal methodology was employed. This method considers the entire dataset to understand the underlying factors driving
medicine use.

For the clustering portion of the study, the K-means technique was selected. K-means clustering offers several advantages, including simplicity, computational efficiency, and ease of implementation and scalability for large datasets. It provides clear and distinct cluster assignments, effectively discovers underlying patterns and groupings, and its centroid-based approach helps create well-separated and balanced clusters, making the results easier to interpret and analyze.

Given that the aforementioned techniques did not yield satisfactory results in the forecasting section of the study as illustrated in the result section, an alternative approach was considered. This involved manually pairing all medicines from various hospitals to compare their consumption trends, which might potentially show similarities and clustering possibilities for prediction purposes.

The chosen metrics to evaluate the clustering techniques were the silhouette score and the Davies-Bouldin index, as they are commonly used to assess clustering quality. The Davies-Bouldin Index measures the average similarity between each cluster and its most similar cluster, where lower values show better clustering. The Silhouette Score quantifies how similar an object is to its own cluster compared to other clusters, with values ranging from -1 to 1; higher scores suggest better-defined clusters. These metrics provide objective assessments of clustering performance, aiding in selecting the most suitable clustering algorithm and parameter settings. For the unified approach, the metrics scores for the K-means algorithm are presented in Fig. 5.

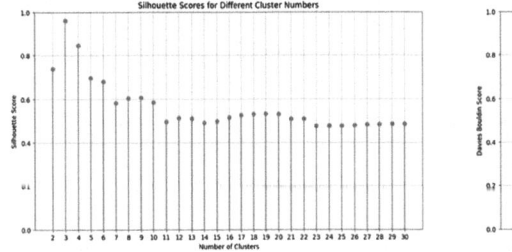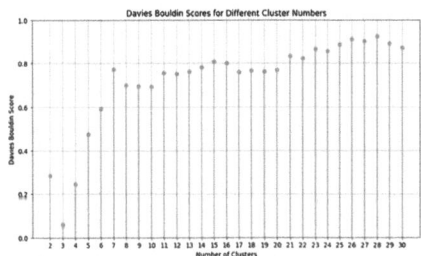

Fig. 5. Metrics scores for the k-means algorithm

The figure shows that the optimal cluster composition occurs with $k = 3$. This insight is valuable for the forecasting step, as it allows for the testing and evaluation of both approaches. For the unified approach or the approach using data separated per hospital, all the 21 medicines were in each cluster, varying by the date or other features of the dataset.

To apply the manual clustering methodology, combinations of medicines and hospitals were created, such as Medicine A from Hospital X paired with Medicine B from Hospital Y. This approach allowed for a visual comparison of trends between the same medicine from different hospitals or different medicines from the same or different hospitals. To find the total number of possible combinations of medicines, we considered two cases: (1) choosing medicines from different hospitals and (2) choosing different medicines from the same hospital. For different hospitals, there are $\binom{4}{2} \times 21^2 = 6 \times 441 = 2646$ combinations. For the same hospital, there are $\binom{4}{1} \times \binom{21}{2} = 4 \times 210 = 840$ combinations. Adding these, the total number of possible combinations is $2646 + 840 = 3486$.

This idea was based on trends observed during the seasonal decomposition in the feature engineering step. Despite varying consumption magnitudes, some medicines exhibited very similar behaviors, prompting an investigation into combining pairs, trios, and quartets. However, as a first investigation, this study focuses on pairs of medicines and their respective performance in the evaluation (forecasting) step.

At this stage, we labeled the inputs from various hospitals based on the clusters generated using different methods. Since we have multiple records for each medicine recorded at different times and with different features, it's common for parts of the data to be grouped into each cluster for all 21 medicines. This occurs because medicine consumption patterns are complex and can vary because of factors like patient demographics, seasons, and treatment approaches. Consequently, one medicine may show different usage patterns across clusters, illustrating how its use varies within the healthcare system.

2.3 Forecasting

For the evaluation method, we implemented random forest regressor models to forecast medicine consumption based on the identified clusters. Random forest regressors are helpful because of their robustness, ability to handle large datasets, and ease of interpretability. The process begins by selecting a single medicine or a set of medicines from the same or different hospitals. The dataset is then divided into a training set (85%) and a test set (15%). Figure 6 illustrates the steps implemented in the forecasting process to evaluate the clusters' quality.

The data, whether from the unified or separated datasets, is used to select either a single medicine or a cluster of medicines. The random forest regressor is initialized with specific parameters and cross-validated using a 5-fold strategy to ensure reliability and prevent overfitting. Grid search is then employed to fine-tune the model by systematically testing different parameter combinations to find the optimal settings. Finally, the fine-tuned model is used to forecast

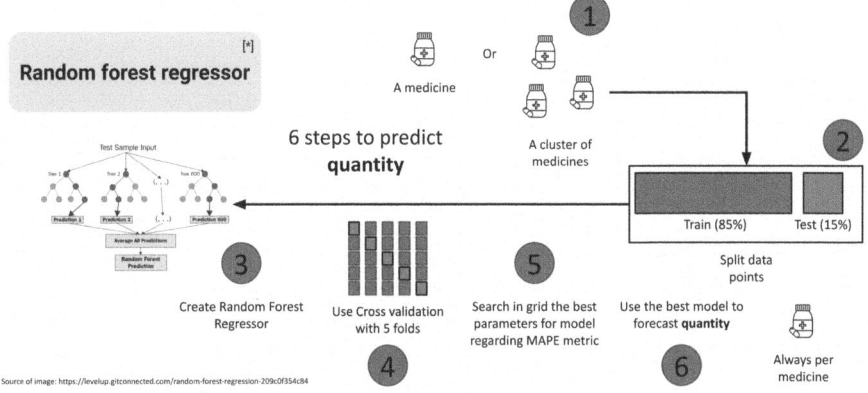

Fig. 6. Process of Forecasting medicine consumption

the medicine quantities in the test set, providing insights into the expected consumption patterns. This method offers an effective and comprehensible approach to accurately predict medicine demand.

To ensure a robust analysis, this study emphasizes the manual clustering technique because of its superior performance in yielding relevant results. The subsequent sections will concentrate on this method. A baseline comparison was established using the Mean Absolute Percentage Error (MAPE) metric, which is particularly well-suited for evaluating forecast models in the context of medicine consumption [5], [18] and availability in hospitals. MAPE provides a clear, intuitive percentage that reflects the average deviation of the forecasts from the actual figures, offering a proportional accuracy that is critical for effective inventory management in healthcare settings. This metric was applied to a curated dataset comprising various medicines across different hospitals, allowing precise evaluation of the clustering technique's effectiveness on a per-hospital basis. Accurate forecasts, showed by a low MAPE value, are essential for hospitals to ensure the right medicines are available when needed, avoiding overstock and minimizing waste.

To facilitate the comparison of results for the various tested medicines, it is crucial to establish a guideline. A baseline was developed by creating a forecasting model for each medicine from each hospital. This baseline serves as a reference point, providing an objective to be achieved. A cluster is considered effective if it outperforms the baseline, showing improved forecasting accuracy.

3 Results and Comparison

3.1 Forecasting Per Hospital and Medicine Without Clustering (Baseline Forecasting)

To facilitate a comparative analysis, the baseline for forecasting medicine consumption was established using the same pipeline as the manual clustering. How-

Table 1. Baseline per hospital

Medicine	Hospital 1	Hospital 2	Hospital 3	Hospital 4
Medicine 1	11.80%	9.20%	**8.60%**	18.00%
Medicine 2	13.10%	12.50%	20.40%	**3.80%**
Medicine 3	13.80%	**13.60%**	29.50%	20.70%
Medicine 4	7.40%	14.50%	**4.20%**	7.10%
Medicine 5	17.40%	19.80%	**13.90%**	21.90%
Medicine 6	12.40%	27.20%	**4.00%**	5.60%
Medicine 7	25.10%	15.90%	**4.90%**	11.40%
Medicine 8	10.80%	9.10%	**8.30%**	26.50%
Medicine 9	10.00%	**4.00%**	9.50%	17.00%
Medicine 10	12.20%	15.60%	11.80%	**9.40%**
Medicine 11	24.20%	**10.50%**	222.10%	19.50%
Medicine 12	**3.10%**	21.30%	9.50%	8.00%
Medicine 13	18.10%	**9.40%**	14.70%	12.30%
Medicine 14	**6.40%**	12.60%	8.40%	16.00%
Medicine 15	19.70%	**17.00%**	38.60%	27.00%
Medicine 16	**9.50%**	33.80%	18.30%	24.20%
Medicine 17	22.70%	**2.90%**	6.30%	11.10%
Medicine 18	**10.90%**	39.10%	17.00%	26.70%
Medicine 19	9.40%	**4.10%**	**4.10%**	7.00%
Medicine 20	25.40%	18.20%	**15.00%**	21.30%
Medicine 21	30.50%	**11.20%**	14.90%	20.20%

ever, it was executed individually for each hospital and specific medicine. The outcomes of this process are systematically presented in Table 1, detailing the baseline results for each hospital, from the 21 medicines.

The table illustrates the variance in forecasting accuracy for medicine consumption across four hospitals, measured by MAPE. The metric values exhibit a broad range, from a low of 3.80% to a high of 222.10%. Specifically, Hospital 1 demonstrates moderate forecasting accuracy, while Hospital 2 achieves the most consistent and reliable results. Hospital 3's data includes an extreme outlier that significantly affects its MAPE value, suggesting an anomaly that requires further examination. In contrast, Hospital 4 consistently experiences higher forecasting errors. The observed discrepancies in MAPE may be attributed to factors such as data volume, demand variability, case complexity, or the forecasting model's performance. This analysis is confined to the available data and does not account for external factors that could influence the results.

3.2   K-means Clustering Forecasting

Using clustering methods and forecasting the consumption of medicine in different hospitals offer several benefits. Clustering helps identify patterns and group similar data points, simplifying the complex and varied consumption behaviors of medicines. This allows for more targeted analysis and a better understanding of how different factors influence medicine usage. Forecasting, on the other hand, provides hospitals with predictive insights into future medicine needs, enabling more efficient inventory management and reducing the risk of shortages or overstock. Together, these techniques improve resource allocation, optimize supply chains, and support more effective and proactive healthcare planning, ultimately enhancing patient care and operational efficiency in hospitals.

Several tests were conducted using different feature combinations. The most significant results for the clustering technique were obtained using all 12 original features. One-hot encoding was applied to categorical features, and the seasonal decomposition features were excluded as they did not yield good MAPE results compared to other feature compositions. The unified dataset containing the inputs of the four hospitals was used in this experiment.

As mentioned in the previous section, since the data inputs are from different time periods, it is expected that each medicine is clustered into more than one cluster. This is because there are multiple factors to consider beyond just the medicine used itself.

Table 2 that shows the MAPE results from different clusters using the *K-means* technique shows none achieved acceptable performance. As mentioned earlier, metrics for evaluating different values of K for clustering determined that three clusters were optimal, but not the only option. Different values of K were tested, and for values greater than three, some clusters had too few data points to allow for effective forecasting, leading to their exclusion. Analyzing the cluster compositions revealed all medicines had data points distributed across each cluster. This was expected since multiple entries from different dates with varying variables can influence cluster assignment. For example, Medicine A in month X might belong to one cluster, while the same medicine in month Y might belong to another because of seasonal effects or other factors. Accurate predictions for medicine logistics in hospitals are crucial: underestimation risks stock-outs, while overestimation impacts the facility's budget. Various cluster numbers were tested, including four clusters corresponding to the four hospitals, but this approach did not yield good metrics compared to others and was thus deemed unsuitable.

Given these results, it became clear that exploring other clustering techniques is necessary. Manual clustering emerged as a potential method to identify similarities between medicines in a straightforward manner.

Table 2. Table of Medicines and MAPE per Cluster using *K-means*

Medicine	Cluster 0	Cluster 1	Cluster 2
Medicine 1	4190%	74%	92%
Medicine 2	308%	159%	295%
Medicine 3	1021%	110%	162%
Medicine 4	33%	50%	33%
Medicine 5	4395%	62%	603%
Medicine 6	1786%	93%	90%
Medicine 7	136%	400%	66%
Medicine 8	323%	208%	117%
Medicine 9	1721%	97%	21%
Medicine 10	404%	39%	197%
Medicine 11	37500%	815%	339%
Medicine 12	1709%	36%	34%
Medicine 13	238%	300%	92%
Medicine 14	1491%	27%	74%
Medicine 15	1832%	23%	2699%
Medicine 16	523%	58%	541%
Medicine 17	197%	200%	65%
Medicine 18	3734%	649%	7370%
Medicine 19	1937%	118%	57%
Medicine 20	9604%	35%	21%
Medicine 21	1690%	170%	149%

3.3 Pair Clustering Forecasting Using Trend Pattern

For this part of the work, the time series features created with seasonal decomposition were used, with the dataset with the hospitals separated, calculating individually the trends of each medicine for each hospital and then applying the manual pair clustering technique. For some hospitals there are some months without inputs and for this reason, the range of data was used from November 2017 to March 2019.

From 3486 potential medicine pair combinations, not all were considered appropriate candidates for testing and evaluating forecasting performance. Selection was therefore focused on pairs exhibiting the most similar trend patterns.

Among all the tested pairs, we selected five pairs as they represent the potential of the technique and the different combinations of medicines from the same hospital or different hospitals (Table 1). Similarities are observed based on their visual representation of the trends. Even some pair had different magnitudes, they had similar behavior. Moreover, some pairs, even that they are from different hospitals, they have common behaviors. Within this manual process, only top five pairs were selected and are presented in Table 3. The aim is to analyse each of these pairs to understand why they are grouped together.

Table 3. Example of Pairs of Medicines and Hospitals

Cluster	Medicine A	Hospital A	Medicine B	Hospital B	MAPE A	MAPE B
1	Medicine 3	1	Medicine 2	1	**3.20%**	**8.40%**
2	Medicine 15	1	Medicine 4	4	**3.30%**	**9.30%**
3	Medicine 15	1	Medicine 13	3	**2.10%**	**8.30%**
4	Medicine 20	1	Medicine 20	3	**1.80%**	**7.10%**
5	Medicine 9	1	Medicine 9	2	**8.30%**	**4.70%**

For the first pair in Table 3, the analysis covered the period from November 2017 to January 2019. The pronounced similarity in consumption patterns for the two medicines (Medicine 3 and medicine 2) within the same hospital (Hospital 1) suggests a reliable forecast. As detailed in the preceding section, the input data for these medicines was combined and processed through the forecasting pipeline. The resulting MAPE values were 3.20% for Medicine 3 and 8.40% for Medicine 2 within the test dataset, in contrast with the baseline values of 13.80% and 13.10% respectively. These outcomes may be attributed to factors such as seasonality and the demographic characteristics of the patient population at Hospital 1, which influence the consumption rates of both medicines. Figure 7 provides a visual representation of the trend for the first pair.

The second pair under examination in Table 3 includes two distinct medicines from separate hospitals. Given this context, the previously considered factors of seasonality and hospital size are unlikely to be the primary influences on the observed similarities in consumption trends. It is important to note that the analysis period remains consistent with that of the first pair, spanning from November 2017 to January 2019. This uniformity ensures that the comparison across different pairs is methodologically sound. The consumption trends for this second pair, which may suggest other underlying factors such as prescribing habits, patient demographics, or even regional health policies, are depicted in Fig. 8. A deeper investigation into these trends could provide valuable insights into the factors driving medicine consumption patterns across different hospital facilities.

The comparative analysis of the second pair yields mixed results. For Medicine 15, the MAPE is encouraging (3.30%), markedly better than the baseline's (19.70%). This suggests that the forecasting model performs well for this medicine at Hospital 1. In contrast, Medicine 4 from Hospital 4 shows a MAPE of (9.30%), which is not as favorable, especially when compared to its baseline of (7.10%). This discrepancy shows that the model may not be as effective for this medicine, signaling a need for further investigation and potential model adjustments. Figure 9 illustrates three other pairs of medicines with their trends.

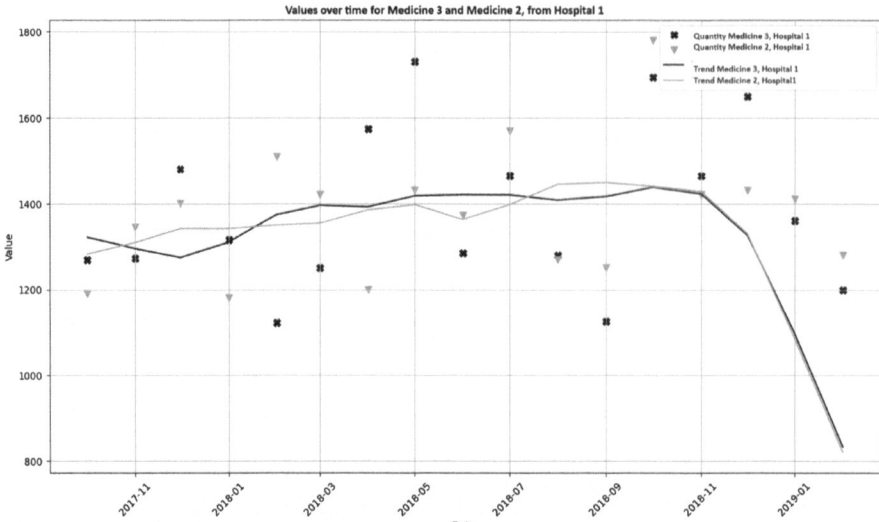

Fig. 7. Trends comparison between first pair

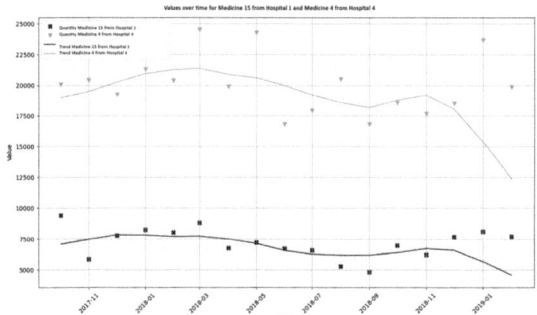

Fig. 8. Trends comparison between second pair

The forecasting results for the third pair are notably impressive (Fig. 9a) medicine 15 of Hospital 1 demonstrates a MAPE of (2.10%), which is a significant improvement compared to the baseline MAPE of (19.70%). Additionally, Medicine 13 from Hospital 3 achieves a MAPE of (8.30%), also surpassing the baseline's (14.70%). These results highlight the effectiveness of the forecasting model for both medicines, with substantial enhancements over the established baselines.

The analysis of Medicine 20 presented in Fig. 9b from different hospitals (1 and 3) reveals that combining the data leads to a MAPE metric that outperforms the baseline for both institutions. Specifically, for Hospital 1, the baseline MAPE is (25.40%), which is significantly higher than the (1.80%) achieved when using the paired data. Similarly, Hospital 3 shows a baseline MAPE of (15.00%),

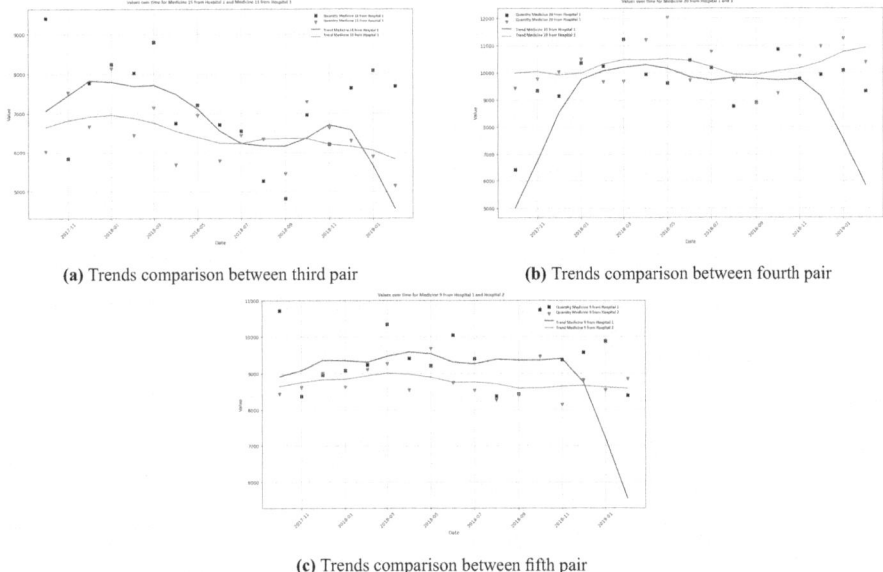

(a) Trends comparison between third pair   **(b)** Trends comparison between fourth pair

(c) Trends comparison between fifth pair

Fig. 9. Comparison of trends between different pairs

compared to (7.10%) with the paired data. These improved results from using combined data support the hypothesis that there are underlying factors contributing to the similarity in medicine consumption trends across different hospitals. Identifying these factors could be instrumental in developing more accurate combined forecasting models, which consider the shared influences on medicine consumption.

Figure 9c displays the consumption trends for Medicine 9 at hospitals 1 and 2. The forecasting results show an improvement for Hospital 1, with the MAPE decreasing from (10.00%) to (8.30%). However, Hospital 2 experienced a slight increase in MAPE from (4.00%) to (4.70%). This marginal difference at Hospital 2 raises considerations about the trade-offs involved in optimizing forecast accuracy for one medicine at the expense of another. It prompts a careful evaluation of whether the gains in precision for one hospital justify the minor loss in another, ensuring that the overall prediction of medicine consumption remains robust.

Many pairs were examined, yet the five showcased in this analysis were telling. They provide some comprehensive comparison between the baseline forecasts and those obtained using the paired data approach, alongside manual clustering. These examples serve to illustrate the potential benefits and challenges of integrating data across different contexts to enhance forecasting models.

The results from the K-means (and other tested clustering techniques) did not yield satisfactory outcomes, likely because of insufficient data and the inherent complexity of medicine consumption patterns. The limited dataset may not have provided enough variability to form distinct clusters effectively, leading to poor predictive performance. To address this, manual pair clustering was explored as an alternative, allowing for the identification of similarities between medicines based on domain knowledge, rather than relying solely on automated algorithms. However, this approach also has limitations, such as the focus on only pairing medicines, which might not capture the full spectrum of relationships.

Additionally, the study compared unified and separated approaches to clustering. The unified approach, which combined data from all hospitals, did not produce as good results as the separated approach, where data from each hospital were treated independently. The separated approach allowed for more tailored clustering that better reflected the unique consumption patterns of each hospital. Based on these findings, it is recommended to investigate further manual clustering in combination with a separated approach, as this method demonstrated more accurate forecasting of medicine consumption. Future work should aim to gather more extensive and diverse datasets to enhance the clustering process and further validate these methods.

Therefore, the proposed approach is hardly applicable in reality in the current state. Additionally to the suggestions of improvements made above, It will be interesting to analyse other variables that could determine the variations in consumption.

4   Conclusion

Investing in medicine consumption forecasting is crucial due to its significant impact on hospital logistics costs, particularly in public hospitals with high patient demand where efficient resource allocation is critical. Although various forecasting methods have been explored in previous studies, the Random Forest Regressor has proven to be the most suitable for our dataset and context. By meticulously formatting, treating, and engineering features from the raw data, we transformed it into actionable insights. This enabled the application of clustering methods to streamline the number of forecasting models, facilitating more generalized forecasts and the potential to extend these predictions to new hospitals using existing data.

While the classical clustering technique K-means was evaluated, it did not produce satisfactory results. An alternative approach involving seasonal decomposition and focusing on consumption trends for each hospital and medicine led to the manual pairing of medicines. This approach raised a pivotal question: Does grouping medicines with similar trends inherently lead to superior forecasting outcomes? The findings from this study suggest that, in certain instances, such groupings do indeed result in improved MAPE metrics, indicating the presence of latent factors that enhance prediction accuracy. Consequently, further research is needed to uncover these factors.

Attempts to extend the clustering to include trios and quartets of medicines were also made. However, these did not yield better results for the majority of combinations tested. Given the time-intensive nature of manual clustering, it was not feasible to determine definitively whether incorporating more diverse data could yield improved outcomes.

Looking ahead, future research should consider methodologies like Dynamic Time Warping (DTW), which has demonstrated promise in clustering time series data and has garnered positive results in existing literature. Exploring DTW and other advanced techniques could provide deeper insights into the complex patterns of medicine consumption, leading to even more accurate and effective forecasting models.

Acknowledgements. This work has been partially supported by the MIAI Multidisciplinary AI Institute at the Univ. Grenoble Alpes: (MIAI@Grenoble Alpes - ANR-19-P3IA-0003).

References

1. Aptel, O., Pourjalali, H.: Improving activities and decreasing costs of logistics in hospitals: a comparison of us and French hospitals. Int. J. Account. **36**(1), 65–90 (2001)
2. Beldek, T., Konyalıoğlu, A.K., Akdağ, H.C.: Supply chain management in healthcare: a literature review. In: Durakbasa, N.M., Gençyılmaz, M.G. (eds.) ISPR -2019. LNME, pp. 570–579. Springer, Cham (2020). https://doi.org/10.1007/978-3-030-31343-2_50
3. Bertolotti, F., Schettini, F., Ferrario, L., Bellavia, D., Foglia, E.: A prediction framework for pharmaceutical drug consumption using short time-series. Expert Syst. Appl. **253**, 124265 (2024)
4. Cateau, D., Bugnon, O., Niquille, A.: Evolution of potentially inappropriate medication use in nursing homes: retrospective analysis of drug consumption data. Res. Soc. Adm. Pharm. **17**(4), 701–706 (2021)
5. Chicco, D., Warrens, M.J., Jurman, G.: The coefficient of determination r-squared is more informative than SMAPE, MAE, MAPE, MSE and RMSE in regression analysis evaluation. PeerJ Comput. Sci. **7**, e623 (2021)
6. Fu, W., Simonoff, J.S.: Unbiased regression trees for longitudinal and clustered data. Comput. Stat. Data Anal. **88**, 53–74 (2015)
7. Ghousi, R., Mehrani, S., Momeni, M., Anjomshoaa, S.: Application of data mining techniques in drug consumption forecasting to help pharmaceutical industry production planning. In: Proceedings of the 2012 International Conference on Industrial Engineering and Operations Management, pp. 3–6 (2012)
8. Hajjem, A., Bellavance, F., Larocque, D.: Mixed effects regression trees for clustered data. Stat. Probab. Lett. **81**(4), 451–459 (2011)
9. Hamzehlou, M.: System dynamics model for an agile pharmaceutical supply chain during COVID-19 pandemic in Iran. PloS ONE **19**, e0290789 (2024)
10. Jimenez, F., Palma, J., Sanchez, G., Marın, D., Palacios, M.F., López, M.L.: Feature selection based multivariate time series forecasting: an application to antibiotic resistance outbreaks prediction. Artif. Intell. Med. **104**, 101818 (2020)
11. Koala, D., Yahouni, Z., Alpan, G., Si Mohand, D.: Correlation analysis of factors impacting health product consumption in French hospitals. IFAC-PapersOnLine **55**(10), 895–900 (2022)

12. Koala, D., Yahouni, Z., Alpan, G., Frein, Y.: Factors influencing drug consumption and prediction methods. In: CIGI-Qualita : International Conference on Industrial Engineering, Grenoble (2021)
13. Lim, S.S.Y., Phouratsamay, S.L., Yahouni, Z., Gascard, E.: Medicine consumption demand forecasting in French hospitals using seasonal auto-regressive integrated moving average (SARIMA) models. In: 8th International Conference on Control, Automation and Diagnosis (ICCAD'24), Paris, France (2024)
14. Babai, M.Z., Boylan, J.E., Rostami-Tabar, B.: Demand forecasting in supply chains: a review of aggregation and hierarchical approaches. Int. J. Prod. Res. **60**(1), 324–348 (2022)
15. Mizan, T., Taghipour, S.: Medical resource allocation planning by integrating machine learning and optimization models. Artif. Intell. Med. **134**, 102430 (2022)
16. Mousa, B.A., Al-Khateeb, B.: Predicting medicine demand using deep learning techniques: a review. J. Intell. Syst. **32**(1), 20220297 (2023)
17. OCDE: Health at a Glance 2013: OECD Indicators. OECD Publishing, Paris (2013)
18. Ramirez-Alcocer, U.M., Hernandez-Resendiz, J.D., Leal, E.T.: Evaluation of deep learning network architectures for medicine expenditure prediction in the healthcare domain. In: Applied Intelligence for Medical Image Analysis, pp. 179–199. Apple Academic Press, Palm Bay (2024)
19. Speiser, J.L.: A random forest method with feature selection for developing medical prediction models with clustered and longitudinal data. J. Biomed. Inform. **117**, 103763 (2021)
20. Uthayakumar, R., Priyan, S.: Pharmaceutical supply chain and inventory management strategies: optimization for a pharmaceutical company and a hospital. Oper. Res. Health Care **2**(3), 52–64 (2013)
21. Volland, J., Fügener, A., Schoenfelder, J., Brunner, J.O.: Material logistics in hospitals: a literature review. Omega **69**, 82–101 (2017)
22. Vélez, D., Phouratsamay, S.L., Yahouni, Z., Alpan, G.: Predicting medicine demand fluctuations through Markov chain. In: 12th International Workshop on Service Oriented. Holonic and Multi-agent Manufacturing Systems for Industry of the Future, pp. 329–340. Bucharest, Romania (2022)
23. Wang, X., Smith, K., Hyndman, R.: Characteristic-based clustering for time series data. Data Min. Knowl. Disc. **13**, 335–364 (2006)

A Decision Support System of the Configuration of a Supermarket in a Components Company for the Automotive Industry

Telma Pereira(✉) ⓘ, José Oliveira ⓘ, and António Vieira ⓘ

ALGORITMI Research Center, University of Minho, Campus Gualtar,
4710-057 Braga, Portugal
telmapereira7@outlook.com

Abstract. The present study took place in the industrial environment of a company that is part of the automotive industry. The characteristics of this type of industry require company to constantly optimise the configuration of its warehouses. The aim of this paper is to present an algorithm that allows the company to (re)configure the location of items in the Central Shelf Supply System (CSSS), which is the main supplier of parts for production lines. The algorithm was developed in Visual Basic.NET and operates sequentially, considering the characteristics of each item, providing a solution for the distribution of items in the CSSS, considering the balance of picking workload and ergonomic conditions of the picking operation. To evaluate the performance of the proposed solution for items location in CSSS, a simulation tool was developed using SIMIO. This tool demonstrated the capability to simulate different real-world scenarios in a virtual environment efficiently, quantifying important performance indicators. Two scenarios were considered when modelling the configuration of the CSSS system. Scenario 1 was modelled considering the locations of the items in the CSSS, while Scenario 2 was modelled taking into account the locations of the items proposed by the developed algorithm. With this simulation tool, it is now possible to easily assess over time whether the current item location solution can be maintained or needs adjustment. This developed simulation solution also enables the creation and testing of alternative layouts.

Keywords: Decision support system · Digital twin · Heuristics · Logistics · Simulation · Warehouse

1 Introduction

This study was developed in an industrial context of an important company that is part of the automotive components industry. This industry is characterised by a wide variety of products and frequent technical changes. This dynamic results in a very wide range of components used in production, requiring the company's warehouses to be managed appropriately. According to Gu, Goetschalckx and McGinnis [1] warehouses are an essential component for any supply chain and in order to remain competitive, companies

© The Author(s), under exclusive license to Springer Nature Switzerland AG 2025
M. Dassisti et al. (Eds.): IN4PL 2024, CCIS 2372, pp. 173–188, 2025.
https://doi.org/10.1007/978-3-031-80760-2_11

must optimize this logistics process. In general, this study focuses on optimizing and redefining the process currently used in the Central Shelf Supply System (CSSS), which is the main supermarket to supply components to production lines.

The objective of this study was to create an algorithm that allows the company to configure the location of items in the CSSS. This algorithm was implemented in Visual Basic.NET (the programming language used by the company) and adopts constructive heuristic strategies, with the aim of finding effective solutions for item allocations in this supermarket. The algorithm was enhanced throughout the project in order to improve operational efficiency on the one hand and to provide significant benefits in terms of ergonomics on the other. In terms of ergonomics, efforts were made for the algorithm to reduce physical strain on workers by ensuring, for example, that frequently used and heavier items are conveniently located. By achieving this, we are effectively proposing a Decision Support System (DSS) for the warehouse problem, which encompasses a heuristic and a simulation model.

According to Gu, Goetschalckx and McGinnis [2] simulations are a distinct approach for evaluating the performance of a warehouse design. Analysis of the results obtained by a simulation tool can be used to improve the performance of any type of warehouse, including supermarkets in a company [3]. The SIMIO simulation software was chosen for modelling and studying this supermarket because it is one of the best proposals currently available [4]. Furthermore, SIMIO is a program that, in addition to 2D animation, also supports 3D animation, both fully integrated with the modelling process [3, 5].

Simulation models comprise robust DSSs, since they allow decision-makers to test alternatives in a model, rather than in the real system. Concretely, in our case this means that users can test alternative layouts, either manual altered or the result of specific heuristics (which is the case herein described). Furthermore, it can also be argued that the herein proposed simulation model comprises a digital twin of the warehouse problem, since it mimics the activities, events and flows of goods and information that occur in the real system, and since it uses real data originated from said system [6–9].

This paper is structured as follows. Section 2 analyses literature related to the concept of a supermarket in a company, storage policies, optimization, simulation, and examples of work related to simulation in warehouses and the integration of simulation with optimization. Section 3 describes CSSS's warehousing process and summarizes the methodology used throughout the study. Section 4 explores the algorithm developed and presents the simulation model developed. Section 5 presents and discusses the results obtained during the simulation experiments. Finally, Sect. 6 summarizes the main conclusions and limitations of the study.

2   Literature Review

A significant challenge for companies is the supply of parts to the production units on the lines. On the one hand, the material must always reach the production lines on time to avoid extremely costly line stoppages. On the other hand, excessive stock on the production lines and/or traffic on the shop floor leads to excessive costs [10].

In order to get around these problems, the supermarket concept has become common [10]. Supermarkets are decentralized storage areas close to production lines and serve as intermediate suppliers of parts required by those same lines [10, 11].

Warehouse managers must decide how and where to allocate items in the warehouse. There are various policies for defining the location of items in a warehouse and the policy used can have a significant impact on the efficiency of handling and moving items within the warehouse and on the warehouse utilization rate [12–14]. The dedicated storage policy, the random storage policy, the full-turnover-based storage policy and the class-based storage policy are some of the policies mentioned by Roodbergen and Vis [14]. In the dedicated storage policy, each item is associated with a fixed location and replenishment of that item always takes place at the same location [12–14]. In the random storage policy, the location of the item in the warehouse is randomly determined at the time of receipt, taking into account empty storage spaces [12–14]. With the full-turnover-based storage policy, frequently requested items are given the most accessible locations [14]. In the class-based storage policy, the available warehouse space is divided into several areas and each item is assigned to one of the defined areas based on its relevance [14]. One of the best-known class-based storage policy strategies is ABC analysis [14]. With ABC analysis, products are classified into three classes: class A, class B and class C. The most relevant products correspond to class A and are allocated to the most accessible locations in the warehouse, products with intermediate relevance correspond to class B and are allocated to locations with an intermediate level of accessibility, and the least relevant products correspond to class C and are allocated to the least accessible locations [12, 14]. According to Carvalho [12] the criteria used to measure the relevance of each product differs from business sector to business sector and from what is intended to be done with the results of the ABC analysis.

In optimization, methods can be categorised into two main approaches: exact methods and approximate methods. Each approach has its own distinct characteristics, advantages, and limitations. The choice between exact and approximate methods depends on the nature of the problem, the computational resources available and the specific objectives of the project [15].

Contrary to exact methods, which are concerned with obtaining the optimum solution, requiring considerably more time, memory and space, approximate methods seek to find viable solutions efficiently, i.e. faster and with more accessible computing resources [16]. For this reason, this study opted to use an approximation optimization method, more specifically heuristics. Heuristic methods use carefully designed functions to explore the set of possible solutions in an insightful way. These methods involve the use of practical rules, educated guesses, intuitive judgments, or common sense [16].

Integrating simulation with optimization is a promising approach to designing and improving a system [17]. For Banks [18] simulation is an experimental method with detailed modelling of a real system, where using visual models and/or graphic animations it becomes possible to describe and analyse the behaviour of the system in relation to various types of changes.

Over the years, the quality of simulation tools has grown and evolved, helping to simplify the process of building, running, analysing and visualizing models [19]. SIMIO was the tool selected for this study as it offers a number of features that were deemed relevant to the project in question, such as the ability to link to external data, the ease with which it provides an integrated 3D animation environment and the flexibility it offers in terms of modelling [20].

Simulation has been the most popular approach to studying warehouse operations, specifically to validate the performance of a certain configuration or the equipment to be used [13]. In the cases presented by Vieira et al., [3, 21] simulation was used to improve the performance of a company's supermarket, reducing time and space costs. Ekren [22] used simulation to evaluate the performance of a storage and retrieval system for autonomous vehicles according to various predefined design scenarios. Vieira et al., [23] integrated simulation with optimization in order to improve the performance of a production line for a particular company. In this study, the results of the optimization model developed were used in a simulation model to estimate performance indicators such as waiting times, travel times and utilization rates.

On the other hand, simulation has also been used to study alternatives from an ergonomic perspective, albeit these cases are rarer. Such an example can be found in the work of Afonso et al., [24] who used simulation to test the inclusion of automatically guided vehicles that could reduce the workload on workers. Another example includes the work of Zhang et al., [25] who used simulation to investigate how order picking systems can reduce the daily workload of human order pickers. Despite these cases, the use of simulation to test alternatives from an ergonomics perspective is rare in literature, despite the benefits that can be achieved. As a result of the analyses of literature, and to the best of the authors' knowledge these studies do not focus on the specific problem we are targeting, i.e., ergonomic concerns in a warehouse picking problem.

3   Problem Description

This section introduces the problem under investigation, providing a comprehensive description of the PW-CSSS storage system's operation. It delves into the intricacies of the system's functionality and examines the layout of the CSSS in relation to the various types of boxes utilised.

3.1   Description of the Operation of the PW-CSSS Storage System

The CSSS warehouse is supplied by the PW warehouse. In the PW-CSSS storage system there are four different rack alignments: alignment 2, alignment 3, alignment 4 and alignment 5. Between alignments 2 and 3 and alignments 4 and 5, there are two aisles which are subdivided by a conveyor into two work zones for CSSS operations, making a total of four work zones. Only one employee works in each work area, and they are separated by a conveyor whose function is to transport the items collected by the employees to the picking area. Figure 1 shows how the CSSS is positioned in relation to the PW, noting that there is a union of both warehouses, with the same rack containing not only the PW but also the CSSS.

The CSSS has total capacity of 2300 product references, and the PW has a capacity of 537 pallets.

3.2   Description of the CSSS Layout in Relation to the Different Types of Boxes

When storing items at CSSS there are some variations in the boxes that are used, i.e. there are items that are stored in Small Euro Stacking Boxes (20 cm width, 30 cm length

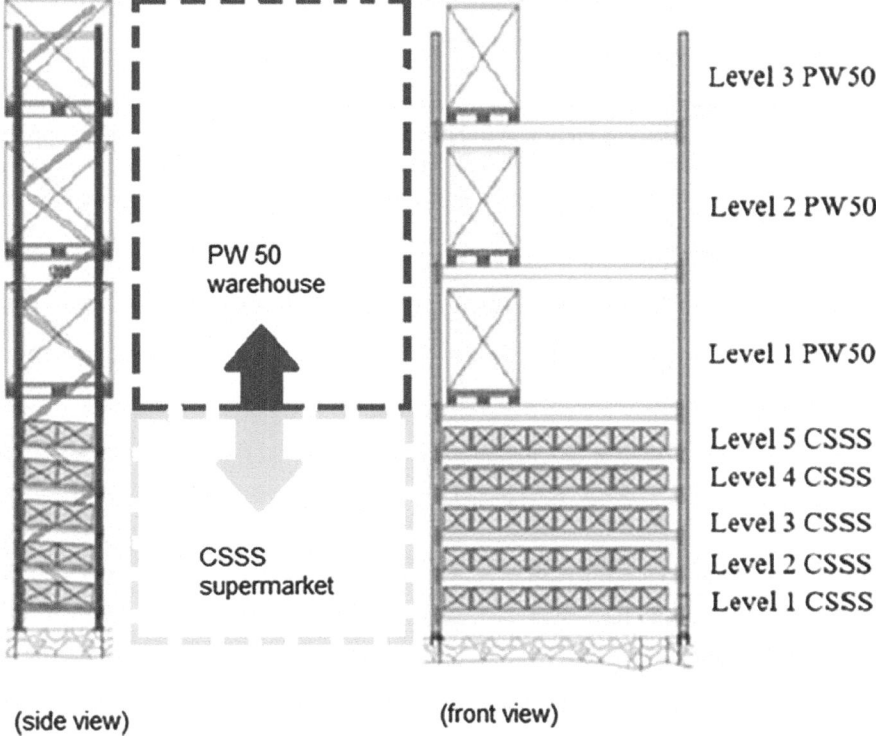

Fig. 1. Location of the CSSS in relation to the PW.

and 10 cm height), Big Euro Stacking Boxes (30 cm width, 40 cm length and 20 cm height) and in their Original Boxes.

This variation between the types of boxes exists for several reasons. Firstly, having places for small boxes increases the number of possible CSSS locations and the fact that there are items with low consumption or low volume justifies the use of these boxes. Secondly, there are also items that must be stored in their original box, due to customer demands or even to avoid damage due to their fragility. These items are known as "mandatory original box items". Finally, the majority of CSSS locations are designed for boxes with maximum dimensions of 30 cm in width, 100 cm in length and 30 cm in height. As there are original boxes with measurements exceeding these values, these items need to be made into big euro stacking boxes. Throughout this paper, all original boxes that have measurements equal to or less than a 30 cm width, 100 cm length and 30 cm height are referred to as "on-size" original boxes, otherwise they are "off-size" original boxes.

The four different box possibilities have been grouped into three categories based on their measurements and CSSS has its own places in its layout for each of these categories. Figure 2 shows a scheme of CSSS layout, where each block associated with each alignment represents a rack and each rack has a box category associated with it.

Category 1 refers to the original "off-size" boxes, Category 2 includes the original "on-size" boxes and the big euro stacking boxes and Category 3 refers to the small euro stacking boxes.

When it is mentioned that each rack has an associated box category, it means that the space between the locations and the number of levels varies. Racks designed to supply Category 1 boxes have four or five levels (yellow blocks), racks designed to supply Category 2 boxes have five levels (blue blocks) and racks designed to supply Category 3 boxes have eight levels (pink blocks).

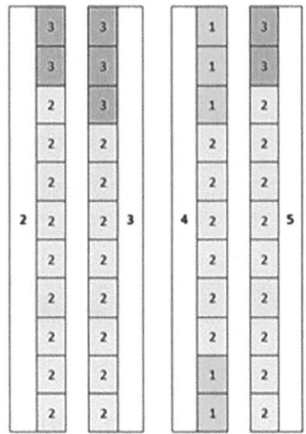

Fig. 2. CSSS layout considering the three categories of boxes.

4   Development of the Decision Support System

This section explains how the DSS was developed detailing the creation of the algorithm for product allocation in the company's CSSS and the implementation of the simulation in modelling the CSSS system configuration. Additionally, this section provides a summary of the methodology used in the project's development.

4.1   Adopted Approach for the Decision Support System

During this study, an optimisation algorithm was developed using heuristic methods in order to allocate items in the CSSS. A simulation tool was used to model the CSSS system, using the results of the algorithm as input. By analysing the results of this simulation tool, it has become possible to draw conclusions that enable decision-making. Figure 3 provides an overview of the methodology used to carry out this study.

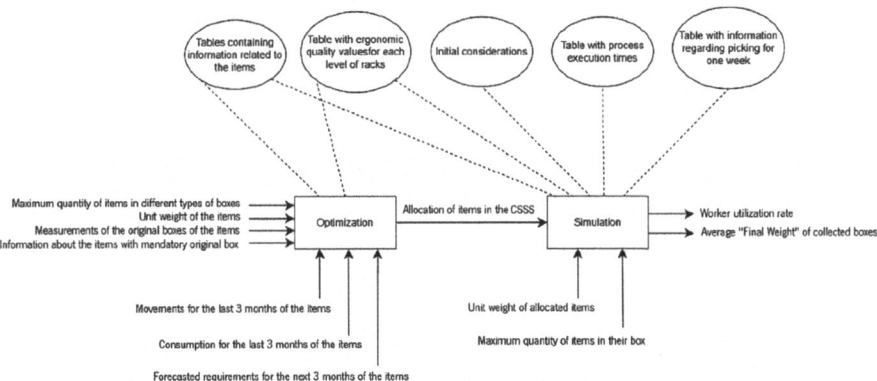

Fig. 3. Illustration of the adopted approach for the Decision Support System.

4.2   Allocation of Items in CSSS

This section describes in detail the development of the algorithm for allocating products in the company's CSSS. The algorithm was programmed in Visual Basic.NET, using Microsoft Visual Studio.

Required Inputs for the Algorithm

The data collected in relation to the items that can be supplied to the CSSS is shown in Table 1. Table 2 shows the variables calculated and needed to develop the algorithm.

Table 1. Collected data.

Abbreviation	Data Description
-	Item part number
W_{Item}	Unit weight of the item in grams
$Q_{OrigBox}$	Maximum quantity of the item in an original box
$Q_{SmallBox}$	Maximum quantity of the item in a small euro stacking box
Q_{BigBox}	Maximum quantity of the item in a big euro stacking box
-	Width of the original box in centimetres
-	Length of the original box in centimetres
-	Height of the original box in centimetres
-	Item with mandatory original box
$C3$	Consumption for the last 3 months of the item
$M3$	Movements for the last 3 months of the item
$FR3$	Forecasted requirements for the next 3 months of the item

Table 2. Calculated variables.

Abbreviation	Description
CM	Consumption per movement
FM3	Forecasted movements for the next 3 months
SB3	Forecast of the quantity of small euro stacking boxes used in the next 3 months
BB3	Forecast of the quantity of big euro stacking boxes used in the next 3 months
OB3	Forecast of the quantity of original boxes used in the next 3 months

The following formulas show how each of the above values was calculated.

$$CM = \frac{C3}{M3} \tag{1}$$

$$FM3 = \frac{FR3}{CM} \tag{2}$$

$$SB3 = \frac{FR3}{Q_{SmallBox}} \tag{3}$$

$$BB3 = \frac{FR3}{Q_{BigBox}} \tag{4}$$

$$OB3 = \frac{FR3}{Q_{OrigBox}} \tag{5}$$

One of the aims of this algorithm is to improve the ergonomic situation of the employees working at the CSSS, so it was necessary to give an ergonomic quality value to each of the levels based on their height. Throughout this paper, the terminology used to refer to this ergonomic quality value will be "quality". When the rack has five levels, level 1 and level 5 have a "quality" value of 0, level 2 has a "quality" value of 1 and levels 3 and 4 have a "quality" value of 2. In the case of racks intended for small euro stacking boxes, levels 1, 7 and 8 have a "quality" of 0, level 2 has a "quality" of 1 and levels 3, 4, 5 and 6 have a "quality" value of 2. Finally, for racks with four levels, level 1 has a "quality" of 0, level 2 has a "quality" of 1 and levels 3 and 4 have a "quality" value of 2.

Description of the Algorithm Developed

By using historical data and certain characteristics of the items, as well as the particularities of the CSSS facilities, the algorithm proposes a product distribution solution that takes into account not only the ergonomic conditions of the workers, but also the balance of the workload. The algorithm adopts constructive heuristic strategies and was developed with the aim of guiding the product allocation process at CSSS in an efficient and systematic way. The algorithm works sequentially and is divided into three stages, one for each category of box, guaranteeing proper fulfilment of the restrictions associated with assigning each type of box to a convenient place. Each stage of the algorithm has been subdivided into steps and Fig. 4 summarises each of them for each stage.

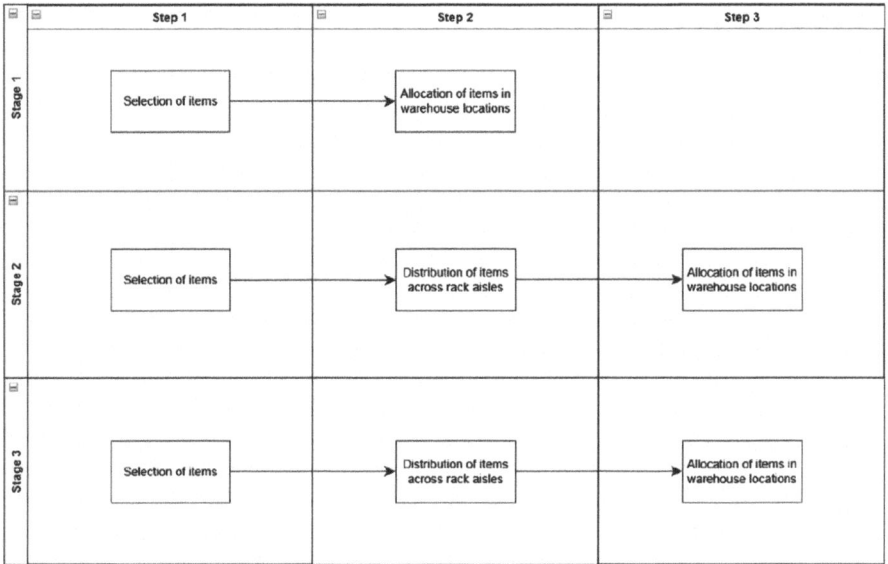

Fig. 4. Summary of the different steps in each stage of the algorithm.

Stage 1 – Allocate Items with Category 1 Boxes

This stage of the algorithm that was developed to allocate the items in the locations destined for the Category 1 boxes is divided into two steps. The first step involves selecting the items that have the right characteristics to be allocated to the locations destined for Category 1 boxes. The second step involves allocating the previously selected items to the locations.

In selecting the items, the first to be chosen were the mandatory original box items and "off-size" items. After this selection and taking into account the number of locations still available for Category 1 boxes, the remaining items were chosen, whether they had an "off-size" or "on-size" original box. The items with the highest OB3 values were chosen.

In the second step of this first stage, the following expression was used:

$$W_{Item} \times Q_{OrigBox} \times 0{,}5 + FM3 \times 0{,}5 \tag{6}$$

The values from the calculations resulting from this mathematical expression were used to allocate the items to the locations. This allocation followed a very specific rule: in descending order, the items with the highest values were allocated to the locations with "quality" levels equal to 2. When these places ran out, they were allocated to the locations with "quality" levels equal to 1 and, finally, to the locations with "quality" levels equal to 0. This allocation is carried out from the locations closest to the picking zone to those furthest away.

The logic used in this second step is similar to that of the class-based storage method with ABC analysis. In this case, the levels of the racks are also classified (according to their "quality") and depending on the relevance of the items, they are allocated to each location taking into account the class of the level, i.e. the "quality" of the level. However, in this allocation defined by the algorithm developed, the traditional ABC analysis with the Pareto rule is not applied, as the ABC classification was not made directly to the items taking into account their total, but to the warehouse levels considering the total number of locations in each level taking into account their "quality" value.

Note that when calculating expression (6), the weight of the boxes and the forecasted movements were given equal importance, because it was important to CSSS employees not only that the heaviest boxes were not at the highest or lowest levels, but also that they weren't items with a lot of movements, so that they didn't have to force themselves into bad postures several times a day.

Stage 2 – Allocate Items with Category 2 Boxes

Contrary to the first stage of the algorithm developed, this second stage, which serves to allocate the items in the cells destined for the Category 2 boxes, is divided into three steps. The first step involves selecting the items that have the right characteristics to be allocated to the locations destined for Category 2 boxes. The second step involves distributing the items among the alignments, since the four CSSS alignments have capacity for this type of item. The third and last step is to allocate the items to the locations.

Items with the original "off-size" boxes had to follow in the algorithm as big euro stacking boxes, while items with the original "on-size" boxes continued to be associated with those same boxes.

In the first step of this stage, the BB3 and OB3 values of the items were sorted in descending order. Taking into account the number of locations available for Category 2 boxes, the same number of items were selected, these being the ones with the highest BB3 or OB3 values. Selecting in this way ensures that the items with the highest consumption are chosen from a wide range of possible items to be allocated to the CSSS.

Once the items had been selected, the second step of this second stage of the algorithm began and in this step an alignment was assigned to each item.

Mathematical expressions (7) and (8) were used in this second step.

$$BB3 \times 0,5 + FM3 \times 0,5 \qquad (7)$$

$$OB3 \times 0,5 + FM3 \times 0,5 \qquad (8)$$

Mathematical expressions (7) and (8) were constructed taking into account the work of CSSS and PW employees. BB3/OB3 considers the work of PW operators and FM3 considers the work of CSSS employees. The higher the BB3/OB3 value for any given item, the higher the forecast for the number of out-of-stock boxes for that item and, consequently, the more often the PW operators need to replenish those boxes. The value of FM3 defines the number of times CSSS employees need to travel to the item's location. The values in expressions (7) and (8) were ordered in descending order and, following this order, the distribution of the items in the alignments began with the first item being assigned to alignment 2, the second to alignment 3, the third to alignment 4, the fourth to alignment 5, the fifth to alignment 2 and so on. By assigning them in this way, an attempt was made to ensure a balance of work in the alignments. This process of distributing the items among the alignments was divided not only by the alignments, but also by the "quality" of the levels. The number of locations that each alignment has with a "quality" level of 2 was counted, then with a "quality" level of 1 and finally with a "quality" level of 0. Items were allocated alignment by alignment, but when the locations of "quality" equal to 2 in a given alignment were exhausted, the allocation continued for the other alignments and only returned to the alignment that finished first when all the locations of "quality" equal to 2 in the other alignments were exhausted. Then the process would resume allocating items to the "quality" locations equal to 1 and finally to the "quality" locations equal to 0.

After assigning the items to a specific alignment, the algorithm proceeded to the third step of this second stage, where the items were allocated to the locations. The process of this allocation is similar to the process of allocating boxes in the first stage of the algorithm, with the only difference being that the expression used ((9) or (10)) depends on the type of box used.

$$W_{Item} \times Q_{BigBox} \times 0,5 + FM3 \times 0,5 \tag{9}$$

$$W_{Item} \times Q_{OrigBox} \times 0,5 + FM3 \times 0,5 \tag{10}$$

Stage 3 – Allocate Items with Category 3 Boxes

Just like the second stage of the developed algorithm, this third stage, which serves for the allocation of items in the locations destined for Category 3 boxes, is divided into three steps: item selection, distribution of items across alignments, and allocation of items to locations.

The first step of this third stage of the developed algorithm follows the same logic as the first step of Stage 2. Considering the number of locations still available for Category 3 boxes, the same number of items was selected, which are those with the highest values of SB3.

The second step of this third stage follows the same logic as the second step of Stage 2. In this case, the items were distributed across alignments 2, 3, and 5, also taking into account the available spaces in each alignment based on the "quality" of the levels. The mathematical expression used to assist in the process of assigning items to alignments was as follows:

$$SB3 \times 0,5 + FM3 \times 0,5 \tag{11}$$

The third and final step of this third stage of the developed algorithm follows a similar logic to the second step of Stage 1 and the third step of Stage 2, with the only difference being that, in this case, only the FM3 values of the items were considered and not the weight of the boxes, since small euro stacking boxes do not present a detrimental weight from an ergonomic point of view.

4.3 Simulation

Simulation, using the SIMIO software, was employed to model the current CSSS system and the proposed new system. Thus, two different simulation scenarios were created. Scenario 1 takes into account the current data regarding the locations of the items in the CSSS alignments. Scenario 2 uses the data concerning the item locations provided by the output of the developed optimization algorithm. In summary, the only difference between the two scenarios lies in the input data utilized. Regarding the modelling of the systems, this is carried out in exactly the same way. Scenario 1 serves as validation of the model, while Scenario 2 is one of the alternatives that can be studied with this tool.

The location of the items in the warehouse alignments, the ergonomic quality value of the levels to which each item belongs, the data regarding the weights of the items, the association of process execution times, and the exact and real picking times that occurred during a week of work in the X, were indispensable input data for the development of modelling this system. During the modelling of the current CSSS system, multiples distinct processes were developed, of which some types can be distinguished. The first type of process that can be highlighted was modelled with the aim of assigning a numerical value to all boxes allocated in the warehouse.

The second type of process that can be highlighted is represented in Fig. 5 and served to define the entire process of picking items in the CSSS.

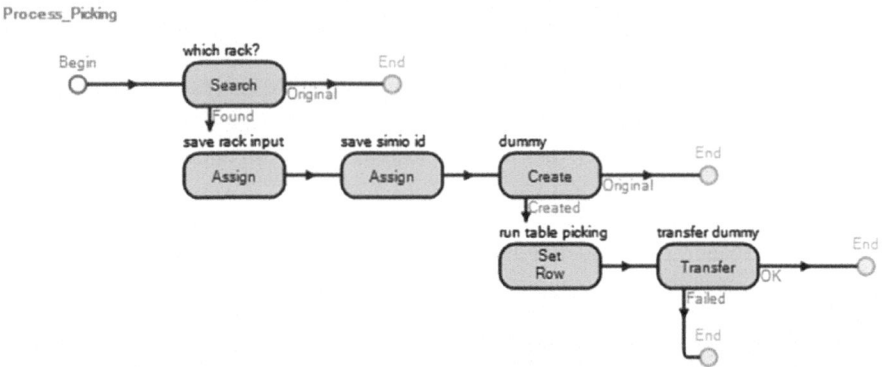

Fig. 5. Modelled process to define the picking process of items.

The next process aims to generate statistical data for each alignment and is modelled as shown in Fig. 6. The statistical data that this process will allow to extract is related to the "quality" of the levels and the weight that the workers are bearing during the picking process of the items.

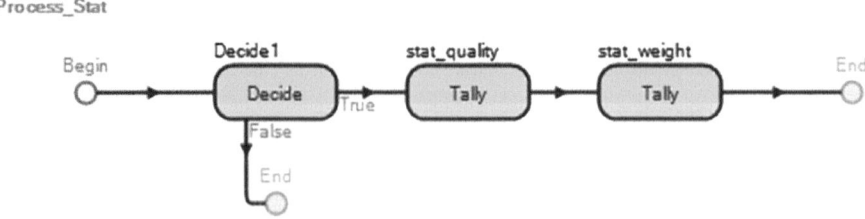

Fig. 6. Example of the modelled process to extract statistical data.

The last process that can be highlighted was modelled with the aim of causing a delay in the workers tasks. With this delay, the workers take a certain time to load the entity and only release it at the end of that time. Figure 7 represents an example of how this process was modelled.

Process_Delay_Worker1

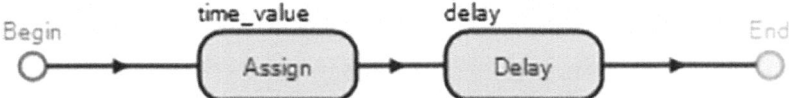

Fig. 7. Example of the modelled process to delay the workers tasks.

5   Results

The implications of transitioning between the current system state (Scenario 1) and the potential future system state of CSSS (Scenario 2) were analysed and evaluated in detail, providing solid data and critical insights through the SIMIO tool for future strategic decision-making by the company. Performance metrics considered include worker utilization rate and the average Final Weight of the boxes picked for each alignment. The Final Weight is defined as the weight that workers bear when picking up the box for item retrieval, considering that this weight may increase depending on the ergonomic quality value of the level to which the item belongs.

The results regarding worker utilization rate, analysed based on 30 replications, are presented in Table 3. The first scenario demonstrated a more satisfactory balance in worker tasks compared to the second scenario. As shown in Table 3, in Scenario 1, the worker utilization rate ranged from 68.53% to 74.12%, while in Scenario 2, the variation was between 58.27% and 95.60%. In the case of the second scenario, although a balance in worker tasks is observed for workers 2, 3, and 4, worker 1, operating in alignment 2, exhibits a significantly higher utilization rate, standing out as an exception to this balance.

Regarding the average Final Weight of the picked boxes per alignment, Scenario 2 showed better results compared to Scenario 1. Table 3 displays the results of both scenarios for each alignment. It is noteworthy that Scenario 2 only presents worse results for alignment 2, and this may be related to the excessive workload that worker 1 in this second scenario exhibited.

Figure 8 shows how the developed simulation model looks in 3D visualisation.

Table 3. SIMIO results.

Worker Utilization Rate (%)	Scenario 1	Scenario 2
Worker 1	70,5	95,6
Worker 2	72,2	66,3
Worker 3	74,1	58,3
Worker 4	68,5	61,7
Average Final Weight	Scenario 1	Scenario 2
Alignment 2	4455	5583
Alignment 3	7337	5519
Alignment 4	6980	4802
Alignment 5	5997	4898

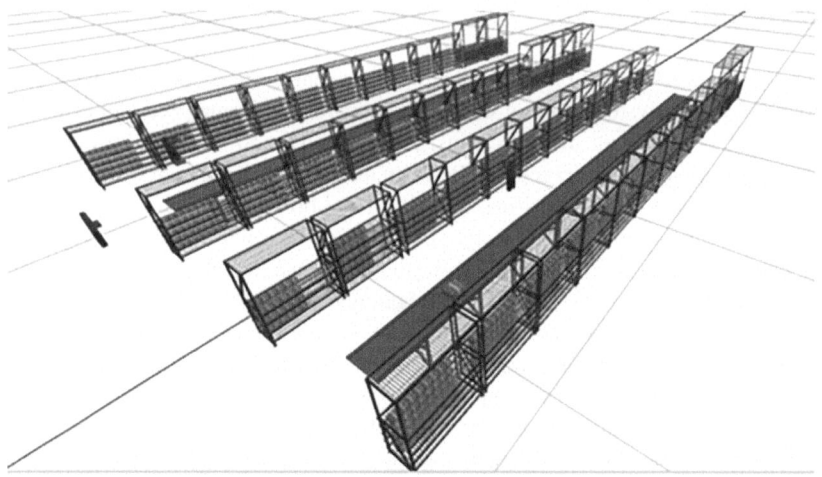

Fig. 8. 3D visualisation of the model.

6 Conclusions

The algorithm developed generates a solution for distributing items in the CSSS, the main supermarket of an important company that operates in Portugal in the automotive sector. The algorithm, developed in Visual Basic.NET, functions sequentially by taking into account the characteristics of each item. It offers a solution for item distribution within the CSSS, aiming to balance the picking workload and improve the ergonomic conditions of the picking operation.

The SIMIO software was used to simulate both the existing CSSS system and the proposed new system. Thus, two different simulation scenarios were developed. Scenario 1 considers the current data on the locations of items within the CSSS alignments.

Scenario 2 employs the data on item locations generated by the newly developed optimisation algorithm. Based on the analysis of the results from Scenario 1, it is understood that in this scenario, there is an excellent balance in the workload of the employees. From the results obtained in Scenario 2, it can be concluded that the workload balance was maintained, although not as efficiently as observed in Scenario 1, as one of the employees exhibited a very high utilization rate compared to others. Regarding the ergonomic conditions of the employees, comparing with Scenario 1, Scenario 2 presented better results concerning the average weight of the picked boxes, considering that this weight varies according to the ergonomic quality value of the levels to which the items belong. Thus, it can be proven that Scenario 2 ensures a better balance between the weight of the boxes and the ergonomic quality value of the levels, compared to Scenario 1.

In addition to enhancing worker ergonomics, the implementation of this algorithm provides the company with the ability to continuously update the optimization of item management in the warehouse. This process is interesting from the optimization and efficiency perspective if used in the medium and long term, rather than a short-term operational perspective.

Regarding the limitations of the project, there were two major limitations. One of them relates to the lack of data on the characteristics of several items, which are used as input in the algorithm. The second limitation is related to the picking data provided by the company and used in the simulation. These data belong to a temporal space of only one week, which proves to be insufficient, considering that the algorithm was developed based on data covering a period of 3 months. These limitations are directly related to the developed algorithm and, consequently, to Scenario 2, and may be limiting or even impairing its results.

Acknowledgements. This work has been supported by FCT – Fundação para a Ciência e Tecnologia within the R&D Units Project Scope: UIDB/00319/2020.

References

1. Gu, J., Goetschalckx, M., McGinnis, L.F.: Research on warehouse operation: a comprehensive review. Eur. J. Oper. Res. **177**(1), 1–21 (2007). https://doi.org/10.1016/j.ejor.2006.02.025
2. Gu, J., Goetschalckx, M., McGinnis, L.F.: Research on warehouse design and performance evaluation: a comprehensive review. Eur. J. Oper. Res. **203**(3), 539–549 (2010). https://doi.org/10.1016/j.ejor.2009.07.031
3. Vieira, A., et al.: Simulation model generation for warehouse management: case study to test different storage strategies. Int. J. Simul. Process Model. **13**(4) (2018)
4. Dias, L.M.S., Vieira, A.A.C., Pereira, G.A.B., Oliveira, J.A.: Discrete simulation software ranking – a top list of the worldwide most popular and used tools. In: Proceedings of the 2016 Winter Simulation Conference, pp. 1060–1071 (2016)
5. Houck, D., Whitehead, C.: Introduction to Simio. In: Winter Simulation Conference, pp. 3802–3811. Association for Computing Machinery (2019)
6. Coelho, F., Relvas, S., Barbosa-Póvoa, A.P.: Simulation-based decision support tool for in-house logistics: the basis for a digital twin. Comput. Ind. Eng. **153** (2021)
7. Qi, Q., et al.: Enabling technologies and tools for digital twin. J. Manuf. Syst. **58**, 3–21 (2021)

8. Tao, F., Zhang, M.: Digital twin shop-floor: a new shop-floor paradigm towards smart manufacturing. IEEE Access **5**, 20418–20427 (2017). https://doi.org/10.1109/ACCESS.2017.275 6069

9. Ferreira, W.P., Armellini, F., De Santa-Eulalia, L.A.: Simulation in industry 4.0: a state-of-the-art review. Comput. Ind. Eng. **149** (2020)

10. Emde, S., Boysen, N.: Optimally locating in-house logistics areas to facilitate JIT-supply of mixed-model assembly lines. Int. J. Prod. Econ. **135**(1), 393–402 (2012). https://doi.org/10. 1016/j.ijpe.2011.07.022

11. Battini, D., Boysen, N., Emde, S.: Just-in-Time supermarkets for part supply in the automobile industry. J. Manage. Control **24**(2), 209–217 (2013). https://doi.org/10.1007/s00187-012-0154-y

12. Carvalho, J.C.: Logística e Gestão da Cadeia de Abastecimento, 3 edn. Edições Sílabo (2020)

13. Gagliardi, J.-P., Renaud, J., Ruiz, A.: A simulation model to improve warehouse operations. Winter Simulation Conference, pp. 2012–2018 (2007). https://doi.org/10.1145/135154 2.1351899

14. Roodbergen, K.J., Vis, I.F.A.: A survey of literature on automated storage and retrieval systems. Eur. J. Oper. Res. **194**(2), 343–362 (2009). https://doi.org/10.1016/j.ejor.2008. 01.038

15. Alvelos, F.: Investigação operacional – Modelos determinísticos de optimização, Métodos e Software (Versão 0.1) (2009)

16. Desale, S., Rasool, A., Andhale, S., Rane, P.: View of heuristic and meta-heuristic algorithms and their relevance to the real world_ a survey. Int. J. Comput. Eng. Res. Trends **2**(5), 296–304 (2015)

17. Zúñiga, E.R.: Facility layout design with simulation-based optimization. A holistic methodology including process, flow, and logistics requirements in manufacturing. Doctoral Dissertation (2020)

18. Banks, J.: Introduction to Simulation. In: Winter Simulation Conference, pp. 7–13 (1999)

19. Pegden, C.D.: SIMIO: a new simulation system based on intelligent objects. In: Winter Simulation Conference, pp. 2293–2300 (2007)

20. Vieira, A., Figueira, J.R., Fragoso, R.: A multi-objective simulation-based decision support tool for wine supply chain design and management under sustainability goals. Expert Syst. Appl. **232** (2023). https://doi.org/10.1016/j.eswa.2023.120757

21. Vieira, A., Dias, L.S., Pereira, G.B., Oliveira, J.A., Carvalho, M.S., Martins, P.: Automatic simulation models generation of warehouses with milk runs and pickers. In: Proceedings of the 28th European Modeling and Simulation Symposium, pp. 231–241 (2016)

22. Ekren, B.Y.: Performance evaluation of AVS/RS under various design scenarios: a case study. Int. J. Adv. Manuf. Technol. **55**(9–12), 1253–1261 (2011). https://doi.org/10.1007/s00170-010-3137-x

23. Vieira, A., Guilherme, E., Oliveira, J.A., Dias, L.M.S., Pereira, G.A.B.: Combining simulation and optimization models on a production line problem: a case study. ALGORITMI Research Center (2019)

24. Afonso, T., Alves, A.C., Carneiro, P., Vieira, A.: Simulation pulled by the need to reduce wastes and human effort in an intralogistics project. Int. J. Ind. Eng. Manage. **12**(4), 274–285 (2021). https://doi.org/10.24867/IJIEM-2021-4-294

25. Zhang, M., Grosse, E.H., Glock, C.H.: Ergonomic and economic evaluation of a collaborative hybrid order picking system. Int. J. Prod. Econ. **258** (2023). https://doi.org/10.1016/j.ijpe. 2023.108774

A Distributed Framework for Cooperative Scheduling of Production, Transportation, and Maintenance Using Multi-Agent Systems

Yassir Haoudi[(⊠)] [ID], Agnès Letouzey [ID], and Xavier Desforges [ID]

Laboratoire Génie de Production, Université de Technologie Tarbes Occitanie Pyrénées, 65016 Tarbes, France
yassir.haoudi@doctorant.uttop.fr, {agnes.letouzey, xavier.desforges}@uttop.fr

Abstract. Manufacturing systems often face conflicting demands between production, maintenance, and transport services, as the activities of each can disrupt the operations of the others. To address these conflicts and ensure a harmonized workflow, this paper introduces an advanced multi-agent system with three distinct SCEP (Supervisor, Customers, Environment and Producers) models for production, maintenance, and transport. The objective is to facilitate distributed joint scheduling of these three critical areas, with considerations about the health state of the machines. This approach allows the integrated scheduling of production, transport, and predictive maintenance activities based on real-time health assessments of the machines. By doing so, the system aims at resolving operational conflicts among the services, ensuring that all stakeholders of these three domains collaborate effectively towards a common goal.

Keywords: Joint production scheduling · Distributed scheduling · Transportation · Predictive maintenance · Supply chain · Cloud manufacturing

1 Introduction

The fierce competition among industrial companies forces them to adapt to market changes, diversify their products and services, and automate their manufacturing equipment. These market dynamics, along with growing customer demands and expectations, require companies to efficiently manage and process different customer orders, particularly in a make-to-order manufacturing strategy, which will improve productivity and operational efficiency on the production floor. This depends on well-organized production processes that are driven by manufacturing orders, which specify in detail the products to be manufactured, the quantities required and the appropriate lead times for producing finished or semi-finished products according to a predefined sequence of activities. Operational excellence in a workshop cannot be achieved without a well-designed scheduling function.

M. Dassisti et al. (Eds.): IN4PL 2024, CCIS 2372, pp. 189–201, 2025.
https://doi.org/10.1007/978-3-031-80760-2_12

Scheduling, which largely depends on the execution of these activities, allows the precise allocation of available resources, such as machines, materials, and personnel, to requested production tasks over a certain planning horizon, while respecting production deadlines and maintaining high quality of finished products [1]. To be truly effective, scheduling must be supported by strategic resource management and a proactive maintenance policy.

Although production tasks are performed by machines, it is essential that these resources are in good condition to perform the necessary functions. Many scheduling problems assume that machines are available, whereas in reality it is important to consider that machines may become unavailable for reasons such as unexpected breakdowns and maintenance [2]. Thus, maintenance activity impacts production scheduling according to the maintenance policy adopted by the company. The emergence of new techniques from artificial intelligence and the Internet of Things (IoT) has prompted companies to shift to a predictive maintenance policy [3]. Through advanced diagnostic technologies and predictive analysis, predictive maintenance needs on-line assessment of machine health, making it easier to detect, isolate and identify precursor faults, and to monitor and predict fault evolution to develop appropriate maintenance plans [2].

Considering the state of resources and the scheduling of maintenance tasks is an essential factor in creating efficient production scheduling. Over the last few decades, there has been a growing interest in the joint scheduling of production and maintenance, in contrast to the past when the scheduling of both activities was treated individually as part of an interdependent approach. The interdependent approach optimizes one parameter by considering another parameter as a constraint, whereas all decision variables are treated simultaneously for global problem solving, which proves to be effective.

The modern industrial environment involves broader and more complex industrial processes that include multi-products, for multiple objectives, and in geographically distributed sites, where sites use the intermediate products of other sites to manufacture the products of the company [4]. This means that an order can be processed jointly at different sites. From the transport to the end of production activities, there are two interdependent supply chain functions that literature often treats in an uncoordinated approach leading to solutions that are often unsatisfactory. Thus, production scheduling problems should be joined with the classical Vehicle Routing Problems (VRP) to integrate production and transport activities at the operational level. The need to integrate production and transport becomes very important especially when it comes to the management of operations spread across various locations. For example, research focusing on omni-channel retailing [5], has shown the relevance of logistics in a way that is coordinated in real time, thus, reducing the lag that exists when product dispatch through various channels is concerned. This implies that, there should be a smooth interrelation of production and transportation processes, so that there are no delays in making deliveries and no wastage of time in waiting to carry out certain tasks.

Well organized production and transport operations can enhance the efficiency Concept. Previous research, for example, the investigation of two-echelon supply chains with grey revenue sharing contracts [6], has shown the importance of contractual agreements in optimizing supply chain interactions. These agreements balance pricing and competition, ultimately improving cooperation between manufacturers and distributors.

Therefore, a well-integrated supply chain, which coordinates production and maintenance activities up to delivery, ensures efficient operation and smooth flow of operations and resource utilization optimization.

The objective of our work is to develop a generic method for jointly scheduling production, transport, and maintenance in a job shop configuration for sites and machines with considerations about their health states.

This article addresses a distributed production network, which must operate cooperatively with a transport and maintenance network. For this reason, we propose a Multi-Agent System (MAS) that can adapt to different scheduling approaches and model various services of the manufacturing system. The MAS consists of a group of agents of different natures (physical, functional) that are autonomous and interact according to modes of cooperation, competition, or coexistence. The use of this approach allows for resolving conflicts among agents in complex scheduling problems through negotiation techniques.

The integration of diverse systems is also seen in the context of cloud manufacturing, which provides much larger scale by integrating the capabilities and resources of a wide supplier network. This model virtualizes and shares resources with multiple users and consumers [7], allowing for more dynamic and adaptable task distribution. This distribution is based on real-time availability and skills across the cloud, and it must handle not only production but also services, maintenance, and transportation in an integrated manner. This system heavily relies on cloud technology, Internet of Things (IoT) systems, and big data solutions to connect and synchronize distributed resources [7]. In contrast, scheduling in cloud manufacturing transforms these challenges into opportunities. Thanks to cloud technology, manufacturing, maintenance, and transportation resources can be managed much more dynamically. Cloud manufacturing enhances visibility and control over processes by integrating and synchronizing resources and tasks through a centralized virtual platform. This capability to manage resources from multiple suppliers in real-time not only improves flexibility but also the responsiveness of the entire production system.

This paper is then organized as follows. Section 2 briefly presents some related works. Section 3 is devoted to the description of the considered problem is formulated and modelled by an UML (Unified Modeling Language) class diagram. In Sect. 4, the MAS model used to solve the problem is presented. First, the different agents are introduced, then the communication protocol of these agents is described. Finally, we conclude and give some perspectives to our work in Sect. 5.

2   Related Works

To our knowledge, no research has been dedicated to the joint scheduling of production, transport, and predictive maintenance activities in the distributed job shop context. However, some studies have addressed integrated approaches to production and maintenance scheduling. For instance, Q. Liu et al. [8] proposed an integrated decision model that coordinates predictive maintenance decisions, based on prognostic information such as machine degradation and fictive age, with scheduling decisions for a single machine to minimize production and task delay costs. Mifdal et al. [9] considered the impact of the production rate on system degradation in their optimal production and maintenance plan. Qiu et al. [10] examined the influence of customer orders on the deterioration of production machines and modeled various dependencies among machines in a single model, aiming to develop a joint optimization approach for production and conditional maintenance in made-to-order manufacturing systems.

Several studies have also explored integrated production scheduling with transport in centralized, distributed, or multi-site environments. Gharaei and Jolai [11] investigated parallel multi-site manufacturing using a multi-agent system where different agents have different goals: customers aim to minimize delivery delays, distributors focus on reducing transportation costs, and manufacturers strive to minimize inventory costs. Each production site is equipped with identical machines and homogeneous vehicles with capacity constraints. Yağmur and Kesen [12] considered a job shop environment with a heterogeneous fleet of vehicles, where each customer order goes through several operations and is handled by multiple vehicles across multiple trips. The problem was formulated using a mixed-integer linear programming (MILP) method and solved using the Augmented ε-Constraint method for small-sized instances. For larger problems, they used metaheuristics like Pareto local search and the NSGA-II genetic algorithm, with NSGA-II outperforming Pareto local search on large datasets.

In the context of cloud manufacturing, service suppliers, manufacturers, maintainers, transporters and customers have a certain autonomy enabling them to apply their own decision criteria according to their own performance indicators, while collaborating to achieve a common goal. Consequently, this leads to favour a distributed approach based on MAS, as it encompasses architectures and patterns capable of handling complex production systems, such as the cyber-physical production systems [13]. This work presents various examples regarding agent autonomy for decision-making and task execution. For example, the self-control architecture indicates that sub-agents such as the High-Availability Agent and the Rescheduler Agent work independently to manage tasks such as safety, fault tolerance, and resource scheduling. Therefore, MAS generally remain a promising approach for scheduling and control of complex manufacturing systems [14], and in particular for our investigation of joint scheduling of production, maintenance, and transportation, due to the numerous potential advantages of distributed scheduling mentioned in [15]. In this context of distributed scheduling, SCEP (Supervisor, Customers, Environment, Producers) seems a promising framework, among other distributed approaches, and it has been implemented in various contexts, the integration of which is sought here. The SCEP model [16], based on indirect cooperation among agents (customers, producers, supervisor) through an environment (blackboard), relies on a negotiation protocol derived from Contract Net. The model allows for the processing of flexible manufacturing sequences, various resources, and can incorporate specific objectives and constraints for each agent. The interest of methods based on the SCEP model lies in the quality of the solution provided as well as in the execution time.

SCEMP, proposed in [17], is an extension of the SCEP model. It introduces new maintenance agents and enhances the capabilities of production agents to assess the current and future health status of their machines and to schedule operations based on this health status. This approach helps in scheduling maintenance based on the machines' anticipated needs, reducing conflicts between production and maintenance activities, to incorporates the maintenance needs into the production schedule. Regarding the transport scheduling, Memon et al. [18] developed multi-agent framework based on SCEP for collaborative transportation planning, the model, named POVES (Path Finder, Order, Vehicle, Environment, and Supervisor), aims to optimize the use of transport resources by grouping several transport orders for each effective movement, where companies often outsource their logistics needs to third-party logistics (3PL) companies to reduce costs and improve efficiency. The goal is to plan transport activities by indirect collaboration between order agents and vehicle agents, assisted by a Path Finder agent.

The presented approach consists of a sort of fusion of those previous developments for the distributed joint production, maintenance and transport scheduling.

Notwithstanding the efforts devoted to improvements in scheduling methodologies, a significant research gap persists regarding the joint scheduling of activities related to production, transport, and maintenance in a distributed job shop environment. Most existing literature treats these processes separately, and when interactions are accounted for, the dependencies are often neglected. For instance, when machines' health status continuously feeds into the schedules, the literature fails to address them jointly. This ultimately results in suboptimal efficiency, downtime, and misalignment within the supply chain, leading to missed deadlines or excess stock (i.e., work-in-process or excess inventory).

The primary research questions guiding this work are:

- How can joint production, transport, and maintenance scheduling be conducted to alleviate disruptions and inefficiencies in a distributed job shop?
- How can real-time machine health updates be incorporated into a joint scheduling algorithm to optimize resource utilization?
- In this work, we aim to address these gaps by developing a model that jointly schedules these three key activities to enhance operational efficiency.

In the next section, we give a detailed description of our problem and the purpose of our study.

3   Problem Description

In our study, the central element of production is the Manufacturing Order (MO), which is characterized by a start date and an end date. Its processing involves a sequence of manufacturing tasks that refer to a specific routing. Each manufacturing task requires one or more activities (cutting, drilling, etc.). The machine must have all the necessary functionalities to perform the activities required by a task.

Each manufacturing task (TF) has an execution duration that includes setup and internal transport times. As the machine is composed of several components, its performance depends on their conditions.

Each machine component is characterized by a health state (condition) that deteriorates with use. To avoid unexpected failures and to increase the machine's availability, we use methods developed in the field of system health assessment and forecasting to estimate the Remaining Useful Life (RUL) of components.

With data from the PHM (Prognostic and Health Management) module, we assess the operational conditions of components and calculate the probability of failure. Each component has a predefined risk threshold above which the probability of failure is high, triggering a request for a maintenance task (TM), as the component will be unable to execute the manufacturing task sequence under acceptable conditions with a too high probability. This probability helps to schedule production and maintenance tasks and to distinguish between available components and those that need maintenance [19].

To carry out the requested TFs, the associated resources and competencies are required, including maintenance personnel and repair tools. As with production, the maintenance task can only be completed by a maintainer with the appropriate skills for the component. The TM scheduling is handled by the maintainer in response to the producer's needs, but the latter can refuse the TM proposals because of production or transport constraints.

In our study, we focus on the joint scheduling of production, transport, and maintenance, which involves multi-site scheduling based on several production sites, each with its own production resources and activities. Each site processes a set of customer orders (MOs), and each MO can be processed on different sites if the activities linked to the TFs sequence of the MO require machine functionalities that exist on different sites. In this case, the in-process products of the MO will be transported between sites due to the machine's competence or availability.

Like a manufacturing order, a transport order or request is triggered by the producer at a site when one or more TFs in an MO require activities not present at this site. The semi-finished product must then be transported to another competent site that has a machine with the required functionalities. The objective is to establish delivery routes to supply the next plant that will continue the production process, leading us to the VRP. This problem has several variants [20], and the one that interests us is the VRP with pickup and delivery (PDP), and particularly the One-to-One category, where each product has only one origin and one destination. The transport order is therefore characterized by information about the pickup point (origin) and destination, with a start and end date. It contains a sequence of transport tasks, each associated with an activity, and one activity may require multiple Transport Tasks (TTs).

The activity designates the route taken between the pickup point and the delivery point and represents a segment of transport Each activity requires a vehicle t, characterized by its capacity, functionalities, and skills, to be performed.

To summarize, each triggered MO may include TFs scheduled on machines from different sites, which means TTs must be considered, along with maintenance tasks if one or more machine components require a maintenance activity.

This integrated approach aims to optimize the scheduling of production, maintenance, and transport activities by creating a responsive and flexible system that adjusts to the on-line assessed conditions of the machinery, thereby enhancing overall operational efficiency and reducing conflicts between the interconnected activities.

The complexity of this distributed system is modelled using the UML class diagram (see Fig. 1), providing a structured visual representation of the interactions and dependencies among the different elements of the system.

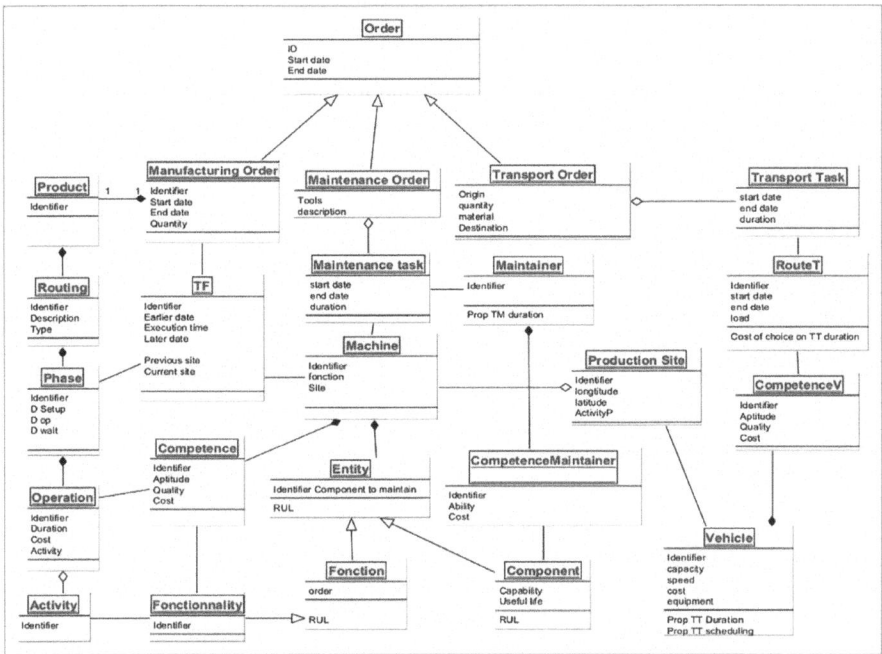

Fig. 1. Functional UML diagram modelling.

To solve our problem, we propose the SCEMPT model made of three improved SCEP models.

4   SCEMPT Model

4.1   Model Description

Our joint scheduling approach for production, transport, and maintenance relies on a MAS model because it aims at the collaboration of these three activities. None of these activities individually have the skills and knowledge to comprehensively solve the whole problem, so we need to gather the knowledge and reasoning abilities of several kinds of agents. Our MAS model is based on the SCEP model [16], where communication between the agents is done indirectly via a blackboard. Our proposed model introduces cooperation between three models:

- SCEMPT, made of a Supervisor, Customers, an Environment, Virtual Maintainers, Producers, Virtual Transporters,
- SCET made of a Supervisor, Customers, an Environment, Transporters.
- SCEM made of a Supervisor, Customers, an Environment, Maintainers.

As presented in Fig. 2, the first model primarily manages production scheduling, the second one handles transport scheduling, and the third one is dedicated to maintenance scheduling. Cooperation within each model occurs through the blackboard-like environment, where agents submit and retrieve information required to solve their sub-problems.

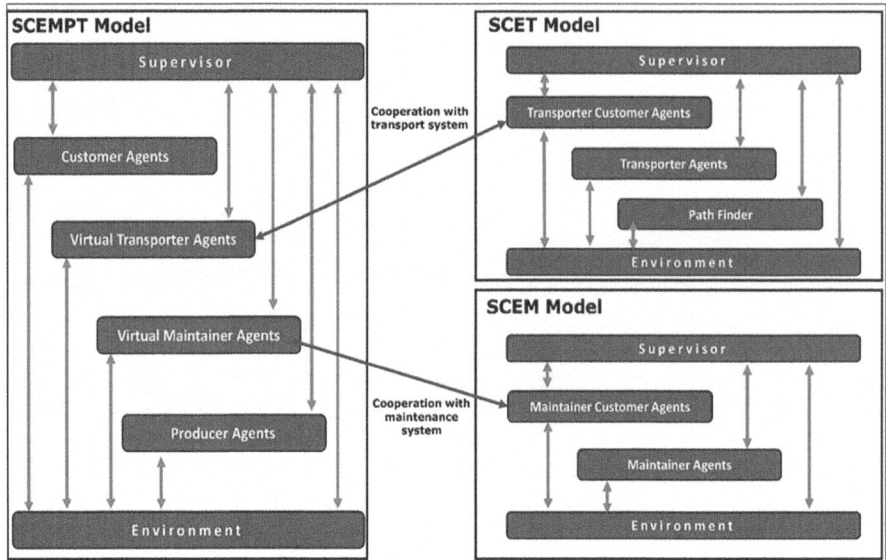

Fig. 2. SCEMPT Model Architecture.

SCEMPT Agents Description. The Supervisor Agent controls and grants access to the environment for other agents, triggering the cooperation cycle between them.

- Each Customer Agent corresponds to one manufacturing order (MOi), containing a sequence of TFs, following an order predetermined by the production range. A customer agent ensures that the MO execution does not starts earlier than its earliest start date (Ri) and demands to be delivered not later than its latest due date (Di). Each TF must begin only after the preceding task has been completed. Each TF contains information about the production site identifier.
- A Producer Agent corresponds to a machine (Mj), managing its associated functionalities, capabilities, and health status as described in [17]. It schedules the TFs on its list according to its objective and scheduling method. Because every producer has an objective (e.g., minimizing total tardiness of jobs, minimizing total cost), each producer schedules the TFs using its own scheduling rules such as First-In-First-Out (FIFO), Shortest Processing Time (SPT), or Longest Processing Time (LPT) depending on the production environment. These rules allow the producer agents to complete TFs scheduling. The producer agent constantly monitors the machine's condition by calculating the probabilities of failure. When the risk of failure of a component is too

high and will potentially disrupt the scheduling of TFs, the agent initiates a request for a TM for this component.

- Virtual Maintenance Agents manage cooperation between the producer and the maintainer in the SCEM model. They receive maintenance requests from the producers and request potential and effective proposals for each requested TM from the SCEM maintainer, then communicate these proposals back to the producers for planning purposes. The virtual agent approach has also been used in [21] based on the SCEP model, but with the addition of a distributor in a DSCEP architecture, mainly to address scheduling problems involving shared resources for an enterprises network.
- Virtual Transport Agents, as virtual maintenance agents, act as an intermediary between the producers and the transporters in the SCET model. The producers make a TT requests to account for their durations in the scheduling. The virtual transport agents send these requests to the transporter customers to obtain potential and effective proposals, allowing the producers to decide which transport resources to use.

SCEM Model Description. The model consists of a supervisor, maintenance customers, an environment, and maintainers. This model behaves similarly to the SCEP described in [16], but instead of relying on producer resources, it utilizes maintainer resources. These maintainers schedule the list of TMs based on the methods they implement and the skills they possess. Each maintainer prioritizes the list of TMs using the FIFO Rule, repairing the machines in the order the requests are received.

Nevertheless, given a situation in which the health of the machine is critical, the maintainer may rearrange its scheduled TMs to prioritize the most urgent repairs, minimizing down time.

In this model, the virtual maintainers from SCEMPT become customer maintainers. They receive maintenance requests from the virtual maintenance agents and forward them to the maintainers through the environment. They then receive proposals from the maintainers and send them back to the virtual maintainer.

SCET Model Description. SCET consists of a simplified version of POVES [18] without producer and transport companies agents and their interoperability interfaces with the collaborative environment. Like SCEM this model engages transporters who represent the transport resource associated with a vehicle. each transporter (vehicle) proposes positions during the auction across the environment.

In the SCET, each virtual transporter in the SCEMPT becomes a transport customer who receives transport requests, including information on origin, destination and product identifier. The system also provides information on transporters, corresponding to vehicles, as well as on the transport network.

The Pathfinder gathers information from the transport customer about the vehicle's current location, transport requests, and the details of the delivery, including the origin, destination, and the type of product being transported.

Based on the information received, Pathfinder analyzes the transport network and, by means of Dijkstra's algorithm, calculates the best possible route for each transport order, finding the shortest path. In graph theory, the transport network is a fully connected graph, and this algorithm finds the path that is least costly in distance, time, or another important factor in a very efficient way. With this calculation, every conceivable route between origin and destination is taken into account for the optimal course of the transport process.

SCEMPT introduces an indirect cooperation between SCET and SCEM. The collaboration protocol between them and between the agents is described by the UML sequence diagram (see Fig. 3).

4.2   Collaboration Protocol

At the beginning of the production cycle, the supervisor activates the customer agents and requests other agents to wait. These agents then launch their bids for Manufacturing Orders (MOs) within an environment composed of TFs. Each TF is represented by an object indicating information such as the desired completion date, otherwise known as the desired position, processing duration contingent on the machine's state, the skills required to perform the task, and the identifier of the production site responsible for its processing. Once the tasks are issued, the clients become idle, allowing the supervisor to activate the producer to intervene and make suitable proposals based on his competencies relative to the assigned tasks. The producer agent reads the TF information displayed in the environment and only proposes plans for those that are compatible with its machine's competencies. It schedules the TFs considering the health status of its machine, schedules its list of TFs according to its method and criteria, and calculates their EPs and PPs.

The EP for each TF is calculated by considering all the TFs in the list, i.e., the less favourable proposal, while the PP is estimated by considering the best possible proposal for each task within the environment. If a machine is unable to perform a TF due to a functionality that will be unavailable, the producer initiates maintenance request for the faulty components that will fail, thereby announcing a TM also associated with an object in the environment with its desired position. The supervisor then activates the virtual maintainer who manages the interoperability between the SCEMPT and SCEM distribution models to facilitate collaboration between the two planning systems. In the SCEM model, each maintainer reads the information of the TMs written in the environment and proposes EPs and PPs suitable according to their skills. Each producer then reviews the TM proposals made by the maintainer, accepting those where the EPs and PPs positions coincide, or choosing the less distant proposal from their Wished Position WP. Each production cycle must schedule at least one TF to avoid dead end.

Similarly, a transportation need can be triggered if a TF of a MO whose previous TF is processed by a different production site from the one of the producer agent, needs to be transferred. As in the previous approach, the supervisor activates the virtual transporter who manages the communication between the SCEMPT and SCET models, receiving a transport order with the desired position from the producer. Any transport request initiated by the producer is displayed in the environment in the SCET model, enabling the transport customer to ask the navigation system to propose the best possible route associated with each request. The transporter agents (vehicles) select tasks that match their activities and schedule the tasks according to their own rules of priority and capacity and propose EPs and PPs. After the vehicles have completed their scheduling, they record their proposals in the environment for evaluation by the transport customer and

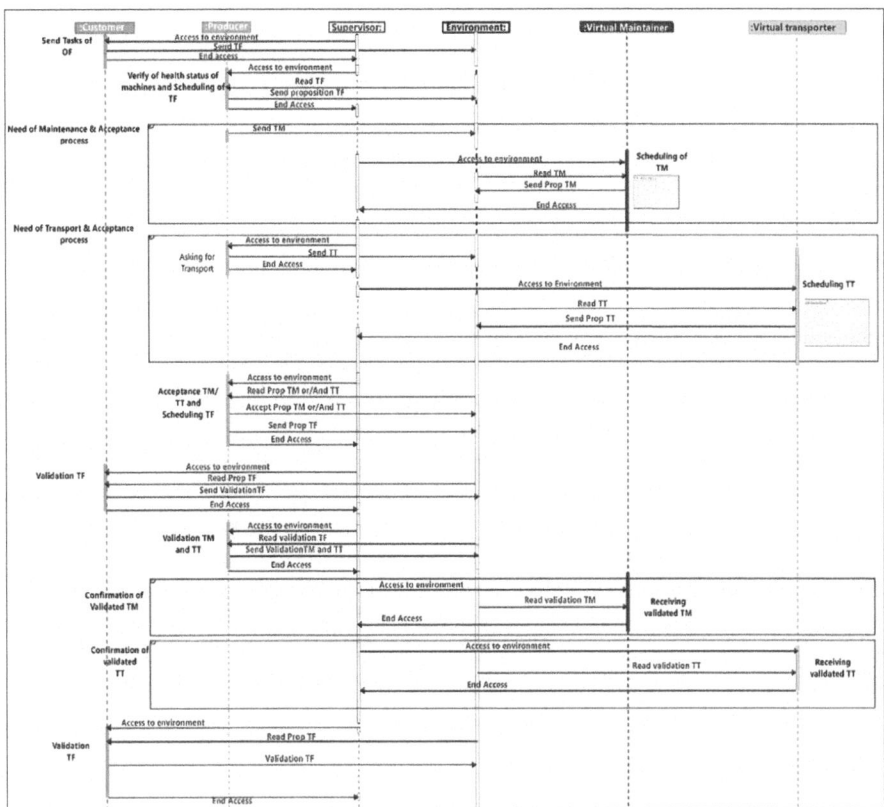

Fig. 3. Sequence diagram of SCEMPT Model.

the producer agent in the SCEMPT model. Each producer compares the proposed EPs and PPs with their desired positions and validates the best proposal (when the EP and the PP are the same). Otherwise, the task is retained for the next scheduling cycle.

Finally, the supervisor agent reactivates the customer agents to review the TF proposals made by the producer agent. Similar to the acceptance phase of TF and TT, each customer validates the best proposal provided the EP and PP positions are equivalent, otherwise, they prefer to wait for a possible proposal for the next scheduling cycle. It is important to note that each scheduling cycle must plan at least one TF and can plan at most one TF for each customer agent. At the end of this phase, the tasks retained by the customers then move to the "validated" state. The supervising agent reactivates the producer agents to be aware of the validations made by the customer agents, in order to decide whether or not to validate the TMs accepted during the current production cycle.

Each producer agent who wins a bid integrates the corresponding task into its planning, and a contract is thus assigned between the customer who requested the TF and its producer. Naturally, if none of a producer's proposals are selected, it is not necessary to perform the TMs requested by this producer during the current production cycle. Conversely, a validation process for TMs is initiated to decide whether an TM accepted by a producer should be validated or abandoned. Similarly, for the validation of transportation tasks during the production cycle, each producer agent integrates the TT into its schedule based on the TFs that are validated by the customer. If none of these proposals are retained, there will be no need to initiate transportation to process the TF during the current production cycle. Therefore, in each scheduling cycle, at least one TF from a given MO must be validated in order to move to the next cycle.

5 Conclusion

In this study, we presented a new SCEMPT model aimed at improving the joint scheduling of production, transportation, and maintenance activities in the context of cloud manufacturing. This model relies on a multi-agent system to provide efficient coordination and communication between different scheduling agents. Using the proposed framework and conception, the SCEMPT model uses communication protocols and agent functionality to optimize resource allocation and task execution, paving the way for significant advances in the way production, maintenance, and transportation activities are coordinated and executed.

Our future work will be focused on implementing the SCEMPT model in a real simulated environment, to evaluate its effectiveness in real-time scheduling scenarios. We expect to investigate various strategies for validation of transport and maintenance (TM) tasks, as well as meta-heuristic approaches to further optimize task scheduling.

References

1. Ehm, J., Freitag, M.: The benefit of integrating production and transport scheduling. Procedia CIRP **41**, 585–590 (2016). https://doi.org/10.1016/j.procir.2015.12.143
2. Zhu, T., Ran, Y., Zhou, X., Wen, Y.: A survey of predictive maintenance: systems, purposes and approaches. arXiv:1912.07383 (2024)
3. Lee, J., Ni, J., Singh, J., Jiang, B., Azamfar, M., Feng, J.: Intelligent maintenance systems and predictive manufacturing. J. Manuf. Sci. Eng. **142**(110805) (2020). https://doi.org/10.1115/1.4047856
4. Sauer, J., Appelrath, H.J.: Integrating transportation in a multi-site scheduling environment. In: Proceedings of the 33rd Annual Hawaii International Conference on System Sciences, p. 9. IEEE (2000)
5. Liu, P., Hendalianpour, A., Feylizadeh, M., Pedrycz, W.: Mathematical modeling of vehicle routing problem in omni-channel retailing. Appl. Soft Comput. **131**, 109791 (2022). https://doi.org/10.1016/j.asoc.2022.109791
6. Hendalianpour, A., Hamzehlou, M., Feylizadeh, M.R., Xie, N., Shakerizadeh, M.H.: Coordination and competition in two-echelon supply chain using grey revenue-sharing contracts. Grey Syst. Theory Appl. **11**(4), 681–706 (2021). https://doi.org/10.1108/GS-04-2020-0056
7. Liu, Y., Wang, L., Wang, X.V., Xu, X., Zhang, L.: Scheduling in cloud manufacturing: state-of-the-art and research challenges. Int. J. Prod. Res. **57**(15–16), 4854–4879 (2019). https://doi.org/10.1080/00207543.2018.1449978
8. Liu, Q., Dong, M., Chen, F.F.: Single-machine-based joint optimization of predictive maintenance planning and production scheduling. Robot. Comput. Integr. Manuf. **51**, 238–247 (2018). https://doi.org/10.1016/j.rcim.2018.01.002

9. Mifdal, L., Hajej, Z., Dellagi, S.: Joint optimization approach of maintenance and production planning for a multiple-product manufacturing system. Math. Probl. Eng. 2015 (2015). https://doi.org/10.3182/20140824-6-ZA-1003.02161

10. Qiu, S., Ming, X., Sallak, M., Lu, J.: Joint optimization of production and condition-based maintenance scheduling for make-to-order manufacturing systems. Comput. Ind. Eng. **162**, 107753 (2021). https://doi.org/10.1016/j.cie.2021.107753

11. Gharaei, A., Jolai, F.: An ERNSGA-III algorithm for the production and distribution planning problem in the multi-agent supply chain. Int. Trans. Oper. Res. **28**(4), 2139–2168 (2021). https://doi.org/10.1111/itor.12654

12. Yağmur, E., Kesen, S.E.: Bi-Objective Coordinated Production And Transportation Scheduling Problem With Sustainability: Formulation And Solution Approaches. Int. J. Prod. Res. **61**(3), 774–795 (2023). https://doi.org/10.1080/00207543.2021.2017054

13. Cruz Salazar, L.A., Ryashentseva, D., Lüder, A., Vogel-Heuser, B.: Cyber-physical production systems architecture based on multi-agent's design pattern—comparison of selected approaches mapping four agent patterns. Int. J. Adv. Manuf. Technol. **105**(9), 4005–4034 (2019). https://doi.org/10.1007/s00170-019-03800-4

14. Kang, S.G., Choi, S.H.: Multi-agent based beam search for intelligent production planning and scheduling. Int. J. Prod. Res. **48**(11), 3319–3353 (2010). https://doi.org/10.1080/00207540902810502

15. Shen, W., Wang, L., Hao, Q.: Agent-based distributed manufacturing process planning and scheduling: a state-of-the-art survey. IEEE Trans. Syst. Man Cybern. Part C (Appl. Rev.) **36**(4), 563–577 (2006). https://doi.org/10.1109/TSMCC.2006.874022

16. Archimede, B., Coudert, T.: Reactive scheduling using a multi-agent model: the SCEP framework. Eng. Appl. Artif. Intell. **14**(5), 667–683 (2001). https://doi.org/10.1016/S0952-1976(01)00025-2

17. Bencheikh, G., Letouzey, A., Desforges, X.: An approach for joint scheduling of production and predictive maintenance activities. J. Manuf. Syst. **64**, 546–560 (2022). https://doi.org/10.1016/j.jmsy.2022.08.005

18. Memon, M.A., Letouzey, A., Karray, M.H., Archimède, B.: Collaborating multiple 3PL enterprises for ontology-based interoperable transportation planning. In: Mertins, K., Bénaben, F., Poler, R., Bourrières, JP. (eds.) Enterprise Interoperability VI. Proceedings of the I-ESA Conferences, vol. 7, pp. 319–329. Springer, Cham (2014). https://doi.org/10.1007/978-3-319-04948-9_27

19. Desforges, X., Diévart, M., Archimede, B.: A prognostic function for complex systems to support production and maintenance co-operative planning based on an extension of object oriented Bayesian networks. Comput. Ind. **86**, 34–51 (2017). https://doi.org/10.1016/j.compind.2017.01.002

20. Parragh, S.N., Doerner, K.F., Hartl, R.F.: A survey on pickup and delivery problems. J. für Betriebswirtschaft **58**, 21–51 (2008). https://doi.org/10.1007/s11301-008-0033-7

21. Archimede, B., Letouzey, A., Memon, M.A., Xu, J.: Towards a distributed multi-agent framework for shared resources scheduling. J. Intell. Manuf. **25**(5), 1077–1087 (2014). https://doi.org/10.1007/s10845-013-0748-8

The Role of Actor's Creative Self-efficacy in AI Enabled Value Creation

Tuomas Hongisto[✉] and Jyri Vilko

LUT School of Engineering Sciences, LUT-University, Kauppalankatu 13,
45100 Kouvola, Finland
{tuomas.hongisto,jyri.vilko}@lut.fi

Abstract. Researching creativity remains crucial despite the growing use of AI, as human creativity drives innovation, problem-solving, and value creation in ways that AI alone cannot replicate. This study examines the impact of Solution-Focused (SF) coaching on individuals' creative self-efficacy (CSE) within AI-enabled environments. Core findings indicate that SF coaching significantly enhances CSE by increasing participants' awareness of their creative potential and cognitive abilities related to creativity. The study reveals that a clear coaching structure, personalized tools, and the quality of the coach-client relationship and interaction are essential for maximizing the benefits of SF coaching. These findings underscore the importance of fostering human creativity alongside AI to achieve dynamic and human-centric value creation in modern organizations.

Keywords: AI · Coaching · Collaborative innovations · Creativity · Creative · Self-Efficacy · Dialogue · Digital transformation · Industry 5.0 · Innovation · Organizational creativity · Self-Efficacy · Solution-Focused coaching · Value creation

1 Introduction

The increasing use of artificial intelligence (AI) technology, including generative AI tools, in organizations is becoming more apparent [1]. As these systems become more integrated into organizational practices and processes, it is also essential to focus on areas where humans excel. One such area is the ability to think differently, which distinguishes humans from other living things [2].

The integration and interaction of human work with AI presents new challenges and opportunities, especially in knowledge-intensive domains where AI capabilities overlap with those of humans [3]. While AI and robots are taking over many routine jobs, employees are increasingly engaged in creative and innovative tasks that leverage uniquely human skills. These abilities, such as sensorimotor skills, intuition, critical analysis, judgment, collaboration, creativity, social sensitivity, and problem-solving, are crucial in the 21st century to cope with industry transformation. [4].

It is unavoidable that the skills expected from individuals will change as change pressure increases in the future and adaptation to the evolving world becomes crucial

[2]. In a future of human–AI co-creative processes, where generative AI becomes more mainstream in creative endeavors, humans' ideation proficiency and a refined artistic filter, rather than pure mechanical skill, may become the focal skills required [5]. For example, it is argued that in the creative industries, including advertising, publishing, IT, and design, the successful adoption of generative AI lies in finding the delicate balance between maintaining human ingenuity and reaping the benefits of technological innovation [6].

It can be stated that one aspect of human ingenuity is creativity: the truly original and imaginative aspects of creativity, which involve human emotion and intention, remain a distinct human capability [7] as AI lacks the raw emotional depth and human experiences [8]. However, in organizations creativity has been seen as unrecognized phenomena. It has been described vague and slippery concept [8, 9]. There are also various preconceived notions and myths about creativity. Without scientific evidence, creativity is often linked to intelligence or the arts, considered to have something to do with magic, and thought to be based on personality [10]. These myths imply that creative abilities are static and innate, thus discouraging the belief that creativity can be cultivated through effort and learning. This kind of view means fixed-creative mindset; in general, creative mindset refers to beliefs about the stable-versus-malleable character and the nature of creativity [11].

Despite these fixed assumptions, it is possible to develop creativity by enhancing individuals' belief in their own creative productivity [12]. One relevant concept in this regard is creative self-efficacy (CSE). It is defined as "the belief one has the ability to produce creative outcomes" [13]. CSE is derived from Bandura's broader concept of self-efficacy, explained as a person's belief in their ability to successfully perform specific tasks or roles in particular settings [14].

Self-efficacy and creative performance have a likely relationship. It is suggested that self-efficacy beliefs are a key motivational component of individual creative action [15]. Further, it has been shown that CSE positively and significantly is related to creative performance [13]. According to Bandura, the reason for this relationship is the nature of creative work: innovativeness requires a firm sense of efficacy to persist in creative efforts when they demand prolonged investment of time and effort, progress is discouragingly slow, the outcome is highly uncertain, and creations are socially devalued when they are too inconsistent with existing customs [14].

Since CSE is an important factor of creative behavior and performance, it would be assumed that efforts to enhance belief in one's creative abilities should be a central component facilitating creative outcomes in the workplace. This assumption drives us to cognitive behavioral science. In the context of psychotherapy, utilizing cognitive modelling can bring out an individual's erroneous thoughts and beliefs, which they can actively assess while reinforcing beneficial thoughts by transforming less useful ones into more useful ones [16].

The focus in this study are the unique capabilities of humans in the realm of creativity. Study finds out how person's CSE can be developed with cognitive modeling. More specifically, it aims to determine **how solution-focused (SF) coaching affects an individual's CSE**. SF coaching refers to strength-based approaches that emphasize people's resilience, strengths, and resources and how these can be utilized in the pursuit of goals and the enactment of purposeful positive change [17]. The core of the research is to find out **what impact does SF coaching have on participant's CSE** and **how do various factors of the coaching process influence outcomes**.

Empirically this research is the first of its kind study to investigate the relationship between SF coaching and CSE. Further, it draws insights for the young field of the coaching research by completing entire coaching sessions with five different participants; in this research area there is a need for realistic coaching sessions instead of laboratory or partial study [18]. The study is conducted as a multiple case study, which according to Yin, refers to empirical research that investigates a contemporary phenomenon deeply within its real-life context, where the boundaries between the phenomenon and context are not clear [19].

2 Theoretical Background

The concept of value lies at the heart of human activities [2]. This chapter delves into how AI-human integration and interaction intersect to shape organizational dynamics and value creation. It explores how AI technologies augment decision-making and operational efficiency, complementing human creativity in achieving organizational goals such as increased productivity and enhanced customer experiences. Despite AI's capabilities, human creativity driven by intrinsic motivation and expertise remains pivotal for innovation in dynamic environments.

In the context of innovation, the chapter examines the role of CSE in fostering individual and organizational creativity. CSE, rooted in beliefs about one's ability to produce creative outcomes, influences how individuals leverage their creative potential within collaborative settings. Additionally, it underlines the relevance of SF coaching in guiding organizations through industrial transformation.

In summary, this chapter explores how leadership, AI-human integration, and interaction mutually influence each other. Specifically, it examines how creativity and CSE play pivotal roles in this dynamic interplay. The chapter emphasizes the significance of SF coaching in enhancing individuals' CSE within the context of AI integration and leadership practices.

2.1 Individual's Creativity in AI Based Value Creation

Productivity and efficiency benefits of AI can only be realized through intentional and functional collaboration between humans and the technology [1]. This collaboration refers to augmented intelligence, which means a process or application that combines the unique capabilities of both humans and AI technologies to enhance decision-making outcomes in organizational systems [20]. In AI-human collaboration value creation is defined as the impact of augmented intelligence systems on organizational performance and capability that is aligned with their strategic goals [20]. For example, the use of machine learning and AI in business intelligence allows organizations to process large volumes of data efficiently, uncover hidden patterns, make accurate predictions, and helps businesses understand customer behavior, personalize experiences, and create targeted marketing campaigns, leading to higher customer engagement, loyalty, and revenue growth [21]. Overall, AI–based value creation includes a broad range of organizational goals such as efficiency in decision making, teamwork in information and knowledge exchange, increased productivity, cost reduction, and improved customer experiences [20].

On the contrary, companies also need to innovate, meaning they must consistently and swiftly develop new value propositions to survive in dynamic market conditions. The need to innovate underscores the necessity for every company to actively pursue value creation to foster a productive and innovative workplace. [22] This can be related to organizational creativity which can be considered as the process of introducing the tools that will provide an environment for the creation of some innovative phenomena in the corporate structure, including the creativity of the employees [24]. It is supported that organizational creativity plays crucial role in AI-oriented enterprises having a positive effect both innovation and operational performance [2]. While AI brings its own unique capabilities, it is important to recognize the enduring value of human ingenuity and imaginative creativity [7]. Organizations will need creative people to find instruments to increase organizational creativity in order to survive and be flourishing in the future [2].

According to Amabile, creativity involves generating a novel and appropriate response, product, or solution to an open-ended task [23]. This means that the response must not only be new but also fitting and valuable to the task at hand. Additionally, the task must be heuristic, lacking a single obvious solution. Ultimately, creativity is judged by those familiar with the domain in which the response is produced.

In her componential theory of creativity, creativity is influenced by three within-individual components: domain-relevant skills (expertise in the relevant field), creativity-relevant processes (cognitive and personality traits that encourage novel thinking), and task motivation (intrinsic interest and enjoyment in the activity). The external component is the surrounding environment, particularly the social environment. [25] According to the theory, creativity peaks when an intrinsically motivated person with high domain expertise and strong creative thinking skills operates in a supportive environment [23].

Comparing to AI, human's creativity stands out in many ways: Generative AI tools lack the ability to harness human creativity, curiosity, and compassion [8], and may struggle to replicate the deeply personal and emotionally nuanced aspects of human expression [7]. Further, humans mark superiority over large language models (LLM) in social intelligence tasks [26]. Also, AI output can be inaccurate, less useful, and degrades human performance when operating outside of the technological frontier [3].

Overall, human unique capabilities should be central to creative processes, with AI serving as a collaborative tool to spark new ideas, streamline workflows, and accelerate creativity [6]. Within the framework of Amabile's theory [25], AI should enhance creativity-relevant processes – it can augment and enhance human creativity rather than replace it [7].

2.2 Creative Self-efficacy in Collaborative Innovations

Creativity research is moving beyond the exclude of traditional psychology and shifting away from an individual-centric approach [27]. Instead, it views creativity as emerging from the interactions between individuals and their situations. [28]. Based on meta-analysis, extensive interaction is significant for the creativity of teams and groups [29]. Further, creativity is no longer seen as solely a mental process; the social aspect is now considered inherent to creativity, which is viewed as emerging from interactions [30]. This idea is better understood through the "dialectical model" of creation, which integrates different perspectives through dialogue [31]. According to Isaacs dialogue can be defined as a continuous collective inquiry into the processes and assumptions that form everyday experience [32]. Dialogue aims to reveal the field of meaning shaped by collective tacit thinking that constructs an individual's worldview, from which various frames and action options emerge [32].

These arguments underline the importance of social environment in creative process. Maintaining an organizational climate that supports change and encourages creativity is a fundamental goal for managers as the environment in which organizations operate changes and becomes increasingly competitive [33]. In the future, the greatest strength of organizations will be their intellectual capital, comprised of creative people and innovative ideas. Successful organizations will distinguish themselves from competitors by motivating employees to continually enhance their intellectual capabilities. [2] The ongoing digital revolution, marked by rapid technological advancements, has paved the way for innovative collaboration among companies, organizations, and governments of all sizes [6].

One way to motivate employees to enhance intellectual capabilities is to support their self-efficacy development. In the school context, self-efficacy has appeared to be a highly effective predictor of students' motivation and learning [34]. Comparing to fixed personal traits, CSE is a dynamic and changeable belief which is related to individual's curiosity [11]. In general. Self-efficacy, as a performance-based measure of perceived capability, is conceptually and psychometrically distinct from related motivational constructs like outcome expectations, self-concept, and locus of control [34].

Regarding the challenges of innovation, self-efficacy plays a crucial motivational role in individual achievement [14]. Humans need a sense of perseverance to overcome obstacles they may encounter on their path to success. For example, persistence is one of the factors that enables creative thinking [9]. Self-efficacy fosters this sense by promoting positive outcome expectations [15]. Additionally, an optimistic sense of self-efficacy enhances psychological well-being and goal attainment [14].

Various factors influence efficacy beliefs. These beliefs are dynamically shaped by a person's past performance history with similar tasks, as well as by socio-psychological circumstances in the performance setting, such as physiological state (e.g., feeling tired vs. energized), social persuasion (e.g., receiving encouragement from trusted sources), and vicarious experiences (e.g., observing relatable models) [14]. Additionally, there are other socio-psychological and material aspects of the performance setting to consider. These include creative affordances provided by physical objects in the environment (e.g., generating various uses for a object), current and past relational interactions with individuals in the environment (e.g., encounters with a bully), and even dialogical aspects (e.g., internal dialogue with real or imagined conversational partners) [35].

CSE has many different roles in the dynamics of creativity related phenomena. Firstly, based on meta-analysis, CSE and creative results have a consistent and moderately strong relationship [36]. Secondly, CSE acts as a moderator between an individual's creative expectations and positive creative outcomes [36]. Additionally, individuals with high CSE showed a stronger relationship between creative expectations and participation in creative work compared to those with low CSE [37]. Organizational factors can enhance this relationship: the results of the study indicated that workplace demands for creativity can increase the creativity of individuals with high CSE [38] Furthermore, CSE can act as a moderator between individual and group resources: it positively influences how individuals utilize resources from the group in creative activities [36].

Thirdly, empirical evidence shows that CSE serves as a significant mediator between creativity and other factors [36]. From a motivational perspective CSE mediated the effects of learning orientation on creativity [39]. The same study also found that it mediated the effects of transformational leadership on employee creativity. Regarding job characteristics, CSE mediated the effects of tasks requiring problem-solving skills on creativity, particularly when intrinsic motivation was high [40].

The impact of CSE is primarily cognitive, increasing an individual's awareness and focus on creativity-enhancing behaviors [36]. It has been observed that CSE affects partly in radical creativity increasing environment scanning [41]. However, CSE clearly has cognitive foundations, it is also possible that it serves as an affective influence on creativity, generating certain emotions or states of mind [36]. For example, CSE can act as a mediator between the feeling of optimism and innovative behavior [42].

2.3 The Relevance of Solution-Focused Coaching in Industrial Transformation

Despite the rising use of AI, it is still uncertain how these new digital applications transform industrial work [43]. However, digital transformation is a process that leads to disruptive changes in companies and affects all business processes. This means that leaders should have the ability to manage both the digital transformation process and the new digital organization that is emerging. [44] For example, middle managers in the digital era must step up their role of supporting, enabling and coaching people to use the available digital tools, and are expected to facilitate the organization [45]. Leader's strong support for digital transformation can facilitate worker adoption of AI [46]. Additionally, motivation is crucial for successfully managing digital transformation. In this context, leaders should act as motivating coaches throughout the digital transformation process. [44].

From this perspective, coaching leadership and coaching in general are essential tools to lead organization in the waves of digital transformation. More importantly, coaching can be a major factor in Industry 5.0 leadership practices, as explained later. In general, Industry 5.0 is defined by a re-found and widened purposefulness, going beyond producing goods and services for profit [47]. The wider purpose constitutes three core elements: human-centricity, sustainability, and resilience.

A human-centric approach in industry prioritizes core human needs and interests in the production process. Instead of asking what can be done with new technology, the focus is on what technology can do for us. Rather than requiring workers to adapt to rapidly evolving technology, technology is used to adapt the production process to the workers' needs, such as guiding and training them. Workers are viewed not as costs but as investments, allowing both the company and the worker to develop. This approach values human capital by investing in employees' skills, capabilities, and well-being, rather than merely balancing worker costs with financial revenue. [47].

These insights reflect with the definition of a SF approach, which is a strengths-based practice that emphasizes individuals' resources and flexibility and how these can be utilized in deliberate positive change [48]. As the Industry 5.0 is placing the wellbeing of the industry worker at the center of the production process [47], the client is in the center of coaching process: In SF coaching, the fundamental belief is that people are more likely to change and achieve their goals quickly if they utilize their own resources and solutions. Therefore, coach's role is to encourage them to find what works for them, reinforce their solutions, and ask how they could expand their repertoire of solutions. [49].

In general, there is different approaches and methods regarding to coaching [50]. However, all these approaches have a common similarity: a systematic process designed to promote development related to cognition, emotions, or behavior; intended for healthy individuals; a personalized and tailored approach; aimed at encouraging clients to take responsibility for their lives; based on the growth of awareness and accountability; skills of listening and questioning; a collaborative and equal relationship; to create a relationship in which the client takes responsibility for their own choices, and; to access the individual's inner creativity by utilizing their knowledge, experience, and intuition [50]. Overall, one key feature is central to most approaches: focusing on achieving a clear goal rather than analyzing the problem [50].

Coaching follows a certain process. For example, GROW-model consist of four different steps as a process: setting **goals**, mapping the current **reality**, creating **options**, and the **will** to implement the chosen course of action [51]. However using a certain model, the process should be allowed to vary. For instance, eliciting positive emotions during the process did not negatively impact goal achievement; instead, it enhanced positive emotions while reducing negative ones [52]. Overall, processes and models are not coaching in themselves; the effectiveness arises from the coach's awareness and responsibility, which are generated through active listening and powerful questioning within the process [51].

The effectiveness of SF practices is supported by empirical evidence. In meta-analysis, the SF approach proved to be an effective method for treating internal behavioral disorders, such as depression, self-concept, and self-esteem [53]. In group therapy context, SF approach increased children's perceived sense of self-efficacy [54]. Furthermore, comparing problem-focused and solution-focused approaches in coaching showed that solution-focused questions were a more effective way to enhance clients' overall self-efficacy [18, 55] It is noteworthy that when using the SF approach, a greater number of coaching sessions did not lead to stronger positive effects [56].

In general, the effectiveness of coaching depends upon different factors. According to Killburg, there are eight different factors that affect how well the coaching process achieves its objectives: client's commitment to the path of progressive development; coach's commitment to the path of progressive development; characteristics and the client's problems and issues; structure of the coaching containment; client-coach relationship; quality of coaching interventions; adherence protocol; and organizational settings [57]. In the other point of view, the effectiveness has nine different elements:

the learning relationship is at the core of change; the client decides the agenda and is resourceful; the coach facilitates learning and development; the context; the outcome is change and action; the used model provides movement and direction for the process; coach's skill development to release client's potential and deliver results; the coach as a person; and ethical practices [58].

There is evidence for the development of general self-efficacy through coaching. Leaders' self-efficacy has improved with coaching interventions lasting four months [59] and one year [60]. Furthermore, leaders' self-efficacy has improved with just six coaching sessions [61]. Employees' self-efficacy increased when leaders coached them in interventions lasting five days [62] and six months [63].

The effects of coaching on self-efficacy are multifaceted. As mentioned earlier, self-efficacy can be modified, and its building blocks include successful experiences, vicarious learning, verbal persuasion, physical and psychological states, and internal dialogue. According to the literature, these factors are an essential part of coaching. For example, the goal of coaching is to increase the coachees' self-awareness and sense of responsibility for change, thereby encouraging learning, goal achievement, and ultimately improving performance [51, 60]. This assumption is based on the coaching mindset that all individuals could achieve their goals [51].

It is suggested that the impact of coaching is based on the development of the individual's cognitive processing [60]. Coaching enhances client's self-reflection by challenging destructive and harmful thought pattern that are injurious to self-efficacy [64]. Through coaching, clients could respond more positively and constructively to their experiences [60]. In practice, clients should be encouraged to recognize and understand the patterns in their minds that shape their thinking and behavior, and harmful thought patterns should be replaced with constructive and productive thinking [64].

3   Research Design

3.1   Methodology

The study is conducted as a multiple case study, which refers to a research situation where the study includes multiple cases that are examined. Compared to a single case study, evidence obtained from multiple cases can be considered more compelling and robust. [19].

The sample is chosen with random selection. The purpose is to avoid systematic biases in the sample and achieve a representative sample that allows for generalization for the entire population [65]. This approach reduces the risk of bias in the results due to the homogeneity of the target group, even though demographic factors do not influence the relationship between creativity and CSE [66]. The typical sample size criteria cannot be applied when determining the number of cases in a multiple case study [19]. However, the sample's size is decisive for generalization [65]. With five, six, or more repetitions, the research results can be considered more reliable and robust compared to studies with only two or three cases [19]. In this study, the sample consists of five participants, both male and female, with diverse backgrounds: an entrepreneur, an artist, two adult students, and a business manager.

3.2 Research Process and Data

A single case study progresses through three stages: initial assessment, coaching process, and conclusion. During the initial assessment, participant is contacted and explained how the process will be conducted. At the end of this phase, participant fills out coaching agreement, defines their goals for the process, and commits to participating in the study. Before the first meeting, participant completes a CSE questionnaire.

The coaching process itself includes three 60-min sessions, spaced about one to two weeks apart. For each session, the participant prepares a topic to discuss in advance. The coaching process follows the GROW model, and participants are given homework assignments, which may vary according to their needs. Common assignments include the creativity index survey, the strengths survey, and keeping a journal of their creative successes. In the final stage, the participant completes the CSE questionnaire again, and the interview is conducted.

There are several things to consider when measuring CSE. Firstly, the questionnaire should be future oriented (e.g. "I'm confident that I will..."). Secondly, the measures should capture respondents' confidence (e.g., "How sure are you that you can..."). Thirdly, by using broader response scales, such as 1–100, scale restriction or inflated self-assessments are avoided. [35] The used questionnaire is based on Abbott's dissertation, measuring an individual's CSE through themes of creative thinking and creative activity [67].

One of the most important sources of information in a case study is the interview. Its benefits include its focus, allowing direct attention to the subject being studied. Additionally, it is insightful, providing causal inferences and explanations. [19] In this study the thematic interview is conducted in the end of process. The interview consists of three phases: warm-up questions, main questions, and conclusion. The warm-up questions ask for general information about the participants, such as their current job description and how creativity manifests in their life. Following this, the main questions proceed first exploring the sources of the participant's CSE. Then, answers are sought regarding changes in CSE and their causes. The second main question theme is to examine various factors of the coaching process and their impact on the participant's experience of the process. Finally, the interview concludes by asking if the participant has anything else to add.

The interviews have been interpreted by thematic analysis. According to Aronson [68] thematic analysis consists of the following stages:

1. Collecting data from audio recordings or interviews.
2. Identifying patterns within this data.
3. Expanding and explaining these patterns.
4. Grouping related patterns into sub-themes.
5. Constructing an argument for the selection of themes by reviewing relevant literature.
6. Using themes to construct a narrative that aids in understanding the research process outcomes.

After data collection, Aronson suggests that the subsequent stages of thematic analysis involve analyzing the data: first identifying recurring patterns, then explaining and expanding upon these patterns, and next grouping them into sub-themes. The next step is to construct a coherent argument for the selection of themes. This is achieved by connecting the data to established theories. Returning to the literature provides the interviewer with information to draw conclusions from the interviews. Following this, the researcher is prepared to formulate themes to develop the narrative. [68].

4 Results and Analysis

The results are demonstrated in two phases. Firstly, the changes of CSE are presented showing the changes that have occurred in CSE when comparing the initial and final survey. Secondly, the reasons for these changes are explored based on the data of interviews.

4.1 Variation in Creative Self-efficacy

In only two statements, no participant experienced any change. Overall, in the last three statements, which measured personality, there was practically no change. This can be explained by the already high CSE ratings of the participants. For the last statement, one participant's initial survey rating was 50 points, with a change of 60 percent. In the other three statements, each participant's rating was at least 75 points (see Table 1).

In statement 14, there was a change for all participants except the third one. The lack of change can be explained by the third participant's understanding of the nature of the question and the high self-rating in the initial survey: "At first glance, the question may seem manipulative. I like to network without conscious ulterior motives, so my self-assessment is high." For other participants, the positive change indicates an affective and cognitive shift: their emotional state and beliefs in their creative abilities improved positively. Interviews revealed that participants experienced this change as an increase in relaxation and self-confidence. According to Ford, strong positive self-efficacy beliefs, such as self-confidence, can enhance an individual's creativity [15].

In this case, the enhancement is seen in the confidence in one's creative abilities, which can convince others of their creativity.

A significant change occurred also in statement 8 for all participants except the fourth one. This is partly explained by the fact that the fourth participant had already rated statement at 75 points in the initial survey. The change in statement 8 reflects the development of ideation skills, supported by changes in statements 1 and 4. Overall, this development indicates changes in the participant's cognition related to creative processes. According to Amabile, in the cognitive process of creativity, an individual should be able to think broadly and flexibly in combining information and be able to break beliefs related to perceptions and performance [23].

CSE development varied among different participants in other statements. The reason for the lack of development or negative changes in certain areas was mainly due to the already high level of confidence. Also, participants said that the statements were quite open-ended and multifaceted, making it difficult to form precise evaluations, and the assessments could vary depending on one's mood.

Table 1. The changes of CSE.

Statement	Participant 1			Participant 2			Participant 3			Participant 4			Participant 5		
	start	end	%	start	end	%	start	end	%	start	end	%	start	end	%
1. Come up with many possible solutions to a problem	80	100	25 %	40	60	50 %	33	80	142 %	80	95	19 %	60	70	17 %
2. Arrive at a variety of conclusions given a difficult situation	90	90	0 %	50	70	40 %	75	60	−20%	60	80	33 %	60	60	0 %
3. Come up with different kinds of responses, not just different responses	70	80	14 %	40	50	25 %	75	75	0 %	60	90	50 %	80	80	0 %
4. Answer problems in different ways, each of which are unique and special	60	80	33 %	50	60	20 %	65	75	15 %	30	80	167%	40	50	25 %
5. Think of ways to defend a 'crazy' thought, by thinking back on what you already know	80	100	25 %	60	70	17 %	50	75	50 %	70	90	29 %	60	80	33 %
6. Talk to your friends about wild ideas, and make them sound reasonable	50	90	80 %	60	70	17 %	80	80	0 %	90	85	−6%	80	88	10 %
7. Tell stories based on dreams you had, even if you need to fill in answers	40	90	125 %	60	70	17 %	75	75	0 %	90	75	−17%	80	90	13 %
8. Be the first in a group to come up with an original suggestion	70	90	29 %	30	70	133 %	20	60	200 %	75	85	13 %	60	80	33 %
9. Arrive at a novel solution before other people	50	90	80 %	70	80	14 %	20	50	150 %	85	90	6 %	50	60	20 %
10. Make sense of something you want to learn to do	90	100	11 %	70	90	29 %	90	90	0 %	70	85	21 %	100	100	0 %
11. Start to learn to do something, even if there are obstacles to doing so	70	100	43 %	90	90	0 %	90	90	0 %	45	78	73 %	50	100	100 %
12. Teach yourself how to do something new	80	100	25 %	80	80	0 %	90	90	0 %	50	88	76 %	50	90	80 %
13. Create a novelty that people will choose, over other novelties available	80	80	0 %	60	80	33 %	50	70	40 %	95	95	0 %	70	90	29 %
14. Network with people to convince them that what you made is the best	30	100	233 %	40	50	25 %	75	75	0 %	40	90	125 %	50	90	80 %
15. Be motivated to come up with new ideas	90	100	11 %	90	90	0 %	75	85	13 %	95	100	5 %	100	100	0 %
16. Have fun coming up with new ideas, after having learned from others	90	100	11 %	100	90	−10%	90	80	−11%	80	95	19 %	100	100	0 %
17. Sustain wonder about something, even after working with it for years or decades	90	90	0 %	50	80	60 %	90	90	0 %	95	98	3 %	100	100	0 %

4.2 Results of the Interviews

The sources of CSE generally supported the claims in the literature (see Table 2). There were differences in the sources of CSE among the participants, reflecting the diversity of these sources. Of Bandura's [14] four sources, three appeared directly in at least one participant. Additionally, the fourth source, verbal persuasion, was evident in the fourth participant in such a way that its absence acted as a factor weakening CSE. Among the sources identified by Beghetto and Karwowski [35], inner speech was found in two participants. For the fifth participant, this inner speech refers to concept of dialogue between creativity and the self [69]. Furthermore, one source of CSE for the fifth participant did not appear directly in the literature: the participant's internal drive and feeling that creativity is a part of one's life. This feeling strengthened the participant's ability beliefs affecting "compelling need to create".

The obstacles of creativity were primarily based on the social environment, which for respondents meant two different factors: close personal relationships and cultural norms. These observations align with Amabile's view that intrinsic motivation is significantly influenced by the social environment [23]. This includes all external incentives shown to undermine intrinsic motivation, as well as various other environmental factors that can act as barriers to intrinsic motivation and creativity. Furthermore, according to Ford's theory, creating shared understanding impacts creative activity [15]. In the participants' cases, the social environment limited creativity through the scarcity of schemas, such as the mental model of the lack of creativity in engineers, and promoted habits through automatic problem interpretation, such as "one cannot make a living as an artist." In other point of view these observations of the social environment refers to Csikszentmihalyi's systems model of creativity, where culture is seen as a system that regulates human consciousness, including thoughts, emotions, beliefs, and intentional actions [70]. In this case, these norms and attitudes negatively affected the participants.

The changes experienced by the participants can be linked to Farmer and Tierney's [36] analysis, which suggests that CSE directly influences creative activity: for one participant, the development of self-efficacy led to more boldly presenting ideas, while for another participant, it manifested as increased "propellor-headedness." The observations further support the role of CSE as a moderator between creative expectations and positive creative outcomes. Strengthened beliefs in their creativity led participants to act more creatively and achieve positive creative results. For the first participant, this development was evident in more active participation in facilitating creativity-enhancing interactions. For the second participant, it was the courage to present own ideas. For the third participant, it appeared in sparring with colleagues, and for the fourth participant, facilitating meetings with customers. These observations support the argument, that high CSE increases participation in creative work [37]. In other words, increased CSE encouraged participants to believe they could produce valuable creative outcomes, motivating them to engage more actively in creative processes.

The changes experienced by the participants can be linked to Farmer and Tierney's [36] analysis, which suggests that CSE directly influences creative activity: for one participant, the development of self-efficacy led to more boldly presenting ideas, while for another participant, it manifested as increased "propellor-headedness." The observations further support the role of CSE as a moderator between creative expectations and positive creative outcomes. Strengthened beliefs in their creativity led participants to act more creatively and achieve positive creative results. For the first participant, this development was evident in more active participation in facilitating creativity-enhancing interactions. For the second participant, it was the courage to present own ideas. For the third participant, it appeared in sparring with colleagues, and for the fourth participant, facilitating meetings with customers. These observations support the argument, that high CSE increases participation in creative work [37]. In other words, increased CSE encouraged participants to believe they could produce valuable creative outcomes, motivating them to engage more actively in creative processes.

The participants' results also partially support previous empirical evidence suggesting that CSE acts as a significant mediator between creativity and other factors [36]. For

Table 2. Categorized summary of the interviews.

Categories	Participant 1	Participant 2	Participant 3	Participant 4	Participant 5
Sources of CSE	Experiences	Vicarious learning, psychological state	Vicarious learning, psychological state	Experiences, inner dialogue	Experiences, inner dialogue, gut feeling
Obstacles of creativity	Social norms	Social norms, beliefs, experiences	Social norms	Social norms, fixed mindset	Social environment, beliefs
Change during process	Networking with other, understanding of the multidimensionality of life	Courage to bring out own ideas	Inventiveness	Finding strengths and clarity about the future	Focusing on career and taking care of yourself
Exact transition	Affective and cognitive: relaxation, increased awareness	Affective and cognitive: increased awareness and confidence	Cognitive: increased awareness, creative mindset	Affective and cognitive: increased awareness and confidence	Affective and cognitive: increased awareness and confidence, expansion of thought
Relevance of coaching	Initiating change, spotting alternatives	Increased reflection, creativity became visible	Increased reflection	Reflection and feedback have increased self-esteem	Initiating change, increased reflection
Structure of coaching	Clear and straightforward	Meetings more closely	Meetings less often	Clear and suitably dense	The need for more meetings
Homework	Journal was useful	Journal was useful, others not	Useful	Useful, how to make sure they are done?	Journal was useful
Coach's performance	The guidance was suitably relaxed	Logical, the guidance was suitably relaxed	The guidance was suitably relaxed	Sturdy guidance, easy to "jump in"	Kind but guidance control
Relationship	Warm-hearted, confidence	Warm-hearted, confidence, openness, sincerity	Equality	Openness, confidence, relaxation	Warm-hearted, confidence, empathy, compassion

(continued)

Table 2. (*continued*)

Categories	Participant 1	Participant 2	Participant 3	Participant 4	Participant 5
Interaction	Dialogical, fluent	Dialogical, simple, active listening	Dialogical, respectable, confidential, fluent	Dialogical, simple, fluent, insightful	Dialogical, simple, fluent
Participant's readiness for chance	Life experience, motivation, curiosity	Motivation	Openness	Life experience, openness, curiosity	Life experience, openness, motivation

the fifth participant, this change was concretely visible in the development of learning orientation [39], demonstrating a commitment to improving own skills by deciding to pursue further art studies. Furthermore, the participants' results confirmed Farmer and Tierney's view that the impact of CSE is primarily cognitive, increasing an individual's awareness and focus on creativity-enhancing behaviors [36]. This was evidenced by each participant mentioning increased awareness as an important change resulting from the development of CSE. Additionally, other clear cognitive changes were observed in all participants except the second one. These changes included an expanded concept of creativity, self-reflection questioning thought patterns, and the adoption of a creative mindset or growth mindset.

The results also provide hints of suggestion that CSE serves as an affective influence on creativity, generating certain emotions or states of mind [36]. Participants reported increased self-confidence during the process, which may indicate the emotion or state of mind presented by Farmer and Tierney [36]. On the other hand, self-confidence, or confidence in one's creativity, is the core of CSE, making it potentially meaningless to distinguish it as a separate emotion or state of mind. Additionally, other affective impacts were also evident: participants 1 and 4 reported positive emotions, such as increased relaxation and playfulness, because of the process.

Concrete changes in internal motivation were mainly evident in the fifth participant. This was reflected by motivation to apply for further art studies and an increased sense of resilience compared to before. Similar clear changes were not observed in other participants during the interviews. However, it should be noted that the interviews did not directly ask if participants experienced changes in intrinsic motivation.

The coaching process acted as a driver of change in various ways. The most significant factor was the initiation of change and the emergence of reflection. Reflection was characterized as occurring both during and outside coaching sessions. This directly refers to view that effective coaching enables reflection, which leads to change and produces valuable outcomes [58]. In other words, this perception supports the argument that coaching sessions serve as a catalyst for changes that occur in the client's real world [58].

The emergence of reflection and its impact on creativity can be explained using Hargadon and Bechky's collective model of creativity [71]. According to the theory, reflective reframing occurs in situations where individuals in social interactions reinterpret what they already know. Creativity moves to a collective level when everyone's contributions not only shape others' subsequent contributions but also give new meaning to previous inputs from others. Recognizing potentially relevant new ideas and insights and reframing problematic situations require participants to consciously consider these contributions and alter their previous understanding of both the problem and the relevant solution. [71].

The coaching structure was generally perceived as effective. Suggestions for improvement were related to the number and scheduling of coaching sessions. These suggestions varied, so the results do not provide a clear indication of how the structure could be improved without new research to test these suggestions. Regarding structure, the creativity journal as a homework assignment was unanimously found to be beneficial and had a concrete impact on increasing participants' awareness. In other words, homework formed a process that created opportunities for success and reinforced achievements through effort [64]. The creativity journal demonstrated early improvements in performance. Other homework assignments received mixed feedback, and their benefits were not clear.

All participants gave positive feedback on coach's approach. The second participant found a few questions too challenging to understand. Based on the interviews, coach's guidance approach ensured that sessions stayed on topic without being overly directive. This approach facilitated reflection and placed the participant at the center of the process. In the effective coaching, the client should be at the center of the process, with the coach's goal being to help the client clarify what they want and how to achieve their goals using their own resources [58]. Being at the center helps the client commit to the learning process and achieve their goals.

The client-coach relationship was deemed successful for each participant. Participants' views on the quality of the relationship strongly resonated with Kilburg's theory of effective coaching, which emphasizes the importance of the client-coach relationship [57]. Additionally, participants considered the relationship significant for enabling change. These experiences reflect Connor and Pokora's model, which places the relationship at the core of coaching [58]. The essential point is that learning, and change occur in relation to the coach, rather than being driven by specific coaching models. The results suggest that the coaching was dialogic and partnership-based, as characterized by Connor and Pokora [58].

Each participant described the interaction as dialogic in some way. Significant observations included ease and simply, forward flow, smoothness, fluentness, and active listening. Additionally, the fourth and fifth participants noted how the interaction facilitated insights. According to them, the interaction led the participant to independently discover solutions to problems without external suggestions. These observations align with the view of dialogue aiming to produce insight and convey change in the formative "ground" from which experience arises [72].

Key factors in participants' readiness for change were openness, life experience, and motivation. According to Kilburg's model, each of these characteristics are a key factor in client's commitment [57].

5   Discussion and Conclusions

The aim of the study was to investigate how SF coaching affects an individual's CSE. The first research question examined the impacts of SF coaching on the participants' CSE. In all cases each participant's CSE improved through coaching. The results confirmed that CSE can be enhanced by adjusting beliefs. This change was unique for each participant, although there were similarities. The most significant and consistent changes occurred in ideation and networking. The personality related to creative activity did not develop significantly, mainly due to an already high level of self-confidence in the assessed statements.

The most significant factor in the impact of coaching on CSE was the development of cognition. For participants, this meant increased awareness, which supports the observation about the impact of CSE on cognition [36]. On the other hand, the results suggested that coaching increased the participant's awareness, which enabled the development of CSE. In other words, increased awareness strengthened CSE rather than the other way around. In addition to awareness, coaching influenced other cognitive factors and affective factors, promoting CSE either directly or indirectly.

The second research question explored how different elements of the coaching process affect the outcomes. The structure of coaching should be clear and guided, allowing the participant to "immerse" in the process. Homework assignments that engage the participant and demonstrate performance improvement support the development of self-efficacy. The coach's approach should enable participant reflection and centrality, which is essential for their learning process and goal achievement. The tools used should be tailored to each participant, and the process should deviate as necessary. The goal is to build and maintain the client's self-confidence [51].

Both theory and empirical evidence indicated that the relationship between the client and the coach is a key factor in enabling change. The learning relationship is built around trust, where the coach's human side is essential for creating an equal partnership. Furthermore, it is crucial that the coach can consider the client's context and, if necessary, interrupt the planned activity to focus on what is important for the client at that moment.

Interaction should be dialogical, enabling the client's internal reflection and the resulting insights. The foundation for dialogue is the coach's active listening. According to Isaacs to foster dialogue, the person should interrupt automatic thought patterns, observe their own thinking, listen to their own listening, and avoid the urge to act as an expert improving or developing other's views [32].

When the client is at the center of coaching, they must be motivated to achieve their goals. Additionally, openness and life experience are factors that facilitate change.

The research task was to find out how SF coaching affects an individual's CSE. In summary, based on the two research questions, it can be concluded that the coaching process has acted as a cognitive and affective exploration of one's internal processes and assumptions, enabling reflection. Coaching has changed and expanded the participants' beliefs and emotions related to creativity, which were previously influenced by various factors in the social environment.

Coaching has functioned as collaborative creative process. In this respect, coaching has created a collective process, as per Hardagon and Bechky's [71] theory, enabling reflective reframing. This is strongly linked to Isaacs' definition of dialogue, which can be seen as a continuous collective inquiry into the processes and assumptions that form everyday experience [32]. Furthermore, according to Isaacs, dialogue aims to reveal the field of meaning shaped by collective tacit thinking, which constructs an individual's worldview from which various frameworks and action options emerge [32].

In this regard, coaching has brought participants' mental models and beliefs to the surface, and through the process, borrowing from famous theoretical physicists Bohm the flow of meaning has enabled the emergence of new understanding [73]. All this has been built around the building blocks of effective coaching, centered on the learning relationship model of Connor and Pokora [58]. Participant's learning and change have occurred in relation to the coach, where the effect has been enabled by a dialogical and partnership-based relationship.

5.1　Implications for Research and Practice

This study highlighted the importance of human's creativity in the era of AI. Also, this research has contributed new scientific value by shedding light on the effects of SF coaching on individual CSE. The study was the first of its kind to examine the impact of SF coaching on CSE. Additionally, it provided valuable insights for the emerging field of coaching research by elucidating how different elements of the coaching process influence outcomes. The study also explored the collective emergence of creativity and identified factors that influence the relationship between creativity and interaction.

From a leadership and organizational perspective, the research demonstrated that coaching is an effective tool for influencing individuals' beliefs. Leaders should recognize and provide opportunities for coaching within the organization to fully leverage employees' personal strengths and creative resources. Despite the digital transformation, organizations should invest in training leaders in coaching skills to be better to guide and support their subordinates towards enhanced creative performance. Promoting a coaching leadership style can also improve team dynamics and both creativity and innovation capacity bringing organizations towards Industry 5.0 and human-centric approach.

Organizations should also incorporate "creativity stop points" into their strategies—moments or processes where employees can pause their routine tasks and focus on practicing and developing creativity. Leaders should also understand the impact of the social environment on creativity and foster a culture that supports and encourages creative thinking and action. This involves openness to new ideas, a permissive attitude towards failure, and constructive feedback that helps employees recognize and utilize their creative potential.

5.2　Limitations and Further Research

There are several limitations to consider. Firstly, the researcher participated actively to coaching process by being a coach for each participant. This can cause biases to the methodology by distorting data and the results. Despite this, the research has strived for objectivity. For instance, the latest studies and practices on the subject have been utilized when developing metrics and surveys. Also, the credibility of the participants' results was reinforced by consistent observations from the literature that aligned with the empirical data.

Secondly, the validity of the results is limited by the significance of the relationship between the coach and the client for the effectiveness of coaching. Although this study demonstrated the recurrence of certain phenomena across different cases related to CSE and SF coaching, the results might not be the same if conducted by a different coach and client.

Thirdly, the significant limitation was the duration of the process. The limitations of the three 60-min sessions, spanning a total of approximately four weeks, overshadow the assessment of long-term effectiveness. It is unclear whether the effects are permanent or not.

In the future, it would be beneficial to study group coaching. It could offer an interesting perspective on developing creativity at the team level. Reflecting and cross-pollinating ideas within a group can accelerate individual learning processes and strengthen experiences of CSE. Group coaching generates broader discussion and interaction, which can expand individuals' viewpoints and deepen their understanding of their own creative processes.

Referring to limitations, it would be worthwhile to investigate how longer-term coaching programs promote participants' development and support the sustainability of changes. Such research can determine the progress participants can achieve during a six-month or longer coaching process and how these changes integrate into their professional and personal lives. Long-term coaching provides an opportunity for deeper self-examination and consolidation of insights, which can be critical for the development of CSE. Through this research, the long-term cost-effectiveness and impact of coaching interventions can also be evaluated. Currently, there is no clear consensus in the research field on the optimal duration of a coaching process.

References

1. Bankins, S., Ocampo, A.C., Marrone, M., Restubog, S.L.D., Woo, S.E.: A multilevel review of artificial intelligence in organizations: implications for organizational behavior research and practice. J. Organ. Behav. **45**(2), 159–182 (2021)
2. Pinarbasi, F., Cakir, F.S, Gültekin, D.G., Yazici, M., Adiguzel, Z.: Examination of the effects of value creation, intellectual property and organizational creativity on artificial intelligence focused enterprises. Bus. Process Manage. J. **30**(1), 317–337 (2024)
3. Dell'Acqua, F., et al.: Navigating the jagged technological frontier: field experimental evidence of the effects of AI on knowledge worker productivity and quality. Harvard Business School Technology & Operations Management, Working Paper No. 24-013 (2023)
4. Chuang, S.: Indispensable skills for human employees in the age of robots and AI. Eur. J. Training Dev. **48**(1/2), 179–195 (2022)
5. Zhou, E., Lee, D.: Generative artificial intelligence, human creativity, and art. PNAS Nexus **3**(3), 1–8 (2024)
6. Abdalla, S., Mogaji, E., Elhanna, A., Dwivedi, Y.: The impending disruption of creative industries by generative AI: opportunities, challenges, and research agenda. Int. J. Inf. Manage. **79** (2024)
7. Hutson, J., Lively, J., Robertson, B., Cotroneo, P., Lang, M.: Of techne and praxis: redefining creativity. In: Creative Convergence. Springer Series on Cultural Computing, pp. 21–36. Springer, Cham (2024). https://doi.org/10.1007/978-3-031-45127-0_2

8. Carroll, N.: Are we inventing ourselves out of our own usefulness? Striking a balance between creativity and AI. AI & Society (2024)
9. Amabile, T.M.: Creativity and Innovation in Organizations. Harvard Business School, Background Note, pp. 396–239 (1996a)
10. Dawson, P., Andriopoulos, C.: Managing Change, Creativity and Innovation. SAGE Publications Ltd, London (2014)
11. Karwowski, M.: Creative mindsets: measurement, correlates, consequences. Psychol. Aesthet. Creat. Arts 8(1), 62–70 (2014)
12. Mathisen, G.E., Bronnick, K.S.: Creative self-efficacy: an intervention study. Int. J. Educ. Res. 48(1), 21–29 (2009)
13. Tierney, P., Farmer, S.M.: Creative self-efficacy: its potential antecedents and relationship to creative performance. Acad. Manag. J. 45(6), 1137–1148 (2002)
14. Bandura, A.: Self-Efficacy: The Exercice of Control, 4th edn. W. H. Freeman and Company, New York (2000)
15. Ford, C.M.: A theory of individual creative action in multiple social domains. Acad. Manag. Rev. 21(4), 1112–1142 (1996)
16. Creed, T.A., Reisweber, J., Beck, A.T.: Cognitive Therapy for Adolescents in School Settings. Guilford Press, New York (2011)
17. Grant, A.M.: The solution-focused inventory: a tripartite taxonomy for teaching, measuring and conceptualising solution-focused approaches to coaching. The Coaching Psychologist (2011)
18. Braunstein, K., Grant, A.M.: Approaching solutions or avoiding problems? The differential effects of approach and avoidance goals with solution-focused and problem-focused coaching questions. Coaching Int. J. Theory Res. Pract. 9(2), 93–109 (2016)
19. Yin, R.K.: Case Study Research: Design and Methods, 4th edn. SAGE, Los Angeles (2009)
20. Raftopolous, M., Hamari, J.: Human-AI collaboration in organisations: a literature review on enabling value creation. Research Paper (2023)
21. Bharadiya, J.: Machine learning and AI in business intelligence: trends and opportunities. Int. J. Comput. 48(1), 123–134 (2023)
22. Ogunkoya, O.A.: Value creation and innovation performance of Nigeria manufacturing firm. Int. J. Adv. Stud. Bus. Strat. Manage. 7(1), 1–17 (2019)
23. Amabile, T.M.: Componential Theory of Creativity. Harvard Business School, Working Paper, 12-096 (2012)
24. Duan, Q.: A study of the influence of learning organization on organizational creativity and organizational communication in high tech technology. Eurasia J. Math. Sci. Technol. Educ. 13(6), 1817–1830 (2017)
25. Amabile, T.M.: Creativity in Context. Westview Press, Boulder, CO (1996)
26. Wang, J., et al.: Evaluating and modeling social intelligence: a comparative study of human and AI capabilities. arXiv (2024)
27. Poutanen, P.: Complexity and Collaboration in Creative Group Work. Unigrafia, Helsinki (2016)
28. Sawyer, R.K.: Individual and group creativity. In: Kaufman, J.C., Sternberg, R.J. (eds.) The Cambridge Handbook of Creativity, pp. 366–380. Cambridge University Press, New York (2010)
29. Hülsheger, U.R., Anderson, N., Salgado, J.F.: Team-level predictors of innovation at work. A comprehensive meta-analysis spanning three decades of research. J. Appl. Psychol. 94(5), 1128–1145 (2009)
30. Glăveanu, V.-P.: How are we creative together? Comparing sociocognitive and sociocultural answers. Theory Psychol. 21(4), 473–492 (2011)
31. Harvey, S.: Creative synthesis: exploring the process of extraordinary group creativity. Acad. Manag. Rev. 39(3), 324–343 (2014)

32. Isaacs, W.N.: Taking flight: dialogue, collective thinking, and organizational learning. Organ. Dyn. **22**(2), 24–39 (1993)
33. Hu, H., Gu, Q., Chen, J.: How and when does transformational leadership affect organizational creativity and innovation? Critical review and future directions. Nankai Bus. Rev. Int. **4**(2), 147–166 (2013)
34. Zimmerman, B.J.: Self-efficacy: an essential motive to learn. Contemp. Educ. Psychol. **25**, 82–91 (2000)
35. Beghetto, R.A., Karwowski, M.: Toward untangling creative self-beliefs. In: Karwoski, M., Kaufman, J.C. (eds.) The Creative Self: Effect of Beliefs, Self-Efficacy, Mindset, and Identity, pp. 3–22. Academic Press, London (2017)
36. Farmer, S.M., Tierney, P.: Considering creative self-efficacy: its current state and ideas for future inquiry. In: Karwoski, M., Kaufman, J.C. (eds.) The Creative Self: Effect of Beliefs, Self-Efficacy, Mindset, and Identity. Academic Press, London (2017)
37. Carmeli, A., Schaubroeck, J.: The influence of leaders' and other referents' normative expectations on individual involvement in creative work. Leadersh. Q. **18**(1), 35–48 (2007)
38. Robinson-Morral, E., Reiter-Palmon, R., Kaufman, J.: The interactive effects of self- perceptions and job requirements on creative problem solving. J. Creative Behav. **47**, 200–214 (2013)
39. Gong, Y., Huang, J., Farh, J.: Employee learning orientation, transformational leadership, and employee creativity: the mediating role of employee creative self-efficacy. Acad. Manag. J. **52**(4), 765–778 (2009)
40. Zhou, Q., Hirst, G., Shipton, H.: Promoting creativity at work: the role of problem-solving demand. Appl. Psychol. Int. Rev. **61**, 56–80 (2012)
41. Jaussi, K.S., Randel, A.E.: Where to look? Creative self-efficacy, knowledge retrieval, and incremental and radical creativity. Creat. Res. J. **26**(4), 400–410 (2014)
42. Li, C.-H., Wu, J.-J.: The structural relationships between optimism and innovative behavior: understanding potential antecedents and mediating effects. Creat. Res. J. **23**(2), 119–128 (2011)
43. Wahlström, M., Tammentie, B., Salonen, T.-T., Karvonen, A.: AI and the transformation of industrial work: hybrid intelligence vs double-black box effect. Appl. Ergon. **118** (2024)
44. Klein, M.: Leadership characteristics in the era of digital transformation. Bus. Manage. Stud. Int. J. **8**(1), 883–902 (2020)
45. Nadkarni, S., Prügl, R.: Digital transformation: a review, synthesis and opportunities for future research. Manage. Rev. Q. **71**, 233–341 (2021)
46. Brock, J.K.U., von Wangenheim, F.: Demystifying AI: what digital transformation leaders can teach you about realistic artificial intelligence. Calif. Manage. Rev. **61**(4), 110–134 (2019)
47. Breque, M., De Nul, L., Petridis, A.: Industry 5.0 – towards a sustainable, human-centric and resilient European industry. European Commission, Directorate-General for Research and Innovation, Luxemburg (2021)
48. Grant, A.M., Cavanagh, M.J., Kleitman, S., Spence, G., Lakota, M., Yu, N.: Development and validation of the solution-focused inventory. J. Posit. Psychol. **7**(4), 334–348 (2012)
49. O'Connell, B., Palmer, S., Williams, H.: Solution Focused Coaching in Practice. Routledge, London, New York (2012)
50. Ives, Y.: What is 'Coaching'? An exploration of conflicting paradigms. Int. J. Evid. Based Coaching Mentoring **6**(2), 100–113 (2008)
51. Whitmore, J.: Coaching for Performance, 5th edn. Nicholas Brealey, London (2017)
52. Grant, A.M., O'Connor, S.A.: Broadening and building solution-focused coaching: feeling good is not enough. Coaching Int. J. Theory Res. Pract. **11**(2), 165–185 (2018)
53. Kim, J.: Examining the effectiveness of solution-focused brief therapy: a meta-analysis. Res. Soc. Work. Pract. **18**(2), 107–116 (2008)

54. Kvarme, L., Helseth, S., Sørum, R., Luth-Hansen, V., Haugland, S., Natvig, G.K.: The effect of a solution-focused approach to improve self-efficacy in socially withdrawn school children: a non-randomized controlled trial. Int. J. Nurs. Stud. **47**(11), 1389–1396 (2010)

55. Grant, A.M.: Making positive change: a randomized study comparing solution-focused vs. problem-focused coaching questions. J. Syst. Ther. **31**(2), 21–35 (2012)

56. Theeboom, T., Beersma, B., van Vianen, A.E.M.: Does coaching work? A meta-analysis on the effects of coaching on individual level outcomes in an organizational context. J. Posit. Psychol. **9**(1), 1–18 (2014)

57. Kilburg, R.R.: Facilitating intervention adherence in executive coaching: a model and methods. Consult. Psychol. J. Pract. Res. **53**(4), 251–267 (2001)

58. Connor, M., Pokora, J.: Coaching and Mentoring at Work: Developing Effective Practice, 3rd edn. McGraw Hill, London (2017)

59. Evers, W.J., Brouwers, A., Tomic, W.: A quasi-experimental study on management coaching effectiveness. Consult. Psychol. J. Pract. Res. **58**(3), 174 (2006)

60. Moen, F., Allgood, E.: Coaching and the effect on self-efficacy. Organ. Dev. J. **27**(4), 69–82 (2009)

61. MacKie, D.: The effects of coachee readiness and core self-evaluations on leadership coaching outcomes: a controlled trial. Coaching Int. J. Theory Res. Pract. **8**(12), 1–17 (2015)

62. Xanthopoulou, D., Bakker, A.B., Demerouti, E., Schaufeli, W.B.: Work engagement and financial returns: a diary study on the role of job and personal resources. J. Occup. Organ. Psychol. **82**(1), 183–200 (2009)

63. Pousa, C., Mathieu, A.: Is managerial coaching a source of competitive advantage? Promoting employee self-regulation through coaching. Coaching: An International Journal of Theory, Research and Practice, 8(1), 20–35 (2015)

64. Malone, J.W.: Improving self-efficacy through coaching. Organ. Dev. J. **19**(2), 27–36 (2001)

65. Flyvbjerg, B.: Case Study. In: Denzin, N.K., Lincoln, Y.S. (eds.) The Sage Handbook of Qualitative Research, 4th edn., pp. 301–316. Sage Publications, Thousand Oaks, California (2011)

66. Haase, J., Hoff, E.V., Hanel, P.H.P., Innes-Ker, Å.: A meta-analysis of the relation between creative self-efficacy and different creativity measurements. Creat. Res. J. **30**(1), 1–16 (2018)

67. Abbott, D.H.: Constructing a creative self-efficacy inventory: a mixed methods inquiry. ETD collection for University of Nebraska-Lincoln (2010)

68. Aronson, J.: A pragmatic view of thematic analysis. Qual. Rep. **2**(1), 1–3 (1995)

69. Glăveanu, V.P.: Creativity as a sociocultural act. J. Creative Behav. **49**(3), 165–180 (2015)

70. Csikszentmihalyi, M.: Creativity: a systems approach. In: Runco, M. A., Albert, R. S. (eds.) Theories of Creativity, pp. 190–214. Sage, Newbury Park, CA (1990)

71. Hargadon, A.B., Bechky, B.A.: when collections of creatives become creative collectives: a field study of problem solving at work. Organ. Sci. (Providence, R.I.) **17**(4), 484–500 (2006)

72. Isaacs, W.N.: Toward an action theory of dialogue. Int. J. Public Adm. **24**(7–8), 709–748 (2001)

73. Bohm, D., Peat, D.F.: Science, Order and Creativity, 1st edn. Routlegde, New York (2010)

Building Realistic Environment from Computer Vision Approach Applied to Manufacturing Simulation in the Digital Twin Context

Marcelo Rudek$^{(\boxtimes)}$ ⓘ, Ana P. R. Valle, and Ricardo Bertolin

Pontifical Catholic University of Paraná (PUCPR), Curitiba, Paraná, Brazil
marcelo.rudek@pucpr.br

Abstract. Digital twins to manufacturing simulation require a complete virtual representation of the environment for immersive human interactions. From computer vision techniques, it is possible to model the respective real scenery based on a set of digital images. This paper addresses a strategy to create virtual layouts through 3D reconstruction from photogrammetry. The main context is to help humans to be trained using synthetic information, preparing their actions to perform the respective real operations of productive processes as aligned with industry 5.0 requirements. Here we present a selection of the emerging technologies categorized to perform the shop-floor layout digitalization as a first stage of a digital twin creation of a real industrial scenario as a starting point to the industrial metaverse architecture. Also, we present an experimental digitalization operation of a complex scenery and the respective discussion about its use in manufacturing simulation.

Keywords: Digital twin · Computer vision · 3D reconstruction · Metaverse · Manufacturing · Simulation

1 Introduction

This paper describes a project to create a virtual model in the context of Digital Twin (DT) for interactive and immersive simulations, replicating a physical environment in the virtual space realistically in terms of appearance and functionality. The scope is in the field of education in engineering applying simulations as an active learning methodology to train and prepare students well qualified to act as human-in-the-loop in the industry 5.0 productive environment.

The problem to be solved involves virtually using the Automation Laboratory (LAS) of PUCPR University, through the development of a digital twin of a specific shopfloor, intended for experiments. To achieve this objective, existing methods in the field of virtual environments and simulation were tested and compared, including state-of-the-art approaches and available tools, considering three main pillars as developing support: (i) 3D reconstruction of the physical world. (ii) digital twin. (iii) metaverse.

M. Dassisti et al. (Eds.): IN4PL 2024, CCIS 2372, pp. 223–235, 2025.
https://doi.org/10.1007/978-3-031-80760-2_14

One of the main technological aspects relevant to this problem is computer vision [1]. Accurately capturing visual data from the physical environment requires the application of advanced image processing and video analysis techniques to perform de 3D reconstruction. This includes the use of cameras and specific sensors, such as LiDAR, to collect information about the environment structure, object detection, and movement tracking [2, 3].

According to [4] the Digital Twin refers to a virtual representation of a real-world object, system, or process. A digital representation is created using real-time data or information collected over time. We observe in the literature the concept of Digital Twin is applied in various sectors such as engineering, healthcare, smart cities, transportation, etc., but with different interpretations, since the simplest DT is only a digital representation (mirroring) until a complete bidirectional communication system and interactivity between real and virtual. Anyway, all approaches have digitalization as a preliminary step. In the industrial context, the DT is still a novelty to instruct operators and facilitate the acquisition of new skills from the realistic interaction with a fully reconstructed environment [5].

The metaverse [6] integrates all the previous concepts, linking immersive technologies and DT, together with the industrial internet of things (IIoT), artificial intelligence (AI), cloud computing, and cyber-physical systems (CPS). The metaverse also represents a merging of the physical and virtual worlds and can be considered an expansion of the Digital Twin.

The research problem is illustrated in the Fig. 1. From a real site, for instance, a Fanuc 200iC as highlighted in Fig. 1(a) can be modeled to a simulation platform as a virtual model (b) to be virtually handled.

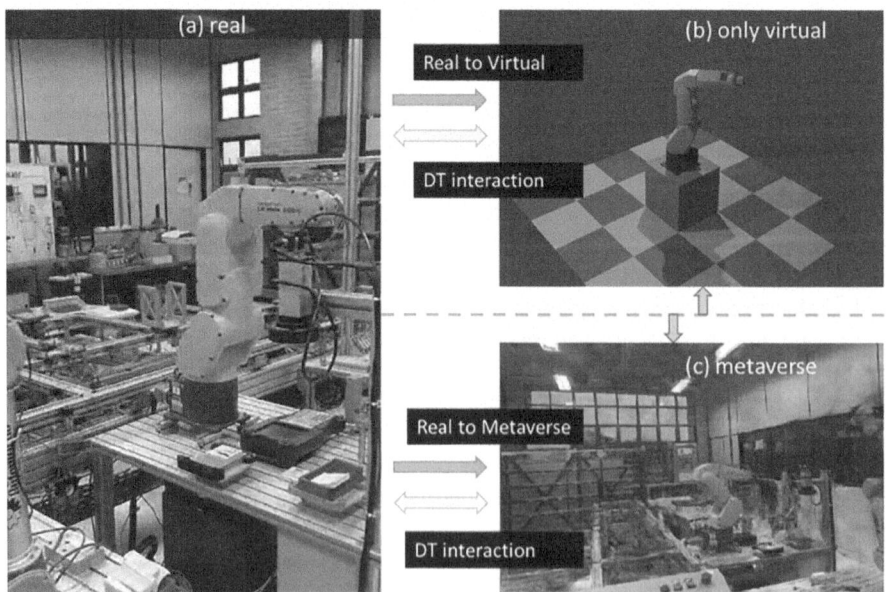

Fig. 1. The context research and research problem illustration.

In Fig. 1, the (a) to (b) path is a DT interaction in both directions viewed as only a virtual representation. The (a) to (c) path is a DT interaction between the Real environment and the metaverse. The path (a) to (c) comprehends the digitalization process, which is our scope here. Thus, we also have a linkage between (b) and (c).

Thus, the purpose of this research is to explore the computational elements required for virtual operation of one of the robots in the laboratory (on the side of the virtual twin) by building those pillars. The development will serve as the basis for a tool for simulating experiments as if they were being conducted in a real environment. Realistic simulation is an activity present in the current context of so-called smart factories and allows for planning and operation tests to be carried out without interfering with the real part of the process.

The relevance of this area of study lies in the ability to provide a more dynamic and accessible teaching and research experience by accurately mirroring the physical environment and enabling users to conduct experiments remotely. Its application in the industrial environment aims at increasing productivity, reducing rework, and lowering compliance costs.

1.1 Background and Definitions

The three main topics aborded in this work are widely covered in recent works, as well as very consolidate in literature. Then here we put the more commonly adopted interpretation of them.

Photogrammetry. Photogrammetry is based on multiple images captured from different positions of an RGB camera, and it involves essential concepts for 3D reconstruction such as stereo vision and triangulation [7]. Stereo vision is essential for depth estimating, as addressed by [8], who describes it as the ability to interpret disparities between images captured from different positions to perceive three-dimensionality. Triangulation is a fundamental principle that allows determining the three-dimensional coordinates of points based on their projections in two or more images.

Digital Twin. The Digital Twin (DT) is the name given to a dynamic virtual model of a system, process, or service [9–11]. However, it is not standardized, and definitions vary depending on the context and application, but in general, DT is composed of a) physical devices in the real world, b) the digital model in the virtual world, and c) data and connected information interconnecting these two spaces. Inside this context, Mixed Reality (MR = Augmented Reality + Images) provides that natural human abilities are expanded by computer vision systems that help to think or make decisions. In this trajectory, components are sought to cover two premises: 1) create digital simulations (cyber) from synthetic datasets [12] of the real world (physical) through a prescriptive model, when it serves to create an object based on the model. And, 2) provide learning so that human interaction experiences and skills are measured and adapted for human-machine interfaces, providing training according to individual capabilities [13].

Metaverse. The metaverse represents a merging of the physical and virtual worlds [6]. The proposal is to create interactions between people within a fictional universe or in a simulation of the real world. In addition to socialization, this enables the exchange of emotional, sensory, and learning experiences [14]. In this way, the definition is consonant with the industry 5.0 paradigm. This is because it is a way of creating "versions" of the real world within the virtual world with human interaction. In this interactive ecosystem, devices are used to simulate and recreate situations. In this sense, the industrial metaverse refers to the work options that begin to form around the use of virtual reality [15]. It can be applied to predict the behavior of machines and their components and allows testing of products, optimizing resources and efforts used in finalizing and developing projects. The new reality also means that physical tests are simplified and simulated in different ways before a manufacturing procedure [16].

Following those all perceptions about immersive necessities, we proposed a method to DT x Metaverse linkage presented in the next section.

2 The Proposed Method

2.1 The Conceptual Model

The fundamental pillars of virtual simulation introduced in Sect. 1 were now expanded to explain their inner conceptual elements. We rearranged them into three layers as in Fig. 2, in order to improve the visualization of the levels of an interconnected matrix.

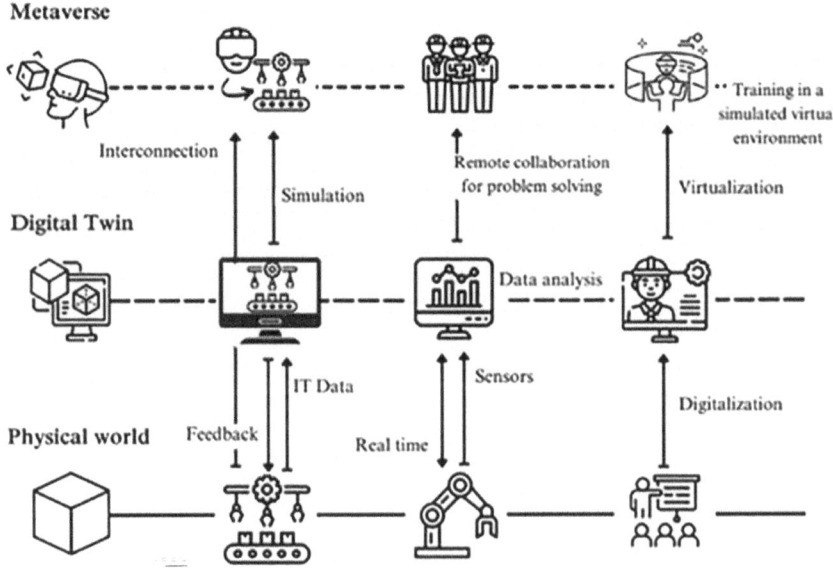

Fig. 2. The layers of the conceptual model represent the main interconnections of the virtualization matrix.

According to Fig. 2, the basis and more elementary level is obviously the physical world layer, and inside of the same line is represented the process to be mapped and associated training with real human interaction. The second level from bottom-up visualization is the Digital Twin layer formed by 2 bidirectional connected columns compound by sensors providing data interchanging and feedback in real-time, and a third column representing the digitalization process as a unidirectional path with the level below. The superior layer is the metaverse level. The model shows the interconnection between the 2nd and 3rd levels compound by simulation, remote collaboration and virtualization. Here, as scope delimitation, we are focused to describe in the next sections the digitalization and virtualization stages to build the virtual model.

2.2 The Digitalization Process

The photogrammetry tolls are already implemented in some mobile apps. It facilitates the scanning process because these devices have cameras and Lidar sensors embedded. Thus, we can use them to build proof of concepts (PoCs) and prototyping. By moving the device around the scenery we collect the sequenced image frames as the input to triangulation-based reconstruction. A set of a hundred images collected are capable of making a digitalized environment. Once the digitalization process is performed, the cloud of points generated, and respective texture information (pixel's colors) can be exported to the next step: virtualization.

2.3 The Virtualization Process

The virtualization process deals with rebuilding the cloud of points from digitalization in an interactive environment. There are many solutions already applied to perform this step, and we select a reduced set based on the criteria of license availability in our university. The evaluation of them is presented in the next section.

3   The Computational Resources Analysis

In order to obtain more complete information about the different existing simulation environments, we selected some of the more commonly applied to build the virtual replicas of a scene. Table 1 lists some examples of such software commonly applied to industrial simulation and academic research. The idea is to compare their key applications and make a relationship between advantages and disadvantages. The interest is to select a low-cost solution as a strategy to be employed in our research.

From Table 1, the systems indicated are the ones nowadays available in the university, and we were able to test them. According to [17], Blender is an open-source software and has the advantage of many tutorials providing, plugins and resources from a community of developers, offering versatility to animation and rendering tools. The Coppelia Sim is applied to robotic simulation and provides a realistic physics simulation to accurate representation of robotic behaviors, and also offers APIs for customizations and integration with external systems. The Gazebo simulator is also open-source offering robot operating system integration with realistic physics to simulations. The Pybullet solution is in the class of open-source environments with large community contributions very frequently used to real-time simulations and machine learning integration. The Unity 3D is a complete platform that incorporates the capacity to develop to mobile, consoles and VR/AR devices support. And, it has vast pre-made assets, various plugins, and tools to conduct easy prototyping. The last cited in Table 1, the Unreal Engine, due real-time rendering allow us for interactive and immersive experience, and it has a large developers community and structured support. In the Table 1, the (*) marked options are fully covered by other systems such as (Siemens Teknomatix, Arena, Flexsim).

Table 1. Selected simulation environments, adapted from [17].

Key Application \ System	Blender	Coppelia SIM	Gazebo	PyBullet	Unity 3D	Unreal Engine
Robotic Simulation	o	•	•	•	o	o
Augmented and virtual reality					•	•
Animation	•	•	•	•	•	•
Simulation		•	•	•	•	o
Game development	•				•	•
Virtual Prototyping	o		o		o	•
Architectural visualization	•				•	•
Training and Education	o	•			•	
Digital Manufacturing*	o	o	o	o	o	o
Product Lifecycle Management (PLM)*	o		o		o	
Factory Simulation*	o	o	o		o	

Legend (o partial / • full)

For a low-cost strategy, we in this moment did not focus to a dedicated solution as Siemens Teknomatix or Arena, but we tried adapting the open-source solutions for our application. By considering the potential and resources available we choose to develop the virtual environment on Unity solution. Thus, we conduct an experiment as described in the next section.

4   The Application Example

The application example describes a reconstruction process based on photogrammetry, illustrated as Fig. 3.

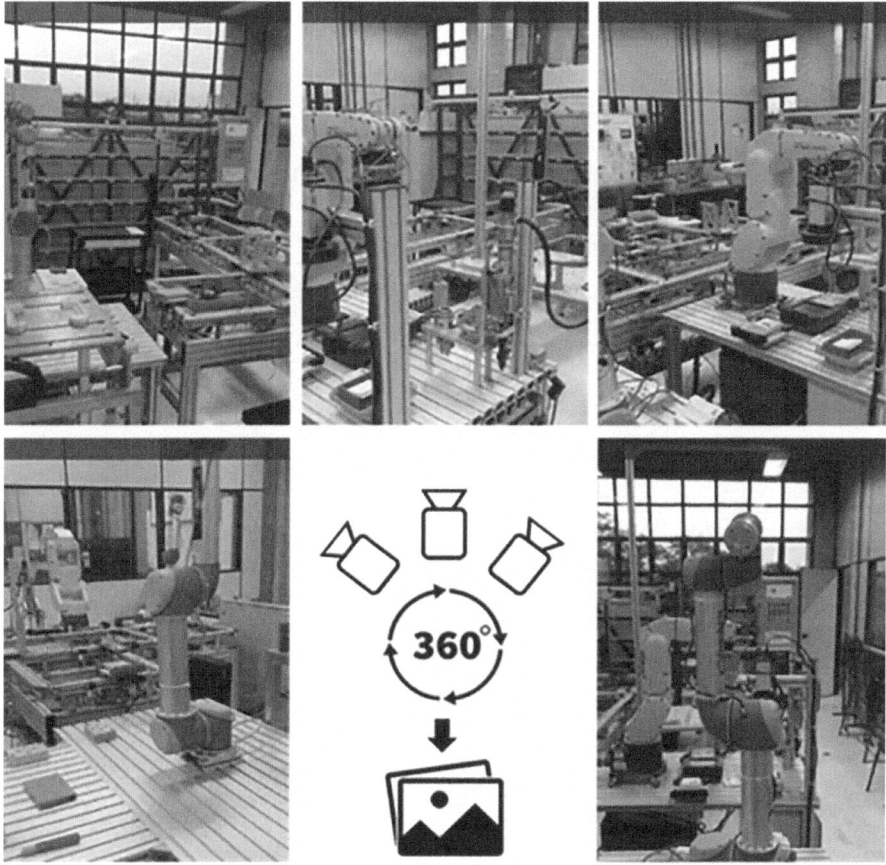

Fig. 3. The N views samples to image capture sequence from PUCPR-LAS.

To use this approach, we need first to collect the image sequences, regarding the photogrammetry needs a lot of images taken while the camera is moving around the object/environment. The Fig. 3 shows a set of selected frames form the laboratory of systems automation (LAS) extracted from a video capture using a smartphone. The figure illustrates the image complexity due presence of different equipment, robots, devices, cables, tables, etc.

The process of virtual model reconstruction was developed applying Polycam software [18, 19], using only 150 image frames of the LAS Laboratory of the university, and the respective virtual model is presented in Fig. 4.

The photogrammetry process applied in Polycam's reconstruction system represents the 3D data as polygonal meshes with corresponding image textures by the 3D Gaussian Splatting method [20]. It represents a 3D scene as millions of particles called 3D Gaussians. Thus, each 3D Gaussian comes with its respective position, orientation, scale, opacity, and view-dependent color.

(a)

(b)

Fig. 4. The mapped environment. (a) the real laboratory image and (b) its respective virtual model.

From the visual comparison between images (a) and (b), we observe the similarity level of realism which makes it possible to identify the main structures and equipment. The aspect ratio is kept similar in the virtual twin image. Also, the environmental conditions of illumination are replicated giving a sense of realism. However, details of objects are lost during reconstruction, causing lots of distortions in the virtual image. The virtual image can be freely rotated, and depending of position the details quality of visualization changes.

From Fig. 5, the images (a), (b), and (c) present the user interaction from the Hololens viewpoint, where the virtual robotic arm is commanded to a specific movement. Also, the images (d), (e), and (f) present the same virtual robotic arm representation into the

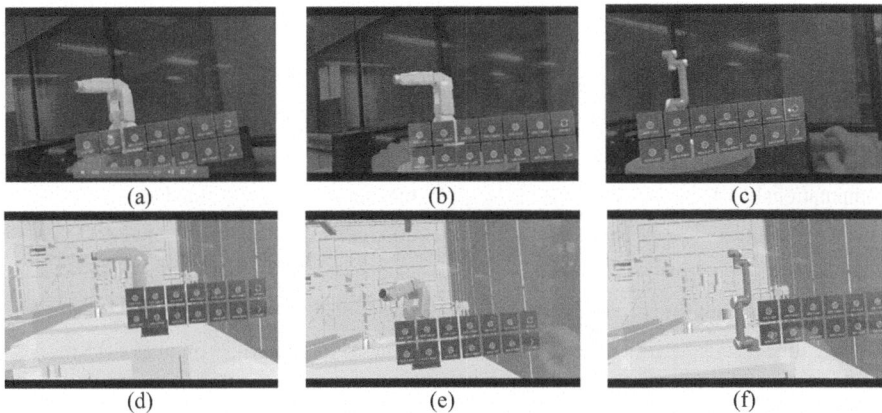

Fig. 5. The virtual projection of robot and user interaction commands.

Unity environment inside the laboratory sketch structure. It shows that both VR and AR can be set to simulated operation. Figure 6 presents the tested robotic operation of a robot picking a virtual box inside the Unity environment. We evaluated the main characteristics of visual quality among manual reconstruction and photogrammetric reconstruction. Table 2 presents the comparing evaluation of the model built only virtual, and its respective models by photogrammetry.

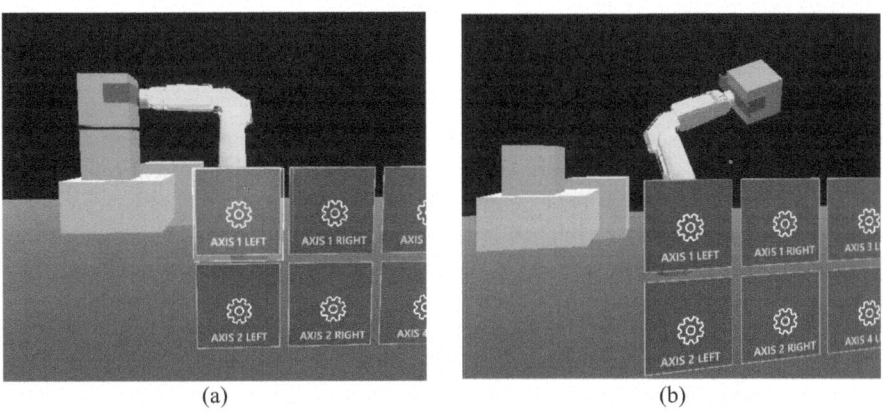

Fig. 6. The simulated picking operation in the virtual projection.

Table 2 shows a comparative analysis of photogrammetric and non-photogrammetric models. It is observed that model #3, which uses photogrammetry with splatting technology, achieves the greatest realism. However, all tested modeling modes have the possibility of improvements, with the model non-photogrammetry being dependent on knowledge in rendering. On the other hand, the non-photogrammetric model is efficient in processing and customization but significantly compromises realism and scales. Table 3 evaluates the configuration and export experience within Unity and compatibility

Table 2. Comparative analysis of photogrammetric and non-photogrammetric models.

Criteria	Model #1 (manual build)	Model #2 (photogrammetry)	Model #3 (gaussian)
Realism	low	median	high
Computational cost	low	median	median
Samples quantities	n/a	200 images	200 images
Final Quality	partial	median-low	median-high
HoloLens2 compatibility	yes	yes	limited
Building time	hours (8 h ~ 10 h)	minutes (~15 min)	minutes (~15 min)

Table 3. Evaluation of the configuration and export experience within Unity and compatibility with HoloLens2.

Criteria	Unity/MRTK	HoloLens2 (Emulator)	HoloLens2 (Device)
Configuration facilities	low	median	median
System requirements	median	high	median
Application stability	median	low	median
Extern tools integration	yes	not	yes
Exporting facilities	high	median	median
Post-exported adjustments	yes	yes	not

with HoloLens2. It is seen that configuring the MRTK tool in Unity presents challenges, especially due to system requirements and the need for integration with other tools (Windows Development Kit, for example). The biggest loss of stability is seen in the integration into the emulator, which points to positioning errors and lack of stability due to the tool itself, making it necessary to generate corrections to function properly and then export to the device model.

Figure 7 presents the final reconstructed model of the laboratory based on best-evaluated reconstruction methods and tools. In this picture, we joined the virtual UR5 robotic arm and a virtual box inside the 3D environment. The user wearing a Hololens can virtually walk inside the laboratory and command the movements of the robot. Thus, all operations can be performed by users located in any place everywhere.

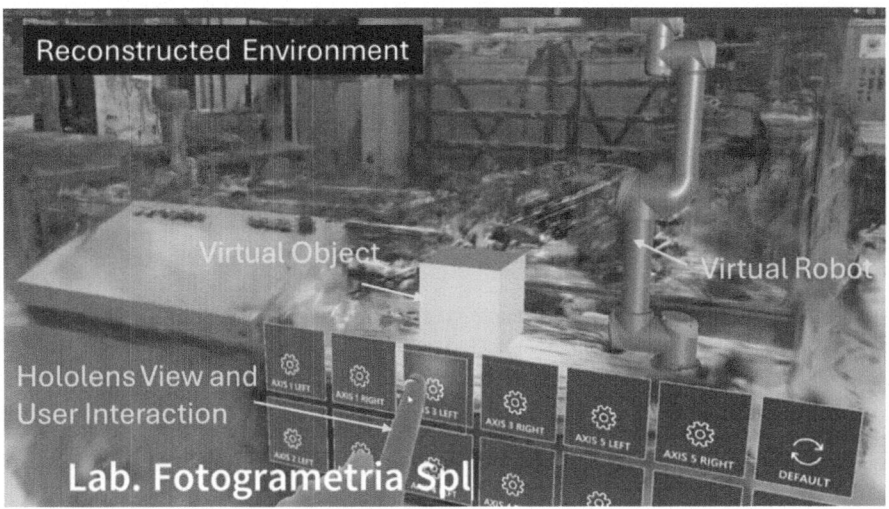

Fig. 7. The final reconstructed environment saw into Hololens.

5 Conclusion

The text presented a conceptual model for the virtualization step for DT x Industrial Metaverse creation. We named three layers as fundamental part of model, as: the physical world, the digital twin and the metaverse. From the model of Fig. (2), we described the main interconnection among all elements inside of a matrix shape arrangement. From all parts of that arrangement, we focused on the digitalization process applied to virtual 3D modeling as a preliminary step to the digital twin and metaverse creation.

Also, we explored in the literature the most common tools to be applied of creation of the virtual side of the Laboratory of System Automation (LAS) to didact use in the university. From several development environments, we checked which of them was more suitable for our experiment and chose Unity as a preliminary tool for testing. After 3D generation from Polycam reconstruction software by 3D Gaussian Splatting approach, we got a 3D virtual replica, and the quality was discussed in comparison with the real image.

The research is ongoing and the next stage we are going to put the human interactivity to act with the digital model. So, by this way as future work, we will explore the teaching-learning inside the metaverse viewpoint.

Disclosure of Interests The authors have no competing interests to declare that are relevant to the content of this article.

References

1. Silva, R.L., Canciglieri Junior, O., Rudek, M.: A road map for planning-deploying machine vision artifacts in the context of industry 4.0. J. Ind. Prod. Eng. **39**(3), 167–180 (2022)
2. Lyons, N.: Deep learning-based computer vision algorithms, immersive analytics and simulation software, and virtual reality modeling tools in digital twin-driven smart manufacturing. Econ. Manage. Financ. Markets Woodside **17**(2), 67–81 (2022)
3. Tadeja, S.K., Lu, Y., Rydlewicz, M., et al.: Exploring gestural input engineering surveys of real-life structures in virtual reality using photogrammetric 3D models. Multimed. Tools Appl. **80**, 31039–31058 (2021)
4. Wang, Y., Wang, X., Liu, A. et al.: Ontology of 3D virtual modeling in digital twin: a review, analysis, and thinking. J. Intell. Manuf., 1–51 (2023)
5. Martínez-Gutiérrez, A., Díez-González, J., Verde, P., Perez, H.: Convergence of virtual reality and digital twin technologies to enhance digital operators' training in Industry 4.0. Int. J. Hum. Comput. Stud. **180**, 1–14 (2023)
6. Lv, Z., Fridenfalk, M.: Digital twins for building industrial metaverse. J. Adv. Res., 1–8 (2023). (in press)
7. Kurka, P.R.G., Rudek, M.: Three-dimensional volume and position recovering using a virtual reference box. IEEE Trans. Image Process., 573–576 (2007)
8. Ruijun, L., Haisheng, L., Zhihan, L.: Modeling methods of 3D model in digital twins. CMES – Comput. Model. Eng. Sci. **136**(2), 985–1022 (2023)
9. Jones, D., Snider, C., Nassehi, A., Yon, J., Hicks, B.: Characterizing the digital twin: a systematic literature review. CIRP J. Manuf. Sci. Technol. **29**(A), 36–52 (2020)
10. Minerva, R., Lee, G.M.: Digital twin in the IoT context: a survey on technical features, scenarios, and architectural models. Proc. IEEE **108**(10), 1785–1824 (2020)
11. Leng, J., et al.: Digital twins-based remote semi-physical commissioning of flow-type smart manufacturing systems. J. Clean. Prod. **306**, 1–15 (2021)
12. Jianyang, G., et al.: Efficient dataset distillation via minimax diffusion. arXiv:2311.155 29v2[cs.CV], pp. 1–26 (2024)
13. Yue, Y., Pai, Z., Chengxi, L., Lihui, W.: A state-of-the-art survey on augmented reality-assisted digital twin for futuristic human-centric industry transformation. Robot. Comput. Integr. Manuf. **81**, 1–21 (2023)
14. Moro, C.: Utilizing the metaverse in anatomy and physiology. Anat. Sci. Educ. **16**(4), 574–581 (2023)
15. Kaluza, A. et al.: Implementing mixed reality in automotive life cycle engineering: a visual analytics based approach. (26) CIRP Life Cycle Engineering (LCE) Conference. Procedia CIRP **80**, 717–722 (2019)
16. Lee, J., Kundu, P.: Integrated cyber-physical systems and industrial metaverse for remote manufacturing. Manuf. Lett. **34**, 12–15 (2022)
17. Rudek, M., Valle, A.P.R., Bertolin, R., Szjeka, A.L., Canciglieri Jr, O.: A computer vision approach to build manufacturing simulation models in the digital twin context. In: IFIP 21st International Conference on Product Lifecycle Management, PLM 2024, pp. 1–11 (2024)
18. Polycam. https://poly.cam/tools/gaussian-splatting. Accessed 14 Feb 2024
19. Valandro, R., Nogueira, J.C., Rudek, M.: A method to interactive simulations of industrial environments based on immersive technologies. In: Danjou, C., Harik, R., Nyffenegger, F., Rivest, L., Bouras, A. (eds.) Product Lifecycle Management. Leveraging Digital Twins, Circular Economy, and Knowledge Management for Sustainable Innovation. PLM 2023. IFIP Advances in Information and Communication Technology, vol. 701, pp. 91–109. Springer, Cham (2024). https://doi.org/10.1007/978-3-031-62578-7_9

20. Luiten, J., Kopanas, G., Leibe, B., Ramanan, D.: Dynamic 3D Gaussians: tracking by persistent dynamic view synthesis. In: 3DV International Conference on 3D Vision, 2024, arXiv preprint arXiv:2308.09713 (2024)

21. Sivov, N.Y., Shmatko, E.V., Poroykov, A.Y.: Estimating the feasibility of images simulation in unity 3D for sub-pixel processing algorithms. IEEE Wave Electronics and its Application in Information and Telecommunication Systems (WECONF), St. Petersburg, Russian Federation, pp. 1–4 (2023)

22. Steed, C., Kim, N.: Deep active-learning-based model-synchronization of digital manufacturing stations using human-in-the-loop simulation. J. Manuf. Syst. **70**, 436–450 (2023)

23. Yang, Y., Deb, S., He, M., Kobir, M.H.: The use of virtual reality in manufacturing education: state-of-the-art and future directions. Manuf. Lett. **35**, 1214–1221 (2023)

Towards a Process-Based Industry 5.0 Maturity Model: A Feasibility Study in Supply Chain

Sara Himmiche[✉] [iD], Jean-Luc Maire, Jose-Fernando Jimenez, Magali Pralus, and Laurent Tabourot

SYMME Laboratory, Université Savoie Mont Blanc, Annecy, France
{Sara.Himmiche,Jean-Luc.Maire,Jose-Fernando.Jimenez, Magali.Pralus,Laurent.Tabourot}@univ-savoie.fr

Abstract. A focus on sustainability, resilience, and human-centricity is necessary to implement the global vision of Industry 5.0. However, assessing the readiness of these pillars within the business processes of an organization remains a significant challenge. This paper addresses this gap by providing a comprehensive and process-based maturity model in Industry 5.0 context. The model adopts a top-down approach assessing the maturity of business processes at different layers and focusing on the formalization of practices and their correlation with maturity levels. The applicability of the model is demonstrated through its instantiation to the supply chain process category, with a focus on the schedule production process. Furthermore, the paper explores the integration of AI-based techniques to automate the creation of maturity grids and streamline the assessment process. Overall, the results of this paper highlight the prescriptive characteristic of the proposed maturity model, providing a robust framework to guide organizations towards a step-by-step transition through the Industry 5.0 vision.

Keywords: Industry 5.0 · Maturity model · Business processes · Practices · Supply chain

1 Introduction

The global industrial context has been continuously evolving over the past few years. The development of new technologies and the large-scale digitization of industrial processes have been the core of the fourth industrial revolution. The focus on technologies in Industry 4.0 has led to a partial exclusion of the human aspect from being the center of Industry [1]. This has given rise to a debate about the place that humans should or will have to occupy in industry but more widely on the planet. To respond to this challenge, the combination of the three existing principles of resilience, sustainability, and human has inspired the emergence of Industry 5.0 [2]. As such, Industry 5.0 (I5.0) advocates industrial resilience while respecting the limits of the planet and placing human well-being at the center of industrial processes [3].

Industry 5.0 has been the subject of numerous scientific articles, most of which analyze its origins [4], while others list its main differences from Industry 4.0 [5].

M. Dassisti et al. (Eds.): IN4PL 2024, CCIS 2372, pp. 236–249, 2025.
https://doi.org/10.1007/978-3-031-80760-2_15

Industry 5.0 is not positioned as a chronological evolution of Industry 4.0, nor as an alternative to Industry 4.0 [2].

Its purpose is to introduce a value-based industry vision based on the fundamental pillars of human-centricity, sustainability, and resilience.

The transition to I5.0 brings many new challenges. In [2], the acceptance of its values and the measurement of their social and environmental impacts are defined as an important challenge. Therefore, I5.0 brings various changes to the known industrial and social systems. This can be seen as a barrier to the acceptance and adoption of this value-driven transformation. Furthermore, the lack of a clear set of guiding principles and objectives in current research is a serious handicap to initiating effective changes in the industrial world [6].

This paper contributes to address the challenge of comprehensiveness and acceptance of the I5.0 principles by organizations. In the literature related to I5.0, conceptual frameworks and global analyzes are used to link the different aspects of I5.0 [5, 7]. However, it does not provide a clear vision of how these aspects are embedded in the real business processes of an organization. Therefore, this paper initiates the development of a prescriptive and holistic Maturity Model (i.e. MM). The proposed model enables a global overview of the I5.0 pillars and their mapping to industrial business processes. In fact, the use of MMs has shown its strengths in several areas, including Industry 4.0 [9]. In fact, a MM first allows for a global view of a context. However, its main objective is to assess the maturity level of an organization along one or more dimensions, based on well-defined indicators and their associated evaluation criteria [10]. Furthermore, and based on the assessment provided by the MMs, a diagnosis or roadmap can be proposed to guide organizations to progress within the values of I5.0.

The proposed model is validated through its application to the Supply Chain process category. In fact, Supply Chain remain a critical process category for organizational operations, encompassing all activities necessary for the design, production and distribution of goods and services. In literature, Supply Chain activities are explored in the context of Industry 5.0 with the emergence of the definitions of resilient, human-centric, and sustainable Supply Chain [8].

This paper is organized as follows. In the next section, the background of MMs and their exploration in Industry 5.0 are presented. Then, the conception of the MM is discussed in Sect. 3. In Sect. 4, the feasibility of the proposed MM in Supply Chain is demonstrated and insights into evaluation perspectives are provided. Finally, the conclusions and perspectives are drawn in Sect. 5.

2 Background and Related Work

The concept of maturity models has been extensively explored in various domains to assess and enhance organizational capabilities. This section introduces necessary background on maturity models and their limitations in the context of I5.0. Following this overview, a discussion will address these limitations and outline the related research question.

2.1 Maturity Models

In a general context, the term "maturity" denotes a state of completeness or perfection, suggesting progress in the development of a system [11]. Thus, to achieve a maturity state of an organization, the objective is to continuously increase its capability regarding the context, over time, and towards a target state. Therefore, MMs allow one to identify, for a given context, the dimensions that enable the organization to progress in a defined area. For this purpose, maturity levels are defined and measured. They can be quantitative or qualitative, discrete or continuous [10].

In the literature, several types of MMs are defined. In [10], the type of MM is referred to as a design principle. In fact, the authors categorize MMs according to their purpose of design: basic, descriptive, or prescriptive (see Table 1).

Table 1. Types of Maturity Models.

Type	Description	I5.0 Example
Basic	Gives the basic information about the domain of applicability, maturity dimensions, and levels	I5.0 Meta Model [7]
Descriptive	Describe the evaluation criteria and their level of granularity	RMA assessment tool [12]
Prescriptive	Gives improvement guidelines enforced with decision methodology	---

The interesting aspect of this categorization is that it highlights the possible evolution of a basic MM to a descriptive or prescriptive MM.

2.2 Maturity Models in Industry 5.0

Maturity Models find their roots in software engineering and project management, with several models such as the Capability Maturity Model (CMM) [11] and Business Process Maturity Models (BPMM) [12]. Over time, MMs have transcended these origins to become applicable in various domains, including, but not limited to, information technology, business processes, sustainability, healthcare, and education, as presented in [13]. More recently, MMs have been used in various studies related to Industry 4.0 context [9, 11, 13]. Together, these studies highlight a discernible shift towards the incorporation of MMs as valuable tools for the assessment and development of organizational capabilities within the dynamic landscape of the fourth industrial revolution.

In I5.0, understanding the requirements and outcomes came with the development of frameworks. For example, the author in [5] proposed a framework for Industry 5.0 based on a literature review. This framework links resilience, sustainability, and human centricity through performance metrics such as efficiency, productivity, resilience, and viability. In [8], the Industry 5.0 framework is oriented toward the evolution of a human-centric, sustainable, resilient, and supply chain.

These frameworks give a high-level structure to provide guidelines and principles. However, their objective is not to evaluate the performance of an organization. More recently, the use of MMs in the context of I5.0 has been explored by [14] through a systematic literature review. In this study, the authors highlight that no MMs are used in the I5.0 context. Therefore, their study is based on 24 MMs developed to integrate Industry 4.0 concepts and linked to the pillars of I5.0. Moreover, the authors state that the MMs studied are basic or descriptive. Therefore, there is a real gap in the development and use of prescriptive MMs in this context. However, the literature review proposed in [14] is limited. In fact, in the same year, several research studies on MM were initiated in the context of 5.0. For instance, [7] proposes a metamodel to define the key elements and relationships needed to design a new I5.0 maturity assessment model. In [12], the authors present the development of a Resilience Maturity Assessment tool to assess the maturity of supply chain resilience in manufacturing SMEs in the context of Industry 5.0. The proposed models are classified in (Table 1).

2.3 Discussion and Research Question

Maturity models (MMs) have garnered significant attention in the context of I5.0. However, the existing models have limitations, as they are often non-prescriptive and lack explicit guidance on the subsequent steps that organizations should take to enhance their maturity levels. Furthermore, many of these models tend to focus on generic assessment criteria that can be subjectively interpreted by different organizations.

These statements led us to the following research question.

RQ: *How to guide organizations through the I5.0 pillars using prescriptive MMs?*

Addressing this research question involves developing MMs that not only assess, but also provide clear and actionable recommendations, aligned with the specific pillars of Industry 5.0: sustainability, resilience, and human-centricity.

3 Towards Industry 5.0 Maturity Model: A Process-Based Approach

To answer the research question (RQ), this section presents a description of the suggested MM. The development of this model follows the conception steps detailed in [15]. These steps structure the development of the MM with an iterative loop to guarantee the verification and validation of the model.

The proposed model is inspired by the Business Process Maturity Model (BPMM). The objective of the BPMM is to assess the maturity level of business processes in an organization. To achieve this objective, the authors in [16] propose a holistic approach that considers six major success factors of an organization (i.e. Strategic alignment, governance, methods, IT, people, and culture). These factors are defined as dimensions of the BPMM. Their model also presents five maturity levels answering whether the processes are mature or not towards these six success factors. Furthermore, the final element of the model is the organizational units that identify the processes examined.

The main limit of BPMM is that it focuses on only six success factors that can overlook other relevant aspects or emerging trends that could affect the maturity of the process. Moreover, the proposed maturity levels are focused on whether the success factor is considered or not in the process which led to an oversimplified evaluation that does not consider the incremental advancements and intermediate improvements.

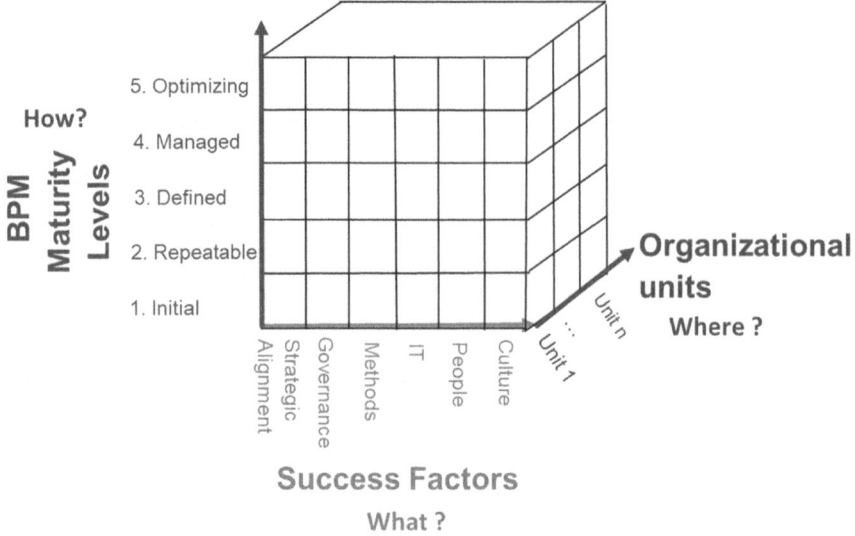

Fig. 1. BPMM elements.

From this model (see Fig. 1), we conclude three major questions to be answered during the conception process of our MM:

- What ? What are the dimensions of the MM that are going to be explored ?
- Where ? What are the organizational units where the dimensions are going to be explored ?
- How ? How to assess the dimensions throughout the organizational units?

From the study of these questions, we have designed an enhanced MM in the context of I5.0 that answers these three questions and answers the limits of the BPMM.

The I5.0 MM is presented through the following answers (See Fig. 2):

- What ? The main context of the model is I5.0, therefore, three dimensions are defined: Sustainability, Resilience, and Human-centricity.
- Where ? The organizational units are linked to the process-based approach. They are identified from a standard framework and are structured into 3 layers.
- How ? The maturity levels enable the analysis of practices adopted by the organization in these processes. The purpose here is to assess the level of practices used within each process and across the three dimensions.

This model offers several advantages. First, it establishes the relationship between the I5.0 dimensions, an organization's processes, and its practices. Second, the focus

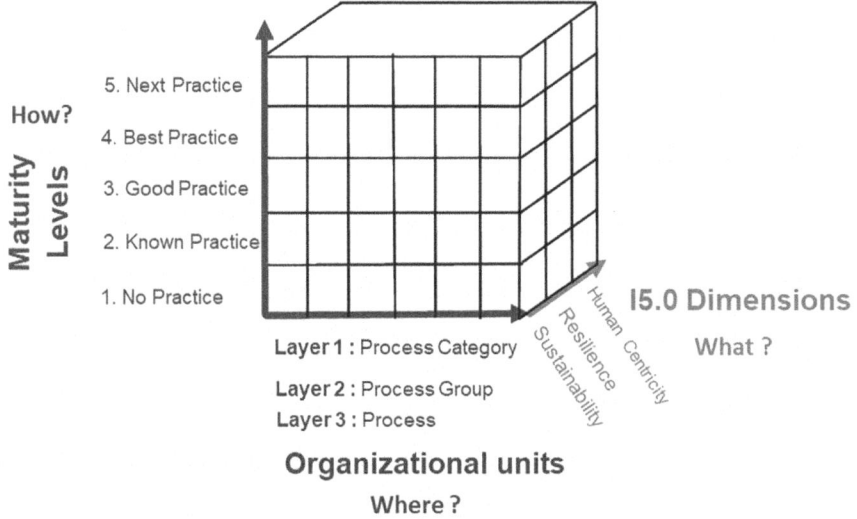

Fig. 2. I5.0MM elements.

on processes provides a common ground for all organizations to begin to apply the model. Finally, the benefit of the practice assessment is that it allows the organization to identify these practices, if any, and develop them within its processes. The I5.0 MM is then classified as prescriptive. The three axes of this model are described in detail below.

3.1 I5.0 Maturity Model Dimensions

The MM aims to evaluate organizations from several dimensions. In the context of I5.0, the dimensions refer to the three value-based pillars introduced in the literature.

Dimension 1: Human-Centricity
This dimension focuses on how organizations focus their processes on human resources from various perspectives (human-machine interactions, ergonomics, well-being, skills, etc.) [2]. There are many criteria for this dimension that need to be considered to achieve the main goal of an inclusive human environment, where the global well-being of people is a priority in all the organization's processes.

Dimension 2: Resilience
The second dimension of the MM presents the resilience of processes. Rather than considering geopolitical characteristics and natural emergencies in all organizational processes, this dimension treats the robustness of processes through ongoing and upcoming, global, and intern, changes [12].

Dimension 3: Sustainability
This dimension covers the aspect of sustainability in all processes of an organization. More specifically, this dimension considers the triple bottom line (TBL) of a sustainable organization [8]. The TBL highlights three sustainability objectives: Economic, Social, and Environmental.

3.2 I5.0 Maturity Model Organizational Units

Given the prescriptive objective of the I5.0 MM, the adopted approach considers all processes in the organization and guides their practices as they progress towards the values of I5.0. Therefore, several frameworks allow the mapping of business processes.

For the design of this MM, the generic and open access "Process Classification Framework (PCF)" is considered.

This framework was created in 1992 from the collaboration between a group of industry members and the American Productivity and Quality Center (APQC). Originally intended as an improvement tool, it has since evolved into the broad taxonomy it is today, allowing for a cross-industry framework [17]. The PCF structures the processes into a distinct hierarchy that goes from the category of processes to the activities and tasks of the process (see Fig. 3).

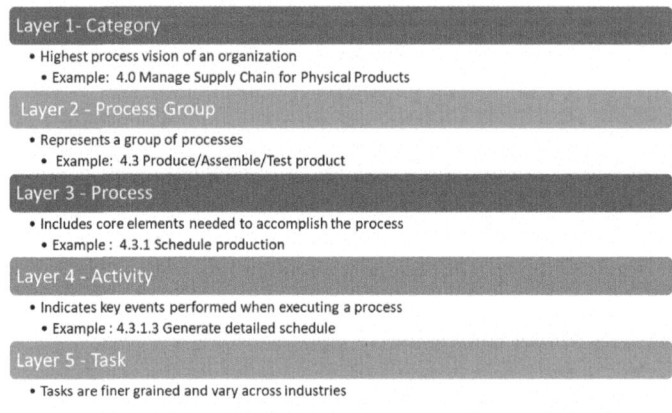

Fig. 3. Description of the PCF hierarchy given by [17].

In I5.0 MM, the PCF hierarchy is considered from the category level down to process. In fact, to ensure that the model remains independent from any domain-specific activities and tasks, both layers 4 and 5 are excluded from the maturity assessment. However, the final layers can be integrated in the roadmap when necessary. In fact, to improve the maturity of a process, it is important to identify which activities and tasks should be modified or changed. This approach provides the organization with a clear roadmap outlining specific actions to be implemented.

For each layer of the PCF, the following question arises: What are the criteria for assessing maturity across the dimensions of I5.0 MM?

The first layer provides a global view and description of the I5.0 dimensions within process categories. The second layer, which consists in process groups gives a more detailed view that enables both the description and assessment of maturity for each I5.0 dimension in each process group.

Finally, the third layer of the PCF introduces the prescriptive aspect of the I5.0 MM by refining the analysis of maturity for each process. The objective is to understand the implementation of each dimension in the process, along with its associated metrics. At this stage, the MM can be used to identify the processes requiring improvement and to propose a corresponding roadmap for the organization.

The PCF presents a total of 13 categories, 71 process groups, 344 processes, and 1281 activities. Although the number of processes described is very high, the PCF hierarchy makes it easier to go for a personalized application of the MM through the layer approach.

3.3 I5.0 Maturity Levels

The first step towards the assessment of maturity through I5.0 MM is to identify the Key Performance Indicators (KPIs) linked to each dimension and each process. However, more than finding these KPIs, the question asked is 'What is the impact of practices on these KPIs and inversely ?'.

In fact, for the I5.0 MM to be perspective, we have focused the maturity levels on the practices adopted in a process. A practice is the set of actions and methods within an organization that enable the achievement of goals. Analyzing practices within processes provides insight into the overall maturity from an I5.0 vision. Processes are usually linked to performance indicators. This allows the questioning of the practices that can improve these indicators and the performance of the process. In the case of this MM, the objective is to go beyond the usual KPIs defined in a process to KPIs linked to the I5.0 dimensions. Before identifying these KPIs, a classification of practices according to maturity levels is proposed.

The identification and classification of practices remains a challenge for organizations. In fact, it is difficult to arrive at a clear and precise definition of a "best practice" or a "good practice". Although a few definitions have been put forward, most of them are limited to giving a very general meaning to the term "practice". In addition, they provide only a limited number of indications on the criteria to be used to qualify this practice as the best. The Chevron company proposed a first classification of industrial practices, in which four types of practice were identified [18]:

- a "Good Idea", a practice that is intuitively known to have a positive impact on the company's overall performance. Therefore, it is not associated with quantifiable data that can help demonstrate its effectiveness.
- a "Good Practice", a practice that has been implemented very locally in the company, in the form of a technique, method or process, and whose effectiveness for the company has been demonstrated. It is closely linked to the context in which it is implemented, and its reuse concerns very similar application frameworks.
- a "Local Best Practice", a practice that is considered the best for a large part of the company, and whose effectiveness has been quantitatively demonstrated. It can be generalized to different contexts and used for internal benchmarking.
- an "Industry Best Practice", a practice that has been judged to be the best in relation to other practices used internally or externally, and whose effectiveness has been quantitatively proven. It can be adapted to other companies, including those in other sectors.

Drawing inspiration from this classification of practices, we have chosen five levels of practice of an organization towards the dimensions of I5.0 MM and linked them with the KPIs of the process (Table 2).

Table 2. Maturity levels of I5.0 MM.

Level	Designation	Description
1	No Practice	No KPIs or practices related to the I5.0 dimensions have been identified
2	Known Practice	The practices are listed based on a ground analysis
3	Good Practice	A list of KPIs is identified and linked to practices for their improvement
4	Best Practice	Practices have been optimized with the comparison of KPIs using an internal benchmark
5	Next Practice	Future practices are anticipated collectively to maintain and improve I5.0 KPIs

The five maturity levels given will be instantiated to evaluate the maturity of a process through the three dimensions of I5.0.

4 Application to Supply Chain Process Category

In this section, the feasibility of the proposed I5.0 MM in the supply chain category is explained with a focus on the process layer.

Out of the 13 process categories discussed in the previous section, our focus lies on the fourth category: 4.0 Manage Supply Chain for Physical Products. The I5.0 MM is then deployed over the three layers (see Fig. 4) with a focus on the Resilience dimension.

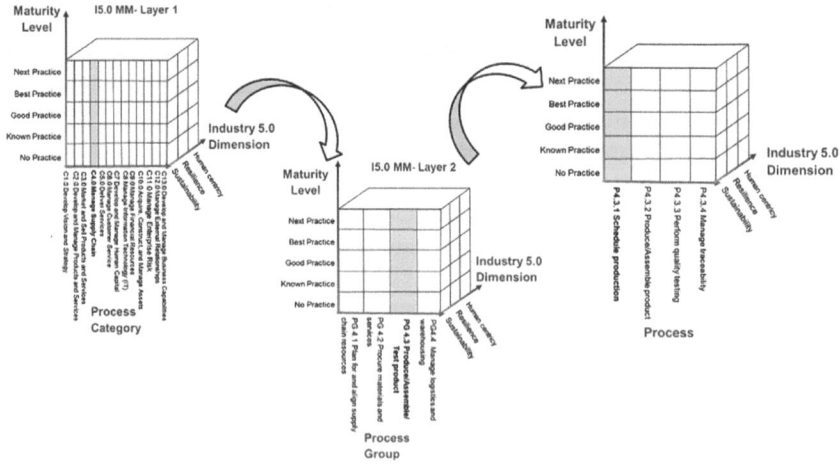

Fig. 4. I5.0 MM application through the 3 layers of the PCF.

4.1 Deployment of the I5.0 MM in the Supply Chain Process Category

The first application of the MM comes with the definition of each dimension and maturity level for this category. In the first layer, an overview is provided, along with an explanation of what is resilience, sustainability, and human-centricity for this process category. The definitions and strategic outcomes of Resilient Supply Chain, Sustainable Supply Chain, and Human-Centric Supply Chain are outlined in [8]. Specifically, a Resilient Supply Chain is defined as a flexible and agile system that can respond to operational perturbations, maintaining the required operations under normal and abnormal conditions. From this definition, the interpretation of the maturity level at this layer is given in (Table 3).

Table 3. Maturity levels in Resilience dimension for the process category: 4. Manage Supply Chain for Physical Products.

Level	Description	Example
1	No resilience practices or KPIs are identified for this category	Perturbations such as geopolitical tensions are listed, yet no practices or KPIs are identified
2	Practices are identified and listed	Perturbations like geopolitical tensions are considered. Practices for handling these perturbations are listed. For instance, Practice 1: Scenario Planning and Risk Analysis
3	The list of measured KPIs is identified	For Practice 1, an identified KPI could be the 'Scenario Implementation Time (SIT)'
4	An internal benchmark is conducted in the organization to compare KPIs and identify Best Practices	For SIT KPI: compare different implementation times for different scenarios in different units (exp:3.8 days for unit 1–2.5 days for unit 2). This comparison leads to the best practice (linked to 2.5 days). For instance, an evolution of Practice 1: Standardize scenarios with faster SIT
5	An external benchmark is conducted to identify the next practices	For Practice 1, the next practice can be: Monitor and predict geopolitical KPIs to decrease SIT

The second layer details the process groups of this category. In this case, four process groups are identified in the cross-industries PCF: "4.1 Manage supply chain for physical products", "4.2 Procure materials and services", "4.3 Produce/Assemble/ Test product", and "4.4 Manage logistics and warehousing". The maturity among the I5.0 dimensions is then detailed. However, a comprehensive assessment of maturity often requires a deeper analysis of specific processes defined in the third layer. Consequently, the maturity evaluation at this level may correlate with the maturity of individual processes in layer 3, rather than being solely determined at the process group level.

In the last layer of the I5.0 MM, the objective is to provide organizations with a prescriptive approach to evaluate and improve their maturity. In fact, metrics are more precise for assessing maturity levels, but also from the evaluation result, the organization can target one or more processes and one or more dimensions.

For instance, for the third process group (4.3), four processes are expressed in the PCF: "4.3.1 Schedule production,4.3.2 Produce/Assemble product, 4.3.3 Perform quality testing, and 4.3.4 Maintain production records and manage lot traceability".

When choosing the process "4.3.1 schedule production process", the question to answer before deploying the MM at this level is "What are resilience, sustainability, and human-centricity for a scheduling process ?".

In schedule production, resilience is a property that measures the ability to re-optimize the scheduling objective after the occurrence of perturbations [19].

Sustainable production scheduling is defined as an approach to balance trade-offs between conflicting objectives defined in the TBL [20].

Finally, human-centricity for this process is more challenging to define. In fact, several axes have been identified in the literature [8]. In this case, two aspects are considered. First, humans should be considered in the scheduling loop, especially in the decision-making process, to ensure ethical decisions and enable efficient human-machine interaction. The second aspect is skill development that ensures the consideration of novel scheduling techniques related to resilience, sustainability, and human-machine collaboration.

Table 4. Maturity levels in resilience dimension for Process: 4.3.1 Schedule Production.

Level	Description	Example
1	No resilience practices or KPIs are identified for this process	The process is subject to perturbations, yet no practices or KPIs are identified
2	Practices are identified and listed	Perturbations such as breakdowns are considered with the identification of related practices. For instance, Practice 1: The use of preventive maintenance
3	The list of measured KPIs is identified	For Practice 1, KPI 1 could be the Failure Rate
4	An internal benchmark is conducted in the organization to compare KPIs and identify Best Practices	For KPI 1: comparing the failure rates of different units (exp:15%-10%). This comparison leads to the best practice (linked to the 10% value). For instance, an evolution of Practice 1: Use Predictive maintenance rather than preventive one
5	An external benchmark is conducted to identify possible evolutions of best practices to next practices	For Practice 1, the next practice can be: the integration of an AI based Predictive maintenance

In (Table 4), an instantiation of maturity levels in the resilience dimension is given for the process 4.3.1 Schedule Production.

The strength of a general description of maturity levels, as given in (Table 4) is to decrease the number of maturity grids that can be used for the assessment of maturity. Moreover, it allows the gathering of important information about the type of KPIs linked to resilience, sustainability, and human centricity and the related practices to these KPIs. In addition, this model allows the continuous questioning of practices from the organizational point of view, leading to a roadmap to be followed for continuous improvement of maturity in the I5.0 context.

4.2 AI Based Evaluation Perspectives

The layers of I5.0 MM are numerous, depending on the number of process categories, process groups, and processes, as mentioned in the last subsection. Usually, MM is assessed through maturity grids that indicate the maturity level and dimension for each layer. Creating a maturity grid that includes all three layers of the maturity model would be very complex and time-consuming for organizations. Therefore, a first approach is to create a customized assessment according to the organization's specific needs and ambitions. The aim is to encourage organizations to embrace an Industry 5.0 vision based on values step by step.

Furthermore, the assessment process could be automated to allow for the customization of questionnaires and the processing of results. In fact, using AI-based techniques is the main evaluation perspective to automatically generate maturity grids and assess maturity results. Indeed, the NLP and clustering algorithms are promising for the evaluation of maturity from the proposed I5.0 MM (See Fig. 5).

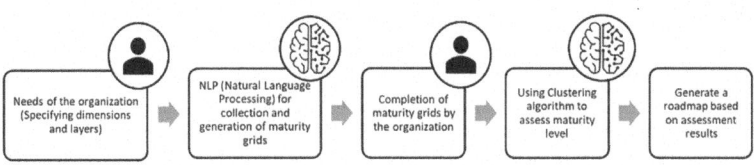

Fig. 5. Steps of the evaluation perspective of the I5.0 MM.

5   Conclusion and Perspectives

This paper has developed a comprehensive maturity model tailored to I5.0. This model answers the challenge of acceptance and integration of I5.0 values in the processes of organizations. The novelty of this model is its ability to link the I5.0 dimensions (Human centricity, Resilience and Sustainability) to the business processes of an organization and their level of practices. Moreover, the layer structure of the PCF allows for a detailed understating of the process maturity within an organization.

To demonstrate the feasibility of this model, this article focuses on the supply chain process category, examining the schedule production process. Through this example, the demonstration of how the three layers of PCF can be used for customizing the deployment of the proposed I5.0 MM. Moreover, it guides organizations through a top-down approach to finally evaluate a precise process. This example also shows an instantiation of maturity levels through the resilience dimension for the schedule production process. Moreover, it shows how KPIs can be linked to practices at each maturity level.

The complexity of the proposed model relies on its multiple process categories, groups, and individual processes. Thus, creating maturity grids is complex and time consuming. Therefore, this paper suggests an evaluation perspective powered by AI based techniques. The objective is to automate the creation of customized maturity grids aligned with the specific needs of each organization and to efficiently assess the maturity levels in each layer of the I5.0 MM.

Several perspectives have emerged from this research. Initially, we will proceed with the implementation of this maturity model to additional processes with a focus on the Supply Chain category, and with particular emphasis on those that are most influenced by the three fundamental aspects of I5.0. Another perspective relies on the development of a software tool to automate the assessment of the maturity and give recommendations on the practices to be deployed based on the evaluation perspective proposed in this paper. Finally, since the aim of the model is to be prescriptive, it is important to propose a roadmap based on the maturity model assessment. This roadmap will help the organization target its next steps towards I5.0.

Disclosure of Interests. The authors have no competing interests to declare that are relevant to the content of this article.

References

1. Grabowska, S., Saniuk, S., Gajdzik, B., Gajdzik, B.: Industry 5.0: improving humanization and sustainability of Industry 4.0. Scientometrics **127**(6), 3117–3144 (2022). https://doi.org/10.1007/s11192-022-04370-1
2. Breque, M., De Nul, L., Petridis, A.: Industry 5.0: towards a sustainable, human centric and resilient European industry. Publications Office of the European Union, LU (2021). https://data.europa.eu/doi/https://doi.org/10.2777/308407
3. Xu, X., Lu, Y., Vogel-Heuser, B., Vogel-Heuser, B., Wang, L.: Industry 4.0 and Industry 5.0—Inception, conception and perception. J. Manuf. Syst. **61**, 530–535 (2021). https://doi.org/10.1016/j.jmsy.2021.10.006
4. Akundi, A., Euresti, D., Luna, S., Ankobiah, W., Lopes, A., Edinbarough, I.: State of Industry 5.0—Analysis and identification of current research trends. Appl. Syst. Innov. **5**, 27 (2022). https://doi.org/10.3390/asi5010027
5. Ivanov, D.: The Industry 5.0 framework: viability-based integration of the resilience, sustainability, and human-centricity perspectives. Int. J. Prod. Res. **61**(5), 1683–1695 (2022). https://doi.org/10.1080/00207543.2022.2118892
6. Leng, J., et al.: Industry 5.0: prospect and retrospect. J. Manuf. Syst. **65**, 279–295 (2022). https://doi.org/10.1016/j.jmsy.2022.09.017
7. Caggiano, M., Semeraro, C., Dassisti, M.: A Metamodel for designing assessment models to support transition of production systems towards Industry 5.0. Comput. Ind. **152**, 104008 (2023). https://doi.org/10.1016/j.compind.2023.104008

8. Villar, A., Paladini, S., Buckley, O.: Towards supply chain 5.0: redesigning supply chains as resilient, sustainable, and human-centric systems in a post-pandemic world. Oper. Res. Forum **4**, 60 (2023). https://doi.org/10.1007/s43069-023-00234-3

9. Hajoary, P.K., Ma, A., Garza-Reyes, J.: Industry 4.0 maturity assessment: a multi-dimensional indicator approach. Int. J. Product. Perform. Manag. **73**(4), 981–1004 (2023). https://doi.org/10.1108/ijppm-07-2022-0325

10. Poeppelbuss, J., Roeglinger, M.: What makes a useful maturity model? A framework of general design principles for maturity models and its demonstration in business process management. In: ECIS 2011 Proceedings, p. 28 (2011). https://aisel.aisnet.org/ecis2011/28

11. Schumacher, A., Erol, S., Sihn, W.: A maturity model for assessing industry 4.0 readiness and maturity of manufacturing enterprises. Procedia CIRP **52**, 161–166 (2016). https://doi.org/10.1016/j.procir.2016.07.040

12. Thomassen, M., Henriksen, B.: Resilience maturity assessment in manufacturing supply chains. In: Proceedings of the CPSL, pp. 947–956 (2023). https://doi.org/10.15488/15294

13. Dikhanbayeva, D., Dikhanbayeva, D., Shaikholla, S., Suleiman, Z., Turkyilmaz, A.: Assessment of Industry 4.0 maturity models by design principles. Sustainability **12**(23), 9927 (2020). https://doi.org/10.3390/su12239927

14. Hein-Pensel, F., et al.: Maturity assessment for Industry 5.0: a review of existing maturity models. J. Manuf. Syst. **66**, 200–210 (2023). https://doi.org/10.1016/j.jmsy.2022.12.009

15. Becker, J., Knackstedt, R., Pöppelbuß, J.: Developing maturity models for IT management. Bus. Inf. Syst. Eng. **1**, 213–222 (2009). https://doi.org/10.1007/s12599-009-0044-5

16. Rosemann, M., De Bruin, T.: Application of a holistic model for determining BPM maturity. In: Akoka, J., Favier, M., Comyn-Wattiau, I. (eds.) Proceedings of the 3rd Pre-ICIS Workshop on Process Management and Information Systems, pp. 1–17. Association for Information Systems, CD ROM (2004)

17. Process Frameworks—APQC. https://www.apqc.org/process-frameworks

18. O'Dell, C., Grayson, C.J.: If only we knew what we know: identification and transfer of internal best practices. Calif. Manage. Rev. **40**, 154–174 (1998). https://doi.org/10.2307/41165948

19. Wang, B., Zheng, P., Yin, Y., Shih, A., Wang, L.: Toward human-centric smart manufacturing: A human-cyber-physical systems (HCPS) perspective. J. Manuf. Syst. **63**, 471–490 (2022). https://doi.org/10.1016/j.jmsy.2022.05.005

20. Abedini, A., Li, W., Badurdeen, F., Jawahir, I.S.: A metric-based framework for sustainable production scheduling. J. Manuf. Syst. **54**, 174–185 (2020). https://doi.org/10.1016/j.jmsy.2019.12.003

A Multi-objective Genetic Algorithm Approach for Multi-component Products Recovery and Remanufacturing Planning

Latifa Belhocine[1]([✉]) [iD], Mohammed Dahane[1] [iD], and Mohammed Yagouni[2]

[1] LGIPM, Université de Lorraine, 57000 Metz, France
lbelhocine@cesi.fr, mohammed.dahane@univ-lorraine.fr
[2] LaROMAD, USTHB, Algiers, Algeria
myagouni@usthb.dz

Abstract. The remanufacturing process has gained recognition primarily for its effectiveness in addressing environmental concerns related to End-Of-Life (EOL) and End-Of-Use (EOU) products. Consequently, a growing number of companies specialise in remanufacturing various product types. This practice not only prolongs product lifespan but also reduces manufacturing costs. This paper examines the challenges encompassing all stages of the remanufacturing process: product recovery, transportation, and remanufacturing operations for customers with similar product types over a finite horizon. The problem involves planning the recovery of used products for remanufacturing and grade enhancement. The main decisions include selecting customers for product recovery and replacement, optimising transportation for used product retrieval, and making decisions for the post-remanufacturing grade. The objective is to minimise both economic and environmental costs. To address this, we propose an NSGA-II (Non-dominated Sorting Genetic Algorithm) based multi-objective solution approach to tackle this problem.

Keywords: Remanufacturing · Electronic products reconditioning · Multi-components products · Product performance · Multi-objective · NSGA-II

1 Introduction

Despite the opportunities of industrialisation, its negative environmental impacts are evident, with industries consuming raw materials, emitting gases, and using large amounts of energy. Remanufacturing, however, presents a promising solution. It refurbishes used products to like-new conditions, reclaiming energy and materials and reducing waste, which aligns with the principles of the circular economy [7,18].

Surveys have shown significant remanufacturing activities. The North American Remanufacturing Industry Survey (2012) identified over 7000 companies in

North America [12], and a European study found 7200 remanufacturing firms [13,14].

Research demonstrates that remanufacturing has economic, environmental, and social benefits. It reduces waste, consumes less energy, and lowers carbon emissions [8]. For example, remanufacturing can reduce production costs by up to 50%, energy usage by 60%, and raw material consumption by 70% [15]. The Automotive Remanufacturers Association in Europe estimates that remanufacturing saves up to 88% of materials by reusing up to 80% of the original components.

Remanufacturing is more ecologically beneficial than producing new products or recycling end-of-life products, saving 56% of energy and reducing CO_2 emissions by 53%. For instance, remanufacturing efforts have prevented around 8.3 million metric tons of CO_2 emissions and diverted 2.3 million metric tons of waste from landfills in Europe [13].

The remanufacturing process typically involves three main stages [1]:

– Recovery of used products.
– Disassembly, cleaning, inspection, reconditioning/replacement, reassembly, and
   testing.
– Redistribution of remanufactured products.

Used products are returned to remanufacturing centres for refurbishment, disassembly, and component replacement or reconditioning. The remanufactured products are then redistributed, often at lower prices or directly to customers.

Product deterioration depends on various factors, such as usage frequency. For example, a gaming computer deteriorates faster than one used for office work. Additionally, product performance affects lifespan: a lower-performing product will likely reach its end of life sooner.

Governments are increasingly recognising the benefits of remanufacturing. A comparative study showed that government subsidies related to carbon emissions could boost consumer interest in remanufactured products, improving product quality and growing the industry [17]. Some manufacturers have adopted long-term leasing models, allowing customers to acquire new products without concern for end-of-life disposal, as the original manufacturer retrieves and remanufactures them [11].

This article considers the remanufacturing process over a finite horizon:

– Products are in use by customers.
– At each period, decisions are made about how many products to recover, which are then replaced with products from stock.
– Recovered products are disassembled into components, and remanufacturing improves the grade of each component, thus enhancing the total grade of the product.
– The remanufactured products replace the recovered ones in the next period.

To this end, we present in the next Sect. 2 a state-of-the-art summarising the main works related to the considered problem. Then, we present a detailed problem description in Sect. 3. Section 4 explains the steps of the proposed solution approach. Section 5 presents and discusses the results of implementing the solution approach. Finally, we conclude this article with the last section.

2   State-of-the-Art

Remanufacturing is a cost-effective and environmentally friendly option for managing end-of-life products, helping to reduce waste, energy consumption, and raw material usage. As part of the circular economy, it poses challenges in economic impact, stock management, and supply chain coordination. Researchers have focused on solving the lot-sizing problem in remanufacturing, which aims to minimise costs while considering stock and resource utilisation constraints.

Early research [6], introduced the economic lot-sizing problem in remanufacturing and proved its NP-hardness for specific cost structures. This foundational work spurred further research incorporating additional objectives like environmental costs, carbon emissions, and material dissipation.

Recent studies have advanced dynamic lot-sizing models for remanufacturing systems. Th authors in [4] considered multi-level products and proposed heuristics to minimise setup and inventory costs. Other studies [9] tackled carbon emissions and delivery time in production decisions using algorithms like the Discrete Krill Swarm. The authors in [20] assessed remanufacturing's impact on material dissipation, finding significant reductions in material loss compared to recycling.

In the context of electric vehicles, [16] demonstrated the environmental benefits of remanufacturing lithium-ion batteries, reducing energy consumption and greenhouse gas emissions. In [19], proposed using the Internet of Things for real-time scheduling in remanufacturing engines, optimising cost, energy consumption, and resource management.

Sustainability evaluation methods, like the emergy-based approach in [10], have been proposed to assess remanufacturing's environmental impact. In [5], the authors explored greenhouse gas mitigation in remanufactured alternators, focusing on life cycle assessment, reliability, and technical criteria. The authors in [2] examined the environmental implications of manufacturing and remanufacturing regarding energy use, emissions, and transportation, incorporating penalties under the European Union Emissions Trading System to minimise total costs.

Remanufacturing research has expanded to integrate environmental and economic factors, addressing real-world complexities and advancing sustainable production methods.

Based on the studies above, we observe a significant emphasis on addressing economic and environmental considerations in remanufacturing decisions. Most of these studies focus on the lot-sizing problem within remanufacturing, often in conjunction with scheduling or inventory management. In contrast, our research holistically addresses the entire remanufacturing process, encompassing all stages from product recovery to redistribution. Moreover, a vital contribution of this work is the explicit consideration of the product's internal structure. Accordingly, the contributions of this work are twofold:

1. A joint consideration of recovery, transport, remanufacturing, and distribution decisions:
   - How many products are recovered?
   - Which product should be recovered? From which customer?
   - What is the path to collect the product to be recovered?
   - What is the grade to reach for each recovered product?
   - Which product should be assigned to which customer?

The product lot-sizing problem involves determining how many products (currently in use by customers) should be recovered at each period. To address this problem, we consider:

- **Customer Selection and Product Assignments.** Identifying the optimal set of products to be recovered and replacing them with the recovered products involves integrating the assignment problem between products and customers.
- **Travelling Salesman Problem (TSP).** Since recovered products must be transported to the remanufacturing centre, we include the TSP to optimise transportation.
- **Product Grade Improvement.** Each recovered product has a specific grade. We aim to determine the target grade after remanufacturing to improve the product's condition.

Two critical parameters in our study are:

- **Product Performance.** This percentage indicates the product's condition compared to a new one after a given period of use.
- **Customer Usage Profile.** This percentage reflects a customer's average usage of a product relative to its maximum usage.

The objective is to minimise total economic and environmental costs. We propose solving this multi-objective problem using an adapted NSGA-II (Non-dominated Sorting Genetic Algorithm) metaheuristic, enhanced with TOPSIS (Technique for Order of Preference by Similarity to Ideal Solution) for sorting the Pareto front solutions.

3 Problem Description

3.1 Problem Components

The Product. An electronic product (such as smartphones, televisions,...) can be defined by its structure. A set of components characterises the structure. Figure 1 illustrates the example of a smartphone made of several components, such as CPU, camera, battery, etc.

The relationships between a product and its components are defined as follows:

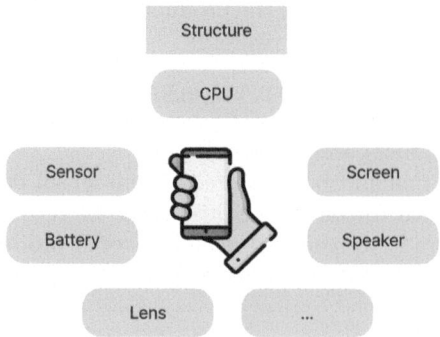

Fig. 1. Product structure: the smartphone case

– **Component Characteristics.** Each component is characterised by its importance and performance. Importance measures the component's usage in the product, while performance estimates the component's state compared to a new one. Performance decreases with use, and the total product performance is expressed in grades, using sub-intervals corresponding to different grades.
– **Example.** Consider a smartphone, which includes components like the battery. The battery's importance is high because the smartphone cannot function without it. Compared to a new battery, the battery's performance and its importance index affect the smartphone's overall performance. Any malfunction in a component impacts its performance index and, consequently, the product's overall performance.

The Customer. In the studied problem, a customer is the product's user. This user profile, represented by the frequency with which the customer uses his product, influences the performance of the components (the more severe the profile, the more critical the decay). If we take the example of a smartphone battery, the more a customer uses the smartphone with a severe profile, the faster its battery performance index decreases.

3.2 The Recovery and the Remanufacturing of Used Products

We consider the problem of recovering and remanufacturing products over a finite horizon to minimise economic and environmental costs. It involves three main decisions:

– **Customer Selection.** Determine which customers' products will be collected and replaced with better-graded products from stock.

- **Product Transport.** Optimise the pathway for transporting recovered products from the selected customers.
- **Product Remanufacturing.** After customer selection and transport optimisation, decide on the remanufacturing operations to improve the performance of recovered products, ensuring the new grade is higher than the recovery grade.

Key parameters for the remanufacturing plan over the fixed periods include:

- **Product Characteristics.** Each product consists of components with specific performance levels, affecting the overall product grade.
- **Customer Behaviour.** The frequency with which customers use their products impacts the product's performance, causing it to degrade over time. Higher usage leads to a lower performance grade.
- **Period Profile.** The duration of each period affects product performance over time, influencing remanufacturing decisions.

In summary, a customer's product usage frequency (0% to 100%) affects its performance during each period. It impacts product selection for recovery, transport decisions, and the grades to which products will be remanufactured.

4 Solution Approach

A solution includes planning product recoveries over the entire horizon over each period. In addition to the recovery stage, we are also interested in the remanufacturing operations that will be applied to the recovered products. At the same time, we consider the transport optimisation to the subset of customers potentially selected for recovery at each period. The objective of the problem is the minimisation of economic and environmental costs. Since we are dealing with a problem with two objectives, we have adopted a multi-objective evolutionary algorithm, NSGA-II, because of its recognised effectiveness.

We will explain the coding used to apply the main steps of NSGA-II described in [3]. The general idea of the algorithm is presented in Fig. 2.

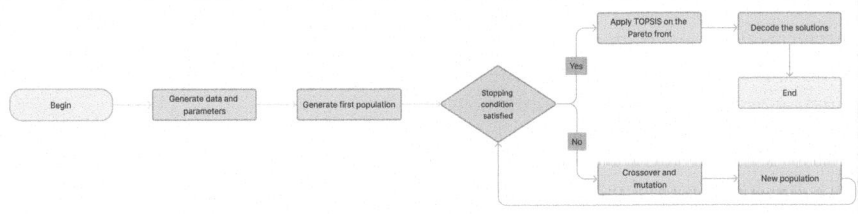

Fig. 2. Solution approach scheme

4.1   Step I: Data and Parameters Generation

In this step, the data and parameters of the problem and the NSGA-II algorithm, such as population size, mutation probability, stopping condition, etc., are generated. The user determines the number of products, customers, periods, components, and initial stock.

The components parameter depends on the type of products used by the customers. It is, therefore, specific to each type of product (we consider in our problem only one type of product). The component importance parameter is initialised at 100% for all products (because we consider new products).

The duration of the periods is chosen according to the type of products considered in the study. For example, the recovery times for televisions will be different than for smartphones.

The symmetrical distances matrix between one customer and another and between the customers and the remanufacturing centre is generated.

Regarding the parameters of the NSGA-II algorithm, the population size, the mutation probability, and the stopping condition are first set.

4.2   Step II: Population Generation

In this step, the first population of parents is constructed. This population will contain several individuals, each generated according to a coding.

The coding we have chosen to construct an individual (a solution to our problem) is defined as follows:

- A table is considered with three times the number of rows as the customers and as many columns as the number of periods.
- In the first part of the table, a random order for the customers is generated for each column using the following steps:
  - Initialise the period as 1.
  - Loop through the periods. For each period:
    * Loop through the customers and assign a number between 1 and the number of unassigned customers.
  - Move to the next period and repeat the process until all periods are processed.
- In the second part of the table, random real numbers between 0 and 1 are generated for each element.
- The third part follows the same process as the first part, generating random customer orders for each column.

According to the previous steps, the interpretation of the generated table allows for building a feasible solution to the problem. The decoding procedure is processed according to the steps described below:

- **Product Assignment and Stock Management.** The system first evaluates the performance of each product being used by customers. Customers are visited in a predefined order, and each customer is assigned the first available product from stock that performs better than the one they currently use. The stock is updated, and the old product is collected for remanufacturing. This process continues until there are no more products in stock.

– **Remanufacturing Operations.** The collected products are remanufactured. Each product's performance is upgraded according to a formula from a coding table, and the stock levels are adjusted to include the remanufactured products. The process is repeated for all recovered products.

– **Hamiltonian Cycle for Customer Visits.** A Hamiltonian cycle (a route that visits each customer once) is constructed based on the order of customers to be visited. The remanufacturing centre is the starting and ending point, and customers are visited in the order specified for that period.

The process is repeated for all columns (periods) of the coding table.

4.3   Step III: Selection, Crossover, and Mutation

This part will describe the selection, crossover, and mutation operations.

– **Selection.** The objective function values (total cost and carbon footprint) are calculated for each solution. Solutions are ranked into non-dominated fronts, with the first front containing the best solutions (not dominated by others). A rank is assigned to each individual based on their front, and fitness is inversely proportional to the rank. Higher fitness increases the likelihood of selection for crossover.

– **Crossover.** Two individuals are selected, and a crossover point ω is chosen. A new "child" solution is generated by combining columns from both parents. The resulting table is processed to ensure feasible random orders.

– **Mutation.** With a probability $p_{mutation}$, two randomly chosen columns in the coding table are swapped to introduce variation in the solution.

4.4   Step IV: Next Generation Definition

Before selecting the individuals for the next "parents" population, the objective function values of the "children" population are calculated. The combined population of "parents" and "children" is sorted into non-dominated fronts.

– If the number of solutions in the current front is less than the desired population size, all individuals in that front are added to the next generation, and the process moves to the next front.

– If the number of solutions exceeds the population size, the crowding distance for individuals in the current front is calculated.

– Individuals with the highest crowding distance are selected one by one until the new generation's population size is filled.

4.5   Step V: Termination Condition

If the termination condition is satisfied, then the algorithm stops. Otherwise, go to step III.

4.6   Solution Approach Illustration

In the following, we will explain steps I and II, the mutation and crossover operations from step III of the algorithm described above, to illustrate and explain the proposed solution approach functioning over one iteration.

Data and Parameters Generation. As parameters of the NGSA-II algorithm, we chose a mutation probability of $\frac{1}{3}$. We consider only two individuals from the population. We can limit the number of iterations to be completed for the algorithm's stopping condition. In the case of this example, we are not going to set any stopping condition because we apply only one iteration.

As parameters of the problem, we consider 4 periods, 5 products, 3 customers, 5 grades (Table 1), 3 components. Table 2 represents the components' importance.

Table 1. Grade/performance relation

Grade	1	2	3	4	5
Interval	[8.0;1]	[0.6;0.8[	[0.4;0.6[	[0.2;0.4[	[0;0.2[

Table 2. Components' importance

Component	1	2	3
Importance	0.29	0.33	0.38

The initial stock is equal to 2 (there are two new products available in stock initially).

For the economic and ecological costs related to stock:

– The storage cost per unit of time is 3% of the value of the stored product. The cost of manufacturing a new product has a value of 50. The best grade is the first grade. The storage cost is calculated based on these parameters.
– The storage carbon footprint per unit of time is 1% of the carbon footprint from manufacturing a new product. The carbon footprint for manufacturing a new product is 0.01

We consider the following set $\{1, 2, 3, 4\}$ where we have 3 cities. The fourth one refers to the remanufacturing centre.

The calculation of the economic and environmental cost of transport is based on the average consumption of cars, so we have:

We have calculated the other data according to the following functions:

- A logarithmic function depending on the frequency of usage is used to calculate the rate of decrease in a component's performance.
- A function that calculates the difference in performance before and after remanufacturing operations is used to determine the rate of decrease in a component's remanufacturability.
- A function that calculates the grade based on performance is used.
- Functions that evaluate changes based on the grade after remanufacturing operations, considering performance before and after, are used.
- Functions that calculate costs related to disposal and CO_2 emissions, based on a performance period and performance, are used.
- A logarithmic function combining the frequency of usage and performance is used to measure the usage carbon footprint.

We assume we have 3 different usage profiles for the customers' use of the products. The first profile corresponds to the low frequency of usage (from 0 to 0.33), the second corresponds to the medium frequency of usage (from 0.34 to 0.66), and the last corresponds to the high frequency of usage (from 0.67 to 1). We assume that customers 1, 2, and 3 represent profiles 1, 2, and 3, respectively.

Table 3. Frequencies of usage

customer \ Period	1	2	3	4
1	0.27	0.16	0.31	0.08
2	0.62	0.47	0.58	0.36
3	0.69	0.85	0.96	0.73

Each component's performance and remanufacturability are initialised to 1 (100%).

Products 1, 2, and 3 are assigned to customers 1, 2, and 3.

Population Generation. Now that all the data, problem parameters, and the solution algorithm have been defined, we proceed to population generation.

Table 4 represents a generated individual. Before interpreting the coding, we will calculate the performance of each component after a period of use Table 5 (Table 3).

The interpretation of the coding used for the Parent 1 proceeded period per period as follows:

Table 4. Example of a chromosone

customer \ Period	1	2	3	4
1	1	2	1	2
2	2	1	3	1
3	3	3	2	3
1	0,38	0,48	0,49	0,10
2	0,64	0,76	0,69	0,66
3	0,72	0,58	0,75	0,41
1	3	2	1	3
2	1	1	3	1
3	2	3	2	2

Table 5. Components' performance after one period of use for Parent 1

Product \ Component	1	2	3	π_{i1}
1	0,95	0,94	0,93	0,94
2	0,90	0,88	0,87	0,88
3	0,89	0,87	0,85	0,87

- According to the order of visit of the customers (from row 1 to row 3 and considering the first column only), we start with customer 1, then customer 2, and finally customer 3 (because the position is 1 for customer 1, 2 for customer 2 and 3 for customer 3).
- After a period of use, product 1 in customer 1's possession achieves a performance of 0.94. We will check if a product's performance in the stock is better than product 1. Two products (4 and 5) are available in stock and are new (performance equal to 1). Therefore, product 4 (with the smallest index) is assigned to customer 1, and product 1 (previously used by this customer) is to be recovered.
- Product 2 is used by customer 2 and achieves a performance of 0.88 after one period of use. The only product available in stock has a performance of 1 (higher than the performance of product 2). Product 5 is assigned to customer 2, and product 2 is to be recovered.
- Since there are no more products in stock, customer three is not visited, so he keeps the product 3 that he already has.
- From the previous operations, we deduce the set of customers whose products are recovered in the first period, to which we add the remanufacturing centre. We will later construct a Hamiltonian cycle.
- We now move on to remanufacturing operations: Products 1 and 2 will be refurbished and have 0.94 and 0.88 performance, respectively. We consider the first column of the Parent 1 table and rows 4, 5, and 6 to determine the performance after the remanufacturing operations. As customer 1 used

product 1 to calculate its new grade, we will multiply the box corresponding to the intersection of row 4 (customer 1's row for the second part of the coding table) and column 1 (period 1) by the product's recovery. We then apply the upper floor function to the resulting number. The grade to be achieved after remanufacturing is 1; in terms of performance, we take the upper bound of the interval representing grade 1 (performance equal to 1). Then, the performance to be achieved for each component is 1. Following the same procedure for product 2, the performance to be achieved after its remanufacturing is 1 (even for the components).

- Concerning constructing the Hamiltonian cycle, we rely on the last three rows of the coding table of Parent 1, considering only the first column to extract the information on the order to follow for the recovery of the products. Starting from the remanufacturing centre, we pick up the product of customer 2, then the one used by customer 1 to return to the remanufacturing centre.
- At this point, we calculate the remanufacturability of each component of each product recovered and remanufactured in period 1. For the other products, the remanufacturability index does not change (equal to 1).
- Once we reach the end of the first period, we calculate the economic cost generated by each of the performed operations.

By following the same procedure for the other periods (2, 3, and 4), the results obtained are summarised in the following tables:

- In Table 6, we have the assignment of the products to the customers such that in the initialisation period, the products 1, 2, and 3 are assigned respectively to customers 1, 2, and 3. Then, after one period, we recover products 1 and 2 from customers 1 and 2, replacing them with products 4 and 5, respectively. In the second period, products 4 and 5 are recovered from customers 1 and 2 and are replaced by products 2 and 1, respectively. In the third period, products 2 and 3 were recovered from customers 1 and 3 and replaced by products 4 and 5 respectively. In the last period, the products 4 and 1 are recovered from customers 1 and 2 and replaced by 3 and 2, respectively.
- Table 7 shows the total performances of the products through the periods. For example, product 1 is new at the beginning. After one period of use, its performance reaches 0.94. It is recovered and remanufactured and has a performance equal to 1 in the second period. It is used during two periods, reaching a performance equal to 0.94 at the end of the last period. Table 9

Table 6. Customers \ products assignment

Customer \ Period	0	1	2	3	4
1	1	4	2	4	3
2	2	5	1	1	2
3	3	3	3	5	5

Table 7. Products performance

Product \ Period	0	1	2	3	4
1	1	0.94	1	0.95	0.94
2	1	0.88	1	0.97	1
3	1	0.87	0.76	0.68	1
4	1	1	0.97	1	0.99
5	1	1	0.93	1	0.95
1	1	0.94	1		

Table 8. Components performance

Product	Component \ Period	0	1	2	3	4
1	1	1	0.95	1	0.95	0.95
	2	1	0.94	1	0.95	0.94
	3	1	0.93	1	0.94	0.93
2	1	1	0.90	1	0.97	1
	2	1	0.88	1	0.97	1
	3	1	0.87	1	0.96	1
3	1	1	0.89	0.8	0.73	1
	2	1	0.87	0.76	0.68	1
	3	1	0.85	0.73	0.64	1
4	1	1	1	0.98	1	0.99
	2	1	1	0.97	1	0.99
	3	1	1	0.97	1	0.99
5	1	1	1	0.94	1	0.96
	2	1	1	0.93	1	0.95
	3	1	1	0.92	1	0.94

gives more details and shows the performances of each component of the products.

- Table 9 represents the remanufacturability index of the products through the periods. For example, product 1 starts with a total remanufacturability (equal to 1), it reaches 0.98 after the first remanufacturing at the end of the first period, and then it reaches 0.95 in the last period after the second remanufacturing. Table 10 gives more details and shows the evolution of remanufacturability at the component level for each product.
- Tables 11 and 12 represent the economic and environmental costs, respectively, and show the storage, remanufacturing, transport operations, and total costs. Since no product is disposed of in any period, the disposal costs are equal to 0 (Table 8).

Table 9. Products remanufacturability

Product \ Period	0	1	2	3	4
1		1	0.98	0.98	0.98	0.95
2		1	0.96	0.96	0.94	0.94
3		1	1	1	0.89	0.89
4		1	1	0.99	0.99	0.98
5		1	1	0.98	0.98	0.98

Table 10. Components remanufacturability

Product	Component \ Period	0	1	2	3	4
1	1		1	0.99	0.99	0.99	0.97
	2		1	0.98	0.98	0.98	0.96
	3		1	0.97	0.97	0.97	0.94
2	1		1	0.97	0.97	0.96	0.96
	2		1	0.96	0.96	0.95	0.95
	3		1	0.95	0.95	0.93	0.93
3	1		1	1	1	0.92	0.92
	2		1	1	1	0.89	0.89
	3		1	1	1	0.86	0.86
4	1		1	1	0.99	0.99	0.98
	2		1	1	0.99	0.99	0.98
	3		1	1	0.99	0.99	0.98
5	1		1	1	0.98	0.98	0.98
	2		1	1	0.98	0.98	0.98
	3		1	1	0.97	0.97	0.97

Table 11. Economic costs

Costs \ Product	1	2	3	4
Storage	9	4.5	2.25	1.12
Remanufacturing	9	5	18.5	8
Transport	6.9	6.9	5	6.9

Table 12. Environmental costs

Costs \ Product	1	2	3	4
Storage	0.003	0.0015	0.00075	0.0004
Remanufacturing	0.001	0.001	0.004	0.002
Transport	0.02	0.02	0.015	0.02

Crossover and Mutation. We first determine a crossover point (a randomly generated number amongst 1, 2 or 3). We assume this number is 1, so the crossover point is between column 1 and column 2 of Parent 1 and 2. The crossover is done according to the scheme presented in Fig. 3.

The mutation occurs with a probability of $\frac{1}{3}$. We must pick a real random number between 0 and 1 to apply it. If this number exceeds the mutation probability, then the Child does not change. Otherwise, the mutation is done by inverting two columns (chosen randomly) of the child table.

5   Numerical Experimentation

After explaining the behaviour of our proposed approach in the previous section, we now present the execution results for a small instance, with the relevant parameters detailed in Table 13. The data related to the components were generated randomly. We opted to test our algorithm on small instances to focus on illustrating the product recovery and remanufacturing planning process. Our problem, along with the proposed solution approach, involves several parameters, and as the number of these parameters increases, the complexity of the planning grows substantially. Additionally, it is important to note that the execution of the algorithm is computationally efficient, requiring only a few seconds to generate the results.

Table 14 presents the Pareto front obtained at the last iteration composed of four solutions.

Then, we will apply the TOPSIS method to give an order to the solutions of this Pareto front, considering three cases :

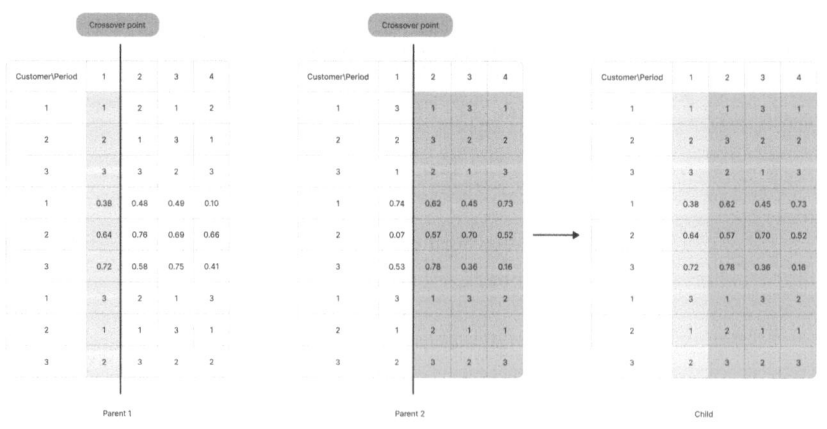

Fig. 3. Crossover scheme

Table 13. NSGA-II and problem parameters

NSGA-II parameters	
Population size	6
Mutation probability	0,15
Iteration number	8
Problem parameters	
Number of customers	7
Number of periods	6
Number of products	10
Number of components	3
Number of grades	5

Table 14. Pareto front

Solutions	Total cost	Total CO_2e
1	852,66	0,93
2	918,77	0,90
3	1010,61	0,86
4	926,19	0,87

- Since our problem has two objectives, we will assign a weight to each objective to apply the TOPSIS method. In the first case, we will give a weight of 0.75 to the first objective. The weight assigned to the second objective is then 0.25.
- In the second case, we give the same weight to the two objectives (0.50).
- In the third case, the weights are 0.25 and 0.75 for the first and the second objective, respectively.

The order given by TOPSIS indicates that solution 1 is the best in all three cases (Table 15).

Table 15. TOPSIS order for the solutions of the Pareto front

Cost	CO_2e	Order
0,5	0,5	1-2-3-4
0,25	0,75	1-2-3-4
0,75	0,25	1-2-3-4

According to the orders given by testing the TOPSIS method, we will present the recovery and remanufacturing planning obtained in solution 1. We first present in Table 16 the product assignment to the customers through the 6 periods.

Table 16. Products assignment to the customers

Periods	0	1	2	3	4	5	6
Customer 1	1	1	4	4	4	4	4
Customer 2	2	9	9	8	8	8	8
Customer 3	3	3	3	6	6	6	6
Customer 4	4	8	2	1	1	1	9
Customer 5	5	10	10	10	9	5	3
Customer 6	6	6	5	5	2	2	2
Customer 7	7	7	7	7	3	10	10

Period 0 is an initialisation period during which all the products are assigned to the customers. Since we have 7 customers and 10 products available, we assign 7 products to the customers, and the three remaining ones are used for replacement. As shown in Table 16, in the first period, products 2, 4 and 5 are recovered and replaced by products 9, 8 and 10, respectively.

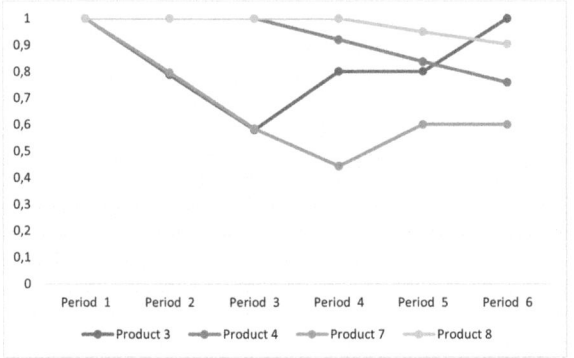

Fig. 4. Performance evolution for products 3, 4, 7 and 8

In Fig. 4, we present the evolution of the performance for products 3, 4, 7 and 8 through the considered horizon. We have chosen to graph the performance of these products in particular because they represent many possible cases. We plan to remanufacture all these products at different times; for example, for product 4, the first remanufacturing operation is carried out as soon as the first recovery is made. These results show that these operations extend their performance regardless of when the products are remanufactured.

Figure 5 shows the evolution over time of the performance of the components of product 3 to explain the components' performance in more detail. After 3 periods of usage, product 3 is recovered and remanufactured. According to the solution given by our solution approach, the remanufacturing operations improve the performance of each component to the second-best grade (0.8). Then, the product is used in the fifth period, and the performance of the components decreases. The product is recovered and remanufactured to the best grade following the decision made in the proposed solution approach. For the recovery, the approach gives a Hamiltonian cycle. The results for the transportation are shown in Fig. 6. The recovery figures show that 2 products were recovered in the last period. This is because product 7 was available in stock in the last period and has a performance of 0.6. None of the products to be recovered according to the decisions made by NSGA-II has a weaker performance than product 7, so a recovered product can be replaced.

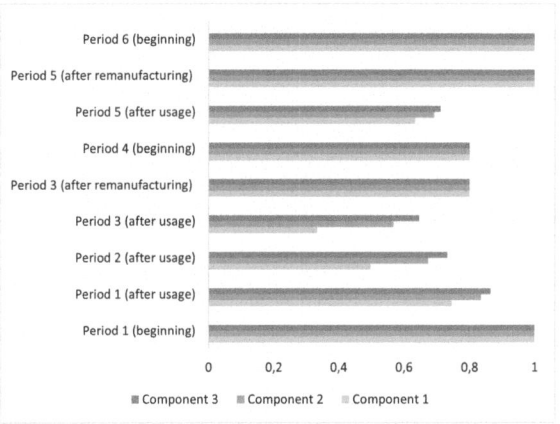

Fig. 5. Performance evolution for products 3, 4, 7 and 8

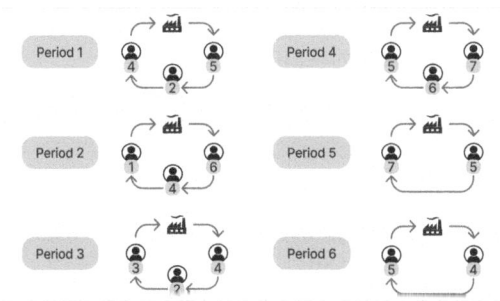

Fig. 6. Hamiltonian cycles for solution 1

6   Conclusion

This paper explores the economic and environmental benefits of remanufacturing by integrating three well-known problems: the lot-sizing problem, the allocation problem, and the traveling salesman problem. The goal is to develop an optimal remanufacturing strategy that extends product life while minimising economic and environmental costs. Key points include determining which products to recover and in what quantities, ensuring continuity in product use by replacing recovered products with those available in stock and optimising the transport route for recovered products by considering the remanufacturing centre as the start and end point of the tour between selected customers.

An adaptation of the NSGA-II metaheuristic is used to solve the problem. Results from tests on a small instance are presented, including Pareto front solutions, ordered using the TOPSIS method, and a recovery and remanufacturing plan for the instance.

It should be noted that no direct comparison with existing solution approaches from the literature has been conducted. This is due to the novelty of the problem formulation and the specific environment considered in this work, which, to the best of our knowledge, has not been addressed from this perspective in previous studies.

References

1. Acerbi, F., Sassanelli, C., Terzi, S., Taisch, M.: A systematic literature review on data and information required for circular manufacturing strategies adoption. Sustainability **13**(4), 2047 (2021)
2. Bazan, E., Jaber, M.Y., El Saadany, A.M.: Carbon emissions and energy effects on manufacturing-remanufacturing inventory models. Comput. Ind. Eng. **88**, 307–316 (2015)
3. Deb, K., Agrawal, S., Pratap, A., Meyarivan, T.: A fast elitist non-dominated sorting genetic algorithm for multi-objective optimization: NSGA-II. In: Schoenauer, M., et al. (eds.) PPSN 2000. LNCS, vol. 1917, pp. 849–858. Springer, Heidelberg (2000). https://doi.org/10.1007/3-540-45356-3_83
4. Doh, H.H., Lee, D.H.: Dynamic lot-sizing for remanufacturing systems with multi-level structured products and components commonality. Appl. Math. Model. **125**, 789–808 (2024)
5. Fatimah, Y.A., Biswas, W.K.: Remanufacturing as a means for achieving low-carbon SMEs in Indonesia. Clean Technol. Environ. Policy **18**(8), 2363–2379 (2016)
6. Golany, B., Yang, J., Yu, G.: Economic lot-sizing with remanufacturing options. IIE Trans. **33**(11), 995–1004 (2001)
7. Golinska-Dawson, P., Kübler, F.: Sustainability in Remanufacturing Operations. Springer, Cham (2017). https://doi.org/10.1007/978-3-319-60355-1
8. Liao, H., Deng, Q., Wang, Y., Guo, S., Ren, Q.: An environmental benefits and costs assessment model for remanufacturing process under quality uncertainty. J. Clean. Prod. **178**, 45–58 (2018)
9. Liu, C., Zhou, W.: Production decision optimization for iron and steel scrap remanufacturing considering carbon emission and delivery time. Complexity **2021** (2021)

10. Liu, C., et al.: Emergy based sustainability evaluation of remanufacturing machining systems. Energy **150**, 670–680 (2018)
11. Liu, J., Mantin, B., Song, X.: Rent, sell, and remanufacture: the manufacturer's choice when remanufacturing can be outsourced. Eur. J. Oper. Res. **303**(1), 184–200 (2022)
12. Lund, R.T., Hauser, W.: The Database of Remanufacturers. Boston University, Boston (2012)
13. Nasr, N.: Remanufacturing in the Circular Economy: Operations, Engineering and Logistics. Wiley, New York (2019)
14. Parker, D., et al.: Remanufacturing market study, report from the horizon 2020 project: Ern-European remanufacturing network. Grant Agreement (645984) (2015)
15. Wang, H., Jiang, Z., Zhang, X., Wang, Y., Wang, Y.: A fault feature characterization based method for remanufacturing process planning optimization. J. Clean. Prod. **161**, 708–719 (2017)
16. Xiong, S., Ji, J., Ma, X.: Environmental and economic evaluation of remanufacturing lithium-ion batteries from electric vehicles. Waste Manag. **102**, 579–586 (2020)
17. Xu, Y., Liu, C., Wei, F., Zhao, S., Mao, H.: The influence of government subsidies on remanufacturers' production decisions, considering product quality, customer purchase intention, and carbon emissions. J. Clean. Prod. 141130 (2024)
18. Zhang, X., Xu, L., Zhang, H., Jiang, Z., Cai, W.: Emergy based intelligent decision-making model for remanufacturing process scheme integrating economic and environmental factors. J. Clean. Prod. 125247 (2020)
19. Zhang, Y., et al.: The 'internet of things' enabled real-time scheduling for remanufacturing of automobile engines. J. Clean. Prod. **185**, 562–575 (2018)
20. Zhang, Z., Matsubae, K., Nakajima, K.: Impact of remanufacturing on the reduction of metal losses through the life cycles of vehicle engines. Resour. Conserv. Recycl. **170**, 105614 (2021)

Reinforcement Learning for Optimizing Routing in the Production Supply of Matrix Production Systems

Florian Ried[(✉)] [iD], Simon Niederdränk [iD], and Johannes Fottner [iD]

Chair of Materials Handling, Material Flow, Logistics, Technical University of Munich, Boltzmannstr. 15, 85748 Garching, Germany
florian.ried@tum.de

Abstract. Matrix production systems offer the flexibility to meet an increasingly individualized and volatile customer demand. However, production supply processes within these systems have rarely been investigated in detail despite playing an integral role in their performance. Contributing to closing this research gap, this work utilizes reinforcement learning for routing in the production supply of matrix production systems. In particular, it focuses on dispatching orders to the vehicles and scheduling the orders within a route. Various constraints are considered to simulate a realistic setting, including order time windows, vehicle battery limitations, and a vehicle capacity allowing to transport multiple items at once. A reinforcement learning framework is conceptualized and implemented, assigning orders to vehicles based on various route construction heuristics. Its observation space contains abstract information about current orders of the matrix production supply environment and specific data on the vehicles for the reinforcement learning agent to select both a vehicle and a heuristic. The action and observation spaces are complemented by a multi-criteria reward function, prompting the agent to learn not to violate any constraints of the environment while simultaneously choosing actions that lead to the most cost-effective routes after route optimization. The reinforcement learning route constructor approach is trained and deployed on a discrete-event simulation of a matrix production system, which is connected to the reinforcement learning framework via a socket interface. The approach has proven to be successful by outperforming two non-reinforcement learning heuristics for route construction.

Keywords: Reinforcement learning · Dynamic pickup-and-delivery problem · Matrix production systems · Routing

1 Introduction

Managing increasing market dynamics has become a common challenge in today's economy. Concurrently, there is a trend toward individualizing mass-produced goods, known as mass personalization [1]. This results in a need for flexible manufacturing systems, with Matrix Production Systems (MPS) being a specific form [2]. Consisting of multiple independent production stations connected by a flexible transport system, they can respond to changing demands both qualitatively and quantitatively due to their modular nature, while also improving efficiency and performance of production sites [3]. The complexity of such production systems can be managed by facilitating communication and interconnectedness among the system's elements, as promoted by the concept of Industry 4.0, alongside a digital transformation and the intelligent automation of processes [3, 4]. In addition to rising complexity in production planning and scheduling, production logistics experiences an equal increase in complexity. Production logistics, also referred to as production supply, in MPS requires a flexible approach to dynamic changes in the production environment and material flow to maximize efficiency and prevent disruptions to the manufacturing processes [5].

To address the challenges posed by dynamic production supply environments, various types of automated vehicles, in the context of this work collectively referred to as Autonomous Mobile Robots (AMR), are utilized to transport goods, as they offer flexibility and a high degree of automation [6]. To efficiently deploy the vehicles to fulfill the transport requests and avoid delays in production, the Vehicle Routing Problem (VRP) describing the logistical objective and constraints of production supply must be solved for the respective MPS. On the control level, applying Reinforcement Learning (RL), a subset of machine learning, seems to be a suitable solution to efficiently dispatch transport requests to AMR. This method involves a software agent interacting with its environment to learn to make the best decisions based on the current state of the environment. As it does not require pre-existing training data but generates it through the training process, RL is particularly effective in dynamic environments and can adapt to changes over time [7]. This makes RL a promising approach to address the challenges encountered in the production supply of MPS. The research question addressed in this paper is therefore how to design an RL-based routing approach for MPS and how it compares to conventional routing approaches.

In the following, the state of the art of production supply in MPS, as well as that of RL and its application in production supply are presented. Subsequently, the underlying problem is described and an RL approach for route construction aiming to improve the performance of production supply by optimizing the dispatching of transport orders to is presented. Its effect on the performance is evaluated by comparing it to two alternative dispatching approaches, using discrete-event simulation.

2 State of the Art

2.1 Production Supply in Matrix Production Systems

MPS, a type of flexible manufacturing systems, consist of multiple independent manufacturing and assembly stations connected by a highly automated transport system, allowing for flexible transport between any pair of stations [2, 8]. With each station offering complementary and redundant functionalities compared to other stations, these systems are designed to provide flexibility for mass individualization by enabling high adaptability for producing numerous product variants simultaneously [5]. Thus, they offer a promising alternative to current high-throughput, low-flexibility manufacturing systems [9]. Their approach fundamentally changes both the production process and production logistics, demanding material supply concepts to match the production's flexibility requirements as each product can take an individual route of production stations, depending on the required operations [10]. Due to lot sizes down to one for individualized products, the number of transport operations within the system increases and product transport and material supply are caused to overlap, as the products serve as supply for corresponding machines [11].

Several approaches exist for optimizing the layout and production planning of MPS. Benfer et al. [12] compare the performance of a genetic algorithm and a simulated annealing approach, which both aim to optimize the entire matrix production setup. The same goal is pursued by Czarnetzki et al. [2], who utilize RL for optimizing a matrix production layout. A modular approach to designing the production supply of an MPS is developed by Fries et al. [10], who rely on certain modules to be combined to suit the individual system characteristics.

Filz et al. [13] analyze different routing concepts for flexible manufacturing systems and conclude that using flexible autonomous vehicles for matrix production supply shows the best results compared to tugger trains or a shopping basket system. Bányai et al. [14] formulate the mathematical model of a cyber-physical MPS, which is to be optimized regarding its logistics. Their literature review shows that clustering and genetic algorithms are most often used for improving material handling in manufacturing, and that linear programming, integer linear programming and mixed integer linear programming can also be used to optimize logistics processes in manufacturing systems. Furthermore, they propose a multiphase optimization algorithm for assigning transport requests to vehicles, which includes the clustering of supply-requests, routing, and scheduling.

The underlying VRP of MPS is a Pickup-and-Delivery Problem (PDP). VRP in general can be characterized as optimization problems, with a given set of transport requests and fleet of vehicles. The objective is to determine a set of vehicle routes that fulfill the transport requests with the given fleet in the required time at minimum cost [15]. The PDP in MPS consists of point-to-point transports, as each transport request represents the movement of a good between two specific locations, from the pickup to the delivery location. Every production station can serve both as a source as well as a sink for transport requests. Since new transport requests continuously arise during operations and are therefore unknown before, in MPS a dynamic variant of the PDP has to be solved [15].

2.2 Reinforcement Learning

As the dynamic PDP with its constraints is an NP-hard problem, an exact solution cannot be obtained within a reasonable time frame, except for very small systems [16, 17]. Instead, oftentimes non-optimal heuristics or algorithms are used. As RL proved itself to be effective in successfully optimizing VRP of similar use cases, it may also be a promising approach to improve the production supply of MPS. RL is a subset of the broader field of machine learning. RL problems are modeled as stochastic Markov processes, which implies that future system states depend solely on the current state without being influenced by past states [18]. In RL, an agent interacts with its environment by selecting an action a from an action space A at each timestep t. The selected action is then executed in the environment. The decision for an action is based on a state observation s from a set of states S, which is provided to the agent by the environment. In response to the executed action, the agent receives a reward r and an updated state observation [7]. This interaction is depicted in Fig. 1.

RL has become popular after demonstrating its performance in the games of chess and Go, showing its ability to solve complex optimization problems and to handle complex solution spaces [19, 20]. It is therefore also used for solving various types of VRP in contexts like goods and people transportation. RL is often applied to optimize routes for the classical VRP, as demonstrated by Lu et al. [21], who specifically address the capacitated Vehicle Routing Problem (CVRP) and a "Learn to Improve" algorithm to optimize its solutions. Nazari et al. [22] and Kalakanti et al. [23] propose frameworks for solving the CVRP by using a policy gradient algorithm and Q-learning, respectively, while Li et al. [24] modify the problem by applying Deep Reinforcement Learning (DRL), a combination of RL and neural networks, to solve the CVRP for a heterogeneous fleet of vehicles.

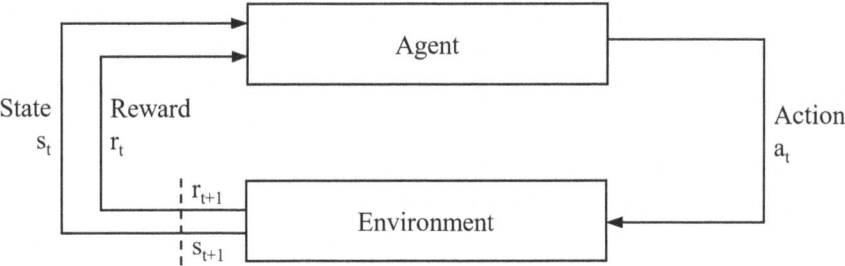

Fig. 1. RL interaction loop, adapted from Ding et al. [25].

Besides optimizing the classical VRP, RL is also applied to the PDP, which occurs in the MPS environment of this research. An approach for solving the PDP using DRL and hybrid pointer networks for transport logistics is presented by Alharbi et al. [26]. A similar use case is presented by Zong et al. [27], who utilize a multi-agent RL approach to improve cooperation between the capacitated vehicles and thus minimize the total travel distance. Garces et al. [28] also employ a multi-agent RL approach, aiming to optimize the route planning of autonomous taxis in San Francisco while considering the stochastic nature of incoming service requests. This way, future requests are predicted to reduce waiting times for customers. Adi et al. [29, 30] focus on the transport of containers between various terminals of a seaport using trucks. They propose both a single-agent DRL algorithm and a multi-agent approach. The objectives are to reduce the number of empty truck trips and to minimize truck waiting times.

2.3 Reinforcement Learning for Production Supply

The potential of RL for manufacturing is immense, as it offers the ability to continuously improve both manufacturing as well as production supply processes. Feldkamp et al. [31] explore modular production systems in the automotive industry, with each product being assigned to a particular AMR from start to finish of production. A DRL approach to minimize makespan and delay ratios for scheduling AMR on a flexible shopfloor is presented by Hu et al. [32], where the agent learns to select from a list of heuristics to assign orders to the AMR. Malus et al. [33] implemented a multi-agent RL approach to optimize order dispatching to a fleet of AMR in production supply, which can only carry a single order at a time. Xue et al. [34] developed an approach, in which the AMR exchange data on machine states and current orders to decide their allocation to the vehicles. Moreover, the approach by Zhou et al. [35] aims to minimize delays and energy consumption to promote environmentally friendly manufacturing environments. However, due to the unique characteristics of MPS that have not been investigated by any of the sources above, these findings do not translate directly to this particular type of production system and therefore only serve as indication, not ready-made solutions.

3 Problem Description

Current research in MPS primarily focuses on layout and production planning. In contrast, there are very few existing studies on logistics processes in MPS, and none that utilize RL to manage routing tasks in MPS. To address that research gap, this paper aims to assess the potential of RL algorithms for this purpose. It addresses the dispatching of requests to AMR, and thus the construction and optimization of routes. For this purpose, an RL framework considering the complexity and high dimensionality of production supply in MPS was developed, including a meaningful action and observation space and a framework for rewarding the agent to support the learning of favorable routing decisions. Special attention is given to the various constraints typical of real-world production supply environments. For all PDP, this includes ensuring that each pickup request is fulfilled before its corresponding delivery request and that the same vehicle fulfills both the pickup and the delivery request of an individual order. This specific environment additionally considers AMR with a finite capacity greater than one. This allows AMR to carry multiple loads at a time, providing opportunities for route optimization by varying the sequence of the assigned orders. Furthermore, time constraints are considered, which include a hard beginning of the time windows, meaning that goods cannot be picked up beforehand, and a soft ending, penalizing delays in the objective function when missing the end of a time window. Moreover, constraints regarding the power supply of the AMR are incorporated, including battery charge limits, route length restrictions, and the necessity for vehicles to recharge.

A possible objective function for optimizing the production supply of such MPS is introduced by Ried et al. [36] and applied in this research. It includes three factors for optimization: delays of the transport orders, travel times of the vehicles, and the development of a charging strategy for the AMR by penalizing removing vehicles from charging before their battery is full. The value of this objective function quantifies the cost of a route to compare routing alternatives.

4 Reinforcement Learning Approach for Route Construction

This approach applies RL to order dispatching in the production supply of MPS, aiming to optimize the construction of routes. As stated above, the capacity of the vehicles is greater than one, giving the opportunity to optimize the sequence in which the transport requests are fulfilled within a route. The RL agent's aim is to learn how to allocate orders to the vehicles, which are then optimized, trying to minimize the overall costs of the routes. Therefore, the RL route constructor is coupled with a Hill Climbing algorithm, which is executed after completing the action chosen by the agent but before returning the reward, as Fig. 2 shows.

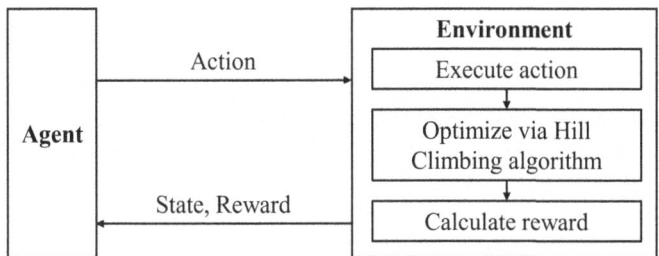

Fig. 2. Sequence of the RL framework.

During the operation of an MPS, sometimes a high number of open transport requests can accumulate. To avoid this from resulting in high-dimensional action and observation spaces, that complicate the RL agent's process to understand relations between action and observation space parameters, a lower-dimensional approach is chosen: Instead of selecting specific orders, the agent learns to select from a set of route-constructing heuristics for an AMR.

To ensure a timely optimization of the constructed routes and to maintain flexibility within order allocation, each AMR has a maximum number of assigned routes, limiting the route length of the vehicles.

4.1 Observation Space

The observation space of the route constructor framework defines the structure of each state observation given to the agent. It provides abstract information on the current system state to enable decision making. It consists of relevant and expressive parameters given to the agent in every state observation:

– Average travel time: This indicator provides the average travel times from each pickup to the delivery location of all unassigned orders.
– Battery level per AMR: The current battery level of each AMR allows the agent to select vehicles that have sufficient charge or to prioritize charging when necessary.
– Open pickup and delivery requests per station: This parameter indicates the number of unassigned requests per workstation, separated by pickup and delivery. It helps the agent to understand the workload of each station.
– Orders delayed: This Boolean value provides information on whether there are any unassigned delayed orders.
– Status per AMR: This parameter indicates the status of each AMR, specifically the number of orders assigned to each vehicle or if a vehicle is currently charging in the depot. This information helps the agent to manage the workload distribution among vehicles and to learn to comply with the maximum route length.

– Travel times of each AMR: This set of parameters provides the travel times of every AMR to each workstation, assisting in minimizing travel times.

Including these parameters in the observation space enables the agent to gain valuable insights into the simulation state, thereby facilitating informed decision-making for route assignment.

4.2 Action Space

The action space of the RL framework defines the actions the RL agent can select to be executed within the environment to influence the system state and, in this use case, to assign orders to the vehicles. In the chosen approach, the agent selects both a route construction heuristic and an AMR, to which the heuristic assigns an order. Over time, it learns to select the best heuristic and vehicle for each system state. Both pieces of information are encoded into a single action value. The agent can choose from the following set of six heuristics:

– First-In-First-Out (FIFO): Assigns the earliest created unassigned order to the selected AMR.
– Earliest-Deadline-First (EDF): Assigns the unassigned order with the earliest deadline to the selected AMR.
– Nearest-Order-First (NOF): Assigns the unassigned order closest to the selected AMR.
– Shortest-Travel-Distance (STD): Assigns the unassigned order with the shortest distance between pickup and delivery location to the selected AMR.
– Most-Pickups-Location (MPL): Assigns the unassigned order from the working station with the most pickup requests to the selected AMR.
– Most-Deliveries-Location (MDL): Assigns the unassigned order from the working station with the most delivery requests to the selected AMR.

Furthermore, the agent can select an action referring to no heuristic and no vehicle, therefore deciding not to assign any order to any AMR. This action is to be chosen if no transport request can be assigned, as either no unassigned orders are available, or no requests should be assigned, as every AMR's route reached its maximum route length.

To determine whether to assign an order, the agent considers the individual AMR's status and battery charge to assume its readiness for additional tasks. Furthermore, the presence of open orders at each station is a cue to identify upcoming transports. In the event of delays in transport requests, the agent might prioritize assignments based on the earliest deadlines by using EDF. Regarding route transport times, STD selects the shortest travel path and thus balances the average travel times parameter. The NOF heuristic assigns orders based on proximity to an AMR, utilizing the given travel times of each AMR to every workstation in the observation space. Meanwhile, MPL and MDL are employed to level the load of pickup and delivery locations as well as distribute multiple orders across stations by considering both the number of open requests per station and the distance to these stations from the observation space. The FIFO heuristic is an option commonly employed for scheduling tasks, characterized by its simplicity. It is therefore included despite not being directly influenced by any of the observation space parameters.

4.3   Reward Structure

The reward structure of the route constructor framework plays a crucial role in guiding the agent's decision-making process towards efficient order dispatching. It includes both penalties for violating constraints or prerequisites, and bonuses for achieving desirable outcomes.

A penalty is given when choosing not to assign an order despite unassigned orders being available and at least one AMR having a route that is not of maximum length. Additionally, a penalty is imposed if the agent attempts to assign an order to an AMR that has already reached its maximum order limit. Lastly, a penalty is given if the route constraints of the selected AMR's route are not met after the orders have been assigned. When assigning a transport request to an AMR, the previous route is expected to fulfill all constraints and the pickup and delivery requests are added to the end of the route. This ensures that the AMR's route maintains a valid order sequence, with pickups preceding their corresponding deliveries and the capacity of the vehicle not being exceeded. However, the battery constraints of the vehicles must also be considered. After completing a route, the AMR's battery must not fall below a predetermined threshold to ensure it can return to the depot for charging. Therefore, the route constructor agent estimates the battery reserve of each AMR before assigning additional orders. If the calculated battery reserve for the completed route falls below the predetermined threshold after the assignment, a penalty is incurred, and the order is not assigned.

The agent receives a bonus for successfully assigning a transport request to a vehicle. The amount of this bonus depends on the predicted delays and the duration of the route affected by the agent's action after applying the Hill Climbing optimization to it. The bonus is reduced if an AMR is withdrawn early from charging to fulfill a new transport request, aligning with the objective function's aim to identify efficient charging strategies. Additionally, if an order without delay is assigned while delayed orders are available, the reward is decreased to encourage the agent to prioritize the timely completion of orders.

5   Experimental Results

In order to evaluate the performance of the RL approach, this research utilizes a discrete-event simulation model of an MPS, implemented in Siemens Plant Simulation and connected to the RL framework using a socket interface. The simulated production environment layout consists of eight production stations, one goods receipt and one goods issue, all connected by bidirectional paths. AMR handle the transport of components between stations. Furthermore, there are two depots, to which the AMR return for charging after finishing their routes.

A Deep Q-Network algorithm is proposed for the agent. It uses two neural networks as nonlinear approximators for the action-value function Q, which defines the value of each action a when chosen in a given state s [7, 18]. The Q-network estimates the Q-value for the current state, while the target network provides the Q-values for future states. At each timestep, a temporal difference error is computed using the current reward, the Q-network, and the target network. This temporal difference error is used to update the weights of the Q-network. Periodically, after a certain number of timesteps, the target network is synchronized with the Q-network. During training, the weights of the neural networks are optimized to maximize the rewards for the agent as it interacts with the environment [18].

The trained RL agent is then deployed on the RL environment and executes the routing for the simulation. It is compared to two non-RL approaches implemented directly in the Plant Simulation model, namely to a static and a dynamic EDF approach. The static EDF approach begins by assigning open orders to the first AMR from a list of all vehicles until no open orders are left or the vehicle meets range restrictions due to the enlargement of the route. Then, the order assignment continues with the next vehicle. The routes of all vehicles that new orders have been assigned to are optimized by a Hill Climbing algorithm and executed entirely before new orders can be assigned to the vehicle. In contrast, the dynamic EDF approach is triggered every time a new transport request arises. It compares the additional route costs assigning the request to each AMR would cause, already considering a Hill Climbing algorithm for route optimization. The order is then assigned to the vehicle with the lowest additional costs.

Figure 3 compares the accumulated route costs per episode of the RL route construction approach to the static and dynamic EDF route constructors, with each episode spanning four hours of simulated time.

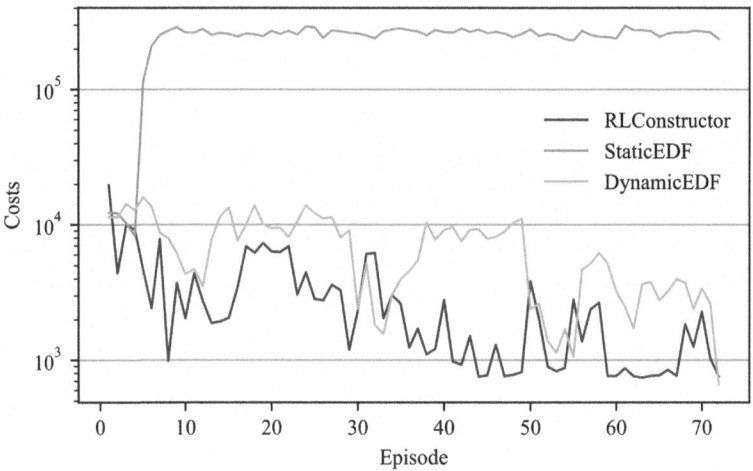

Fig. 3. Costs comparison of the RL route constructor approach.

The results demonstrate that the RL route constructor approach outperforms both the static and the dynamic EDF algorithm. While the static EDF approach offers route costs fluctuating around 250,000, the EDF and RL approaches show improved results. Even though the dynamic EDF algorithm directly considers the route costs as a criterion for assigning the open orders to the vehicles, the RL route constructor approach performs better overall, as only a limited number of episodes show higher route costs than those of the dynamic EDF algorithm. Therefore, the conceptualized and implemented RL route constructor approach can be regarded as very efficient. The chosen parameters in the observation space and the chosen heuristics in the action space provide the agent with sufficient information and agency to improve the route construction process.

Moreover, once trained, RL offers advantages over common routing approaches in terms of computing times. As the computational times for common heuristics and algorithms increase with growing complexity or upscaling of the system, the RL approach can provide a more efficient solution after training.

6 Conclusion

This paper presents the first attempt to apply RL-based route construction to the production supply of MPS to improve logistics performance by identifying efficient routes for the AMR. In our approach, the RL agent learns to select both a route construction heuristic and a vehicle that the heuristic assigns an order to. These actions are complemented by an observation space providing the agent with abstract information about the orders and specific data on the vehicle. Moreover, an MPS-specific reward structure is introduced, supporting the agent to learn to assign orders to the AMR and resulting in low overall route costs without violating any constraints. The experimental results demonstrate the potential of the trained Deep Q-Network. This indicates that the agent effectively extracts and utilizes important information from its environment to select the best actions in return. Future research could investigate replacing the Hill Climbing route optimizer with an RL-based approach for route optimization, resulting in a multi-agent RL approach to further minimize route cost and improve logistics performance.

Disclosure of Interests. The authors have no competing interests to declare that are relevant to the content of this article.

References

1. Schumacher, S., Bauer, D.: Autonome produktion. In: Bauernhansl, T. (ed.) Handbuch Industrie 4.0, pp. 95–122. Springer, Heidelberg (2023). https://doi.org/10.1007/978-3-662-58532-0_164
2. Czarnetzki, L., Laflamme, C., Halbwidl, C., Günther, L.C., Sobottka, T., Bachlechner, D.: Optimisation of matrix production system reconfiguration with reinforcement learning. In: Seipel, D., Steen, A. (eds.) KI 2023. LNCS, vol. 14236, pp. 15–22. Springer, Cham (2023). https://doi.org/10.1007/978-3-031-42608-7_2
3. Kellner, F., Lienland, B., Lukesch, M.: Produktionswirtschaft. Springer, Heidelberg (2022). https://doi.org/10.1007/978-3-662-65803-1
4. Schaffer, J., Weidenbach, M.: Agentenbasierte Steuerung Fahrerloser Transportsysteme im Umfeld von Industrie 4.0. In: ten Hompel, M., Bauernhansl, T., Vogel-Heuser, B. (eds.) Handbuch Industrie 4.0, pp. 143–169. Springer, Heidelberg (2020). https://doi.org/10.1007/978-3-662-58530-6_100
5. Adam, D.: Flexible Fertigungssysteme. Gabler Verlag, Wiesbaden (1993)
6. Wehking, K.-H.: Entwicklung und Eingrenzung. In: Wehking, K.-H. (ed.) Technisches Handbuch Logistik 1, pp. 3–34. Springer, Heidelberg (2020). https://doi.org/10.1007/978-3-662-60867-8_1
7. Rebala, G., Ravi, A., Churiwala, S.: An Introduction to Machine Learning. Springer, Cham (2019). https://doi.org/10.1007/978-3-030-15729-6

8. Arnold, D., Isermann, H., Kuhn, A., Tempelmeier, H., Furmans, K.: Handbuch Logistik. Springer, Heidelberg (2008). https://doi.org/10.1007/978-3-540-72929-7
9. May, M.C., Schmidt, S., Kuhnle, A., Stricker, N., Lanza, G.: Product generation module: automated production planning for optimized workload and increased efficiency in matrix production systems. Procedia CIRP **96**, 45–50 (2021)
10. Fries, C., Wiendahl, H.-H., Assadi, A.A.: Design concept for the intralogistics material supply in matrix productions. Procedia CIRP **91**, 33–38 (2020)
11. Filz, M.-A., Herrmann, C., Thiede, S.: Simulation-based data analysis to support the planning of flexible manufacturing systems. SNE **30**, 131–137 (2020)
12. Benfer, M., Heyer, V., Brützel, O., Liebrecht, C., Peukert, S., Lanza, G.: Analysis of meta-heuristic optimisation techniques for simulated matrix production systems. Prod. Eng. Res. Dev. **18**, 159–168 (2024)
13. Filz, M.-A., Gerberding, J., Herrmann, C., Thiede, S.: Analyzing different material supply strategies in matrix-structured manufacturing systems. Procedia CIRP **81**, 1004–1009 (2019)
14. Bányai, Á., et al.: Smart cyber-physical manufacturing: extended and real-time optimization of logistics resources in matrix production. Appl. Sci. **9**, 1287 (2019)
15. Irnich, S., Toth, P., Vigo, D.: Chapter 1: The family of vehicle routing problems. In: Toth, P., Vigo, D. (eds.) Vehicle routing: Problems, methods, and applications, pp. 1–33. SIAM Society for Industrial and Applied Mathematics; Mathematical Optimization Society, Philadelphia (2014)
16. Savelsbergh, M.W.P., Sol, M.: The general pickup and delivery problem. Transp. Sci. **29**, 17–29 (1995)
17. Lenstra, J.K., Kan, A.H.G.R.: Complexity of vehicle routing and scheduling problems. Networks **11**, 221–227 (1981)
18. Lapan, M.: Deep Reinforcement Learning Hands-On. Packt, Birmingham, Mumbai (2020)
19. Silver, D., et al.: Mastering the game of Go with deep neural networks and tree search. Nature **529**, 484–489 (2016)
20. Silver, D., et al.: A general reinforcement learning algorithm that masters chess, shogi, and Go through self-play. Science **362**, 1140–1144 (2018)
21. Lu, H., Zhang, X., Yang, S.: A learning-based iterative method for solving vehicle routing problems. In: International Conference on Learning Representations (2020)
22. Nazari, M., Oroojlooy, A., Snyder, L.V., Takáč, M.: Reinforcement learning for solving the vehicle routing problem. In: Proceedings of the 32nd International Conference on Neural Information Processing Systems, NIPS 2018, pp. 9861–9871 (2018)
23. Kalakanti, A.K., Verma, S., Paul, T., Yoshida, T.: RL SolVeR Pro: reinforcement learning for solving vehicle routing problem. In: 2019 1st International Conference on Artificial Intelligence and Data Sciences (AiDAS), pp. 94–99 (2019)
24. Li, J., et al.: Deep reinforcement learning for solving the heterogeneous capacitated vehicle routing problem. IEEE Trans. Cybern. **52**, 13572–13585 (2022)
25. Ding, Z., Huang, Y., Yuan, H., Dong, H.: Introduction to reinforcement learning. In: Dong, H., Ding, Z., Zhang, S. (eds.) Deep Reinforcement Learning, pp. 47–123. Springer, Singapore (2020). https://doi.org/10.1007/978-981-15-4095-0_2
26. Alharbi, M.G., Stohy, A., Elhenawy, M., Masoud, M., Khalifa, H.A.E.-W.: Solving pickup and drop-off problem using hybrid pointer networks with deep reinforcement learning. PLoS ONE **17** (2022)
27. Zong, Z., Zheng, M., Li, Y., Jin, D.: MAPDP: cooperative multi-agent reinforcement learning to solve pickup and delivery problems. In: Proceedings of the 36th AAAI Conference on Artificial Intelligence, AAAI 2022, vol. 36 (2022)
28. Garces, D., Bhattacharya, S., Gil, S., Bertsekas, D.: Multiagent reinforcement learning for autonomous routing and pickup problem with adaptation to variable demand. In: 2023 IEEE International Conference on Robotics and Automation (ICRA), pp. 3524–3531 (2023)

29. Adi, T.N., Iskandar, Y.A., Bae, H.: Interterminal truck routing optimization using deep reinforcement learning. Sensors **20** (2020)
30. Adi, T.N., Bae, H., Iskandar, Y.A.: Interterminal truck routing optimization using cooperative multiagent deep reinforcement learning. Processes **9** (2021)
31. Feldkamp, N., Bergmann, S., Strassburger, S.: Simulation-based deep reinforcement learning for modular production systems. In: 2020 Winter Simulation Conference (WSC), pp. 1596–1607 (2020)
32. Hu, H., Jia, X., He, Q., Fu, S., Liu, K.: Deep reinforcement learning based AGVs real-time scheduling with mixed rule for flexible shop floor in industry 4.0. Comput. Ind. Eng. **149** (2020)
33. Malus, A., Kozjek, D., Vrabič, R.: Real-time order dispatching for a fleet of autonomous mobile robots using multi-agent reinforcement learning. CIRP Ann. **69**, 397–400 (2020)
34. Xue, T., Zeng, P., Yu, H.: A reinforcement learning method for multi-AGV scheduling in manufacturing. In: 2018 IEEE International Conference on Industrial Technology (ICIT), pp. 1557–1561 (2018)
35. Zhou, B., Lei, Y.: The pickup and delivery hybrid-operations of AGV conflict-free scheduling problem with time constraint among multi-FMCs. Neural Comput. Appl. **35**, 23125–23151 (2023)
36. Ried, F., Oefinger, V., Henß, A., Fottner, J.: Routing requirements in matrix production systems. In: Wissenschaftliche Gesellschaft für Technische Logistik (ed.) Logistics Journal (2023)

An Innovative Fault Detection Robotic Tool for Overhead Cranes in Industries: Magnetic Wheel Modelling and Experimental Validation

Arun Kumar Yadav$^{(\boxtimes)}$ and Janusz Szpytko

AGH University of Krakow, Krakow, Poland
aruyad1@gmail.com, szpytko@agh.edu.pl

Abstract. In this paper, we present the innovative robotic tool design and modelling, validation of a new family of climbing robots that are capable of adhering to vertical surfaces through permanent magnetic wheels. The robotic system is composed of two modules, a sensing module, and magnetic wheel module which are arranged in a sandwich configuration, with the surface to climb interposed between them. To perform the inspection task, few magnetic wheeled climbing robots have been proposed for many industrial applications of ferromagnetic structures. To achieve a reliable system, good payload abilities, and minimize the power consumption of robot, the design of magnetic circuit and calculation of adhesion forces of magnetic wheel are drive factor to achieve all these. In this paper a four permanent wheeled robot is proposed to climb on the bridges and girders of the overhead cranes for health monitoring. An improved design of magnetic wheel is presented in this paper. Finite element method is performed on the wheel to get the magnetic flux distribution and calculate the attractive forces between the wheels and inspection area. By the simulation distribution of magnetic flux lines were compared on the plane inspection area and a curved concave and convex surface. By keeping the main objective of recognizing the fault into the ferromagnetic structures a wireless robotic system is proposed for the overhead cranes.

Keywords: Crack detection · Nondestructive testing · Climbing robot · Wheeled robot · Magnetic adhesion · GMR sensor

1 Introduction

Now a day with increase in demand of overhead cranes in industries, it is necessary to perform the health monitoring of overhead cranes. Traditionally visual inspection method is mostly in use for the inspection of surface defects of overhead cranes. Some NDT (nondestructive techniques) such as eddy current (EDT), magnetic flux (MFT), ultrasonic testing, are also some methods employed for the structural health monitoring of heavy steel structures. Availability of inspector and cost of inspection also influence the process of heavy steel structures such as overhead cranes. As the inspection target is always located at a few meters of heights, it is crucial task to access the inspection area with heavy inspection devices. To access the inspection area at some height, scaffolding and

M. Dassisti et al. (Eds.): IN4PL 2024, CCIS 2372, pp. 282–295, 2025.
https://doi.org/10.1007/978-3-031-80760-2_18

aerial working platforms are in use [2]. From safety point of view and economical point of view these methods to access the target are not so effective. A manual inspection method for surface inspection has some major drawbacks such as low operating efficiency, safety issues, poor inspection quality [3]. Overhead cranes are in many industries working into hazardous environment and to perform the surface inspection can cause operator's death. Therefore, for an automated inspection, an unmanned vehicle for continuous inspection of heavy steel structures of overhead crane is essential to enhance safety of human and efficiency by minimizing the cost and errors in calibration [1]. Overhead cranes bridges are made up of ferromagnetic steel mounted on a heavy steel frame structure. As these cranes work into a harsh environment, this environmental changes causes the structures suffered from many problems such as corrosions, fatigue cracks and metal loss. In order to keep overhead cranes working for longer time, it is necessary to perform inspection of surfaces on regular intervals by performing nondestructive techniques. This study mainly focuses to develop an autonomous mobile robot for inspection of overhead crane bridges. To perform the climbing operation many technologies have been developed by researchers [4]. For a climbing operation on steel surface a proper adhesion mechanism, contributes a major role. It provides adhesive forces to generate required friction for keeping the weight of the robot and also contributes in movement to the robot with high velocity and maneuverability. Currently for all climbing robots, a variety of adhesion - locomotion methods are available depending upon the required payload capacity. To achieve high capacity of payload, mobility, and high velocity, for the inspection of ferromagnetic structures, permanent magnet wheeled type locomotion is mostly preferable for climbing robots [5]. In climbing operation of robot on overhead crane bridges magnetic technique is well - advised efficient method to attain good results as compared to other adhesion locomotion.

At present many inspection robots with magnetic adhesion mechanism and crawler wall climbing robots have been proposed and applied in many industries such as oil and gas tank inspection, steel pipes inspection, and many structural inspections [6, 7]. In case to achieve high reliability, payload capacity and minimize the power consumption of the robot, it is necessary to perform the calculation of the magnetic circuit design and attractive force.

In the past years for wall climbing robots some permanent magnetic track components were designed for oil tanks and weld line inspection. In that permanent magnets were used for locomotion of robot [8]. Fumin Gao et al. [9] presented a magnetic crawler climbing detecting robot based on metal magnetic memory testing technology.

N.J Montas [10] designed a robot Mobile robot with failure inspection system for ferromagnetic structures using magnetic memory method. The prototype proposed for NDT can detect geometric defects in the range of millimeters, producing changes in the density of the magnetic field in the order of thousands of μ.

The creation of a robot for monitoring of overhead crane girders is crucial in this research initiative since it aims to enhance the safety and efficiency of industrial operations. Overhead crane bridges are largely utilized in various sectors such as manufacturing, construction, and transportation, but they are susceptible to wear and tear, corrosion, and structural defects that can adversely affect their performance and reliability.

Presently, the method of inspection of overhead crane bridges is manually done by human workers. This method is tedious, time-consuming, costly, and hazardous.

However, a robot tool that can autonomously navigate and inspect the overhead crane bridges would offer several advantages over the manual method. First and foremost, it would reduce the human exposure to high-risk environments and potential accidents. Second, it would enhance the precision and rate of inspection, and thus, allows prompt and early assessment, evaluations, detection and prevention of failures. And finally, use of robot for detection would be swift and economical via eradicating the need for scaffolding, ladders, or other conventional equipment hitherto used. Therefore, this research study is justified by its potential to enhance the quality and safety of industrial operations that rely on overhead crane bridges. It is expected that stakeholders in the manufacturing, transportation and other allied sectors may find the outcome of the study useful particularly in policy and decision making.

The paper is segmented as follows: A conceptual design of robot with four permanent magnetic wheels for climbing on overhead crane bridges to perform the surface inspection is presented. In other section of this paper some other designed permanent magnetic wheel are presented for climbing Next FEMM method is shown for the particular wheel to calculate the magnetic field intensity. An optimal design of selected wheel is presented to achieve the adhesion forces on curved as well as plane surface.

2   Type of Inspection Robots

In the field of professional service robots, inspection robots are one of the newest innovations. Automation of surveillance and inspections in locations where inspectors are unable to reach and where the inspection site is hazardous to human health is accomplished through the use of inspection robots. As a result, inspection robots contribute a significant role in the handling and inspection of these potentially hazardous places. Robots are classed in a variety of ways, depending on where they are intended to function. Inspection robots are primarily grouped into four categories from the standpoint of the market:

1. remotely operated vehicles (ROV);
2. unmanned aerial vehicles (UAV);
3. unmanned ground vehicles (UGV);
4. autonomous underwater vehicles (AUV).

After conducting a thorough analysis and reviewing several previous research articles, it was discovered that traditional inspection techniques are still used for overhead cranes. Flexibility was lacking in earlier research on robotic system design for inspecting steel structures. An irregular, concave, or curved surface makes inspection difficult. Robots in the past could only inspect a plane's surface. The accuracy and dependability of the results were the second issue found during the literature review. More accurate results couldn't be obtained because of the lift – off effect during calibration. Despite decades of research, it is clear from a closer look at the literature that traditional inspection methods, such as visual inspection, are still used for overhead crane inspection. It has been determined through careful reading of the literature that non - destructive technique (NDT) methods with some automation technology are not currently being used.

In this research, a climbing four-wheeled robot with permanent magnets for an overhead crane has been developed, and an automated NDT method using a GMR sensor array for crack detection has been implemented on that robot. The novel aspect of this research is the adaptable robot design, which enables it to climb on plane, curved, and inverted surfaces while reducing lift-off values. The accuracy of the data produced by the specially crafted GMR sensor array is another novel feature. The system is user - friendly and interactive thanks to the ability to stream live video and display live graphs on an Android mobile device. Cost reduction, dependability, and safety that this automated solution will provide to industries are three more promising research areas.

In recent years, several authors have suggested inspection robots, but reachability and inspection quality have been the key limitations. Historically, the majority of designed devices could only examine horizontal surfaces. In addition, the inspection was confined to surface flaws and did not include subsurface flaws or fractures. Another drawback of the previously designed inspection system was that it was not real-time and could only inspect a certain surface thickness.

In this research work, the magnetic wheel robotic tool was created exclusively for the inspection of overhead crane bridges and girders, primarily container-loading cranes at seaports. The robot's adaptable structure and degree of freedom allow it to maneuver on horizontal, vertical, and inverted surfaces. The Giant magneto resistance (GMR) sensor array contributes to the inspection of the inspection area's surface, sub-surface, and corrosion. A real-time monitoring feature and live video streaming make this robotic system for the inspection of overhead cranes more precise and efficient. This robot may be used instead of overhead cranes to check any steel structure, including steel bridges, ship superstructures, and other similar structures. Nonetheless, the major function of this robot is to examine the overhead crane's structure for cracks.

3   Design and Analysis of Robotic Magnetic Wheels

It is evident from reading the literature on magnetic wheels that little weight and simplicity of design are necessary for smooth steering and tilting at any angle. Reading this study, which has been discussed by other authors, makes it clear that the design of the wheels should be straightforward and lightweight. After considering all relevant elements, the design of a magnetic wheel using two neodymium magnets and ferromagnetic rings is shown in Fig. 1.

An innovative method for creating an efficient magnetic wheel is presented in this section. The robot's ability to climb is mostly dependent on its wheels. A lot of research has been done on the magnetic wheel's construction. In this case, the magnetic wheels are provided for two purposes: first, as a climbing aid, and second, as a magnetic field generator for a non-destructive flaw diagnosis technique. When developing the magnetic wheel, it is necessary to keep the weight of the magnetic wheel as light as possible. And the magnetic field created by the wheels should be strong during wheel rotation. To attach to the bridge's surface, it must provide adequate adhesion and friction forces to prevent slipping. This necessitates the deployment of a permanent magnet made of Neodymium Iron Boran (NDFeB) of type N48 to attain all of these attributes. A revolutionary magnetic wheel design is provided to address the significant drop in adhesion force that occurs

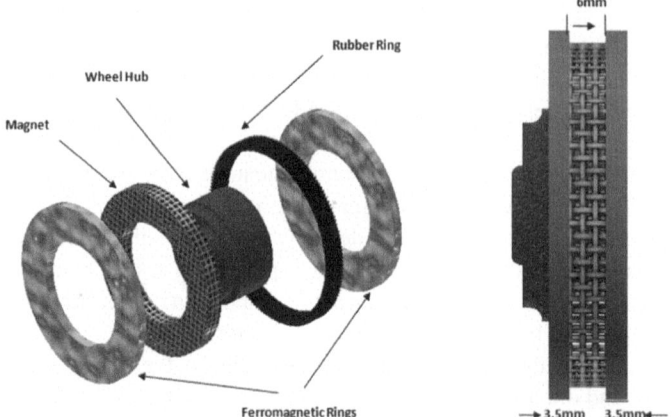

Fig. 1. Exploded view of magnetic wheel assembly of magnetic wheel.

when the wheel is coated with rubber tape. Despite its small size, the wheel can pull a robot weighing between 5 and 6 kg by creating an attracting force of 4.4 kgf. Knowing the overall weight of the robot enables you to estimate the adhesion and frictional forces.

Calculation of Magnetic Flux Simulation for the Final Wheel Design
The adhesion forces, frictional forces, size, and weight of the projected magnetic wheel were all determined through a series of tests. The adhesion forces between the wheel and the surface area must be determined. Adhesion forces need to be strong enough to hold a 5 kg robot with all of its sensors and inspection equipment attached. To find the density of magnetic flux and the flow of magnetic field lines, a simulation was run on the magnetic wheel, Fig. 2.

The wheel and 10-mm-thick steel plate were subjected to a finite-element analysis. The resultant magnetic flux and adhesion force among the steel plate and wheel are shown in Fig. 2. In the picture, the point where the wheel makes contact with the steel surface is where the magnetic flux is at its highest. This designed wheel prototype can generate an adhesion force of up to 169 N, which is sufficient to support a load of up to 15 kg. A magnet and a steel surface need to be in physical touch with one another in order to create this adhesion force. In Fig. 3 are the computed results of adhesion forces between the magnet and wheel.

There are no magnets in direct contact with the steel surface since only the 3.5 mm thick ferromagnetic rings on the wheel's sides come into interaction with the testing area. In this instance, the wheel's adhesion force holding a 7 kg robot in place is 64.9 N. This forced adhesion is produced by one of the robot's four magnetic wheels. This implies that a maximum of 26.12 kg might be supported by the four adhesion forces acting together. For clarity and understanding, the dimensions of the robots have been presented in Table 1. This is an overview of how these wheels will be carrying a robot with the below-mentioned dimensions.

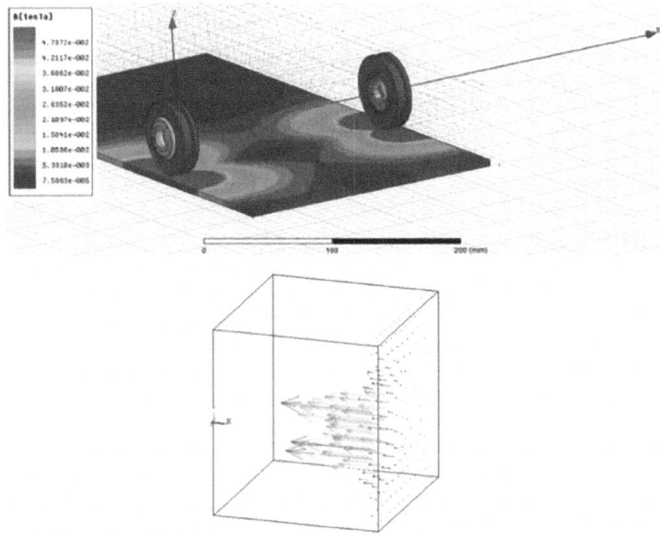

Fig. 2. The Finite Element method is performed on the wheel for adhesion force and magnetic flux density.

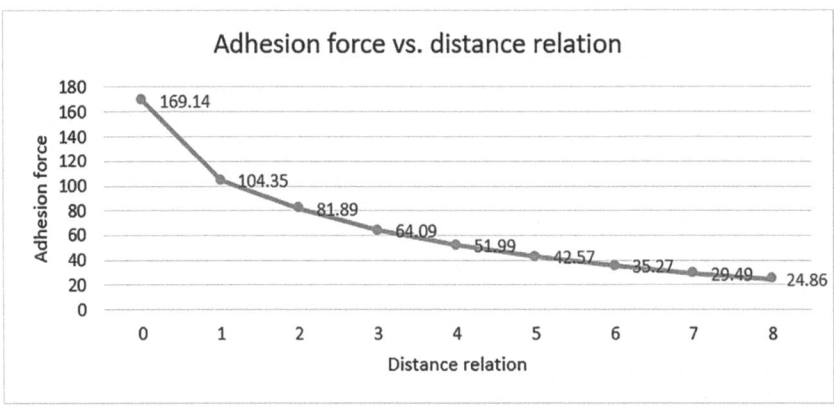

Fig. 3. Adhesion forces between a magnet and a wheel.

4   Experimental Testing and Simulation of Magnetic Wheels

To design a robot for the inspection of overhead crane bridges, some special requirement such as smooth movement on concave and convex surface, obstacles such as bolts and nuts, and high adhesion ability is necessary to be considered during the design. Here a robot with flexible joint for overhead crane bridges inspection is presented in Fig. 4.

The robot equipped with magnetic wheels has simple driving mechanism and greater mobility as compared to the legged and tracked drive mechanism. The front and rear axle of robot act as driving source equipped with two geared DC motors. The flexible

Table 1. Dimensions of the designed robot.

Parameter	Value
Length	35 cm
Width	25 cm
Height	15 cm
Control operations	2.4 GHZ Remote Control Unit
Drive	4 motors, 4 WD
Approx. total weight	4 kg (approx.)

joint between the structures have servo motor to bend the structure so robot can cross 90 degree corners. The middle joint enables robot to adaptively work on concave and convex surface overhead crane bridges. The total weight of the robot is approximately 4.5 kg including the light weight body of robot, magnetic wheels, servo motors, Sensors, electrical devices, navigation and cameras.

This paper is mainly concentrating on the magnetic wheels of the inspection robot. Magnetic wheels are responsible to generate enough adhesion forces for the designed robot. In this study several configurations of permanent magnets were studied to generate a constant magnetic field. By employing the novel permanent magnet in the design of magnetic wheel as proposed in this paper a reliable and efficient magnetic wheel is developed. An NdFeB magnet can provide a great adhesion force that corresponds to more than 100 times its own mass. For an improved design of magnetic wheel, magnet poles should face to steel surface. The designed wheel consists three ferromagnetic steel rings of thickness 2 mm, 2 mm and 10 mm on both side of the wheel and two neodymium magnets of thickness 5 mm.

To make the more magnetic lines pass through the thick steel ring of thickness 10 mm, it is placed in middle of the two ferromagnetic rings of thickness 2 mm. In this case permanent magnet faces three steel surfaces and these ferromagnetic rings get highly magnetized as they are in direct contact with magnet. By doing this two magnetic close loop circuit can be established between the magnet and steel surface and more magnetic lines will pass through steel surface. Passage of more magnetic lines through steel surface generates 2 times more adhesion forces. Second advantage of this designed wheel is that as the magnet and steel surface are not in direct contact with each other so chances of corrosion and metal loss are less.

For calculation of magnetic field analysis such as material properties, loads apply, element attribution and magnetic boundaries finite element method is employed. 2D model of model for magnetic flux lines on wheel was performed in FEMM and for 3 D model ANSYS Maxwell software was use.

To perform the analysis of magnetic field it is necessary to define the material properties. As the wheel consists of a silicon rubber covering and aluminum central hub so for nonmagnetic components relative permeability was considered 1.0 in the air medium.

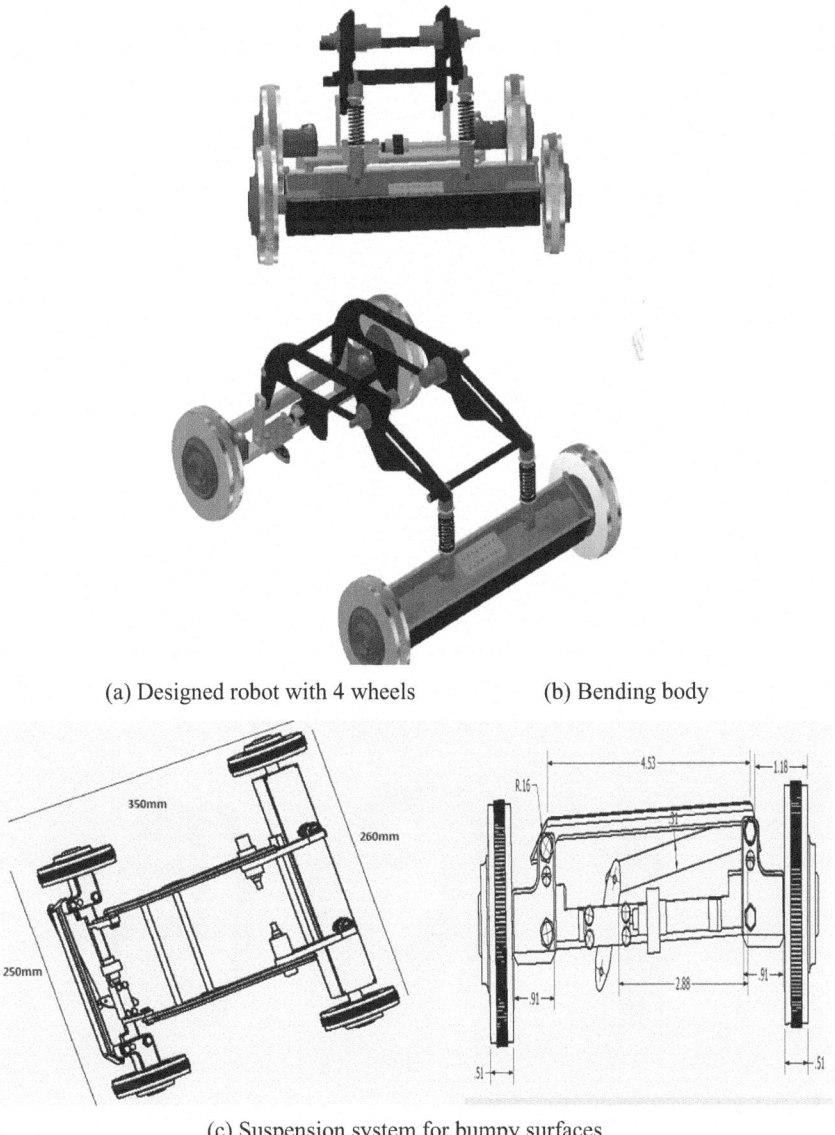

(a) Designed robot with 4 wheels   (b) Bending body

(c) Suspension system for bumpy surfaces

Fig. 4. Robot with flexible joint for overhead crane bridges inspection.

For the inspection surface of stainless steel, the relative permeability is approximately 2000 and 1000.

The most important step is to decide the material for the permanent magnet. Permanent magnets are categorized in four category: neodymium iron boron (NDFeB), Samarium cobalt (SmCo), alnico, and ceramic or ferrite magnets. NDFeB types of magnet are composed of rare earth metal and high coercive force. They have high energy product range, up to 50 MGOe because of this property a high energy product can be designed compact and small in size. NDFeB magnet of grade N42 is considered for the magnetic wheel design of its property of being light in weight and higher strength. Some of the properties of used magnet N42 is presented in Table 2.

Table 2. Characteristics of Neodymium magnet (N42).

Grade N42 magnet	
Diameter	30 mm
Thickness	5 mm
Remanence	1300 BR mt
Normal coercivity	950 kA/m
Mass energy product	318 kJ/m^3

In FE method arrangement the magnetic ring of NDFeB acts as an excited component to apply loads with magnetic boundary. As the magnetic wheel consists of two magnets and three ferromagnetic steel rings, it forms two closed magnetic circuit. High relative permeability steel, permanent magnet, silicon rubber layer and inspection area are part of the FE method and contributes in calculation of flux density and magnetic forces. Some results of FE method on the designed wheels are presented in Fig. 5.

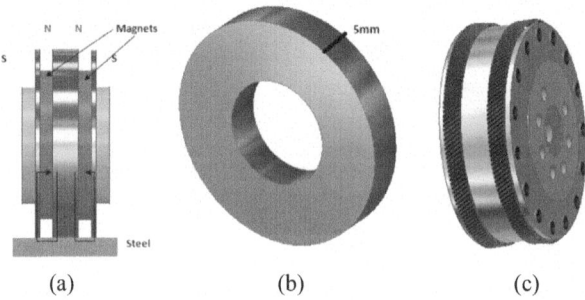

(a)   (b)   (c)

Fig. 5. Designed wheels: (a) the 1st designed magnetic wheel, (b) magnetic ring of 5 mm thickness, (c) modified designed wheel.

Some of the designed wheels in Inventor 3D software are presented in Fig. 6a to Fig. 6c. Minor changes in the design of the magnetic wheels induce major changes in adhesion forces.

The first designed wheel has one neodymium N42 permanent magnet sandwiched between two ferromagnetic rings of stainless steel. To keep the weight low, motor shaft hub is made up aluminum. 1st designed wheel is light in weight and very compact in design but lacking behind in adhesion forces as compare to other two designed wheels. To enhance the adhesion forces in next design, 16 small magnets are embedded into the wheel instead of using a single ring of permanent magnet. By doing that a considerable increase in adhesion forces was achieved. Due to higher number of magnets and complicated design and arrangement of magnets, the wheel weight was heavier. In 3rd design of wheel to generate more adhesion forces and keeps the weight of low neodymium N42 magnets are placed in between three ferromagnetic rings. For a smooth climbing operation, wheel should have to generate enough friction so it can avoid the slippage. To produce enough friction a rubber layer of varying thickness places on the magnetic wheel. Some experiments and simulation action were performed for the calculation of adhesion force and frictional force.

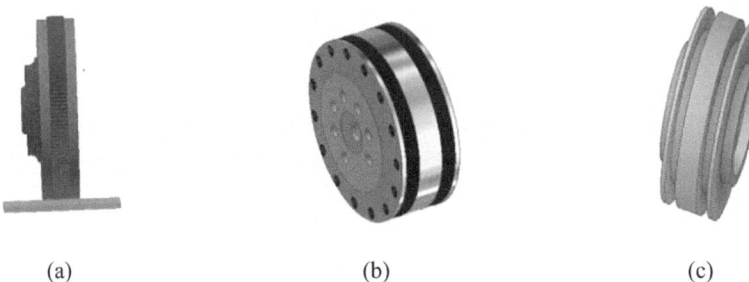

(a)   (b)   (c)

Fig. 6. Inventor 3D designed magnetic wheel. (a) single magnet wheel with rubber covering (b) 16 hollow magnetic wheel with aluminum hub, (c) double magnet wheel with aluminum hub.

In the testing process of adhesion and frictional forces wheels are placed on a ferromagnetic surface area of varying thickness from 1mm to. A pull force applied on the wheel by using a digital gauge meter. When the applied force become more than the adhesion force, the wheel start detaching from the steel surface. During the experiment on the designed wheel, permanent magnet is magnetized axially. Some major properties such as effect of air gap on adhesion force, effect of varying thickness on the adhesion forces, calculation of tilt angle and adhesion force are studied in the experimental form. To avoid the slippage or roll off the wheels' coefficient of friction has been studied. Figure 7 represents the adhesion forces of three different magnetic wheels on the steel surface of varying thickness.

Lift off effect has been performed on the three designed wheels. From the below graph it is investigated that with the increase in the lift off value, adhesion forces decrease gradually and becomes near to zero when the lift off value is greater than 6mm. After the experimental result it is clear that wheel 3, adhesion force is less affected by the change in lift off values as compared to other two wheels (Fig. 8).

In case of tilting of wheel at some angle decrease in the adhesion force occurs. This decrease in adhesion force can result into slippage of robot from the surface. According to simulation performed in magnetic field simulation software, considerable decrease in adhesion forces can be seen in the below graph when the wheel tilted at some angel. Increase in tilt angel of wheel results decrease in adhesion force of wheels (Fig. 9, Table 3).

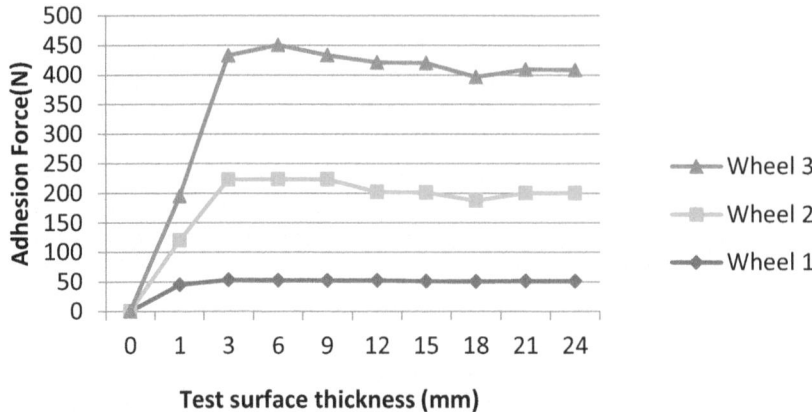

Fig. 7. Relation between adhesion forces and test surface thickness.

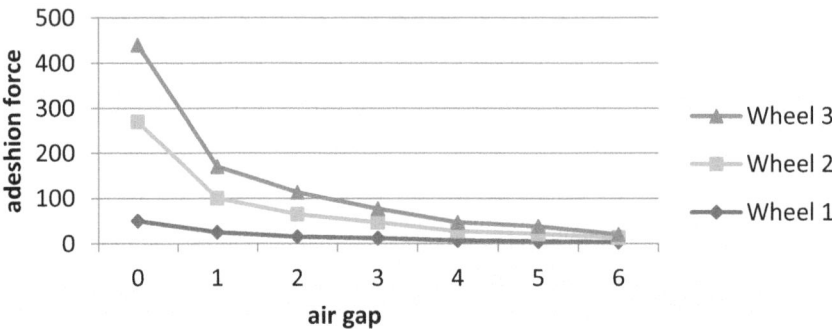

Fig. 8. Relation between the adhesion force and lift off value.

Extensive simulations were performed to signify the ability of magnetic wheel in avoiding the slip off and enhancing the robot climbing performance. The results of adhesion force and traction of magnetic wheel are already presented in Fig. 7, 8. These results of simulations and experiments on three designed wheels demonstrate the relation of adhesion force and thickness of the inspection area, relation between the tilt angel and adhesion force, and relation between the adhesion force and lift off value. To make the climbing operation of robot more reliable some experiments were performed on the designed wheels with varying inspection thickness.

The robot was tested on the smooth and uneven surface created using obstacles like sharp corners, concave and convex shape and weld joints. The robot was able to climb over all these obstacles that validate the effective design of robot and magnetic wheels.

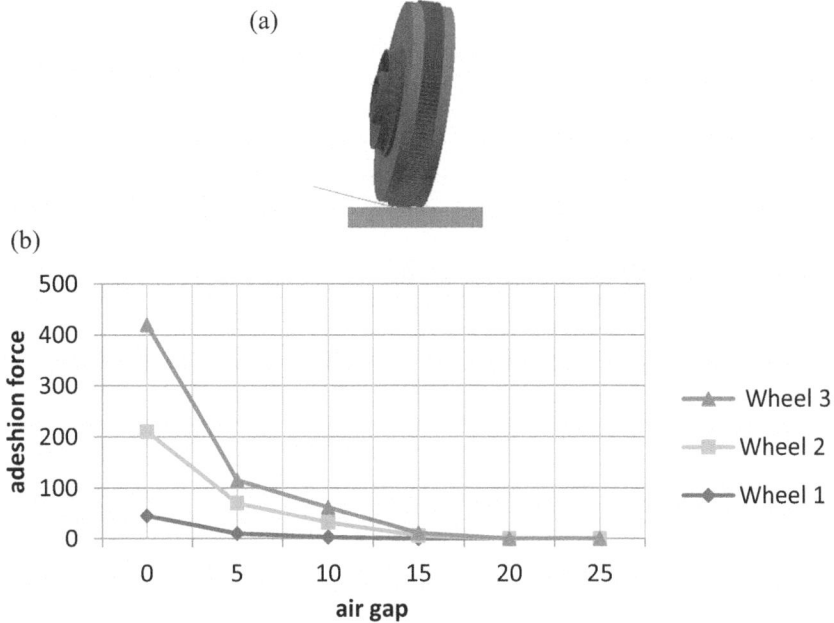

Fig. 9. Relation between the adhesion force and lift off value: (a) tilting of wheel on inspection area, (b) relation between the tilt angle and adhesion forces.

Table 3. Adhesion force comparison of three magnetic wheels.

Parameters	Weight (gm)	Adhesion force on 1mm thickness surface (N)	Adhesion force on 3 mm thickness surface (N)	Adhesion ratio (N/gm) for 1 mm thickness	Adhesion ratio (N/gm) for 3 mm thickness
wheel 1	275	45	53	0.163	0.192
wheel 2	225	75	170	0.333	0.755
wheel 3	180	75	210	0.416	1.166

5 Conclusion

This study introduces a novel approach for detecting corrosion and cracks on the bridges of overhead cranes by combining a GMR sensor with a flexible climbing robotic framework. The mobility flexibility given by this robot design enables considerably quicker, more secure, and more complete inspections to be performed at a lower cost.

A magnetic-based GMR sensor array mounted on a climbing robot is proposed for detecting corrosion and fracture inspection on overhead crane steel bridges.

This research work presents a various distinct design for magnetic wheels that can be used on the climbing robot. The fundamental issue of magnetic wheel design in past research was to keep the wheel light while yet providing appropriate adherence and friction force. Previous studies always covered the magnetic wheel's tread with a rubber tire to boost its friction coefficient. The adhesion force, however, drops noticeably due to the rubber tire's increased friction coefficient. An innovative magnetic wheel design is introduced to address this issue. When a magnetic circuit is combined with a rubber tire with a serrated tread, the adhesion force and friction coefficient are greatly improved. The magnetic wheel, as demonstrated in the studies, can create an adhesion force equivalent to 26 its own weight, and the coefficient of friction can be increased to 0.7–0.85. The wheel is under 200 g in weight.

The portability, light weight, and responsive control of these robots are significant benefits. System designs include those for driving, steering, bending, twisting, and suspension. The robot is capable of achieving a remarkable variety of obstructions, including stairs, slanted and sloping walls, and bolts. The robot can now manoeuvre around concave curves thanks to a bending technology that incorporates an active-passive compliant joint. The robot weighs only 4.5 kg and measures 35 cm by 25 cm by 15 cm. To verify the robot's mobility and identify its limits, experimental testing is carried out in the real world. The robot can travel at a top speed of 0.32 m/s and can travel at a steady 0.18 m/s on average. The highest bolt that can be overcome by the robot is 30mm. We arrived at the anticipated output of this research work, which is an entirely novel approach for crane girder inspection. A novel way for damage identification in overhead crane girders has been devised using the robot as a tool and GMR sensing, a non-destructive testing methodology. The primary goal of this study was to provide a solution and approach for automating the inspection process. The objective of the research was achieved by combining a flexible-structure robot with four magnetic wheels and an array of GMR sensor.

References

1. Guan, S., Zhu, Z., Wang, G.: A review on UAV-based remote sensing technologies for construction and civil applications. Drones 6(5), 117 (2022)
2. Song, W., et al.: Design of permanent magnetic wheel – type adhesion –locomotion system for water-jetting wall- climbing robot. Adv. Mech. Eng. 10, 1–11 (2018)
3. Liu, Z., Wu, L., Liu, Z., Mo, Y.: Quality control method of steel structure construction based on digital twin technology [version 1; peer review: 1 approved, 1 approved with reservations]. Digit. Twin 3(5) 2023. https://doi.org/10.12688/digitaltwin.17824.1
4. Zhang, X., Zhang, M., Jiao, S., Zhang, X., Li, M.: Optimization design and parameter analysis of a wheel with array magnets. Symmetry 15, 962 (2023). https://doi.org/10.3390/sym1505 0962
5. Albitar, H., Dandan, K., Ananiev, A., et al.: Underwater robotics: surface cleaning technics, adhesion and locomotion systems. Int. J. Adv. Robot. Syst. 13 (2016)
6. Hu. J., Han X.: A magnetic crawler wall-climbing robot with capacity of high payload on the convex surface. Robot. Autom. Syst. 148(12), 103907 (2021). https://doi.org/10.1016/j. robot.2021.103907
7. Özgür, A., YaŞar, C.F.: Autonomous climbing robot for tank inspection. Procedia Comput. Sci. 158, 376–381 (2019). ISSN 1877-0509. https://doi.org/10.1016/j.procs.2019.09.065
8. Zhu, L., Zheng, X.: Design of a curved surface adaptive permanent magnet wall climbing robot. J. Phys. Conf. Ser. 2405, 012028 (2022). https://doi.org/10.1088/1742-6596/2405/1/ 012028

9. Fumin, G., et al.: Magnetic crawler climbing detection robot basing on metal magnetic memory testing technology. Robot. Autom. Syst. **125**, 103439. https://doi.org/10.1016/j.robot.2020.103439

10. Montes de Oca-Mora, N.J., Woo-Garcia, R.M., Juarez-Aguirre, R., et al.: Mobile robot with failure inspection system for ferromagnetic structures using magnetic memory method. SN Appl. Sci. **3**, 853 (2021). https://doi.org/10.1007/s42452-021-04833-9

Current Trends and Future Challenges to Put Circular Manufacturing in Practice

Yasamin Eslami[1]([✉]), Chiara Franciosi[2], Maroua Nouiri[1], Adriana Giret[3], Elisa Negri[4], and Pascale Marangé[2]

[1] Nantes Université, École Centrale de Nantes, CNRS, LS2N, UMR 6004, 44000 Nantes, France
yasamin.eslami@ec-nantes.fr, maroua.nouiri@univ-nantes.fr
[2] Université de Lorraine, CNRS, CRAN, 54000 Nancy, France
{chiara.franciosi,pascale.marange}@univ-lorraine.fr
[3] VRAIN - Universitat Politènica de València, Valencia, Spain
agiret@dsic.upv.es
[4] Department of Management Economics and Industrial Engineering, Politecnico di Milano, Milan, Italy
elisa.negri@polimi.it

Abstract. Addressing Sustainable Development issues in the industrial sector is a hot topic in the existing literature. Different production and consumption strategies have been introduced as drivers for sustainable development in manufacturing such as Circular Economy (CE). It covers a prominent position in boosting sustainable development. The adoption of the CE concept to manufacturing leads to Circular Manufacturing (CM). Different strategies and approaches have been investigated toward the transition to a Circular Manufacturing System (CMS). Although abundant studies have been focused on the adoption of CM strategies in manufacturing systems, the literature still lacks an overview of the challenges raised through this implementation in practice. To address this gap, the present study centres around looking through various definitions of CM, different methodologies and frameworks to adopt CM strategies and finally the challenges faced in putting these strategies into practice.

Keywords: Circular manufacturing · Circulation economy · Sustainable development · digitalisation

1 Introduction

Nowadays, sustainable development is of interest in many sectors. It is the development that meets the needs of the present without compromising the ability of future generations to meet their own needs. Our society is asked to urgently cope with the increased need for resource consumption due to the growth of the population. Thus, assessment of environmental, social and economic impacts is a must. Industrial companies aim to deal with sustainability issues while using new production and consumption strategies rather than linear strategies. This requires re-thinking current ways of producing, providing and using materials and products.

Circular Economy (CE) has been introduced as the most promising sustainable paradigm (Ellen MacArthur Foundation, 2012). The concept has received a great deal of attention from both industry and academia [1]. It is defined as a model of production and consumption, which involves sharing, leasing, reusing, repairing, refurbishing and recycling existing materials and products as long as possible. Thus, the product's life cycle is extended, its disposal is postponed, and consequently, it moves towards a more sustainable path. When the concept of CE is adapted to the manufacturing sector, it is called "**Circular Manufacturing**" (CM) [2]. To ensure the CM concept, different strategies are adaptable beyond CE. CM strategies have been studied in the literature alongside technologies that can support the adaptation. The authors in [3] did a literature review on the role of Industry 4.0 tools and technologies in adopting CM approaches. In their study, they have developed a framework to represent the barriers identified in the adoption of CE with the potential use of I4.0 technologies. The same authors, put their focus in [4] on the social benefits gained by adapting CM in manufacturing organisations, especially when it comes to the integration of I4.0 technologies.

Despite the general agreement to move toward a CM system, no exhaustive work gives a holistic view of the CM concept and CM strategies and highlights the related challenges. The literature still neglects how the approaches and technologies can be applied to get a concrete deployment of CM. To fill the gap, this paper presents a representative literature review that focuses on challenges and trends presented in scientific works in adopting CM, focusing on two main research questions:

RQ1. 'What are the approaches/methodologies/tools/frameworks recommended to date to adopt Circular Manufacturing strategies in practice?
RQ2. 'What are the challenges/issues a manufacturing firm can face while enabling Circular Manufacturing?'

To investigate the research queries, this article first looks at the existing definitions of CM in the literature. Afterwards, the research methodology is presented in Sect. 3. Section 4 discusses the results of the two research questions (RQ). Consequently, Sect. 5 concludes the findings and offers a future research agenda.

2   Content Description: What is Circular Manufacturing?

Before going through the RQs and having a better overview of the challenges and trends, it is necessary to understand how CM is intended from the point of view of several researchers over the years. To that point, the CM definitions and the discussions around the topic were extracted from the papers and reported in the following.

In 2013, Takata.S, [5] started to talk about CM and he proposed the concept of maintenance-centred CM, highlighting the relevance of maintenance engineering, diagnosis, restoration and upgrading technologies for enabling the CM. Later, several authors started to see CM as the integration of CE principles in manufacturing systems. In particular, the authors in [2] studied, identified and clustered the CE strategies manufacturers adopted and called them CM strategies. Coherently, Acerbi et al. [6] stated that the CE paradigm is transferred to manufacturing companies through the adoption of CM strategies. These strategies include remanufacturing, reuse, recycling, closed-loop supply chain and reverse logistics, industrial symbiosis, disassembly, circular design practices, resource efficiency and cleaner production, waste management and servitization. In the same direction, [7] affirmed that CE practices in manufacturing industries are often called CM and represent industrial tasks in which the CE principles are integrated. They declared that the classic 3R strategies of recycling, remanufacturing, and reusing, among the CM strategies, are the ones that help the manufacturing industry close the loop towards sustainability.

According to [8], the manufacturing industry needs to implement Circular Manufacturing Systems (CMS), where the products are designed intentionally to be used for multiple life cycles. Indeed, their point of view is more focused on the product level, particularly the relevance of correctly designing products to implement CMS. They considered as a reference the definition of CMS provided by the Ellen MacArthur Foundation (2012), in which products, components and materials have to be kept at the highest utility and value at all times. The authors in [9] also considered the concept of CMS, previously provided by [10], which refers to "systems that are designed intentionally to close the loop of products/components, preferably in their original form, through multiple lifecycles".

Another definition is provided by [11], who stated that CM is "a manufacturing system in which products, modules, parts, and materials (collectively called items) are reused and recycled as much as possible so that we can decrease the number of resources and environmental load for providing functionalities to the customers and increase profits".

Summarising, different definitions of CM are provided in the literature with different points of view and perspectives (product, process, system) based on the research conducted by several researchers. However, a shared definition of the concept of CM was not found. Whatever the definition, it emphasises several recovery cycles and the need to consider account all the micro, meso and macro levels. However, the definition does not say how to put CM into practice.

3   Research Methodology

To answer the research questions, a representative review of the literature was carried out using the keyword "circular manufacturing" (the search was run by indicating the words circular manufacturing in quotes "" to consider only papers that presented the two words one after the other within title/abstract/keywords). As mentioned above, the literature review is not a systematic analysis of the existing studies including implicit or explicit application of CM and its strategies. This study is a representative review and will focus on direct applications of CM strategies in manufacturing systems. Therefore, the articles whose direct focus and implications were not on CM strategies application were considered excluded from this study. The methodology is shown in Fig. 1.

4   Discussion on the Results

The following sections show the findings after investigating the final 23 papers selected and analysed to answer two main research questions.

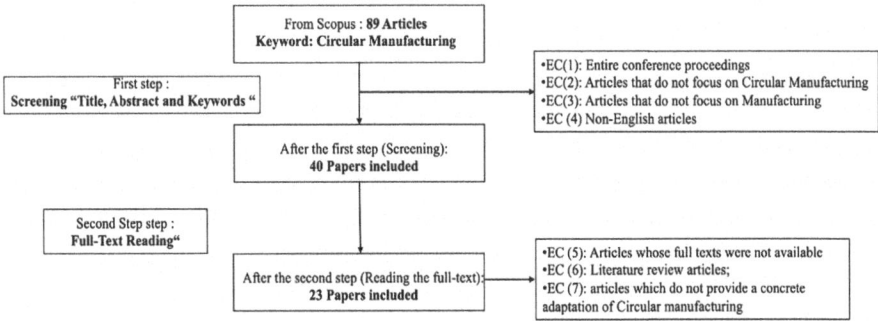

Fig. 1. Literature review process.

RQ1. What are the Approaches/Methodologies/Tools/Frameworks Recommended to Adopt CM in Practice?

To analyse the practical application of CM, this study focuses on the contributions of the selected papers on three aspects: the acceptance of this new production method, the design and analysis of products and processes and, finally, the tools and methods used for the implementation of CM.

Acceptance of the New Production Model. Some authors focus on how to adopt the classical business model characterised by a take-make-use-dispose approach to a circular model in which materials and energy remain in a restorative system [12]. Still, at the business level, Asif, F. et al. [8] discuss the positioning of CM concerning the strategic positioning of "product leadership", "customer intimacy", and "operational excellence"; in particular, the focus is on understanding which CE strategy is most appropriate for each product module.

Design and Analysis of Products/Processes for CM. Industry 4.0 has opened the way to the CPS (Cyber-physical system) paradigm that allows intelligent, autonomous, self-aware systems to rapidly and flexibly communicate, coordinate and collaborate, which is one of the core capabilities the CM can benefit from the most, from a financial and environmental point of view [13]. In particular, authors in [14] proposed using CPS to support rapid reconfiguration and improvement of the system.

Concerning the technological point of view, [2] extracted the technologies that can be used to support the physical implementation of CM strategies from the literature, such as additive manufacturing, waste recovery technologies, cloud manufacturing and digital technologies empowered by I4.0 (IoT). Many digital technologies play a significant role in allowing, supporting or augmenting the capabilities for the adoption of CM [15]. Finally, [3] sets the basis for a tool to support manufacturing companies in defining circular business practices enabled by Industry 4.0 technologies.

Furthermore, simulation, in its many natures, has been considered a powerful tool to analyse the impact of various CM strategies and to select the best scenario or alternative for CM implementation. In particular, simulation allows us to understand the evolution in time of phenomena and parameters, which is of particular importance for the lifecycle perspective that CM practices must keep, and deal with the complexity of circular industrial systems, where single actors are autonomous agents and where decisions of one actor impact on the decision of the other actor(s). For example, [9] proposed a hybrid simulation approach that includes agent-based simulation, discrete event simulation and system dynamics to estimate the lifecycle cost, revenues, and environmental impact of a CMS. Also, the studies in [11] showed the use of lifecycle simulation for CM flow management.

Among the key digital technologies, AI is one of the most promising tools to support implementing applications that foster Sustainable Development Goals (SDG). There has been significant growth in applying these technologies to CM in recent years, and policymakers are increasingly interested in AI as a key supporter in achieving SDG in almost every application field.

In [6], a thorough literature review is presented from which pertinent conclusions are derived, and a coherent understating of how AI can foster the achievement of CM ambitions at different adoption scales (i.e. micro, meso, macro) is depicted. Successful AI applications have shown great opportunity in enabling product and process-based circularity since they ensure traceability and management along the entire product lifecycle [16]. Meso-level AI can provide efficiency and effectiveness in supporting collaboration among entities built on reliable data [17]. Starting from the micro level, AI technologies can aid in tracking, in real-time, huge amounts of complex data, which enables support for the decision-making process (at the macro level) in pursuing the right path relying on the contextual situation and optimising a set of SDGs [18].

Information Technologies for the CM Implementation. Traditional technologies in the realm of ICT are mentioned by literature to have great importance in the collection, analysis, traceability, sharing and visualization of data across company, supply chain and lifecycle phases: information systems such as PLM, CAD, CRM, MRP, ERP, Eco-agent information system, Recycling and Environmental information system play a vital role when a company wants to implement any CM strategy (such as remanufacturing, recycling etc.) [2]. Depending on the various maturity levels of the information system implemented in the company and their use for CM strategies, a roadmap of future steps to progress even more in this respect is provided by [4]. The work in [12] investigates the specific role a company's Master Data has for the implementation of CM strategies, but the investigation could also be extended to other types of data. The elaboration of data is at the core of specific research articles, where the contribution evolves around the use of methodologies or algorithms for CM. For instance, authors in [7] discussed the use of DEMATEL (a method for identification of cause-effect chain components of complex systems, to analyse the interrelationships of barriers for blockchain technology implementation for CM. Additionally, [6]focused on process mining and genetic algorithms for energy-aware disassembly.

RQ 2. What are the Challenges/Issues a Manufacturing Firm can face while enabling Circular Manufacturing?

Following the previous RQ, this section aims to discuss the challenges/issues that a manufacturing firm can face while enabling Circular Manufacturing (RQ2), in the same categories as before: Readiness to accept and sustain this new production model, challenges for designing products and/or process for CM, and the information technologies required to monitor the CM implementation.

Readiness to Accept and to Sustain. One of the issues in terms of implementing the CM paradigm is the presence of CE or sustainability culture in the system. Studies showed that the transition through CM or CE in a system is more accepted and supported in systems that prioritize circularity and sustainability in their system and are more adapted to a continuous state of adjustment, reviewing actions and operations redesigning procedures and reinventing mindsets [13]. Additionally, [15] mentioned that "awareness about CE" as an enabler of Sustainable CM plays a critical role in implementing Sustainable CM alongside governess rules and customer pressure on CE. Therefore, infrastructure availability and cultural acceptance through the transition are among the first challenges a system might face while implementing CM practices.

On the other hand, authors in [13] discuss financial investment as a challenge for the implementation. Through the surveys they have run, they found out that CM shows long-term financial benefits as well as environmental benefits. However, environmental benefits are more tangible in shorter terms rather than financial ones. The implementation generally is accompanied by high investment costs in the short term but benefits in the long term due to energy cost reduction. Therefore, the system's commitment to the implementation not only leads to improving energy efficiency and environmental protections but also to financial gain.

Additionally, some challenges were also observed in sustaining the transition and keeping committed to the implementation of CM. Authors in [10] discuss the role of IoT development in implementing the CM paradigm, however, that will be accompanied by fully connected machines and the risk of invasion of personal information. Therefore, systems are faced with the issue of "customer acceptance" even after the implementation. Additionally, [13] claim that the commitment of the top management to the CM initiatives and ensuring consistency in practising the implemented frameworks play an important role in sustaining the CM strategies; even though they might face negative financial feedback or discontinuation or even substitution of some products that are still profitable. In this way, long-term environmental and economic benefits appear which comply more with the societal demand and promote more sustainable solutions.

Design and Analysis of Products/Processes for CM. Designing the CM based on stakeholders' needs acquires new challenges related to product, process, design, analysis method, and technology. Some challenges for the CM implementation at the product level are related to the design of circular products [8], i.e. designing products that can either extend their lifespan or be looped back into the system for reuse. However, the design of products for several lifecycles is not a standard practice and there are not many methods that can support designers towards this direction [8].

On the other hand, when the product reaches the end of life, some critical issues for decision making in the reconditioning processes are highlighted regarding the level of uncertainty related to the condition of the item [6]. Therefore, fully automated decision-making is still not possible, and it is needed to put the human in the loop.

Challenges at the process level, from a technical point of view can be mentioned. For example, [10] discussed the challenge related to the need to establish an ICT (information and communication technology) infrastructure enabling the management and sharing of information, as well as real-time communication among stakeholders, to enable the CM business model. However, from the point of view of [10], the big challenge is not the technical one, but more "the customers' acceptance of fully connected machine with the risk of invasion of personal information".

Another challenge identified by [9] is related to the assessment of the economic and environmental impact of the adoption of circular business models. Even if they proposed a tool to identify which business model configuration allows the maximisation of lifecycle revenues and the minimization of the environmental impact, they also pointed out that the main limitation of their study is related to the chosen method, i.e. a multi-method simulation modelling, which implies that the findings of their study are limited to the assumptions and model boundaries to perform the simulation study. Therefore, challenges remain and [9] reported that future research can be related to the extension of the simulation tool to link features of business model strategies to product design and supply chain configurations considering that the interrelations among these elements influence the system performance.

Information Technologies for the CM Implementation. Observing products and the CM process requires essential information, which presents several challenges. First of all, an efficient Information System approach and a tailored AI-supported complexity management mechanism can aid the system developer and system monitor in overcoming many challenging and complex issues for enabling CM. In [19], the authors identified key challenges in exchanging and sharing data appropriately, together with EIS interoperability issues. To overcome this challenge, special attention should be given to standard data format exchange protocols and initiatives such as International Data Spaces[1]. In [12], the information flow is identified as a key aspect when implementing CM efficient applications. In this work, the authors recognise the fundamental aspect of understanding the role of each piece of data for each strategy of CM and each lifecycle phase. Identifying and understanding master data is a fundamental element and of critical importance to maintaining effective CM strategies. Another important aspect associated with implementing Information Systems for CM is data visibility and accessibility, especially for long, complex supply chains.

In [9], the increased complexity associated with closing the loop of physical and information flows due to a high number of lifecycles of different products is highlighted as another challenge in CM development. They propose a multi-level architectural Information System for tackling complexity based on autonomous interacting agents and hybrid simulation. A similar approach based on different abstraction levels is proposed by [20], where distributed AI technology is used to design and develop Intelligent Manufacturing Systems; in this approach, specific tailored guidelines are provided to help the engineer reduce the information system complexity. Different scenarios that prioritise CM-related features are described as key modelling and development templates. Moreover, the SDGs optimization workflow proposed by [18] is also seamlessly integrated into the proposed scenarios.

---

[1] (https://internationaldataspaces.org/).

5   Conclusions

The recent technological advancements pose two challenges related to the relationship between digital technologies and CM. On one hand, researchers tried to investigate how digital technologies can support the solution of CM-related problems or barriers; on the other hand, researchers also analysed how the technology advancement can bring new opportunities for an improved and even novel CM pursuing of strategies. Alongside technological challenges, performance measurement challenges or cultural challenges of acceptance of a mindset change, literature also mentions human-related challenges such as the availability of proper capabilities and competencies of people. This article focused on both sides, through two raised research questions. First, throughout the study, it tried to find a common definition got CM, and then the efforts to implement CM strategies were studied in three main domains acceptance, product/process design and analysis and information technologies. Finally, the implementation of CM strategies was looked through concerning the challenges it might face in the three observed domains. However, the presented work is non-exhaustive and can be a beginning path to future studies more detailed in the studied domain, regarding the usability of I4.0 technologies and their complementary to support circular manufacturing transition in a digitalized context. In addition, further study would be oriented to a more systematic and in-depth study of the literature to define managerial insights needed to put CM into practice through real industrial use cases. On the other hand, there is still a gap to be addressed to put industrial symbiosis configurations connecting different organisations. Additionally, the direct and/or indirect effects of CM strategies toward sustainable manufacturing might be investigated in future works.

Acknowledgement. This study was carried out thanks to supports provided for the authors:
- MICS (Made in Italy – Circular and Sustainable) Extended Partnership and received funding from the European Union Next-Generation EU (PIANO NAZIONALE DI RIPRESA E RESILIENZA (PNRR) – MISSIONE 4 COMPONENTE 2, INVESTIMENTO 1.3 – D.D. 1551.11-10-2022, PE00000004).
- ANR (Agence Nationale de la Recherche) EasyRESCHED project [Grant number ANR-23-CE10-0009] sponsored by the National Research Agency (ANR).
- PULSAR project sponsored by the « Académie des jeunes chercheurs en Pays de la Loire».

References

1. Moreno, M., Court, R., Wright, M., Charnley, F.: Opportunities for redistributed manufacturing and digital intelligence as enablers of a circular economy. Int. J. Sustain. Eng. **12**, 77–94 (2019). https://doi.org/10.1080/19397038.2018.1508316
2. Acerbi, F., Taisch, M.: A literature review on circular economy adoption in the manufacturing sector. J. Clean. Prod. **273** (2020). https://doi.org/10.1016/j.jclepro.2020.123086
3. Spaltini, M., Acerbi, F., Taisch, M.: Development of an industry 4.0-oriented tool supporting circular manufacturing: a systematic literature review. In: Noël, F., Nyffenegger, F., Rivest, L., Bouras, A. (eds.) PLM 2022. IFIPAICT, vol. 667, pp. 609–619. Springer, Cham (2023). https://doi.org/10.1007/978-3-031-25182-5_59

4. Acerbi, F., Spaltini, M., Taisch, M.: Industry 4.0 enabling technologies supporting the social sphere of circular manufacturing. Presented at the Proceedings of the Summer School Francesco Turco (2022)

5. Takata, S.: Maintenance-centered circular manufacturing. Procedia CIRP **11**, 23–31 (2013). https://doi.org/10.1016/j.procir.2013.07.066

6. Acerbi, F., Sassanelli, C., Terzi, S., Taisch, M.: A systematic literature review on data and information required for circular manufacturing strategies adoption. Sustainability **13**, 1–27 (2021). https://doi.org/10.3390/su13042047

7. Govindan, K.: Tunneling the barriers of blockchain technology in remanufacturing for achieving sustainable development goals: a circular manufacturing perspective. Bus. Strategy Environ. **31**, 3769–3785 (2022). https://doi.org/10.1002/bse.3031

8. Asif, F.M.A., Roci, M., Lieder, M., Rashid, A., Mihelič, A., Kotnik, S.: A methodological approach to design products for multiple lifecycles in the context of circular manufacturing systems. J. Clean. Prod. **296**, 126534 (2021). https://doi.org/10.1016/j.jclepro.2021.126534

9. Roci, M., et al.: Towards circular manufacturing systems implementation: a complex adaptive systems perspective using modelling and simulation as a quantitative analysis tool. Sustain. Prod. Consum. **31**, 97–112 (2022). https://doi.org/10.1016/j.spc.2022.01.033

10. Asif, F.M.A., et al.: A practical ICT framework for transition to circular manufacturing systems. Procedia CIRP **72**, 598–602 (2018). https://doi.org/10.1016/j.procir.2018.03.311

11. Asai, K., Nishida, D., Takata, S.: Life cycle simulation system as a tool for improving flow management in circular manufacturing. Presented at the November 1 (2020)

12. Andersen, T., Bressanelli, G., Saccani, N., Franceschi, B.: Information systems and circular manufacturing strategies: the role of master data. In: Kim, D.Y., von Cieminski, G., Romero, D. (eds.) APMS 2022. IFIPAICT, vol. 664, pp. 26–33. Springer, Cham (2022). https://doi.org/10.1007/978-3-031-16411-8_4

13. Liu, Y., Farooque, M., Lee, C.-H., Gong, Y., Zhang, A.: Antecedents of circular manufacturing and its effect on environmental and financial performance: a practice-based view. Int. J. Prod. Econ. **260**, 108866 (2023). https://doi.org/10.1016/j.ijpe.2023.108866

14. Assuad, C.S.A., Leirmo, T., Martinsen, K.: Proposed framework for flexible de- and remanufacturing systems using cyber-physical systems, additive manufacturing, and digital twins. Presented at the Procedia CIRP (2022)

15. Garg, D., Mustaqueem, O.A., Kumar, R.: Sustainable circular manufacturing in the digital era: analysis of enablers. In: Phanden, R.K., Mathiyazhagan, K., Kumar, R., Paulo Davim, J. (eds.) Advances in Industrial and Production Engineering. LNME, pp. 541–554. Springer, Singapore (2021). https://doi.org/10.1007/978-981-33-4320-7_48

16. Cioffi, R., Travaglioni, M., Piscitelli, G., Petrillo, A., Parmentola, A.: Smart manufacturing systems and applied industrial technologies for a sustainable industry: a systematic literature review. Appl. Sci. **10**, 2897 (2020). https://doi.org/10.3390/app10082897

17. Niu, S., Zhuo, H., Xue, K.: DfRem-driven closed-loop supply chain decision-making: a systematic framework for modeling research. Sustainability **11**, 3299 (2019). https://doi.org/10.3390/su11123299

18. Giret, A., Trentesaux, D., Prabhu, V.: Sustainability in manufacturing operations scheduling: a state of the art review. J. Manuf. Syst. **37**, 126–140 (2015). https://doi.org/10.1016/j.jmsy.2015.08.002

19. Polenghi, A., Acerbi, F., Roda, I., Macchi, M., Taisch, M.: Enterprise information systems interoperability for asset lifecycle management to enhance circular manufacturing. Presented at the IFAC-PapersOnLine (2021)

20. Botti, V., Giret, A.: ANEMONA: A Mulit-agent Methodology for Holonic Manufacturing Systems (2008)

Enhancing Human – Robot Collaboration in the Industry 5.0 Framework with Physics-Informed Neural Networks: Application to Collision Detection

Francesco G. Ciampi[1,2](✉) , Thierno M. L. Diallo[2] , Faïda Mhenni[2] ,
Stanislao Patalano[1] , and Jean-Yves Choley[2]

[1] Department of Industrial Engineering, University of Naples Federico II, 80125 Naples, Italy
francesco.ciampi@isae-supmeca.fr
[2] Quartz Laboratory (EA7393), ISAE-Supméca, 3 rue Fernand Hainaut,
93400 Saint-Ouen, France

Abstract. In the context of rapidly evolving technology and increased attention to social and environmental dimensions, the industrial sector is transitioning from Industry 4.0 to Industry 5.0. This new paradigm emphasizes human centrality in highly automated environments, necessitating the exploration of collaboration mechanisms between humans and robots. This study investigates the application of Physics-Informed Neural Networks (PINNs) to enhance Human-Robot Collaboration (HRC). PINNs integrates the traditional data-driven approach based on machine learning models with a prior physical knowledge of the system, providing a valuable solution when data are scarce or physical models are too complex or incomplete. The study first focuses on the main aspects of interest in the field of HRC through a state-of-the-art analysis, evaluating the application of Physics-Informed Neural Networks (PINNs) in HRC and robotics. It then delves into the definition of PINNs and their implementation. Finally, as a proof of concept, the model is applied to a case study concerning collision detection in a 6 DoF robotic arm. This is achieved by predicting the joint currents and comparing them with the measured values to identify the contribution due to external forces such as collisions. The results demonstrate that the PINNs model outperforms a traditional neural network, achieving an average error below 10%. Additionally, the collision detection application shows an f1_score of 0.80, indicating strong performance.

Keywords: Industry 5.0 · Human-robot collaboration · Collision detection · Physics-informed neural networks · Physics-informed machine learning

1 Introduction

Over the last decade, industry has undergone significant transformations, particularly through digitalization [1]. Although we are in the midst of the fourth industrial revolution, the concepts of Industry 5.0 are already being widely explored [2]. Industry 5.0

M. Dassisti et al. (Eds.): IN4PL 2024, CCIS 2372, pp. 305–318, 2025.
https://doi.org/10.1007/978-3-031-80760-2_20

shifts the focus towards sustainability from economic, ecological, and social perspectives, emphasizing the integration of human cognitive abilities with the efficiency of automation [3]. This new paradigm prioritizes human roles and seeks to enhance collaboration between humans and robots. The study of Human-robot Collaboration (HRC), therefore, becomes one of the cornerstones of this new industrial era [4]. In addition, the HRC is often associated with the term Cobot (COllaborative roBOT), a robot designed to work in collaboration with humans that relies mainly on dexterity, versatility, and easy programming [5].

Despite extensive progress in enhancing collaborative robotics, the research still faces many topics concerning HRC and cobots. A primary focus regards the Human-Robot Interaction (HRI), especially concerning physical contact and safety. Unlike traditional industrial robots confined by barriers, cobots, in fact, operate in close proximity to humans, necessitating robust safety measures. This includes prediction capabilities to anticipate potential impacts, collision avoidance strategies, and collision detection systems coupled with quick response mechanisms [6]. In addition, research also investigates the cognitive capabilities of cobots such as learning modes or programming [7], as well as the design of suitable workspaces [8] to ensure optimal collaboration between humans and robots. Many of these studies involve the use of advanced sensors, vision systems, and more recently machine learning to enhance the safety measures and the performances.

In this study, therefore, the HRC is investigated in order to exploit the applicability of an emerging methodology of applied mathematics, the Physics-Informed Neural Networks (PINNs). PINNs are a category of neural networks designed to solve supervised learning tasks while respecting the physical laws described by general nonlinear partial differential equations (PDEs) [9]. These networks are assignable to a broader category of models, the Physics-Informed Machine Learning (PIML), which seeks to combine the strengths of both data-driven and physics-based methodologies. PIML is particularly valuable in scenarios where traditional modelling approaches underperform or are unfeasible. This often occurs when there is only partial knowledge of the system's underlying physics, or when there is an insufficient amount of data to train accurate machine learning models [10]. This work, therefore, focuses on understanding whether and how PINNs can be applied to one or more aspects of the HRC. As a proof of concept, a case study about collision detection has been chosen. Specifically, the work of Czubenko et Al. (2021) [11] is taken as reference. It implements a data-driven approach for collision detection using a CURA6 prototype cobot in the experiments. The dataset[1] they provided is used for the implementation and validation of the PINN model.

The remainder of this paper is organized as follows. Section 2 summarizes the state of the art on HRC, focusing mainly on machine learning and PINNs applications. In Sect. 3, the PINN methodology is analysed. Section 4 presents the case study. Finally, Sect. 5 provides some concluding remarks and insights for future works.

---

[1] https://www.kaggle.com/datasets/intema/cooperative-robot-collisioncurrent-dataset.

2 Related Works

The literature on Human Robot Collaboration in industrial context encompasses an extensive range of research topics, classified and detailed in several review papers [12–14]. Below, a brief overview of these topics is presented:

- *Human-Robot Interaction (HRI) and Safety*: it covers several aspects such as safety standards, collaborative operating modes, and risk analysis. The category encompasses both physical HRI and contactless HRI.
- *Cognitive robotics and robot programming*: this category addresses learning processes, programming approaches implemented for cobots and studies on human actions recognitions or vocal commanding.
- *Human – Robot Interfaces*: it covers the studies on Virtual Reality (VR), Augmented Reality (AR) or other technologies for enhanced interfaces.
- *Collaborative systems design*: it regards studies on design of collaborative workspaces, implementation of control logics and sensors, task allocation or task planning.

These topics are recurrent in the literature regarding HRC. Li et al. (2024) [15], for instance, analyses the Human-Robot interaction in detail, focusing on safety standards and implementation approaches. Ren et al. (2023) [16], instead, reviews the evolution of human-machine collaborative decision-making based on cognitive intelligence. Concerning human – robot interfaces, Costa et al. (2022) [17] reviews 32 papers on the use of AR in human-robot collaboration. Finally, Rega et al. (2021) [18] explores the critical role of layout design in ensuring safe and efficient Human-Robot Collaboration (HRC).

In order to understand how PINNs can address one or more of these topics, this study analyses first how machine learning models are applied in HRC. For this purpose, the work of Semeraro et al. (2023) [19] is taken as a reference. It provides a comprehensive overview of machine learning applications in HRC, analysing interaction tasks, sensing systems, human and robot roles, and modelled variables. However, it does not compare machine learning approaches with traditional physics-based methods in terms of performance or application areas. In addition, the work of Mukherjee et al. (2022) [20] focuses the research on the industrial sector. The detailed review suggests several insights for application, but it also highlights that in using machine learning for industrial HRC there is an inherent limitation due to the deterministic nature of the problem. Overall, it emerges that there is a growing interest in the use of data-driven models in HRC and that all the discussed topics can be addressed by choosing the most suitable model.

Regarding the applications of PINNs in HRC, three recent publications have been found in the literature. The work of Yang et al. (2023a) [21] implements an hybrid version of PINNs for parameter estimation in a physical human-robot interaction model. The PINN model combines a Recurrent Neural Network with the Runge-Gutta method and is validated on a real cobot. It demonstrates the applicability of this model in the context of cobots but focuses only on their modelling without addressing other aspects of HRC. In Yang et al. (2023b) [22], instead, they apply a similar hybrid PINN methodology (H-PINN) for parameter estimation of cobot joints. In this paper, they focus more on comparing the H-PINN with classical PINNs and Grey-box models. However, the application remains within the context of robot dynamics without going into the details of collaborative operations. Finally, the work of Lee (2023) [23] proposes PINNs for catching point prediction in contactless delivery between two cobots. The approach is based on a deep learning framework combined with information on the physics of the system, such as environmental constraints, throwing physics and robot dynamics. It presents a comprehensive case study, and the validity of the model is demonstrated experimentally. In this case, the focus is precisely on collaboration, which, however, is between two robots and does not consider the aspects of a shared human-robot environment.

These works clearly show the potential of a hybrid approach such as PINNs in the field of collaborative robotics and highlight how the interest in this methodology is growing. However, based on the number and the year of the publications, it is clear that these works are at an early stage of research. Moreover, they focus mainly on robot dynamics. This aspect suggests that PINNs have greater potential when the integration of physical knowledge provides a significant advantage, such as in the modelling of deterministic systems. Therefore, among the four categories analysed, it results from the literature that PINNs are mostly applied into the first category, i.e. Human-Robot Interaction and Safety. This is also due to the presence of a wider literature on PINNs in the field of robotics, which provides interesting insights when switching from robot modelling to cobot modelling. Among these works, for example, Nicodemus et al. (2022) [24] proposes PINNs for Model Predictive Control (MPC) of multi-link manipulators and Sun et al. (2022) [25] applied the Physics Informed Recurrent Neural Networks (PIRNN) for the indirect sensing of soft pneumatic actuators. Moreover, Liu et al. (2024) [26] discusses the application of physics-informed neural networks to modelling and controlling complex robotic systems, validating the approach through real-world experiments with a soft robot. Topics, methodologies and physical knowledge proposed by these articles are also applicable in collaborative environments.

3   Introduction to PINNs

The Physics-Informed Neural Networks (PINNs), introduced by [9], can be generally described as a Machine Learning-based approach that enhances the classical data-driven methodology through the use of a prior physics knowledge of the system. The process of integrating prior knowledge in machine learning involves several aspects to be defined, such as the choice of the ML model, the representation of the prior knowledge and the point of integration [27]. Every combination of these three aspects leads to different results. The vanilla version of PINNs, for example, is based on Artificial Neural Networks (ANN) and integrates the physics knowledge in the definition of the loss function, using general non-linear Partial Differential Equations (PDE). In addition to this one, many other versions have been developed, such as the already mentioned PIRNN and H-PINN. Among these versions, some use more complex machine learning models to integrate time dependencies while others integrate physics into the architecture of the neural network. This article, however, is not intended to analyse the different versions nor to propose a new methodology, therefore only the vanilla PINNs are considered.

In order to provide a comprehensive framework, a general formulation is presented in this section, referring to the work of [28]. In Sect. 4, however, the physics of the system is discussed in more details and the general equations presented are specialised on the case study. As already mentioned, PINNs address problems described by general nonlinear partial differential equations (PDEs), The PDE equation is represented in a general form in (1).

$$F(u(z); \gamma) = f(z) \; in \; W \tag{1}$$

where F is a nonlinear differential operator, $u(z)$ represents the unknown solution, γ are parameters associated with the physics, and $f(z)$ is the function describing the data. The domain Ω is a subset of n-dimensional space $\mathbb{R}^n$, and $z := [x_1, \ldots, x_{n-1}, t]$ represents the space-time coordinate vector.

Alongside this, PINNs may incorporate physical knowledge in terms of boundary conditions or constraints, as shown in (2).

$$B(u(z)) = g(z) \; on \; \partial W \tag{2}$$

where ∂W denotes the boundary of the domain W. The operator B represents arbitrary initial or boundary conditions related to the problem, and $g(z)$ represents the boundary function.

Equations (1) and (2) provide a general formulation of the physics that is integrated into the PINNs. Considering the machine learning model, instead, a Neural Network defined by a set of parameters θ is implemented to predict the function $u(z)$, yielding an approximation as defined in (3).

$$\hat{u}_\theta(z) \approx u(z) \tag{3}$$

where the first term represents the NN-based approximation with the set of parameters θ. The Neural Network needs to be trained to approximate the PDEs and the boundary conditions by identifying the optimal θ. This is achieved by minimizing a loss function that contains a term obtained from the PDEs $\mathcal{L}_F(\theta)$, another based on the boundary conditions $\mathcal{L}_B(\theta)$, and a third one $\mathcal{L}_D(\theta)$ that represents the standard loss function of Neural Networks based on labeled data. Each one of them is weighted according to expert knowledge or optimization processes. Thus, the optimal parameters θ^* are determined as shown in (4).

$$\theta^* = \underset{\theta}{\text{argmin}}(\omega_F \mathcal{L}_F(\theta) + \omega_B \mathcal{L}_B(\theta) + \omega_D \mathcal{L}_D(\theta)) \tag{4}$$

The three loss functions can be defined, for instance, using the Mean Squared Error (MSE). Specifically, MSE_D can be calculated comparing u_θ with the labeled data while MSE_F and MSE_D may represent the errors obtained by replacing u with u_θ respectively in the PDEs and in the boundary conditions. Figure 1 shows a general scheme of PINN.

Although studies are recent on this methodology, there are already some tools in the literature that simplify the implementation of PINNs by providing predefined functions. Among these, a major contribution is provided by DeepXDE [29]. This tool is available on Python 3.0.

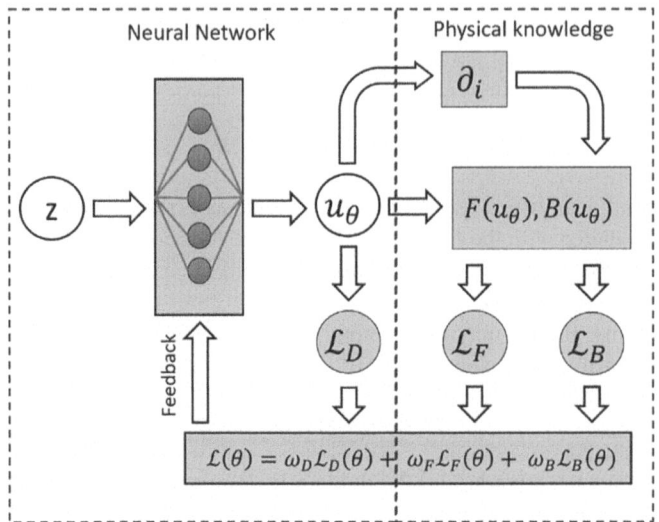

Fig. 1. Physics-Informed Neural Network framework.

4 Application of PINNs to Collision Detection

4.1 Case Study Definition

To exploit the application of PINNs in collaborative robotics, a case study regarding the collision detection is presented. The collision analysis is, in fact, widely addressed in the HRC [30], and regulated by some main standards: the ISO 10218-1 (2011) [31] and ISO 10218-2 (2011) [32], concerning the safety requirements for industrial robots, and the ISO\TS 15066 (2016) [33], focusing on collaborative robots. These guidelines led to the development of different approaches to fulfil some of the requirements in collision analysis, such as pre-collision strategies, contact detection and post-collision response. The collision detection strategies can be classified in two main categories: the ones using exteroceptive sensors and the ones using only proprioceptive sensors. The first case includes mostly contact sensors, whose measurements allow collisions to be detected if pressure or force values exceed limits defined by regulations. The second case refers to measurement strategies based on the dynamic modelling of the robot [34]. A detailed description of collision detection approaches is proposed in Park and Park (2023) [35]. The standard model-based approaches analysed in this work are the energy observer-based estimation of external power and estimation of external joint torque, that can be performed using a direct approach, a velocity observer, and a momentum observer. Application of it can be found in literature [36, 37]. For what concern ML-based approaches, reference is made to the work of Czubenko e Kowalczuk (2021) [11]. Their model defines a collision detection strategy based on Neural Networks. The model is applied to the prediction of the current for each joint and the results are compared with the sensor data. The obtained error is partly due to the accuracy of the model and partly due to anomalies such as a collision. Appropriate calibration of threshold values allows to distinguish between the two types of errors and detect an eventual collision.

Therefore, considering this work and the data provided to support it, the objective of this study is to apply the PINNs instead of a traditional ML-based approach.

The cobot under consideration is a 6 DoF CURA6 robot prototype (Cooperative Universal Robotic Assistant 6) developed by Intema. The prototype is manually assembled, hence, the correct estimation of the physical parameters (e.g. mass distribution) results in the resolution of a non-trivial inverse problem and, although several solutions are available nowadays, it necessarily implies an increased complexity of the model. This penalizes physical approaches in favour of data-driven ones. At the same time, the system is deterministic, so there is an ideal case for the application of PINNs.

The dynamic of the robot can be defined with the general Eq. (5).

$$M(q)\ddot{q} + C(q, \dot{q})\dot{q} + g(q) + \tau_f = \tau_d \tag{5}$$

where q, $\dot{q}$, $\ddot{q}$ are respectively position, speed and acceleration vectors, $M(q)$ represents the Inertia matrix, $C(q, \dot{q})$ the matrix of Coriolis and centrifugal forces, $g(q)$ the gravity force vector, and τ_f is the joint friction. Finally τ_d represents the sum of the joint torque produced by the motors and the external torque. The system thus defined has several unknown parameters difficult to identify. Different formulations allow the definition of the minimum number of them, useful for an analytical-experimental identification process. In this case, however, the use of the PINNs allows a simplified or partial mathematical formulation using, for instance, the dynamic of general rotational systems as in (6).

$$J_i\ddot{\theta}_i + c_i\dot{\vartheta}_i + k_i\theta_i = \tau_i \qquad i = [1,6] \tag{6}$$

This equation is a strong approximation as it does consider the joints as isolated systems and the parameters as static but gains value in a hybrid model such as PINNs. Moreover, it is possible to consider the relationship between the torque and the motor current, defined as in (7).

$$\tau = k_t I \tag{7}$$

where k_t is the torque constant and I is the current. Substituting Eq. (6) into Eq. (5) and reducing the number of parameters leads to (8).

$$A_i\ddot{\theta}_i + B_i\dot{\vartheta}_i + C_i\theta_i = I_i \qquad i = [1,6] \tag{8}$$

where, for the i-th joint, there are 3 unknown parameters (A_i, B_i, C_i), identifiable during the PINN training process.

The implementation of this model consists of two parts. In the first, the model is used for parameter estimation where an inverse problem is solved using training data. In the second, instead, the model with the previously calculated parameters is used to detect collisions. For the latter point, the criteria to detect collisions are based on the considerations made in [11]. Specifically, when the model performs the prediction of the currents, the error is analysed and two reference thresholds are defined to determine whether this error is due to the model accuracy or to collisions. The first threshold is defined through the Standard Deviation (SD) while the second is a constant gap, as shown in Eqs. (9) and (10).

$$\left|I_{real} - I_{pred}\right| < \gamma * SD(I_{real}, I_{pred}) \tag{9}$$

$$\left|I_{real} - I_{pred}\right| < T \tag{10}$$

The choice of γ and T allows the thresholds to be adjusted. In the case of γ, it defines the percentage of values within the threshold ($\gamma = 2.57$ corresponds to the 99%). The Standard Deviation, instead, is defined through the Root Mean Square Error (RMSE). The same KPI has been normalized (NRMSE) and used in the evaluation of prediction accuracy to compare values on different scales, as shown in (11).

$$NRMSE = \frac{1}{I_{max} - I_{min}} \sqrt{\frac{1}{N} \sum_{i=1}^{N} \left(I_{real} - I_{pred}\right)^2} \tag{11}$$

In the application of PINNs, a Fully-connected Neural Network (FNN) has been built with two hidden layers of 50 neurons, learning rate of 0.01, tanh as activation function and Adam as optimizer. The model has been implemented with DeepXDE library on Python 3.0. Moreover, a model based on Multi-Layer Perceptron (MLP) is used as a benchmark. The model uses the same architecture as the one proposed for PINNs and thus allows us to understand the actual advantage obtained by using a hybrid model. The device used for the simulations has the following characteristics: CPU Intel® Core™ i7-13700H, GPU NVIDIA® GeForce RTX™ 3060, RAM 16 GB.

4.2 Parameter Estimation

For parameter estimation, various operating conditions have been evaluated, varying between different speed limits and payloads. Around 660 samples from each operating condition have been used. Table 1 shows the results in terms of error on the current prediction, once the optimal parameters are found. The results are compared with the ones obtained by using the MLP model. The use of NRMSE standardizes the scale and shows that accuracy is not particularly affected by load. On the other hand, for PINNs, there is a reduction in accuracy as speed increases, due mainly to the physical model which does not consider joints' coupling and results in an excessive approximation for high rotational speeds. Moreover, it is also clear that joint 1 tends to have a greater error than the others. To further investigate the error, Fig. 2 shows the current prediction for joint 1 in the case of 401g of payload. It is clear from the graph that the error, although considerable, is mainly due to the rapid fluctuation of the variable under consideration and not to the trend, which is well captured.

The PINN model generally outperforms the MLP model across different joints and conditions (speed and load) in terms of lower error values, especially in joints 4, 5, and 6, where the approximation due to the chosen physical model is of minor relevance. In conclusion, the average error of the PINN model is well below the 10%.

Table 1. NRMSE of the current prediction (A) for different speed limit (with 0g load) and different loads (with 10% speed).

Speed	Model	Joint 1	Joint 2	Joint 3	Joint 4	Joint 5	Joint 6
10%	PINN	**0.099**	**0.041**	**0.079**	**0.073**	**0.102**	**0.111**
	MLP	0.151	0.043	0.086	0.086	0.138	0.147
30%	PINN	0.183	**0.042**	**0.041**	**0.056**	**0.097**	**0.112**
	MLP	**0.143**	0.056	0.069	0.088	0.133	0.145
50%	PINN	0.165	0.049	**0.032**	**0.054**	**0.100**	**0.102**
	MLP	**0.140**	**0.044**	0.076	0.105	0.128	0.132
70%	PINN	0.157	0.079	0.091	**0.080**	**0.096**	**0.086**
	MLP	**0.118**	**0.070**	**0.078**	0.092	0.129	0.123
Load	Model	Joint 1	Joint 2	Joint 3	Joint 4	Joint 5	Joint 6
401g	PINN	**0.089**	**0.051**	**0.030**	**0.057**	**0.108**	**0.097**
	MLP	0.143	0.054	0.066	0.062	0.148	0.139
1086g	PINN	**0.080**	**0.051**	**0.039**	**0.032**	**0.055**	**0.096**
	MLP	0.137	0.074	0.062	0.082	0.131	0.142
2832g	PINN	**0.080**	**0.016**	**0.029**	**0.035**	**0.071**	**0.107**
	MLP	0.137	0.065	0.060	0.065	0.079	0.131
4652g	PINN	**0.097**	**0.016**	**0.028**	**0.036**	**0.071**	**0.107**
	MLP	0.143	0.045	0.063	0.055	0.108	0.149
	Model	Joint 1	Joint 2	Joint 3	Joint 4	Joint 5	Joint 6
Average	PINN	**0.119**	**0.043**	**0.046**	**0.053**	**0.088**	**0.102**
	MLP	0.139	0.056	0.070	0.079	0.124	0.139

4.3   Collision Detection

Once the parameters have been defined, the developed model has been used for collision detection. 1000 samples from each case have been used. The results are shown in Table 2 for joint 1 with different speed limits and payloads. They are obtained by imposing as conditions $\gamma = 3$ (99% of values inside the threshold) and T = 2A. In addition, a tolerance of ± 0.01 on timestamp has been imposed, to avoid that a peak of current could be considered more than once. For the metrics, it has been preferred to ignore accuracy because of the large number of true negative. Recall, precision and f1_score, instead, have been considered, as shown in (12).

$$Precision = \frac{TP}{TP + FP} \quad Recall = \frac{TP}{TP + FN} \quad f1_{score} = \frac{2 * (Precision * Recall)}{(Precision + Recall)} \tag{12}$$

For further clarification, the graph of the current prediction in the case of speed 60% is shown in Fig. 3. It also shows the thresholds used for detection. The model correctly identified four collisions out of five. In addition, the tolerance on timestamps prevented

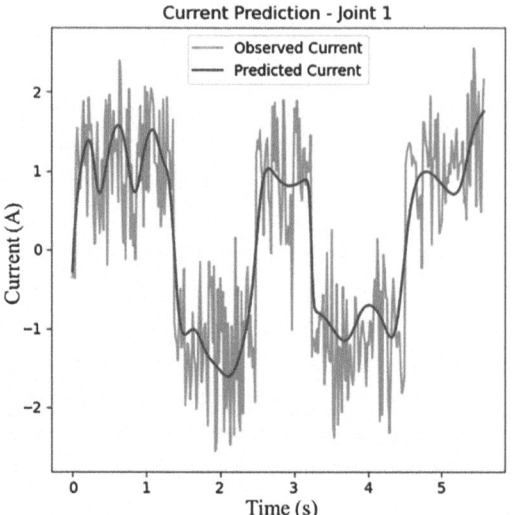

Fig. 2. Current prediction for joint 1 with 401g of payload.

Table 2. Confusion matrix and metrics for collision detection. TP is true positive, FP is false positive, TN is true negative and FN is false negative.

Speed	TP	FP	TN	FN	Precision	Recall	f1_score
10%	4	1	–	1	0,80	0,80	0,8
30%	3	2	–	2	0,60	0,60	0,6
50%	3	0	–	2	1,00	0,60	0,75
60%	4	0	–	1	1,00	0,80	0,89
Load	TP	FP	TN	FN	Precision	Recall	f1_score
401g	3	2	–	1	0,60	0,75	0,67
1086g	3	0	–	2	1,00	0,60	0,75
2832g	5	1	–	0	0,83	1,00	0,91
4652g	5	0	–	0	1,00	1,00	1,00
Total	30	6	–	9	0.83	0.77	0.80

the assignment of several FP for the last collision. Overall, the results show a f1_score of 80% and a precision of 83%, in line with the findings of Czubenko e Kowalczuk (2021) [11], that found a f1_score of 85% or Sharkawy e Aspragathos (2016) [38], that found a precision of 84%. The advantage in the application of PINNS, however, is the considerable reduction in the complexity of the machine learning model (FNN is one of the simplest model) and in the amount of data used (around 10% of the original datasets).

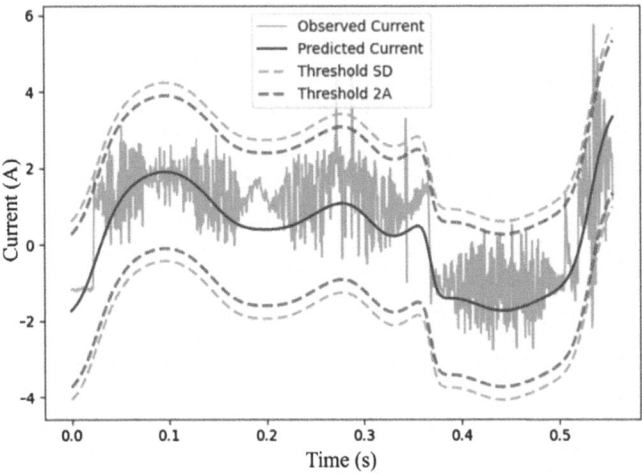

Fig. 3. Collision detection for joint 1 in the case of 60% speed.

5   Conclusions

The Physics-Informed Neural Networks (PINNs) are a type of neural network enhanced through the integration of physical knowledge into the system. The aim of this work was to assess their applicability in the field of Human-Robot Collaboration (HRC), a topic widely discussed in the new Industry 5.0 paradigm. The HRC, therefore, has been investigated to find the main applications of machine learning approaches and PINNs, and to identify the category that best suits these models. Afterwards, the PINN methodology has been presented and applied to a case study on collision detection in collaborative workspaces. This involved using PINNs to predict joint currents and comparing these predictions with measured data to identify variations due to external forces, such as collisions. The results obtained show that the model outperforms a traditional machine learning approach with an average error in prediction below 10%. Additionally, an F1 score of 0.80 in collision detection highlights the model's applicability in deterministic systems with less data than traditional ML models and with simplified physics compared to purely physical models, without sacrificing accuracy and robustness. Future work will explore an improvement in the physics models and the implementation of different types of neural networks. Another promising direction is in the application of PINNs to non-deterministic aspects, such as the analysis of human behaviour in HRC.

Disclosure of Interests.   The authors have no competing interests to declare that are relevant to the content of this article.

References

1. Zizic, M.C., Mladineo, M., Gjeldum, N., Celent, L.: From Industry 4.0 towards Industry 5.0: a review and analysis of paradigm shift for the people, organization and technology. Energies **15**, 5221 (2022). https://doi.org/10.3390/en15145221
2. Nahavandi, S.: Industry 5.0—a human-centric solution. Sustainability **11**, 4371 (2019). https://doi.org/10.3390/su11164371
3. Möller, D.P.F., Vakilzadian, H., Haas, R.E.: From Industry 4.0 towards Industry 5.0. In: 2022 IEEE International Conference on Electro Information Technology (eIT), pp. 61–68 (2022). https://doi.org/10.1109/eIT53891.2022.9813831
4. Demir, K.A., Döven, G., Sezen, B.: Industry 5.0 and human-robot co-working. Procedia Comput. Sci. **158**, 688–695 (2019). https://doi.org/10.1016/j.procs.2019.09.104
5. Matheson, E., Minto, R., Zampieri, E.G.G., Faccio, M., Rosati, G.: Human-robot collaboration in manufacturing applications: a review. Robotics **8**, 100 (2019). https://doi.org/10.3390/robotics8040100
6. Lasota, P.A., Fong, T., Shah, J.A.: A survey of methods for safe human-robot interaction. Found. Trends® Robot. **5**, 261–349 (2017). https://doi.org/10.1561/2300000052
7. Castro, A., Silva, F., Santos, V.: Trends of human-robot collaboration in industry contexts: handover, learning, and metrics. Sensors **21**, 4113 (2021). https://doi.org/10.3390/s21124113
8. Di Marino, C., Rega, A., Pasquariello, A., Fruggiero, F., Vitolo, F., Patalano, S.: An interactive graph-based tool to support the designing of human–robot collaborative workplaces. Int. J. Interact. Des. Manuf. IJIDeM. (2023). https://doi.org/10.1007/s12008-023-01607-y
9. Raissi, M., Perdikaris, P., Karniadakis, G.E.: Physics-informed neural networks: a deep learning framework for solving forward and inverse problems involving nonlinear partial differential equations. J. Comput. Phys. **378**, 686–707 (2019). https://doi.org/10.1016/j.jcp.2018.10.045
10. Karniadakis, G.E., Kevrekidis, I.G., Lu, L., Perdikaris, P., Wang, S., Yang, L.: Physics-informed machine learning. Nat. Rev. Phys. **3**, 422–440 (2021). https://doi.org/10.1038/s42254-021-00314-5
11. Czubenko, M., Kowalczuk, Z.: A simple neural network for collision detection of collaborative robots. Sensors **21**, 4235 (2021). https://doi.org/10.3390/s21124235
12. Villani, V., Pini, F., Leali, F., Secchi, C.: Survey on human–robot collaboration in industrial settings: safety, intuitive interfaces and applications. Mechatronics **55**, 248–266 (2018). https://doi.org/10.1016/j.mechatronics.2018.02.009
13. Hentout, A., Aouache, M., Maoudj, A., Akli, I.: Human–robot interaction in industrial collaborative robotics: a literature review of the decade 2008–2017. Adv. Robot. **33**, 764–799 (2019). https://doi.org/10.1080/01691864.2019.1636714
14. Kumar, S., Savur, C., Sahin, F.: Survey of human-robot collaboration in industrial settings: awareness, intelligence, and compliance. IEEE Trans. Syst. Man Cybern. Syst. **51**, 280–297 (2021). https://doi.org/10.1109/TSMC.2020.3041231
15. Li, W., Hu, Y., Zhou, Y., Pham, D.T.: Safe human–robot collaboration for industrial settings: a survey. J. Intell. Manuf. **35**, 2235–2261 (2024). https://doi.org/10.1007/s10845-023-02159-4
16. Ren, M., Chen, N., Qiu, H.: Human-machine collaborative decision-making: an evolutionary roadmap based on cognitive intelligence. Int. J. Soc. Robot. **15**, 1101–1114 (2023). https://doi.org/10.1007/s12369-023-01020-1
17. Costa, G.D.M., Petry, M.R., Moreira, A.P.: Augmented reality for human-robot collaboration and cooperation in industrial applications: a systematic literature review. Sensors **22**, 2725 (2022). https://doi.org/10.3390/s22072725
18. Rega, A., et al.: Collaborative workplace design: a knowledge-based approach to promote human-robot collaboration and multi-objective layout optimization. Appl. Sci. **11**, 12147 (2021). https://doi.org/10.3390/app112412147

19. Semeraro, F., Griffiths, A., Cangelosi, A.: Human–robot collaboration and machine learning: a systematic review of recent research. Robot. Comput. Integr. Manuf. **79**, 102432 (2023). https://doi.org/10.1016/j.rcim.2022.102432

20. Mukherjee, D., Gupta, K., Chang, L.H., Najjaran, H.: A survey of robot learning strategies for human-robot collaboration in industrial settings. Robot. Comput. Integr. Manuf. **73**, 102231 (2022). https://doi.org/10.1016/j.rcim.2021.102231

21. Yang, X., Zhou, Z., Li, L., Zhang, X.: Collaborative robot dynamics with physical human–robot interaction and parameter identification with PINN. Mech. Mach. Theory. **189**, 105439 (2023). https://doi.org/10.1016/j.mechmachtheory.2023.105439

22. Yang, X., Du, Y., Li, L., Zhou, Z., Zhang, X.: Physics-informed neural network for model prediction and dynamics parameter identification of collaborative robot joints. IEEE Robot. Autom. Lett. **8**, 8462–8469 (2023). https://doi.org/10.1109/LRA.2023.3329620

23. Lee, H.: Physics-based cooperative robotic digital twin framework for contactless delivery motion planning. Int. J. Adv. Manuf. Technol. **128**, 1255–1270 (2023). https://doi.org/10.1007/s00170-023-11956-3

24. Nicodemus, J., Kneifl, J., Fehr, J., Unger, B.: Physics-informed neural networks-based model predictive control for multi-link manipulators. IFAC-Pap. **55**, 331–336 (2022). https://doi.org/10.1016/j.ifacol.2022.09.117

25. Sun, W., Akashi, N., Kuniyoshi, Y., Nakajima, K.: Physics-informed recurrent neural networks for soft pneumatic actuators. IEEE Robot. Autom. Lett. **7**, 6862–6869 (2022). https://doi.org/10.1109/LRA.2022.3178496

26. Liu, J., Borja, P., Della Santina, C.: Physics-informed neural networks to model and control robots: a theoretical and experimental investigation. Adv. Intell. Syst. **6**, 2300385 (2024). https://doi.org/10.1002/aisy.202300385

27. Kim, S.W., Kim, I., Lee, J., Lee, S.: Knowledge Integration into deep learning in dynamical systems: an overview and taxonomy. J. Mech. Sci. Technol. **35**, 1331–1342 (2021). https://doi.org/10.1007/s12206-021-0342-5

28. Cuomo, S., Di Cola, V.S., Giampaolo, F., Rozza, G., Raissi, M., Piccialli, F.: Scientific machine learning through physics–informed neural networks: where we are and what's next. J. Sci. Comput. **92**, 88 (2022). https://doi.org/10.1007/s10915-022-01939-z

29. Lu, L., Meng, X., Mao, Z., Karniadakis, G.E.: DeepXDE: a deep learning library for solving differential equations. SIAM Rev. **63**, 208–228 (2021). https://doi.org/10.1137/19M1274067

30. Haddadin, S., Albu-Schaffer, A., De Luca, A., Hirzinger, G.: Collision detection and reaction: a contribution to safe physical human-robot interaction. In: 2008 IEEE/RSJ International Conference on Intelligent Robots and Systems, Nice, pp. 3356–3363. IEEE (2008). https://doi.org/10.1109/IROS.2008.4650764

31. International Organization for Standardization: ISO 10218-1:2011. Robots and Robotic Devices -Safety requirements for industrial robots - Part 1: Robots (2011)

32. International Organization for Standardization: ISO 10218-2:2011. Robots and robotic devices - Safety requirements for industrial robots - Part 2: Robot systems and integration, (2011)

33. International Organization for Standardization: ISO\TS 15066:2016. Robots and Robotic Devices: Collaborative Robots (2016)

34. Heo, Y.J., Kim, D., Lee, W., Kim, H., Park, J., Chung, W.K.: Collision detection for industrial collaborative robots: a deep learning approach. IEEE Robot. Autom. Lett. **4**, 740–746 (2019). https://doi.org/10.1109/LRA.2019.2893400

35. Park, K.M., Park, F.C.: Collision Detection for Robot Manipulators: Methods and Algorithms. Springer, Cham (2023). https://doi.org/10.1007/978-3-031-30195-7

36. Li, Y., Li, Y., Zhu, M., Xu, Z., Mu, D.: A nonlinear momentum observer for sensorless robot collision detection under model uncertainties. Mechatronics **78**, 102603 (2021). https://doi.org/10.1016/j.mechatronics.2021.102603

37. Tian, Y., Chen, Z., Jia, T., Wang, A., Li, L.: Sensorless collision detection and contact force estimation for collaborative robots based on torque observer. In: 2016 IEEE International Conference on Robotics and Biomimetics (ROBIO), Qingdao, China, pp. 946–951. IEEE (2016). https://doi.org/10.1109/ROBIO.2016.7866446
38. Sharkawy, A.-N., Aspragathos, N.: Human-robot collision detection based on neural networks. Int. J. Mech. Eng. Robot. Res. 7, 150–157 (2016). https://doi.org/10.18178/ijmerr.7.2.150-157

AI-Driven Smart Air Conditioning System for a Sustainable and Energy-Efficient Industrial Future

Cherifa Nakkach[1(✉)] and Yvan Picaud[2]

[1] Orange Innovation Tunisia, Sofrecom Tunisia, Tunis, Tunisia
cherifa.nakkach@sofrecom.com
[2] Orange Innovation, Lannion, France

Abstract. This paper examines short-term predictions of industrial air-conditioning loads using the data from smart meters. Using IoT, data can be collected from sensors that measure temperature, humidity, and other relevant parameters. This enables real-time monitoring of environmental conditions. We present a comprehensive architecture for an energy-efficient and sustainable solar air conditioning system for an efficient industrial future. To optimize operational efficiency and reduce energy costs, this system must predict energy consumption. Various machine learning models were explored and tested, including Convolutional Neural Networks - Long Short-Term Memory (CNN-LSTM), Recurrent Neural Networks (RNN), Gated Recurrent Units (GRU) and TimeGPT to identify the most effective approach for energy prediction. RMSE and MAPE metrics showed that the TimeGPT model outperformed all other models in terms of accuracy and reliability in forecasting energy consumption. TimeGPT's results provide evidence that industrial environments can improve their energy efficiency and sustainability by using the TimeGPT model. In addition to better energy management, this approach reduces costs and reduces carbon footprints. Energy consumption can is therefore predicted to optimize air conditioner operation, plan preventive maintenance, detect potential problems, and take corrective action to reduce the unnecessary consumption of energy.

Keywords: Energy consumption prediction · Industry · Air conditioner · RNN · CNN-LSTM · GRU · TimeGPT

1 Introduction

We are living in the "perfect energy storm" of the 21st century, when energy prices are volatile, the environment is changing, and energy supply and security are threatened. As the century progresses, energy will become one of the greatest challenges mankind will face. All vital components of human society are powered by fossil fuels, such as coal, petroleum, and natural gas [1]. Energy demand is expected to double or even triple by 2050 due to growing populations and expanding economies in developing nations. There have already been concerns raised about possible supply difficulties, depletion of energy resources, and acceleration of environmental impacts such as global warming, and climate change. Globally, fossil fuels account for 80% of energy production, leaving dreadful environmental impacts [2]. Fuel demand is increasing around the world, leading to undesirable conditions such as acidification, global warming, air pollution, and land degradation [3]. And there is no doubt that energy sustainability is one of the most pressing socioenvironmental concerns of our time [4]. Alternatively, and from a socio-economic sustainability perspective, having affordable energy, particularly electricity, and capacity in energy systems are integral components of socio-economic equality. Collectively, these concerns underscore the importance of energy sustainability and the need to increase energy efficiency and eliminate energy waste while simultaneously ensuring energy availability is more accessible, economically viable, and environmentally friendly [5]. Known as Industry of the future, industry 5.0 will bring immense opportunities for energy sustainability [6]. As part of industry of the future, the entire industrial value chain is digitalized and integrated. As a result of vertical integration of intelligent production systems and horizontal integration of value chain members, modern digital technologies such as the Industrial Internet of Things (IIoT), the Internet of People (IoP), the Internet of Services (IoS), and Cyber-Physical Production Systems (CPPS) have led to the development of new business models and global value-creation networks.

A power management system's intelligent power consumption prediction is a complex and crucial task. National energy development policies are heavily influenced by it. In industries, air conditioners are among the biggest power consumers. Energy is transferred from space-air to defined space, to make that defined space cooler than its natural surroundings. The purpose of air conditioning is to improve the quality of the air within a defined space, both in terms of temperature and humidity, and therefore to create a healthy and suitable environment. Due to this, industries consume high amounts of energy. Due to global warming, the outdoor temperature has also increased significantly over the past few years during the summer season. To meet the harsh environmental challenges, the cooling system's capacity is ordinarily not designed to handle these changes. Thus, an insufficient cooling capacity increased electrical consumption, and higher maintenance costs would result. As traditional electrical energy sources became scarcer and more expensive, researchers investigated the design and applications of air conditioners to achieve suitable conditions in industries using normal processes and methods. When operating at high ambient temperatures, air conditioner compressor power consumption can be reduced to improve system performance. The advantages of solar energy include its inexhaustibility, pollution-free nature, along with limited regional restrictions. As far as energy resources go, solar energy is the most abundant. It is increasingly replacing non-renewable energy sources. Solar photovoltaic technology has been evolving rapidly since 1990, with continuous improvements in photovoltaic performance and constant price drops of solar modules, its usage has increased. During operation, air conditioners with solar power directly driven method convert solar power to air conditioner compressor by means of solar power generation and new cooling technologies. As an added benefit, the excess power can be used to charge the battery at night or during cloudy days, reducing the grid's energy costs significantly. As a result, solar powered air conditioners offer unparalleled benefits when compared to conventional air conditioners, both in terms of energy savings and emission reductions.

Thus, to reduce energy consumption and ensure efficient use of solar energy, this article proposes AI-driven air conditioning system. As for the remainder of the paper, Sect. 2 discusses related works that deal with energy prediction models. As a result of this section, a brief overview of the proposed energy forecasting system is presented. In Sect. 4, we present the three machine learning models we have trained and tested. In Sect. 5, the model's performance evaluation is presented, and its main results are discussed. The paper concludes with Sect. 6.

2 Related Works

Sustainable development goals and Industry 4.0 are the main promoters of sustainable development. In this study, we explain how industry of nowadays may contribute to energy sustainability as part of this research topic. Data-driven, semi-physical, and physical methods are used to predict industries air-conditioning energy consumption [7]. By using geometrical information and the industries's thermal properties, physical and semi-physical methods estimate the industries's energy demand. It is important, however, to have a thorough understanding of industries thermal dynamics to determine several physical parameters using the physical and semi-physical methods [8]. In [9], the authors develop and simulate an energy-efficient and sustainable advanced liquid desiccant dehumidification air-conditioning system. Buildings with this system are able to reduce their electricity consumption while maintaining comfortable temperatures inside. It consists of a counterflow packed bed absorber and regenerator, as well as flat plate solar collectors. During the cooling process, the strong desiccant solution and processed air are cooled by evaporative coolers and cooling towers. As a result of simulations conducted on three consecutive sunny summer days in Sydney, the proposed system achieved an average daily thermal efficiency of 0.5–0.55 and generated 73.4% of the thermal energy needed for thermal regeneration. In [10], A transient analysis of a solar desiccant cooling system integrated with a counter-flow Maisotsenko cycle heat transfer system to cool hot and humid buildings in this paper is presented. Based on the experimental data, the developed model is validated with the highest deviation of 4.50%. RA1 is a mixture of 100% indoor and 100% outdoor air. RA2 is a mixture of 75% outdoor and 25% indoor air. RA3 is a mixture of 50:50 indoor and outdoor air. A higher ratio of outdoor air in the return air decreases the COP and the cooling capacity of the system, while higher supply and regeneration temperatures increase them. RA1 shows approximately half the solar fraction of RA3, whereas RA3 shows approximately two-thirds. In [11], the work aims to propose a grid-independent, hybrid wind-solar air-conditioning model that will meet room cooling demand in the future. There is a 1.5 kW, 48 V, BLDC motor drive system driving this model, which has a 0.3 ton capacity. As compared to the conventional model, the BLDC-based model improves the energy efficiency from 13 to 20%, and it costs 952 dollars. It is analyzed how much energy can be generated at the proposed location under a range of weather conditions using a virtual 4kW hybrid model. As shown in this analysis, solar energy contributes 69.4% in winter and 57% in summer to the total generation of energy. In [12], A new model was introduced for predicting energy consumption in homes, utilizing a hybrid approach that combines LSTM with DELM (featuring seven hidden layers). Its prediction performance was successfully compared to other statistical models. The results from training and testing demonstrate that our model excels in energy consumption prediction, with an MAE of 0.42, an R-squared of 1.1, and an RMSE of 1.23. The proposed model, with its modified DELM architecture, outperforms other models and can be applied to various IoT applications, including smart cities, homes, buildings, and grids. Because data-driven methods can solve nonlinear problems in a faster and more efficient way, air-conditioning energy consumption models have been widely used to estimate air conditioning energy consumption. Dynamic environments and future conditions have been sufficiently considered [13]. Data science has often used machine learning (ML) to overcome predicaments related to energy management [14]. In [15], authors introduce the concept of smart scheduling and energy consumption management of a single-machine manufacturing setup, using a 3D printer as the focal point. In order to plan production, the system combines real-time data on energy usage with weather-based forecasts of solar power production. The SARIMA and XGBoost models were selected for the testing and evaluation phase due to their superior accuracy compared to the other models. Both models seem to effectively capture the overall trend of actual power production, though with differing levels of precision. According to [16], this paper uses a conventional smart meter to predict short-term AC load in residential buildings. An energy disaggregation methodology separates AC load from smart meter's aggregate consumption at each time step. A prediction algorithm is developed based on the obtained air-conditioning load and corresponding historical weather data. Various machine learning algorithms are used to make hour-ahead and day-ahead predictions, including Artificial Neural Networks, Support Vector Machines, and Random Forests. It has been shown that Random Forests provide the best hour-ahead and day-ahead predictions, respectively, with R2 scores of 87.3% and 83.2%.

3 Solar Air Conditioning System and Methodology

3.1 Solar Air Conditioning System

The purpose of air conditioning systems is to keep homes and offices at a comfortable temperature. Medical applications of it are also numerous. A common feature of a home is an HVAC system [17]. Most offices and commercial industries also use them. Air conditioning system systems heat, cool, and control airflow. Using this method, the air is distributed to the places that need to be cooled or heated. Climate-controlled areas are especially useful when temperatures are extreme. The use of solar air-conditioning systems (as shown in Fig. 1) allows for energy-saving thermal comfort in residential and office buildings. Rather than using vapor compression, such systems utilize desiccant dehumidification. Using low-grade energy (solar energy) to heat air is used for dehumidifier regeneration and for adsorption-based chilling.

3.2 Methodology

In this section, we introduce the methodology adopted to forecast energy consumption of our solar air conditioning system. As shown in Fig. 2, we follow a set of steps.

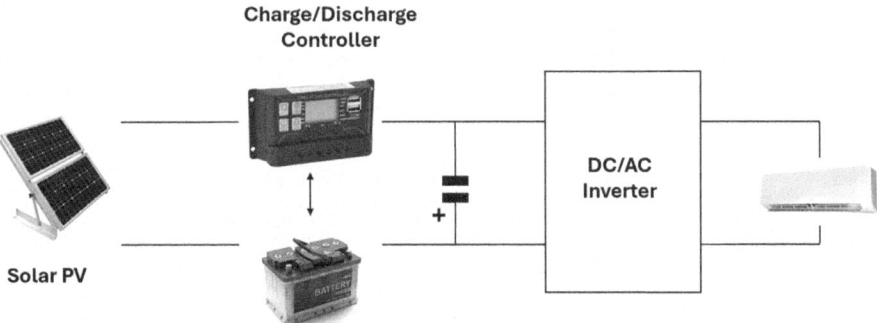

Fig. 1. Solar air conditioning system.

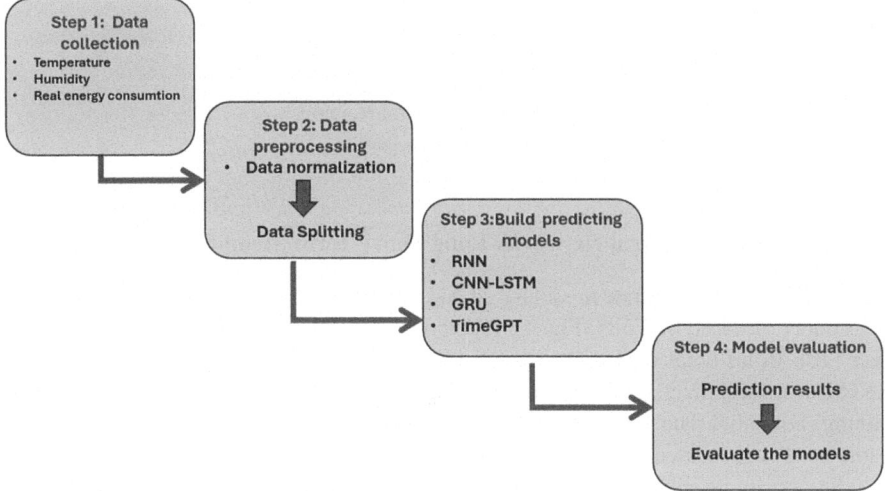

Fig. 2. Proposed methodology.

4 Machine Learning Models Description

The purpose of this section is to briefly describe the proposed machine learning models for predicting energy consumption of air conditioning system.

4.1 Recurrent Neural Network (RNN)

RNN is a type of neural network designed to work with sequential data, such as time series or natural language data [18]. They are a powerful and robust type of neural networks and belong to the most promising algorithms of the moment because they are the only ones to have internal memory. Many other deep learning algorithms [19], such as RNNs, have been around for a long time. Although they were originally developed in the 1980s, their real potential has only been realized in recent years thanks to the increase in available computing power, the huge amount of data we now have, and the invention of LSTM. In addition to memorizing important information about the data that they have received, RNNs (as shown on Fig. 3) are able to predict the future very accurately because of their internal memory.

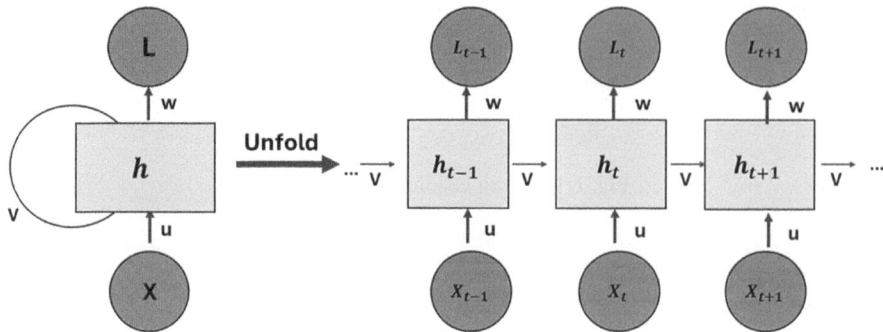

Fig. 3. Recurrent Neural Network.

4.2 Convolutional Neural Networks-Long Short-Term Memory (CNN-LSTM)

CNN-LSTM is a multivariate model based on CNN that extracts main features from time series data processed by CNN (Fig. 4). Prediction results are calculated using the LSTM layer [20]. In artificial recurrent neural networks (RNNs), Long Short-Term Memory (LSTM) is a specialized model that models sequential or temporal aspects of data. When training sequential data, original RNN models often experience vanishing or exploding gradients. As presented in Fig. 4, LSTM model introduces three gates in each cell, including an input gate, an output gate, and a forget gate, which can detect temporal changes in long sequential data. For this reason, it has been widely used for analyzing text, videos, and time series.

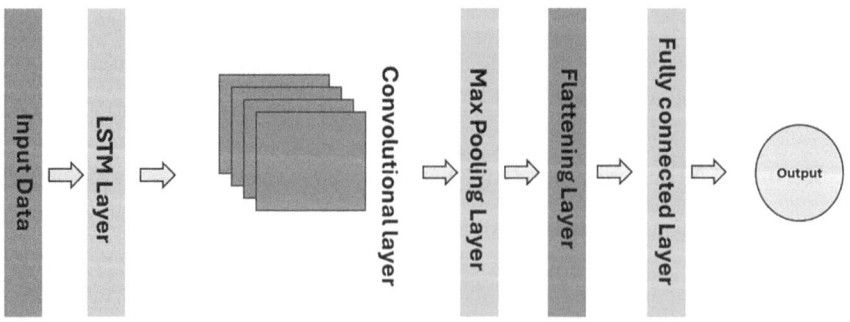

Fig. 4. The structure of LSTM-CNN model.

4.3 Gated Recurrent Unit (GRU)

GRU are improved variations of RNN based on recurrent neural networks with gated recurrent networks. Such as the LSTM, the GRU's internal structure consists of an input gate and a forget gate, except it combines them into an update gate. Two gates are included in this model: an update gate, which controls how much previous information is incorporated into the current state; and a reset gate that determines whether previous information will be attributed to the current state [21]. GRU unit is shown in Fig. 5.

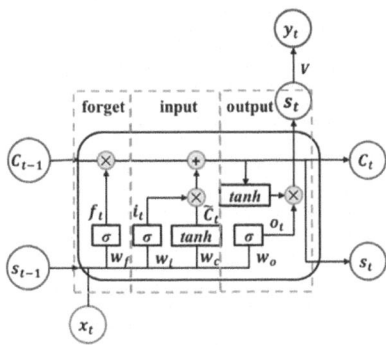

Fig. 5. GRU unit.

4.4 Time Generative Pre-trained Transformer (TimeGPT)

TimeGPT is constructed using a transformer architecture with attention mechanisms, like LLMs. As shown in Fig. 6, the architecture consists mainly of positional encoding (PE), multi-head attention, and CNN, which incorporates residual connections and layer normalizations to prevent gradient degradation and speed up algorithm convergence [22]. With TimeGPT, historical values are leveraged to generate forecasts, and local PE is incorporated to improve input representation. A linear layer is then applied to the decoder's output to forecast values. A decoder maintains its autoregressive property by shifting the input sequence one position to the right of its previously generated tokens. As shown in Fig. 6, using sine-cosine positional coding, the Positional Encoding has the responsibility of assigning positional information to each feature in order to enable the model to comprehend the sequential information in the input features.

5 Results and Discussion

5.1 Dataset

Obtaining data is an essential step because all subsequent steps rely on it. In data collection, all relevant data is gathered from the available sources. It has been collected from June 2023 to December 2023. It contains 10400 instances. As shown in Table 1, this

Target variable
+
Events
+
Additional variables

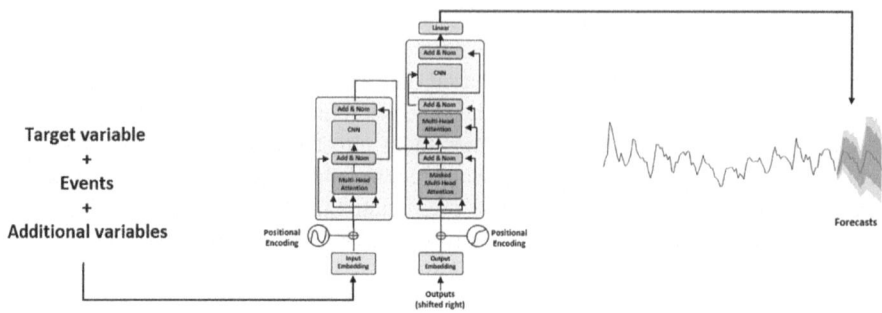

Fig. 6. Architecture of TimeGPT.

dataset contains 4 variables. It consists of two parts: As a training set, 70% of the data is selected. The test set consists of 30% of the data set and is used for evaluating the performance of the detector. Each epoch consisted of 350 steps, which were run over all training images in each epoch.

Table 1. Dataset with its attribute description.

Attribute	Unit	Symbol
Date	Days/months/years	D
Temperature	°C	T
Humidity	g/kg	H
Electricity	kWh	E

Then, cleaning and filtering data is essential before using it. To conduct this study, we collected raw power flow data from a power grid under study. Due to the high level of data quality in this work, the proposed machine learning models can be trained and tested to predict power flow directions. After collecting data, preprocessing is the next step. A data preprocessing step is essential for any type of deep learning model since it can improve the model's accuracy by improving the data quality and extracting valuable information. In this study, datasets are collected from different sources with different scales and units (Fig. 7).

It is possible that these differences in datasets can affect the performance during the learning process, and even worse, they may increase the generalization error. This problem was thus avoided by scaling or normalizing all variables. Our study used the min-max normalization method for numerical scaling. This equation shows how to convert the original value into a normalized value.

$$x' = \frac{x - \min(x)}{\max(x) - \min(x)} \tag{1}$$

In this equation, x' is the normalized value of x, x is the original value, $\max(x)$ is the maximum value of x, while $\min(x)$ is the minimum.

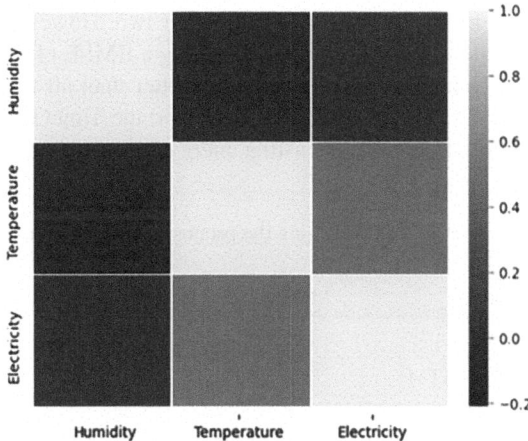

Fig. 7. Confusion matrix: Variable correlation.

5.2 Models' Performance Indicators

Metric scores are crucial to assessing and measuring energy prediction model performance and accuracy. We selected the evaluation metrics based on recommendations from studies and reports about predictive cases. There are three metrics to measure these errors: RMSE and MAPE as shown in Eq. 2 and Eq. 3. These metrics can be expressed in the following equations.

$$RMSE = \sqrt{\frac{\sum_1^N (zt - \widehat{zt})}{N}} \tag{2}$$

$$MAPE = \sqrt{\frac{\sum_1^N |zt - \widehat{zt}|}{N}} \tag{3}$$

In this formula, zt represents the actual value, $\widehat{zt}$ represents the predicted value, yy represents the mean value of y, and N represents the number of observations. Data from the original study were used to calculate the evaluation metrics in the Results and Discussion section. Normalized values were converted by inverse min–max scaling algorithms presented in Eq. (1).

5.3 Discussion

This study examined four machine learning models for predicting energy use: the Recurrent Neural Network (RNN), the Convolutional Neural Network - Long Short-Term Memory (CNN-LSTM), the Gated Recurrent Unit (GRU) and TimeGPT. To evaluate the models' performance, Root Mean Square Error (RMSE) and Mean Absolute Percentage Error (MAPE) metrics were used. Based on the results in Table 1 and Fig. 8, the RNN model produced an RMSE of 111.57 and a MAPE of 17.87, which is the highest prediction error among the tested models. A CNN-LSTM model achieved an RMSE of

63.55 and a MAPE of 15.65, outperforming the other two. However, the GRU model performed better than the other two models, achieving a RMSE of 78.76 and a MAPE of 12.06. Finally, the TimeGPT model performed better than all models, achieving a RMSE of 64.32 and a MAPE of 11.64. We recommend the TimeGPT model due to its superior accuracy and reliability in forecasting energy consumption (Table 2).

Table 2. Metrics for evaluating the proposed model's accuracy.

Model	RMSE	MAPE
RNN	111.57	17.87
CNN-LSTM	63.55	15.65
GRU	78.76	12.06
TimeGPT	64.32	11.64

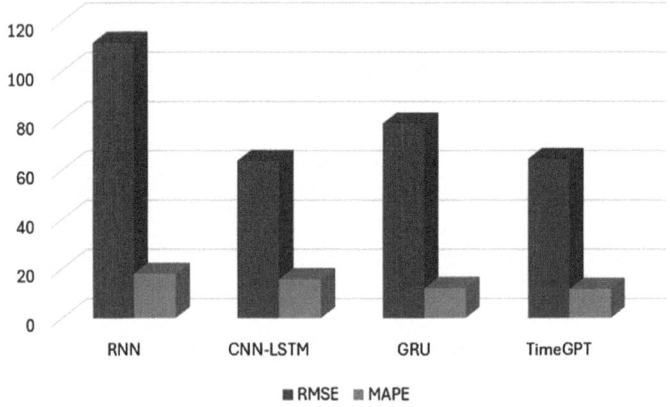

Fig. 8. Comparison of results.

Using the collected dataset, we present our model's forecasting results in Fig. 9.

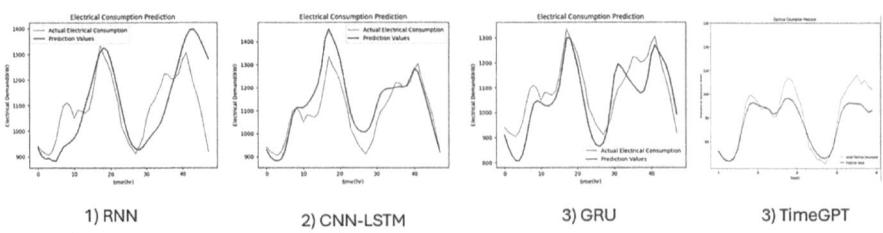

1) RNN   2) CNN-LSTM   3) GRU   3) TimeGPT

Fig. 9. Actual and predicted output using RNN, CNN-LSTM, GRU and TimeGPT.

Loss over time is the most common way to illustrate a learning curve. Loss is our measure of model error. We therefore expect our model's performance to improve as our loss decreases. The process of learning is illustrated in Fig. 10.

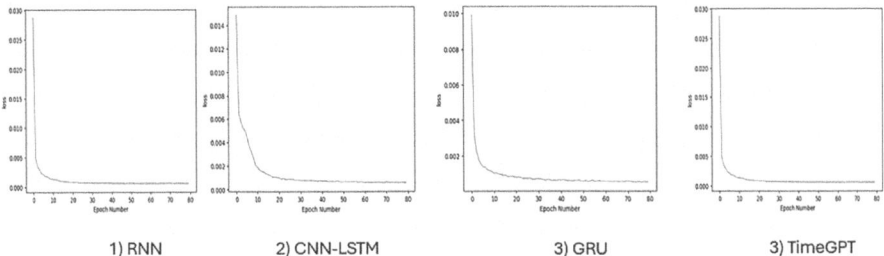

| 1) RNN | 2) CNN-LSTM | 3) GRU | 3) TimeGPT |

Fig. 10. Loss function for RNN, CNN-LSTM, GRU and TimeGPT.

6 Conclusion

A growing number of renewable energy systems are being deployed and growing rapidly, increasing the complexity of the energy exchange. Solar PV power generation was predicted using deep learning models developed in this study. Through RMSE and MAPE analysis, accuracy was verified. In this paper, we present a strategy for assessing and comparing machine loads. Furthermore, we introduced for deep learning models to compare results of prediction. TimeGPT is the most appropriate model for our proposed solution. This study investigated the prediction of energy consumption in smart air conditioning systems using the TimeGPT model. We sought to develop an accurate and efficient method for forecasting energy usage in smart industries so that energy management could be enhanced, and operational efficiency could be optimized. In addition to its ability to accommodate temporal dependencies, the TimeGPT model is also effective at handling sequential data. TimeGPT performed better than traditional methods and other machine learning models in our experiments, predicting energy consumption patterns with a high degree of accuracy. Using the TimeGPT model, smart air conditioning systems can be predicted with more accuracy. By applying it, energy practices can become more sustainable, resource management can be improved, and user comfort can be enhanced. Soon, it may be possible to further refine the model, include additional features such as weather data and occupancy patterns. Industries will become smarter and more energy-efficient with our proposed smart system using TimeGPT model.

References

1. Fanchi, J.R.: Energy In The 21st Century: Energy In Transition. World Scientific (2023)
2. Schernikau, L., Smith, W.H.: Climate impacts of fossil fuels in today's electricity systems. J. South. Afr. Inst. Min. Metall. **122**(3), 133–145 (2022)
3. Atedhor, G.O., Atedhor, C.N.: Contexts of sustainable development risk in climate change and anthropogenic-induced bushfire in Nigeria. Sci. Afr., e02271 (2024)

4. Phillis, A., Grigoroudis, E., Kouikoglou, V.S.: Assessing national energy sustainability using multiple criteria decision analysis. Int. J. Sustain. Dev. World **28**(1), 18–35 (2021)
5. Kim, J., et al.: Energy, material, and resource efficiency for industrial decarbonization: a systematic review of sociotechnical systems, technological innovations, and policy options. Energy Res. Soc. Sci. **112**, 103521 (2024)
6. Nguyen, H.D., Tran, K.P.: Artificial intelligence for smart manufacturing in industry 5.0: methods, applications, and challenges. In: Tran, K.P. (ed.) Artificial Intelligence for Smart Manufacturing. SSRE, pp. 5–33. Springer, Cham (2023). https://doi.org/10.1007/978-3-031-30510-8_2
7. Weng, K.: Data-driven model predictive control of buildings. Diss. Cardiff University (2020)
8. Boodi, A., et al.: Building thermal-network models: a comparative analysis, recommendations, and perspectives. Energies **15**(4), 1328 (2022)
9. Mohaisen, A.K., Ma, Z.: Development and modelling of a solar assisted liquid desiccant dehumidification air-conditioning system. Build. Simul. **8**, 123–135 (2015)
10. Karami, M., Delfani, S., Noroozi, A.: Performance characteristics of a solar desiccant/M-cycle air-conditioning system for the buildings in hot and humid areas. Asian J. Civ. Eng. **21**, 189–199 (2020)
11. Mohanasundaram, A., Valsalal, P.: Design of a wind-solar hybrid energy air conditioning system using BLDC motor for the Indian home environment. Electr. Eng. **105**(3), 1717–1728 (2023)
12. Nakkach, C., Zrelli, A., Ezzedine, T.: Long-term energy forecasting system based on LSTM and deep extreme machine learning. Intell. Autom. Soft Comput. **37**(1) (2023)
13. Sun, Y., Haghighat, F., Fung, B.C.M.: A review of the-state-of-the-art in data-driven approaches for building energy prediction. Energy Build. **221**, 110022 (2020)
14. Ahmad, T., et al.: Data-driven probabilistic machine learning in sustainable smart energy/smart energy systems: key developments, challenges, and future research opportunities in the context of smart grid paradigm. Renew. Sustain. Energy Rev. **160**, 112128 (2022)
15. Moussi, K., Nakkach, C., Picaud, Y.: AI-powered energy optimization: advancing industry 4.0 with smart forecasting for 3D printing and solar panels. In: Automation, Robotics & Communications for Industry 4.0/5.0, p. 238 (2024)
16. Manivannan, M., Najafi, B., Rinaldi, F.: Machine learning-based short-term prediction of air-conditioning load through smart meter analytics. Energies **10**(11), 1905 (2017)
17. Yau, Y.H., Rajput, U.A., Badarudin, A.: A comprehensive review of variable refrigerant flow (VRF) and ventilation designs for thermal comfort in commercial buildings. J. Therm. Anal. Calorim., 1–27 (2024)
18. Park, M.K., et al.: Predictive model for PV power generation using RNN (LSTM). J. Mech. Sci. Technol. **35**(2), 795–803 (2021)
19. Nakkach, C., Zrelli, A., Ezzeddine, T.: Deep learning algorithms enabling event detection: a review. In: 2nd International Conference on Industry 4.0 and Artificial Intelligence (ICIAI 2021). Atlantis Press (2022)
20. Pu, Z., et al.: A hybrid Wavelet-CNN-LSTM deep learning model for short-term urban water demand forecasting. Front. Environ. Sci. Eng. **17**(2), 22 (2023)
21. Khodaverdian, Z., et al.: An energy aware resource allocation based on combination of CNN and GRU for virtual machine selection. Multimedia Tools Appl. **83**(9), 25769–25796 (2024)
22. Liao, W., et al.: TimeGPT in load forecasting: a large time series model perspective. arXiv preprint arXiv:2404.04885 (2024)

A Framework for Resilient Integration of Industry 4.0 Components into Production Systems

Héctor Hostos[1,2(✉)] 🆔, Virginie Goepp[1] 🆔, and Patrick Sondi[2] 🆔

[1] ICube - INSA Strasbourg, 24 bd de la Victoire, 67084 Strasbourg Cedex, France
{hector.hostos,virginie.goepp}@insa-strasbourg.fr
[2] CERI SN - IMT Nord Europe, Rue Guglielmo Marconi,
59650 Villeneuve-d'Ascq, France
patrick.sondi@imt-nord-europe.fr

Abstract. Industry 4.0 has made possible the integration of new technologies, also called 4.0 components, into production systems in order to enhance their productivity and performance in general. However, this integration has brought new types of risks that have to be mitigated to avoid production systems to stop operating due to a failure of the 4.0 components. In this context, resilience, defined as the capability and ability of an element to return to a stable state after a disruption, represents a promising domain to explore. For industrial systems and Industry 4.0, current works dealing with resilience focus on specific types of disruptions and technologies without providing a general framework. This article proposes a general framework to integrate 4.0 components into production systems in a resilient manner. The framework is inspired by the concepts of resilience in socio-ecological systems in an attempt to provide production systems the ability to overcome unexpected disturbances and persist in time. This includes the adaptation of the concepts of *state variables, stability landscape* and the aspects of resilience (*resistance, latitude and precariousness*). It has a service-oriented architecture that connects the 4.0 components to all the services that they enable in the production system. This allows to define several system states according to the service levels enabled by the 4.0 components. The potential use of the framework is illustrated on the Internet of Things (IoT) as a specific 4.0 component.

Keywords: Manufacturing systems · Industry 4.0 · Industry 5.0 · Resilience · Internet of Things · Framework · Service oriented architecture

1 Introduction

The implementation of new technologies in industrial production has recently led to a new era of digitization known as Industry 4.0. This term was introduced in 2013 by the German government as an initiative to secure the future

© The Author(s), under exclusive license to Springer Nature Switzerland AG 2025
M. Dassisti et al. (Eds.): IN4PL 2024, CCIS 2372, pp. 331–349, 2025.
https://doi.org/10.1007/978-3-031-80760-2_22

of their manufacturing industry [19]. Since then, many industries have bene-fited from the technological breakthroughs to improve the performance of their production systems. For example, the development of ultra-high-speed Internet access made possible the emergence of cloud computing, enabling the pooling of storage and processing resources for ever-greater volumes of data. The Internet of Things (IoT) allowed the massification of sensors to get data from processes that were otherwise unmeasurable, and which are used for traceability or pre-dictive maintenance. Additive manufacturing has increased the level of product customization. Artificial intelligence has impacted the manufacturing industry from several subdomains. One of them is computer vision, which has been widely used to automate detection and classification tasks in an efficient manner.

Nonetheless, the integration of such a wide range of technological options, to which we will refer to as 4.0 components, into the existing production systems is also generating new vulnerabilities since these components import the risks associated with their technologies into factories. For instance, the introduction of connected objects with low levels of administration and security represent a cybersecurity risk. Furthermore, the increased dependence on the Internet can cause production stoppages in the case where a cut-off leads to the loss of access to the Cloud. This is particularly troublesome in factories where these techno-logical components are not mandatory for production, but have been introduced there in order to enhance efficiency.

This rises the question of the factory resilience, namely, the ability of the pro-duction system to return to a stable operation after disruptions such as a failure of all or part of these 4.0 components. Most of the operational proposals app-roach resilience from their specific angle. Managers focus on business continuity plans in case of crisis [25], and technicians mostly investigate fault tolerance and cybersecurity [9], while those from the institutional side focus more on raw mate-rials accessibility and data sovereignty in the cloud [8]. However, very little work addresses resilience as a broader topic instead of a technology-specific approach. The concept of resilience has been gaining importance in the industrial domain. In fact, it is one of the three pillars, together with sustainability and human centricity, that are proposed by the European Commission in a new paradigm known as Industry 5.0 [7], in an effort to go beyond a purely profit-driven app-roach for the development of the industry.

In order to develop an approach of resilience that is integrated into the design of the production system, and that evolves with it whatever the crisis, we pro-pose taking inspiration from nature. As a first step to achieve this global target, we propose to adapt the concepts related to resilience as formalized for socioe-cological systems for industrial systems. Such concepts comprise, among others, the system states, the stability landscape [3,10,15] and the aspects of resilience (resistance, latitude, precariousness and panarchy) as detailed in [29]. The under-lying objective is to provide production systems with the ability observed in socioecological systems to overcome unexpected disturbances and persist in time. Complementary, as the first building block towards an operational and practical framework based on these concepts, we also propose a service-oriented architecture that connects the 4.0 components to all the services that they enable in the production system. This allows to define several system states according to the service levels enabled by the different 4.0 components and in turn to make the production system able to deal with disturbances.

This paper is organized as follows. Section 2 reviews the background and related works that integrate the resilience concept into the industrial systems domain and makes a focus on ecological resilience as a means to cope with resilient integration of 4.0 components. Section 3 develops the general framework using a service-oriented architecture and adapting the notion of *state variables, stability landscape* stemming from ecological resilience to our context. In Sect. 4, we illustrate the use of the preliminary framework taking IoT as an application example. Section 5 discusses possible interpretations of the aspects of ecological resilience (*resistance, latitude and precariousness*) to the integration of 4.0 components. Finally, Sect. 6 discusses, concludes and gives future research directions.

2 Background and Related Works

2.1 Resilience in Industrial Systems

Since the first conception of resilience in the domain of ecology [18], the term has been adopted in multiple disciplines so that to date there is no universal definition. However, the work of Bhamra et al. [4] extracts a common meaning from the most notable definitions of resilience in the literature and associates the concept with *"the capability and ability of an element to return to a stable state after a disruption"*.

Resilience has been already addressed in the domain of industrial systems. Goepp et al. [12] review the position of resilience in the context of Industry 4.0. They show three research streams found in the literature. The first one corresponds to the tools for handling specific disruptions, mostly applied to supply chain. The second stream is the impact of the Industry 4.0 technologies on companies' resilience. The third, and less developed stream, is the formulation of frameworks integrating resilience in the management of production systems.

Morisse et al. [22] introduce the house of resilience as a holistic approach to help managers to implement resilience when transiting towards Industry 4.0 in their organizations. However, it is a very high level and conceptual framework that has been extended in Goepp et al. [13] to enhance its applicability.

Fiksel [10] proposes a framework to design resilient and sustainable enterprise and industrial systems. He remarks that traditional engineering practices try to anticipate and respond to known disruptions but may be vulnerable to unforeseen factors. Therefore, the framework inherits properties from biological and social systems, which enables the industrial systems to have a continuous response after external disruptions. However, again this framework is not easily applicable.

Zhu et Ruth [32] address the resilience of industrial eco-systems. These authors defined it as "an approach for industrial production and consumption based on recycling, use of by-products, and life cycle consideration". They focus on eco-efficiency. It arises as a characteristic of industrial eco-systems based on material and energy reduction without affecting the goods and services supplied. They use a network model that portrays the dependencies among several firms. The application of the model to two case studies shows that industrial eco-systems with high inter-dependency may exhibit high eco-efficiency but are less resilient given the rapid propagation of disruptions.

Ruiz-Puente et Bayona [24] model a network of manufacturing companies as suppliers, receivers and processes in analogy with a supply chain. They define the industrial symbiosis as the implementation of synergies among companies in search of benefit in their environmental, economic and social coexistence. Among the assessments performed on the model, they measure the resilience by adapting concepts from socio-ecological systems. This model is not conceived for a single production system but to model a network of systems.

The review of the current works that deal with resilience in Industry 4.0 and industrial systems shows that the available frameworks are not easily applicable when companies are integrating the 4.0 components into their production systems. However the resilience concepts from the ecological domain exhibit interesting features that should make the systems able to deal with unforeseen disruptions. In the next section we propose to review them.

2.2   Ecological Resilience

Holling introduced first the concept of resilience back in 1973 [18] for ecological systems. There, the author explores the behavior of natural systems as they are profoundly affected by external and unexpected changes. He proposes that the behavior of ecological systems can be defined by two properties: resilience and stability. In this context, he defines resilience as a measure of the ability of the system to absorb changes and still persist. Since this first conception, the term of resilience has been adopted by multiple disciplines giving rise to *engineering resilience* and *ecological resilience* and a set of related concepts.

Ecological Resilience Vs. Engineering Resilience. According to [17] *engineering resilience* and *ecological resilience* are two unveiled faces of resilience. The first one concentrates on the stability of the system near an equilibrium state. Thus, the design of engineering systems is fail-safe, namely, it focuses on optimizing its performance under certain operating conditions whose margin of variation is usually narrow, but the efficiency is maximized. The engineering resilience is then linked to resist the effects of disturbances and the speed to return to the equilibrium state. The second one considers that the system may adopt several regimes of behavior instead of a single equilibrium steady state. These kind of systems exhibit other kind of attributes such as unpredictability, change and persistence. In this case, closer to ecological systems, the resilience represents the ability of the system to absorb disturbances without changing the essence of its function, thus leading to persistence in time.

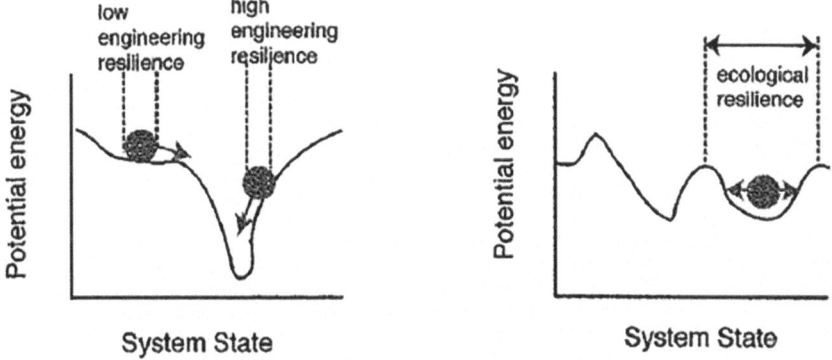

Fig. 1. Two stability landscapes to represent the resilience in engineering systems (left) and ecological systems(right). Taken from [15]

Ecological Resilience Related Concepts. In order to illustrate and differentiate engineering and ecological resilience, Gunderson et al. [15] use stability landscapes as shown in Fig. 1. The x and y axis represent the state of the system and the potential energy kept by the system respectively.

Therefore, the curve represents the potential energy for each possible system state, namely, the stability landscape. The ball represents the system state in a given time and it can be moved along the landscape by disturbances.

The shape of the landscape is given by the controlling variables of the system. The left side of Fig. 1 depicts how systems with high engineering resilience exhibit a high slope in its stability landscape, which leads the system rapidly towards a single equilibrium state. Given this slope, it is also seen that once the system achieves the equilibrium state, disturbances need to be much stronger to take the system out of such state.

On the contrary, systems with low engineering resilience exhibit a low slope which causes a slower return to equilibrium and makes easier for disturbances to act on the system state. The right side of Fig. 1 shows that the ecological resilience is related to the width of a stability basin. However, it is also noticeable that this landscape may have more than one equilibrium state. Therefore, even if the system leaves one equilibrium state, it can go to another one with a similar level of potential energy.

A subsequent proposal was made by Walker et al. [29] in order to further characterize resilience in socio-ecological systems. To do so, they propose (see Fig. 2) a more sophisticated version of the stability landscape as a surface in a three dimensional space. The additional dimension with respect to Fig. 1 recalls the fact that the state of the system may be given by more than one variable. Therefore, if there are n state variables, the state space is the n-dimensional space of all possible combinations of the amounts of these n state variables.

The concept of basin is more specifically called "basin of attraction" to designate all the initial states that tend the system towards the equilibrium state

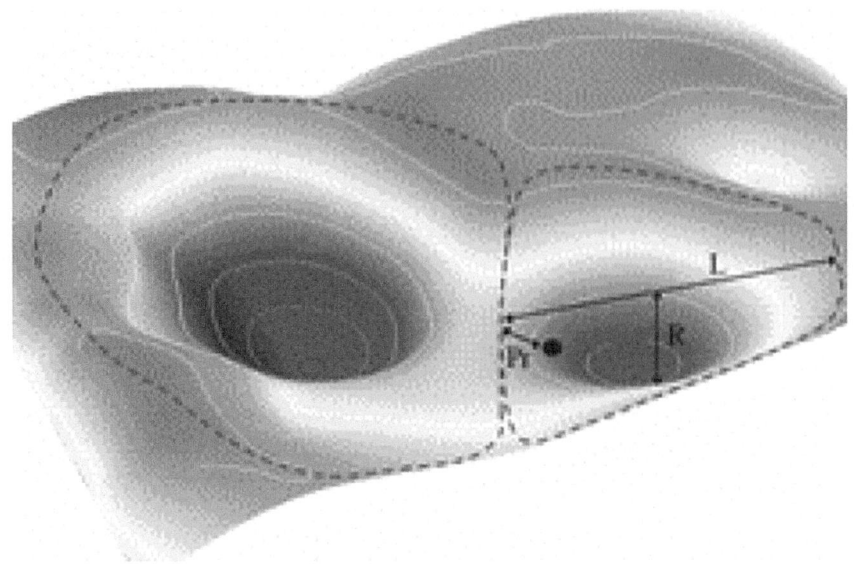

Fig. 2. Three-dimensional stability landscape with multiple basins of attraction. One of the basins shows the aspects of resilience (L. R and Pr). Taken from [29]

also called "attractor". This means that there is one equilibrium state per basin of attraction. The dotted contours in Fig. 2 represent the boundary of each basin of attraction.

Furthermore, Walker et al. [29] introduce the aspects of resilience, enabling to measure the resilience level of a given socio-ecological system, as follows:

- Latitude (L in Fig. 2): the width of a basin of attraction. It represents the maximum amount that the system can be changed without "falling" into another basin of attraction.
- Resistance (R in Fig. 2): the depth of a basin of attraction. It represents the ease of difficulty of moving the system out of its equilibrium state.
- Precariousness (Pr in Fig. 2): the distance between the current state of the system and the boundary of the basin of attraction. It represents how close the system is to reach the threshold and to enter to another basin.
- Panarchy (Pa): the influence that the systems at scales above and below the scale of interest have on the other three aspects of resilience.

All the concepts we have described above can, in our view, provide a sound basis for working out a general framework for resilient integration of 4.0 components. However, to be applicable, all concepts have to be adapted to the specificity of our application context and integrated into a practical architecture. Next section details the architecture of the framework and how it is linked with the concepts of ecological resilience.

3   A General Framework for Resilient Integration of 4.0 Components

3.1   Adaptation of Resilience Related Concepts

The key idea to retrieve from ecological systems is the fact that multiple equilibrium states improve the ability of the system to persist in time in the face of disruptions, namely, they increase its resilience. Likewise, we can define multiple equilibrium states for the operation of the production system so that it is able to change from one state to another in the face of disruptions. This will be reflected on the continuity of the operation. Even if only one of the equilibrium states represents the desired performance, the others may represent the operation under sub-optimal conditions. Thus, the operation in a degraded but controlled state is privileged over a full stop of the operation.

The discussion therefore moves to how to adapt the concepts of ecological resilience to the design of production systems that are upgraded with 4.0 components. The following subsections introduce the framework and its architecture that we propose as the means to implement 4.0 components in a resilient manner.

3.2   A Framework Based on Services

Generally, a 4.0 component is introduced in a production system in order to provide a new service or participate in the improvement of a set of existing services. Therefore, we propose a service-oriented architecture (SOA) as a first approach towards a framework for resilient production systems. SOA is a paradigm that comes from software engineering and it is defined as a way of thinking in terms of services, service-based development, and the outcomes of services [14]. In our field of application, this means that we focus on the services that the 4.0 components provide to the production system instead of the components themselves. In this way, the resilience of the production system can be defined independently from the fact that the service is provided by a single component or by a combination of several components, some of which may not be 4.0 components. For each service, there must be a clear definition of service levels that represent the performance level of such service.

Figure 3 depicts the proposed architecture with its two main components: the 4.0-Component Management System (4CMS) and the Service Management System (SMS). Both systems are intended to be part of the production system, which, in turn, comprises many other subsystems that are not shown in the figure for the sake of simplicity. The 4CMS stores the information related to each 4.0 component like its features. It also contains the live and historical status data. For example, each component is registered, unregistered, updated, diagnosed, etc. The SMS registers each service enabled by the components. It is also aware of its live status, conditions and levels.

3.3   Relation Between Services and 4.0 Components

The relationship between the 4CMS and the SMS is given by the dependence that each service has on the features offered by the components. One component

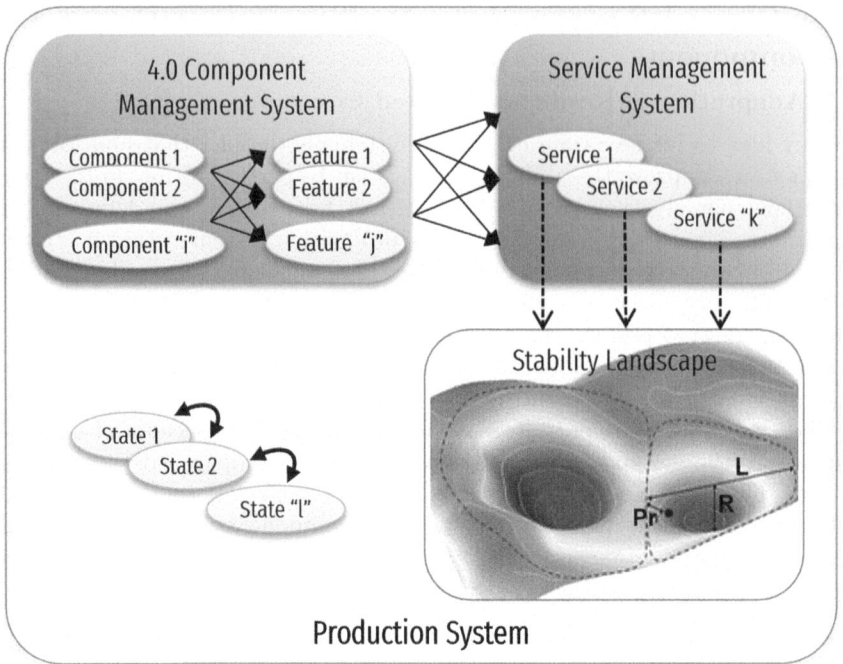

Fig. 3. Service-oriented architecture for the resilient integration of 4.0 components into production systems.

may have one or more features that, in turn, can contribute to one or more services simultaneously. Conversely, one service may depend from one or more features of components at the same time.

Let $C = \{c_1, c_2, ..., c_i, ..., c_n\}$ and $F = \{f_1, f_2, ..., f_j, ..., f_m\}$ respectively the set of n components and m features, and let $S = \{s_1, s_2, ..., s_k, ..., s_r\}$ a set of r services. In addition, let V_{f_j} an ordered set of distinct values $(V_{f_j} = \{v_1, v_2, ..., v_u\})$ which characterize the feature f_j. It contains all the different modes in which a feature f_j can be provided by every existing components supporting it.

It is first possible to express a set of modes V_{f_j,c_i} at which any component c_i provides the feature f_j as a function from $CX\{f_j\}$ towards the set of subsets $\mathcal{P}(V_{f_j})$ of the set of modes V_{f_j} related to the feature considered f_j, as follows:

$$V : CX\{f_j\} \rightarrow \mathcal{P}(V_{f_j})$$
$$(c_i, f_j) \rightarrow V(c_i, f_j) = V_{f_j,c_i} \tag{1}$$

Indeed, although a component c_i may support several different modes of a given feature f_j, it cannot necessarily supply all of its existing modes. Therefore, the subset of the modes of a feature f_j supported by the component c_i, $V_{f_j,c_i} = \{v_{min,c_i}, ..., v_{l,c_i}, ..., v_{max,c_i}\}$, is obviously a subset of V_{f_j} (see Eq. 1).

From every modes of feature f_j supported by a component c_i, it may be useful to identify a reference mode Z_{f_j,c_i} which represents the best mode of f_j supported by c_i. Since V_{f_j} is an ordered set, depending on the feature considered, such a best mode should be either the first or the last element in the subset V_{f_j,c_i}. It could be defined as follows:

$$
\begin{aligned}
Z_{f_j,c_i} &= \max V_{f_j,c_i} = v_{max,c_i} \, or \\
Z_{f_j,c_i} &= \min V_{f_j,c_i} = v_{min,c_i}
\end{aligned}
\tag{2}
$$

Consequently, it is possible to compare any couple of components c_p and c_q regarding a given feature f_j by comparing their respective modes Z_{f_j,c_p} and Z_{f_j,c_q} for this feature. Therefore, let C_t a subset of t available components of C ($C_t \subseteq C$ and $t \leq n$) that are the only admitted for providing a feature f_j. It is possible to express that, at any moment, at least one of these components provides this feature at its best (highest or lowest, depending on the feature) available mode as follows:

$$
\begin{aligned}
Z_{f_j,best} &= \max\{Z_{f_j,c \in C_t}\}(Z_{f_j,best} \leq \max V_{f_j}) \, or \\
Z_{f_j,best} &= \min\{Z_{f_j,c \in C_t}\}(Z_{f_j,best} \geq \min V_{f_j})
\end{aligned}
\tag{3}
$$

However, this does not allow choosing among different available components, nor determining if a component replacing another will perform worse or better regarding a specific feature for every targeted services. Indeed, it should be noticed that a feature does not contribute to two different services with the same importance. Therefore, the service level associated to the mode of a given feature for one service is not necessarily the same for another service. Thus, it is necessary to introduce a relation between the values of the level of a service with those of the mode of any feature. Let W denotes that relation, it can be defined for any feature f_j as follows:

$$
\begin{aligned}
W : SX\{f_j\} &\rightarrow \mathbf{N}^{|V_{f_j}|} \\
(s_k, f_j) &\rightarrow W_{s_k,f_j} = \{g(v_1), g(v_2), ..., g(v_u)\}
\end{aligned}
\tag{4}
$$

where g is a function that associates each mode of the feature f_j in V_{f_j} with a level of the service s_k for this feature. It should be noticed that contrary to V_{f_j} values that are all distinct from each other, W_{s_k,f_j} values may not be necessarily distinct. Indeed, it is obvious that for some services, upgrading a feature above a certain mode may not necessarily change the level of the service supplied.

In summary, for any feature f_j supplied through a component c_i, it is possible to build a table that reports the relation between the feature modes V_{f_j,c_i} supported by that component and the associated service levels W_{s_k,f_j} achieved through it, and denoted as $W_{s_k,f_j,c_i} - \{g(v_{min,c_i}), ..., g(v_{l,c_i}), ..., g(v_{max,c_i})\}$. However, it may happen that a higher feature mode leads to counter performance and decreases the service level. Therefore, $g(v_{min,c_i})$ is not necessarily lower than $g(v_{max,c_i})$.

Consequently, in order to choose among two components c_p and c_q regarding a given feature f_j for a service s_k, it may not be sufficient to compare Z_{f_j,c_p} and Z_{f_j,c_q}, but it may be necessary to compare the service levels respectively achieved by both components W_{s_k,f_j,c_p} and W_{s_k,f_j,c_q} for the feature f_j.

Table 1. Service levels according to feature modes obtained through a component

Component c_i	Feature f_j					
Services	Modes V_{f_j} of feature f_j supported by component c_i					
	not supported	v_{max,c_i}	... v_{l,c_i}	... v_{min,c_i}	not supported	
Service 1		W_{s_1,max,c_i}	... W_{s_1,l,c_i}	... W_{s_1,min,c_i}		
Service 2		W_{s_2,max,c_i}	... W_{s_2,l,c_i}	... W_{s_2,min,c_i}		
...			...			
Service k		W_{s_k,max,c_i}	... W_{s_k,l,c_i}	... W_{s_k,min,c_i}		

3.4 Relation Between Service Levels and System States

The SMS works as an interface between the 4CMS and the production system as the current service levels will dictate the state of operation of the production system. It is in the SMS that the adaptation of the resilience concepts takes place. The first step in this adaptation is to define the state variables that will shape the stability landscape. Those values must describe the state of the production system at a given time. They must be measurable, practical and interpretable by the managers of the production system. We propose that each service corresponds to one state variable. The values that each state variable can take are given by the service levels already defined for each service. Therefore, if there are n services provided by the 4.0 components to the production system, the stability landscape becomes the *n-dimensional* space of all possible combinations of the service levels from those n services.

4   Application to IoT as a 4.0 Component

We chose IoT as a 4.0 component to illustrate the potential application of the proposed framework. However, it is worth mentioning that the framework is intended to be used with any other 4.0 component that aims at improving the service levels of the production system. The following subsections will describe an example in which a production system is equipped with IoT cameras to improve its services of *traceability* and *quality control*. For this, we review the use of IoT in industrial applications, propose the adaptation of the architecture for IoT devices and examine the relationships within the internal systems of the architecture.

4.1   IoT and Its Industrial Applications

The International Telecommunication Union (ITU) defines the IoT as "a global infrastructure for the information society, enabling advanced services by interconnecting things based on existing and evolving interoperable information and communication technologies" [26]. Here, a thing refers to an object from the physical or virtual world, which is capable of being identified and integrated into communication networks [26]. In practical terms, IoT enables objects, like vehicles or home appliances to connect to a network and exchange data [27].

With the development of Industry 4.0, IoT has played an important role in the manufacturing sector. Real-time data acquisition from machines, processes, and business environments brought new opportunities to the operation of manufacturing enterprises, which requires numerous types of decision-making [5]. The amount of data generated when adopting IoT in manufacturing opens the way for new data-driven strategies that support the companies in optimizing its performance [23]. Moreover, energy management, proactive maintenance and connected supply chain represent potential applications for future development [31]. IoT solutions have been already employed in multiple sectors to enhance services in production systems like predictive maintenance [6], traceability [20], energy management [28], safety [11] and quality control [21].

4.2   Application of the Framework for IoT Devices

Figure 4 shows an adaptation of the framework for an example of a production system characterized by two services: *traceability* and *quality control*. The former refers to the capability of the production system to track raw materials, components or finished products during the production processes. The latter

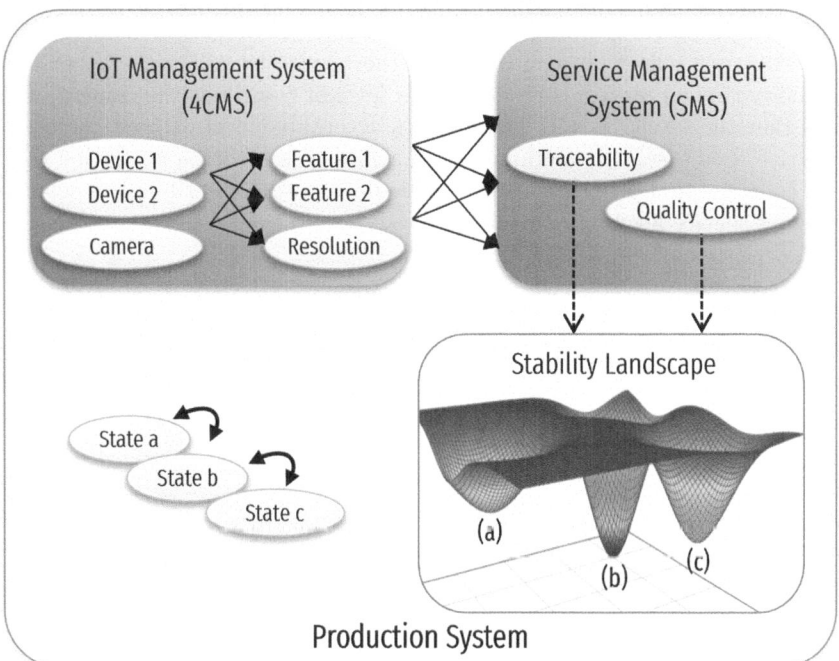

Fig. 4. Application of the framework on IoT within a production system with two services.

ensures that the products meet specified quality standards and customer expectations. Both services have a service level defined in the range from 1 to 10. The two services can be located inside the SMS. They act as the interface between the features provided by the 4CMS and the operation of the production system modeled as a stability landscape.

As the 4.0 component chosen was IoT, the 4CMS corresponds in this case to an IoT management system. In practice, these systems are typically provided by the vendors of IoT solutions to manage multiple types of IoT devices. For our purpose, one of the devices is a *camera* and one of its features is the *resolution*, which enables the services listed in the SMS.

4.3   Defining Service Levels

In accordance with Table 1 detailed in Sect. 3.3, Fig. 5 shows the relationship between the feature *resolution* (f_j) of the component *camera* (c_i) and the corresponding services, which are *traceability* (s_1) and *quality control* (s_2). It can be noticed how the device enables different levels of service according to different modes ($V_{f_j,c_i} = \{v_{min,c_i} = $ "No image", ..., $v_{l,c_i} = $ "2K", ..., $v_{max,c_i} = $ "8K"$\}$) of the feature *resolution*. The service levels (W_{s_k,f_j}) of this example have been predefined as integer numbers in the range from 1 to 10 ($W_{s_k,f_j} = \{g(v_1) = 1, ..., g(v_i), ..., g(v_u) = 10\}$). It is observed that the service level for *traceability* ranges from 2 to 8. When the camera is absent, the service level falls to 2. Moreover, even though the camera offers resolutions higher than 2K, it does not reflect on an increase in the service level. On the other hand, the quality control service is rendered at a level of 6 without the camera, which means that the service is still offered at an acceptable level without the need of the device. Likewise, the maximum level achieved is 8 with a resolution of 2K, which confirms that a higher feature mode does not necessarily allow achieving the higher service level.

		Feature (e.g.: Resolution)				
		8K	4K	2K	720	No image
Service	Traceability	8	8	8	5	2
	Quality Control	3	5	8	7	6

Fig. 5. Relationship between the feature Resolution of the IoT device Camera with the services Traceability and Quality Control.

4.4   Relation Between Service Levels and System States

Figure 4 also shows a possible stability landscape formed by the combination of all possible service levels. Further details of this landscape can be extracted from Fig. 6. Three basins of attraction can be identified and therefore three equilibrium states labeled as (a), (b) and (c). Such states are defined by the duples of service levels (2,6), (8,8) and (8,3) respectively. The deepest equilibrium state (b) represents the set of service levels at which the production system is desired to operate. In other words, the service *traceability* operates at a service level 8 and *quality control* at a service level 8. The other equilibrium states (a) and (c) are predefined modes of operation in case a specific disruption prevents the system from operating in state (b). If the production systems fails to operate in one of its equilibrium states, managers must strive to bring the system back to one of its equilibrium state.

In addition, a service may depend on several features from several components. However, for this example, we assume that each service depends just on one feature from a single component. In this case, we can establish a link between the feature *resolution* and the equilibrium states in Fig. 6. The absence of the camera represents the equilibrium state (a), the operation at a 2K resolution represents the equilibrium state (b) and the resolution 8K represents the equilibrium state (c). In practice, this means that the desired resolution of operation is 2K. However, there might be different kinds of disruptions, like a shortage in the supply chain that makes the cameras unavailable or a technical glitch in the firmware that forces the operation in 8K resolution. In such cases, the production system is able to continue its operation in equilibrium states (a) or (c) respectively until a solution is found.

5   Towards the Adaptation of the Aspects of Resilience

So far, we have developed a general framework to adapt the concepts related to socio-ecological resilience to production systems. These concepts include the state variables, the stability landscape, its basins of attraction and equilibrium states. The next step forward consists in adapting the aspects of resilience, that according to [29] are the latitude, resistance, precariousness and panarchy. These aspects should have an interpretation in our application domain that allows the managers to make informed decisions with respect to the operation of the production system. Here are a few proposals for adapting three aspects of resilience to production systems, based on the framework developed in this paper.

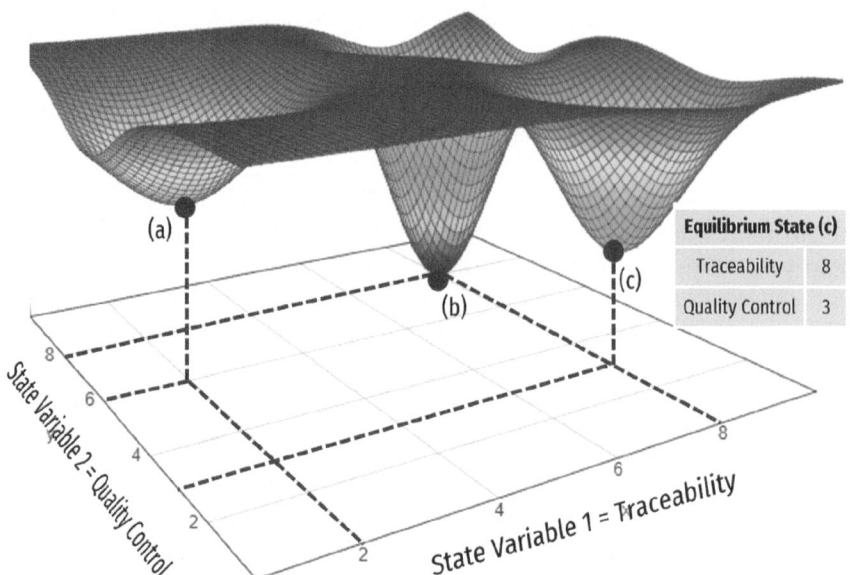

Fig. 6. Illustration of a potential stability landscape for two services and three basins of attraction.

5.1   Adaptation of Latitude and Precariousness Aspects

Returning to the definitions of Sect. 2.2, the latitude measures the width of each basin of attraction and it refers to the change in state variables required to move the system state from one basin to another. In our application domain, where the state variables are the services offered by the 4.0 components, latitude would be the amount that a service level may change without leading the production system into another behavioral regime, i.e. another basin of attraction.

This raises the question of defining basin boundaries. We propose that these boundaries correspond to the service level thresholds, which, if crossed, can represent a loss for the service provider. These thresholds are generally found in the service level agreements (SLAs) that are established at the time of service creation between the service provider and the consumer, which can be internal or external to the production system. For example, the SLA of a given service whose level is measured from 0 to 100 may state that the service is normally provided if the service level is above 90. It is degraded if the service level is between 70 and 90, and it is not functional below 70. In the two last cases the service consumer is entitled compensation from the service provider. Three basins of attraction are identified here by the intervals $(0, 70)$, $(70, 90)$ and $(90, 100)$. Their latitudes therefore correspond to the difference between their limits, i.e. 70, 20 and 10 respectively. Similarly, precariousness reflects how close the system is to reaching the threshold and entering into another basin of attraction. Therefore, for the above example, we can deduce that if system state is currently at a service level of 92, the precariousness is 2, as this is the minimum change to cross the boundary of the current basin. Likewise, if the service level were 85, the precariousness would be 5 since it is the distance to the nearest service level threshold.

5.2 Adaptation of Resistance Aspect

The aspect of resistance, defined as the depth of a basin of attraction, opens room for different interpretations in the production systems domain. However, any interpretation and related implementation should respect the original definition of the ease or difficulty of moving the system out of its equilibrium state. We propose to link the resistance of a basin to the penalties that the manufacturing organization has to incur when its production system operates in this basin of attraction. These penalties could be extracted from the SLAs, internal agreements, insurance contracts, standards or laws. The relationship of resistance would be inversely proportional to penalties, so that a deep basin of attraction means a desired point of operation with low or zero penalties. Therefore a shallow basin of attraction represents higher costs and important penalties, which should prompt managers to take the necessary actions to move the state of the production system to a deeper basin of attraction. However, the resistance of a basin is not the only aspect to consider for the resilience of a system. The latitude also plays an important role since it influences the slope of the basins. A wider basin is more resilient than a narrow one. Also a system with multiple basins of attraction is more resilient that a single-basin system [10].

Therefore, it is possible to manage the resilience of production systems by following three practical measures to be implemented during the design stage of the system. First, to increase the margin of operation of the services, the basins of attraction have to be as wide as possible. Second, to negotiate the penalties when the production system is not operating in the preferred basin of attraction (the one with the best performance for which the 4.0 component is designed), the basins of attraction have to be as deep as possible. These two measures can be managed at the time of establishing the SLAs with the service consumers. Finally, the third and most important measure is to have several modes of operation predefined, namely several basins of attractions.

Regarding the fourth aspect of resilience called panarchy, we do not propose a specific interpretation for it since, unlike the other aspects of resilience, panarchy does not have a direct relationship with the stability landscape.

6   Discussion and Conclusions

This paper develops a general and practical framework that allows organizations to integrate resilience when upgrading their production systems with technologies from the Industry 4.0. Several concepts of resilience from socio-ecological systems, such as the stability landscape, were adapted in the framework. This allows to model the behaviour of the production system in terms of the status of its services.

To support this modelling a service-oriented architecture has been proposed. It separates the management of the 4.0 components and the management of their services. This separation is important from the resilient perspective given that the production system should be able to replace one of its 4.0 components as long as the related service levels can be maintained or even enhanced. This will provide the production system with independence from specific vendors, products or technologies.

The proposal was illustrated with IoT to show how a production system would be able to anticipate the degradation or unavailability of a service provided by such a 4.0 component in the face of disruptions. The framework is intended to cover the production systems against the effects that unforeseeable events may have on the services that the 4.0 components provide to the production system. However, those events may impact also other components of the production system different than the 4.0 ones. In this case, an extended version of the framework should be formulated.

In spite of the parallels established between the socio-ecological and the industrial production systems, it is also important to highlight a fundamental difference by adopting the concepts related to ecological resilience. For example, in ecological systems the equilibrium state is achieved by the internal dynamics of the system without the intervention of external actions. On the contrary, in production systems, the equilibrium states are achieved and maintained by the actions that the managers take.

The stability landscape that describes the different modes of operation of the production system should serve as a tool to support managers' decisions. However, the use of the framework should not depend heavily on the graphical representation of the stability landscape as this becomes unfeasible for more than two state variables, namely, two services. On the contrary, the measurement and the interpretability of the aspects of resilience should be straightforward and they should not be constrained if the quantity of services increases.

The stability landscape, the services and the service levels introduced in Sect. 4 corresponds to arbitrary examples. Their values, when applying the framework in a real scenario, should result from a systematic method that may be subject of future work. This method should incorporate, among others, the definition of services, service levels, their relationship with the features of the components. It may also include features from existing work on the systematic transformation of production systems such as [30]. Enterprise architecture also exhibits promising features to be included since this subject has already been linked with the transformation of production systems [16] and with resilience [1].

Although we have proposed an interpretation of three aspects of resilience, i.e. resistance, latitude and precariousness, in the industrial domain of production systems, the future method should also include the way to measure these aspects. This will provide production managers with additional quantitative information useful to guide the design of the basins. Similarly, it is worth exploring further metrics of resilience that have been reviewed in enterprise context [2].

Given the definition of panarchy as the influence that systems at other scales have on the other three aspects of resilience, it may be a matter of future analysis to link the panarchy with the relationship between the 4.0 components, the legacy components of the production system and the components external to the production system.

Of course, the framework and its related method have to be applied on a real testbed as a way of validation that allows to show both their relevance and their improvement points.

Disclosure of Interests. The authors have no competing interests to declare that are relevant to the content of this article.

References

1. Aldea, A., Iacob, M.E., Wombacher, A., Hiralal, M., Franck, T.: Enterprise architecture 4.0-a vision, an approach and software tool support (2018). https://doi.org/10.1109/EDOC.2018.00011
2. Aldea, A., Vaicekauskaitė, E., Daneva, M., Piest, J.P.S.: Assessing resilience in enterprise architecture: a systematic review. In: 2020 IEEE 24th International Enterprise Distributed Object Computing Conference (EDOC), pp. 1–10. IEEE (2020)
3. Beisner, B.E., Haydon, D.T., Cuddington, K.: Alternative stable states in ecology (2003). https://doi.org/10.1890/1540-9295(2003)001[0376:ASSIE]2.0.CO;2
4. Bhamra, R., Dani, S., Burnard, K.: Resilience: the concept, a literature review and future directions (2011). https://doi.org/10.1080/00207543.2011.563826
5. Bi, Z., Da Xu, L., Wang, C.: Internet of things for enterprise systems of modern manufacturing. IEEE Trans. Industr. Inf. **10**(2), 1537–1546 (2014)
6. Civerchia, F., Bocchino, S., Salvadori, C., Rossi, E., Maggiani, L., Petracca, M.: Industrial internet of things monitoring solution for advanced predictive maintenance applications. J. Ind. Inf. Integr. **7**, 4–12 (2017)
7. European Commission and Directorate-General for Research and Innovation, Breque, M., De Nul, L., Petridis, A.: Industry 5.0 - towards a sustainable, human-centric and resilient European industry. Publications Office of the European Union (2021). https://doi.org/10.2777/308407
8. Gaia-X European Association for Data and Cloud: Gaia-x architecture document (2021). https://gaia-x.eu/
9. Espinoza-Zelaya, C., Moon, Y.: Resilient cyber-manufacturing systems under cyber attacks. In: ASME International Mechanical Engineering Congress and Exposition, vol. 85567, p. V02BT02A011. American Society of Mechanical Engineers (2021)
10. Fiksel, J.: Designing resilient, sustainable systems. Environ. Sci. Technol. **37**(23), 5330–5339 (2003)
11. Gnoni, M.G., Bragatto, P.A., Milazzo, M.F., Setola, R.: Integrating IoT technologies for an "intelligent" safety management in the process industry. Procedia Manuf. **42**, 511–515 (2020)

12. Goepp, V., Berrah, L., Caillaud, E.: A literature review on resilience approaches in the industry 4.0 context. In: Borangiu, T., Trentesaux, D., Leitão, P., Berrah, L., Jimenez, J.F. (eds.) SOHOMA 2023. SCI, vol. 1136, pp. 547–558. Springer, Cham (2024). https://doi.org/10.1007/978-3-031-53445-4_45

13. Goepp, V., Berrah, L., Drira, E., Chaabane, S.: Towards a framework to position resilience and industry 4.0. IFAC-PapersOnLine **55**(10), 2258–2263 (2022)

14. The Open Group SOA Working Grooup: Service-oriented architecture (2007)

15. Gunderson, L.H., Holling, C.S., Lowell, J.P., Peterson, G.D.: Resilience of large-scale resource systems. In: Resilience and the Behavior of Large-Scale Systems, vol. 60 (2002)

16. Hostos, H.: An evaluation-aware method for transforming a production system into a cyber-physical production system. Master's thesis, Universidad de Los Andes (2023)

17. Holling, C.S.: Engineering resilience versus ecological resilience. Eng. within Ecol. Constraints **31**(1996), 32 (1996)

18. Holling, C.S.: Resilience and stability of ecological systems. Annu. Rev. Ecol. Syst. **4**, 1–23 (1973)

19. Kagermann, H., Wahlster, W., Helbig, J.: Securing the future of German manufacturing industry initiative industrie 4.0 implementing the strategic recommendations for final report of the industrie 4.0 working group (2013)

20. Lin, J., Shen, Z., Zhang, A., Chai, Y.: Blockchain and IoT based food traceability for smart agriculture. In: Proceedings of the 3rd International Conference on Crowd Science and Engineering, pp. 1–6 (2018)

21. Liu, Y., Han, W., Zhang, Y., Li, L., Wang, J., Zheng, L.: An internet-of-things solution for food safety and quality control: a pilot project in China. J. Ind. Inf. Integr. **3**, 1–7 (2016)

22. Morisse, M., Prigge, C.: Design of a business resilience model for industry 4.0 manufacturers. In: Americas Conference on Information Systems (2017)

23. Mourtzis, D., Vlachou, E., Milas, N.: Industrial big data as a result of IoT adoption in manufacturing. Procedia CIRP **55**, 290–295 (2016)

24. Ruiz-Puente, C., Bayona, E.: Modelling of an industrial symbiosis network as a supply chain (2017)

25. Russo, N., Reis, L., Silveira, C., Mamede, H.S.: Framework for designing business continuity - multidisciplinary evaluation of organizational maturity. In: 2021 16th Iberian Conference on Information Systems and Technologies (CISTI), pp. 1–4 (2021). https://doi.org/10.23919/CISTI52073.2021.9476297

26. Sector, ITU Telecommunication Standardization: Recommendation ITU-T Y. 2060: Overview of the internet of things. Series Y: Global information infrastructure, internet protocol aspects and next-generation networks-Frameworks and functional architecture models, pp. 2060–201206 (2012)

27. Shafiq, M., Gu, Z., Cheikhrouhou, O., Alhakami, W., Hamam, H.: The rise of internet of things: review and open research issues related to detection and prevention of IoT-based security attacks. Wirel. Commun. Mob. Comput. **2022**(1), 8669348 (2022)

28. Shrouf, F., Miragliotta, G.: Energy management based on internet of things: practices and framework for adoption in production management. J. Clean. Prod. **100**, 235–246 (2015)

29. Walker, B., Holling, C.S., Carpenter, S.R., Kinzig, A.: Resilience, adaptability and transformability in social-ecological systems. Ecology Soc. **9** (2004). https://doi.org/10.5751/ES-00650-090205

30. Wu, X., Goepp, V., Siadat, A., Vernadat, F.: A method for supporting the transformation of an existing production system with its integrated enterprise information systems (EISS) into a cyber physical production system (CPPS). Comput. Ind. **131**, 103483 (2021)
31. Yang, C., Shen, W., Wang, X.: The internet of things in manufacturing: key issues and potential applications. IEEE Syst. Man Cybern. Mag. **4**(1), 6–15 (2018)
32. Zhu, J., Ruth, M.: Exploring the resilience of industrial ecosystems. J. Environ. Manag. **122** (2013). https://doi.org/10.1016/j.jenvman.2013.02.052

A Reinforcement Learning Algorithm for Dynamic Job Shop Scheduling

Laura Alcamo$^{(\boxtimes)}$, Giulia Bruno, and Niccolò Giovenali

Politecnico di Torino, 10129 Torino, Italy
s315375@studenti.polito.it

Abstract. The job shop scheduling problem, a notable NP-hard problem, requires scheduling jobs with multiple operations on specific machines in a predetermined order. A strong assumption is that all the information of the manufacturing environment is known in advance and there is no modification during the scheduling process. However, the real-world environment is significantly affected by uncertainties. The dynamic job shop scheduling is a variant of the job shop scheduling problem in which the scheduling environment is subject to changes over time including variations in job arrival times, processing times, machine breakdowns, resource availability and job priority. To address this issue, this paper presents a single-agent reinforcement learning algorithm, which implements a proximal policy optimization that uses masking to reduce the search space and improve efficiency. The algorithm was tested in both deterministic and dynamic environments and compared to traditional scheduling methods. The results demonstrate that the proposed approach is comparable to traditional methods in deterministic cases and outperforms them in dynamic environments. These findings emphasize the potential of reinforcement learning in addressing and optimizing complex scheduling challenges.

Keywords: Job shop scheduling · Dynamic job shop scheduling · Industry 4.0 · Combinatorial optimization · Reinforcement learning · Artificial intelligence

1 Introduction

Efficient job scheduling is crucial for optimizing production processes in a wide range of industries including manufacturing industries, logistic and transportation sectors and healthcare settings. These industries are faced with the task of optimally scheduling tasks and allocating resources to boosts operational efficiency and cut expense.

In manufacturing sectors such as automotive, electronics, and aerospace, efficient job scheduling is crucial for optimizing production processes. Effective scheduling minimizes production time, reduces costs, and enhances overall productivity by ensuring the optimal use of resources like machines, tools, and

M. Dassisti et al. (Eds.): IN4PL 2024, CCIS 2372, pp. 350–366, 2025.
https://doi.org/10.1007/978-3-031-80760-2_23

manpower [1]. Similarly, in logistics and transportation, job scheduling applications include scheduling vehicles, routes, and deliveries to ensure timely and cost-effective operations. Healthcare settings also benefit from job scheduling by optimizing patient appointments, resource allocation, and staff schedules, ultimately improving the quality-of-care delivery. Even service industries like call centers and utilities management rely on efficient job scheduling to maintain high service standards and operational efficiency.

In the era of Industry 4.0, characterized by the integration of digital technologies into manufacturing and industrial practices, job scheduling has gained significant importance. Industry 4.0 leverages technologies such as the Internet of Things (IoT), big data analytics, artificial intelligence (AI), and cyber-physical systems that enable the collection and processing of vast amounts of data in real-time, which is essential for dynamic and adaptive scheduling [2].

Reinforcement learning (RL), a subfield of AI, has emerged as a powerful tool in this context. RL involves training agents to make decisions by interacting with their environment to maximize cumulative rewards. This capability makes RL particularly well-suited for complex, dynamic, and stochastic scheduling scenarios where traditional methods often struggle. By learning from ongoing operations, RL algorithms can adapt to changing job priorities, machine availability, and other unforeseen variables, providing more efficient and responsive scheduling solutions.

This research focuses on the job shop scheduling problem (JSSP) and its dynamic variant (DJSSP) that hold a prominent position in scheduling literature.

Traditional methods for solving JSSP, such as dispatching rules and heuristics, often fall short in dynamic and unpredictable environments. These methods typically lack the adaptability required to respond to changes in job priorities and machine availability, leading to suboptimal scheduling decisions.

Recent advancements in artificial intelligence, particularly in reinforcement learning, have shown promise in addressing complex optimization problems. RL algorithms can autonomously learn optimal policies through interactions with their environment, making them well-suited for dynamic and stochastic scheduling scenarios [3].

This work explores the application of a single-agent reinforcement learning algorithm to both the deterministic and dynamic variants of the Job Shop Scheduling Problem. The primary objective of this research is to evaluate the efficiency and adaptability of the proposed RL algorithm in optimizing scheduling solutions under varying conditions of variability and uncertainty. The algorithm's performance is benchmarked against traditional scheduling methods, including First-Come First-Served (FCFS), Shortest Processing Time (SPT), and Genetic Algorithms (GA), to demonstrate its comparative advantages.

The remainder of this paper is structured as follows: a detailed description of the problem we aim to solve and the current state of art are presented respectively in Sect. 2 and 3. Section 4 introduces the Masked PPO algorithm, outlining its design and implementation while Sect. 5 presents the results of our experiments, demonstrating the efficacy of the proposed approach. Finally, Sect. 6 concludes the paper and discusses potential future work directions.

2   Problem Description

This section delves into the intricacies of the Job Shop Scheduling Problem, a complex combinatorial optimization problem that is fundamental to operational research.

The discussion begins with the deterministic version of JSSP, which serves as the classical representation of the problem under fixed conditions. Following this, the Dynamic Job Shop Scheduling Problem is explored, introducing variability and uncertainty to reflect more realistic manufacturing scenarios. This exploration provides a foundation for understanding the challenges and methodologies addressed in the subsequent research.

2.1   Deterministic Job Shop Scheduling

The Job Shop Scheduling Problem is a widely studied combinatorial optimization problem in the operational research and management field [4].

JSSP is classified as NP-hard, meaning that it belongs to a class of computationally difficult problems for which no polynomial-time algorithm exists to guarantee finding the optimal solution. This complexity arises from the need to explore a vast search space to identify the best schedule among all possible combinations [9].

The classical form of the problem, known as deterministic, consists of a finite set of n jobs, denoted as $J = \{ J_1, J_2, ..., J_n \}$, and a finite set of m machine, denoted as $M = \{ M_1, M_2, ..., M_m \}$. Each job J_k involves an ordered sequence of m_k operations, denoted as $O = \{ O_1, O_2, ..., O_{m_k} \}$, with each operation to be executed on a machine. These operations are characterized by their start time, denoted as t, and processing time, denoted as τ. The problem incorporates capacity constraints, meaning that each machine can only handle one operation at a time, and each job can only be processed on one machine at a time [8].

The resolution of the problem requires finding the optimal operation sequence in relation to an objective function. Some common objective functions described in [10], include:

- Makespan minimization. The makespan is the completion time of the last job to leave the system [9].
- Total weighted completion time minimization. The weighted completion time represents the total holding or inventory cost incurred by the schedule.
- Maximum of lateness minimization. The lateness relative to a job is the difference between its completion time and its due date which is positive in case the job is completed late and negative in case the job is completed early.

Despite there being several theoretical objective functions that embody different industrial criteria, the most widely used objective function in academic research is the minimization of the maximum makespan C_{max} which can be expressed as follow:

$$C_{max} = max(t_{ik} + \tau_{ik}) : \forall J_t \in J, m_k \in M \qquad (1)$$

Its adoption is justified by an ease in the problem formulation and its mathematical handling [8].

2.2   Dynamic Job Shop Scheduling

The strong connection of the job shop scheduling problem with the real-world manufacturing and production environments has led researchers to explore several variants of the problem with increasing complexity and uncertainty.

The deterministic Job Shop Scheduling problem, in fact, can be further complicated with different combinations of constraints and problem settings. This approach aims at addressing all possible real-world scenarios effectively.

Dynamic Job Shop Scheduling, specifically, is a variant of the job shop scheduling problem in which the scheduling environment is subject to changes over time including variations in job arrival times, processing times, machine breakdowns, resource availability and job priority [5].

In this research, the dynamic job shop scheduling problem is characterized by:

- variability in job arrival times: job arrivals are governed by a uniform distribution. Specifically, at each time step, a random number of jobs is introduced into the system. Each arriving job is assigned a type based on a uniform random selection from the available job types.
- variability in processing times: the processing time for each job at each station is determined randomly following a uniform distribution. The time is set to vary within a range from half of its standard value to one time and a half its standard value.

This stochastic process ensures a realistic and variable workflow, simulating the unpredictable nature of real-world manufacturing environments.

3   Literature Review

Over time, various approaches and algorithms have been developed to tackle Job Shop Scheduling Problems [8]. The resolution methods can be broadly categorized into four groups: exact methods, heuristic methods, metaheuristic methods, and other methodologies.

Exact methods involve algorithms or approaches that aim to find the optimal solution by exhaustively exploring the entire solution space or using rigorous mathematical formulations. While these methods guarantee optimality, they often face scalability issues due to the exponential growth of the solution space as the problem size increases. When finding the optimal solution is computationally infeasible, heuristic methods are employed to identify a satisfactory solution within a reasonable timeframe. Metaheuristic methods, on the other hand, are designed to efficiently explore large solution spaces to find near-optimal solutions in a practical amount of time. Since the late 1990s, different techniques were implemented for the resolution of the JSSP, such as hybrid methods, multiagent systems and artificial intelligence algorithm.

Reinforcement learning algorithms have become a significant focus in tackling job shop scheduling and its variants due to their ability to adapt and optimize in complex, dynamic environments. Deep reinforcement learning (DRL) approaches, in particular, have shown promising results by leveraging neural networks to handle large state and action spaces effectively. This capability allows DRL to capture intricate patterns and dependencies within the scheduling problem, making it well-suited for real-world JSSP and DJSSP scenarios where the number of possible states and actions can be vast.

In the context of JSSP, researchers have explored several approaches leveraging different algorithms, state representations and reward functions to allow for stable learning approaches and long term strategies exploitation. Zhao et al. [11] introduced Q-learning as a foundational approach, focusing on iterative improvements through action-value updates based on observed rewards. Traditional reinforcement learning relies on value functions or policy representations, which can become unmanageable as scheduling problems increase in complexity. To address this issue, Tassel et al. [12] and Moon et al. [13] employed deep reinforcement learning methods, specifically proximal policy optimization and deep Q-network algorithms. DRL uses deep neural networks to process high-dimensional input data (such as job and machine states) and output optimal actions (such as job scheduling decisions) with increased efficiency and stability.

Given the dynamic nature of the environment, the dynamic job shop scheduling problem has been primarily tackled with deep reinforcement learning approaches to effectively manage the evolving nature of scheduling requirements. One prominent contribution by Zhao et al. [14] involves the adaptation of deep Q-networks, which utilize deep neural networks to approximate optimal action-value functions where the action set is composed of ten heuristic dispatching rules. Another notable strategy exploited by Zhang et al. [15] includes Proximal Policy Optimization characterized by increased stability and fast optimization speed ensuring adaptation to changing scheduling conditions.

This study proposes an innovative approach to the Dynamic Job Shop Scheduling Problem utilizing Maskable Proximal Policy Optimization [6]. To achieve improved perfomances, the strategy proposed integrates the strengths of state-of-art approaches with several innovative features.

Unlike traditional approaches that employ large and complex action spaces, this method simplifies the decision-making process by integrating priority dispatching rules with action masking. This reduction in search space ensures the agent focuses on relevant and feasible decisions, enhancing learning efficiency and accelerating convergence. This contrasts with methods like the Q-learning, which often struggle with large action spaces.

The state representation in this approach is streamlined compared to others that rely on high-dimensional state spaces. Employing a matrix-based representation facilitates faster decision-making and enhances adaptability to more complex environments, where traditional reinforcement learning methods might become overwhelmed by the intricacies of the job and machine states.

Finally, the use of an event-based control mechanism, which activates the agent only when necessary, contrasts with the fixed interval updates common in other approaches. This selective activation conserves computational resources and allows for more responsive scheduling, making this approach more adaptable and efficient in handling the unpredictability of real-world manufacturing scenarios.

These innovations collectively offer significant advantages over traditional methods, improving efficiency, adaptability, and performance in dynamic job shop scheduling.

4 Maskable PPO Algorithm

This section explores how the Maskable PPO algorithm is employed to optimize job shop scheduling, delving into its components and adaptations, including the environment setup, state and action representations, and reward structure.

4.1 Job Shop Scheduling Environment

The Job Shop Scheduling Problem environment can be formulated as a sequential decision-making problem, often framed as a Markov Decision Process (MDP). This approach allows the application of reinforcement learning algorithms to train an agent to learn optimal scheduling policies.

In our study, we have opted for a single-agent reinforcement learning framework, where a single agent is responsible for making scheduling decisions for all machines within the job shop. This choice simplifies the problem structure, reduces coordination complexity, and leverages the agent's global view of the job shop for more effective optimization. By interacting iteratively with the scheduling environment, the agent learns to adapt to dynamic changes and unforeseen disruptions, aiming to minimize idle times and enhance overall production efficiency.

Unlike traditional Reinforcement Learning (RL) frameworks that rely on fixed time intervals or a predefined number of steps for updates, our approach leverages event-based control, where the agent's internal clock advances only when a new machine becomes available.

4.2 Proximal Policy Optimization

The Proximal Policy Optimization (PPO) algorithm is a widely used reinforcement learning method known for its stability and effectiveness in training deep neural networks. It builds upon traditional policy gradient methods by introducing a clipped objective function that regulates policy updates. This clipping mechanism ensures that the policy does not change too drastically between updates, thereby enhancing stability during training [16].

In our research, we leveraged the implementation of PPO, represented in Fig. 1, provided by Stable Baselines3 [7], a library recognized for its robust implementations of reinforcement learning algorithms. Specifically, we employed the MaskableActorCriticPolicy, which is a variant of the actor-critic architecture capable of handling environments with masked actions, such as those found in multi-agent settings or tasks with variable action spaces.

PPO's approach to optimization strikes a balance between exploration and exploitation, making it suitable for tasks requiring both robust learning and efficient policy updates. By using Stable Baselines3, we benefited from a straightforward implementation process and the assurance of working with a reliable framework designed to support standardized reinforcement learning experiments.

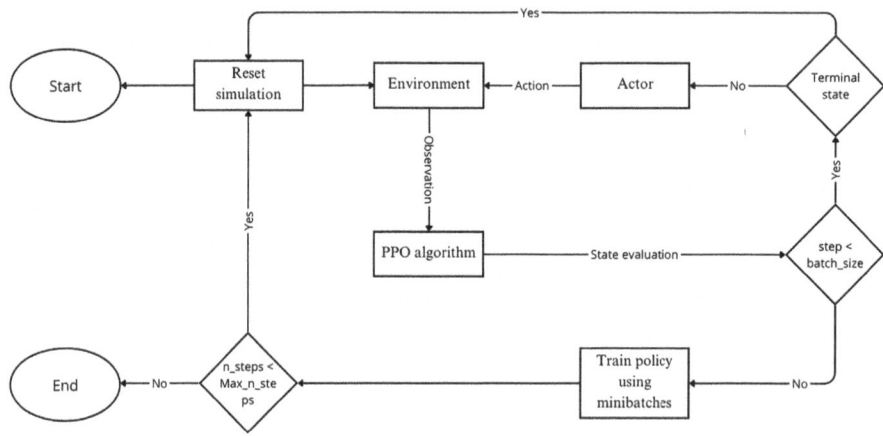

Fig. 1. Flowchart representation of the Proximal Policy Optimization algorithm.

4.3   State Representation

State representation is crucial in the application of reinforcement learning to the Job Shop Scheduling Problem. It encodes the status of the job shop environment and presents it to the RL agent.

In this study, the state is represented as a matrix, where each row corresponds to a machine and each column corresponds to a job. Entries in the matrix are binary values: '0' indicates that the job is not in the machine's queue, while '1' signifies that the job is present in the queue. This dynamic representation updates in real-time to reflect changes as jobs are processed and new jobs arrive.

The simplicity and clarity of this matrix- based representation facilitate efficient decision-making, learning, and interaction within the job shop environment, ensuring that the agent can effectively prioritize actions to maintain optimal job flow (Fig. 2).

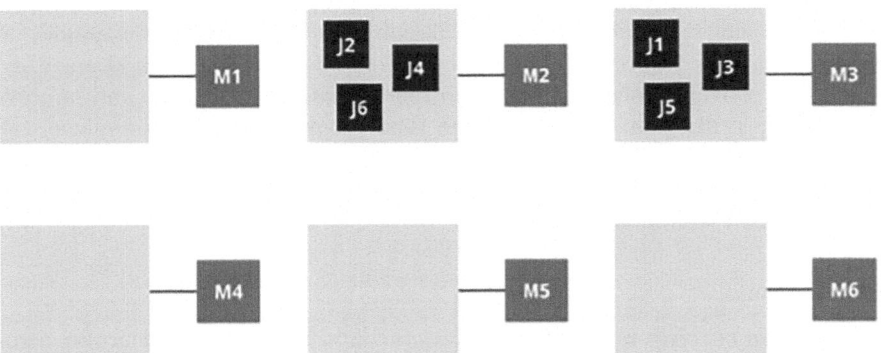

Fig. 2. Initial ft06 state representation.

4.4 Action Representation

Action representation defines the set of actions available to the RL agent, determining how it can influence the job scheduling process. In this study, the action space is simplified by focusing on specific scheduling strategies rather than all possible actions. The selected actions include:

- Choosing the job with the longest total processing time remaining across all machines: this strategy prioritizes jobs that require the most work to complete, ensuring that these more complex jobs are scheduled earlier, potentially reducing their impact on the overall job shop flow.
- Choosing the job with the highest number of remaining steps: this strategy focuses on jobs that have the most steps left in their processing sequence which doesn't necessarily coincides with a highest remaining processing time. By addressing these jobs first, the agent can help to reduce bottlenecks that may arise from jobs that are still far from completion.
- Choosing the null action: this action allows the agent to opt for no immediate scheduling decision, which can be useful in scenarios where delaying a decision might lead to a more optimal scheduling arrangement in subsequent steps.

This strategy-based action space reduces computational complexity and allows the agent to explore and learn effective scheduling policies more efficiently.

The implementation of an action masking function [6] aims to enhance the efficiency of decision-making in our agent. It restricts the agent from choosing illegal or suboptimal actions, thereby reducing the search space and ensuring that decisions are always contextually appropriate. This approach improves the learning process and accelerates convergence to an optimal scheduling policy. Specifically, action masking serves two main purposes in our study: first, it reduces the complexity of the decision-making process by eliminating illegal actions, allowing the agent to focus more effectively on relevant choices. Second, it prevents the selection of non-optimal actions that would not contribute to an optimal schedule, such as idle actions when machines are available or choosing less efficient strategies when only one job is in the queue. For example, we enforce that the null action (standing by) is only permissible when at least one machine is actively processing a job, preventing wasteful idle time and improving machine utilization. Similarly, when there's only one job in the queue, the agent automatically selects the strategy of scheduling the job with the longest remaining processing time across all machines, optimizing decision-making in such simplified scenarios.

4.5   Reward

Designing an effective reward function is crucial in reinforcement learning algorithms for job-shop scheduling, as it guides the agent towards optimal schedules. A well-designed reward function should incentivize behaviors that maximize the objective function, provide timely feedback, and balance complexity with clarity.

Rather than the traditional makespan metric, the reward strategy explored in this study is proposed by Tassel et al. (2021) [12] and is centered on the concept of scheduled area. The reward function $R(s, a)$ calculates the difference between the duration of the scheduled operation p_{aj} and the idle time introduced on machines:

$$R(s, a) = p_{aj} - \Sigma_{m \in M} empty(s, s') \qquad (2)$$

where $empty(s, s')$ measures the idle time on machine m during the transition from state s to s'.

The goal of the reward function is to minimize the scheduled area on a Gantt chart, reducing idle time on machines and maximizing their utilization. In the training experiments, it is possible to observe a consistent inverse relationship between the mean makespan of solutions found and their cumulative reward. This correlation underscores the effectiveness of the reward function in guiding the agent towards scheduling solutions that optimize both machine usage and overall efficiency.

5   Results

In the results section of this paper, we present a comprehensive evaluation of the proposed algorithm.

The section is structured to first assess the algorithm's performance in a deterministic environment comparing it with traditional methods. Following this, we evaluate the algorithm in a dynamic environment across three different scenarios: Dynamic Job Arrival, Variability in Processing Times, and a combination of both Dynamic Job Arrival and Variability in Processing Times.

5.1 Performance Evaluation in Deterministic Environment

The proposed algorithm has been tested it against a series of JSSP established benchmark problems collected in the OR library [17] and its performance has been compared with traditional methods including priority dispatching rules (FIFO, LPT, SPT), and a genetic algorithm [18].

This approach is crucial for several reasons. Firstly, benchmark problems provide a standardized platform to assess the effectiveness, robustness, and efficiency of the algorithm, ensuring that the results are comparable and reproducible. Furthermore, by comparing the performance of our algorithm with traditional methods, we can objectively determine its relative strengths and weaknesses. This comparison not only highlights areas where our algorithm excels but also identifies potential limitations, thereby providing a balanced and thorough assessment of its practical utility.

Such rigorous testing and comparison are essential to validate the algorithm's real-world applicability and to demonstrate its potential advantages over existing solutions.

The primary metric for comparison is the makespan, which is the total time required to complete all jobs. Benchmark problems are associated to specific optimal makespan. Table 1 summarize the results for three benchmark problems demonstrate that the proposed reinforcement learning approach consistently outperforms traditional priority dispatching rules (FIFO, LPT, SPT) and achieves makespans that are comparable to those obtained by the genetic algorithm (GA).

Table 1. Performance of Algorithms in a Deterministic Job Shop Scheduling Environment.

Instance	OPT	FIFO	LPT	SPT	GA	Maskable PPO
ft06 (06x06) [19]	55	65	77	88	55	55 timesteps = 55000
ft10 (10x10) [19]	930	1184	1295	1074	994	1103 timesteps = 100000
la01 (05x10) [20]	666	772	822	751	667	666 timesteps = 100000

5.2 Performance Evaluation in Dynamic Environment

To assess the performance of the proposed algorithm in a dynamic environment, the maskable PPO algorithm has been trained on a dynamic version of the ft06 problem for a total of 55,000 timesteps.

The hyperparameters of the Maskable PPO model have been meticulously tuned to optimize performance for the job shop scheduling problem. A learning rate of 3e−4 and a clip range of 0.2 ensure stable and rapid learning. A gamma value of 0.99 focuses on long-term rewards. An entropy coefficient of 0.01 fosters exploration, while a value function coefficient of 0.5 ensures a balance between policy and value improvements. A maximum gradient norm of 0.5

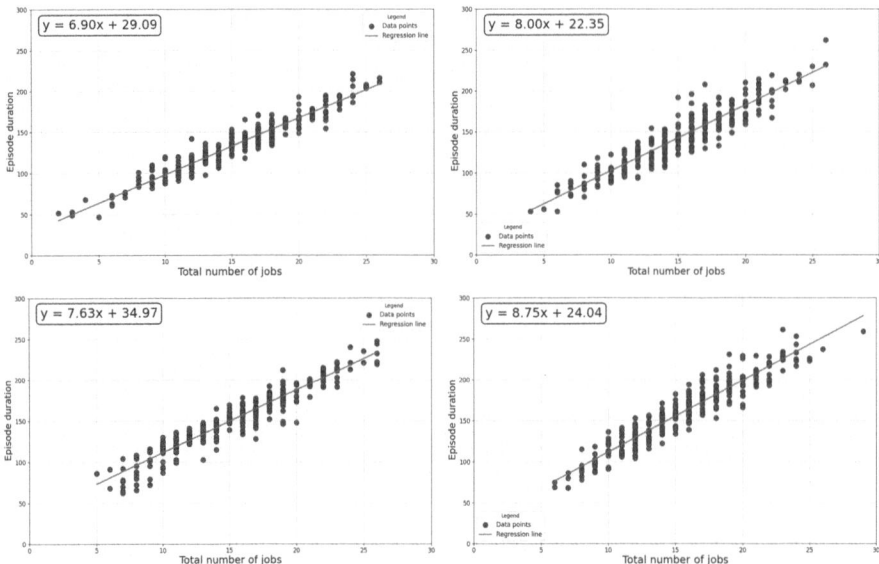

Fig. 3. Comparison of Algorithm Performance in Case 1: Top-left: maskable PPO performance, Top-right: FIFO performance, Bottom-left: SPT performance, Bottom-right: LPT performance.

prevents gradient explosion, and a GAE lambda of 0.95 balances bias and variance for accurate updates. To capture diverse scenarios, 2048 steps per update are used, and a batch size of 64 is chosen to balance computational efficiency and generalization. Running 10 epochs per update allows for thorough learning without overfitting. The problem maintains the job types and processing times of the deterministic scenario, introducing elements of dynamism. Subsequently, 300 episodes were run to evaluate the effectiveness of the learned scheduling policy.

The problem maintains the job types and processing time of the deterministic scenario, introducing elements of dynamicity. Subsequently, 300 episodes has been run to evaluate the effectiveness of the learned scheduling policy. For the purpose of comparison, 300 episodes were also run using three commonly used heuristics for dynamic scheduling scenarios: First-In-First-Out, Shortest Processing Times, and Longest Processing Times. The makespan, or the total time required to complete all jobs, was recorded for each episode under each scheduling strategy. The test has been conducted in three different cases: job arrival randomicity, variability in processing times, and both randomicity in job arrival and variability in processing times.

Case 1: Dynamic Job Arrival. The first dynamic environment scenario involves the variability in job arrival times which are governed by a uniform distribution.

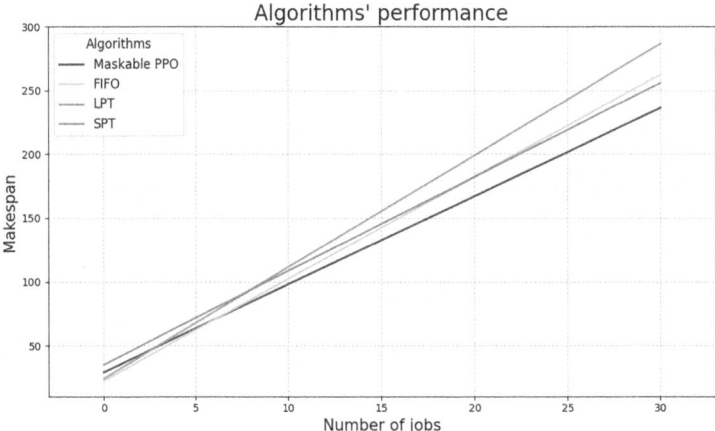

Fig. 4. Comparison of algorithms' performance - Case 1.

Figure 3 and 4, for each episode, the total number of jobs that entered the system and the episode duration (makespan).

The points in the graphs have been interpolated to show the episode duration trend in relation to an increasing number of jobs entering the plant. Notably, the coefficient of the line on the PPO performance graph is lower compared to other methods, indicating that Maskable PPO achieves a lower makespan per episode in comparison to the other methods for the same number of total jobs in the system. This underscores the algorithm's superior efficiency and effectiveness in dynamic scheduling environments.

Case 2: Variability in Processing Times. The second dynamic environment scenario involves the variability in job processing times which is determined by a uniform distribution.

Figure 5 and 6 depict, for each episode, the total workload of the system and the episode duration. The workload is defined as the sum of the processing times of each job entered in the system on each machine. The points in the graphs have been interpolated to show the episode duration trend in relation to an increasing plant workload.

Not only the coefficient of the line on the PPO performance graph is lower compared to other methods, indicating that Maskable PPO achieves a lower makespan per episode in comparison to the other methods, but the graphs shows a significantly reduced variability of episodes' duration by using Maskable PPO algorithm instead of other methods.

Case 3: Dynamic Job Arrival and Variability in Processing Times. The third dynamic environment scenario constitute a combination of the two cases above involving variability in both job arrival and job processing times.

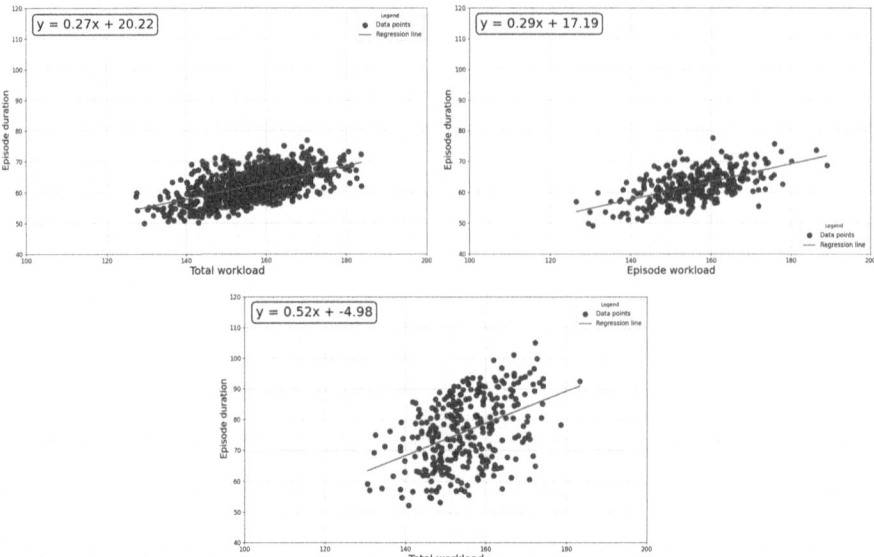

Fig. 5. Comparison of Algorithm Performance in Case 2: Top-left: maskable PPO performance, Top-right: FIFO performance, Bottom-left: SPT performance, Bottom-right: LPT performance.

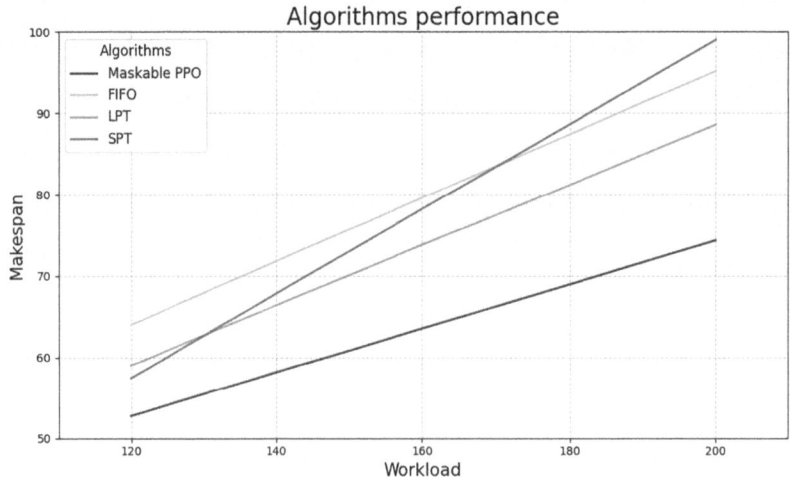

Fig. 6. Comparison of algorithms' performance in case 2.

Figure 7 and 8 depict, for each episode, the total workload of the system and the episode duration. The points in the graphs have been interpolated to show the episode duration trend in relation to an increasing plant workload.

As for the cases above, the Maskable PPO algorithm continues to outperform FIFO, SPT, and LPT showing a coefficient of the line that is lower compared to other methods and highlighting its robust scheduling capabilities in highly dynamic environments.

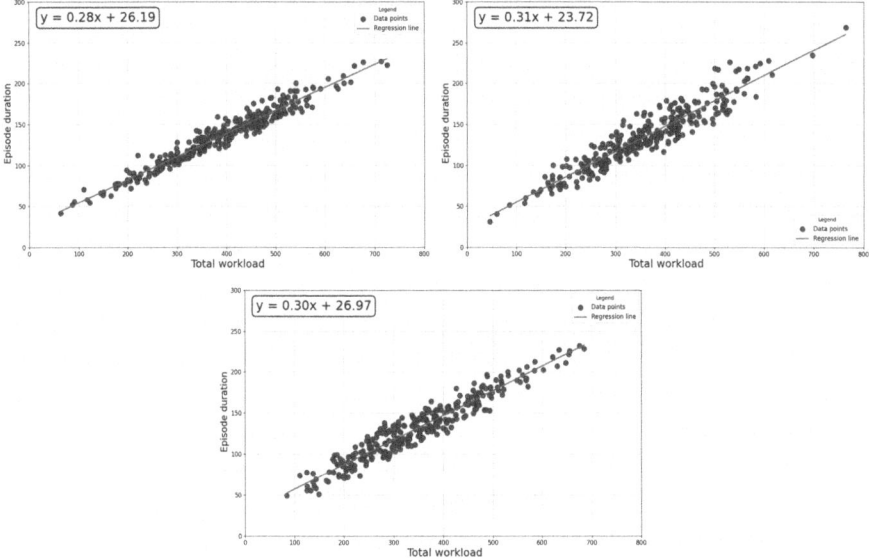

Fig. 7. Comparison of Algorithm Performance in Case 2: Top-left: maskable PPO performance, Top-right: FIFO performance, Bottom-left: SPT performance, Bottom-right: LPT performance.

Overall, the results clearly indicate that the Maskable PPO algorithm outperforms priority dispatching rules in all tested scenarios, demonstrating its ability to effectively handle the dynamic job shop scheduling problem. By leveraging event-based control and action masking, the Maskable PPO algorithm makes more informed and strategic scheduling decisions, leading to a significant reduction in makespan compared to FIFO, SPT, and LPT rules. These findings highlight the potential of reinforcement learning, in optimizing scheduling policies for dynamic job shop environments. The algorithm's adaptability to changing conditions and its ability to avoid illegal and non-optimal actions contribute to its superior performance.

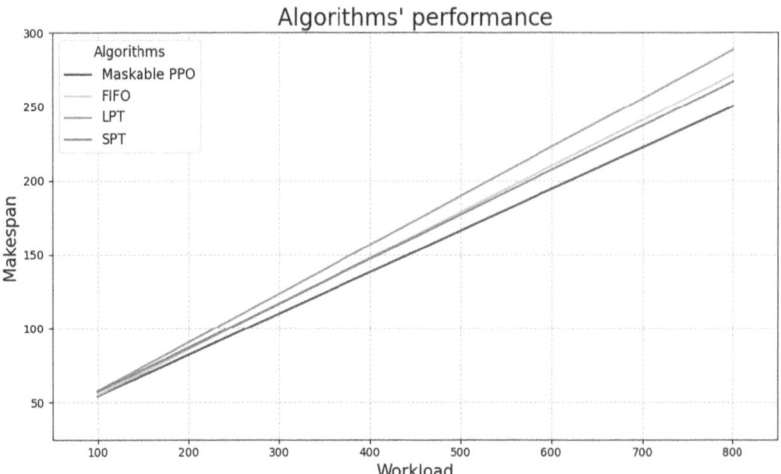

Fig. 8. Comparison of algorithms' performance in case 3.

6   Conclusion

In this paper, we introduced a single-agent reinforcement learning approach to tackle the Job Shop Scheduling Problem, assessing its performance in both deterministic and dynamic environments.

The proposed method leverages maskable proximal policy optimization to enhance scheduling efficiency. In deterministic scenarios, the Maskable PPO algorithm consistently achieved optimal or near-optimal makespans, demonstrating performance on par with the Genetic Algorithm and surpassing traditional heuristic methods. This highlights its capability to effectively manage fixed scheduling tasks. In dynamic environments, characterized by random job arrivals and variability in processing times, the Maskable PPO algorithm excelled by adapting swiftly to changing conditions and making informed, strategic scheduling decisions. Its adaptability and robust decision-making process resulted in superior performance compared to conventional approaches like priority dispatching rules. These findings emphasize the significant potential of reinforcement learning, particularly the Maskable PPO algorithm, in addressing and optimizing complex scheduling challenges across various industrial contexts.

Future work will focus on refining the algorithm to further enhance its performance and adaptability. One area of improvement involves testing various reward functions to better align the reinforcement learning process with specific scheduling objectives, such as minimizing energy consumption or balancing workload across machines. Additionally, exploring multi-agent reinforcement learning approaches could provide a more robust solution by enabling collaboration and competition among agents, thereby improving overall scheduling efficiency and adaptability in complex manufacturing environments. Another promising direction is the integration of advanced optimization techniques, such as metaheuristic algorithms or hybrid methods that combine reinforcement learning with traditional optimization approaches. This could help in overcoming local optima and achieving better global performance. Moreover, implementing adaptive learning rates and more sophisticated exploration-exploitation strategies could lead to more efficient learning and faster convergence.

To bridge the gap between theoretical optimization and practical implementation, future research will explore the development of digital twin solutions. The primary motivation for this approach lies in the need to create more adaptive and responsive manufacturing systems able to enhance operational efficiency, reduce downtime, and improve decision-making in a rapidly changing manufacturing landscape. By expanding the Maskable PPO algorithm integrating it with the physical machines in the manufacturing plant, a real-time scheduling solution can be created. This digital twin approach will enable continuous monitoring and optimization of the scheduling process, allowing for immediate adjustments based on real-time data from the production floor.

In summary, future research will focus on enhancing the reinforcement learning algorithm through improved reward functions, multi-agent approaches, and hybrid optimization techniques. Additionally, the integration of digital twin solutions promises to provide a seamless and adaptive real-time scheduling system, significantly improving operational efficiency and responsiveness in dynamic manufacturing environments.

Disclosure of Interests. The authors have no competing interests to declare that are relevant to the content of this article.

References

1. Del Gallo, M., Mazzuto, G., Ciarapica, F.E., Bevilacqua, M.: Artificial intelligence to solve production scheduling problems in real industrial settings: systematic literature review. Electronics **12**(23), 4732 (2023). https://doi.org/10.3390/electronics12234732
2. Kriouich, M., Sarir, H.: Artificial intelligence application in production scheduling problem systematic literature review: bibliometric analysis, research trend, and knowledge taxonomy. SN Oper. Res. Forum **5**(2), 1–24 (2024)
3. Kayhan, B.M., Yildiz, G.: Reinforcement learning applications to machine scheduling problems: a comprehensive literature review. J. Intell. Manuf. **34**(3), 905–929 (2023)
4. Baker, K.R., Trietsch, D.: Principles of Sequencing and Scheduling. Wiley (2013)
5. Renke, L., Piplani, R., Toro, C.: A review of dynamic scheduling: context, techniques and prospects. In: Toro, C., Wang, W., Akhtar, H. (eds.) Implementing Industry 4.0. ISRL, vol. 202, pp. 229–258. Springer, Cham (2021). https://doi.org/10.1007/978-3-030-67270-6_9
6. Huang, S., Ontañón, S.: A closer look at invalid action masking in policy gradient algorithms (2020). arXiv preprint arXiv:2006.14171
7. Raffin, A., Hill, A., Gleave, A., Kanervisto, A., Ernestus, M., Dormann, N.: Stable-baselines3: reliable reinforcement learning implementations. J. Mach. Learn. Res. **22**(268), 1–8 (2021)

8. Jain, A.S., Meeran, S.: Deterministic job-shop scheduling: past, present and future, Department of Applied Physics and Electronic and Mechanical Engineering, University of Dundee, Dundee, Scotland, DD1 4HN, UK (1998)

9. Pinedo, M.L.: Scheduling: Theory, Algorithms, and Systems, Stern School of Business. New York University, NY, USA (2008)

10. Abdolrazzagh-Nezhad, M., Abdulla, S.: Job shop scheduling: classification, constraints and objective functions, world academy of science, engineering and technology. Int. J. Comput. Inf. Eng. (2020)

11. Liu, Z., et al.: A graph neural networks-based deep Q-learning approach for job shop scheduling problems in traffic management. Inf. Sci. **607**, 1211–1223 (2022)

12. Tassel, P., Gebser, M., Schekotihin, K.: A reinforcement learning environment for job-shop scheduling (2021). arXiv preprint arXiv:2104.03760

13. Moon, J., Yang, M., Jeong, J.: A novel approach to the job shop scheduling problem based on the deep Q-network in a cooperative multi-access edge computing ecosystem. Sensors **21**(13), 4553 (2021). https://doi.org/10.3390/s21134553

14. Zhao, Y., Wang, Y., Tan, Y., Zhang, J., Yu, H.: Dynamic jobshop scheduling algorithm based on deep Q network. IEEE Access **9**, 122995–123011 (2021)

15. Zhang, Z., et al.: A deep Q-network for job-shop scheduling in smart factories. IEEE Trans. Ind. Inf. **17**(5), 3346–3354 (2021)

16. Schulman, J., Wolski, F., Dhariwal, P., Radford, A., Klimov, O.: Proximal policy optimization algorithms (2017). arXiv preprint arXiv:1707.06347

17. Beasley, J.E.: OR-Library (1990). https://www.people.brunel.ac.uk/~mastjjb/jeb/info.html

18. Ombukiet, B.M., Ventresca, M.: Local search genetic algorithms for the job shop scheduling problem. Appl. Intell., 99–109 (2004)

19. Fisher, H., Thompson, G.L.: Probabilistic learning combinations of local job-shop scheduling rules. In: Muth, J.F., Thompson, G.L. (eds.) Industrial Scheduling, Prentice Hall, Englewood Cliffs, New Jersey, pp. 225–251 (1963)

20. Lawrence, S.: Resource constrained project scheduling: an experimental investigation of heuristic scheduling techniques (Supplement), Graduate School of Industrial Administration. Carnegie-Mellon University, Pittsburgh, Pennsylvania (1984)

A Blockchain-Powered Framework for Traceable and Secure Pharmaceutical Delivery with Crowdsourced Logistics

Kadim Lahcen Nadime[(✉)], Jamal Benhra, Rajaa Benabbou, and Salma Mouatassim

ENSEM, University Hassan II, Casablanca, Morocco
nadime.kadim@gmail.com

Abstract. Current pharmaceutical last-mile delivery systems often rely on outdated manual processes and paper-based documentation, leading to significant inefficiencies and security vulnerabilities. This paper proposes a comprehensive framework that leverages smart contracts, blockchain technology, and crowdsourcing to enhance the traceability and security of pharmaceutical deliveries. By utilizing blockchain, the framework automates order processing, tracking, and delivery, ensuring a transparent and tamper-proof record of each transaction. Additionally, the framework incorporates a flexible, crowd-sourced model for selecting carriers through a competitive bidding mechanism, improving efficiency and responsiveness. Our research includes a site visit to a drug distribution company to analyze the existing delivery process and identify critical issues. Based on these insights, we developed a solution that integrates digital and physical tracking measures, such as reusable drug packaging with sensors. The solution was tested locally in a simulated blockchain environment to validate its functionality. The paper emphasizes the need for tailored studies to address international regulatory differences and ethical implications in implementing a blockchain-based pharmaceutical delivery system. This approach not only simplifies the delivery process but also ensures enhanced visibility, reliability, and accountability across the supply chain.

Keywords: Pharmaceutical supply chain · Blockchain · Last-mile delivery · Smart contracts · Urban logistics · Crowdsourcing · Traceability

1 Introduction

The distribution of pharmaceutical products is a critical component of healthcare, characterized by its complexity and the stringent requirements for managing sensitive medications [1]. Unlike typical goods, pharmaceuticals often require specialized conditions throughout their transit, including temperature control and protection from light and humidity, to maintain their efficacy [2]. This complexity is compounded by the necessity for timely delivery, especially for medications critical to ongoing patient care or those with short shelf lives.

Unlike other industries, the pharmaceutical sector is subject to stringent regulatory requirements to ensure the safety and efficacy of medications. Pharmaceuticals often

M. Dassisti et al. (Eds.): IN4PL 2024, CCIS 2372, pp. 367–384, 2025.
https://doi.org/10.1007/978-3-031-80760-2_24

require specific storage conditions, such as temperature control, to prevent degradation during transport, and any failure in maintaining these conditions could lead to ineffective or dangerous drugs. Moreover, pharmaceutical deliveries must be timely, as delays in critical medications can have life-threatening consequences. These unique challenges necessitate specialized supply chain solutions that differ from those used in less sensitive industries like consumer goods or electronics.

Despite the essential nature of these deliveries, the pharmaceutical sector faces significant challenges [3, 4]. Errors, delays, and inefficiencies are common, potentially leading to severe consequences, including adverse health outcomes from misdelivered or delayed medications. These issues not only jeopardize patient health but also contribute to the high costs associated with pharmaceutical logistics, exacerbated by the need for specialized transportation and skilled handling.

In response to these challenges, this paper proposes a framework that utilizes blockchain technology and smart contracts, integrated with a crowdsourcing approach to enhance the traceability and security of pharmaceutical deliveries. Smart contracts play a vital role in perishable supply chains, where precise delivery timing and conditions are essential to ensure the effectiveness and safety of products [5]. Unlike traditional systems that rely heavily on manual processes and are prone to errors, this framework aims to automate and secure the delivery process from start to finish. By recording every transaction on a blockchain, the proposed system ensures that each step in the medication's journey is transparent and immutable, greatly reducing the risks of counterfeit drugs entering the supply chain and ensuring that medications are delivered accurately and on time.

Furthermore, the use of smart contracts offers a level of accountability previously unattainable in traditional delivery models. These contracts execute automatically based on predefined conditions [6], providing a clear, tamper-proof record of each party's responsibilities and actions throughout the delivery process. This not only enhances security but also streamlines the resolution of disputes and the enforcement of compliance.

By integrating these technologies with a decentralized crowdsourcing model for carrier selection and management, the proposed framework promises to revolutionize pharmaceutical logistics. It aims to reduce costs, improve efficiency, and significantly enhance the quality of service in pharmaceutical deliveries, setting a new standard for reliability and safety in the healthcare sector.

This paper explores the theoretical foundations of this framework, compares it with existing models, and discusses the potential benefits and challenges of its implementation. It seeks to contribute to the ongoing discourse on technological innovation in drug distribution and provide actionable insights for stakeholders considering the adoption of advanced technologies in their logistics operations.

This article is organized as follows: Sect. 2 provides a review of relevant literature and current research advancements. Section 3 details the methodology used and supply chain implementation strategy. Section 4 describes our proposed framework. Section 5 the solution design and implementation. Section 6 discusses the research findings, highlighting the practical advantages and limitations of our approach. Finally, Sect. 7 concludes the article by summarizing the key discoveries and insights.

2   Literature Review

The integration of blockchain technology in the pharmaceutical supply chain has been extensively explored due to its potential to enhance traceability, security, and efficiency across various stages of drug management and distribution. While blockchain technology has found applications across various industries, its use in the pharmaceutical sector is particularly crucial due to the need for traceability and the prevention of counterfeit medications. Unlike industries where traceability may improve operational efficiency, in the pharmaceutical supply chain, it is essential for ensuring patient safety and complying with stringent regulatory standards. The use of blockchain in non-financial sectors, particularly in the pharmaceutical supply chain, is exemplified by Bocek et al. [7], who detail a start-up's application of IoT and blockchain technology to monitor environmental conditions during drug transport, ensuring compliance and enhancing supply chain efficiency. The pivotal role of blockchain in improving drug traceability and transparency is also emphasized by Panda and Satapathy [8], who discuss the decentralized nature of blockchain which facilitates systematic updates and validations, thereby ensuring drug authenticity and reducing fraud.

The challenges of managing near-expiry drugs in pharmaceutical inventories have been addressed through innovative blockchain applications such as "PharmaBlock," described by Mirdad, Khan, and Hussain [9]. This system not only ensures efficient management but also integrates an early warning system to optimize drug disposal, thereby reducing waste and enhancing supply chain responsiveness.

A comprehensive framework for pharmaceutical supply chains, incorporating blockchain to ensure the integrity and traceability of drugs, is presented by Bapatla, Mohanty, and Kougianos [10]. Their approach, termed "PharmaChain 3.0," utilizes a novel product serialization mechanism that tracks drugs through a secure barcode system integrated with blockchain, enhancing the transparency and security necessary for compliance with health regulations.

Aslam et al. [11] focus on leveraging the Ethereum platform to develop a tractability system for pharmaceutical products, which aims to address the asymmetric information problem in pharmaceutical supply chains by providing end-to-end traceability. Similarly, Abdallah and Nizamuddin [12] propose a blockchain framework for the online sale of pharmaceutical products, emphasizing decentralized operations that enhance transparency and trust between stakeholders.

The application of blockchain to combat counterfeit drugs is a significant theme in recent studies. Kordestani, Oghazi, and Mostaghel [13] identify how smart contracts on blockchain platforms can be effectively utilized to prevent the entry of counterfeit drugs into the supply chain. This is further supported by the development of "PharmaChain," discussed by Bapatla et al. [14], which provides a transparent and secure pharmaceutical supply chain, significantly reducing the risks associated with counterfeit medications.

The operational aspects of blockchain applications in pharmaceutical logistics are illustrated through various studies. Samonte et al. [15] demonstrate how blockchain technology can improve performance metrics such as throughput and latency in pharmaceutical logistics. Omidian and Omidi [16] discuss the broader impacts of blockchain across the drug life cycle, noting its potential to significantly improve management practices from drug discovery through to distribution and disposal.

Konapure and Nawale [17] describe a specific blockchain-based system architecture for pharmaceutical supply chains, which ensures improved traceability and data provenance, facilitating secure and transparent drug tracking. The utility of blockchain in managing drug supply chain integrity in a smart hospital context is explored by Jamil et al. [18], highlighting the use of Hyperledger Fabric for secure transaction management.

Blockchain's role in addressing security challenges in the pharmaceutical industry is further elaborated by Uddin [19], who introduces a blockchain-enabled system designed to combat the threat of counterfeit drugs effectively. Similarly, Musamih et al. [20] discuss an Ethereum-based approach that ensures secure, transparent, and immutable transaction histories, crucial for pharmaceutical traceability.

Dwivedi, Amin, and Vollala [21] propose a secure information sharing protocol within pharmaceutical supply chains, utilizing blockchain to enhance data integrity and participant authentication. This is supported by the work of Sylim et al. [22], who develop a blockchain-based pharmacosurveillance system aimed at reducing the incidence of counterfeit drugs in the market.

Further discussions on the implementation and challenges of blockchain in supply chain management are provided by Di Ciccio et al. [23], who emphasize the need for full traceability in multi-peer environments. Kim and Laskowski [24] explore the potential of ontologies in enhancing blockchain's effectiveness for provenance in complex supply chains. [25] propose a system utilizing smart contracts to streamline logistics activities, specifically targeting transport operations between distributors and clients, aiming to eliminate intermediaries and enhance organization, security, and distribution times.

Despite these advancements, there remains a significant gap specifically concerning the integration of crowdsourcing logistics models within the blockchain framework for pharmaceutical delivery. Most studies focus on conventional supply chain mechanisms or explore blockchain in isolation without addressing the potential of a decentralized workforce of couriers.

While existing studies effectively demonstrate how blockchain enhances transparency and traceability in pharmaceutical and other logistics-related supply chains, they primarily focus on conventional applications of blockchain for static delivery systems and centralized management practices. For instance, studies by Nadime et al. [26] and Moudaa et al. [27] explore decentralized delivery systems using blockchain to improve transparency and efficiency in e-commerce logistics and last-mile deliveries, respectively. However, these applications do not fully exploit the dynamic interaction possibilities of real-time, crowdsourced delivery systems specifically tailored to pharmaceutical logistics.

Furthermore, the potential for blockchain to interact dynamically with crowdsourced delivery systems based on geographic data and immediate availability has not been thoroughly investigated. Ducrée et al. [28] and Li et al. [29] discuss the broader concept of blockchain-enabled crowdsourcing platforms that can decentralize various aspects of technology development and supply chain management. These platforms utilize blockchain to create a more transparent, secure, and participatory environment, leveraging the "Wisdom of the Crowds" and enhancing collaboration across diverse stakeholders. Yet, these studies stop short of applying these concepts to the unique challenges of pharmaceutical deliveries, where real-time data and rapid response capabilities are crucial.

Moreover, there is a gap in exploring how these innovative blockchain and crowd-sourcing frameworks can be adapted to the specific needs of pharmaceutical logistics, which require not only traceability and security but also high responsiveness and adapt-ability to sudden changes in demand and supply conditions. The pharmaceutical sector, with its stringent requirements for timely and secure delivery of medications, presents unique challenges that could benefit significantly from the integration of blockchain technology with a crowdsourced, geographically aware delivery system.

This gap points to the need for further research into how blockchain can be effectively integrated with real-time, dynamic crowdsourcing mechanisms to optimize pharmaceu-tical deliveries. Such systems could significantly enhance the efficiency, reliability, and adaptability of the pharmaceutical supply chain, particularly in scenarios demanding rapid adjustments to delivery routes and schedules based on immediate logistical require-ments. This paper aims to bridge this gap by proposing a framework that combines the robust traceability and security features of blockchain with the flexibility and scalability of crowdsourced delivery systems, tailored specifically for the pharmaceutical industry.

3   Supply Chain Implementation

Our research methodology for this framework emphasizes a theoretical approach grounded in an extensive review of current practices and potential innovations in phar-maceutical supply chains. We propose a model that integrates blockchain technology, smart contracts, and crowdsourcing to address critical challenges in the pharmaceutical last-mile delivery sector.

First, we conducted a site visit to a drug distribution company to analyze the cur-rent drug delivery process. From this analysis, we identified critical issues and built a framework to address them, enhancing traceability and security. Our model leverages blockchain and smart contracts, and uses crowdsourcing to improve carrier selection and reduce delivery times.

Next, we developed the solution and tested it locally by simulating a blockchain environment. This testing allowed us to validate the model's functionality and effective-ness in a controlled setting. This approach ensures our proposed model is both practical and ready for real-world implementation.

Figure 1 depicts the two-echelon pharmaceutical supply chain model structured around a central drug distribution company in the context of our case study. This setup reflects the flow of pharmaceutical products from multiple laboratories (providers) to various healthcare entities (clients), such as pharmacies and hospitals.

- **Echelon1 (Supplier):** This echelon is composed of three separate laboratories or providers, each serving as a source of pharmaceutical products. They are responsible for manufacturing and supplying medications to the drug distribution company. Their role in the supply chain is critical, as they are the starting point of the drug's journey, ensuring that the products are produced according to industry standards and regulatory requirements.

- **Echelon2 (Clients):** The clients in the second echelon consist of two pharmacies and a hospital, all of which receive pharmaceutical products from the drug distribution company. They represent the last mile of the delivery process, where the medications are dispensed to the final consumer – the patients.

3.1 The Drug Distribution Company

At the core of the supply chain is the drug distribution company, which acts as an intermediary between the suppliers (laboratories) and the clients (pharmacies and hospitals). It is responsible for the critical functions of receiving, storing, and managing the inventory of pharmaceutical products. The company also takes charge of the order fulfillment, ensuring that the pharmacies and the hospital receive the correct medications in a timely and secure manner.

In our case study, this company would implement a solution involving blockchain and smart contracts. The aim is to increase the traceability and security of the drugs as they move through the supply chain. Each medication would be associated with a unique digital identifier upon leaving the laboratory, which would then be tracked through the blockchain as it moves through the distribution company and onto the pharmacies and hospital. Smart contracts would automate and validate each step of the process, from receipt of the goods at the distribution center to their final delivery, ensuring compliance and efficiency. Crowdsourcing is used to optimize delivery logistics, with carriers bidding on delivery tasks, adding a layer of flexibility and cost efficiency to the last-mile delivery to the clients.

The drug distribution process in our framework is reimagined to leverage advanced technologies and innovative logistics approaches, ensuring high standards of efficiency, security, and compliance are maintained. Key stages of the process include:

Reception and Storage Area: This initial stage involves the receipt of pharmaceutical products, where each item is scanned and entered into a blockchain ledger, providing an immutable record of the product's entry into the supply chain. Advanced verification techniques ensure the authenticity and proper storage conditions of received items.

Upon arrival, products are immediately logged into a blockchain database, ensuring that each unit's unique data, such as expiry date, batch number, and compliance certificates, are securely recorded. This immutable record supports the effective management of stock and prevents the introduction of counterfeit drugs into the supply chain.

Order Fulfillment Area: In this critical phase, blockchain technology helps in tracking inventory levels in real time, while smart contracts automate the order fulfillment process. Medications are picked and packed based on digital orders, with each step logged to ensure accuracy and accountability.

Utilizing IoT devices, each package is tracked from picking to packaging. Smart contracts trigger alerts if any discrepancies arise, ensuring immediate corrective actions. This automated oversight significantly reduces human error and increases processing speed.

Expedition Area: Final checks are automated through smart contracts, which confirm that the packaged orders meet all required criteria before leaving the facility. The dispatch process incorporates a dynamic bidding system for carrier selection, that allows the drug

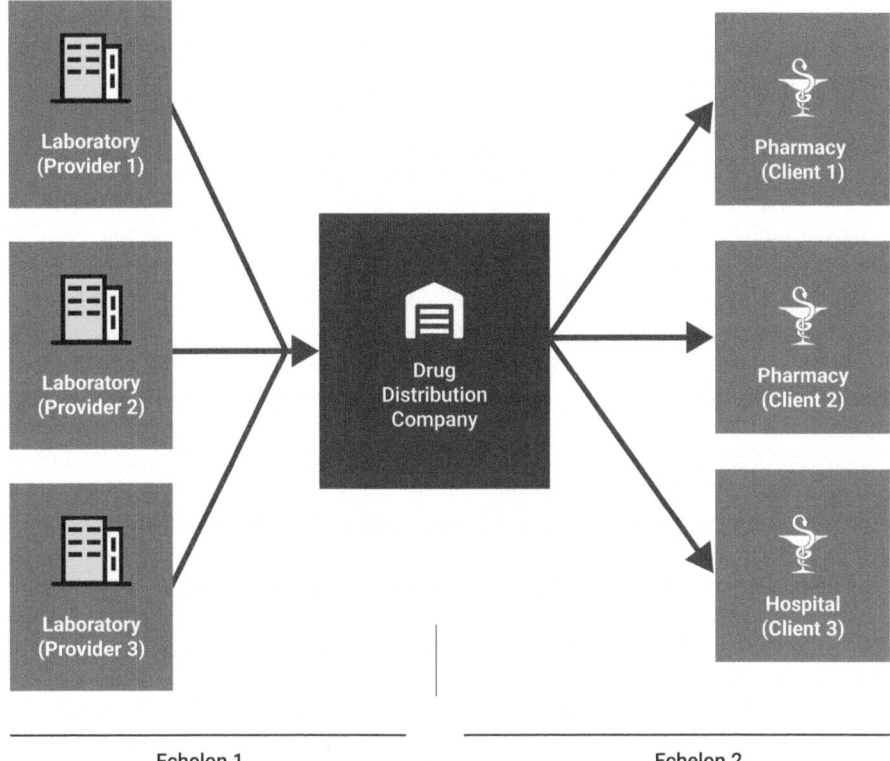

Echelon 1   Echelon 2

Fig. 1. Pharmaceutical Supply Chain Network.

distribution company to optimize carrier selection by takinf into account carrier metrics and history.

As orders are prepared for dispatch, smart contracts verify that all conditions for safe and compliant transport are met. The system selects carriers based on predefined criteria such as cost, delivery speed, and carrier reliability, recorded via previous blockchain entries. This process not only streamlines logistics but also enhances transparency and trust among stakeholders.

3.2 Pharmaceutical Delivery Process Workflow

The pharmaceutical delivery process using the blockchain-powered framework intro-duces several critical improvements over traditional systems, both in the workflow and interactions among the various actors involved. In a conventional supply chain, much of the process relies on manual coordination, centralized management, and paper-based tracking, which often leads to delays, inefficiencies, and errors. By contrast, this blockchain-based system automates several key steps, provides real-time transparency, and enhances security through immutable records.

The process begins when a pharmacy places an order for a batch of medications through the blockchain-enabled system. This order is automatically recorded as a smart contract on the blockchain, containing essential details such as the type of medication, the quantity, the destination, and specific delivery conditions like temperature control. Once the order is placed, the system initiates the selection of a carrier using a crowdsourcing approach. Registered carriers on the platform receive notifications about the new delivery task and are invited to submit their bids. These bids typically include the proposed cost of delivery, the estimated delivery time, and whether the carrier can meet the required delivery conditions, such as providing refrigerated transport if necessary.

The bids submitted by carriers are evaluated based on several factors, including the carrier's previous performance, proximity to the pick-up location, and the overall cost-effectiveness of the offer. The company then reviews these bids, taking into account the criteria provided by the system, and selects the carrier that best meets the delivery requirements. Once the carrier is chosen, the pharmaceutical distribution company prepares the medications for dispatch. The medications are packed in containers equipped with IoT sensors that monitor temperature and humidity, ensuring that the environmental conditions during transport meet the necessary requirements for maintaining the efficacy of the drugs. Each package is assigned a unique digital identifier, or token, on the blockchain, which allows it to be tracked throughout the delivery process. The blockchain records the creation of this digital token, linking it to the smart contract that governs the order and its delivery details.

After the carrier picks up the package, the system begins real-time monitoring of the delivery. The IoT sensors embedded in the containers transmit live data on the package's location, temperature, and humidity to the blockchain. This information is automatically recorded, providing an immutable and transparent log of the delivery's progress. Should any issues arise, such as a deviation in temperature from the required range, an alert is generated by the system and logged on the blockchain for later review. This ensures that any anomalies are immediately addressed and traceable.

When the carrier arrives at the pharmacy and delivers the package, the recipient uses a mobile application to confirm the delivery. This verification involves scanning the digital token associated with the package, checking the environmental conditions during transit, and confirming that the delivery met all the specified requirements. If the delivery conditions are satisfactory, the smart contract automatically finalizes the transaction, releasing the payment to the carrier and officially completing the delivery. Every interaction, from the order's placement to the final delivery confirmation, is securely recorded on the blockchain, creating a tamper-proof audit trail. This trail ensures full visibility and accountability for both the pharmaceutical company and the pharmacy, facilitating easier dispute resolution and ensuring compliance with regulatory standards.

4 Framework Overview

The framework aims to establish a fast, secure, and traceable shipping system for decentralized drug distribution utilizing smart contracts. This goal is achieved through a series of interconnected implementation steps, as outlined in Fig. 2. Starting from mobile applications for driver traceability and IoT integrated containers for product traceability, the framework progresses through tracking and routing APIs to ensure real-time monitoring. Smart contracts provide insured traceability, culminating in a proof of delivery, thus ensuring the efficiency and security of the drug distribution process.

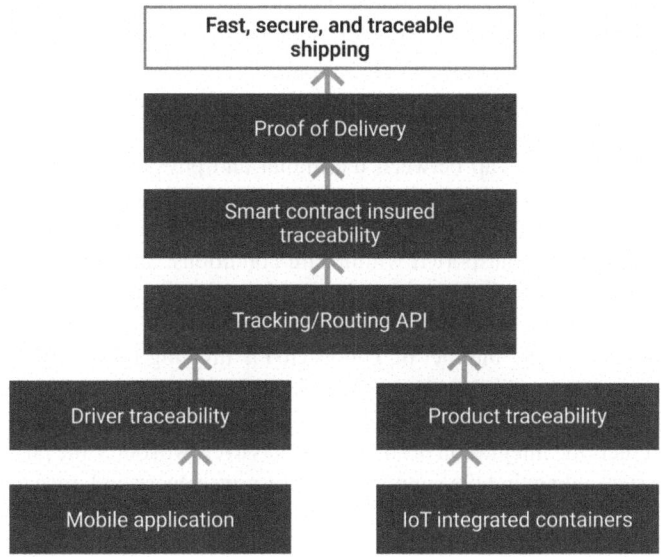

Fig. 2. Integrated Decentralized Drug Distribution Framework.

The proposed framework introduces an integrated architecture that underpins a decentralized drug distribution system utilizing smart contracts. Figure 3 outlines the structure of this system across several interconnected layers.

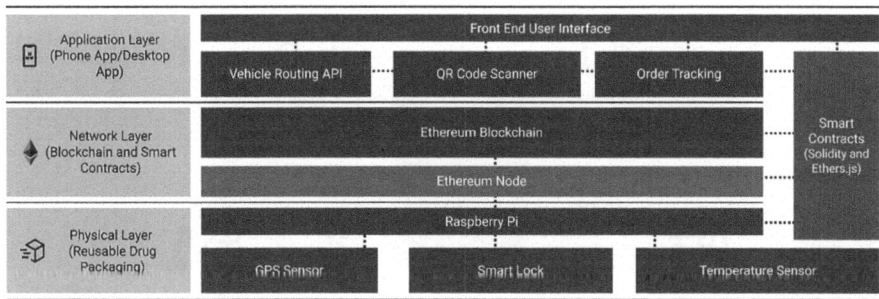

Fig. 3. Integrated Architecture of Blockchain-Enabled Pharmaceutical Delivery Framework.

Application Layer: At the user interaction level, the application layer includes mobile and desktop applications. This interface allows stakeholders, including pharmacies, distribution centers, and carriers, to interact with the system for various operations like order placement and tracking.

Network Layer: This layer is the core of the blockchain infrastructure, consisting of Ethereum Blockchain and associated nodes. It is here that smart contracts, written in Solidity and using libraries such as Ethers.js, are deployed. These contracts manage the logic for transactions, carrier bidding, and delivery verification.

Physical Layer: At the base, the physical layer represents the actual drug packages equipped with technology to make them part of the IoT (Internet of Things). It includes GPS sensors for location tracking, blockchain integrated smart locks to detect and log package opening, Raspberry Pi as a small-scale computer for processing, and temperature sensors to ensure drugs are kept within safe conditions.

This layer bridges the gap between the digital and physical realms, enabling the tracking of medications beyond mere digital transactions. By embedding smart sensors such as GPS for real-time location tracking, temperature sensors to monitor and ensure the drugs are stored and transported within safe conditions, and smart locks to detect and record the opening of packages, the physical layer provides an additional security measure against tampering and environmental deviations. These smart packages become integral components of the Internet of Things (IoT), allowing for the physical state of the drug products to be continuously monitored and logged, complementing the digital oversight provided by blockchain technology.

Figure 4 depicts the integration of smart contracts to crowdsource the pharmaceutical last-mile logistics, enhancing the supply chain's responsiveness and traceability.

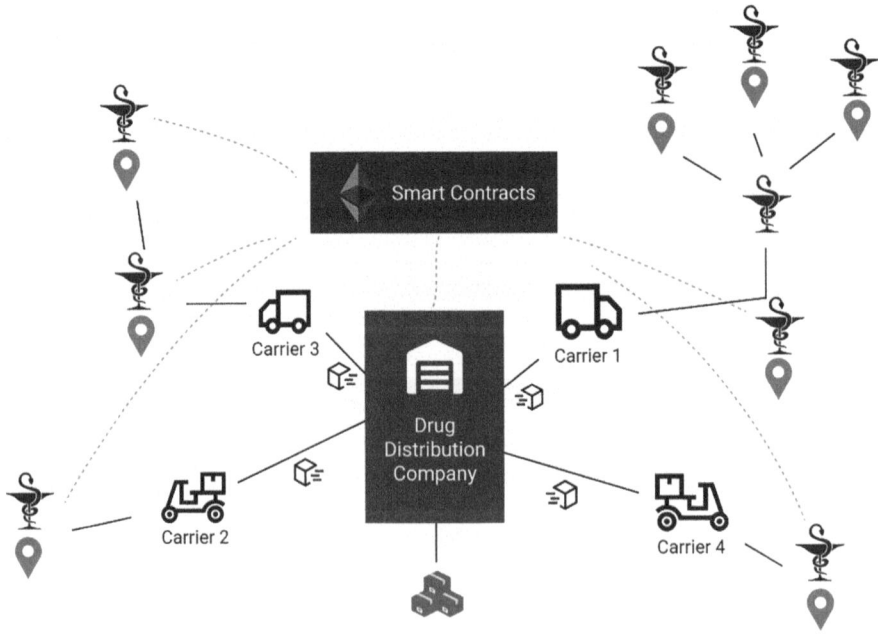

Fig. 4. Decentralized Pharmaceutical Delivery Network with Smart Contract Integration.

In the proposed framework, crowdsourcing plays a crucial role within the pharmaceutical supply chain, especially when aligned with the capabilities of blockchain and smart contracts. Traditional delivery systems, often mired in manual processes and paper trails, face challenges in maintaining the accuracy and timeliness of pharmaceutical deliveries. Such processes are susceptible to errors and lack the capacity for real-time package tracking, thereby delaying issue resolution and delivery schedules.

The envisioned framework suggests integrating smart contracts into the supply chain, notably within a crowdsourcing context. These contracts, supported by a blockchain infrastructure, have the potential to enhance the security and traceability of deliveries significantly. By converting physical transactions to digital records, smart contracts offer an immutable ledger of each step in the delivery process, ensuring that every package is traceable from reception through to final delivery.

In this model, carriers partake in a bidding system, which is an advanced feature tailored for pharmaceutical deliveries. Each medication is represented as a digital token, tied to an order that defines the requirements for its distribution, including destination and delivery conditions. As orders emerge, reflecting the intricate demands of pharmaceutical transport, the drug distribution company launches a bidding process to identify the most suitable carrier. The call for bids invites carriers to present their delivery proposals, which are assessed through an automated and transparent system managed by the smart contracts.

Carriers' proposals encompass a delivery price and a timeline, with estimates that dynamically account for their location relative to the order's pickup point. The selection of a carrier is then determined by a smart contract, based on cost-effectiveness and ability to adhere to the delivery timeline. Upon selection, the smart contract formalizes the delivery agreement, thereby initiating the delivery process. This approach not only ensures efficient assignment of deliveries by focusing on cost and timeliness but also fortifies traceability, with each delivery step being documented on the blockchain.

When an offer is selected by the drug distribution company, it signifies the establishment of a contractual agreement between the order and the chosen carrier. This marks the commencement of the delivery task in accordance with the terms set out. Presumably, this entire process, from the creation of the product token to the final choice of the carrier, is logged within the blockchain framework, ensuring that each transaction is secure, transparent, and verifiable. Thus, the integration of smart contracts with crowdsourcing mechanisms not only optimizes the selection and validation of delivery agents but also provides an enhanced level of traceability essential in the tightly regulated realm of pharmaceutical distribution.

5 Solution Design and Deployment

Our proposed smart contract solution is designed to seamlessly integrate into the existing infrastructure of a drug distribution company, enhancing traceability and security at each operational stage. Utilizing Ethereum-based digital assets, such as ERC-721 tokens, products are represented as unique, non-fungible tokens (NFTs), ensuring that each item can be individually tracked and verified throughout its journey. Figure 5 illustrates the different layers of our solution built on the Ethereum blockchain.

During the development and testing phase, the Hardhat framework was instrumental in creating a robust environment for building and evaluating our smart contract system.

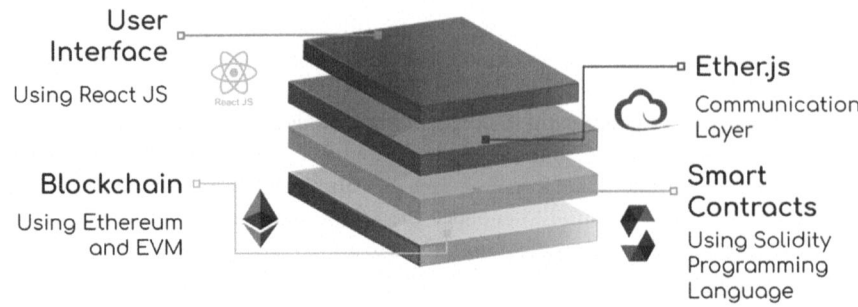

Fig. 5. Blockchain-Enabled Pharmaceutical Last-Mile Solution Design.

By leveraging Hardhat, we could meticulously develop each component represented in the system's design—the Carrier, Company, Customer, Order, Offer, Bid, and Product—as discrete, testable modules within the Ethereum ecosystem.

Figure 6 depicts the smart contract architecture, illustrating the interaction between various roles and functionalities within the system. For example, the Carrier can register itself to the system through the addCarrier function, while the Company can create a new Order specifying details such as product information, destination and desired delivery timeframe.

We also simulated a local blockchain environment, where we could deploy and interact with our smart contracts. This enabled us to conduct comprehensive unit testing, ensuring each function performed as intended, adhering strictly to the prescribed business logic. Integration testing followed, where the interactions between these modules were tested. For instance, the flow from a Carrier placing a bid for an Order, a Company choosing an Offer, to updating the OrderStatus and processing Payments, was scrutinized for seamless operation.

Upon passing these initial tests, we engaged in end-to-end testing with real-world scenarios to validate the system's functionality in a setting that closely mirrors live operation. Through Hardhat's network-agnostic testing capabilities, we were able to ensure that our smart contracts would operate correctly on the Ethereum mainnet. This approach to development and testing was critical for affirming that our blockchain solution was ready for deployment, poised to enhance transparency, efficiency, and traceability within the pharmaceutical supply chain.

A modern and intuitive user interface was developed using React.js, focusing on delivering an experience that embodies simplicity and intuitiveness, tailored to meet the diverse needs of all users within the supply chain network. With a clean and modern aesthetic, the UI offers seamless interaction with the blockchain-enabled system, emphasizing clarity and ease of navigation (Fig. 7).

Across all user interfaces, the system incorporates features that allow for convenient data viewing and editing, with blockchain transactions processed transparently in the background. This not only fosters trust in the system's data integrity but also ensures frictionless experience for editing and updating information on the blockchain.

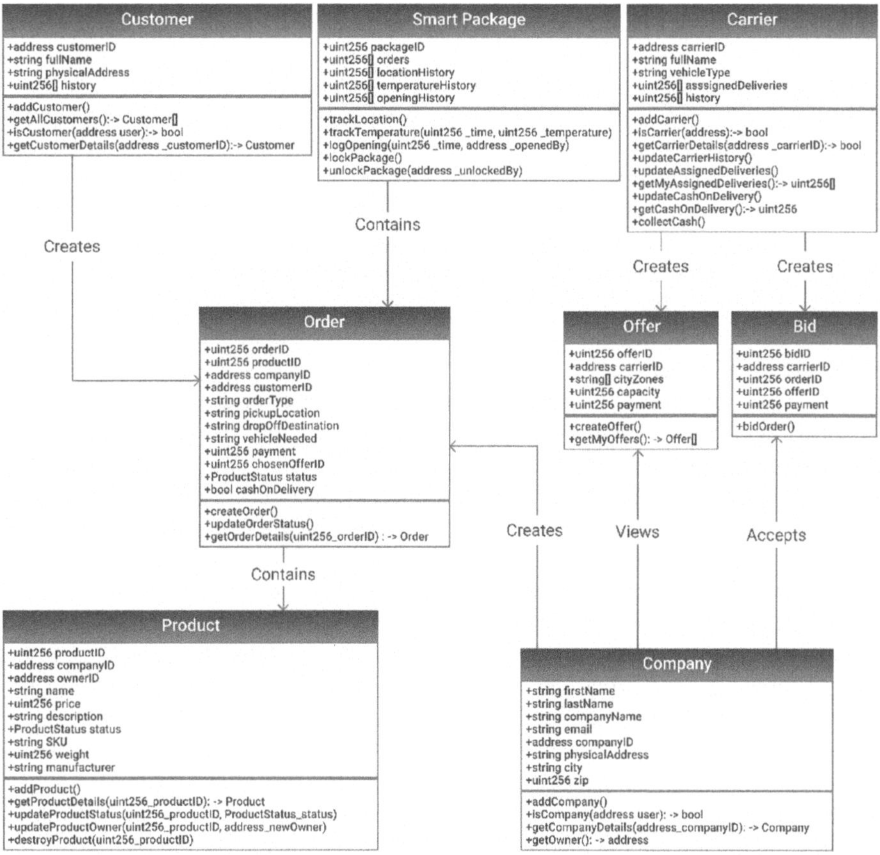

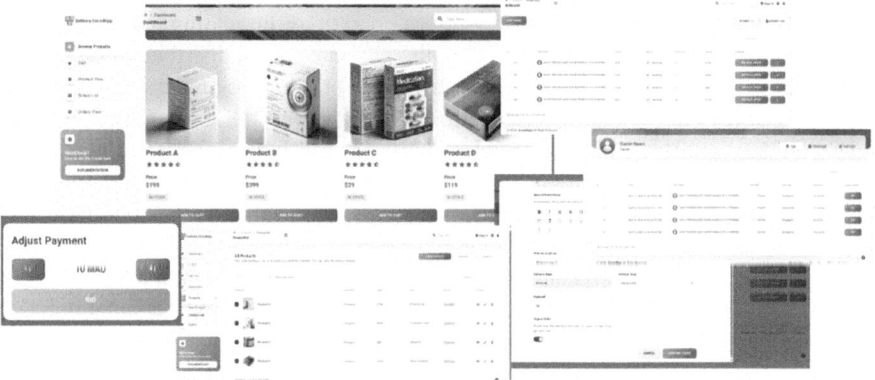

Fig. 6. Class Diagram of the Proposed Solution.

Fig. 7. User Interface of the Proposed Solution.

6 Discussion

The results obtained in this study demonstrate a significant advancement in pharmaceutical logistics by integrating blockchain technology, smart contracts, and crowdsourcing. Compared to previous models, this framework offers enhanced traceability, security, and efficiency in last-mile delivery. Unlike conventional systems, which often rely on manual tracking and centralized management, our decentralized approach minimizes human error and speeds up decision-making. By securing each transaction on a blockchain, this framework ensures data integrity and provides a tamper-proof audit trail. The study not only validates the functionality of blockchain-based delivery systems but also extends their application to real-time crowdsourcing, something largely unexplored in prior literature.

This paper employs a framework that harnesses the power of smart contracts, blockchain, and crowdsourcing within pharmaceutical last-mile deliveries. This trifecta of technological innovation presents a stark contrast to traditional models burdened by manual operations and paper-based tracking, which often result in inefficiencies and heightened susceptibility to errors. Theoretically, this study expands on the use of blockchain technology in supply chain management by demonstrating its effectiveness in highly regulated environments like pharmaceutical logistics. The integration of smart contracts for real-time bidding and tracking introduces a new level of automation that significantly improves decision-making processes. Managerially, the framework offers practical solutions for pharmaceutical companies and logistics service providers, helping them meet regulatory requirements while optimizing costs and delivery times. By leveraging crowdsourced carriers and blockchain's immutable records, organizations can reduce errors, improve accountability, and streamline last-mile delivery operations.

Smart contracts, as part of this proposed framework, play an instrumental role in addressing the challenges of traceability and accountability in the supply chain. By automating transactional processes and maintaining a permanent, unalterable record of each step in a medication's journey, smart contracts can significantly reduce the risks associated with counterfeit drugs and ensure timely and accurate deliveries. The automation inherent in these contracts also streamlines operations, mitigating the potential for human error and enhancing the reliability of the pharmaceutical distribution process.

In addition to the digital improvements, the framework suggests integrating a physical layer of reusable drug packaging equipped with various sensors. This addition not only aligns with the digital tracking provided by smart contracts but also ensures the physical aspects of drug delivery are monitored. Such measures are crucial in maintaining the quality and safety of medications, as they provide real-time data on the conditions and handling of pharmaceuticals throughout their transit.

The utilization of a crowdsourced model for carrier management is a leap towards optimizing logistics and delivery timeframes. This model allows for a competitive and transparent bidding process for carriers, fostering an environment where efficiency is paramount. The integration of such a model showcases the potential for a more agile and responsive pharmaceutical supply chain that caters to the dynamic needs of healthcare providers and patients alike.

In many traditional pharmaceutical delivery systems, carriers are bound by long-term contracts negotiated to ensure reliability, predictability, and adherence to regulatory requirements. These long-term relationships provide a stable framework for delivery, particularly for recurring shipments or specialized transportation needs (e.g., refrigerated transport for sensitive medications). However, while long-term contracts offer stability, they often lack flexibility in responding to dynamic changes in demand, location, or delivery urgency. This is where the proposed bidding scheme in the blockchain framework offers a complementary solution.

The proposed system does not intend to replace long-term contracts but rather to operate alongside them. In fact, the two approaches can coexist within the same blockchain-powered environment, leveraging the strengths of each. For example, when a delivery task arises, the system could first check whether a pre-existing long-term contract carrier is available to handle the shipment. If so, the delivery could be automatically assigned to the contracted carrier through a smart contract, streamlining the process and ensuring compliance with the pre-negotiated terms. The blockchain framework would still provide the necessary traceability and security, ensuring that the carrier adheres to all conditions stipulated in the long-term agreement, such as timely delivery and specific transport requirements.

However, in situations where the contracted carrier is unavailable, overloaded, or not positioned to efficiently handle the delivery, the bidding scheme could be activated. This would allow other carriers registered on the platform to submit real-time bids for the task, ensuring that deliveries are not delayed and the system remains responsive to immediate needs.

While this study demonstrates the feasibility of a blockchain-enabled pharmaceutical delivery system, several limitations remain. First, the testing environment was simulated, which may not fully capture the complexities of large-scale implementation. Future studies should include real-world pilot tests across diverse geographic regions. Second, regulatory variations across countries pose a challenge to universal adoption. Collaborative efforts with regulatory bodies are essential to create standardized protocols for blockchain use in pharmaceutical logistics. Finally, although the crowdsourcing model improves flexibility, ensuring security and reliability of freelance couriers requires further refinement.

Despite the promising advancements offered by integrating smart contracts, blockchain technology, and crowdsourcing into the pharmaceutical supply chain, there are notable challenges and limitations to fully implementing such a solution. The complexity of transitioning from established systems to a new technological framework cannot be underestimated. Organizations may encounter resistance due to the reluctance to adopt new technologies and the significant investment required for system overhauls.

Furthermore, there are concerns related regulatory compliance, and the need for widespread industry standardization. The highly regulated nature of the pharmaceutical industry presents significant hurdles. Crowdsourcing must be managed securely, and while blockchain and smart contracts can help, ensuring compliance with strict regulations is complex. Additionally, the regulatory landscape varies from country to country, making it difficult to create a one-size-fits-all regulatory framework. Therefore, multiple separate studies should be conducted to account for these differences and develop tailored solutions. The ethical and legal implications of this framework need further study, and a comprehensive regulatory framework should be developed to support our solution, ensuring it meets industry standards and legal requirements for real-world implementation.

The technical infrastructure required to support blockchain and smart contracts is substantial, and there is a current lack of expertise in the market to develop and maintain these systems effectively. Therefore, realizing the full potential of blockchain and smart contracts in pharmaceutical distribution demands targeted investments in technical infrastructure and a strategic approach to cultivating specialized expertise.

Although this study focuses on pharmaceutical logistics, the proposed framework is applicable to other industries that require high levels of traceability and security. For instance, the framework could be adapted for perishable food logistics, where real-time monitoring of temperature and delivery conditions is equally critical. Similarly, industries handling high-value electronics or luxury goods could benefit from blockchain's tamper-proof records and crowdsourcing's cost-efficiency, improving their supply chain transparency and security.

7   Conclusion

This paper has presented a novel framework for pharmaceutical last-mile delivery that leverages blockchain technology, smart contracts, and crowdsourcing. By integrating these innovative approaches, the proposed system offers significant improvements over traditional delivery methods. The framework ensures enhanced traceability, bolstered security, and streamlined efficiency throughout the pharmaceutical supply chain.

The proposed framework offers a multitude of advantages. By leveraging blockchain technology, smart contracts, and crowdsourcing, the system enhances medication traceability through a tamper-proof record of every step in the supply chain. This transparency allows for swift identification of potential problems. Additionally, smart contracts and tamper-evident sensor-equipped packaging significantly improve security by minimizing human error and tampering risks. Finally, the framework promotes efficiency through crowdsourced carrier selection, optimizing delivery routes and costs, while automated processes streamline order fulfillment and logistics management. Overall, this framework represents a major advancement in pharmaceutical logistics, prioritizing security, traceability, and efficiency to revolutionize critical medication delivery and ultimately improve patient care within a more robust healthcare system.

Further research is warranted to explore the practical implementation of this framework. Pilot studies and real-world testing are crucial to evaluate its effectiveness and identify potential challenges. Additionally, regulatory considerations and industry-wide collaboration are essential for the successful adoption of this technology-driven approach to pharmaceutical last-mile delivery.

References

1. Kumar, N., Jha, A.: Quality risk management during pharmaceutical 'good distribution practices' – a plausible solution. Bull. Fac. Pharm. Cairo Univ. **56**, 18–25 (2018). https://doi.org/10.1016/j.bfopcu.2017.12.002

2. Mambou, E.N., Nlom, S.M., Swart, T.G., Ouahada, K., Ndjiongue, A.R., Ferreira, H.C.: Monitoring of the medication distribution and the refrigeration temperature in a pharmacy based on Internet of Things (IoT) technology. In: 2016 18th Mediterranean Electrotechnical Conference (MELECON), pp. 1–5 (2016)
3. Kohler, J.C., Martinez, M.G., Petkov, M., Sale, J.: Corruption in the pharmaceutical sector: diagnosing the challenges (2016)
4. Khalique, M., Isa, A.H.B.M., Nassir Shaari, J.A.: Challenges faced by Pakistani pharmaceutical industry: an intellectual capital perspective (2012). https://papers.ssrn.com/abstract=203 5214
5. Nadime, K.L., Benabbou, R., Mouatassim, S., Benhra, J.: Blockchain-enabled two-echelon supply chains for perishable products using just in time inventory management: a case study of the dairy industry. In: 2023 3rd International Conference on Innovative Research in Applied Science, Engineering and Technology (IRASET), pp. 01–08 (2023)
6. Wood, G.: Ethereum: a secure decentralised generalised transaction ledger (n.d.). https://eth erplan.com/ethereum-yellow-paper.pdf
7. Bocek, T., Rodrigues, B.B., Strasser, T., Stiller, B.: Blockchains everywhere - a use-case of blockchains in the pharma supply-chain. In: 2017 IFIP/IEEE Symposium on Integrated Network and Service Management (IM), pp. 772–777 (2017)
8. Panda, S.K., Satapathy, S.C.: Drug traceability and transparency in medical supply chain using blockchain for easing the process and creating trust between stakeholders and consumers. Pers. Ubiquit. Comput. 28, 75–91 (2024). https://doi.org/10.1007/s00779-021-01588-3
9. Mirdad, A.R., Khan, A.M., Hussain, F.K.: Smart contracts and marketplace for just-in-time management of pharmaceutical drugs. IJWGS 20, 25–53 (2024). https://doi.org/10.1504/ IJWGS.2024.137553
10. Bapatla, A.K., Mohanty, S.P., Kougianos, E.: PharmaChain 3.0: efficient tracking and tracing of drugs in pharmaceutical supply chain using blockchain integrated product serialization mechanism. SN Comput. Sci. 5, 149 (2024). https://doi.org/10.1007/s42979-023-02510-9
11. Aslam, M., Jabbar, S., Abbas, Q., Albathan, M., Hussain, A., Raza, U.: Leveraging ethereum platform for development of efficient tractability system in pharmaceutical supply chain. Systems 11, 202 (2023). https://doi.org/10.3390/systems11040202
12. Abdallah, S., Nizamuddin, N.: Blockchain-based solution for pharma supply chain industry. Comput. Ind. Eng. 177, 108997 (2023). https://doi.org/10.1016/j.cie.2023.108997
13. Kordestani, A., Oghazi, P., Mostaghel, R.: Smart contract diffusion in the pharmaceutical blockchain: the battle of counterfeit drugs. J. Bus. Res. 158, 113646 (2023). https://doi.org/ 10.1016/j.jbusres.2023.113646
14. Bapatla, A.K., Mohanty, S.P., Kougianos, E., Puthal, D., Bapatla, A.: PharmaChain: a blockchain to ensure counterfeit-free pharmaceutical supply chain. IET Netw. 12, 53–76 (2023). https://doi.org/10.1049/ntw2.12041
15. Samonte, M.J.C., Advincula, D.G.D., Beltran, S.S.S., Obog, A.D.: A performance evaluation on the blockchain-based traceability application of pharmaceutical supply chain: a case study. In: 2023 13th International Conference on Software Technology and Engineering (ICSTE), pp. 87–92 (2023)
16. Omidian, H., Omidi, Y.: Blockchain in pharmaceutical life cycle management. Drug Discov. Today 27, 935–938 (2022). https://doi.org/10.1016/j.drudis.2022.01.018
17. Konapure, R.R., Nawale, S.D.: Smart contract system architecture for pharma supply chain. In: 2022 International Conference on IoT and Blockchain Technology (ICIBT), pp. 1–5 (2022)
18. Jamil, F., Hang, L., Kim, K., Kim, D.: A novel medical blockchain model for drug supply chain integrity management in a smart hospital. Electronics 8, 505 (2019). https://doi.org/10. 3390/electronics8050505

19. Uddin, M.: Blockchain Medledger: Hyperledger fabric enabled drug traceability system for counterfeit drugs in pharmaceutical industry. Int. J. Pharm. **597**, 120235 (2021). https://doi. org/10.1016/j.ijpharm.2021.120235
20. Musamih, A., et al.: A blockchain-based approach for drug traceability in healthcare supply chain. IEEE Access **9**, 9728–9743 (2021). https://doi.org/10.1109/ACCESS.2021.3049920
21. Dwivedi, S.K., Amin, R., Vollala, S.: Blockchain based secured information sharing protocol in supply chain management system with key distribution mechanism. J. Inf. Secur. Appl. **54**, 102554 (2020). https://doi.org/10.1016/j.jisa.2020.102554
22. Sylim, P., Liu, F., Marcelo, A., Fontelo, P.: Blockchain technology for detecting falsified and substandard drugs in distribution: pharmaceutical supply chain intervention. JMIR Res. Protoc. **7**, e10163 (2018). https://doi.org/10.2196/10163
23. Di Ciccio, C., et al.: Blockchain-based traceability of inter-organisational business processes. In: Shishkov, B. (eds.) BMSD 2018. LNBIP, vol. 319, pp. 56–68. Springer, Cham (2018). https://doi.org/10.1007/978-3-319-94214-8_4
24. Kim, H.M., Laskowski, M.: Toward an ontology-driven blockchain design for supply-chain provenance. Intell. Syst. Account. Finance Manag. **25**, 18–27 (2018). https://doi.org/10.1002/ isaf.1424
25. Casado-Vara, R., González-Briones, A., Prieto, J., Corchado, J.M.: Smart contract for monitoring and control of logistics activities: pharmaceutical utilities case study. In: Graña, M., et al. (eds.) SOCO'18-CISIS'18-ICEUTE'18 2018. AISC, vol. 771, pp. 509–517. Springer, Cham (2019). https://doi.org/10.1007/978-3-319-94120-2_49
26. Nadime, K.L., Benhra, J., Benabbou, R., Mouatassim, S.: Automating attended home deliveries with smart contracts: a blockchain-based solution for e-commerce logistics. E3S Web Conf. **469**, 00026 (2023). https://doi.org/10.1051/e3sconf/202346900026
27. Moudaa, S.E., Ibrahim, Y., Kadadha, M., Mizouni, R., Otrok, H., Singh, S.: PackChain: toward a blockchain-based management platform for last-mile delivery. In: 2022 International Wireless Communications and Mobile Computing (IWCMC), pp. 919–924 (2022)
28. Ducrée, J., Gravitt, M., Walshe, R., Bartling, S., Etzrodt, M., Harrington, T.: Open platform concept for blockchain-enabled crowdsourcing of technology development and supply chains. Front. Blockchain **3** (2020). https://doi.org/10.3389/fbloc.2020.586525
29. Li, M., et al.: CrowdBC: a blockchain-based decentralized framework for crowdsourcing. IEEE Trans. Parallel Distrib. Syst. **30**, 1251–1266 (2019). https://doi.org/10.1109/TPDS. 2018.2881735

A Comprehensive Framework Integrating ML, Automation Pyramid, and KPIs for Industry 5.0

Pedro Ponce[1]([⊠]) ⓘ, Brian Anthony[2], Russel Bradley[2], Wenhao Xu[2],
Juana Isabel Méndez[1] ⓘ, and Arturo Molina[3] ⓘ

[1] Institute of Advanced Materials for Sustainable Manufacturing, Tecnologico de Monterrey,
64849 Monterrey, Nuevo Leon, Mexico
{pedro.ponce,isabelmendez}@tec.mx

[2] Department of Mechanical Engineering, Massachusetts Institute of Technology,
Cambridge 02139, USA
{banthony,russelb,wenhaoxu}@mit.edu

[3] Tecnológico Nacional México/Instituto Tecnológico de Tláhuac III, Mexico City, Mexico

Abstract. The manufacturing industry continually seeks advanced technologies to enhance performance per evolving customer requirements. Machine learning (ML) emerges as a pivotal assistive technology essential for strategic integration with Key Performance Indicators (KPIs). Traditionally, KPIs monitor and measure industrial system performance. This paper proposes a framework leveraging KPIs to integrate ML across the automation pyramid in Industry 5.0. The framework enables early detection of malfunctions and areas for improvement, preventing productivity loss. Validated across various industries, the framework demonstrates enhanced operational efficiency, sustainability, and human-centric benefits. Information and Communication Technologies advancements facilitate real-time data collection and analysis, aligning with ISO 22400 standards for manufacturing operations management. ML techniques generate actionable insights crucial for sustainable development in industries such as automotive, which require holistic goal assessments. Industry 4.0 marked a significant shift towards automation and data exchange, leveraging IoT, cloud computing, and big data analytics. Industry 5.0 emphasizes human-machine collaboration, customization, and sustainability, evolving KPIs to include worker satisfaction, customization capabilities, and social and environmental impact metrics. This evolution spans various sectors: manufacturing, pharmaceuticals, retail, e-commerce, high-energy-use industries, and consumer goods. ML minimizes downtime, enhances product quality, optimizes supply chains, and improves worker safety by analyzing data from wearables and sensors. Integrating ML with KPIs in Industry 4.0 and 5.0 enables industries to be more efficient, adaptive, and responsive to market and environmental changes, improving decision-making, operational efficiency, and alignment with business and sustainability goals.

Keywords: Industry 4.0 · Industry 5.0 · Machine learning · Automation · pyramid · KPIs

1 Introduction

The manufacturing industry faces increasing pressure to enhance performance and adapt to evolving customer requirements. This paper addresses the critical need for a robust framework that integrates Machine Learning (ML) with Key Performance Indicators (KPIs) within the automation pyramid, particularly in the context of Industry 5.0. These KPIs have traditionally been used to monitor and measure the performance of industrial systems and the automation pyramid. The proposed framework allows for the strategic integration of machine learning throughout the entire automation pyramid, using KPIs as a reference point within a unified framework. This approach enables early detection of system malfunctions and areas for improvement, thereby allowing for proactive measures to prevent productivity loss. Information and Communication Technologies (ICT) Advancements have further facilitated this integration. ICT allows for the collection and analysis of real-time system data, which aids in implementing and visualizing standard KPIs as defined in the ISO 22400 standard for manufacturing operations management [1]. ML techniques, a key component of our proposed framework, are crucial in generating actionable insights from the data collected. For instance, in the automotive industry, sustainable development necessitates a holistic approach to assessing an organization's goals and activities [2]. When used effectively, KPIs can monitor and measure processes across various management levels, from operations and finance to security and maintenance.

Paulina Gackowiec et al. [3] outline efficiency indicators tailored to the specific needs of the mining industry, particularly within the context of Industry 4.0 and sustainable business performance. Figure 1 depicts the industry evolution; Industry 4.0 marked a significant transition toward automation and data exchange, leveraging technologies like IoT, cloud computing, and big data analytics. In this era, primary KPIs focused on efficiency, speed, and cost reduction. However, Industry 5.0 builds on these technological advancements to underscore the importance of human-machine collaboration, customization, and sustainability. This new paradigm is driving the evolution of KPIs to include metrics related to worker satisfaction, customization capabilities, and social and environmental impact. The MIT FrED project, for example, highlights this shift, as it integrates machine learning and vision technologies to lower production costs and enhance customization, aligning with the evolving Industry 5.0 KPIs that focus on human-machine collaboration and sustainability [4]. A recent study [5] focuses on the "silver" generation, or individuals over 50, examining their attitudes toward work in the Industry 5.0 era. This research provides insights into the importance of understanding value hierarchies and attitudes toward work for effective human capital management in an Industry 5.0 environment. Industry 5.0 offers promising solutions for our planet and its people, emphasizing the need for evolving KPIs to meet new challenges and opportunities [6].

1.1 Industry 4.0 and 5.0

In the context of Industry 4.0 and 5.0, the collaborative use between ML and KPIs is beneficial but also practical and essential for industries to adapt to the evolving technological landscape and meet the changing market demands. The concept of Industry 4.0, which originated in Germany as part of a strategic initiative to enhance industrial automation and data exchange, set the foundation for integrating advanced technologies into manufacturing processes [7]. Industry 5.0, as often misunderstood, should be referred to as a European vision that emphasizes human-machine collaboration, customization, and sustainability, extending the technological advancements of Industry 4.0 [8]. While Industry 4.0 focuses on efficiency and automation through digital transformation, Industry 5.0 prioritizes human-centricity, resilience, and sustainability, ensuring that manufacturing systems are efficient, sustainable, and socially responsible [9].

This integration is a theoretical concept and a practical reality, as several real-world cases illustrate. Imagine a scenario in the automotive or aerospace manufacturing sectors where heavy machinery is pivotal. ML supports predictive maintenance by analyzing sensor data and aligning with KPIs like Overall Equipment Effectiveness (OEE) to reduce downtime. ML identifies production anomalies in the pharmaceutical sector to improve quality and compliance using the First Pass Yield KPI. ML analyzes sales and market trends in retail for effective inventory management, optimizing supply chains through Inventory Turnover KPI. Similarly, energy-intensive sectors like steel or chemical manufacturing use ML to optimize energy consumption by analyzing operational data.

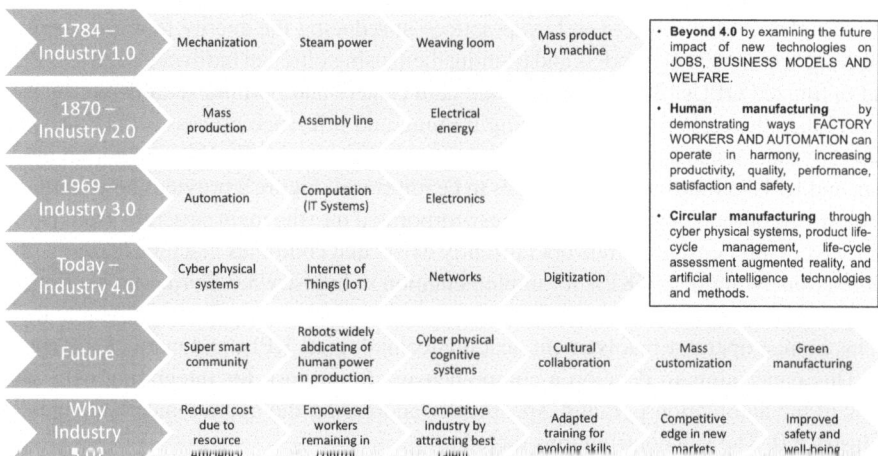

Fig. 1. Industrial Evolution stages.

ML plays is vital for achieving sustainability across industries. In energy, aligning ML with KPIs on consumption and cost can significantly lower bills and carbon footprints. For consumer goods, ML analyzes customer data to offer personalized products, enhancing satisfaction and loyalty when integrated with relevant KPIs. In heavy industries, ML, combined with safety-related KPIs, can analyze wearable and sensor data to proactively address hazards, reducing accidents and improving worker health. Integrating ML with KPIs in Industry 4.0 and 5.0 is essential for better decision-making, efficiency, and sustainability, promising a more adaptive future for industries.

1.2 Machine Learning and KPIs

ML is crucial in advancing manufacturing, particularly in optimizing Laser Powder Bed Fusion for metal additive manufacturing, focusing on quality control and process parameters [10] or for price prediction in agriculture [11]. Research on electrical machine design employs ML to predict KPIs like torque and component costs, enhancing design efficiency and reducing costs [12]. In the energy sector, ML aids in improving renewable energy management, with studies like those by Zhenpeng Yao et al. [13] using ML to accelerate the development of efficient energy systems. Additionally, Giuditta Contini and M. Peruzzini [14] discuss how digitalization can help implement sustainability KPIs across environmental, economic, and social dimensions. Other studies link ML to manufacturing KPIs, such as predicting equipment effectiveness [15] and detecting anomalies [16]. Research also shows ML's capability in forecasting defect-related KPIs [17], and projects like STREAM-0D use KPIs to target zero-defect production [18].

The integration of ML into manufacturing must consider runtime efficiency and the carbon footprint. For example, the energy consumption of ML models, especially during training, has been shown to contribute significantly to CO_2 emissions. Research shows that models like AlexNet can consume up to six times more energy than simpler models like SimpleNet [19]. Moreover, best practices in reducing the energy footprint involve selecting optimized ML models and training them using efficient hardware such as TPUs and optimized GPUs [20]. Efficient cloud data centers and optimized hardware further help reduce the carbon footprint during training and inference processes [21]. Despite these advancements, a comprehensive framework integrating ML, the automation pyramid, and KPIs in Industry 5.0 still needs to be improved. Figure 2 provides how the KPIs based on the automation pyramid can be incorporated into the main structure used. However, no comprehensive framework currently exists that combines machine learning, the automation pyramid, and KPIs for implementation in Industry 5.0. Furthermore, Table 1 compares the essential characteristics of Industry 4.0 and Industry 5.0, highlighting their focus, human operator involvement, leading technologies, KPIs, and main challenges.

This paper aims to develop a comprehensive framework for integrating ML with KPIs in the automation pyramid, specifically addressing the operational challenges in Industry 5.0. The key contributions include:

- Developing a unified framework combining ML, KPIs, and the automation pyramid.
- The framework can be used across multiple industries.
- Demonstration of enhanced operational efficiency, sustainability, and human-centric benefits.

Table 1. Industry 4.0 and 5.0 essential characteristics.

Criteria	Industry 4.0	Industry 5.0
Overview	It focuses on the digitalization and integration of industrial manufacturing and logistics processes. It utilizes smart objects and IoT and merges the physical and virtual worlds [22]	Human operators are involved in several processes while working on manufacturing systems. Industry 5.0 is human-centered, achieved mainly by artificial intelligence, IoT, Digital Twins, and Cobots [23]
Human Operators	Requires a new set of human competencies and may lead to job losses for low-skilled workers [24]	Based on human-machine interaction, the cognitive skills of operators will be more active [25]
Main Technologies	IoT, Cloud, Big Data, AI, Robotics, Blockchain, Autonomous Vehicles, Enterprise Software [26]	ML, cyber-physical, and cognitive systems improve manufacturing processes' efficiency and performance [27]
KPIs	It focuses on operations cycle times, delivery times, time to market new products, quality, and customer involvement [26]	Human-centric design proposes a network to detect the main KPIs in Industry 5.0 (sustainability, resilience, and humancentric) [28]
Main Challenges	Technological, regulatory, and market-related barriers. Strong leadership for digital transformation [22]	Mass customization, green Manufacturing, cultural collaboration [29]

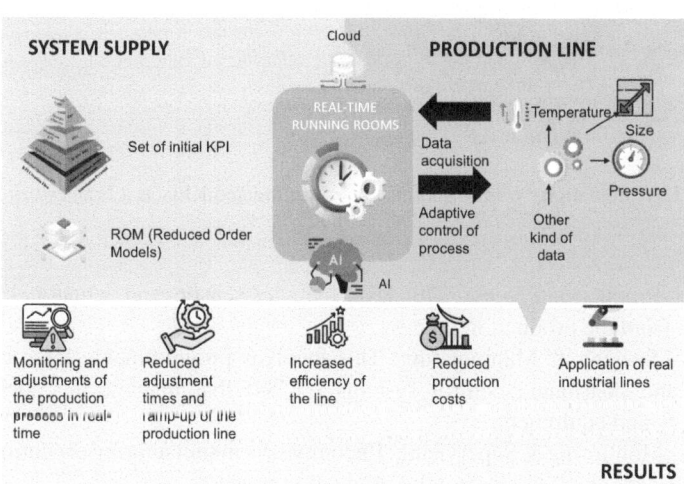

Fig. 2. KPIs based on the automation pyramid in the loop of the STREAM-0D project [18].

2 Proposed Framework

Integrating ML into the automation pyramid and evaluating KPIs significantly enhances a manufacturing company's efficiency, productivity, and decision-making processes. The automation pyramid in manufacturing consists of several layers, each representing different control and data processing levels. Figure 3 illustrates the proposed framework, detailing the integration points of ML within the automation pyramid and the associated KPIs. Thus, from the bottom to the top, these layers are:

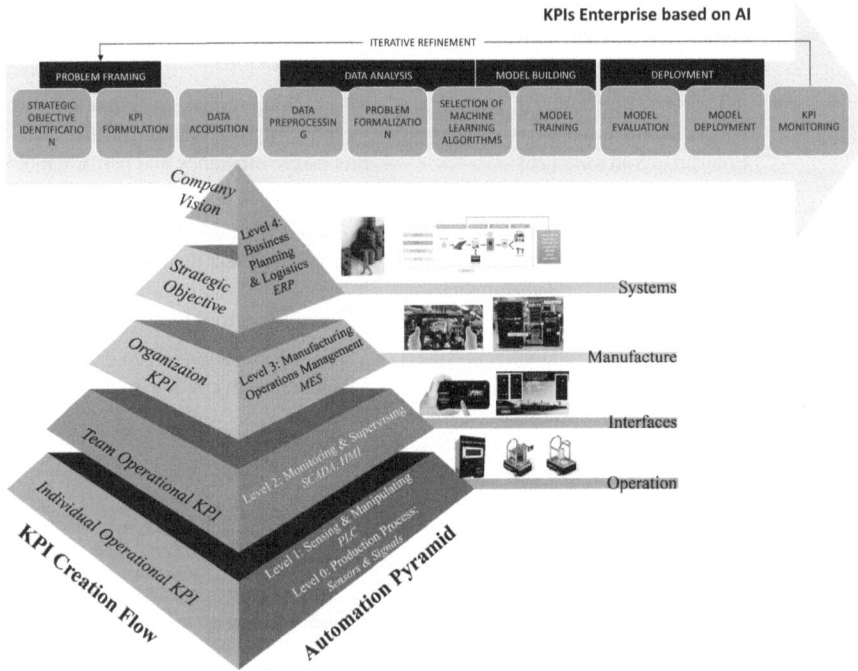

Fig. 3. Automation pyramid and machine learning and KPIs as a Framework [1].

- Level 0—Production Process: This level includes sensors and actuators that collect raw data from the production process.
- Level 1—Sensing & Manipulating: This involves programmable logic controllers (PLCs) and distributed control systems (DCSs) that manage the operations of machinery and equipment.
- Level 2—Monitoring & Supervising: Encompasses manufacturing execution systems (MES) that monitor and control the production process.
- Level 3 - Manufacturing Operations Management: Utilizes enterprise resource planning (ERP) systems for production planning, scheduling, and resource management.
- Level 4—Business Planning & Logistics: This course focuses on business planning and logistics, integrating the entire supply chain and customer relationship management (CRM).

2.1 KPIs

KPIs are specific, measurable values that help evaluate the effectiveness and efficiency of various aspects of the manufacturing process. The common KPIs are shown below:

- Efficiency KPIs: OEE, Cycle Time, Throughput Rate
- Quality KPIs: First Pass Yield, Defect Density
- Cost KPIs: Cost of Goods Manufactured, Variable Cost Per Unit
- Inventory KPIs: Inventory Turnover, Stockouts
- Safety KPIs: Incident Rate, Lost Time Injury Frequency Rate
- Employee KPIs: Productivity, Absenteeism Rate
- Customer KPIs: On-Time Delivery Rate, Customer Retention Rate

2.2 Role of Machine Learning in the Automation Pyramid

Machine learning can be integrated at various levels of the automation pyramid to analyze data and provide actionable insights that align with KPIs [1] (see Fig. 4):

- Level 0: Production Process

  - Predictive Maintenance: ML models analyze sensor data to predict equipment failures, schedule maintenance, and reduce downtime, improving KPIs like Mean Time Between Failures (MTBF) and OEE.

- Level 1: Sensing & Manipulating

  - Process Optimization: ML algorithms optimize control parameters to enhance machine performance and energy usage, directly impacting KPIs related to efficiency and cost.

- Level 2: Monitoring & Supervising

  - Quality Control: ML models analyze production data to identify patterns and detect anomalies, improving quality KPIs like First Pass Yield and Defect Density.

- Level 3: Manufacturing Operations Management

  - Demand Forecasting: ML algorithms predict future product demand based on historical data, market trends, and consumer behavior. This helps optimize inventory levels and production schedules, impacting inventory and cost KPIs.

- Level 4: Business Planning & Logistics

  - Supply Chain Optimization: ML models integrate data from various sources to optimize the entire supply chain, from procurement to delivery, enhancing customer KPIs like On-Time Delivery Rate and Customer Retention Rate.

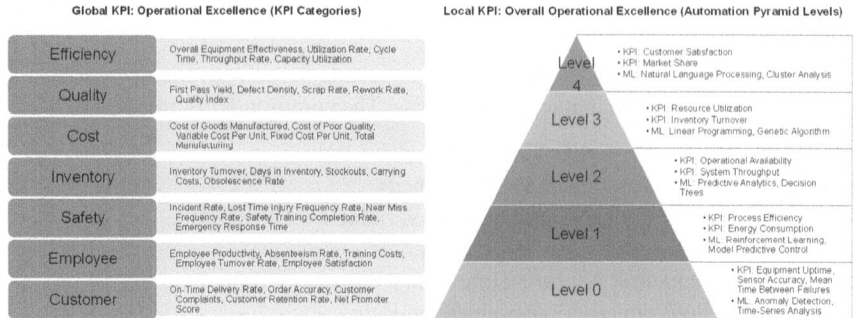

Fig. 4. Global KPIs and partial KPIs in a manufacturing company.

2.3 Evaluating KPIs Using Machine Learning

The evaluation of KPIs using machine learning involves several steps. These steps are presented in Fig. 5 and show step by step how to impact the selected KPIs [30].

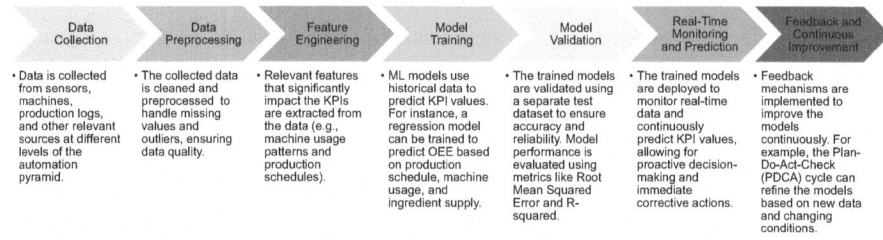

Fig. 5. Steps for impacting selected KPIs.

The automation pyramid structures manufacturing control and data management, utilizing AI, especially ML, to optimize operations and improve KPI outcomes across various levels. From processing production data to enhancing business planning, ML algorithms process sensor data, adjust machine settings, and forecast demand, boosting efficiency, quality, and customer satisfaction. A clear topology ensures that ML algorithms are precisely deployed at optimal levels of the pyramid and evaluated against global KPIs. This allows for flexible and effective enhancements in line with Industry 4.0 and 5.0 standards. Integrated feedback mechanisms continuously identify and correct inefficiencies, while a robust data management strategy maintains data integrity and accessibility, supporting informed decision-making and strategic planning.

The framework presented in Fig. 6 adapts to operational and technological advancements through change management and employee training, enhancing robustness with proactive risk management strategies for technology failures, cybersecurity, and supply chain disruptions to minimize productivity impacts. It incorporates sustainability goals and environmental assessments, making it customizable and scalable for specific factory needs without compromising performance. Integration with external systems like supply chain, customer relationship, and vendor management ensures a holistic approach to manufacturing management.

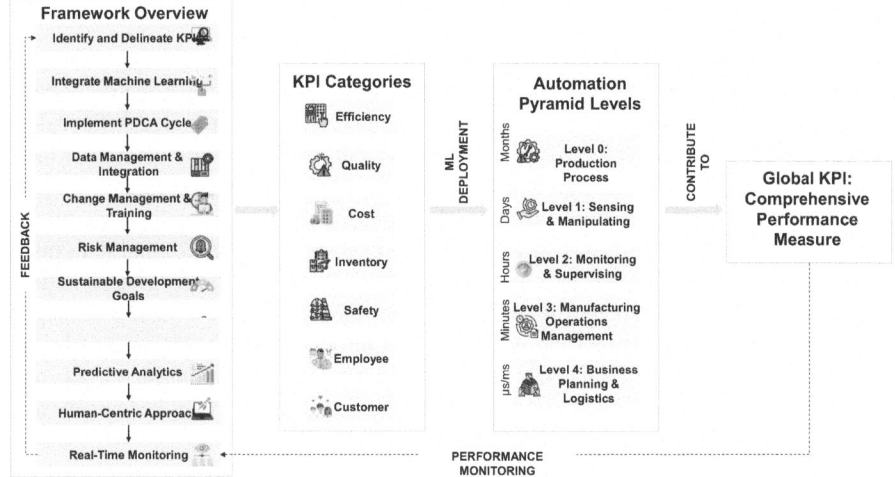

Fig. 6. Proposed framework.

The framework boosts manufacturing responsiveness and efficiency, prioritizes human-centric design for safety and satisfaction, and uses predictive analytics for proactive problem-solving and real-time feedback. This comprehensive approach promotes continuous improvement and supports employee well-being, sustainability practices, and resilience against technological and market changes.

3 Integration of ML in the Manufacturing Framework with a Strategic Focus on Global KPI Impact

ML solutions are tailored to enhance specific KPIs, directly boosting global KPIs by integrating into systems with strategic planning and employee training programs. These solutions reduce defect rates, improve quality, align with cost and sustainability goals in energy management, and enhance supply chain efficiency, impacting inventory and customer satisfaction. The effectiveness of ML is continuously evaluated against global KPIs to ensure alignment with company objectives. Future advancements in AI, ML, and IoT will further optimize these KPIs, driving smarter manufacturing operations. Effective ML integration involves a strategic process including assessment, data infrastructure development, algorithm integration, testing, and ongoing optimization, supported by best practices like iterative development and stakeholder engagement. This approach ensures improvements align with broader organizational goals.

This holistic approach enhances manufacturing by continuously learning and adapting ML algorithms, making operations more efficient and predictive, and aligning with global objectives. The focus on enhancing global KPIs highlights ML's transformative potential in modern manufacturing. Figure 7 illustrates key ML methods, their strategic applications in manufacturing, and recommendations for optimizing their effectiveness. Implementing these methods involves careful planning, continuous monitoring, and regular updates to meet evolving manufacturing needs.

3.1 Limits of the Proposal Using ML

Integrating ML in manufacturing offers benefits but also poses significant challenges. The effectiveness of ML algorithms heavily relies on the availability and quality of data, which can be difficult to maintain in complex manufacturing environments. Poor data quality can result in inaccurate ML predictions, potentially leading to operational inefficiencies or failures. The costs associated with implementing ML, including software, hardware, and data infrastructure, can be prohibitive, especially for smaller enterprises. Additional expenses arise from software updates, system maintenance, and data management. Integrating ML with legacy systems introduces compatibility issues, adding technical complexity and increasing time and financial costs. There is also a skills gap in data science and ML among the workforce, requiring significant training or hiring specialized talent, further increasing operational costs. An over-reliance on ML and automation may reduce critical human oversight and increase risks of cyber-attacks and data breaches due to more connected systems.

ML Method	Application in Manufacturing Strategy	Recommendations
Supervised Learning	Used for predictive maintenance by training on historical data to predict equipment failures.	Regularly update the training data to reflect the latest operational conditions and equipment performance.
Unsupervised Learning	Applied in anomaly detection on production lines to identify unusual patterns or defects without labeled data.	Continuously monitor the output to adjust parameters for better accuracy and relevance.
Regression	Used for quality control by predicting the quality of products based on various input parameters.	Continuously monitor input parameters and model predictions to ensure consistent product quality.
Reinforcement Learning	Optimized for real-time decision-making in automation control systems, adapting to changing conditions.	Implement in a controlled environment first to fine-tune the algorithm before full-scale deployment.
Deep Learning	Employed in quality control for visual inspection using image recognition to identify defects.	Ensure high-quality image data and consider computational requirements for training deep learning models.
Decision Trees	Used for classification tasks in sorting products or optimizing logistics and supply chain decisions.	Regularly prune and maintain the decision trees to prevent overfitting and to keep them relevant to current data.
Random Forests	Applied for more robust and accurate predictions in demand forecasting and inventory management.	Use a diverse data set to train the model and validate its predictions with actual outcomes.
Neural Networks	Utilized for complex pattern recognition in manufacturing processes, such as predicting equipment lifespan.	Invest in high-quality data preprocessing and consider the need for substantial computational resources.
Support Vector Machines (SVM)	Effective in classification tasks for quality assurance, distinguishing between good and defective products.	Choose appropriate kernel functions and parameters to ensure the model's effectiveness in specific tasks.
Natural Language Processing (NLP)	Used in customer service and feedback analysis to gauge customer satisfaction and product feedback.	Continuously update the model with new customer feedback and industry-specific terminology.

Fig. 7. ML methods in the proposed framework.

Ensuring data security and privacy in ML-integrated manufacturing requires robust cybersecurity and intensive data privacy measures. The automation shift raises ethical concerns, including job displacement risks, with broad societal implications. ML systems require regular maintenance, such as updates and retraining, increasing operational costs. While scalable in theory, practical scaling faces challenges as complexity grows with operation size. Additionally, the dynamic nature of manufacturing, with fluctuating market demands, technological advances, and regulatory changes, further complicates ML integration.

ML systems may not adapt quickly to these changes, requiring time for reconfiguration, retraining, and testing. While integrating ML into manufacturing offers significant advantages, it is crucial to approach this integration with a clear understanding of its limitations and challenges. A strategic approach that includes robust planning, continuous assessment, and the flexibility to adapt to changing conditions and technological advancements is essential for successful integration.

4 Connecting the Automation Pyramid and the ML Model Based on KPIs

ML based on KPIs consistently achieves performance metrics. Figure 8 shows how it is applied in each level, significantly improving operational efficiency, waste reduction, and equipment effectiveness, thereby boosting overall performance.

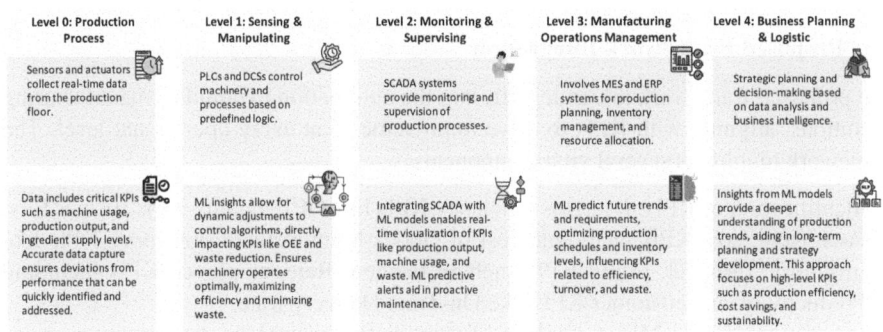

Fig. 8. Flow diagram Automation Pyramid and KPIs.

At Level 0 - Production Process, sensors and actuators collect real-time data on machine usage, production output, and ingredient supply. This data enables quick monitoring, analysis, and correction of performance deviations.

At Level 1—Sensing & Manipulating, PLCs and DCSs control machinery with predefined logic, enhanced by ML models for dynamic adjustments using real-time data. This boosts KPIs like OEE and waste reduction, ensuring optimal machinery operation for maximum efficiency and minimal waste.

At Level 2—Monitoring & Supervising, SCADA (Supervisory Control and Data Acquisition) systems offer detailed monitoring of production processes. When integrated with ML models, these systems enable real-time visualization of KPIs like production output, machine usage, and waste. Predictive alerts from ML models facilitate proactive maintenance and issue resolution, helping consistently meet or exceed KPIs.

At Level 3—Manufacturing Operations Management, MES, and ERP systems manage production, inventory, and resources, enhanced by ML models predicting trends and optimizing schedules and inventory. This improves production efficiency, inventory turnover, and waste management, ensuring efficient resource use.

At Level 4—Business Planning & Logistics, strategic planning and decision-making are enhanced by ML models that analyze data and provide insights into production trends, improving long-term planning and strategy. This focuses on high-level KPIs like production efficiency, cost savings, and sustainability.

5 Case Study: Integrating Machine Learning and KPIs in Manufacturing for Industry 5.0

This case study explores the integration of ML with KPIs within the context of Industry 5.0. The framework aims to enhance performance and sustainability in manufacturing by leveraging advanced technologies to create a human-centric, efficient, and responsive operational environment. The shift from Industry 4.0 to Industry 5.0 emphasizes human-machine collaboration, customization, and sustainability. Traditionally used in monitoring and improving industrial performance, KPIs are evolving to include worker satisfaction, customization capabilities, and social and environmental impact metrics.

5.1 Proposed Framework Integration

The proposed framework integrates ML into the automation pyramid of manufacturing operations, aligning with KPIs to drive improvements at every operational level. The framework highlights several vital components:

1. Identification of KPIs: It targets efficiency KPIs like OEE, quality KPIs such as First Pass Yield, cost KPIs including Cost of Goods Manufactured, inventory KPIs like Inventory Turnover, safety KPIs such as Incident Rate, employee KPIs including Productivity, and customer KPIs like On-Time Delivery Rate.
2. Integration of ML: ML is employed for predictive maintenance to optimize maintenance schedules by predicting equipment failures. In quality control, ML algorithms analyze production data to ensure product quality and reduce waste. ML also enhances demand forecasting by analyzing sales data and market trends, and in energy management, it optimizes energy usage contributing to sustainability.
3. Implementation Strategy:
   (a) Data Infrastructure: Establishes robust data collection and processing capabilities to gather and store data from various sources within the manufacturing environment.
   (b) Customized ML Algorithms: Develops and deploys ML algorithms tailored to address specific KPIs at different levels of the automation pyramid.
   (c) Feedback Mechanisms: Implements the Plan−Do−Check−Act (PDCA) cycle for continuous monitoring and optimization.
   (d) Training and Change Management: Invests in training programs to bridge skills gaps and facilitate the adoption of new technologies.
   (e) Risk Management: Includes structured plans to mitigate risks related to technology failures and cybersecurity threats.
   (f) Sustainability Metrics: Incorporates metrics to assess and manage the environmental impact of manufacturing operations.

6 Integrating Machine Learning and KPIs to Increase Productivity in a Food Manufacturing Company

6.1 Implementing the Proposed Framework

The framework integrates ML into the automation pyramid for food manufacturing operations, aligning with KPIs (OEE, Cycle Time, Throughput Rate, First Pass Yield, Defect Density, Cost of Goods Manufactured, Inventory Turnover, Incident Rate, Productivity, and On-Time Delivery Rate) to enhance functionality across all levels.

ML is used for predictive maintenance, analyzing sensor data to foresee equipment failures, optimizing schedules, and reducing downtime. In quality control, ML algorithms detect patterns to maintain high product quality and minimize waste. ML also improves demand forecasting by analyzing sales data, market trends, and consumer behavior, enhancing inventory management. In energy management, ML optimizes energy usage, contributing to sustainability goals, and it analyzes data from wearables and sensors to identify safety hazards and improve worker well-being.

Implementation involves establishing robust data infrastructure, developing customized ML algorithms, and using the PDCA cycle for continuous optimization [30]. Training programs are essential to bridge skill gaps and ensure smooth technology adoption. Structured risk management plans address technology failures and cybersecurity threats, while sustainability metrics help manage the environmental impact of food manufacturing operations. This framework aims to streamline operations, ensure sustainability, and enhance safety in the food manufacturing process.

6.2 Increasing Productivity in a Food Manufacturing Company

A food manufacturing company integrated ML into its production processes to increase productivity and efficiency. By analyzing production schedules, machine usage patterns, and ingredient supply levels, the ML model provided actionable insights that aligned with KPIs related to production efficiency and cost. This framework guides the integration of ML with KPIs in food manufacturing, enhancing efficiency, quality, and sustainability. This approach aligns with Industry 5.0 principles, ensuring technological advancements contribute to human-centric and eco-friendly manufacturing practices. The following steps describe the implementation of ML:

1. Data Creation or Collection: Collect or create synthetic data based on operational conditions to evaluate the factory's performance in different scenarios. This data includes production schedules, machine usage patterns, and ingredient supply levels, with dependent variables (KPIs) being production output, waste, and OEE. Synthetic data allows for the evaluation of various conditions as a first approach. Thus, synthetic data was created in this paper. Adding random noise to simulate real-world variability is recommended.
2. Data Splitting: Split the dataset into training and testing sets using a 70–30 split.
3. Model Training: Select and train a model, such as linear regression, to predict each KPI based on the production schedule, machine usage, and ingredient supply levels.
4. Model Evaluation: Evaluate the models on the test set, calculating Root Mean Squared Error (RMSE) to measure prediction accuracy.

5. Results Display: Show the RMSE values and model summaries to evaluate the models' performance.

6.3 Regression Model Using ML

Linear regression [27] is a powerful and widely used technique that models the relationship between a dependent variable and one or more independent variables. It is particularly suitable for quantifying these relationships in a manufacturing context due to several key reasons:

- Simplicity and Interpretability:

  - Ease of Understanding: Linear regression provides a straightforward method for predicting the dependent variable based on the values of independent variables. The simplicity of the linear model makes it easy to understand and implement.
  - Interpretable Coefficients: The coefficients in a linear regression model represent the average change in the dependent variable for a one-unit change in an independent variable, holding all other variables constant. This interpretability is crucial for managers and decision-makers who must understand how different factors influence production outcomes.

- Quantifying Relationships:

  - Direct Quantification: Linear regression allows direct quantification of the impact of each independent variable on the dependent variable. For instance, in the context of the food manufacturing company, it quantifies how changes in production schedules, machine usage, and ingredient supply levels affect production output.
  - Insightful Analysis: By examining the magnitude and direction of the coefficients, decision-makers can identify which factors have the most significant impact on production efficiency and cost, enabling targeted improvements.

- Predictive Accuracy:

  - Good Fit for Linearity: If the relationship between the dependent and independent variables is approximately linear, linear regression models can provide accurate predictions. This makes them suitable for many practical applications in manufacturing, where relationships often approximate linearity.
  - Handling Multicollinearity: Linear regression can also reasonably handle multicollinearity (when independent variables are highly correlated), providing reliable estimates of the coefficients. However, care must be taken to address severe multicollinearity through techniques like regularization.

- Versatility and Flexibility:

  - Wide Applicability: Linear regression can be applied to a wide range of problems in manufacturing, from predicting production output to understanding the factors that drive waste and inefficiency.

- Foundation for More Complex Models: Linear regression is a foundational technique for building more complex models. It can be extended to multiple regression, polynomial regression, or more advanced ML algorithms if needed.

• Decision-Making Support:

- Data-Driven Decisions: The gathered insights support data-driven decision-making, helping companies optimize production schedules, machine usage, and ingredient supply to enhance efficiency and productivity.
- Scenario Analysis: Managers can use the model to perform scenario analysis, predicting how changes in input variables might affect production outcomes. They can make informed decisions about resource allocation and process adjustments.

6.4 Model Specification

Equation 1 represents the general form of a linear regression model in which the production_output is modeled as a function of the variables production_schedule, machine_usage, and ingredient_supply. The constant value indicates the inclusion of an intercept term in the model, representing the baseline value of production_output when all independent variables are zero. This equation specifies the structure of the linear regression model, indicating that production_output is influenced by the selected independent variables and an intercept term.

$$production\_output \sim 1 + production\_schedule + machine\_usage + ingredient\_supply \tag{1}$$

Equation 2 expands the general form of the model into a specific instance for the i-th observation. Here, production_output_i is the predicted production output for the i-th observation. $\beta 0$ is the intercept term, representing the baseline production output when all predictors are zero. $\beta 1$ is the coefficient for the production_schedule variable, representing the change in production_output for a one-unit change in production_schedule, holding other variables constant. $\beta 2$ is the coefficient for the machine_usage variable, representing the change in production_output for a one-unit change in machine_usage, holding other variables constant. $\beta 3$ is the coefficient for the ingredient_supply variable, representing the change in production_output for a one-unit change in ingredient_supply, holding other variables constant. ε_i is the error term for the i-th observation, capturing the deviation of the actual production output from the predicted value.

$$production\_output\_i - \beta 0 + \beta 1 \cdot production\_schedule\_i + \beta 2 \cdot machine\_usage\_i + \beta 3 \cdot ingredient\_supply\_i + \varepsilon\_i \tag{2}$$

where:

production_output_i is the predicted production output for the i-th observation.
$\beta 0$ is the intercept term (baseline production output).
$\beta 1, \beta 2, \beta 3$ are the coefficients for the independent variables.

production_schedule_i, machine_usage_i, ingredient_supply_i are the values of the independent variables for the i-th observation.

ε_i is the error term capturing the deviation of the actual production output from the predicted value

Significance of the Coefficients. These coefficients help quantify the impact of each independent variable on the production output, allowing the company to understand and optimize factors influencing productivity. Equation 2 is a regression model that predicts the production output based on the provided independent variables.

- $\beta 1$: Measures the change in production output for each unit change in the production schedule.
- $\beta 2$: Measures the change in production output for each unit change in machine usage percentage.
- $\beta 3$: Measures the change in production output for each unit change in ingredient supply percentage.
- production_output: This is the dependent variable (response variable). It represents the amount of production output in the food manufacturing process.

    - 1: This term represents the intercept in the linear regression model. Including the intercept ensures that the model calculates a baseline production output value when all independent variables are zero. The intercept is crucial as it represents the starting point of the prediction.

- production_schedule: This is an independent variable representing the production schedule, which can have levels such as Low, Medium, and High. It captures the influence of planned production activities on the production output. A higher production schedule typically means a higher planned production capacity, which should positively impact the production output. The production schedule dictates the planned number of production activities, influencing the expected product produced. A well-planned schedule can lead to higher production efficiency and output.
- machine_usage: This independent variable represents the percentage of machinery used. Higher machine usage often leads to higher production output, as more machines are actively involved in manufacturing. This variable helps the model understand how much machine utilization affects the production rate. Also, Machine usage reflects the operational efficiency and capacity of the manufacturing process. Higher machine usage typically correlates with higher production rates as more machines are actively working to produce goods.
- ingredient_supply: Represents the percentage of ingredient supply levels. Adequate supply levels are crucial for maintaining continuous production. If the ingredient supply is low, production may be interrupted or slowed, negatively affecting the output. Conversely, a higher supply level ensures that production can proceed without interruptions, leading to higher output. The availability of ingredients is fundamental to the manufacturing process. Production cannot proceed without an adequate supply, thus directly impacting the production output. Ensuring a steady supply of ingredients helps maintain continuous production flow and maximizes output.

Pseudocode using ML

```
# Function to perform linear regression using gradient descent
function linear_regression_gradient_descent(X, y, alpha, num_it-
erations):
    # Initialize parameters
    m, n = shape(X)  # m: number of observations, n: number of
features (in this case, n = 3)
    beta = [0, 0, 0, 0]  # Initialize coefficients [β0, β1, β2,
β3] to 0
    cost_history = []
    # Perform gradient descent
       for iteration from 1 to num_iterations:
    # Compute the hypothesis
        predictions = X * beta[1:] + beta[0]
    # Compute the error
       errors = predictions - y
 # Compute the cost (Mean Squared Error)
      cost = (1 / (2 * m)) * sum(errors ^ 2)
       cost_history.append(cost)
       # Compute the gradients
       d_beta0 = (1 / m) * sum(errors)
       d_beta1 = (1 / m) * sum(errors * X[:, 1])
       d_beta2 = (1 / m) * sum(errors * X[:, 2])
       d_beta3 = (1 / m) * sum(errors * X[:, 3])
 # Update the coefficients
 beta[0] = beta[0] - alpha * d_beta0
 beta[1] = beta[1] - alpha * d_beta1
 beta[2] = beta[2] - alpha * d_beta2
 beta[3] = beta[3] - alpha * d_beta3
# Optional: print cost every 100 iterations for monitoring
       if iteration % 100 == 0:
       print("Iteration", iteration, "Cost", cost)
     return beta, cost_history
# Main code to run the linear regression
# Assume data is loaded into variables: production_schedule, ma-
chine_usage, ingredient_supply, and production_output
# Combine independent variables into a matrix X
X = concatenate([production_schedule, machine_usage, ingredi-
ent_supply], axis=1)
# Set hyperparameters
alpha = 0.01  # Learning rate
num_iterations - 1000  # Number of iterations
# Call the linear regression function
beta, cost_history = linear_regression_gradient_descent(X, pro-
duction_output, alpha, num_iterations)
# Output the learned coefficients
print("Learned coefficients:", beta)
```

Analysis of Relationships Between Production Variables. This subsection provides a comprehensive overview of the relationships between key production variables. The data and expected relationships presented here are a reference for making initial decisions, which can be further refined by implementing the proposed framework. Figure 9 describes the expected relationship and the rationale behind that expectation.

Figure 10 shows scatter plots from synthetically generated data to visualize the relationships between key variables (production schedule, machine usage, ingredient supply) and KPIs (production output, waste, OEE). Understanding these relationships can help identify the optimal levels of these factors to improve productivity and efficiency in a food manufacturing company. The visualizations also clearly communicate how changes in production schedules, machine usage, and ingredient supply levels impact overall production performance and efficiency.

Variables	Expected	Rationale
Production Output vs. Production Schedule	Positive: Higher schedules lead to higher output	A more intensive production schedule typically means that more resources (labor, machinery, time) are allocated to production activities, leading to increased production output. This relationship is crucial for planning production to meet demand.
Production Output vs. Machine Usage	Positive: Higher machine usage increases output	Machines operating at higher usage levels produce more goods within a given timeframe. However, it is important to monitor machine health to avoid breakdowns due to overuse.
Production Output vs. Ingredient Supply	Positive: Higher supply leads to higher output	A sufficient and timely supply of ingredients ensures that production processes run smoothly without interruptions, leading to higher output. Shortages can cause delays and lower production efficiency.
Waste vs. Production Schedule	Negative: Higher schedules reduce waste	A well-optimized production schedule can lead to more efficient resource use, reducing waste. Overproduction, however, can lead to higher waste due to spoilage or excess inventory.
Waste vs. Machine Usage	Mixed: Both low and high usage might increase waste	Low machine usage can indicate underutilization, leading to inefficiencies and higher per-unit waste. Conversely, very high usage can lead to machine wear and tear, increasing the likelihood of defects and waste.
Waste vs. Ingredient Supply	Positive: Higher supply might increase waste if oversupply	Excessive supply of ingredients can lead to storage issues and spoilage, especially for perishable items. Managing supply levels carefully is essential to minimize waste.
OEE vs. Production Schedule	Positive: Higher schedules increase OEE	An optimized production schedule ensures equipment is used efficiently, reducing downtime and improving performance metrics.
OEE vs. Machine Usage	Positive: Higher usage increases OEE	Effective machine usage maximizes productivity and reduces idle time, directly improving OEE, which measures the overall efficiency of production equipment.
OEE vs. Ingredient Supply	Positive: Higher supply supports better OEE	Adequate ingredient supply ensures continuous production processes, reducing interruptions and enhancing the efficiency of equipment use, thereby improving OEE.
Waste vs. OEE	Negative: Higher OEE reduces waste	Higher OEE means that equipment operates optimally, which usually correlates with lower defect rates and less waste.
Production Output vs. OEE	Positive: Higher OEE increases output	High OEE increases production rates and output as equipment downtime and performance losses are minimized.
Production Output vs. Waste	Mixed: Optimal waste reduction can increase output	Reducing waste generally benefits production output, indicating more efficient processes. However, excessive waste reduction can compromise other production areas, potentially affecting output.

Fig. 9. Summary of Expected Relationships.

1. Predicting Waste - Based on Eq. (1):

$$\text{waste} \sim 1 + \text{production\_schedule} + \text{machine\_usage} + \text{ingredient\_supply}$$

• Estimated Coefficients:

- Intercept: When production_schedule, machine_usage, and ingredient_supply are all zero, the predicted waste is 20.125 units.
- production_schedule: For each unit increase in production schedule level, the waste decreases by 2.15 units, holding other factors constant. This negative relationship indicates that higher production schedules are associated with reduced waste.
- machine_usage: For each percentage point increase in machine usage, the waste increases by 0.10093 units, holding other factors constant. This suggests increased machine usage can lead to higher waste, possibly due to overuse or inefficiencies at higher usage rates.
- ingredient_supply: For each percentage point increase in ingredient supply, the waste increases by 0.20187 units, holding other factors constant. This positive relationship might indicate that surplus ingredients can lead to increased waste

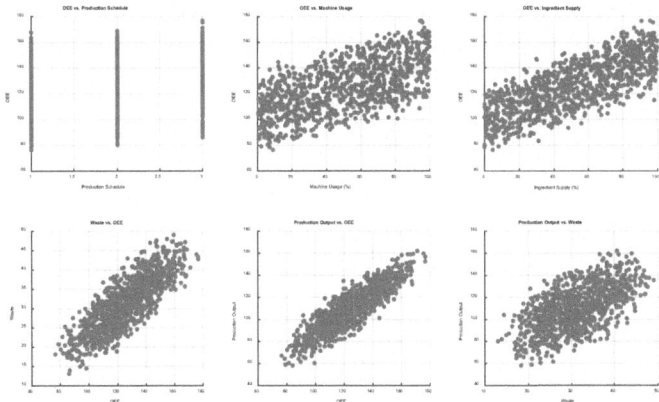

Fig. 10. Scatter plots from synthetically generated data to visualize the relationships between key variables.

The metrics from Table 2 indicate that the model fits the data well. An R-squared value of 0.922 means that the model can explain approximately 92.2% of the variability in waste. The RMSE value of 1.97 reflects the average deviation of the observed values from the predicted values. The high F-statistic and associated p-value confirm the model's overall significance. All p-values are zero, indicating that all predictors are statistically significant at conventional levels.

8. Predicting Overall Equipment Effectiveness (OEE)

OEE $\sim 1 +$ production_schedule $+$ machine_usage $+$ ingredient_supply

- Estimated Coefficients:

  - Intercept: 69.789. In practice, it is unlikely that production schedule, machine usage, and ingredient supply would be zero; this intercept provides a reference point for understanding the additive effects of the independent variables on OEE.

- production_schedule: For each unit increase in the production schedule level, the OEE increases by 5.1333 units, holding other factors constant. This positive relationship indicates that more intensive production schedules are associated with better equipment effectiveness. A higher production schedule likely means that production is planned and executed at a higher capacity, which optimizes the use of equipment and reduces idle time, enhancing OEE.
- machine_usage: This indicates that for each percentage point increase in machine usage, the OEE increases by 0.40205 units, holding other factors constant. Increased machine usage typically implies that machines are utilized more effectively, leading to better performance and reduced downtime. This suggests optimizing machine utilization can significantly enhance equipment effectiveness, provided the machines operate within their optimal performance ranges to avoid wear and tear.
- ingredient_supply: For each percentage point increase in ingredient supply levels, the OEE increases by 0.49561 units, holding other factors constant. Adequate and consistent ingredient supply ensures that production can proceed without interruptions, reducing downtime and improving the efficiency of the manufacturing process. This positive relationship underscores the importance of maintaining a well-managed inventory and supply chain to support continuous production.

Table 2. Standard Error, t-Statistics, p-values and model performance for predicting waste.

Standard Errors (SE)	t-Statistics (tStat) and p-Values	Model Performance
Intercept: 0.26105 production_schedule: 0.092085 machine_usage: 0.002544 ingredient_supply: 0.0025629	Intercept: tStat = 77.092, pValue = 0 production_schedule: tStat = −23.348, pValue = 1.7268e−89 machine_usage: tStat = 39.674, pValue = 7.7592e−181 ingredient_supply: tStat = 78.766, pValue = 0	Number of observations: 700 Error degrees of freedom: 696 RMSE: 1.97 R-squared: 0.922 Adjusted R-squared: 0.922 F-statistic vs. constant model: 2750, p-value = 0

The R-squared from Table 3 indicates that 92.2% of the variability in OEE is explained by the model. This high value suggests that the model fits the data well, capturing most of the variation in OEE through the independent variables. Furthermore, the p-values for all coefficients are effectively zero, indicating that the likelihood that these results are due to random chance is extremely low. The significant coefficients for each variable indicate their substantial influence:

Table 3. Standard Error, t-Statistics, p-values and model performance for predicting OEE.

Standard Errors (SE)	t-Statistics (tStat) and p-Values	Model Performance
Intercept: 0.5544 production_schedule: 0.19557 machine_usage: 0.0054029 ingredient_supply: 0.005443	Intercept: tStat = 125.88, pValue = 0 production_schedule: tStat = 26.248, pValue = 4.3497e−106 machine_usage: tStat = 74.414, pValue = 0 ingredient_supply: tStat = 91.056, pValue = 0	Number of observations: 700 Error degrees of freedom: 696 RMSE: 1.97 R-squared: 0.922 Adjusted R-squared: 0.922 F-statistic vs. constant model: 2750, p-value = 0

- Production Schedule: The positive impact on OEE and the negative impact on waste highlight the importance of efficient production planning. Higher production schedules lead to better equipment effectiveness and reduced waste, optimizing overall production efficiency.
- Machine Usage: The positive coefficients for both OEE and waste suggest that while increased machine usage improves equipment effectiveness, it must be carefully managed to minimize waste. This underscores the need for balanced machine utilization strategies.
- Ingredient Supply: The positive impact on both OEE and waste emphasizes the role of consistent and adequate ingredient supply in maintaining smooth production operations. Proper supply chain management is crucial to minimizing disruptions and maximizing efficiency.

These findings validate the proposal that integrating ML to analyze and optimize production schedules, machine usage, and ingredient supply levels can significantly improve productivity and efficiency in a food manufacturing company. By leveraging ML to monitor and adjust these factors in real-time, companies can achieve substantial gains in production output, reduce waste, and enhance overall equipment effectiveness. Figure 11 shows the actions for each level of the automation pyramid.

7 Discussion

This research paper introduced a novel framework that integrated ML with KPIs within the automation pyramid, catering to the evolving demands of Industry 5.0. As industries transitioned from Industry 4.0, characterized by digital integration, to Industry 5.0, which emphasizes human-machine collaboration and sustainability, the necessity for adaptable, responsive, and efficient systems became paramount. The results of this study highlighted that maintaining an optimal ratio between model execution frequency and input PWM frequency minimized simulation errors, which was critical for deploying RTS technologies on less powerful hardware platforms such as microcontrollers.

Compared to existing studies like those by Paulina Gackowiec et al. [3], which focused primarily on efficiency, speed, and cost reduction in specific industries, this framework embedded ML throughout the automation pyramid. This strategic approach enhanced operational efficiency and addressed broader KPIs, including environmental impact and worker satisfaction—key aspects of the Industry 5.0 paradigm. The integration of Information and Communication Technology (ICT) advancements allowed for leveraging real-time data analytics, enhancing the comprehensiveness absent in many frameworks documented in studies [5] and [14].

The strategic integration of ML across all levels of the automation pyramid presented a significant advantage by enhancing decision-making and operational transparency. It supported practices such as predictive maintenance, aligning with KPIs like Overall Equipment Effectiveness (OEE), which is sporadically seen in existing models [12].

The paper introduced a framework that aligns with Industry 5.0's technological and operational standards, setting a new benchmark for integrating machine learning with KPIs in manufacturing. This significant advancement reflects a deeper understanding

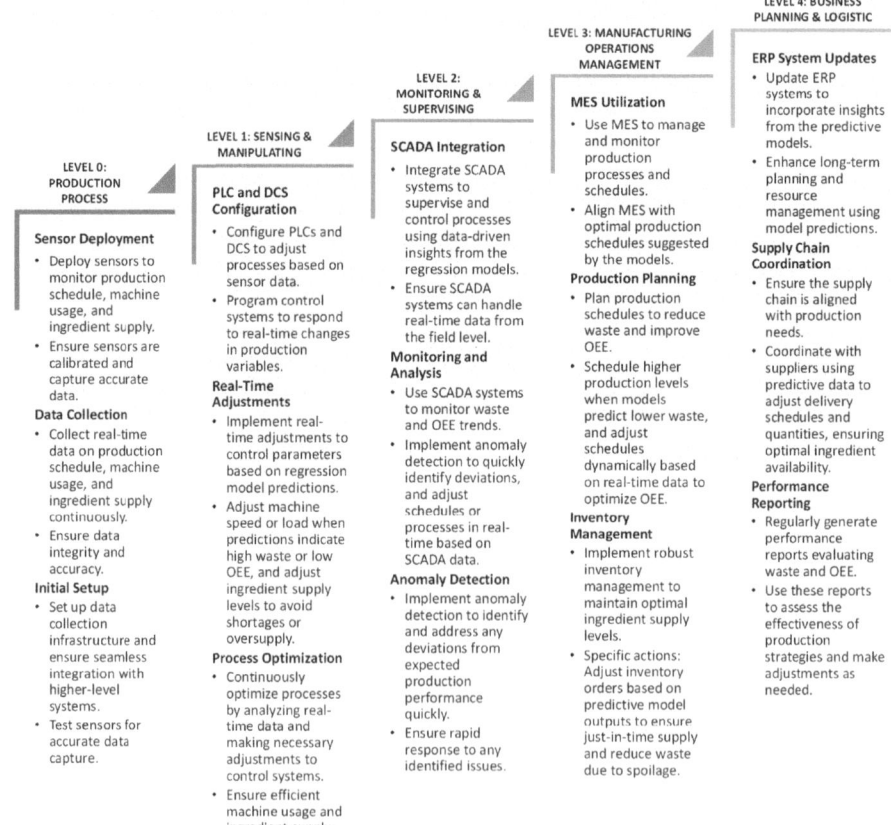

Fig. 11. Actions for Each Level of the Automation Pyramid.

of the interplay between technology and human factors, enhancing industrial efficiency, adaptability, and human-centric operations.

8   Conclusions

The proposed framework integrates ML into the automation pyramid of food manufacturing operations, aligning with various KPIs to drive improvements at every operational level. By focusing on efficiency, quality, cost, inventory, safety, employee performance, and customer satisfaction KPIs, the framework leverages ML for predictive maintenance, quality control, demand forecasting, energy management, and safety.

The case study results demonstrate significant correlations between key variables and KPIs. Higher production schedules are associated with increased production output and reduced waste, indicating more efficient production planning. Increased machine usage improves OEE but must be managed to minimize waste. Adequate ingredient supply supports smoother production processes, enhancing production output and OEE. The linear regression models confirm that production schedule, machine usage, and ingredient supply significantly influence waste and OEE, with high R-squared values indicating strong model fits.

Integrating ML into food manufacturing operations fosters a more efficient, sustainable, and human-centric manufacturing environment, aligning with Industry 5.0 goals. This approach enhances productivity and efficiency, supporting the industry's shift towards more advanced and responsive operational practices.

On the other hand, integrating ML models across the automation pyramid supports a human-centric by improving safety and working conditions through real-time data and predictive maintenance. ML models enhances decision-making by providing data-driven insights, allowing workers and managers to make more informed and effective decisions. Increased efficiency and reduced waste are achieved by optimizing production schedules, machine usage, and inventory levels, which reduces waste and improves overall efficiency, aligning with sustainable practices and reducing environmental impact. Employees are empowered with real-time data and predictive insights, enabling proactive measures, enhancing their roles, and reducing the cognitive burden of manual monitoring and decision-making. Sustainable work practices are supported by optimizing resource allocation and planning, ensuring a balanced workload for employees.

Acknowledgments. The authors acknowledge the technical and financial support of the Institute of Advanced Materials for Sustainable Manufacturing, Tecnologico de Monterrey, Mexico, FEMSA Foundation, and Massachusetts Institute of Technology in producing this work.

Disclosure of Interests. The authors have no competing interests to declare that are relevant to the content of this article.

References

1. Ramis Ferrer, B., Muhammad, U., Mohammed, W.M., Martínez Lastra, J.L.: Implementing and visualizing ISO 22400 key performance indicators for monitoring discrete manufacturing systems. Machines **6**, 39 (2018). https://doi.org/10.3390/machines6030039

2. Wellbrock, W., Ludin, D., Röhrle, L., Gerstlberger, W.: Sustainability in the automotive industry, importance of and impact on automobile interior – insights from an empirical survey. Int. J. Corp. Soc. Responsib. **5**, 10 (2020). https://doi.org/10.1186/s40991-020-00057-z

3. Gackowiec, P., Podobińska-Staniec, M., Brzychczy, E., Kühlbach, C., Özver, T.: Review of key performance indicators for process monitoring in the mining industry. Energies **13**, 5169 (2020). https://doi.org/10.3390/en13195169

4. MIT: A factory for FrEDs at MIT. In: MIT News | Massachusetts Institute of Technology (2022). https://news.mit.edu/2022/factory-for-freds-mit-1005. Accessed 9 Sept 2024

5. Laskowska, A., Laskowski, J.F.: "Silver" generation at work—implications for sustainable human capital management in the industry 5.0 era. Sustainability **15**, 194 (2022). https://doi.org/10.3390/su15010194

6. Tiwari, S., Bahuguna, P.C., Walker, J.: Industry 5.0: a macroperspective approach. In: Handbook of Research on Innovative Management Using AI in Industry 5.0, pp 59–73. IGI Global (2022)

7. Kagermann, H., Helbig, J., Wahlster, W.: Recommendations for Implementing the Strategic Initiative INDUSTRIE 4.0: Securing the Future of German Manufacturing Industry ; Final Report of the Industrie 4.0 Working Group. Forschungsunion (2013)

8. Xu, X., Lu, Y., Vogel-Heuser, B., Wang, L.: Industry 4.0 and industry 5.0—inception, conception and perception. J. Manuf. Syst. **61**, 530–535 (2021). https://doi.org/10.1016/j.jmsy.2021.10.006

9. Mladineo, M., Celent, L., Milković, V., Veža, I.: Current state analysis of croatian manufacturing industry with regard to industry 4.0/5.0. Machines **12**, 87 (2024). https://doi.org/10.3390/machines12020087

10. Sing, S.L., Kuo, C.N., Shih, C.T., Ho, C.C., Chua, C.K.: Perspectives of using machine learning in laser powder bed fusion for metal additive manufacturing. Virtual Phys. Prototyp. **16**, 372–386 (2021). https://doi.org/10.1080/17452759.2021.1944229

11. Deepa, S., Alli, A., Sheetac, G.S.: Machine learning regression model for material synthesis prices prediction in agriculture. Mater. Today Proc. **81**, 989–993 (2023). https://doi.org/10.1016/j.matpr.2021.04.327

12. Parekh, V., Flore, D., Schops, S.: Deep learning-based prediction of key performance indicators for electrical machines. IEEE Access **9**, 21786–21797 (2021). https://doi.org/10.1109/ACCESS.2021.3053856

13. Yao, Z., et al.: Machine learning for a sustainable energy future. Nat. Rev. Mater. **8**, 202–215 (2023). https://doi.org/10.1038/s41578-022-00490-5

14. Contini, G., Peruzzini, M.: Sustainability and industry 4.0: definition of a set of key performance indicators for manufacturing companies. Sustainability **14**, 11004 (2022). https://doi.org/10.3390/su141711004

15. El Mazgualdi, C., Masrour, T., Barka, N., El Hassani, I.: A learning-based decision tool towards smart energy optimization in the manufacturing process. Systems **10**, 180 (2022). https://doi.org/10.3390/systems10050180

16. Shi, J., He, G., Liu, X.: Anomaly detection for key performance indicators through machine learning. In: 2018 International Conference on Network Infrastructure and Digital Content (IC-NIDC), pp 1–5 (2018)

17. Thorström, M.: Applying Machine Learning to Key Performance Indicators. University of Gothenburg (2017)

18. STREAM-0D: Overview of STREAM-0D | Simulation models working in real time. In: STREAM-0D (2016). https://www.stream-0d.com/project/overview/. Accessed 9 Sept 2024
19. Hsueh, G.: Carbon Footprint of Machine Learning Algorithms. Senior Projects Spring 2020, Bard College (2020)
20. Patterson, D., et al.: The carbon footprint of machine learning training will plateau, then shrink. Computer **55**, 18–28 (2022). https://doi.org/10.1109/MC.2022.3148714
21. Lang, S., Engelmann, B., Schiffler, A., Schmitt, J.: A simplified machine learning product carbon footprint evaluation tool. Clean. Environ. Syst. **13**, 100187 (2024). https://doi.org/10.1016/j.cesys.2024.100187
22. Fonseca, L.M.: Industry 4.0 and the digital society: concepts, dimensions and envisioned benefits. In: Proceedings of the International Conference on Business Excellence, vol. 12, pp. 386–397 (2018). https://doi.org/10.2478/picbe-2018-0034
23. Alves, J., Lima, T.M., Gaspar, P.D.: Is industry 5.0 a human-centred approach? A systematic review. Processes **11**, 193 (2023). https://doi.org/10.3390/pr11010193
24. Vrchota, J., Mařiková, M., Řehoř, P., Rolínek, L., Toušek, R.: Human resources readiness for industry 4.0. J. Open Innov. Technol. Mark. Complex. **6**, 3 (2020). https://doi.org/10.3390/joitmc6010003
25. Leng, J., et al.: Industry 5.0: prospect and retrospect. J. Manuf. Syst. **65**, 279–295 (2022). https://doi.org/10.1016/j.jmsy.2022.09.017
26. Tambare, P., Meshram, C., Lee, C.-C., Ramteke, R.J., Imoize, A.L.: Performance measurement system and quality management in data-driven industry 4.0: a review. Sensors **22**, 224 (2021). https://doi.org/10.3390/s22010224
27. Pant, P., Rajawat, A.S., Goyal, S.B., Singh, D., Constantin, N.B., Raboaca, M.S., Verma, C.: Using machine learning for industry 5.0 efficiency prediction based on security and proposing models to enhance efficiency. In: 2022 11th International Conference on System Modeling & Advancement in Research Trends (SMART), pp. 909–914 (2022)
28. Zeb, S., et al.: Industry 5.0 is coming: a survey on intelligent nextg wireless networks as technological enablers (2022)
29. Adel, A.: Future of industry 5.0 in society: human-centric solutions, challenges and prospective research areas. J. Cloud Comput. **11**, 40 (2022). https://doi.org/10.1186/s13677-022-00314-5
30. Realyvásquez-Vargas, A., Arredondo-Soto, K.C., Carrillo-Gutiérrez, T., Ravelo, G.: Applying the plan-do-check-act (PDCA) cycle to reduce the defects in the manufacturing industry. A case study. Appl. Sci. **8**, 2181 (2018). https://doi.org/10.3390/app8112181

A Novel Pipeline for Data Management and Analysis that Integrates Data Lakehouse Architecture into the Aeronautics Industry

Nelson Freitas[1]([✉]) [ID], Diogo Vaqueira[1], Andre Dionisio Rocha[1] [ID], Jose Barata[1] [ID], Fábio Serrano[2], Luís Silva[2], and Manuel Madeira[2]

[1] NOVA School of Science and Technology, Center of Technology and Systems (UNINOVA-CTS), and Associated Lab of Intelligent Systems (LASI), NOVA University Lisbon, 2829-516 Lisbon, Portugal
{n.freitas,andre.rocha,jab}@uninova.pt,
d.vaqueira@campus.fct.unl.pt
[2] Aernnova Aerospace Évora, Parque Da Indústria Aeronáutica De Évora, Herdade De Pinheiro E Casa Branca Lt. A-I, CM1094, 7005-797 Évora, Portugal
{fabio.serrano,luis.silva,manuel.madeira}@aernnova.com

Abstract. Currently, the majority of processes or systems aim to benefit from the data produced by their own or other relevant systems, with the objective of increasing efficiency. This is especially true in the field of industrial systems, where a multitude of devices attempt to publish their metrics and data into the system, often resulting in characteristics that can be classified as big data. However, companies often struggle with the correct and useful utilization of this harvested data. Therefore, this paper focuses on a use case of a data pipeline system with a data lakehouse in an airplane parts factory. The developed architecture shows that with some adjustments to the classic data lakehouse architecture, it is possible to achieve higher parallelism in order to simultaneously store data in the data lake and data warehouse. Additionally, a visualization tool was developed to highlight how metric calculation and outlier detection can be automated or facilitated with the utilization of data, as opposed to manual labor.

Keywords: Big data · Data pipeline · Data lake · Data lakehouse · Data warehouse · Industry · Manufacturing

1 Introduction

In the current day and age, data is being harvested in all matter of processes with the objective of making them more efficient, safer, and more resilient [1, 2]. Specifically, in the industrial processes the usage and collection of this data started to grow exponentially since the beginning of the fourth industrial revolution. From the beginning of 2011 the concept and idea of industry 4.0 allows factories to utilize the power of IoT devices and be able to collect not only data from critical processes but all around the shopfloor [3], able to harvest as much information as possible even if a clear goal is not yet present of what to do with this information.

M. Dassisti et al. (Eds.): IN4PL 2024, CCIS 2372, pp. 410–424, 2025.
https://doi.org/10.1007/978-3-031-80760-2_26

The process of collecting diverse data poses inherent challenges, including managing large volumes of data, real-time processing, and handling different data types [4]. To address these requirements, various concepts have emerged, such as data lake architectures [5] which are repositories designed to store vast amounts of both structured and unstructured raw data. More recently, a hybrid approach called the data lakehouse architecture has gained attention, integrating elements from both data lakes and data warehouses, to leverage their respective strengths [6, 7]. Data warehouses, in contrast, store structured and transformed data from various sources, typically optimized for querying and reporting.

With these challenges and information in mind, the following research question arises: "How can a data management architecture be designed for the aeronautical industry to address the specific needs of data collection, processing, and visualization of industry-related data?".

While still a relatively new concept, the data lakehouse architecture holds significant potential for industrial applications. This paper showcases the practical benefits of implementing such architecture in the aeronautical industry, where there is a need to store raw data while simultaneously leveraging pre-processed information for various purposes.

The paper follows a structured approach with six sections. The first section introduces and contextualizes the paper. Section two provides an overview of the state of the art, focusing specifically on the data aspect of Industry 4.0. In the third section, the architecture is presented in detail. The fourth section showcases a use case and presents the results obtained from implementing the architecture in a real-world scenario. Finally, the fifth section offers conclusions and a brief discussion of the results, followed by the references in the sixth section.

2   Literature Review

2.1   Industry 4.0 and Big Data

With the onset of the fourth industrial revolution, the notion of interconnectedness and internet-enabled communication began to proliferate [8]. This concept, coupled with the advent of cyber-physical systems, where physical components are digitally represented, facilitated seamless communication among various elements, thereby enhancing their automation and autonomy. These concepts also streamlined real-time monitoring and control, enabling the integration of information from various parts of the shop floor and facilitating swift decision-making with network-connected controllers [9].

The implementation of Industry 4.0 has brought invaluable concepts that enable easy and dynamic control of manufacturing processes. However, as previously mentioned, it has also introduced new challenges related to the management and storage of vast volumes of data. With an ever-increasing number of IoT devices, the data generated on a single shop floor is growing exponentially [8]. Furthermore, this data is often heterogeneous and unstructured, meaning that data collected from sensors measuring temperature and data captured by cameras have vastly different formats that must be collected and analyzed [10, 11]. This has highlighted the need to address new challenges associated with data that possess unique characteristics, in order to effectively utilize the harvested data [10, 11]. This new form of extensive or intricate data, which traditional storage and manipulation methods struggle to handle, is collectively referred to as Big Data.

In attempting to classify the type of data described above, researchers have not reached full consensus on the nuances of its classification, typical of a new concept. However, the main characteristics of Big Data have been generally agreed upon and are often explained using a combination of Vs, representing key aspects of this data type [10]:

- Volume – As the term "Big Data" implies, this refers to the substantial size of the dataset, presenting a significant challenge in managing and processing it.
- Velocity – This pertains to the speed at which data is generated. Devices can produce data rapidly, sometimes multiple times per second. When numerous devices are involved in similar tasks, the velocity of data production increases significantly, posing challenges in managing and processing it.
- Variety - This refers to the diversity of data types and formats that are generated by heterogeneous devices. With data coming from various sources, it's common to encounter a wide range of formats and structures, adding complexity to data management and analysis.
- Veracity – This aspect deals with the quality and reliability of the data. Due to various factors such as sensor errors, transmission issues, or data entry mistakes, the veracity of the data may be compromised, leading to inaccuracies or inconsistencies that need to be addressed during data processing and analysis.
- Variability – This characteristic highlight the inconsistency in the structure, format, or arrival rate of the data. Data may vary significantly in terms of its structure, format, or frequency of arrival, posing challenges for data management and analysis.

In order to effectively harness big data, it's essential that not only the storage systems but also every other module, from data generation to data reception, to be prepared. This interconnected chain of activities is collectively referred to as a data pipeline [12]. Therefore, all components of the data pipeline must be equipped to handle big data and its associated attributes. Different methods and frameworks exist for various parts of the data pipeline, each with its own characteristics and challenges [12]. Similarly, various architectures have been developed for data storage, with one of the most commonly associated with big data being the data lake architecture [6–8].

2.2 Data Lake and Warehouse

Some argue that the data lake preceded data warehouses, while others suggest they serve different purposes. However, the fact remains that these two technologies can complement each other, aiming to yield the best results [13, 14]. Therefore, it is essential to take a step back and analyze both concepts to better understand how their combination can lead to something greater.

A data warehouse is a centralized repository for structured, organized, and processed data, typically designed with a specific analytical purpose in mind [15]. In essence, data warehouses use predefined schemas to store large volumes of data collected from various sources. These warehouses can be implemented as relational databases, deployed either on-premises or in the cloud [16].

Data warehousing plays a vital role in business data management by providing decision-makers, such as managers, administrators, and analysts, with tools to make informed decisions more efficiently [17]. Given their widespread use across medium and large enterprises, data warehouses are integral to business intelligence initiatives. Data from operational systems supporting business activities are regularly extracted, transformed, and loaded into the data warehouse environment. Once in the warehouse, data can be queried, analyzed, modified, refined, and enriched using various tools and techniques [15].

Each architecture possesses distinct characteristics. For instance, in the Federated architecture, there exists a uniform view of interconnected data warehouses, allowing for seamless access across disparate data sources [18]. However, the Centralized architecture stands out as a pivotal example, representing the classic and simplest use case of a data warehouse. In this architecture, a single centralized storage system is responsible for storing all acquired data and delivering it to respective systems [19].

Another form of data storage that has been increasingly popular, particularly because it addresses most of the challenges associated with big data, as mentioned previously, is the concept of a data lake.

A data lake commonly serves as a central repository for storing raw, unprocessed data in its original form. It enables businesses to store and process vast amounts of organized, semi-structured, and unstructured data [15]. Data lakes lack a specific organizational structure, and the size and nature of the data they contain can vary greatly. Depending on requirements, a data lake may contain minimal or extensive data. These characteristics provide data lakes with flexibility and scalability [6, 7]. Due to these attributes, many large organizations are adopting this strategy. One of the significant advantages of data lakes is their ability to handle the storage of data from diverse sources without any limitations or predefined structure, a common requirement in the context of the Industry 4.0 industrial revolution.

A plethora of data lake architectures exist, each tailored to specific niches and use cases. However, there are some that broadly represent the concept of a data lake. One of the foundational concepts is the layered data lake architecture (Fig. 1). This architecture, among the earliest used for data lakes, consists of different layers with distinct functions. In Fig. 1a two-layer architecture is depicted, consisting of the landing zone as the initial point of arrival for data, and the raw data layer, which permanently stores the information from the landing zone [5]. While other architectures with more layers, such as transformation or interaction, also exist, the underlying principle remains the same as the two-layer architecture.

It is important to note that the landing zone itself can be loosely described as a data lake, as it often serves as a momentary repository for a multitude of raw files in various formats awaiting processing. Figure 1 illustrates one of the sources as a relational database, alongside several other heterogeneous data sources, highlighting the flexibility and robustness required of the landing zone to reliably manage and process data. Additionally, the landing zone must have sufficient throughput to continuously store and serve data on demand to various software components.

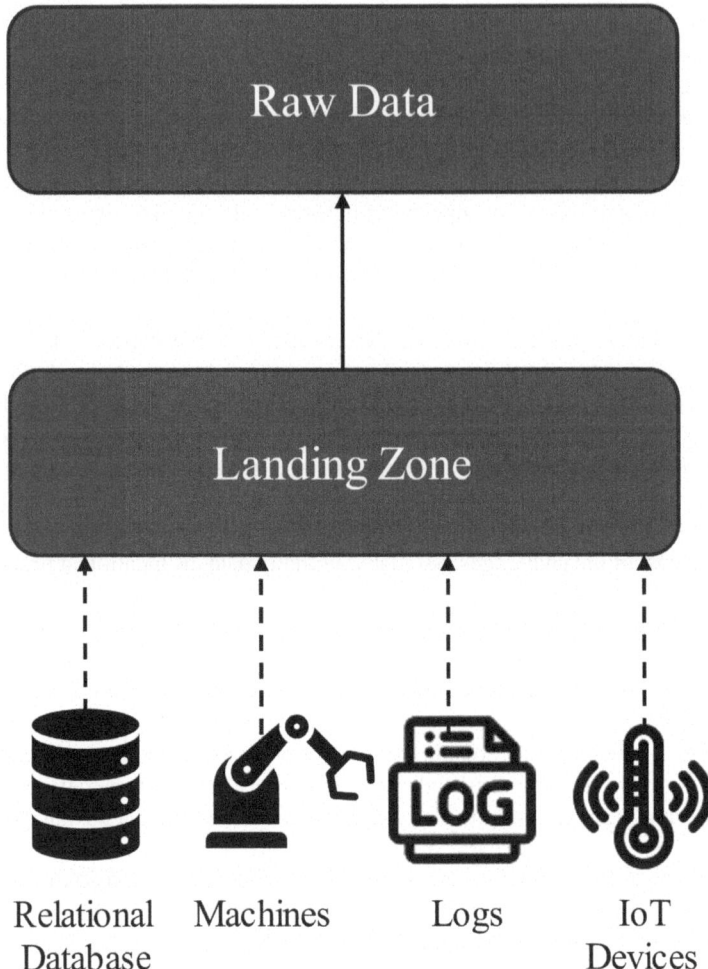

Fig. 1. Two-layered data lake architecture. Adapted from [5].

All these solutions cater to different approaches: data lake for raw storage of data and data warehouse for well-structured and relational data. However, a new concept attempts to amalgamate the best of both worlds, termed as the data lakehouse. The data lakehouse aims to blend the principles of data lake and data warehouse, allowing for the storage of both raw, unprocessed data for future analysis and processed, well-structured, and relational data [5–7]. In Fig. 1 both concepts coexist within the same framework, delineated by respective layers as discussed earlier, enabling the storage of information in the most suitable format for business or research needs. This concept ensures that no information goes to waste, as raw data can be stored before processing, providing valuable insights into the shop floor or decision-makers (Fig. 2).

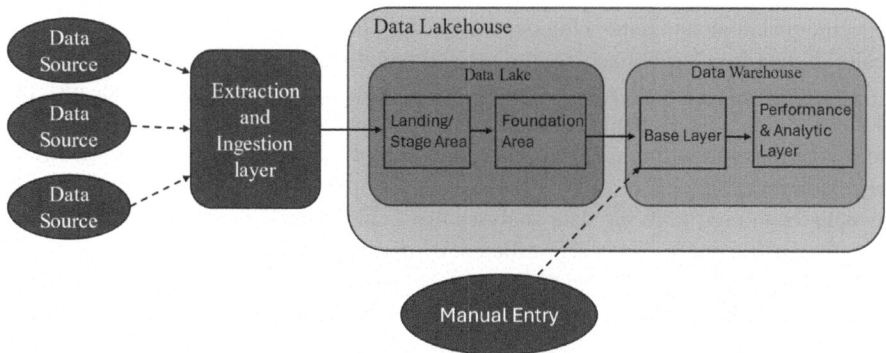

Fig. 2. Data Lakehouse architecture. Adapted from [6].

Table 1 presents a comparison of the three different architectures across various features, helping to highlight both the differences and similarities between the architectures in question.

Table 1. Comparison between data warehouse, data lake and data lakehouse. Adapted from the work present in [13, 14].

Features	Data Warehouse	Data Lake	Data Lakehouse
Data	Structured, Processed	Structured, Semi-Structured, Unstructured, Raw, Processed	Structured, Semi-Structured, Unstructured, Raw, Processed
Processing	Schema-on-write	Schema-on-read	Schema-on-write, Schema-on-read
Storage	Expensive for large data volumes	Designed for low-cost storage	Designed for low-cost storage
Agility	Less agile, fixed configuration	Highly agile, adjustable configuration	Highly agile, adjustable configuration
Security	Mature	Maturing	Maturing

3 Proposed Architecture

The case study involved AERNNOVA Corp., an aeronautical manufacturer based in Évora, Portugal. The company faced a specific challenge where data from each production machine was aggregated into CSV files stored on a central computer within the factory. These CSV files were organized into folders, with each folder corresponding to a specific machine, and data being deposited every hour. While this setup resulted in a wealth of data from each machine, it remained largely unused beyond mere storage.

The primary objective was to leverage the data from the CSV files to generate insightful metrics that factory managers could use for comparison with their own calculations and predictions, providing a deeper understanding of the company's operations. Additionally, the secondary goal was to establish a more appropriate storage solution for this raw data, enabling future big data analyses that could support the factory in areas like predictive maintenance and energy efficiency improvements.

The challenges posed by the company revolved around developing a data pipeline capable of fulfilling the objective of capturing both raw and processed data. To address this, a data lakehouse architecture was employed, drawing inspiration and principles from existing state-of-the-art architectures, but adding some changes to encompass the specific use case, specifically the information does not go directly to the data lake and then to the data warehouse but it is split the landing zone as it acts as a buffer, allowing the processing of information in parallel instead of sequentially. The proposed architecture, used in a real-case scenario to meet the requirements of a manufacturing company, is illustrated in Fig. 3.

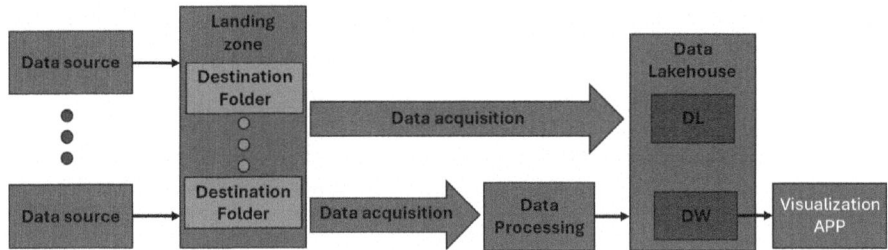

Fig. 3. Proposed architecture.

As depicted in Fig. 3, the data sources publish their data to the central computer. This central computer serves as an initial landing zone, allowing the data to be compartmentalized and organized according to their respective data sources. Once stored in the landing zone, data acquisition software monitors for any new information and transfers it to two designated locations: the data lake and the data processing program.

The raw data is delivered to the data lake directly from the data sources. This data remains unchanged and serves the intended purpose of future utilization by the company, particularly for batch processing. It can be used to train models or infer specifics about processes or machines.

While the raw data is stored in the data lake, a copy of this data is also sent to the data processing unit. The data processing unit then extracts and structures the information contained in the raw CSV files generated by the machines. Subsequently, the processed information, with pre-selected data characteristics, is stored in a data warehouse. With this step completed, the company now has a storage repository for both the raw information, available for future use, and the processed information, which contains the selected characteristics collected from the raw data and is immediately ready for use.

For the final step of the architecture, the company desired a graphical and clear visualization of the selected metrics obtained from the CSV files generated by the machines. Therefore, a visualization application can be connected to the data warehouse, which can provide the chosen metrics for visualization. This setup enables the company to promptly utilize the collected data and compare it to existing metrics, calculations, and thresholds, facilitating the optimization of their production processes.

In Fig. 4 a representation of the data model architecture illustrates how the utilization of the intermediate processes is orchestrated to accomplish the data lakehouse. From the landing zone, two data acquisition processes are initiated. The first process involves converting the information into a JSON object with a specific name, referencing characteristics of the data source. This converted data is then stored directly in a collection within the data lake. Conversely, the process for the data warehouse is more complex. The data needs to be cleansed and selected according to the requisites defined by AERNNOVA Corp., before being stored in the respective tables within the data warehouse.

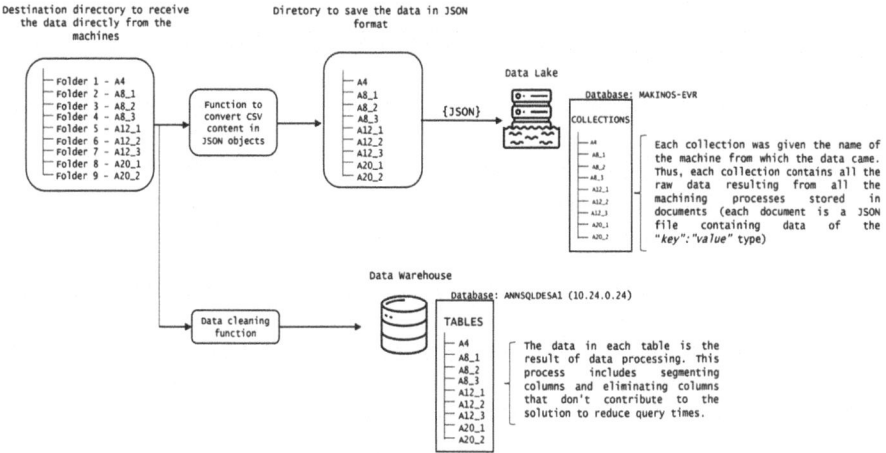

Fig. 4. Architecture data model.

4   Use Case Implementation

In this section, a real case implementation of the data lakehouse concept is explained, detailing its development at the AERNNOVA Corp. center, which primarily focuses on the production of airplane parts. As such, the section is divided in the implementation of the data pipeline and the results, where the proof of concept and real metrics of the implementation can be shown.

4.1   Data Pipeline Implementation

All of the previously mentioned processes that compose the architecture are built upon existing infrastructure at the company. The primary infrastructure comprises the Computer Numerical Control (CNC) machines already installed and operational within the facility. These machines are industrial CNC devices used for machining various airplane parts manufactured by AERNNOVA Corp. They are all connected to a central computer via wiring. While this setup may not offer the utmost flexibility, it provides a certain degree of freedom regarding the placement and expansion of CNC machines on the shop floor. Figure 5, provides a simple representation of AERNNOVA Corp.'s existing setup. The company's unwillingness to modify this setup was a criterion to be considered in the project.

As mentioned earlier, the central computer responsible for storing all the CSV files from the CNC machines serves as a landing zone where the data is initially stored in a temporary manner. However, beyond this point, AERNNOVA Corp. did not had any additional infrastructure implement, and the subsequent modules architecture outlined in Fig. 3 began to be constructed.

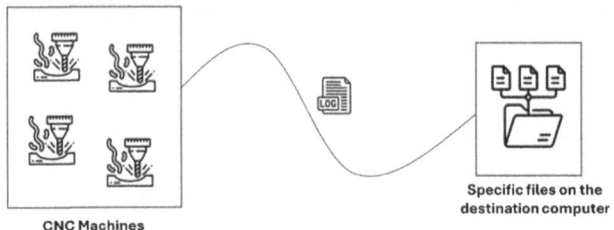

CNC Machines   Specific files on the
                                destination computer

Fig. 5. Infrastructure already built by AERNNOVA Corp.

Before proceeding with any implementation, a flow chart was developed, as shown in Fig. 6. This flow chart served to establish clear and understandable objectives for the tasks ahead. Initially, a mechanism was needed to continually monitor the folders on the central computer (landing zone). This mechanism had to account not only for the creation of new CSV files but also for changes to existing ones. To facilitate manipulation and human readability when stored in the data lake, all CSV files arriving at the landing zone were converted to JSON format. After the creation or alteration of the CSV files, a corresponding JSON file is generated with the same name containing the data from the CSV. This JSON file is then immediately stored in the data lake without any modifications. As for the data warehouse, the data from the JSON file undergoes filtering, cleaning, and processing according to the criteria set by AERNNOVA Corp. before the selected metrics are extracted.

With a combination of the flowchart (Fig. 6) and the proposed architecture (Fig. 3), a data pipeline has been constructed. AERNNOVA Corp. imposed a restriction on the utilization of the data lake, requiring it to be implemented in a cloud database named CosmosDB [20]. The choice for the data warehouse was PostgreSQL [21], mainly because it was a technology the authors were comfortable with and was already being used at AERNNOVA Corp. Additionally, all intermediate programs were developed in Python, including the visualization endpoint made with Python Flask framework, due to the authors' experience with Python and its simplicity. Taking all these points into consideration, the final data pipeline was created, as demonstrated in Fig. 7.

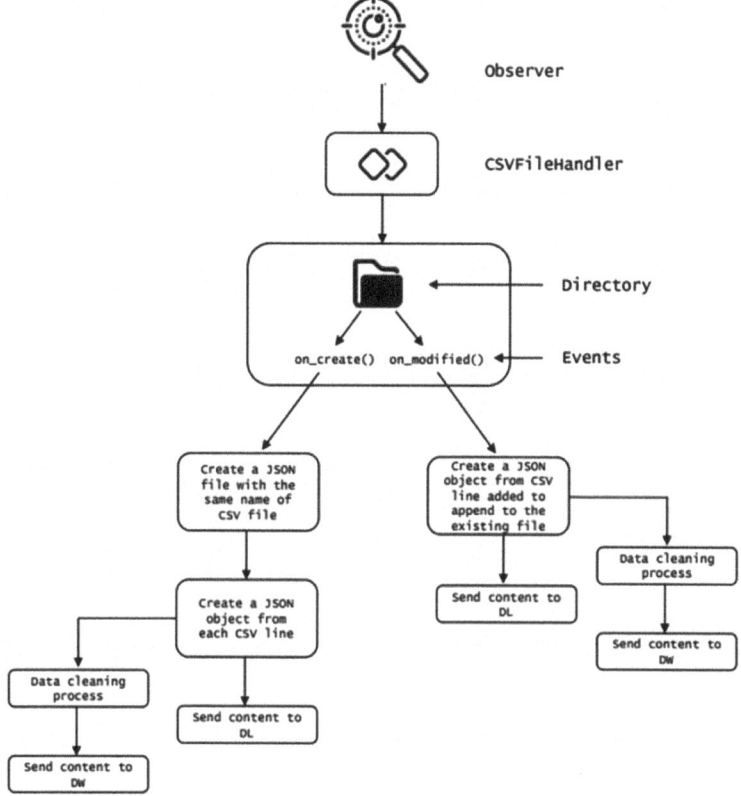

Fig. 6. Data Pipeline flowchart.

Regarding the implementation of the data pipeline, it is important to assess the data model as well. Figure 8 presents the diagram of the data model implemented, providing a clear view of the multitude of data that arrives at the landing zone.

Much of this data may be irrelevant for the current objectives of data visualization at AERNNOVA Corp. In Fig. 8, several fields from the CSV compose the log messages that come from the CNC machines. This data is then transformed into JSON format, with an added ID, and sent directly to the data lake.

In contrast, the data warehouse processes the information by cleaning and structuring it according to the final visualization objectives. It's important to understand that the data warehouse's ultimate objective is to store KPIs and visualizations metrics. However, if the objective shifts to a different type of analysis, the processing phase can be adjusted accordingly, allowing the data warehouse to store data needed for various types of analysis or visualization as required.

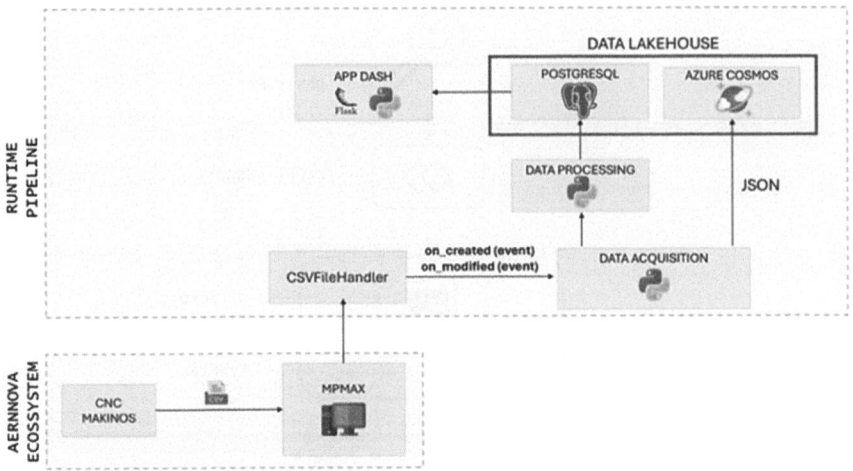

Fig. 7. Data Pipeline implemented in AERNNOVA Corp.

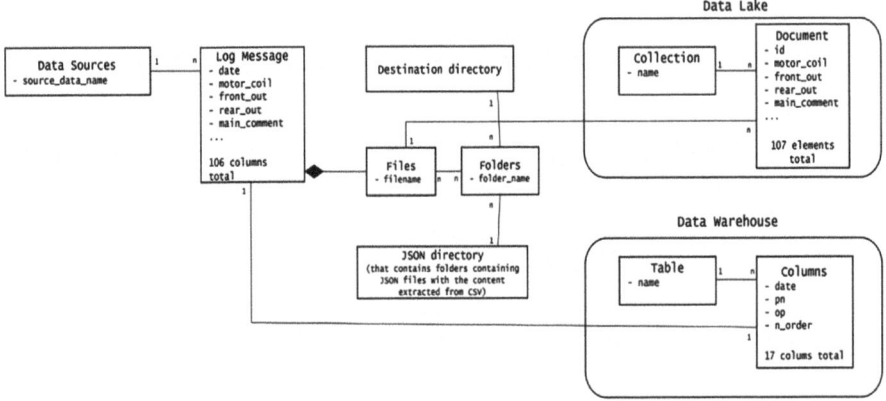

Fig. 8. Data Model implemented in AERNNOVA Corp.

4.2 Proof of Concept

The results can be presented and subsequently divided into three parts. Firstly, the results of the storage in the data lake; then, the results of the storage metrics in the data warehouse. The third result comes from the visualization app, where the KPIs and metrics are displayed.

In Fig. 9, it is possible to see the information stored in the data lake and data warehouse. It is important to note that the data is still organized into collections referring to each machine in the data lake, whereas in the data warehouse, the machine ID serves as the primary identification. It is possible to see the production of each machine their conclusion data, the spindle load, the command speed, among other metrics. These metrics have been previously calculated and separated from the raw data and are the key metrics to make the KPIs and consequently the visualization deemed critical by the company.

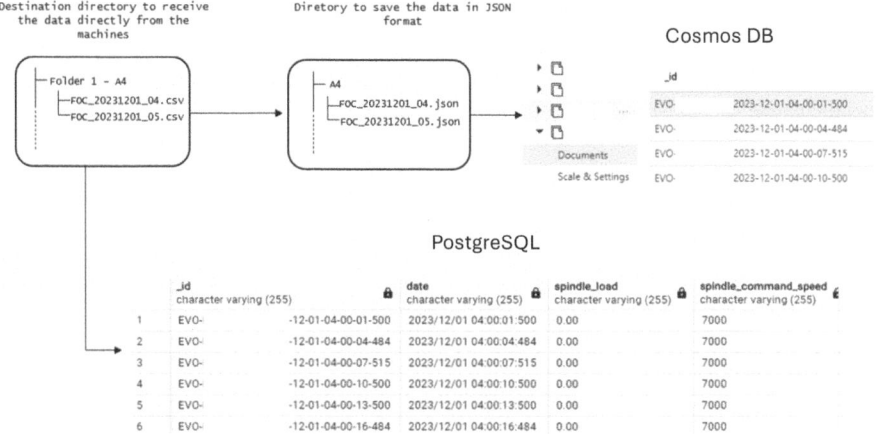

Fig. 9. Results of the implementation of the Data Lakehouse.

For the visualization app, two metrics are particularly important. The first is the performance indicators in percentage, calculated based on the real and theoretical times captured by the machines. Although the specific KPIs cannot be disclosed to protect the company's interests, these metrics are derived from critical information gathered from raw data, which is then stored in a PostgreSQL database. As shown in Fig. 10, one of the project's primary goals has been achieved: automating the metric calculations through the pipeline implementation, which extracts results from a system previously relying on CSV storage.

In Fig. 10, we can see that machine AM.2 exhibits lower performance according to the data harvested and calculated KPIs. Group M1 represents the weighted average of the group, along with some other critical KPIs, while the overall performance indicator reflects the combined performance of all the groups in the factory.

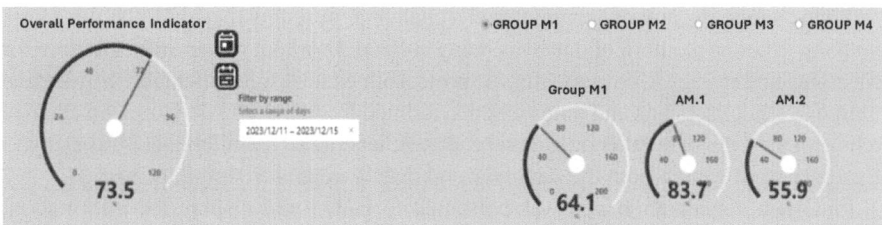

Fig. 10. Visualization app with the production indicators.

The last result concerns the specific choice of a machine, as shown in Fig. 11. This visualization is intended to identify performance results or verify the results of a specific process or part. Figure 11 illustrates a specific problem where the metric between theoretical and actual machine time is abnormally high. As can be seen in Fig. 10, the performance of the machine labelled AM.2 is low, which indicates a problem. With

Fig. 11, it can be concluded that, potentially, the part number labelled 1 was responsible for this problem, since the difference between the theoretical and actual times is around seventeen hours. This indicates that action needs to be taken or that an expected problem was the cause of this situation.

Fig. 11. Visualization app with the production of a specific machine.

5   Conclusions

More data than ever is being collected in industries to enhance understanding of the processes occurring on the shop floor. In an era where efficiency is paramount, this step is crucial. However, increasingly large volumes of data are being harvested without a clear intent for its use, and without clear guidance on how to achieve goals when they arise.

In this paper, the authors encountered a challenge posed by the AERNNOVA Corp. company, where a plethora of data was being collected without proper infrastructure for processing and storage. Consequently, the project aimed to design and establish a pipeline tailored to meet the needs and requirements outlined by AERNNOVA Corp. An adapted architecture of the data lakehouse was proposed, leveraging parallel data processing to efficiently store data in both the data lake and data warehouses simultaneously.

Finally, a visualization app was presented to gather and display the information, generating simple metrics. This app serves as a demonstration of the automation of several manual processes, with potential for further expansion of the project.

With the infrastructure in place, several other data analyses can commence as future work. One such suggestion by both the authors and AERNNOVA Corp. is the utilization of the data in the data lake to train a model capable of advising on predictive projects for the CNC machines. Additionally, there is potential for predictive energy consumption analysis, promoting sustainability on the shop floor. Both of these initiatives carry significant scientific implications and can enhance the efficiency of AERNNOVA Corp.'s manufacturing processes. Concerning the data warehouse, efforts can be made to include all necessary metrics for automatic calculation and to upgrade the visualization interface to encompass not only the data warehouse but also the data lake, thereby creating a comprehensive data lakehouse visualization app.

Implementations of data lakehouses are rarely encountered in the literature. This paper provides a clear example of how a data lakehouse architecture can significantly benefit one of the most rigorous manufacturing processes on the shop floor. It demonstrates the use of specific and appropriate tools for handling various types of data and achieving the goals present in the manufacturing environment.

Acknowledgments. This work was funded in part by Fundação para a Ciência e Tecnologia through the program UIDB/00066/2020 and Center of Technology and Systems (CTS).

Disclosure of Interests. We declare that the authors have no competing interests.

References

1. Qi, C.: Big data management in the mining industry. Int. J. Miner. Metall. Mater. **27**(2), 131–139 (2020). https://doi.org/10.1007/s12613-019-1937-z
2. Brous, P., Janssen, M., Krans, R.: Data governance as success factor for data science. In: Hattingh, M., Matthee, M., Smuts, H., Pappas, I., Dwivedi, Y., Mäntymäki, M. (eds.) I3E 2020. LNCS, vol. 12066, pp. 431–442. Springer, Cham (2020). https://doi.org/10.1007/978-3-030-44999-5_36
3. Malik, P.K., et al.: Industrial internet of things and its applications in industry 4.0: state of the art. Comput. Commun. **166**, 125–139 (2021). https://doi.org/10.1016/j.comcom.2020.11.016
4. Ikegwu, A.C., Nweke, H.F., Anikwe, C.V., Alo, U.R., Okonkwo, O.R.: Big data analytics for data-driven industry: a review of data sources, tools, challenges, solutions, and research directions. Clust. Comput. **25**(5), 3343–3387 (2022). https://doi.org/10.1007/s10586-022-035 68-5
5. Hlupic, T., Orescanin, D., Ruzak, D., Baranovic, M.: An overview of current data lake architecture models. In: 2022 45th Jubilee International Convention on Information, Communication and Electronic Technology (MIPRO), pp. 1082–1087. IEEE, May 2022. https://doi.org/10. 23919/MIPRO55190.2022.9803717
6. Orescanin, D., Hlupic, T.: Data lakehouse - a novel step in analytics architecture. In: 2021 44th International Convention on Information, Communication and Electronic Technology (MIPRO), pp. 1242–1246. IEEE, September 2021. https://doi.org/10.23919/MIPRO52101. 2021.9597091
7. Mazumdar, D., Hughes, J., Onofre, J.: The data lakehouse: data warehousing and more, October 2023. http://arxiv.org/abs/2310.08697
8. Munirathinam, S.: Industry 4.0: industrial Internet of Things (IIOT). In: Advances in Computers, vol. 117, no. 1, pp. 129–164. Academic Press Inc. (2020). https://doi.org/10.1016/bs. adcom.2019.10.010
9. Kagermann, H., Wahlster, W.: Ten years of industrie 4.0. Sci **4**(3), 26 (2022). https://doi.org/ 10.3390/sci4030026
10. González García, C., Álvarez-Fernández, E.: What is (not) big data based on its 7Vs challenges: a survey. Big Data Cogn. Comput. **6**(4), 158 (2022). https://doi.org/10.3390/bdcc60 40158

11. Naeem, M., et al.: Trends and future perspective challenges in big data. In: Pan, J.S., Balas, V.E., Chen, C.M. (eds.) Advances in Intelligent Data Analysis and Applications. SIST, vol. 253, pp. 309–325. Springer, Singapore (2022). https://doi.org/10.1007/978-981-16-5036-9_30

12. Munappy, A.R., Bosch, J., Olsson, H.H.: Data pipeline management in practice: challenges and opportunities. In: Morisio, M., Torchiano, M., Jedlitschka, A. (eds.) PROFES 2020. LNCS, vol. 12562, pp. 168–184. Springer, Cham (2020). https://doi.org/10.1007/978-3-030-64148-1_11

13. Harby, A.A., Zulkernine, F.: From data warehouse to lakehouse: a comparative review. In: Proceedings - 2022 IEEE International Conference on Big Data, Big Data 2022, pp. 389–395. Institute of Electrical and Electronics Engineers Inc. (2022). https://doi.org/10.1109/BigDat a55660.2022.10020719

14. Armbrust, M., Ghodsi, A., Xin, R., Zaharia, M., Berkeley, U.: Lakehouse: a new generation of open platforms that unify data warehousing and advanced analytics (2021)

15. Nambiar, A., Mundra, D.: An overview of data warehouse and data lake in modern enterprise data management. Big Data Cogn. Comput. **6**(4), 132 (2022). https://doi.org/10.3390/bdcc60 40132

16. ur Rehman, K.U., Ahmad, U., Mahmood, S.: A comparative analysis of traditional and cloud data warehouse. VAWKUM Trans. Comput. Sci. **15**(1), 34 (2018). https://doi.org/10.21015/ vtcs.v15i1.487

17. Antunes, A.L., Cardoso, E., Barateiro, J.: Incorporation of ontologies in data warehouse/business intelligence systems - a systematic literature review. Int. J. Inf. Manag. Data Insights **2**(2), 100131 (2022). https://doi.org/10.1016/j.jjimei.2022.100131

18. Kern, R., Kozierkiewicz, A., Pietranik, M.: The data richness estimation framework for federated data warehouse integration. Inf. Sci. **513**, 397–411 (2020). https://doi.org/10.1016/j. ins.2019.10.046

19. Loukiala, A., Joutsenlahti, J.P., Raatikainen, M., Mikkonen, T., Lehtonen, T.: Migrating from a centralized data warehouse to a decentralized data platform architecture. In: Ardito, L., Jedlitschka, A., Morisio, M., Torchiano, M. (eds.) PROFES 2021. LNCS, vol. 13126, pp. 36–48. Springer, Cham (2021). https://doi.org/10.1007/978-3-030-91452-3_3

20. CosmosDB (2024). https://azure.microsoft.com/en-us/products/cosmos-db. Accessed 17 Sept 2024

21. PostgresSQL (2024). https://www.postgresql.org/. Accessed 17 Sept 2024

Multi-agent Path Planning for Logistics Cargo Environment Using LSTM Based Reinforcement Learning

Gun Rae Cho[✉], Sungho Park, Eui-Jung Jung, Hyunseok Shin, So Eun Son, and Yong Choi

Korea Institute of Robotics and Technology Convergence, Pohang 37666, Republic of Korea
{sandman,psh84,ejjung,shin_hyunseok,
smallsilver,potchy0927}@kiro.re.kr

Abstract. In the operation of logistics cargo, temporal efficiency in handling logistics is a critical issue. One solution to enhance this efficiency is the deployment of multiple autonomous ground vehicles (AGVs). This paper proposes a reinforcement learning approach based on Long Short-Term Memory (LSTM) for multi-agent path planning in the logistics cargo environment. When AGVs are treated as moving obstacles to each other, the application of LSTM allows for path planning that aptly addresses changes over time within the environment. Additionally, to solve the well-known problem of the sparse reward in pathfinding, we propose a reinforcement learning architecture for multi-agent path planning that uses the path planning results of a single agent, guided by Q-learning, as the guide path. Furthermore, we have established state variables independent of the number of agents by setting interest window-based state variables, and introduced revisit rewards, effectively resolving the issue of local minima caused by repetitive movement-avoidance behavior between agents. Simulation results, emulating a real-world logistics warehouse environment, demonstrate the proposed technique's capability for effective multi-agent path planning in such settings.

Keywords: Multi-agent path planning · Reinforcement learning · Long-short term memory · Autonomous ground vehicles · Logistics cargo

1 Introduction

The logistics industry, encompassing storage and transportation, is rapidly growing. As the timely management of cargo logistics becomes increasingly critical, robotic systems such as Autonomous Ground Vehicles (AGVs) are being integrated into these environments to enhance efficiency. Employing multiple AGVs presents an effective strategy to boost the temporal efficiency of logistics operations. Multi-agent path planning emerges as a crucial technology for autonomous cargo systems. Yet, while optimal paths for single robots can often be determined using algorithms such as A-star [2, 17], the complexity of state changes in multi-robot scenarios complicates the design of optimal paths. Additionally, logistics warehouses are spaces where storage efficiency and

© The Author(s), under exclusive license to Springer Nature Switzerland AG 2025
M. Dassisti et al. (Eds.): IN4PL 2024, CCIS 2372, pp. 425–439, 2025.
https://doi.org/10.1007/978-3-031-80760-2_27

the efficiency of transporting goods are paramount. To increase storage capacity, it is necessary to consider environmental constraints, such as limiting the width of the travel paths.

In the context of logistics warehouses, the application of reinforcement learning for path planning in multi-robot systems is a compelling area of study. Numerous existing studies corroborate its potential, each contributing nuanced strategies to the discourse. For instance, the work by Yang et al. (2020) [18] introduces a Deep Q-Network (DQN) based reinforcement learning algorithm that employs a collective state vector for all agents. This approach, while innovative, may not scale efficiently for scenarios involving a high number of agents due to the exponential increase in the state space and the consequential demand on the neural network's capacity. Wang et al. (2020) [15] pivot to a Reinforcement Learning (RL) algorithm that leverages Long Short-Term Memory (LSTM) networks. Concurrently, Liu et al. (2020) [10] proposed an evolutionary approach to reinforcement learning, utilizing the Advantage Actor-Critic (A2C) framework. Both studies, however, seem to assume environments with broader passageways that facilitate simultaneous transit of multiple agents, which may not be representative of all warehouse scenarios. Hong et al. (2022) [4] and Hwang et al. (2020) [6] proposed a dynamic Q-learning based algorithm for route guidance specifically tailored to overhead hoist transport systems. Their method is praised for its simplicity and efficacy but is primarily applicable to environments designed for unidirectional traffic flow.

It is evident from these studies that while reinforcement learning holds promise for efficient path planning in multi-robot systems, there remains a need for algorithms that can robustly handle varied and complex environmental constraints typical of real-world logistics warehouses. This includes spaces with limited passageway widths and bidirectional flow, which demand a higher degree of algorithmic flexibility and environmental adaptability. In the logistics warehouse setting, the implementation of multi-agent systems necessitates a path planning capability that can respond to dynamically changing environments. This requirement arises from the fact that multiple agents, when in motion, serve as moving obstacles to one another. Additionally, it is well-documented that the pathfinding issue is prone to the sparse reward problem [16], where significant rewards are only obtained upon reaching the destination, thus complicating the design of rewards that guide actions towards the goal during transit.

Consequently, this paper introduces a multi-agent path planning algorithm for the logistics warehouse environment utilizing reinforcement learning based on Long Short-Term Memory (LSTM) [3,13,15]. The application of LSTM is particularly suitable for environments where multiple AGVs operate and are treated as obstacles to one another, as it can effectively manage state changes over time. The introduction of interest window-based state variables allows for the configuration of state variables that do not depend on the number of AGVs. By securing information on the optimal residual path for a single-agent scenario through Q-learning, and employing this data for guide paths and to verify residual distances, the algorithm overcomes the sparse reward problem [16]. Furthermore, the introduction of rewards related to revisits prevents agents from falling into local minima due to repetitive movement and avoidance behaviors. Finally, the proposed algorithm has been validated through simulations that mimic a real-world logistics warehouse environment.

Fig. 1. Logistics cargo for palletized loads.

2   LSTM Based Learning for Multi-agent Path Planning in Cargo Environment

2.1   Cargo Environment and Problem Definition

The paper focuses on the cargo environment for regular-sized logistics such as palletized loads, as shown in Fig. 1. The logistics cargo house consists of several areas as follows:

- areas for stocking logistics having dual column each of which approachable in opposite direction,
- passageways for logistics movement, and
- other places, e.g., area for AGV stand-by, area for logistics palletizing or depalletizing, and gate for logistics entrance or exit.

It is noteworthy that the stocking capacity is a crucial issue in the logistics cargo; therefore, the passageways are typically designed with a regular width of approximately 3.2 m, which can only accommodate one AGV for storing, retrieving, or moving the logistics.

Logistics handling speed is another significant concern in cargo houses, as logistics are stored and retrieved with temporal efficiency. One of the easiest ways to improve efficiency is to use multiple AGVs. In this case, the path planning problem for multi-agents is critical for improving efficiency and preventing accidents.

Figure 2 depicts the simulation environment utilized in this paper. The white spheres represent the AGVs, the yellow cubes depict the goal positions, the bottom-left corners indicate the areas where the AGVs can stand-by or charge their batteries, and the bottom-middle corner represents the door used for logistics transportation.

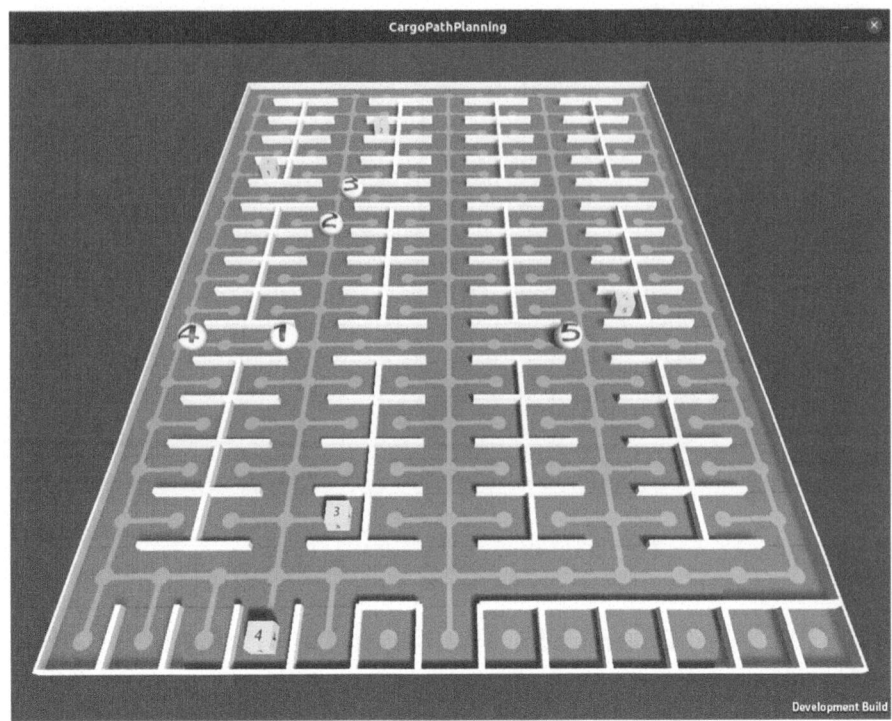

Fig. 2. Cargo environment for the simulation.

2.2 Structure of Reinforcement Learning for Multi-agent Path Planning

The general structure of reinforcement learning is depicted in Fig. 3. In this framework, an agent performs actions within an environment, and as a result, the environment provides changed state variables and rewards based on those actions. Reinforcement learning progresses by maximizing rewards, thereby guiding the agent towards an optimal or near-optimal outcome. In designing algorithms based on reinforcement learning, the essential components include the selection of state variables, the design of rewards, and the configuration and design of the learning model and methodology.

When designing reinforcement learning for multi-robot path planning, the primary considerations can be summarized as follows:

– In terms of state variable design, it is essential to use state variables of a dimension independent of the number of agents. This prevents the increase in dimensionality of state variables and network complexity as the number of agents increases.
– In reward design, addressing the commonly encountered sparse reward problem in path planning is crucial. It is also important to prevent local minima caused by repetitive movement and avoidance behaviors to ensure the learning process converges effectively.
– Regarding the design of the learning model, it is necessary to account for dynamic changes in the environment, such as obstacles. Applying the same model to all robots

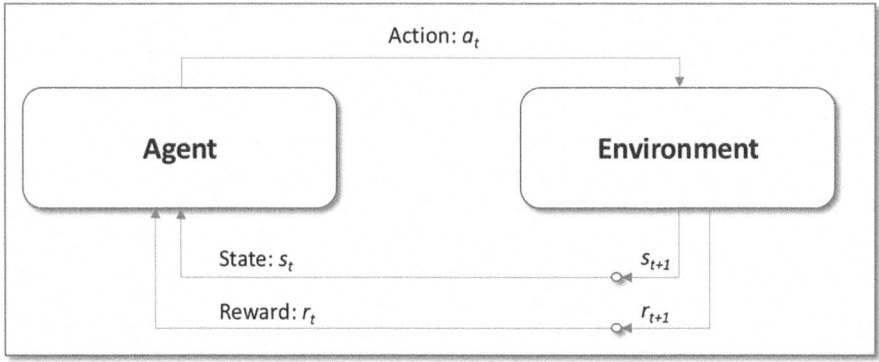

Fig. 3. Structure of reinforcement learning.

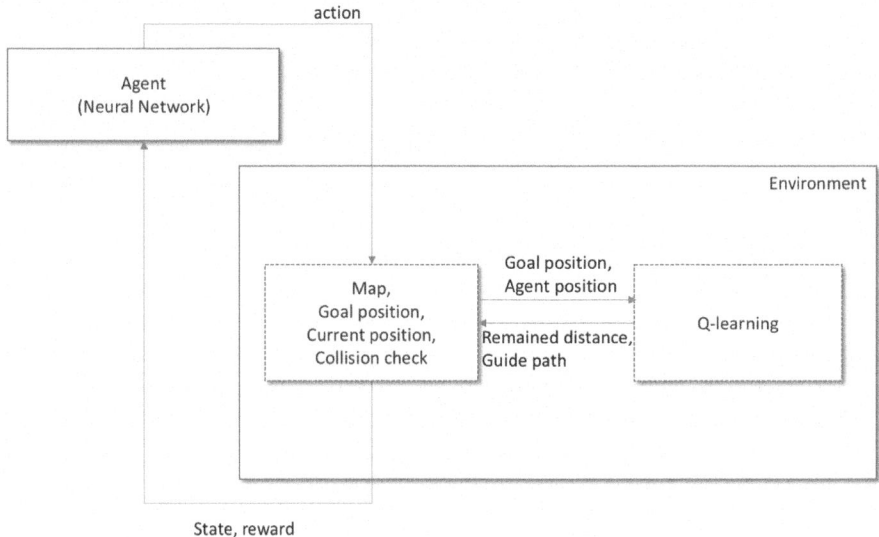

Fig. 4. Reinforcement learning: pre-trained Q-learning is used for generating guide path and obtaining remained distance.

can prevent the increase in the learning cost associated with individual path planning for multiple agents.

Pathfinding problems are prone to the sparse reward problem because significant rewards are only obtained upon reaching the destination [16]. The sparse reward problem makes it challenging to converge the network in reinforcement learning, and research on overcoming this issue is ongoing, as seen in approaches like Never Give Up [1] and Hierarchical Deep Reinforcement Learning [7]. Additionally, in situations with multiple agents operating simultaneously, repetitive movements and avoidance behaviors among robots towards their destinations can occur.

To address the challenges that arise when applying reinforcement learning to multi-robot path planning, this study considers additional state variables beyond the map, agents, and target locations. These additional state variables include the optimal path and remaining distance to the target, assuming a single agent operation. This can be resolved using well-known algorithms such as A-star [2, 17] or Q-learning [5, 11]. By incorporating a routine within the environment that calculates the remaining distance and guide path to the target, and using this information as part of the state information, we aim to address issues related to convergence, such as the sparse reward problem.

The reinforcement learning structure designed in this study is illustrated in Fig. 4. The environment includes a Q-learning component that calculates the guide path and remaining distance information for the case of a single agent operation. This information is used to generate the state and reward provided by the environment. This study has designed a path planning strategy based on Q-learning to calculate the remaining distance to the target. Q-learning, which uses a Q-table to find actions for each state, can reduce computation in the inference stage compared to A-star, which searches for optimal paths. It also allows for the calculation of guide paths for single agent. To this end, we conducted preliminary learning of optimal path planning based on Q-learning for a single agent. While Q-learning is included in the environment in Fig. 4 from a semantic standpoint, in actual implementation, it can be incorporated as a step where the agent modifies the state and reward right before receiving environmental information.

2.3   Design of State Variables

In this study, we introduced the state variables with dimensions that remain constant regardless of the number of agents. As mentioned in the introduction, selecting all agents' states as the state variables would lead to an increase in the dimensionality of the state variables with an increasing number of agents. While managing a few robots might not pose a significant issue, considering cases like KIVA [9], where hundreds to thousands of robots are operated simultaneously, could result in substantial computational costs due to large-dimensional state variables. To design state variables independent of the number of operating agents, this study considered forms like a 2D map image, a method extensively used in reinforcement learning with screen images of Atari games [12] and applied in multi-agents path planning [15]. However, given that an image comprises many pixels and contains a lot of information, this study applied a 2D state variable represented by nodes indicating major points of paths.

The state variables designed in this study can be seen in Fig. 5. A rectangular window area centered around the agent was quantified as state variables, allowing the agent to monitor states within a certain range centered on itself. This is reasonable because states at a significantly far distance from agent's location do not largely impact the current path planning. The state variables for the same time are composed of three channels: i) map information, ii) guide paths and target locations, and iii) obstacle (other agents) locations.

The first channel represents map information, detailing the walls that agents cannot move through at each node. Although map information could be designed as an image, wall information at each node was represented numerically for efficient notation. Each wall's position was assigned a binary characteristic number (1 for a left wall, 2 for an upper wall, 4 for a right wall, 8 for a lower wall), and the combination of these numbers expresses the wall information. Since 1, 2, 4, 8 represent 0x0001, 0x0010, 0x0100, 0x1000 in binary, they can express independent information. Thus, the map information at each node is the sum of the numbers assigned to the wall information on all four sides.

The second channel represents the state information of the agent's position and target location. Since the state information is displayed concerning the window area centered on the agent, the '1' in the middle of the state information denotes agent's position, and '10' denotes the target location. Additionally, a line of '1's connecting the agent to the target location represents the optimal path during single robot operation, which can be generated by methods like A-star or pre-trained Q-learning. Since the state information is set for the window area centered on the agent, the target location may not always be within the window. However, even in such cases, path planning to the target is possible by guiding using the optimal path information for single agent operation.

The third channel provides information about the location of obstacles. Considering situations where multiple agents operate simultaneously, AGVs other than the agent designated are treated as obstacles. As illustrated in Fig. 5, when generating the path for AGV#1, AGV#2 and #3 within AGV#1's window are considered obstacles and marked with '1'. Naturally, besides other AGVs, other obstacles may exist on the path, and their representation can also be added to the states.

By configuring the state variables into three channels (map information, robot/target location information, obstacle information) and considering only the window area centered around the agent, the size of the state variables remains constant regardless of the number of robots operating simultaneously.

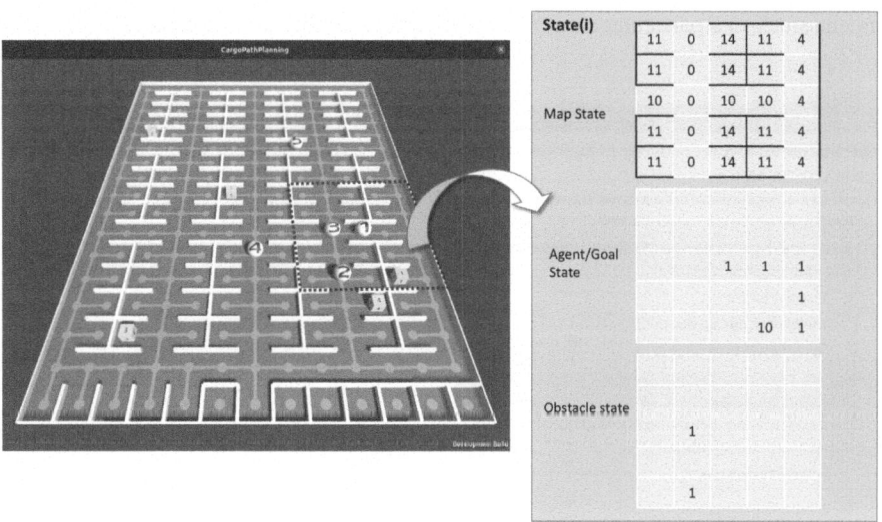

Fig. 5. Definition of the states.

2.4 Design of Rewards

To address the path planning problem for multi-agents, rewards were designed and as four types: i) Action Reward, i) Destination Arrival Reward, iii) Remaining Distance Reward, and iv) Revisit Reward. The designed rewards are summarized in Fig. 6.

Action Reward and Destination Arrival Reward are commonly set rewards in path planning problems. Specifically, by providing a negative reward for each action performed, the Action Reward encourages minimizing the number of actions. Particularly in the design of Action Reward, the reward for stopping actions is set slightly higher than for moving actions to prevent the robot from remaining stationary. Furthermore, a significant negative reward is given for collisions with walls or obstacles to avoid collisions. The Destination Arrival Reward motivates movement towards the destination by offering a substantial positive reward upon arrival.

To tackle the sparse reward problem, a Remaining Distance Reward was introduced. This reward is calculated based on the change in the remaining distance to the destination before and after taking an action, thereby encouraging the choice of actions that decrease the distance to the destination. This method enables the agent to evaluate the effectiveness of its actions towards reaching the destination by determining if they have successfully reduced the remaining distance, thus addressing the sparse reward issue.

Lastly, a Revisit Reward was developed. As depicted in Fig. 7, when all AGVs operate under the same policy, encountering two or more AGVs can lead to a predictable pattern of avoidance and movement. This is particularly noticeable in scenarios like the one studied, where the pathway is narrow, only accommodating one AGV at a time, leading to a cycle of repetitive avoidance and progression due to mutual interference among the AGVs. To address this issue, a reward was established based on the frequency of revisits to each node. The objective is to avoid scenarios where an AGV remains stuck in a particular area of the path, repeating the same actions.

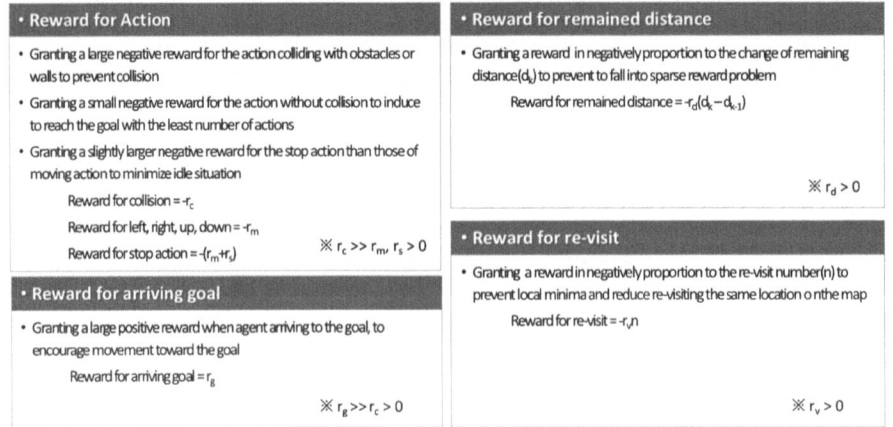

Fig. 6. The design of reward for multi-agent path planning in logistics cargo environment.

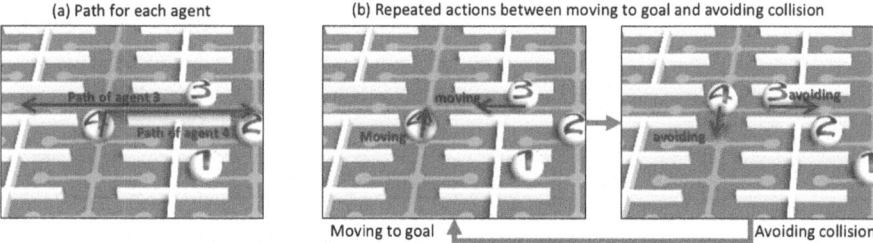

Fig. 7. The case when the agents repeat actions between moving to goal and avoiding collision.

2.5   Design of Learning Network Based on LSTM

In the context of multi-agent path planning, it is reasonable to apply the same policy to all agents. Designing individual algorithms for each agent would increase the number of algorithms needed as the number of agents grows. Moreover, since AGVs move simultaneously for tasks, considering other AGVs as obstacles means that state variables (especially obstacle information) change over time, necessitating consideration in network design. Therefore, this study aims to construct a neural network based on LSTM, capable of handling temporal state changes, improving upon RNN's performance by learning time patterns through long-term and short-term memory.

For multi-agent path planning, the neural network for reinforcement learning should be able to select optimal actions based on state and reward inputs from the environment. This study considers five actions: moving left, up, right, down, and stopping. The selection of optimal actions was based on the Q-values of actions.

The proposed reinforcement learning neural network is illustrated in Fig. 8. To perform multi-agent path planning, the network must: i) accept 2D matrix structure state variables, ii) handle dynamic changes in state, and, iii) select the optimal action through Q-value derivation.

As shown in Fig. 8, a Convolutional Neural Network (CNN) capable of processing 2D matrix state variables was implemented. It extracts 1D array information from state information spanning current time, $t = i$, to past k-steps, $t = i - k$, through CNN. This 1D array information for each time step is input into an LSTM structure, which outputs an array of results. These results are then simplified through a fully connected layer to produce the Q-values for the final action.

The learning technique applied is Double DQN (DDQN) [14], proposed to address the overestimation of action values inherent in traditional DQN. The exploration-exploitation strategy employed is epsilon-greedy, with soft updates [8] applied to target network updates.

3   Simulation

In this study Q-learning was utilized to check the guide path and remaining distance for path planning. The result of Q-learning is then used to design path planning for multi-agent scenarios. In other words, the following two steps are validated through simulation:

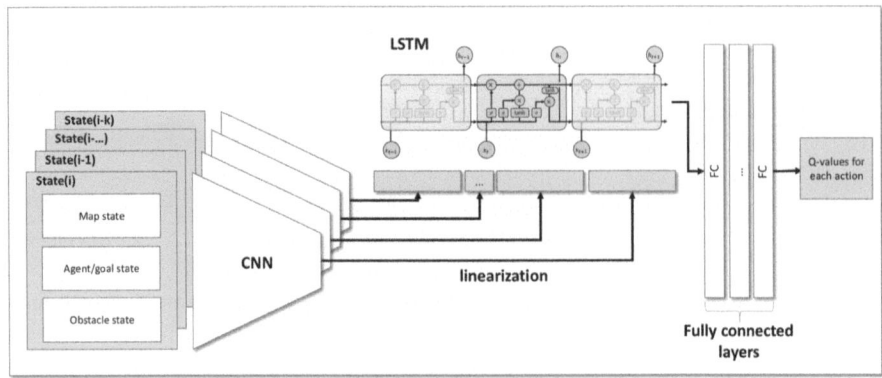

Fig. 8. Design of the neural network using LSTM.

– Learning the shortest path based on Q-learning for a single agent.
– Learning path planning based on LSTM for multiple agents.

3.1 Pre-training of Q-Learning for Single Agent

For generating optimal paths, Q-learning based path planning is pre-trained to create guide paths and calculate remaining distances. The Q-learning based path planning technique for a single agent, a somewhat classical problem, is defined as follows:

– State: agent position, goal position
– Reward: Action Reward, and Destination Arrival Reward
– Action: Five types (left, up, right, down, stop)

The exploration-exploitation strategy employed is epsilon-greedy. Furthermore, to verify whether an optimal path has been generated, the results were compared with those of A-star. Pathfinding results were compared by generating 10,000 random target points, ensuring both Q-learning and A-star used identical target points, of which results are depicted in Fig. 9. From Fig. 9, it can be observed that the number of actions required by Q-learning is equivalent to that of A-star, both averaging 11.54 actions. The results allow for two inferences:

– It can be inferred that Q-learning can derive an optimal path minimizing actions. Although not mathematically verified, this inference is possible as two different algorithms produced equivalent results.
– In the environment used for the simulation, the minimum number of actions for a single agent to reach its destination averages $n_0 = 11.54$.

Since it can be inferred that an optimal solution has been reached for a single robot, the results of Q-learning can be used to calculate each robot's guide path and remaining distance. Here, the guide path indicates the fastest route to the destination if there were no other robots or obstacles, and the remaining distance represents the number of actions needed to follow the fastest route. In this study, the Q-learning based guide path is used as the 'agent/goal state' path in Fig. 5, and the remaining distance is utilized when designing rewards for remained distance in Fig. 6.

The optimal number of actions for a single agent identified through Q-learning can serve as a baseline for evaluating the efficiency of path planning algorithms when extended to multiple agents. It is anticipated that the number of actions to reach the destination will increase for multiple agents as the process of avoiding other AGVs or obstacles is added. Using the average number of actions $n_0 = 11.54$ as a baseline, it is possible to gauge how much this increases compared to a single robot scenario. Naturally, a smaller increase indicates a more efficient multi-agent path planning strategy.

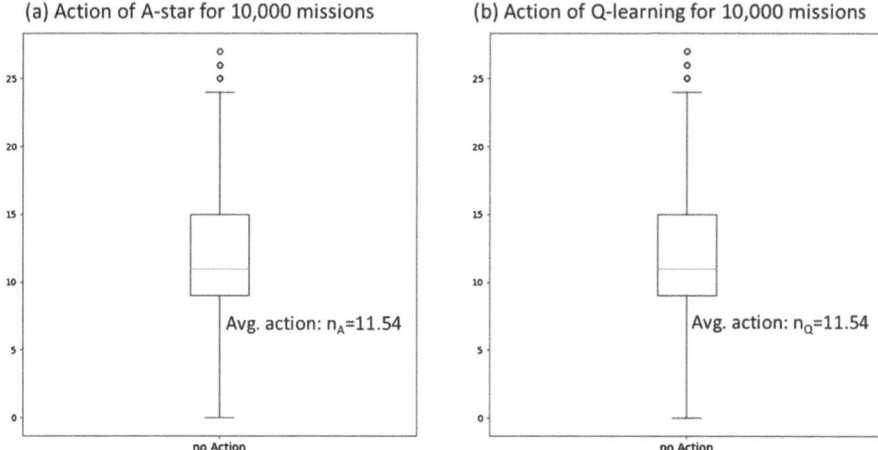

Fig. 9. Box plots of actions: A-star and Q-learning.

3.2   LSTM Based Reinforcement Learning For Multiple Agents

In this study, we demonstrated the performance of the proposed LSTM-based reinforcement learning. As seen in Fig. 2, the network was trained for scenarios where five agents operate simultaneously. The results are illustrated in Figs. 10–12. Figure 10 shows the average number of actions taken to complete 50 missions, indicating that the number of actions decreases as training progresses, thereby demonstrating an improvement in path planning efficiency.

Figures 11–12 present the results observed after training completion, varying the number of agents from two to five. Figure 11 illustrates the average number of actions required for each agent to complete a single mission. As can be seen, the average number of actions slightly increases as the number of agents grows, which is a natural outcome considering multiple agents act as obstacles to each other. Even with five agents operating, the result is commendable, with an average increase of only about 3.12 actions from the baseline (average 11.54 actions for a single agent), totaling an average of 14.66 actions. Figure 12 depicts the number of actions required per mission, considering the simultaneous operation of multiple agents. With five agents working together, there's a reduction to about 2.93 actions, which is approximately a 25.4% of the single agent case (11.54 actions). Although this is slightly higher than the ideal case of no mutual interference among five agents (2.31 actions, 20%), it significantly reduces the operation time compared to a single agent. While it's challenging to theoretically verify the optimality due to the nature of deep learning, considering the given environment and the number of robots, it's a reasonable outcome when frequent avoidance actions are factored in.

For instance, assuming that all actions take an equal amount of time, t_a, and ignoring time spent on other activities such as loading or unloading, a single AGV can complete missions at a rate of $1/(11.54t_a)$ per unit time. In the case when five AGVs are operated simultaneously, they can perform missions at a rate of $5AGVs \times 1/(14.66t_a)$ per unit time, predicting that logistics movement can be approximately 3.94 times faster than single AGV operation. Therefore, using multiple AGVs with proposed path planning algorithm can significantly increase logistics processing efficiency compared to using a single AGV.

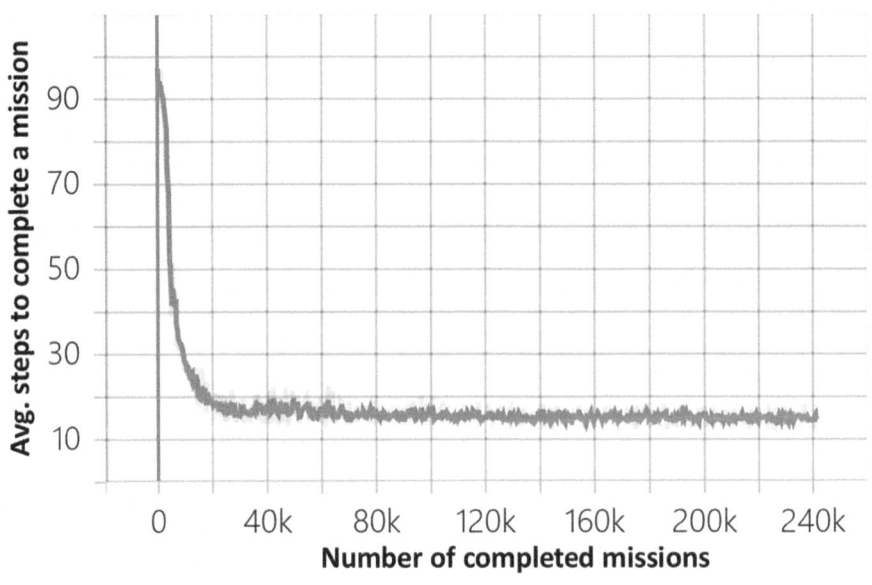

Fig. 10. Averaged number of steps to complete a mission.

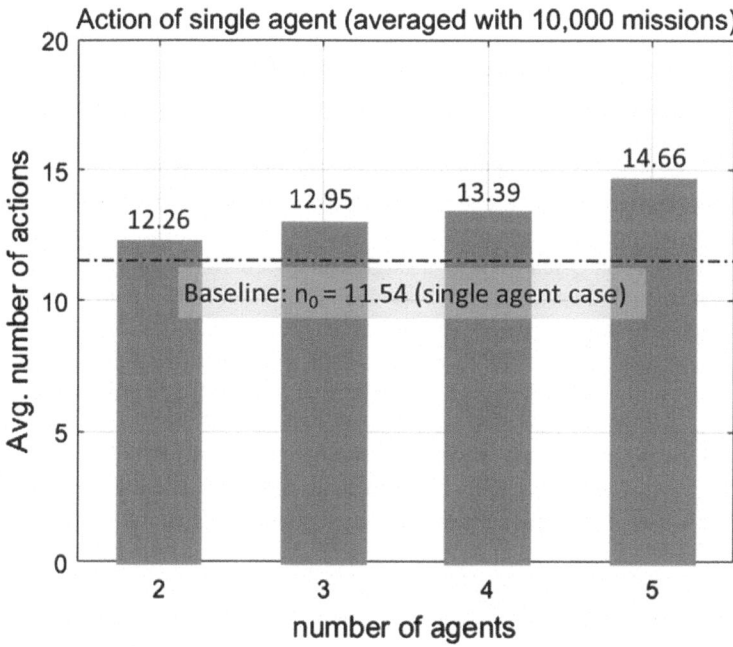

Fig. 11. Averaged actions for each agent to complete a mission.

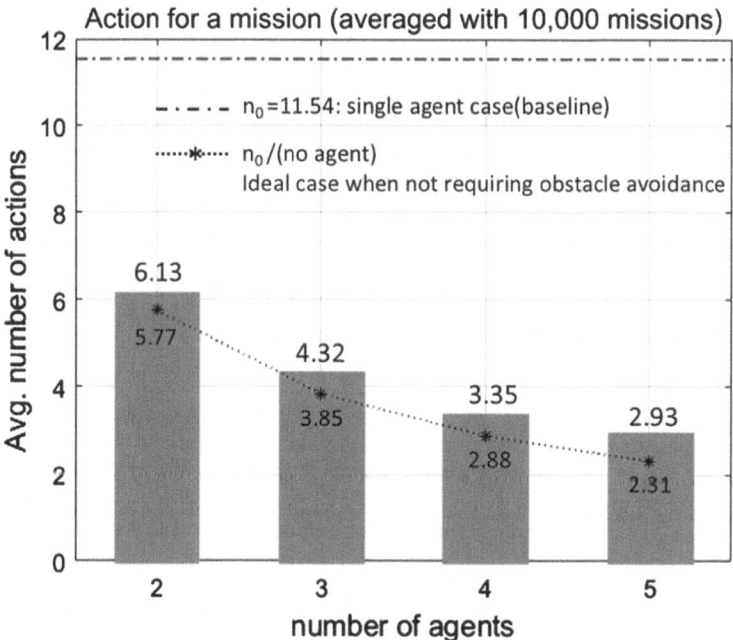

Fig. 12. Averaged actions for a mission: (no. actions)/(no. agents).

4 Conclusion

In this paper, we address the path planning challenge for multiple AGVs to enhance the temporal efficiency of logistics operations within a cargo environment. We introduce a LSTM-based reinforcement learning, designed to manage the highly variable states of a multi-agent system. Utilizing interest window based states ensures the number of states remains constant, even as the number of agents increases. To overcome the sparse reward problem, we employ guide path states and rewards for remaining distance, derived through Q-learning for a single AGV scenario. Additionally, by incorporating revisit-related rewards, we have resolved the issue of local minima arising from mutual avoidance and movement patterns among multiple AGVs. Simulations within an environment that mimics a real logistics warehouse have validated the feasibility of multi-robot path planning using the proposed reinforcement learning approach. When applying five AGVs, we observed an efficiency increase of 3.94 times compared to a single AGV, demonstrating that leveraging multiple AGVs with an LSTM-based path planning approach can significantly boost logistics handling efficiency in warehouses.

Future plans include conducting experiments with multiple robots within a logistics warehouse to further validate the effectiveness of the proposed algorithm. The authors are developing stacker robots capable of transporting and loading palletized goods, which represent an advancement over AGVs. We aim to develop technology for operational testing of multiple robots in real-world settings. The multi-agent path planning developed in this study is expected to provide an effective path planning technique for operating numerous stacker robots.

Acknowledgments. This work was supported by Korea Evaluation Institute of Industrial Technology(KEIT) grant funded by the Korea government(MSIT) (No. 20015420, Development of stacker robot technology for standard pallet rack system having high degree of logistics stacking; partially, RS-2024-00457681, Development of an autonomous robot system for welding inspection process to improve LNG cargo tank manufacturing productivity).

Disclosure of Interests. The authors have no competing interests to declare that are relevant to the content of this article.

References

1. Badia, A.P., et al.: Never give up: Learning directed exploration strategies. arXiv preprint arXiv:2002.06038 (2020)
2. Duchoň, F., et al.: Path planning with modified a star algorithm for a mobile robot. Procedia Eng. **96**, 59–69 (2014)
3. Hochreiter, S., Schmidhuber, J.: Long short-term memory. Neural Comput. **9**(8), 1735–1780 (1997)
4. Hong, S., Hwang, I., Jang, Y.J.: Practical Q-learning-based route-guidance and vehicle assignment for OHT systems in semiconductor fabs. IEEE Trans. Semicond. Manuf. **35**(3), 385–396 (2022)
5. Hu, Y., Yang, L., Lou, Y.: Path planning with Q-learning. J. Phys. Conf. Ser. **1948**, 012038 (2021)

6. Hwang, I., Jang, Y.J.: Q (λ) learning-based dynamic route guidance algorithm for overhead hoist transport systems in semiconductor fabs. Int. J. Prod. Res. **58**(4), 1199–1221 (2020)
7. Kulkarni, T.D., Narasimhan, K., Saeedi, A., Tenenbaum, J.: Hierarchical deep reinforcement learning: integrating temporal abstraction and intrinsic motivation. In: Advances in Neural Information Processing Systems, vol. 29 (2016)
8. Lillicrap, T.P., et al.: Continuous control with deep reinforcement learning. arXiv preprint arXiv:1509.02971 (2015)
9. Liu, Y., Chen, M., Huang, H.: Multi-agent pathfinding based on improved cooperative a in kiva system. In: 2019 5th International Conference on Control, Automation and Robotics (ICCAR), pp. 633–638. IEEE (2019)
10. Liu, Z., Chen, B., Zhou, H., Koushik, G., Hebert, M., Zhao, D.: MAPPER: multi-agent path planning with evolutionary reinforcement learning in mixed dynamic environments. In: 2020 IEEE/RSJ International Conference on Intelligent Robots and Systems (IROS), pp. 11748–11754. IEEE (2020)
11. Maoudj, A., Hentout, A.: Optimal path planning approach based on Q-learning algorithm for mobile robots. Appl. Soft Comput. **97**, 106796 (2020)
12. Mnih, V., et al.: Playing Atari with deep reinforcement learning. arXiv preprint arXiv:1312.5602 (2013)
13. Schlichting, M.R., Notter, S., Fichter, W.: Long short-term memory for spatial encoding in multi-agent path planning. J. Guid. Control. Dyn. **45**(5), 952–961 (2022)
14. Van Hasselt, H., Guez, A., Silver, D.: Deep reinforcement learning with double Q-learning. In: Proceedings of the AAAI Conference on Artificial Intelligence, vol. 30 (2016)
15. Wang, B., Liu, Z., Li, Q., Prorok, A.: Mobile robot path planning in dynamic environments through globally guided reinforcement learning. IEEE Rob. Autom. Lett. **5**(4), 6932–6939 (2020)
16. Wang, W., Wu, Z., Luo, H., Zhang, B.: Path planning method of mobile robot using improved deep reinforcement learning. J. Electric. Comput. Eng. **2022**, 1–7 (2022)
17. Wu, R., et al.: Optimization path and design of intelligent logistics management system based on ROS robot. J. Rob. **2023** (2023)
18. Yang, Y., Juntao, L., Lingling, P.: Multi-robot path planning based on a deep reinforcement learning DQN algorithm. CAAI Trans. Intell. Technol. **5**(3), 177–183 (2020)

Unleashing the Potential of Agility, Resilience and Business Continuity: A Systematic Literature Review

Kunruthai Meechang[1]([✉]) [iD], Margherita Pero[2] [iD], and Khaled Medini[1] [iD]

[1] Ecole des Mines de Saint Etienne, UMR 6158 LIMOS, Henri Fayol Institute,
42000 Saint Etienne, France
kunruthai.meechang@emse.fr

[2] Department of Management, Economics and Industrial Engineering, Politecnico di Milano,
Via Lambruschini 4/b, 20156 Milan, Italy

Abstract. Challenges in the recent business environment have forced manufacturers to adapt production processes while sustaining operational continuity in response to changes in consumer behaviors and the working environment post-pandemic. Even an agile company struggled to survive during COVID-19 due to restriction measures causing supply chain disruption. Thus, there is a need to extend capabilities that allow companies to be fast and flexible despite a crisis. This paper aims to investigate the potential of three manufacturing paradigms, namely agility, business continuity, and resilience, for adverse situations. A systematic literature review has been conducted to analyze existing studies and build a holistic understanding of how they are complemented manufacturing. The results indicate the relevance of the paradigms that strive to survive through changes from different perspectives: agility focuses on quick adaptation, business continuity keeps products or services delivered, and resilience recovers operations from disruptions. Integration of these paradigms is a promising approach to surviving through crisis, adapting manufacturing, and growing competitiveness for future industries. In addition, the enablers for paradigms are identified, including process, strategy, technology, and people. The knowledge gathered from this study enables future researchers to explore an explicit integration from both conceptual and operational points of view.

Keywords: Agility · Business continuity · Resilience · Crisis · Manufacturing

1 Introduction

Dynamic markets and volatility bring industrial challenges and impede manufacturing from achieving their goals as planned. The COVID-19 pandemic has changed global manufacturing by increasing uncertainty in the market and halting logistics worldwide, eventually causing a supply chain disruption [1, 2]. This extraordinary situation complicates consumer habits and operation processes. Consumption of personal protection equipment was at its peak in the healthcare sector [3, 4]. Another increasing demand

M. Dassisti et al. (Eds.): IN4PL 2024, CCIS 2372, pp. 440–455, 2025.
https://doi.org/10.1007/978-3-031-80760-2_28

for electronic devices has caused chip shortages [5]. A reverse impact was found in the food supply chain, in which demand peaked during the early lockdown due to panic behavior, and then sales dropped due to movement restrictions [6]. Looking at the logistics and fashion sectors, they faced severe implications from the limitation of people movement, causing sale losses [1]. Working and supporting customers remotely in the manufacturing sector during this period was challenging as they needed to be physically at work [7]. Manufacturers are required to find new technologies to support customers [8]. The impacts worsened in companies that relied on outsourcing and lean production [9], while the companies that sustained themselves well had a sustainable and resilient supply chain [10]. For instance, Nestle reported growth during the pandemic because its resilient supply chain supported business continuity.

The challenges that companies are currently encountering are beyond demand changes. Regarding the intricacy of the recent business environment, dependence on resources leads to raw material shortages and late delivery [11]. Other crises, such as geopolitics, climate change, cyberattacks, and technological transformation, could obstruct manufacturing performance in the future. Dealing with these problems requires innovative tools, such as information systems and technologies. Agility with technologies can support the timely synchronization of information, data analysis, decision-making, and operations between companies, which is a way to detect changes, adjust operations accordingly, and enhance resilience [12]. Agility studies have been discussed about demand changes from customers [13], lean production [14], and software development [15], while limited attention is paid to production in adverse situations. COVID-19 has awakened manufacturers to consider being agile despite the lockdown. Based on this evidence, we call for greater attention to explore an approach for manufacturing in upcoming unknown environments. In this context, agility, business continuity, and resilience need to emerge as promising approaches to cope with uncertainty, especially in times of discontinuity.

Previous studies have investigated crucial paradigms for manufacturing by highlighting one or more at a time. For example, Ciccullo et al. [16] integrated agility, sustainability, and leanness to meet customer demand while adhering to environmental and social requirements. Similarly, Touriki et al. [17] applied smart, green, resilient, and lean to protect and preserve natural resources, mitigate disruptions, eliminate waste, and create value in manufacturing. Ivanov [18] developed a well-defined framework integrating resilience, agility, and sustainability for viable supply chains to maintain and survive through disruption, but focused on supply chain structure rather than a manufacturing process. Although the pandemic obstructed manufacturing, no study has integrated business continuity to handle operations and product delivery. There is a lack of clarity about how the manufacturer can become agile with continuous operating business and recovery from a crisis.

To overcome this research gap, this study aims to explore agility with business continuity and resilience in a holistic perspective to survive, adapt, and grow in an adverse situation. This novel concept could build competitive manufacturing toward changes while mitigating risk and uncertainties. Therefore, the following research questions are formulated:

- What are the present enablers in developing agility, business continuity, and resilience paradigms in manufacturing?
- What is the relevance of these paradigms?

The remainder of this paper is constructed as follows. Section 2 briefly introduces the background of the three discussed paradigms. Section 3 presents the research methodology used for the literature review. Section 4 presents the general trends in the field with a descriptive analysis. Section 5 responds to the research question by revealing the relevance of the paradigms, their enablers, and integrating opportunities to unleash agility and resilience potential in manufacturing. Section 6 concludes significant findings that could be useful for practitioners and point out research directions.

2 Paradigms Under Study

2.1 Agility

Agility is the capability to sense and thrive on changes in the business environment that may affect production processes [19, 20], focusing on rapid adaptation [21–23] and meeting customer's requirements in terms of price, specifications, quality, quantity, and delivery [24, 25]. Several studies mentioned agility in responding to situations in a well-coordinated adaptation and taking advantage of uncertainty [2, 26–29]. Sharma et al. [30] added that agility maximizes customer service level and minimizes the cost of goods. Previously, it was discussed mainly in the demand changes caused by customers [23, 24, 31, 32]. Since COVID-19, it has been spread in domains such as supply chain disruptions [22, 26, 33] and post-pandemic impacts [1, 7, 8]. In this sense, the critical roles of agility include strengthening information sharing and communication and supply chain reconstruction [34]. Agility is considered as an advanced stage in the process of developing supply chain resilience [22]. However, it is not a static process but rather a continuous process to react faster to changes [35]. While several definitions exist, this study refers to agility as the proactive capability of the company to rapidly sense, adapt, and even take the opportunity from (positive or negative) changes in the business environment.

2.2 Business Continuity

Business continuity has evolved since the 1970s in the disaster recovery [36]. It is defined in ISO22301:2012 as the capability of the organization to continue delivery of products or services at acceptable predefined levels following the disruptive incident [37]. To elaborate, business continuity is to deal with disruption from internal and external organizations, especially for high-consequence risks. Its implementation requires advanced preparation and activities, as well as continuous improvement for up-to-date plans. The objective is to avoid downtime operations, preserve the company's reputation, and increase competitiveness. It is designed to keep the critical operation running as smoothly as possible during disruption. Therefore, this study considers business continuity as an organization's capability to continuously operate and deliver products or services to customers at an acceptable level during a disruption.

2.3 Resilience

Resilience refers to the capability of an organization to withstand, adapt, and bounce back through maintaining critical functions and structures in disruptions [22, 27, 28, 34, 38]. On the other hand, it is the extent to which an organization is prepared to recover from unexpected events to an original or new desirable state [11, 31]. Isip [39] referred to resilience as quickly changing processes, products, systems, and organizational decisions. In manufacturing, resilience implies the reaction to the abnormality as efficiently as possible and prompt recovery [40]. However, it is unfeasible to determine the level of resilience before the disruption [41]. In common, we identify resilience as the capability to withstand disruptions and quickly recover to a normal state or adapt to a better state.

3 Research Methodology

We conducted a systematic review to build on the findings of previous studies. This method serves two objectives, which are to summarize existing research by identifying patterns and gaps and to contribute to theory development with a large amount of data and reliable conclusions [42, 43]. The method of Suering and Muller [43] was adopted, combining three rigorous steps. The first step is the material collection, which involves setting a search strategy for the inclusion and exclusion of papers. Then, descriptive analysis provides an overview of collected papers and research trends, as shown in Sect. 4. Lastly, the thematic analysis, a method of identifying, analyzing, and reporting patterns and themes within data, is selected to present the main findings in categories and allow setting future research paths, as demonstrated in Sect. 5 [16].

In the first step, search keywords and criteria are defined [16]. They are derived from the fact that we aim to investigate an approach related to handling changes in manufacturing in adverse situations. In this context, agility is known for rapidly adapting to changes by adjusting processes [44]. However, agility alone is insufficient for adverse situations [45]. Business continuity is added because it strives to maintain operations and provide products to customers at desirable levels even in crisis [46]. Resilience is included to recover operations back from following disruptions [44]. Boolean operators were combined to connect search keywords. Therefore, the search queries were (agil*) AND (resilien* OR "business continuity") AND (manufactur* OR production) AND (crisis OR disaster OR risk).

The selection criterion for the paper was the presence of agility with business continuity or resilience in manufacturing and crisis. Only English writing and open-access papers were retrieved for comprehensive understanding and information availability. Due to the novelty of the research, publications were limited to journal and conference proceedings. The search period covers 2011–2023 because two significant events, the 2011 Great East Japan Earthquake and the 2011 Thailand floods, caused severe impacts on several industries and the global supply chain [47].

To avoid error and bias, an extraction form is prepared to contain general information (e.g., titles, author names, year of publication), content (e.g., objectives and methods), and findings (e.g., results and gaps). This form facilitates the authors to connect papers and review comprehensive context, leading to emergence and analysis [48]. Based on defined keywords from three databases, 810 papers were found. All papers were first reviewed through titles, abstracts, and keywords. Then, 19 duplicated papers were removed. Next, the full papers were screened to check the content and eliminate irrelevant papers. Consequently, 49 papers are selected, including 13 papers from Scopus, 16 papers from Web of Science, and 20 papers from ScienceDirect. In the final step, a thorough review was conducted to gather data for analysis. This step supported understanding paradigms and elucidated their enablers.

4 Descriptive Results

This section presents the descriptive results from the literature review. The preliminary finding of the publication year is illustrated in Fig. 1. Although we started searching in 2011, no extracted study was found during 2011–2013. There are only a few papers each year between 2014–2019 that fit the research questions. The number of publications increased after 2019, the year of the pandemic. The highest number of relevant papers is in 2022, with 13 papers. About 75% of papers have discussed agility with resilience. The first paper mentioned the three paradigms was found in 2015. However, it did not describe an integration approach for paradigms but positioned relations among them. Only two papers jointly discussed agility and business continuity.

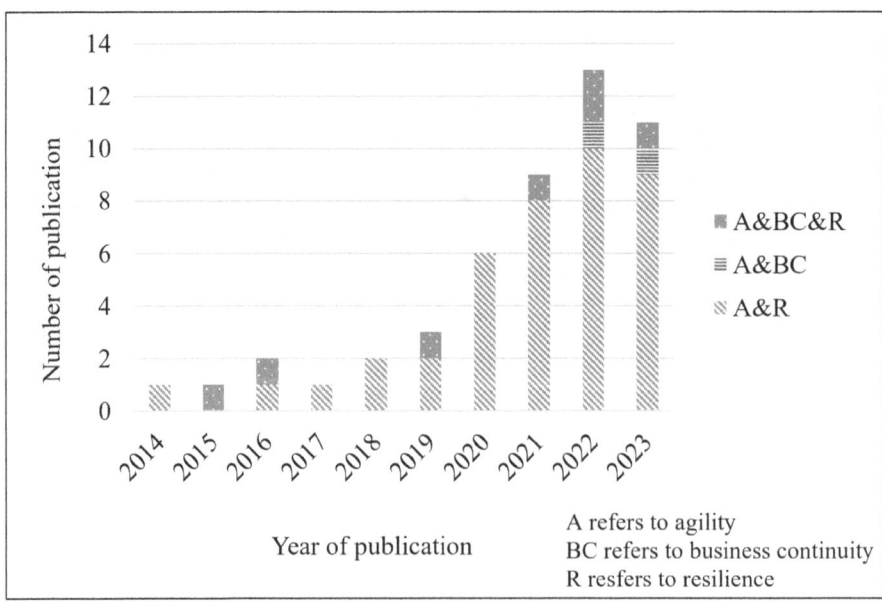

Fig. 1. Distribution of publications for integrated paradigms per year.

Since the current study focuses on the manufacturing domain, it is interesting to explore the type of industry in extracted papers, see Fig. 2a. The healthcare sector has the highest share in publications, followed by the electronics and food and beverage sectors. Five papers included several industries, which showed the different perspectives and effects. On the other hand, 19 papers did not specify a type of industry but discussed it in the general manufacturing context. Looking at the trend of disruptions, supply chain disruption and COVID-19, about 28% each, were the most studied because they affected manufacturers to continue operations and adapt processes in responding to the crisis, followed by demand changes. Due to the recent evolution in embedding technologies into manufacturing, technology disruption was found to be approximately 15%. The global supply chain faces complex issues, and various disruptions have been found, such as environmental issues, floods, cyber security, counterfeit products, earthquakes, and politics, as shown in Fig. 2b. Three papers did not specify the event but discussed disruption in general. These descriptive results show the research trends, indicating an overview of the current study.

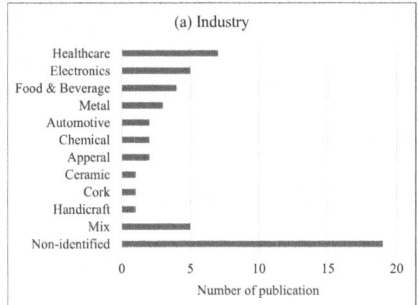 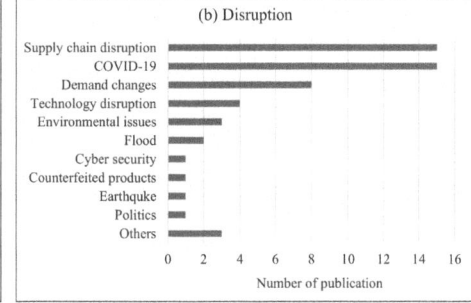

Fig. 2. Distribution of publications (a) per industry and (b) per disruption.

5 Discussion of Paradigms

Based on extracted papers, agility has been applied jointly with business continuity and resilience in several contexts (see Table 1). Therefore, this section begins by illustrating relationships among paradigms. Then, enablers are presented according to four dimensions: process, strategy, technology, and people, following McKinsey's research that demonstrated the fundamental trademarks of an agile organization [49]. The trademarks point out a network of people-centered teams that operate fast decisions enabled by technology. However, this study lacks one fundamental called structure since it is not found in the literature review. Lastly, we discussed in terms of how enablers lead to paradigms and explained integration.

5.1 Relationships

Under investigation of agility, business continuity, and resilience, we discovered three types of relationships: index, support, and synergy. According to the index relationship, agility is an indicator of resilience [5, 20, 26, 39, 50, 51]. In this context, it is a parameter to address manufacturing performance in terms of quality, speed, cost, time, and responsiveness [9] and ensure business continuity [34]. Second, agility is found to be a supporting factor for resilience. It enables a company to sense and respond to disruption, leading to resilience [52]. The agile approaches supporting resilience are, for instance, building network agility for the supply chain's visibility and automation [53] and utilization of technologies for data-driven manufacturing [54]. On the other hand, diversification and delivery are agile approaches to ensure resilience in terms of order fulfillment and changing an order method [41, 55]. Lastly, agility and resilience have a synergy relationship with common features for scenario prediction as they are claimed to deal with unpredicted events and provide the right products at the right time in the ramp-up phase [24].

5.2 Process

This section discusses the processes used for paradigms in manufacturing. Firstly, agility was applied in project management as an interactive and adaptive approach relying on customer short-loop feedback [56]. This method enables interim results and makes resilient management possible. In addition, agile manufacturing is to be fast and able to detect the causes of problems once disruption occurs. Therefore, a well-structured production control process can be executed to depict a self-contained and interactive structure, assessing fault detection and re-configuration, which can bring agility and resilience [23]. Agility has a dominant capability for rapidly adapting productions due to changes in requirements. In a crisis where manufacturers need to adjust production swiftly, ramp-up project management is commonly used for production scaling up and down. Ramp-up processes combine three phases: preparing the team, strategies, and methods, then conducting ramp-up and transfer to production [25], as well as Sprint helped manufacturing to be flexible due to demand peaks during COVID-19 [4]. Looking at the external change, a turbulent market has led to uncontrolled raw materials costs. Manufacturers need to manage risks and keep costs under control. Agile cost-price management determines processes to ensure prices by understanding materials, suppliers, cost drivers, forecasting, and tracking [57]. Besides, managers have to consider safety protocols, secure workers, and work with partners to cope with restriction measures. Crisis management is thus required for quick re-organization [38]. Process enablers address paradigms in various ways, including management, production, cost, and safety. Once they are executed, manufacturers need to evaluate paradigms' performance. This study found evaluation models in three aspects: to assess agility score in the production process [58] and to use agility for resilient evaluation [2, 22, 50]. However, an evaluation of business continuity with other paradigms is neglected.

5.3 Technology

In the digital transformation era, technologies have been increasingly deployed to improve agility and produce diverse sets of products [59]. Their utilization in manufacturing varies based on the company's digital maturity levels. Industry 4.0 (and even 5.0) addresses the inclusion of technology, which raises new opportunities to foster manufacturing paradigms. Implementing Industry 4.0 provides automated solutions against volatile markets [1]. Hsu et al. examined Industry 4.0 on agility to ensure its effects [29]. The results concluded that critical enablers of Industry 4.0, such as information transparency in supply chains, support responding to customer needs quickly, and cooperating with partners to strengthen trust [29]. The synergy of agility and Industry 4.0 drives proactive changes to meet stakeholders' requirements, which unlocks the potential for enhancing agility and resilience. This is a key for production ramp-up to exploit big data, smart products and services, and automated processes [25]. The roadmap of Industry 4.0 presented the implementation process, noting the required actions in sequence for stakeholders [60]. In addition, it indicated technologies as a foundation for agility, flexibility, innovation, and responsiveness, which eventually lead to business continuity. However, detrimental effects on job displacement and energy conservation have brought a negative image of technology [40]; the improvement idea of Industry 5.0 has been introduced for sustainable and resilient manufacturing [40]. To elaborate, Industry 5.0 aims at human-machine collaboration by leveraging technology to enhance human capabilities. It draws on many features of Industry 4.0, such as integrating technology and innovation to promote a sustainable, productive, human-centric, and resilient future industry [40]. While Industry 4.0 focuses on integrating operations and processes across the supply network, Industry 5.0 includes seamless stakeholder involvement [40]. In a crisis, Industry 5.0 provides manufacturing flexibility and agility based on real-time production monitoring and predictability that can better respond to disruptions. Other utilized technologies include blockchain for visibility, authenticity, and traceability [61] and cloud computing for data storage and transformation from various sources [59]. Even agile firms struggled to operate during COVID-19 because they lacked technologies for online business activities [45]. Thus, technology is a crucial enabler.

Modeling and simulation are integral to modern manufacturing, driving innovation, efficiency, and competitiveness by allowing manufacturers to visualize, analyze, and optimize aspects of their operations. For instance, Mensah et al. [62] applied discrete event simulations to understand supply chain behavior under uncertainty and its impacts in order to minimize risk by achieving agility. In production, dynamic modeling was used to visualize data flow and compare the scenarios' performance [27]. The study indicated a timely response to increase resilience using data buffers. Moreover, modeling could analyze the trade-off between the number of partners and reliability, showing the changing percentage of reliability for every additional number of partners [63]. This helps managers to consider their agility and sourcing strategies. While multi-objective programming considers various objectives, it was used to build resilience by minimizing the total cost and the environmental impact and maximizing the value of supply chain resilience [64]. Similarly, Shekarian et al. [65] applied the same method to examine the effects of responsiveness, risk, and cost on supply chain disruption. In brief, modeling and simulation are helpful to understand manufacturing under different conditions and seek suitable strategies.

5.4 Strategy

In COVID-19, the clothing industry discovered risks from supply chain disruption and demand change due to lockdown. This brought a need to balance risk, cost, and agility. Regarding supply chain disruption, strategies include adjusting the sourcing mix to diversify risks and avoid dual sourcing, where two suppliers are located close to one another as it is exposed to greater lockdown disruption [66]. Considering demand disruption, inventory should be relocated to less affected areas, and product supplies should be replenished for flexibility in responding to changes after opening broader. In addition, an agile inventory strategy could mitigate supply chain risk by reserving free capacities for adjusted production in the event of disruption [33]. Other strategies include cost minimization and management culture [32]. Manufacturers must align economic incentives, build trust and collaboration, and identify multiple sourcing to cope with disruption [67].

5.5 People

Embedding the paradigms into manufacturing needs stakeholder collaboration. First, the company's leaders have accountability to set goals and facilitate resources for defined strategies [68, 69]. In a crisis, they take a role in communicating with internal and external stakeholders to make quick decisions for being agile and re-starting operations after a disruption for being resilient [28]. Since building paradigms requires communication, trust, and cross-functional teams, internal collaboration should include various stakeholders from sales, marketing, engineering, logistics, human resources, public relations, equipment procurement, and work safety [11, 56]. Supplier markets at the early stage of COVID-19 were chaotic, and healthcare procurement was in a crisis, needing better coordination [70]. In this case, manufacturers should incorporate local, national, and global stakeholders for emergency preparedness. Plus, cross-organization collaboration supported workforce mobilization due to the demand peak [8]. Local partnerships were claimed to be more agile than re-location out of restriction areas [51]. This way enhances understanding of the market and technology to respond to rapid changes. The government is significant in defining policy and measures to respond to environmental changes. At the same time, they can provide resilience by supporting tax, interest deferral, loans, and digital investments [54]. In addition, cooperation between government, industry, and academics not only recovers production but enables new opportunities by using a knowledge-based system [7].

The above summary table helps practitioners and other researchers understand how discovered enablers enhance paradigms and tackle changes in the business environment, as well as allows them to customize enablers to their manufacturing objectives.

5.6 Integrating Paradigms

This section explains the purpose of paradigm integration and the opportunity for manufacturing towards business environment changes. An integration of paradigms is summarized in Fig. 3. Agility focuses on speed adapting to meet (positive and negative) changes while having the common capability with business continuity to sense and pre-define risks. Agility with business continuity was recognized during COVID-19 since impacts triggered a business decline from restricted measures. Severe effects were workforce movement and limited logistics, eventually causing halted operations [8, 45]. This crisis points to a need to be aware of the discontinuity of manufacturing, as well as to focus on adapting to market uncertainty. The lack of online business activities and technology exacerbates the difficulty in adjusting to the work environment [45]. Therefore, an integrating approach for agility and business continuity is to invest in technology

Table 1. Applications of paradigms.

Applications	Details	A	BC	R
Relationship	Agility as an index of resilience [5, 9, 20, 39, 50-52, 54]	•		•
	Agility as an index of resilience leading to business continuity [34]	•	•	•
	Agility as a supporting factor for resilience [41, 55-56, 69]	•		•
	Agility and resilience as synergetic features [24]	•		•
Process	Agile project management [57]	•		•
	Production planning and control [23]	•		•
	Sprint [4]	•		•
	Ramp-up [25]	•		•
	Cost price management [58]	•		•
	Crisis management [38]	•		•
	Evaluation model: agility score [59]	•		•
	Evaluation model: agility indexes for resilience [2, 22]	•	•	•
Technology	Industry 4.0 [29, 61]	•	•	•
	Industry 5.0 [40]	•		•
	Cloud computing [60]	•		•
	Blockchain [62]	•	•	•
	Digital transformation [70]	•		•
	Technology for flexible working [45]	•	•	
	Simulation: discrete event simulation [63]	•	•	•
	Simulation: dynamic modeling [27, 64], multi-objective programming [65-66]	•		•
Strategy	Inventory management [33]	•		•
	Balancing risk, cost, and agility [67]	•		•
	Risk mitigation [68]	•		•
	Antifragile business ecosystem [32]	•	•	•
People	Local and national government [7, 55]	•		•
	Public health sector and regulatory agencies [8]	•	•	
	Leader [28, 69-70]	•		•
	Sales manager, sales analyst, engineering supervisor, logistics manager [60]	•		•
	Human resource, public relations, marketing, equipment procurement, maintenance, and work safety [41]	•	•	
	Suppliers [8]	•		•
	Customers [60], local partners [52]	•		•
	Academics [7]	•		

to allow flexible working remotely. This way can ensure adaptation in order to deliver products or services to customers even in a crisis.

Agility is the most important capability for supply chain resilience [26, 63]. It drives resilience by utilizing data-driven manufacturing, automated processes, and a visible supply chain, which allows adjusting the operations and taking advantage to create value for products or services. Table 1 presents various enablers to enhance agility and

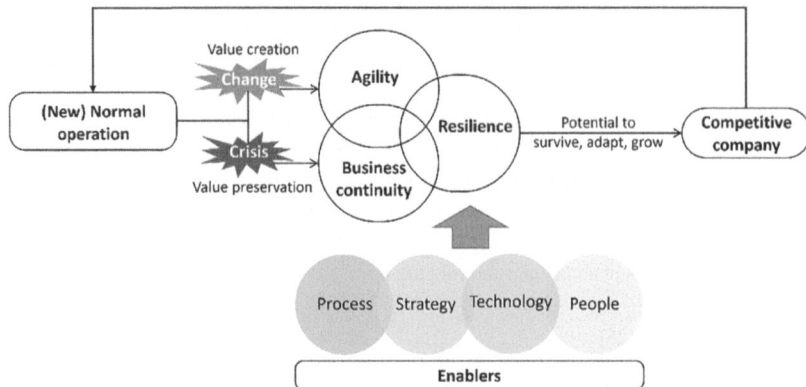

Fig. 3. Integration of paradigms (author's source).

resilience. However, agile methods, such as Lean, can reduce resilience as controlled inventory causes raw material shortages in crisis time [66]. Thus, there is a need to find a balance between agility and resilience. In such a context, balancing strategy and inventory management discussed in the previous section could be helpful in responding to changes while enhancing resilience.

A supply chain prone to risks may impact business operations. Business continuity, as a component of resilience, is the capability to maintain critical operations in disruption. It works on preparing for emergencies and responsive strategies that make it possible to continue operations and deliver products. This helps the company to build back and leads to resilience potential. However, resilience goes beyond recovering to finding a chance and adapting to a new state. The finding enablers that mentioned three paradigms simultaneously are Industry 4.0, blockchain, discrete event simulation, and antifragile business ecosystem since utilizing IoT, AI, and data analytics enables organizations to predict changes, respond rapidly, and adapt based on real-time information [60]. Achieving agility and business continuity is a potential way to build resilience [32, 52]. Nevertheless, there is a gap in the development of the solid integration process.

6 Closing Remarks

Manufacturing has become sophisticated due to dynamic environmental changes and crises, causing manufacturers to struggle to survive. Therefore, this study investigated the necessary capabilities for manufacturing. Agility, business continuity, and resilience were discussed most in situations such as supply chain disruption and COVID-19. The publication trend is obvious after the pandemic. Understanding the paradigms' mechanism indicates their significance in manufacturing. Despite previous studies trying to integrate agile with resilience, only a few studies explored them in adverse situations. Therefore, this study fills a gap by holistically presenting three paradigms focusing on disruption perspectives. From this point of view, each paradigm has different capabilities, but they have a common goal to survive through change. Agility strives to rapidly adapt processes or products to meet stakeholders' requirements. Business continuity aims at operations running and delivering products as planned. These two paradigms drive manufacturing to be resilient and competitive and allow capabilities to sense, adapt, and grow by taking the opportunity. Technology enablers hold important functions in building paradigms, for example, facilitating automated solutions, information transparency, visibility, authenticity, traceability, customer response, cooperation with partners, data storage, and even online operations in a crisis.

To help manufacturers seize opportunities from dynamic changes, we found four dimensions of enablers, which are people who should take responsibility for identified processes and strategies and leverage technology to strengthen paradigms. Agile project management, production planning and control, and SPRINT are the processes that allow manufacturing to have flexibility by obtaining interim feedback, detecting faults, and re-configuration. In a crisis where manufacturers struggle to survive and be competitive, not only is agility required, but it should be balanced with business continuity and resilience. One of the dominant strategies is adopting Lean while balancing risk, cost, and inventory, which minimizes cost and optimizes resources. Industry 4.0 amplifies three paradigms by utilizing technology for transparency and trust. Key integration steps are that manufacturers understand changes and risks to customize enablers depending on objectives and organizational cultures. Then, stakeholder identification, implementation, evaluation, and continuous improvement are run as a cycle to keep the organization's capabilities up to changes. The insights could be helpful for decision-makers in preparing manufacturing for the future industry.

Finally, integrating agility, business continuity, and resilience could be a promising way to manage changes in normal and adverse situations. However, the listed enablers for these paradigms are initial findings, and the proposed integration needs validation. Future studies can be devoted to conducting a rigorous literature review, visualizing and validating the relationships between enablers and paradigms, and evaluating to which extent enablers enhance the paradigms. The tentative methods include surveys and case studies. Exploring enablers in other perspectives, such as psychology and sociology, could be fruitful and contribute to a deeper understanding of how individual behaviors, organizational culture, and human-machine interactions influence paradigms, ultimately helping manufacturing respond better to challenges. In addition, the next potential direction is a solid framework development that illustrates the integration system.

Acknowledgments. This work is partly supported by the German-French Academy for the Industry of the Future through the RAMP-UP II project.

Disclosure of Interests. The authors have no competing interests to declare that are relevant to the content of this article.

References

1. Rinaldi, M., Bottani, E.: How did COVID-19 affect logistics and supply chain processes? Immediate, short and medium-term evidence from some industrial fields of Italy. Int. J. Prod. Econ. **262**, 108915 (2023)

2. Mohammed, A., Yazdani, M., Govindan, K., Chatterjee, P., Hubbard, N.: Would your company's resilience be internally viable after COVID-19 pandemic disruption?: a new PADRIC-based diagnostic methodology. Transp. Res. Part E-Logist. Transp. Rev. **180** (2023)
3. Milzam, M., Mahardika, A., Amalia, R.: Corona virus pandemic impact on sales revenue of micro small and medium enterprises (MSMEs) in Pekalongan city, Indonesia. J. Vocat. Stud. Appl. Res. **2**(1), 7–10 (2020)
4. Vanhooydonck, A., et al.: Case study into the successful emergency production and certification of a filtering facepiece respirator for Belgian hospitals during the COVID-19 pandemic. J. Manuf. Syst. **60**, 876–892 (2021)
5. Dittfeld, H., Donk, D., Huet, S.: The effect of production system characteristics on resilience capabilities: a multiple case study. Int. J. Oper. Prod. Manag. **42**(13), 103–127 (2022)
6. Montenegro, L.D., Young, M.N.: Operational challenges in the food industry and supply chain during the COVID-19 pandemic: a literature review. In: 7th International Conference on Frontiers of Industrial Engineering (ICFIE) 2020, pp. 1–5 (2020)
7. Mezgebe, T.T., Gebreslassie, M.G., Sibhato, H., Bahta, S.T.: Intelligent manufacturing ecosystem: a post COVID-19 recovery and growth opportunity for manufacturing industry in Sub-Saharan countries. Sci. Afr. **19**, 01547 (2023)
8. Cárdenas, A.M., Roger-Dalbert, C.: Learning from agility, partnership and innovation during the Covid-19 pandemic: a perspective from industry. Front. Cell. Infect. Microbiol. **12** (2022)
9. Alkhatib, S. Momani, R.: Supply chain resilience and operational performance: the role of digital technologies in Jordanian manufacturing firms. Adm. Sci. **13**(2) (2023)
10. Kaur, A., Kumar, A., Luthra, S.: Business continuity through customer engagement in sustainable supply chain management: outlining the enablers to manage disruption. Environ. Sci. Pollut. Res. **29**(10), 14999–15017 (2022)
11. Poberschnigg, T., Pimenta, M., Hilletofth, P.: How can cross-functional integration support the development of resilience capabilities? Case Collab. Automot. Ind. Supply Chain Manag. Int. J. **25**(6), 789–801 (2020)
12. Lee, N.C.-A., Wang, E.T., Grover, V.: IOS drivers of manufacturer-supplier flexibility and manufacturer agility. J. Strateg. Inf. Syst. **29**(1), 101594 (2020)
13. Chonko, L.B., Jones, E.: The need for speed: agility selling. J. Pers. Sell. Sales Manag. **25**(4), 371–382 (2005)
14. Alves, A.C., Dinis-Carvalho, J., Sousa, R.M.: Lean production as promoter of thinkers to achieve companies' agility. Learn. Organ. **19**(3), 219–237 (2012)
15. Flora, H.K., Chande, S.V., Wang, X.: Adopting an agile approach for the development of mobile applications. Int. J. Comput. Appl. **94**(17), 43–50 (2014)
16. Ciccullo, F., Pero, M., Caridi, M., Gosling, J., Purvis, L.: Integrating the environmental and social sustainability pillars into the lean and agile supply chain management paradigms: a literature review and future research directions. J. Clean. Prod. **172**, 2336–2350 (2018)
17. Touriki, F.E., Benkhati, I., Kamble, S.S., Belhadi, A.: An integrated smart, green, resilient, and lean manufacturing framework: a literature review and future research directions. J. Clean. Prod. **319**, 128691 (2021)
18. Ivanov, D.: Viable supply chain model: integrating agility, resilience and sustainability perspectives—lessons from and thinking beyond the COVID-19 pandemic. Ann. Oper. Res. **319**(1), 1411–1431 (2022)
19. Terblanche, C., Niemann, W.: Counterfeiting: exploring mitigation capabilities and resilience in South African pharmaceutical supply chains. Acta Commercii **21**(1) (2021)
20. Goodarzi, F., Abdollahzadeh, V., Zeinalnezhad, M.: An integrated multi-criteria decision-making and multi-objective optimization framework for green supplier evaluation and optimal order allocation under uncertainty. Decis. Anal. J. **4**, 100087 (2022)
21. Charles, A.: Improving the design and management of agile supply chains: feedback and application in the context of humanitarian aid (2010)

22. Jorge, V.F., González, D.: Model to assess supply chain resilience. Int. J. Saf. Secur. Eng. **6**(2), 282–292 (2016)
23. Heinicke, M.: Implementation of resilient production systems by production control. Procedia CIRP **19**, 105–110 (2014)
24. Mamaghani, E.J., Medini, K.: Resilience, agility and risk management in production ramp-up. Procedia CIRP **103**, 37–41 (2021)
25. Heraud, J., Medini, K., Andersen, A.-L.: Managing agile ramp-up projects in manufacturing–status quo and recommendations. CIRP J. Manuf. Sci. Technol. **45**, 125–137 (2023)
26. Hsu, C.-H., Yu, R.-Y., Chang, A.-Y., Chung, W.-H., Liu, W.-L.: Resilience-enhancing solution to mitigate risk for sustainable supply chain-an empirical study of elevator manufacturing. Processes **9**(4) (2021)
27. Ribeiro, D., Almeida, A., Azevedo, A., Ferreira, F.: Resilience in industry 4.0 digital infrastructures and platforms. Adv. Transdiscipl. Eng., 390–395 (2021)
28. Evans, S., Bahrami, H.: Super-flexibility in practice: insights from a crisis. Glob. J. Flex. Syst. Manag. **21**(3), 207–214 (2020)
29. Hsu, C., He, X., Zhang, T., Chang, A., Liu, W., Lin, Z.: Enhancing Supply chain agility with industry 4.0 enablers to mitigate ripple effects based on integrated QFD-MCDM: an empirical study of new energy materials manufacturers. Mathematics **10**(10) (2022)
30. Sharma, S., Oberoi, J.S., Gupta, R.D., Saini, S., Gupta, A.K., Sharma, N.: Effect of agility in different dimensions of manufacturing systems: a review. Mater. Today Proc. **63**, 264–267 (2022)
31. García-Reyes, H., Avilés-González, J., Avilés-Sacoto, S.V.: A model to become a supply chain 4.0 based on a digital maturity perspective. Procedia Comput. Sci. **200**, 1058–1067 (2022)
32. Ramezani, J., Camarinha-Matos, L.M.: A collaborative approach to resilient and antifragile business ecosystems. Procedia Comput. Sci. **162**, 604–613 (2019)
33. Lücker, F., Seifert, R., Biçer, I.: Roles of inventory and reserve capacity in mitigating supply chain disruption risk. Int. J. Prod. Res. **57**(4), 1238–1249 (2019)
34. Hsu, C., Zeng, J., Chang, A., Cai, S.: Deploying industry 4.0 enablers to strengthen supply chain resilience to mitigate ripple effects: an empirical study of top relay manufacturer in China. IEEE Access **10**, 114829–114855 (2022)
35. Worley, C.G., Williams, T.D., Lawler III, E.E.: The Agility Factor: Building Adaptable Organizations for Superior Performance. Wiley, Hoboken (2014)
36. Herbane, B.: The evolution of business continuity management: a historical review of practices and drivers. Bus. Hist. **52**(6), 978–1002 (2010)
37. ISO. https://www.iso.org/obp/ui/en/#iso:std:iso:22301:ed-1:v2:en. Accessed 01 June 2024
38. Rapaccini, M., Saccani, N., Kowalkowski, C., Paiola, M., Adrodegari, F.: Navigating disruptive crises through service-led growth: the impact of COVID-19 on Italian manufacturing firms. Ind. Mark. Manag. **88**, 225–237 (2020)
39. Isip, M.I.G.: Adaptive capability of micro agribusiness firms: qualitative evidence from the Philippines. Res. Glob. **5**, 100087 (2022)
40. Ghobakhloo, M., Iranmanesh, M., Foroughi, B., Tirkolaee, E.B., Asadi, S., Amran, A.: Industry 5.0 implications for inclusive sustainable manufacturing: an evidence-knowledge-based strategic roadmap. J. Clean. Prod. **417**, 138023 (2023)
41. Essuman, D., Owusu-Yirenkyi, D., Afloe, W.T., Donbesuur, F.: Leveraging foreign diversification to build firm resilience: a conditional process perspective. J. Int. Manag. **29**(6) (2023)
42. Greenhalgh, T.: How to read a paper: papers that summarise other papers (systematic reviews and meta-analyses). BMJ **315**(7109), 672–675 (1997)
43. Seuring, S., Müller, M.: From a literature review to a conceptual framework for sustainable supply chain management. J. Clean. Prod. **16**(15), 1699–1710 (2008)

44. Gligor, D., Gligor, N., Holcomb, M., Bozkurt, S.: Distinguishing between the concepts of supply chain agility and resilience: a multidisciplinary literature review. Int. J. Logist. Manag. **30**(2), 467–487 (2019)

45. Alo, O., Ali, I., Zahoor, N., Arslan, A., Golgeci, I.: Impression management and leadership in failing or failed business-to-business firms during and post-COVID-19: empirical insights from Africa. Ind. Mark. Manag. **113**, 1–13 (2023)

46. Niemimaa, M., Järveläinen, J., Heikkilä, M., Heikkilä, J.: Business continuity of business models: evaluating the resilience of business models for contingencies. Int. J. Inf. Manag. **49**, 208–216 (2019)

47. Haraguchi, M., Lall, U.: Flood risks and impacts: a case study of Thailand's floods in 2011 and research questions for supply chain decision making. Int. J. Disaster Risk Reduct. **14**, 56–272 (2015)

48. Tranfield, D., Denyer, D., Smart, P.: Towards a methodology for developing evidence-informed management knowledge by means of systematic review. Br. J. Manag. **14**(3), 207–222 (2003)

49. McKinsey. https://www.mckinsey.com/capabilities/people-and-organizational-performance/our-insights/the-five-trademarks-of-agile-organizations/. Accessed 18 Sept 2024

50. Qi, F., Zhang, L., Zhuo, K., Ma, X.: Early warning for manufacturing supply chain resilience based on improved grey prediction model. Sustainability **14**(20) (2022)

51. Shih, Y., Lin, C.: Co-location with marketing value activities as manufacturing upgrading in a COVID-19 outbreak era. J. Bus. Res. **148**, 410–419 (2022)

52. Purvis, L., Spall, S., Naim, M., Spiegler, V.: Developing a resilient supply chain strategy during 'boom' and 'bust.' Prod. Plan. Control **27**(7–8), 579–590 (2016)

53. Magableh, G.M., Mistarihi, M.Z.: Applications of MCDM approach (ANP-TOPSIS) to evaluate supply chain solutions in the context of COVID-19. Heliyon **8**(3) (2022)

54. Dubey, R., Bryde, D., Dwivedi, Y., Graham, G., Foropon, C., Papadopoulos, T.: Dynamic digital capabilities and supply chain resilience: the role of government effectiveness. Int. J. Prod. Econ. **258** (2023)

55. Gunessee, S., Subramanian, N., Ning, K.: Natural disasters, PC supply chain and corporate performance. Int. J. Oper. Prod. Manag. **38**(9), 1796–1814 (2018)

56. Scholz, J.-A., Sieckmann, F., Kohl, H.: Implementation with agile project management approaches: case study of an Industrie 4.0 learning factory in China. Procedia Manuf. **45**, 234–239 (2020)

57. Zamfir, I.: Raw material market disruptions during COVID-19: how agility can create a competitive advantage. In: The International Conference on Business Excellence, pp. 1122–1132 (2022)

58. Ning, A., Tziantzioulis, G., Wentzlaff, D.: Supply chain aware computer architecture. In: The 50th Annual International Symposium on Computer Architecture 2023, pp. 230–244. ACM (2023)

59. Dutta, G., Kumar, R., Sindhwani, R., Singh, R.K.: Overcoming the barriers of effective implementation of manufacturing execution system in pursuit of smart manufacturing in SMEs. Procedia Comput. Sci. **200**, 820–832 (2022) ·

60. Ghobakhloo, M., Iranmanesh, M., Foroughi, B., Tseng, M., Nikbin, D., Khanfar, A.: Industry 4.0 digital transformation and opportunities for supply chain resilience: a comprehensive review and a strategic roadmap. Prod. Plan. Control (2023)

61. Nandi, S., Sarkis, J., Hervani, A., Helms, M.: Redesigning supply chains using blockchain-enabled circular economy and COVID-19 experiences. Sustain. Prod. Consum. **27**, 10–22 (2021)

62. Mensah, P., Merkuryev, Y., Manak, S.: Developing a resilient supply chain strategy by exploiting ICT. Procedia Comput. Sci. **77**, 65–71 (2015)

63. Wu, C., Barnes, D.: Design of agile supply chains including the trade-off between number of partners and reliability. Int. J. Adv. Manuf. Technol. **97**(9–12), 3683–3700 (2018)
64. Mohammed, A., Harris, I., Soroka, A., Nujoom, R.: A hybrid MCDM-fuzzy multi-objective programming approach for a G-resilient supply chain network design. Comput. Ind. Eng. **127**, 297–312 (2019)
65. Shekarian, M., Nooraie, S., Parast, M.: An examination of the impact of flexibility and agility on mitigating supply chain disruptions. Int. J. Prod. Econ. **220** (2020)
66. McMaster, M., Nettleton, C., Tom, C., Xu, B., Cao, C., Qiao, P.: Risk management: rethinking fashion supply chain management for multinational corporations in light of the COVID-19 outbreak. J. Risk Financ. Manag. **13**(8) (2020)
67. Majumdar, A., Sinha, S., Govindan, K.: Prioritising risk mitigation strategies for environmentally sustainable clothing supply chains: insights from selected organisational theories. Sustain. Prod. Consum. **28**, 543–555 (2021)
68. Shin, N., Park, S.: Supply chain leadership driven strategic resilience capabilities management: a leader-member exchange perspective. J. Bus. Res. **122**, 1–13 (2021)
69. Wiechmann, D.M., Reichstein, C., Haerting, R.-C., Bueechl, J., Pressl, M.: Agile management to secure competitiveness in times of digital transformation in medium-sized businesses. Procedia Comput. Sci. **207**, 2353–2363 (2022)
70. Harland, C., et al.: Practitioners' learning about healthcare supply chain management in the COVID-19 pandemic: a public procurement perspective. Int. J. Oper. Prod. Manag. **41**(13), 178–189 (2021)

Accelerating Industry 4.0 and 5.0: The Potential of Generative Artificial Intelligence

Pedro Antonio Boareto[1]([✉]) [ID], Anderson Luis Szejka[1] [ID],
Eduardo Freitas Rocha Loures[1] [ID], Fernando Deschamps[1] [ID],
and Eduardo Alves Portela Santos[2] [ID]

[1] Industrial and Systems Engineering Graduate Program, Pontifícia Universidade Católica do Paraná, Curitiba, Paraná, Brazil
pedroaboareto@gmail.com
[2] Federal University of Paraná, Curitiba, Paraná, Brazil

Abstract. Industry 4.0 (I4.0) integrates technologies like the Internet of Things (IoT), Artificial Intelligence (AI), and robotics to create interconnected, intelligent, and autonomous production environments. This transformation drives innovation and competitiveness but poses challenges, including system integrations, investments, and workforce upskilling. This work explores the potential of Generative Artificial Intelligence (GAI) as an accelerator for I4.0 adoption considering Industry 5.0 (I5.0) requirements, using I4.0 reference architectures and the four key dimensions: Smart Manufacturing (SM), Smart Working (SW), Smart Products and Services (SPS), and Smart Supply Chain (SSC) to guide the analysis. The literature indicates that GAI has been applied in various domains, but there is a gap in comprehensive research to the industrial context. GAI's potential contributions to SM and SW include generating insights, optimizing operations through Digital Twins (DT), predictive maintenance, and enhancing human-machine collaboration, aligning with the I5.0 concept on personalization and human-centric technology solutions. In SPS and SSC, GAI aids in product development, mass customization, production simulation, and inventory control, providing real-time support and improving supply chain efficiency. The paper concludes that GAI holds significant promise for enhancing I4.0 and I5.0. But further research is needed to learn its impact at each organizational level, develop best practices, and address data quality and integration challenges. Future work will involve a systematic literature review to deepen insights into the integration of GAI with I4.0 and I5.0, with a particular focus on the role of DT and their potential to create more connected and cognitive industrial solutions.

Keywords: Industry 4.0/5.0 · Generative artificial intelligence · Reference architecture

1 Introduction

Industry 4.0 (I4.0) signifies a profound evolution in manufacturing and industrial practices through the integration of cutting-edge technologies such as the Internet of Things (IoT), Artificial Intelligence (AI), and robotics [1–4]. The current Industry 5.0 (I5.0)

M. Dassisti et al. (Eds.): IN4PL 2024, CCIS 2372, pp. 456–472, 2025.
https://doi.org/10.1007/978-3-031-80760-2_29

movement focuses on creating a human-centric, sustainable, and resilient manufacturing environment suggesting the integration of advanced technologies like Generative Artificial Intelligence (GAI) and Digital Twin (DT) to enhance cognitive support and collaboration between humans and machines [5–8].

This transformation aims to create intelligent, and autonomous production environments, driving innovation and competitiveness [2, 4, 9]. However, this shift is accompanied by challenges, including the complexity of integrating advanced digital systems, financial investments, and workforce upskilling [10–12]. Exploring challenges is crucial for successfully implementing I4.0 and I5.0.

Despite the potential benefits, many organizations are still in the early stages of adopting I4.0 and I5.0 technologies and still need to prepare for this transformation [10–12]. Reference architectures like the Reference Architectural Model Industry 4.0 (RAMI 4.0), the Industrial Internet Reference Architecture (IIRA), and the LASim Smart Factory Architecture (LASFA) provide structured frameworks to guide industries in this transition. RAMI 4.0 offers a three-dimensional approach addressing layers, hierarchy, and value streams; IIRA focuses on domain-independent adoption of IoT across sectors; and LASFA emphasizes real-time data integration and digital twins for smart factories [13–15].

In parallel, GAI, is emerging with the potential to revolutionize various domains. GAI leverages advanced neural networks like the transformer architecture to create original content, generate code, and function as intelligent assistants [16, 17]. Its applications span diverse fields such as product design, healthcare, and marketing. In the context of I4.0/I5.0, GAI stands out as a potent enabler, accelerating the transformation process by enhancing productivity, and providing valuable insights [5, 18–22].

Integrating advanced digital systems, managing financial investments, and upskilling the workforce are complex challenges in transitioning to I4.0/I5.0. Reference architectures such as RAMI 4.0, IIRA, and LASFA offer structured frameworks to guide industries through this process. Meanwhile, GAI, with its ability to enhance productivity and offer valuable insights, plays a significant role in aligning industrial practices with the core principles of I4.0/I5.0. This paper elucidates in which aspects and how GAI can support I4.0 and I5.0 by aligning its benefits with the principles of these reference architectures. Through various scenarios and insights from existing literature, this paper thoroughly analyzes GAI's role in integrating with smart manufacturing, products and services, smart working approaches, and supply chains, ultimately unlocking new levels of efficiency and competitiveness through using the emergent technology GAI. The paper is structured as follows: Sect. 1 introduces the approach, Sect. 2 provides background on essential concepts, Sect. 3 examines the integration of GAI into I4.0 and I5.0, and Sects. 4 and 5 offer a final discussion and conclusion.

2 Background

2.1 4 Smarts of Industry 4.0

Addressing barriers through targeted research, strategic planning, and supportive policies is crucial for maximizing the benefits of I4.0 across sectors and ensuring sustainable growth. The 4 Smarts framework [25] (see Fig. 1), outlines a maturity evolution for technology implementation, divided into base technologies and front-end technologies.

Base technologies include the IoT, Cloud Computing, Big Data, and AI. These are essential for transforming traditional enterprises into smart ones by integrating the 4 Smart dimensions. Front-end technologies, or the 4 Smarts, drive Industry 4.0 through SM, Smart Working (SW), Smart Supply Chain (SSC), and Smart Products and Services (SPS).

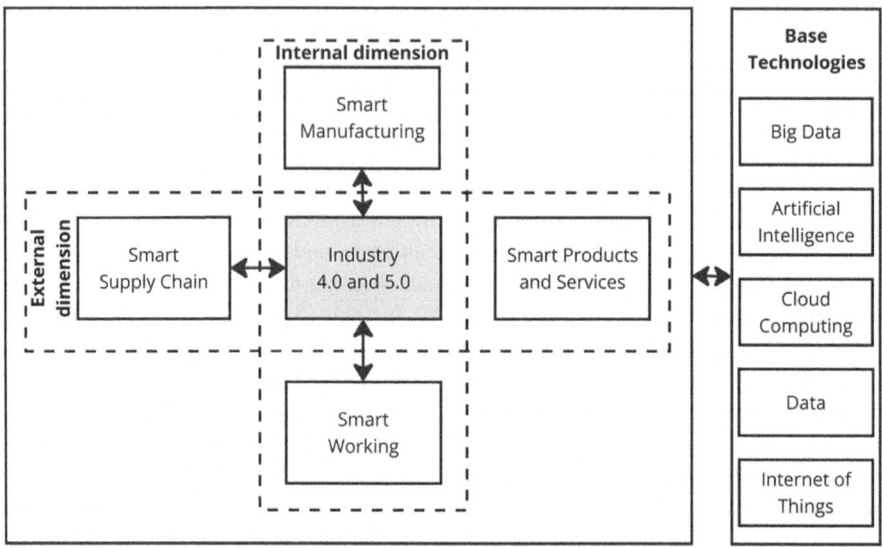

Fig. 1. Front-end Technologies (4 Smarts) – Adapted from [25].

Regarding the internal dimensions, SM involves the integration of manufacturing assets with sensors, computing platforms, communication technologies, and data-intensive modeling. This integration facilitates the creation of cyber-physical systems and enhances production planning and control [25]. SW focuses on enhancing the role of workers in the I4.0 and I5.0 environment. It emphasizes the use of technologies to support decision-making, knowledge management, and worker safety [25]. Under the I5.0 concept SW facilitate mass customization of products and services through integrated technological and social systems, promoting the realization of human creative potential and sustaining more efficient and adaptive organizations [26].

From the external dimensions, SPS encompasses both physical products enhanced with digital technologies and the services provided through these technologies. This dimension reflects the servitization trend, where companies offer services alongside their products to create additional value and generate feedback for continuous improvement [25]. The SSC dimension extends I4.0 technologies to the supply chain, improving information flows and visibility. This dimension enhances efficiency, reduces risks, and enables more responsive and flexible logistics operations [25].

2.2 Reference Architectures for Industry 4.0

Besides the four smarts bringing an overview of dimensions in an organization to organize the maturity in I4.0, reference architecture models provide structured approaches to design, implement, and manage complex industrial systems. These models offer a common language and guidelines that help different stakeholders, from engineers to business strategists, to align their efforts toward achieving the goals of I4.0 [27]. Therefore, this section will explore three main reference architectures (see Fig. 2): the IIRA [14], RAMI 4.0 [15], and LASFA [13].

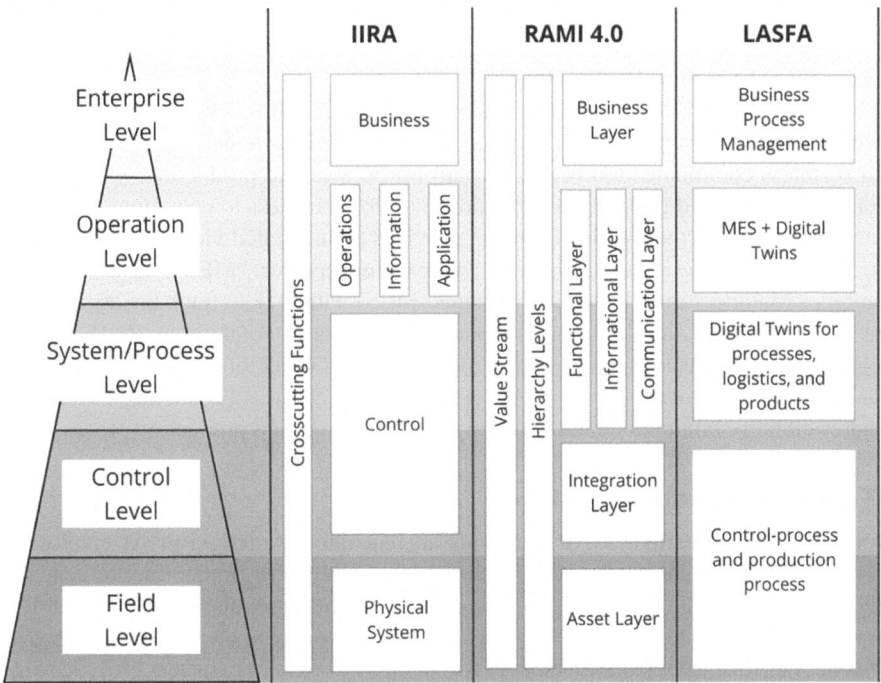

Fig. 2. Main reference architectures overview Adapted from [27]

Industrial Internet Reference Architecture

The IIRA is a comprehensive, domain-independent framework developed by [14]. It is designed to facilitate the adoption of IoT and is organized around four architectural viewpoints: business, usage, functional, and implementation.

The Business Viewpoint defines the business logic and processes for achieving business goals. Implementation Viewpoint addresses the technologies and standards used to implement the system. The Usage Viewpoint focuses on how different users interact with the system. At last, the Functional Viewpoint outlines the system's functional components. Considering seven elements: business, operation, information, application, control physical systems crosscutting functions.

Reference Architectural Model Industry 4.0
The RAMI 4.0 [15] is a domain-specific architecture. It is recognized as the international technical specification and provides a structured approach to implementing I4.0 systems. RAMI 4.0 is represented as a three-dimensional approach, i.e., layers, hierarchy, and value stream, which ensures that all stakeholders have a common understanding of the architecture.

First, the Hierarchy address the functional hierarchy within a factory. The Value Stream manages the lifecycle of products and production processes. The Layers represent different perspectives of the system: business, functional, information, communication, integration, asset.

LAsim Smart Factory Architecture
At last, the LASFA [13] is a two-dimensional architecture. It is designed to address the specific needs of smart factories, focusing on real-time data integration, digital twins, and seamless communication between control processes and production systems. The proposal is structured into four key components, from business to operations.

The "Business Process Management" provides an integrated view of core business processes, facilitating strategic planning and real-time updates. "MES + Digital Twins" combines Manufacturing Execution Systems (MES) with DTs to track the transformation of raw materials into finished products in real-time. "Digital Twins for Processes, Logistics, and Products" creates digital representations of factory processes, logistics, and products. Moreover, "Control-Process Communication + Production Processes" ensures effective communication between control systems and production processes.

2.3   Generative Artificial Intelligence

From another perspective, GAI represents an innovative paradigm in AI employing Advanced Neural Networks (ANNs) architectures such as the Transformer to generate original content, including images, music, and texts, drawing upon vast amounts of data they have been trained on [17, 18]. With GAI lies the ability to understand and predict sequences of tokens, essentially units of text such as words or characters [16]. See [16, 17] for more details on how GAI works.

Within industrial contexts, GAI finds application in diverse domains such as product design, process simulations, and virtual reality scenarios [6, 22, 28–30]. Its pronounced advantages in this realm encompass substantial enhancements in operational productivity by automating creation and prototyping tasks, amplifying efficiency while curbing development timelines. Moreover, GAI facilitates accelerated development cycles and furnishes invaluable business insights, enabling enterprises to discern patterns and trends within vast datasets, propelling innovation, and fostering informed decision-making processes.

2.4 Challenges and Opportunities

The I4.0 and I5.0 transformation demands financial investments, the complexity of integrating advanced digital systems with existing infrastructure, and the up skilling of the workforce to manage and operate these new technologies effectively. These challenges are particularly pronounced for SMEs, which often need more financial resources and technical expertise [1, 10, 11, 27].

The four smarts, i.e., SM, SW, SSC, and SPS, provide a structured approach to harnessing these technologies for optimized production, enhanced worker capabilities, efficient supply chains, and innovative products and services [25, 31]. Therefore, the growth of GAI can significantly augment I4.0 and I5.0 initiatives [6, 18, 22, 32], fitting seamlessly within the framework in each of the four smarts and leveraging key points of the reference architectures like IIRA, RAMI 4.0, and LASFA. This seamless fit of GAI within the four smarts reassures the audience about the compatibility of these technologies. GAI, with its ability to generate original content and simulate processes can enhance product design, process simulations, and virtual reality applications.

By integrating GAI into I4.0 and I5.0 environments, businesses can automate creation and prototyping tasks, accelerating development cycles, and enhancing operational and productivity. This integration facilitates the analysis of large datasets to identify patterns and trends, driving innovation and informed decision-making [6, 18, 22, 32]. Therefore, this paper emphasizes the role of GAI in smart manufacturing, products, and services, smart working approaches, and supply chains, demonstrating how these advanced technologies can unlock new levels of efficiency and competitiveness, fully realizing the transformative potential of I4.0/I5.0.

3 Generative Artificial Intelligence in Industry 4.0 and 5.0

I4.0 and I5.0 introduces numerous challenges, including significant financial investment, the complexity of integrating advanced digital systems into existing infrastructure, and the need for workforce upskilling. Despite these obstacles, I4.0 and I5.0 holds immense potential, which can be systematically understood through the framework of the four smarts [1, 10, 11, 25, 27, 31].

Also, reference architectures for I4.0, such as IIRA, RAMI 4.0, and LASFA, can be organized into five levels of an organization: Enterprise, Operational, System/Process, Control, and Field [27]. The Enterprise Level ERP systems integrate company-wide resources and operations management, supporting strategic decision-making and resource allocation. The Operation Level oversees the entire manufacturing process, from raw materials to finished products. At the System/Process Level, systems integrate data from PLCs to supervise and coordinate processes across multiple devices at the Field Level. The Control Level employs PLCs and PID controllers to manage individual devices. Field Level involves physical entities like machines and sensors on the production floor, where real-time data collection and device control occur.

These architectures map out the key components and interactions necessary for implementing I4.0 technologies. Integrating the four smarts framework with the reference architecture overview and the GAI applications provides a unified perspective on how this technology emerges as a powerful tool that can enhance I4.0 across the organization levels, i.e., the operation to business and in the four smart dimensions.

Therefore, this positional paper aims to explore GAI's detailed contributions to each of the four smarts within the context of the major reference architectures (IIRA, RAMI 4.0, and LASFA) (see Fig. 3). This analysis will highlight GAI's potential to address the challenges of implementing I4.0 and 5.0 and enhance operational efficiency and innovation.

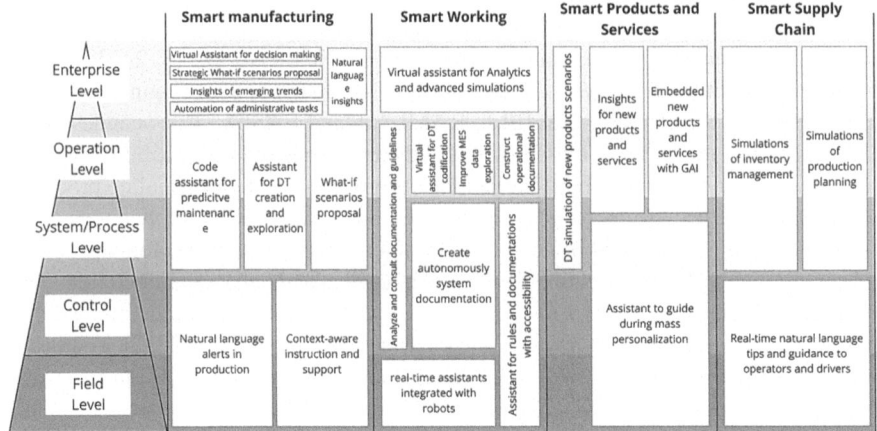

Fig. 3. GAI applications across four smarts and architecture levels.

The upcoming sections will be organized as follows: 3.1 will discuss the applications of generative AI in SM, 3.2 will explore its uses in SW, 3.3 will examine its role in SPS, and 3.4 will cover its impact on SSC. Each section will detail how GAI can be applied within the framework of the critical reference architectures, providing a roadmap for integrating GAI into Industry 4.0 initiatives.

3.1 Generative Artificial Intelligence in Smart Manufacturing

In the view of SM from [22], GAI can play a crucial role in implementing I4.0 and I5.0. Therefore, to improve the SM dimension in support of the above-mentioned reference architectures, GAI presents to be applicable across the five organization levels (see Fig. 4).

At the enterprise level, GAI can enhance and accelerate data analysis and provide valuable insights for strategic planning and decision-making through visual assistants, e.g., PowerBI Assistant, or other high-level visual assistant for management decisions, whereby leveraging large volumes of market data, GAI can identify emerging trends and predict future demands, aiding in the formulation of more robust business strategies and natural language insights [33–35]. To achieve this, GAI processes structured and unstructured data, transforming information into actionable insights. By analyzing patterns, GAI can autonomously generate reports to decision-makers' needs. These systems

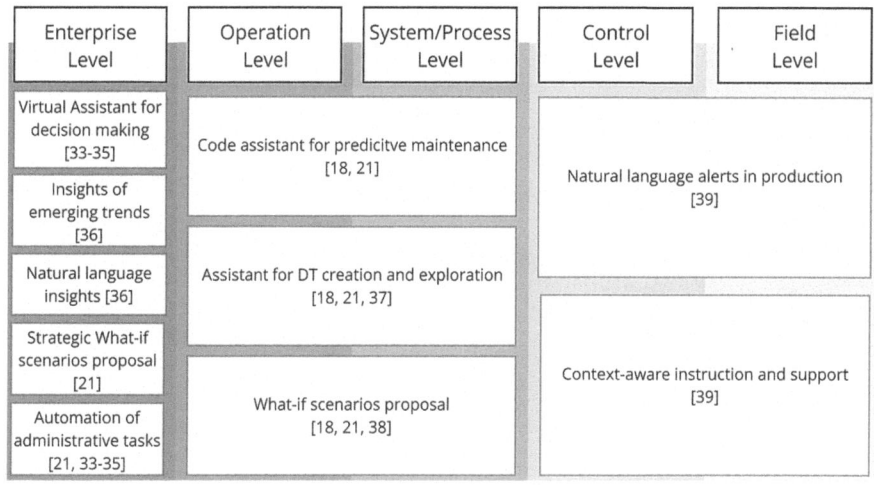

Fig. 4. GAI in SM details.

continuously refine their output by learning from new data inputs, ensuring that insights remain up-to-date and relevant. Additionally, GAI can generate and propose "what-if" scenarios and simulations to predict the impacts of strategic decisions, optimizing business value [21, 36].

From the operational level and system/process, GAI can help during the optimization as a code assistant of production through predictive maintenance, anticipating machine failures before they occur, thus minimizing downtime and repair cost [18, 21, 37]. GAI integrates with IoT devices and existing manufacturing systems, enabling real-time data exchange. This integration allows GAI to detect early signs of equipment degradation and simulate production scenarios based on real-time variables. It also can be used to create and maintain DT processes and products, enabling real-time monitoring, scenario simulation, and continuous optimization [21, 38].

At the Control and Field level, GAI creates a more humanized environment by generating natural language alerts, and AI-powered systems can be programmed to offer detailed, context-aware instructions, enhancing overall productivity and responsiveness in the manufacturing environment as a showcased by [39] that created a solution to enhance telecom customer service. By optimizing knowledge organization and search capabilities, the model significantly improved knowledge recommendation acceptance rates from 15% to 70%.

3.2 Generative Artificial Intelligence in Smart Working

In the SW dimension, GAI is more effective in transforming the way workers do their jobs in I4.0 and I5.0 (see Fig. 5). SW enhances the role of workers by leveraging technologies like virtual and augmented reality, AI, smart glasses, wearables, and cobots to support decision-making, knowledge management, creativity, and worker safety, thereby augmenting their capabilities and improving their work environment [18, 27].

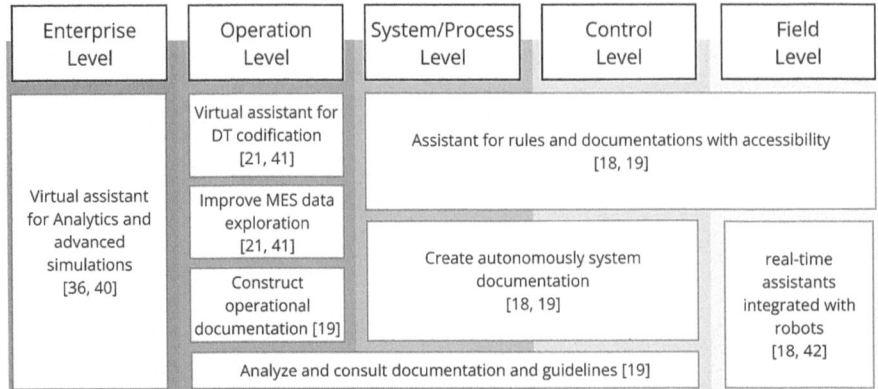

Fig. 5. GAI in SW details.

For Enterprise-level scenarios, GAI offers virtual assistants to help during analytics and advanced simulations, enabling more effective management of strategic data and processes [36, 40]. GAI's ability to autonomously generate documentation, perform complex data analyses, and offer strategic insights. This strengthens data-driven decision-making that is aligned with business goals as defined in the Business Viewpoint of IIRA and facilitates production customization and adaptation to constantly shifting market demands. For example, [40] investigates the capabilities of the GAI in Construction Project Risk Management (CPRM) compared to human experts. Using a mixed-methods approach, it quantitatively and qualitatively assesses responses from 16 Finnish construction industry experts and ChatGPT AI through anonymous peer reviews. The findings reveal ChatGPT's strength in generating comprehensive risk management plans, sur-passing human averages quantitatively.

At the Operational Level, GAI's capability can act as a virtual assistant with cognitive capabilities, e.g., during DT codification and assembling code from MES data, aligning with LASFA's framework [21, 41]. To achieve this, chatbots with GAI embedded can be used. This includes acting as a digital assistant to analyze and construct operational documentation, generating comprehensive views of both operational and informational aspects [19, 21, 41]. By leveraging GAI in these roles, organizations can enhance traceability, streamline production processes, and foster more informed decision-making across all operational tiers. For example, [38] introduces ContextMate, an innovative system designed to enhance the performance of GAI in data analysis tasks by seamlessly integrating contextual information derived from user interactions in desktop environments. It prioritizes real-time interactions with commonly used applications, identifying and prioritizing data analysis tools based on user engagement and task relevance. Evaluation with 18 participants across real-world scenarios demonstrated an impressive 93.0% success rate in completing diverse data analysis tasks, underscoring ContextMate's ability to enhance user accessibility, satisfaction, and task comprehension in data analytics.

From the System/Process and Control level, GAI is pivotal in supporting SW by generating clear and accessible process and system documentation and guidelines [18,

19]. For instance, [19] creates a GAI API documentation solution. Comparative evaluations confirm the method's effectiveness, highlighting its potential to streamline software development processes and pave the way for future advancements in API documentation practices.

At the Field Level, where direct interaction with physical devices and production systems occurs, GAI accelerates the capability to foster a human-machine approach within the framework of Smart Working. To achieve this, by analyzing real-time data streams from wearables, smart glasses, and cobots, GAI can provide workers with on-demand information, recommendations, and decision-making support. It generates real-time assistants that enhance cobots, ensuring direct connections to human activities [18, 42]. This integration reduces errors and risks, improving operational efficiency and minimizing unplanned downtime. [42] creates a vision-language approach to enhance human-robot collaboration (HRC) in manufacturing, leveraging large language models (LLMs) to mitigate communication ambiguity. These advancements promise to streamline industrial processes by improving HRC efficiency despite challenges like computational costs and latency, paving the way for future innovations in industrial automation.

3.3 Generative Artificial Intelligence in Smart Products and Services

By integrating digital technologies into physical products and services, SPS can be significantly enhanced through GAI in Industry 4.0. GAI enables the collection, monitoring, and optimization of user data through IoT, cloud, and AI, fostering the creation of intelligent products and digital services. This integration promotes new business opportunities and customer value, aligning with the service trend where manufacturing companies offer services alongside products for continuous improvement (see Fig. 6.)

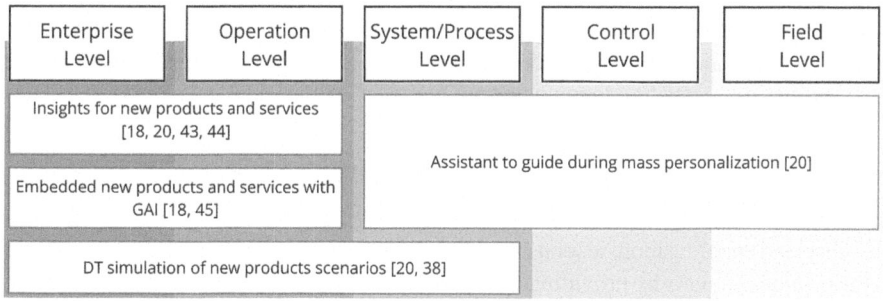

Fig. 6. GAI in SPS details.

GAI contributes to developing innovative products and services at the Enterprise and Operation levels by providing valuable insights through remote assistants, cloud services, and AI-based customer support. GAI can aid in the creation of new products and services with embedded AI, enhancing product capabilities and user experiences [18, 20, 43]. For example, [20] introduces the AI-augmented Multi-modal Collaborative Design (AI-MCD) framework to enhance collaborative design by integrating LLM, GAI, and Mixed Reality (MR). The framework generates professional design prompts, creating precise visual schemes and fostering an interactive, immersive environment. A case study on developing children's educational products highlights its effectiveness. The key innovation is the automatic generation of design proposals, significantly reducing time and resource costs while emphasizing the importance of human-machine interaction.

GAI also supports the creation of DT, enabling real-time monitoring, scenario simulation, and production management of products and processes. These DTs facilitate the optimization of logistics and product management, enhancing operational efficiency [20, 38, 44, 45]. Embedded new products and services with GAI. For example, it demonstrates using LLMs to generate virtual traffic scenarios through natural language descriptions rather than traditional methods like XML files or UI-based editors. By leveraging LLMs, the approach simplifies the creation of traffic scenarios for applications in safety testing, autonomous driver training, and regulatory compliance.

At the System/Process, Control, and Field Levels, GAI supports operators during creating and manufacturing new products. GAI can assist in customizing items and generating hyper-personalizations, ensuring products meet specific customer requirements [20, 42]. For example, [42] proposes a vision-language reasoning approach to enhance Human-Robot Collaboration (HRC) in manufacturing by addressing communication ambiguities. This approach improves HRC performance by leveraging human language cues and visual information. Empirical experiments demonstrate its effectiveness in collaborative assembly tasks. The study highlights the need for lightweight, specialized LLM models and further research into incorporating additional data modalities, compressing models for offline use, and planning long-horizon robotic tasks to tackle complex industrial scenarios.

By processing large volumes of user data collected through IoT devices, cloud platforms, and AI systems, GAI can identify patterns, predict user needs, and generate optimized solutions in real-time. In practical terms, this means GAI can autonomously propose product designs, personalize services, and adapt production workflows to meet specific requirements with minimal human intervention. Through continuous learning from user interactions and feedback, GAI refines its outputs, making it capable of supporting dynamic environments like manufacturing, logistics, and product development.

3.4 Generative Artificial Intelligence in Smart Supply Chain

GAI can significantly enhance the SSC by optimizing information flows, improving visibility, and enabling more responsive and flexible logistics operations. GAI contributes to these improvements by providing advanced data analysis, real-time decision support, and intelligent automation across various organizational levels, ensuring a more efficient and adaptive supply chain (see Fig. 7).

At the Enterprise, Operational, and System/Process Levels, GAI can play a crucial role in enhancing supply chain management. GAI can improve production planning and inventory control by creating real-time simulation models to support decisions to adjust schedules and inventory levels based on current conditions [46–48]. For instance, [46] compares the effectiveness of demand forecasting using the generative language model GPT and the auto ARIMA algorithm in a manufacturing context. Results indicate that ChatGPT outperforms ARIMA in forecast accuracy despite challenges such as manual data input, random interruptions, and the need for additional steps to transfer data

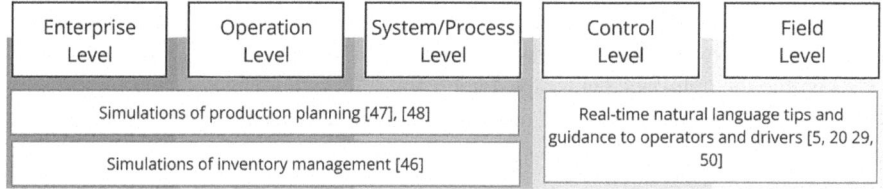

Fig. 7. GAI in SSC details.

from textual outputs to analytical programs. While integrating ChatGPT into existing systems may be complex, it shows potential for improving short- and long-term inventory management accuracy. This enhances flexibility and efficiency, reducing the risk of stockouts or overproduction.

For Control and Field Levels, GAI can act as a virtual assistant, providing real-time, natural language tips and guidance to operators, drivers, and other personnel. This humanized and assertive assistance ensures that workers receive timely updates and support, improving their ability to handle issues and maintain smoothly. By offering real-time support and guidance, GAI ensures that any disruptions in the supply chain are swiftly addressed, minimizing downtime, and maintaining the flow of goods and information [5, 20, 49, 50]. For example, [50] introduces the Context-Aware Visual Grounding (CAVG) model, designed to improve visual grounding in autonomous vehicles (AVs) by accurately interpreting and executing linguistic commands within a visual context. The model shows robustness in challenging scenarios, such as low-light conditions, ambiguous commands, and densely populated environments.

To achieve these benefits, GAI can help to simulate various operational scenarios, and suggest adjustments, e.g., a virtual ChatBot with GAI can help to explore simulation scenarios. Or, through its conversational capabilities, it provides actionable insights in a human-readable format, enabling operators and decision-makers to respond quickly to dynamic changes. This adaptability and real-time support contribute to a more resilient and efficient supply chain, optimizing decision-making at all levels, from enterprise planning to field operations.

4 Discussion

This paper explores the evidence supporting the potential of GAI as an accelerator for I4.0 and I5.0 adoption. This discussion focuses on the four key dimensions, i.e., SM, SW, SPS, and SSC, while employing predominant concepts from reference architecture models like IIRA, RAMI 4.0, and LASFA. The analysis spans five organizational levels: Enterprise, Operational, System/Process, Control, and Field, offering a comprehensive view of GAI's impact across different aspects of industrial operations.

The existing literature provides a varied perspective on the integration of GAI within I4.0 and I5.0 [5, 18–22, 28, 51]. While contributions discuss the application of GAI in specific aspects of the industrial sector, many GAI applications are presented mainly in other domains such as healthcare, marketing, and programming [18, 19, 40]. Though not directly related to I4.0 and I5.0, these studies offer technical insights that can be compared and potentially integrated into industrial applications. Therefore, this paper, based on previously cited frameworks, was capable of identify the usage and integration of GAI within the industrial landscape demonstrates its significant contributions to both internal and external dimensions of organizational operation and explore it's usage (see Fig. 8).

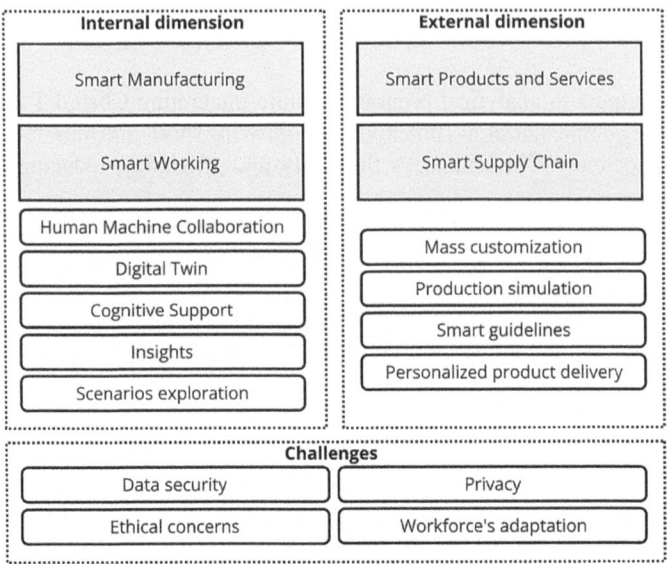

Fig. 8. Main benefits of GAI and challenges.

Internally, GAI assists across the five organizational levels by generating valuable insights, scenarios, and optimizing factory operations through DTs. Also, it enhances the daily activities of operators by fostering a seamless human-machine collaboration with cognitive support. By doing so, GAI positions itself as a pivotal accelerator and enhancer of I4.0 and I5.0 artifacts, promoting a more technology-friendly and accessible environment across all organizational levels. Externally, GAI proves advantageous in generating insights for new product development, enabling mass customization, and simulating production scenarios. It also supports production control with guidelines and support throughout the distribution chain leading to faster and more personalized product delivery without sacrificing efficiency.

However, potential challenges include ensuring data security and privacy, addressing ethical concerns related to AI decision-making, and managing the workforce's adaptation to rapidly changing technological environments. Overcoming these challenges is crucial to fully realizing the benefits of GAI in accelerating the adoption of I4.0 and I5.0. Several strategies can be employed to address these challenges. First, robust data governance frameworks must be developed to ensure data security and privacy across all levels of the organization. This includes implementing encryption, anonymization, and rigorous access controls. Ethical concerns can be mitigated by establishing transparent AI decision-making processes and incorporating human oversight into AI-driven operations, ensuring that your judgment remains a critical part of the decision-making process. Workforce adaptation, a critical barrier, can be addressed through continuous upskilling programs and the integration of AI into training modules, enabling employees to gain hands-on experience with new technologies. Furthermore, fostering a culture of innovation and digital literacy will be essential to smooth the transition toward I4.0 and I5.0. By prioritizing these approaches, organizations can mitigate risks and accelerate GAI's positive impact across their operations.

The paper recognizes certain limitations and outlines future research directions. This study was based on only three reference architectures, which may restrict the scope of the findings regarding the integration of GAI with elements of I4.0 and I5.0. Future research will focus on human-centric and cognitive support aspects of I5.0, particularly how GAI can enhance these areas to improve human-machine collaboration and decision-making. A systematic literature review will be conducted to deepen understanding of how GAI's integration can impact each organizational level and identify key studies that offer insights into the evolving applications of I4.0 and I5.0. Additionally, special attention will be directed toward the role of Digital Twins, examining their potential when combined with GAI's cognitive support capabilities, as these technologies are drivers for accelerating the adoption of smart solutions.

5 Conclusion

This work explored the potential benefits of integrating Generative Artificial Intelligence (GAI) with Industry 4.0/5.0 (I4.0/I5.0), focusing on the four dimensions of Smart Manufacturing (SM), Smart Working (SW), Smart Products and Services (SPS), and Smart Supply Chain (SSC). The analysis, guided by reference architectures like IIRA, RAMI 4.0, and LASFA, spanned five organizational levels, highlighting how GAI can enhance business insights, operational efficiency, and human-machine collaboration, ultimately fostering a more adaptive and productive industrial environment.

GAI, as presented in this paper, has the potential to significantly enhance innovation and efficiency in I4.0 and I5.0, offering substantial contributions across multiple domains. It enhances product customization through advanced data-driven insights, optimizes supply chain management by enabling more responsive and personalized communication, and most importantly, provides critical support for decision-making at all organizational levels. GAI's pivotal role in improving operational efficiency and fostering a more adaptive, connected, and intelligent industrial environment through seamless human-machine collaboration and leveraging decision-making is a testament to its potential. These contributions position GAI as a key enabler in accelerating the transition to a more advanced and sustainable industrial ecosystem.

To further advance research in this field, it is crucial to explore the development of frameworks for effectively implementing GAI across various industrial sectors. This research should focus on optimizing processes through real-time data analysis, enhancing cognitive support with Digital Twins, and improving decision-making at all organizational levels. Equally critical is the need to understand the impact of GAI on workforce adaptation and human-machine collaboration, ensuring a smooth technological transition. Although GAI can be applied across the '4 Smarts' of Industry 4.0, its integration into the context of SW stands out as an emerging area especially relevant to Industry 5.0. Applications such as real-time cognitive assistants for operators and digital assistants in operations to improve accessibility present promising avenues for study. Additionally, research on using GAI in an industrial context must prioritize addressing challenges related to data security, privacy, and ethical concerns by formulating guidelines for transparent and responsible AI decision-making. Developing robust policies and regulatory frameworks will be essential to mitigate risks and ensure that the use of GAI is secure, reliable, and aligned with ethical principles.

Acknowledgments. This paper utilized ChatGPT [52] for English spelling correction and writing [52].

References

1. Ghobakhloo, M.: The future of manufacturing industry: a strategic roadmap toward industry 4.0. J. Manuf. Technol. Manag. **29**(6), 910–936 (2018)
2. Bassi, L.: Industry 4.0: hope, hype or revolution? In: 2017 IEEE 3rd International Forum on Research and Technologies for Society and Industry (RTSI), Modena, Italy, pp. 1–6 (2017)
3. Ustundag, A., Cevikcan, E.: Industry 4.0: Managing the Digital Transformation. Springer Series in Advanced Manufacturing, 1st edn. Springer, Charm (2018). https://doi.org/10.1007/978-3-319-57870-5
4. Li, D.X., Xu, E.L., Li, L.: Industry 4.0: state of the art and future trends. Int. J. Prod. Res. **56**(8), 2941–2962 (2018)
5. Kiangala, K. S., Wang, Z.: An experimental hybrid customized AI and generative AI chatbot human machine interface to improve a factory troubleshooting downtime in the context of Industry 5.0. Int. J. Adv. Manuf. Technol. **132**, 2715–2733 (2024)
6. Yang, J., Wang, Y., Wang, X., Wang, X., Wang, X., Wang, F.Y.: Generative AI empowering parallel manufacturing: building a '6S'; collaborative production ecology for manufacturing 5.0. IEEE Trans. Syst. Man Cybern. Syst., 1–15 (2024)
7. Ali, J.A.H., Gaffinet, B., Panetto, H., Naudet, Y.: Cognitive systems and interoperability in the enterprise: a systematic literature review. Annu. Rev. Control **57**(1), 100954 (2024)
8. Naudet, Y., Panetto, H., Yilma, B.A.: Towards cognitive interoperability in cyber-physical enterprises. IFAC-PapersOnLine **56**, 695–706 (2023)
9. Lu, Y.: Industry 4.0: a survey on technologies, applications and open research issues. J. Ind. Inf. Integr. **6**, 1–10 (2017)
10. Lazarova-Molnar, S., Mohamed, N., Al-Jaroodi, J.: Collaborative data analytics for industry 4.0: challenges, opportunities and models. In: 2018 Sixth International Conference on Enterprise Systems (ES), New York, pp. 100–107. IEEE (2018)
11. Slusarczyk, B.: Industry 4.0 - are we ready? Pol. J. Manag. Stud. **17**(1), 232–248 (2018)
12. Ramanathan, K., Samaranayake, P.: Assessing Industry 4.0 readiness in manufacturing: a self-diagnostic framework and an illustrative case study. J. Manuf. Technol. Manag. **33**(3), 468–488 (2022)
13. Resman, M., Pipan, M., Šimic, M., Herakovič, N.: A new architecture model for smart manufacturing: a performance analysis and comparison with the RAMI 4.0 reference model. Adv. Prod. Eng. Manag. **14**(2), 153–165 (2019)
14. Industry IoT Consortium: The Industrial Internet Reference Architecture (IIRA). https://www.iiconsortium.org/IIRA/. Accessed 07 July 2024

15. DIN SPEC 91345:2016-04: Reference Architecture Model Industry 4.0 (RAMI4.0) (2016)
16. Han, X., et al.: Pre-trained models: past, present and future. AI Open **2**, 225–250 (2021)
17. Lecun, Y., Bengio, Y., Hinton, G.: Deep learning. Nature **521**(7553), 436–444 (2015)
18. Gozalo-Brizuela, R., Garrido-Merchán, E.C.: A survey of generative AI applications. arXiv, Cornell University (2023)
19. Dhyani, P., Nautiyal, S., Negi, A., Dhyani, S., Chaudhary, P.: Automated API docs generator using generative AI. In: 2024 IEEE International Students' Conference on Electrical, Electronics and Computer Science (SCEECS), India, pp. 1–6. IEEE (2024)
20. Xu, S., Wei, Y., Zheng, P., Zhang, J., Yu, C.: LLM enabled generative collaborative design in a mixed reality environment. J. Manuf. Syst. **74**, 703–715 (2024)
21. Mateev, M.: Predictive analytics based on digital twins, generative AI, and ChatGPT. In: Proceedings of World Multi-Conference on Systemics, Cybernetics and Informatics, WMSCI, International Institute of Informatics and Cybernetics, United States of America, pp. 168–174. International Institute of Informatics and Cybernetics (2023)
22. Mondal, S., Das, S., Vrana, V.G.: How to bell the cat? A theoretical review of generative artificial intelligence towards digital disruption in all walks of life. Technologies **11**(2), 44 (2023)
23. Ghobakhloo, M.: Industry 4.0, digitization, and opportunities for sustainability. J. Clean. Prod. **252**, 119869 (2020)
24. Kumar, P., Bhamu, J., Sangwan, K.S.: Analysis of barriers to industry 4.0 adoption in manufacturing organizations: an ISM approach. Procedia CIRP **2021**, 85–90 (2021)
25. Frank, A.G., Dalenogare, L.S., Ayala, N.F.: Industry 4.0 technologies: implementation patterns in manufacturing companies. Int. J. Prod. Econ. **210**, 15–26 (2019)
26. Bednar, P.M., Welch, C.: Socio-technical perspectives on smart working: creating meaningful and sustainable systems. Inf. Syst. Front. **22**(2), 281–298 (2020)
27. Nakagawa, E.Y., Antonino, P.O., Schnicke, F., Capilla, R., Kuhn, T., Liggesmeyer, P.: Industry 4.0 reference architectures: state of the art and future trends. Comput. Ind. Eng. **156**, 107241 (2021)
28. Kulkarni, V., Reddy, S., Barat, S., Dutta, J.: Toward a symbiotic approach leveraging generative AI for model driven engineering, pp. 184–193. IEEE (2023)
29. Sobhanmanesh, F., Beheshti, A., Nouri, N., Chapparo, N.M., Raj, S., George, R.A.: A cognitive model for technology adoption. Algorithms **16**(3), 155 (2023)
30. Badini, S., Regondi, S., Frontoni, E., Pugliese, R.: Assessing the capabilities of ChatGPT to improve additive manufacturing troubleshooting. Adv. Ind. Eng. Polym. Res. **6**(3), 278–287 (2023)
31. Meindl, B., Ayala, N.F., Mendonça, J., Frank, A.G.: The four smarts of industry 4.0: evolution of ten years of research and future perspectives. Technol. Forecast. Soc. Change **168**, 120784 (2021)
32. Kanbach, D.K., Heiduk, L., Blueher, G., Schreiter, M., Lahmann, A.: The GenAI is out of the bottle: generative artificial intelligence from a business model innovation perspective. RMS **12**(3), 345–362 (2023)
33. Maddigan, P., Susnjak, T.: Chat2VIS: generating data visualizations via natural language using ChatGPT, codex and GPT-3 large language models. IEEE Access **11**, 45181–45193 (2023)
34. Wang, Y., et al.: Towards natural language-based visualization authoring. IEEE Trans. Vis. Comput. Graph. **29**(1), 1222–1232 (2023)
35. Mitra, R., Narechania, A., Endert, A., Stasko, J.: Facilitating conversational interaction in natural language interfaces for visualization. In: 2022 IEEE Visualization Conference - Short Papers (VIS 2022), pp. 6–10. IEEE (2022)

36. Bronzini, M., Nicolini, C., Lepri, B., Passerini, A., Staiano, J.: Glitter or gold? Deriving structured insights from sustainability reports via large language models. EPJ Data Sci. **12**(1), 1–15 (2023)

37. Zhong, N., et al.: CASIT: collective intelligent agent system for Internet of Things. IEEE Internet Things J. (2024)

38. Jadoon, A.K., Yu, C., Shi, Y.: ContextMate: a context-aware smart agent for efficient data analysis. CCF Trans. Pervasive Comput. Interact. (2024)

39. Xiaoliang, M., RuQiang, Z., Ying, L., Congjian, D., Dequan, D.: Design of a large language model for improving customer service in telecom operators. Electron. Lett. **60**(10) (2024)

40. Nyqvist, A., Peltokorpi, A., Seppänen, O.: Can ChatGPT exceed humans in construction project risk management? Eng. Constr. Archit. Manag. **31**(13), 223–243 (2024)

41. Fiore, M., Gattullo, M., Mongiello, M.: First steps in constructing an AI-powered digital twin teacher: harnessing large language models in a metaverse classroom. In: 2024 IEEE Conference on Virtual Reality and 3D User Interfaces Abstracts and Workshops (VRW), United States of America, pp. 939–940. IEEE (2024)

42. Fan, J., Zheng, P.: A vision-language-guided robotic action planning approach for ambiguity mitigation in human–robot collaborative manufacturing. J. Manuf. Syst. **74**, 1009–1018 (2024)

43. Ivcevic, Z., Grandinetti, M.: Artificial intelligence as a tool for creativity. J. Creat. **34**(2), 100079 (2024)

44. Güzay, E., Özdemir, E., Kara, Y.: A generative AI-driven application: use of large language models for traffic scenario generation. In: 14th International Conference on Electrical and Electronics Engineering (ELECO), Turkiye, pp. 1–6. IEEE (2023)

45. Holland, M., Chaudhari, K.: Large language model based agent for process planning of fiber composite structures. Manuf. Lett. **40**, 100–103 (2024)

46. Skórnóg, D., Kmiecik, M.: Supporting the inventory management in the manufacturing company by ChatGPT. Logforum **19**(4), 535–554 (2023)

47. Chan, C.C.H., Lin, Y.C., Shih, P.C.: Natural language processing for supply chain with chat GPT. In: 2023 IEEE 5th International Conference on Architecture, Construction, Environment and Hydraulics (ICACEH), Taiwan, pp. 28–31. IEEE (2023)

48. Srivastava, S.K., Routray, S., Bag, S., Gupta, S., Zhang, J.Z.: Exploring the potential of large language in supply chain management: a study using big data. J. Models Glob. Inf. Manag. **32**(1) (2024)

49. Munir, F., Mihaylova, T., Azam, S., Kucner, T.P., Kyrki, V.: Exploring large language models for trajectory prediction: a technical perspective. In: ACM/IEEE International Conference on Human-Robot Interaction, United States of America, pp. 774–778. IEEE (2024)

50. Liao, H., et al.: GPT-4 enhanced multimodal grounding for autonomous driving: leveraging cross-modal attention with large language models. Commun. Transp. Res. **4**, 100116 (2024)

51. Serban, I.V., Sordoni, A., Bengio, Y., Courville, A., Pineau, J.: Building end-to-end dialogue systems using generative hierarchical neural network models. In: 30th AAAI Conference on Artificial Intelligence (AAAI), United States of America, pp. 3776–3784. AAAI Press (2016)

52. OpenAI: ChatGPT – Version 3.5. https://chatgpt.com/. Accessed 20 June 2024

Author Index

The manufacturer's authorised representative in the EU is Springer
Nature Customer Service Centre GmbH, Europaplatz 3, 69115 Heidelberg,
Germany. If you have any concerns regarding our products, please
contact ProductSafety@springernature.com

Printed and bound by CPI Group (UK) Ltd, Croydon, CR0 4YY
29/04/2026
02099544-0016